Reading Hemingway's *The Garden of Eden*

READING HEMINGWAY SERIES

MARK CIRINO, EDITOR

ROBERT W. LEWIS, FOUNDING EDITOR

Reading Hemingway's *The Sun Also Rises*
    H. R. Stoneback

Reading Hemingway's *Men Without Women*
    Joseph M. Flora

Reading Hemingway's *Across the River and into the Trees*
    Mark Cirino

Reading Hemingway's *To Have and Have Not*
    Kirk Curnutt

Reading Hemingway's *The Old Man and the Sea*
    Bickford Sylvester, Larry Grimes, and Peter L. Hays

Reading Hemingway's *A Farewell to Arms*
    Robert W. Lewis and Michael Kim Roos

Reading Hemingway's *Winner Take Nothing*
    Edited by Mark Cirino and Susan Vandagriff

Reading Hemingway's *The Garden of Eden*
    Carl P. Eby

Reading Hemingway's
The Garden of Eden

GLOSSARY AND COMMENTARY

Carl P. Eby

The Kent State University Press

KENT, OHIO

© 2023 by The Kent State University Press, Kent, Ohio 44242
All rights reserved
ISBN 978-1-60635-458-2
Published in the United States of America

No part of this book may be used or reproduced, in any manner whatsoever, without written permission from the Publisher, except in the case of short quotations in critical reviews or articles.

Cataloging information for this title is available at the Library of Congress.

27 26 25 24 23   5 4 3 2 1

This book is for Linda and Paco

CONTENTS

Acknowledgments   ix
Introduction to *The Garden of Eden*   xi
Abbreviations Used in This Book   xxi
Series Note   xxiii
Maps   xxv
Front Matter   3
Book I *(mss. book I)*
   Chapter 1 *(mss. chapter 1)*   9
   Chapter 2 *(mss. chapters 2–3)*   51
   Chapter 3 *(mss. chapter 4)*   64
(mss. book II)
   (mss. chapter 1)   73
Book II *(mss. book III)*
   Chapter 4 *(mss. chapters 1–4)*   81
   Chapter 5 *(mss. chapters 5–8)*   92
   Chapter 6 *(mss. chapters 9–12)*   111
   Chapter 7 *(mss. chapters 13–14)*   139
   Chapter 8 *(mss. chapter 15)*   156
Book III *(not a new book in mss.)*
   Chapter 9 *(mss. chapters 16–17)*   161
   Chapter 10 *(mss. chapters 18–19)*   172
   Chapter 11 *(mss. chapter 20)*   182
   Chapter 12 *(mss. chapter 21)*   188
   Chapter 13 *(mss. chapter 21)*   195
   Chapter 14 *(mss. chapter 22)*   202
   Chapter 15 *(mss. chapter 23)*   204
   Chapter 16 *(mss. chapter 24)*   213
   Chapter 17 *(mss. chapter 25)*   222
   Chapter 18 *(mss. chapter 26)*   227
   Chapter 19 *(mss. chapters 27–28)*   236
   Chapter 20 *(mss. chapter 29)*   247

    Chapter 21 *(mss. chapters 30–31)*   253
    Chapter 22 *(mss. chapters 32–34)*   259
    Chapter 23 *(mss. chapters 35–36)*   265
    Chapter 24 *(mss. chapter 37)*   271
Book IV *(not a new book in mss.)*
    Chapter 25 *(mss. chapters 38–39)*   285
    Chapter 26 *(mss. chapters 40–41)*   296
    Chapter 27 *(mss. chapter 42)*   299
    Chapter 28 *(mss. chapter 43)*   303
    Chapter 29 *(mss. chapters 44–45)*   307
    Chapter 30 *(mss. chapter 46)*   320
Appendix A: The Sheldon Ending   324
Appendix B: The Provisional Ending   334
Appendix C: Dating the Composition of *The Garden of Eden*   337
Works Cited   345
Index   362

ACKNOWLEDGMENTS

I am deeply grateful to my good friend Mark Cirino for the exemplary work he has done as editor for the Reading Hemingway series and for recruiting me to tackle this project, which I have enjoyed immensely. His own volume for this series, on *Across the River and into the Trees,* has been a model, and he has supported me consistently with encouragement, good humor, genuine interest, scholarly insight, wise counsel, and saintly patience. His close reading of my work has been invaluable, and without him this book would not have been possible.

For their support in innumerable small and large ways, I want to thank John Beall, Stephen Gilbert Brown, Don Daiker, Al DeFazio, Paul Hendrickson, J. Gerald Kennedy, Alberto Lena, Miriam Mandel, James H. Meredith, Gail Sinclair, and my many other friends in the Hemingway Society, who are too numerous to name. In particular, I want to thank Kirk Curnutt for his advice and reading, and for the inspiration provided by his volume on *To Have and Have Not* for this series; Suzanne del Gizzo, for her keen editorial eye; Alex Vernon, for a very helpful reading of my manuscript; Debra Moddelmog, for help on thinking about Hemingway, gender, and sexuality; Scott Donaldson, for helping with questions about Archibald MacLeish; Peter Hays, for his wise mentorship; Valerie Hemingway, for her graciousness in answering questions; Sandra Spanier and Verna Kale, for their kind help with Hemingway's letters; Fred Svoboda, for his generosity in sharing his research; Robert Trogdon, for his encyclopedic (and often hilarious) knowledge about Hemingway; and Susan Beegel and Linda Wagner-Martin, for their encouragement and dedication to helping young scholars, which I once was and for which I will be eternally grateful.

I want to thank Hilary Justice, Hemingway Scholar in Residence at the John F. Kennedy Presidential Library in Boston, for her friendship, for sharing ideas, and for spending an afternoon with me cataloging watermarks in the paper of the *Eden* manuscript. I also want to thank Stephen Plotkin, Stacey Chandler, Aimee Wismar, and Emily Mathay at the Kennedy Library, and I am indebted to the John F. Kennedy Library Foundation for an Ernest Hemingway Research Grant. For help answering questions about Hemingway's library at the Finca Vigía in Cuba, I am grateful to Mary Patrick Bogan, former Director of Book Conservation at the Northeast Document Conservation Center, and Grisell Fraga Leal, Directora del

Museo Ernest Hemingway at the Finca. For sharing valuable information from the Ketchum Community Library, I want to thank Jenny Emery Davidson. I am indebted to Tim Murray at the University of Delaware Library, Micaela Teronez at the Knox College Library, Christine Froula and Kevin Leonard at Northwestern University, Brianna Cregle at Princeton's Firestone Library, and Julie Bartlett Nelson at the Calvin Coolidge Presidential Library and Museum. And for work beyond the call of duty, my heartfelt thanks go to Dianna Johnson, Interlibrary Loan librarian at Appalachian State University.

One of the pleasures of writing this book was getting to know the fascinating array of people who helped me to research a dizzying variety of topics. I want to thank Jack Vitek, World Record Coordinator for the International Game Fishing Association, for sharing fishing records for European sea bass. For helping me to track (alas, unsuccessfully) the source of a joke about wing shooting, I am grateful to Pete Blakeley, Chris Batha, and Gary Kramer, all published experts on the topic, and to Cathie Simister, Research Officer at the British Association for Shooting and Conservation. Daniel Rancour-Laferriere helped me with translations of Tolstoy. Bookplate collector Lew Jaffe and art historian Efram Burk helped when I had questions about the history of bookplates. Sedimentologist and paleoenvironmental scientist Cynthia M. Liutkus-Pierce helped me to better understand the terrain around Kenya's Lake Magadi. Andrew Janquitto corresponded with me about the Jelke family's oleomargarine dynasty, and Warren Treadgold helped with a question about the mosaics at Torcello and Ravenna. Gabrielle Motta-Passajou and Jean-François Fournier helped answer questions about the French language, Kyle Stevens helped me with images of Falconetti, Susan Staub helped with paintings by Bosch, and Colin Ramsey helped me to appreciate the beauty and excitement of driving a 1927 Bugatti T35.

I want to thank all of my colleagues and friends in the English Department at Appalachian State University, especially Joseph Bathanti, Jessie Blackburn, Jim Burniston, Leonardo Flores, and Amy Greer. Their support has meant a great deal to me. Many thanks to my graduate research assistants Samantha Hunter, Virge Buck, and Vito Petruzzelli. I want to thank Harrison Brown for the beautiful maps he made for this volume. And I owe a special thanks to my good friend and colleague Tammy Wahpeconiah who listened to me prattle on about wherever my research was taking me.

My deepest gratitude is reserved for my wife and son for their constant love and support. By getting me out of the house and out fly-fishing, Paco helped keep me sane. He also taught me how to use the flight simulator in Google Earth and served as an able bush pilot for several virtual flights across Africa. (We crashed only a few more times than the Hemingways.) I could never have sustained my work on this project for so many years without the loving and infinitely patient and good-humored support of my wife, Linda. Paco and Linda, this book is for you.

INTRODUCTION TO *THE GARDEN OF EDEN*

In their introduction to *The New Hemingway Studies* (2020), reflecting on the 1986 publication of *The Garden of Eden,* editors Suzanne del Gizzo and Kirk Curnutt playfully rewrite Virginia Woolf's famous provocation about the advent of modernism: "On or about May 1986 Hemingway studies changed irrevocably . . ." (10). This, they admit, may be hyperbole; yet it isn't often that a single work—much less a posthumous one—so utterly revolutionizes our understanding of an author of Hemingway's stature. It isn't simply that Hemingway's exploration of gender and sexuality in this novel—even in the truncated and somewhat bowdlerized version published by Scribner's (a mere 40 percent of what Hemingway actually wrote)—stunned readers and early reviewers and forever annihilated the myth of Hemingway as the univocally heteronormative macho man of American literature. The novel, and the more complex understanding of Hemingway that emerged from it, had the power to seismically alter our perception of almost everything that came before it in Hemingway's career. Patterns long hidden in plain sight and ubiquitous in his work suddenly came into sharp focus, inspiring a generation of revisionist Hemingway scholarship, including Kenneth Lynn's 1987 biography of Hemingway, Mark Spilka's *Hemingway's Quarrel with Androgyny* (1990), Nancy Comley and Robert Scholes's *Hemingway's Genders* (1994), Rose Marie Burwell's *Hemingway: The Postwar Years and the Posthumous Novels* (1996), my own *Hemingway's Fetishism: Psychoanalysis and the Mirror of Manhood* (1999), Debra A. Moddelmog's *Reading Desire: In Pursuit of Ernest Hemingway* (1999), Thomas Strychacz's *Hemingway's Theaters of Masculinity* (2003), Richard Fantina's *Ernest Hemingway: Machismo and Masochism* (2005), and Hilary Justice's *The Bones of the Others: The Hemingway Text from the Lost Manuscripts to the Posthumous Novels* (2006). If for no other reason than this, *The Garden of Eden* is a landmark text in the history of twentieth-century American literature.

I do not pretend that *The Garden of Eden* is Hemingway's greatest novel, but I do think it was his bravest and most ambitious. Perhaps also his most interesting. Not only has the book revolutionized our understanding of gender and sexuality in Hemingway's work, it has transformed the way we look at race, colonialism, interspecies relations, self-exploration, memory, creativity, and a dozen other themes in his work. In Catherine Bourne, intrepid erotic explorer and frustrated artist, the novel offers us one of Hemingway's most complex and compelling female characters. In David Bourne, the novel offers us Hemingway's most penetrating analysis of the writer at work—with invaluable and moving insights into the sources, motives, rituals, pitfalls, and costs of creative production. *Eden* powerfully explores the writer's need for self-honesty—and the difficulty of achieving and sustaining it. Though occasionally dismissed by undiscerning readers as a novel merely about suntanning, swimming, and haircuts (admittedly, spiced by a gender-swapping ménage à trois), *The Garden of Eden*—however incomplete, unpolished, self-indulgent, repetitive, and deeply flawed—is a novel of remarkable emotional, intellectual, psychological, and artistic depth.

The kind of research and close reading demanded for a volume like the present one—a project that treats the 60 percent of the *Eden* manuscript left on the cutting-room floor with as much care as it devotes to the Scribner's edition—brings these strengths of the novel into sharper focus, and it cannot help but call attention to aspects of the novel which have until now been comparatively neglected. In writing this volume, I've been struck by Hemingway's meticulous attention—in spite of the occasional poetic license—to historical detail. Whether the subject be horse racing in Hong Kong, varieties of Chanel perfume, translations of Tolstoy, the behavior of pigeons, or the discovery of dinosaur eggs in Mongolia, he writes with a passion for historical detail and accuracy. And his range of reference is immense. In David Bourne, Hemingway created a writer-protagonist who could finally and convincingly give expression to his own wide interests and seemingly encyclopedic knowledge. The result is Hemingway's most allusive and intertextual novel and, with perhaps the exception of *Death in the Afternoon,* his work most deeply engaged with the arts. He gives free rein to his fascination with consumer culture and his passion for food and drink, and as always, he is scrupulous in the evocation and symbolic use of place. With a concern that should interest contemporary ecocritics, he paints a series of fragile Edenic landscapes, all balanced upon a precipice. This novel has given us a new Hemingway, and I hope the present volume will demonstrate how much it still has to teach us.

THE *EDEN* MANUSCRIPT AND THE SCRIBNER'S EDITION

My decision to reach beyond the 70,000 words published by Scribner's, to treat the full 200,000 words that Hemingway actually wrote, entails difficulties. I must often paraphrase content, and I must confine my use of language from the *Eden* manuscript to brief phrases and passages that have already appeared in published scholarship.[1] Yet these concessions are well worth the price. Readers are naturally most curious to read about the full novel Hemingway wrote. A great deal of Hemingway scholarship hinges upon details in the *Eden* manuscript, and we have long needed a volume that systematically and coherently clarifies the relationship between the Scribner's text and material from the *Eden* manuscript for readers without access to the massive, mostly holograph text in the Hemingway Collection at Boston's John F. Kennedy Presidential Library. The present volume attempts to do this—referring to the Scribner's edition wherever possible, but describing significant omissions from the manuscript and clarifying where they would "fit" into the version published by Scribner's. I hope this helps readers to better appreciate the trove of largely untapped riches still hidden in the manuscript: passages that clarify themes in the Scribner's edition or point to themes omitted there; passages that offer us some of the most intricate and highly personal symbolism in Hemingway's work; passages that importantly correct or qualify mistaken impressions produced by the Scribner's edition. I don't mind adding that in the process I hope to save the present volume from obsolescence—for I hope the full *Eden* manuscript will one day be published.

Since few readers have had the privilege of reading the entire manuscript, it makes sense to begin with a brief overview of the novel Hemingway wrote, noting where it departs from the Scribner's edition. *The Garden of Eden* manuscript begins, as does the Scribner's edition, with David and Catherine Bourne honeymooning at Le Grau-du-Roi, on the French Mediterranean. Scribner's editor Tom Jenks is largely faithful to the manuscript in these early chapters, with two important exceptions: (1) he omits the crucial role played by Rodin's statue *The Metamorphoses of Ovid* as an inspiration for the Bournes' erotic adventures, and (2) he significantly mutes the racial overtones Catherine brings to her passion for suntanning. More importantly, before the Bournes journey to Hendaye Plage, as they do next in the Scribner's edition, Book II of the manuscript (omitted in the Scribner's edition) takes us to bohemian Paris and introduces us to another young expatriate couple: the painters Nick and Barbara Sheldon. Inspired, like the Bournes, by Rodin's *Metamorphoses of Ovid,* they too are cutting their hair identically and experimenting with gender and sexuality. When David and Catherine arrive in Hendaye, in what is Book III of the manuscript (Book II of the Scribner's edition), they encounter the Sheldons, who are already friends with David. Catherine is shocked by the beauty of the Sheldons, and Barbara is equally stunned by Catherine, and the eight manuscript chapters set in Hendaye (condensed to two in the Scribner's edition, which omits the Sheldons and repurposes their dialogue) are largely devoted to the encounter between Catherine and Barbara and its resulting sexual tension.

When the Bournes arrive in Madrid, they encounter another of David's friends completely omitted in the Scribner's edition: the travel writer Andrew Murray. A former member of the volunteer ambulance service in World War I, Andy not only knows the Sheldons, but, along with David, he helped Nick to find his art dealer, and everyone knows he is in love with Barbara. Much as David is writing a honeymoon narrative about his adventures with Catherine, Andy is writing a book about the Sheldons. David and Catherine spend a good deal of time with Andy at cafés and restaurants, and he plays an important role in several conversations that appear (without him) in the Scribner's edition. In fact, in the seven manuscript chapters set in Madrid (reduced to three in the Scribner's edition), he plays a much larger role than does David's enigmatic old friend Colonel Boyle, who is retained in the Scribner's edition.

The Scribner's edition is far more faithful to the Bourne plot in the La Napoule section of the novel, when Marita joins the Bournes and David begins writing his African stories. Yet even here, the Scribner's edition deletes long passages focalized through Marita's consciousness, and it misleadingly edits her character to make her a more heteronormative counterbalance to Catherine's restless sexual experimentation. The Scribner's edition departs most drastically from the *Eden* manuscript, though, in its misleading conclusion, which it cobbles together from sentences and phrases from several different chapters of the manuscript to produce the impression that the novel's tensions are largely resolved—and resolved in the service of the conventional. In the Scribner's version, in rewriting his African stories, David restores his damaged identification with his father, recovers a more traditional and stable masculinity, and returns to heteronormativity with a Marita who promises to be his girl, his "good girl," and always his *girl*. In the manuscript, David does, of course, recover and rewrite his African stories—but this doesn't resolve anything. The manuscript just keeps going. David experiences no grand rapprochement with his father's memory, he wants and fully expects Catherine to return, and Marita—who has long wanted to cut her hair to be like the African girl in his stories—gets an ultra-short "African haircut" that "mixe[s] up the genders" (3.45.2). David tells her she doesn't have to do "Catherine things," but she assures him she can be his "girl" and "boy" both because that's how she really is. Where the Scribner's edition patches together two different lines from the manuscript to produce Marita's insistence on her stable girlhood, she is in fact, in the manuscript, noting her transition *back* to girlhood after having just made love with David in a configuration in which they were both boys.

Though the main body of the *Eden* manuscript trails off without a clear ending and with nothing resolved, Hemingway wrote endings for both the Bourne and the Sheldon plots that, well into the composition process, he still intended to use. Narrated by Andrew Murray, the Sheldon ending tells of Andy's springtime encounter with Nick and Barbara in Paris, where they are about to trim their hair identically. He next encounters them in August at Hendaye Plage, soon after he sees David and Catherine in Madrid. The Sheldons have matching shoulder-length haircuts that inspire homophobic anxiety in Nick even though he likes them and claims not to mind that everyone thinks he and Barbara are "queer." Barbara is mentally fragile after her encounter with Catherine earlier that summer, and while Nick busies himself with painting, she initiates an affair with Andy. When Nick, bicycling back from a painting expedition, is killed by a car while she is with Andy, she is devastated by guilt. Trying to care for her, Andy takes her to Venice, where she drowns herself.

What Hemingway called the "provisional ending" of the Bourne plot finds David and Catherine back on a Riviera beach, perhaps a year or two after the events narrated in the rest of the novel. There is no mention of Marita. Catherine is clearly in a fragile state and David is her caretaker. As she basks in the sun, Catherine tries to remember her sexual experiments and better days with David, when they "owned the world," but this Edenic feeling has been lost and her memories are fragmentary and damaged. She has apparently attempted suicide and spent time in a Swiss sanatorium. When she proposes a dip in the sea, she promises not to do anything "comic." David tries to convince her that she will recover, but she doesn't believe him. "Next time will be worse," she predicts *(422.2 1.8)*. She asks David if she can have a "surprise" again "like in the old days," and he agrees *(422.2 1.10)*. She then asks him, if she gets bad again, could she do what Barbara did? David says he couldn't let her, but when she asks if he'd do it with her, he agrees.

A WORD ABOUT FETISHISM

Because erotic fetishism is so central to *The Garden of Eden*—to its action, themes, language, and symbols; because on some level *The Garden of Eden* is *about* fetishistic desire; and because the subject recurs frequently in the pages that follow, an introductory word about it might be helpful here: to briefly define what it is and suggest what it can help us to understand about Hemingway's novel.

Long before I published *Hemingway's Fetishism* (1999), the fact that Hemingway was a hair fetishist was already generally acknowledged by Hemingway scholars. Whether they explicitly used the word *fetish* or not (most didn't), major biographers such as Carlos Baker (1969), Jeffrey Meyers (1985), Michael Reynolds (1986), Kenneth Lynn (1987), and James Mellow (1992)—even Mary Hemingway herself (1976)—all noted Hemingway's lifelong erotic obsession with hair. A glance at his major novels makes it clear. In *The Sun Also Rises* (1926), Brett Ashley wears her hair "brushed back like a boy's" and is even the inventor of this style: "She started all that" (30); Romero eventually asks her to grow it out to become more "womanly," but she refuses (246). During the Alpine idyll in *A Farewell to Arms* (1929), Frederic Henry grows excited as he watches Catherine, reflected in three mirrors, getting her hair waved, and together they plan to trim their hair identically so they can be "just alike only one of us blonde and one of us dark" (299). Marie Morgan's newly waved and bleached hair, in *To Have and Have Not* (1937), excites *Harry* so much that he immediately whisks her off to a hotel. In *For Whom the Bell Tolls* (1940), Robert Jordan gets choked up stroking Maria's cropped head and describes how they can cut their hair identically and admire each other in the mirror, to which Maria responds, "I would look like thee.... And then I would never want to change it" (345). When Colonel Cantwell, in *Across the River and into the Trees* (1950), isn't drinking at *Harry's* Bar or staring at Renata's portrait in the mirror, he is waxing ecstatic over her wind-blown hair. In the restored edition of *A Moveable Feast*, published posthumously in 2009, Ernest and Hadley indulge in "secret pleasures," "cut[ting] each other's hair and let[ting] it grow to the same length"; stroking Hadley's newly cut hair makes Ernest's fingers shake (186, 188). In a chapter Hemingway deleted from the *Islands in the Stream* manuscript (posth.), Thomas Hudson's first wife cuts his hair just like her own so in bed he can become her "girl"—and her "girl," she tells him, "has to be a boy" (JFK Item 112).[2] Such fantasies culminate in *The Garden of Eden* (posth.), where the action of the novel is driven and punctuated by a series of haircuts that turn David and Catherine into mirror images of one another and somehow allow them to swap gender identities in bed.

It has now been twenty-five years since I published *Hemingway's Fetishism,* and I have never been comfortable with the pathologizing connotations of the language used to describe erotic fetishism. I wish I could report that I have found an alternative language, free of links to the coercive and stigmatizing rhetoric of early twentieth-century sexology, but I have not. To some degree, the problem is simply that a systematic explanation of *any* organized psychology inevitably turns it into a "condition," with all that entails. Given the poverty of our language for understanding the range of human sexual experience, the discourse of fetishism, in spite of its problematic connotations, enables a type of understanding—hardly totalizing, but important—that can't be approached through more flexible, contemporary, and non-psychologizing terms such as *queer* and *trans.* The only alternative to it seems to be a form of silence—silence about something that mattered deeply to Hemingway, something central to *The Garden of Eden.*[3]

As Debra Moddelmog has noted, Hemingway was an avid and lifelong reader of sexology, which he found both liberating and confining. As a young man, he responded enthusiastically to Havelock Ellis, in 1920 sending a copy of *Erotic Symbolism* to his friend Bill Smith (Reynolds, *Young* 120); in January 1921, he sent a copy of *Studies in the Psychology of Sex,* which he had "urged unsuccessfully on all his friends," to the woman who would become his first wife, Hadley Richardson, following up in April with three more volumes of Ellis (Reynolds, *Young* 184–85). As David explains about Nick's haircut in the *Eden* manuscript, "Everybody has strange things that mean things to them and we have to understand them" (see *[47:18] 3.7.5).* These things were important to Hemingway. Marita, late in the *Eden* manuscript, thinks, "there must be many people that are like us. . . . Maybe everyone is like us"; no, that can't be, she reflects, but there must be many (3.45.10). Hemingway clearly felt the importance of exploring and expressing his own desire—indeed, of expressing the complexity and range of human desire—and silence on the topic does him no favors. Yet he did push back against the stigmatizing connotations of sexological language. Moddelmog has argued, importantly, that Hemingway (unsuccessfully) resisted sexology's pathologizing tendencies by such strategies as reimagining his characters in tribal or utopian spaces, "replacing sexology's scientific taxonomies with more metaphorical and individualistic possibilities," and replacing words like "perversion" with "variety. . . . infinite variety" (see [244:2] 3.45.4).[4] In this spirit, I hope it is clear that I intend in no way to pathologize or stigmatize fetishism and fetishistic cross-dressing, even if I recognize that the language used to describe it cannot be entirely purged of such associations.

To be sure, in the past twenty-five years the language used to describe fetishism and fetishistic cross-dressing has changed. The word "transvestite," now considered offensive, was replaced with "fetishistic cross-dresser," now almost always shortened to "cross-dresser." (The word "transvestic" has been retained, however, because there is no other adjectival form of "cross-dresser.") The 11th edition of the *GLAAD Media Reference Guide* now labels "cross-dresser" as an "older term that replaced the offensive word 'transvestite'"—but it offers no newer alternative. This important resistance to pathologizing labels and to the confusion and conflation of sexual practices with identities, however, has an effect of erasure—whereas Hemingway's novel clearly aims to make this form of desire visible. (Hemingway's experience and that of his characters in *Eden* fits within the umbrella of what has come to be called bi-gender experience—feeling two genders, sometimes alternatingly, sometimes simultaneously—but that term is capacious and not necessarily synonymous with "cross-dresser.") I have retained the older term "fetishistic cross-dressing" in this volume for several reasons. First, more clearly than the shortened term, it distinguishes between fetishistic cross-dressing, drag, and transgender experience. (Cross-dressers are not drag queens or kings, nor are trangender people cross-dressers.) More importantly, the term "fetishistic cross-dressing" clarifies the essential link to Hemingway's more obvious fetishism and somewhat de-emphasizes the importance of dress. For while Catherine and David Bourne occasionally derive fetishistic satisfaction from dressing identically (see 6:3), what is essential to facilitating cross-gender identification for them and for fetishistic cross-dressers is wearing the fetish. This fetish may be an item of clothing, or a complete set of clothing, but it need not be. In Hemingway's case, and in the case of the Bournes, it was cut or dyed hair. What David Bourne experiences in the mirror when he becomes a "Danish girl" after cutting and dyeing his hair to match Catherine's is no less a form of cross-dressing because it ignores items of traditional female attire. To clarify why this is so, a brief definition of fetishism is in order.

An erotic fetish—as opposed to a Marxist commodity fetish or the anthropological fetishes of so-called primitive religion (and it's important not to confuse and conflate such disparate phenomena)—is an obligatory prop, usually a nongenital body part or an item of clothing with bodily attributes, that is essential for the fetishist's sexual gratification.[5] This in itself might seem simple enough, but as Catherine says of her surprise haircut in *Eden*, "Oh it's very simple but it's very complicated" (11:18). Among other things, the fetish is a tool used to maintain a divided attitude, or disavowal, towards sexual difference—simultaneously acknowledging and denying it. When worn by the partner (fetishism proper), the fetish disavows sexual difference in the partner; when worn by the self, often in front of a mirror (fetishistic cross-dressing), it disavows sexual difference in the self. This helps explain how a haircut can turn Catherine into a "boy," or a "girl and a boy both" (192:25), and how David can become "Catherine" when Catherine becomes "Peter." These double names—David/Catherine and Catherine/Peter—point to a feature central to fetishism and fetishistic cross-dressing: a splitting of the ego along gendered lines. In a moment of cross-gender identification, a fetishistic cross-dresser often gives expression to an alter ego with its own name and attributes of personality. And, because the fetishist and his partner can oscillate between "boyish" and "girlish" positions (Hemingway insists on a binary dichotomy of boy/girl, as opposed to a man/woman or male/female, for these roles), they can make love in any of four possible permutations: boy-girl, girl-boy, girl-girl, or boy-boy. These combinations—particularly the same-sex ones—in their turn are further complicated by disavowal. For the fetishist sometimes recognizes a current of homoerotic desire in the self that he simultaneously tries to deny (often quite homophobically) since he understands himself and his partner to be biologically heterosexual regardless of whatever roles they may play. The "remorse" that David suffers after such combinations (see 68:11) may strike readers as little more than homophobia—a sort of old-fashioned heterosexist moralizing that Catherine dismisses as "thinking in terms of Lutherans and Calvinists and St. Paul" (see *[136:13] 3.23.25bis*)—but this is only half of the picture: because fetishistic desire depends upon a sensation of transgression, it is often paradoxically invested in the so-called rules it must transgress. It is structured by both sides of a divided attitude (see *[5:22] 1.1.3*).

Rooted in infancy—in Hemingway's case, with a mother who tried in many ways to raise Ernest as the identical "twin" of his older sister, Marcelline (almost always with identical haircuts)—the fetish turns trauma into triumph, converting an experience that once threatened the fetishist's gender identity into the prerequisite for a masculinity-confirming erection.[6] Whereas the matching haircuts and pseudotwinning with Marcelline so disturbed a three-and-a-half-year-old Ernest that his mother recorded his fear that Santa Claus wouldn't know if he were a boy or a girl (Lynn 45), Catherine and David Bourne can think of nothing more exciting than identical haircuts that, according to the *Eden* manuscript, make David look like Catherine's "twin brother" (*3.32.12*). Yet far more complicated than a mere triumphant repetition of childhood trauma, the "fetish is a story disguised as an object" (Stoller 155). It is a highly overdetermined symbol and tool used to negotiate and regulate many aspects of the fetishist's identity. These complexities, too numerous and intricate to explore in this introduction, will emerge in separate entries throughout this book, and they will help us to address a wide array of themes, motifs, and symbols in *Eden:* lovers who are mistaken for "brother and sister" (6:6);

characters who claim to be "riven" (183:19); characters who try to merge identities; the Bournes' fascination with mirrors; their obsession with suntanning and fantasies of racial transformation; the characters' attraction to lesbian love and anxiety about male homosexuality; the significance of ivory hair; and the haunting specters of sin, ruin, destruction, and remorse.

I have now been writing about *The Garden of Eden* for almost thirty years, and it still fascinates me. No doubt, this reveals an obsessive strain in my character; yet it also speaks to the depth, complexity, and power of this posthumous novel. Yes, it is deeply flawed—a challenge for readers used to reading only finished works of art—yet its courage and rich beauty are inspiring, and it offers us a glimpse into Hemingway, both as an artist and a man, that could hardly have been imagined before its publication. I hope this volume will help readers to more deeply appreciate what Hemingway's novel has to offer.

NOTES

1. Fortunately, a great many short passages from the manuscript have appeared in published scholarship. The following sources were particularly helpful in this respect: Broer; Burwell; Cheatle; Comley; Comley and Scholes; Eby, *HF* and the several essays listed in the works cited; Fantina; Fleming, "Endings"; Gajdusek; Hermann; Justice; Kennedy; Moddelmog, *Reading*; Nesmith; Roe, *Artist* and "Opening"; Scafella; Schmidt; Solomon; Spilka; Strong, "Go to Sleep"; and Wyatt.
2. For a synopsis of this section of the *Islands* manuscript, see *HF* 263–68.
3. Readers tempted to resist psychoanalytic accounts of fetishism as "dated" should note that alternative accounts are almost nonexistent. More recent psychological models have established themselves, in part, by focusing elsewhere and have little to say about fetishism. Psychoanalytic models remain the best and most current account of fetishism, and I would argue that fetishism remains the paradigm case for psychoanalytic thinking.
4. I am citing here an as yet unpublished essay by Moddelmog. I am grateful for her generosity in sharing this with me and for helping me to think through these issues.
5. Paul Gebhard usefully distinguishes between four levels of fetishistic intensity:

> Level 1: A slight preference for certain kinds of sex partners, sexual stimuli, or sexual activity. The term "fetish" should not be used at this level.
> Level 2: A strong preference for certain kinds of sex partners, sexual stimuli or sexual activity (Lowest intensity of fetishism).
> Level 3: Specific stimuli are necessary for sexual arousal and sexual performance (Moderate intensity of fetishism).
> Level 4: Specific stimuli take the place of a sex partner (High-level fetishism). (qtd. in Gamman and Makinen 38)

At levels three and four, fetishism begins to slide seamlessly into fetishistic cross-dressing.
6. For this aspect of the fetish, see Stoller 27. For the pseudotwinning of Ernest and Marcelline, see Marcelline Hemingway Sanford's *At the Hemingways;* see also Lynn, Spilka, and *HF*.

ABBREVIATIONS USED IN THIS BOOK

ABBREVIATIONS FOR THE WORKS OF ERNEST HEMINGWAY

- ARIT   *Across the River and into the Trees.* Scribner's, 1950.
- BL   *By-Line Ernest Hemingway: Selected Articles and Dispatches of Four Decades.* Edited by William White, Scribner's, 1967.
- CSS   *The Complete Short Stories of Ernest Hemingway: The Finca Vigía Edition.* Scribner's, 1987.
- DIA   *Death in the Afternoon.* Scribner's, 1932.
- DLT   *Dateline: Toronto: The Complete Toronto Star Dispatches, 1920–1924.* Edited by William White, Scribner's, 1985.
- DPDH   *Dear Papa, Dear Hotch: The Correspondence of Ernest Hemingway and A. E. Hotchner.* Edited by Albert J. DeFazio, Missouri UP, 2005.
- EHWW   "Ernest Hemingway." *Writers at Work: The* Paris Review *Interviews: Second Series,* edited by George Plimpton, Penguin, 1977, pp. 215–39.
- FC   *The Fifth Column and the First Forty-Nine Stories.* Scribner's, 1938.
- FTA   *A Farewell to Arms.* 1929. Scribner's, 1995.
- FWBT   *For Whom the Bell Tolls.* Scribner's, 1940.
- GOE   *The Garden of Eden.* Scribner's, 1986.
- GHOA   *Green Hills of Africa.* Scribner's, 1935.
- HMF   *Hemingway and the Mechanism of Fame: Statements, Public Letters, Introductions, Forewords, Prefaces, Blurbs, Reviews, and Endorsements.* Edited by Matthew J. Bruccoli with Judith S. Baughman, U of South Carolina P, 2006.
- IIS   *Islands in the Stream.* Scribner's, 1970.
- Letters 1   *The Letters of Ernest Hemingway, 1907–1922.* Edited by Sandra Spanier and Robert Trogdon, vol. 1, Cambridge UP, 2011.
- Letters 2   *The Letters of Ernest Hemingway, 1923–1925.* Edited by Sandra Spanier et al., vol. 2, Cambridge UP, 2013.
- Letters 3   *The Letters of Ernest Hemingway, 1926–1929.* Edited by Rena Sanderson et al., vol. 3, Cambridge UP, 2015.

Letters 4	*The Letters of Ernest Hemingway, 1929–1931.* Edited by Sandra Spanier and Miriam Mandel, vol. 4, Cambridge UP, 2017.
Letters 5	*The Letters of Ernest Hemingway, 1932–1934.* Edited by Sandra Spanier and Miriam Mandel, vol. 5, Cambridge UP, 202.
MF-RE	*A Moveable Feast: The Restored Edition.* Edited by Sean Hemingway, Scribner's, 2009.
MAW	*Men at War: The Best War Stories of All Time.* Edited by Ernest Hemingway, Wing Books, 1992.
NAS	*The Nick Adams Stories.* Edited by Philip Young, Scribner's, 1973.
SAR	*The Sun Also Rises.* 1926. Scribner's, 1995.
SAR Fac	*The Sun Also Rises: A Facsimile Edition,* part I. Edited by Matthew Bruccoli, Omnigraphics, 1990.
SL	*Ernest Hemingway: Selected Letters, 1917–1961.* Edited by Carlos Baker, Scribner's, 1981.
THHN	*To Have and Have Not.* Scribner's, 1937.
UK	*Under Kilimanjaro.* Edited by Robert W. Lewis and Robert E. Fleming, Kent State UP, 2005.

OTHER ABBREVIATIONS USED

HF	Eby, Carl. *Hemingway's Fetishism: Psychoanalysis and the Mirror of Manhood.* SUNY Press, 1999.
HIW	Hemingway, Mary. *How It Was.* Knopf, 1976.
IndU	Lilly Library, Indiana University, Bloomington.
JFK	Hemingway Collection at the John F. Kennedy Presidential Library and Museum, Boston, MA.
LOC	Library of Congress, Washington, DC.
PUL	Department of Rare Books and Special Collections, Princeton University Library, Princeton, NJ.
UT	Harry Ransom Center, University of Texas at Austin.

SERIES NOTE

All page references in this volume are keyed to the page and line numbers of the first edition of the novel, published by Charles Scribner's Sons in 1986. Chapter 1 begins on page 3, and the final words of chapter 30 end on page 247. Line numbers begin with the first line of each page. Annotations are given a page and line number, separated by a colon. A reference to a passage beginning on the third line on page 17, for instance, would be 17:3.

Because this is a posthumous novel and the Scribner's edition deletes 60 percent of what Hemingway wrote, I have included entries to treat significant deletions from the manuscript. These first indicate in parentheses where the passage would "fit" in the Scribner's edition, then the book, chapter, and page number in the primary *Eden* manuscript in the Hemingway Collection at the John F. Kennedy Presidential Library in Boston (item 422.1). (It should be noted that the division of the novel into books and chapters differs considerably in the Scribner's and manuscript versions. This can be immediately grasped by a glance at the contents page for this volume.) Thus *(163:23) 3.27.26* indicates a passage that comes from book 3, chapter 27, page 26 of manuscript 422.1, and it would fit into the Scribner's edition on page 163 at line 23. (By "fit," I mean that text on line 22 of the Scribner's edition appears before the given manuscript passage, and text on line 24 of the Scribner's edition appears after that passage in the manuscript.) In those few instances when I need to cite a manuscript other than 422.1, I list the manuscript item number. I italicize page numbers and note headings for citations from the manuscript to remind readers that they are from the manuscript, not the Scribner's edition.

Manuscript item 422.4 at the Kennedy Library contains draft pages that originated in the main manuscript (item 422.1) before being discarded. Most are early drafts of passages that Hemingway revised and retained. The Hemingway Collection catalog mistakenly assigns all of these scattered discards to chapters 24 and 25 of the manuscript; they, in fact originated anywhere between chapters 11 and 43 of book 3 of item 422.1. Using clues from action, pagination, repeated language, composition dates, and physical paper, I have been able to identify where each of these discarded pages originated in the main manuscript, and because this information is more useful than the random disorder of the discard folder (item 422.4), I have identified passages from the discard folder as follows: *(57:10) 422.4 3.13.10.*

This numbering means that this is an item that would "fit" in the Scribner's edition on page 57, line 10; it comes from the discard folders (item 422.4) and is numbered page 10, but corresponds to book 3, chapter 13 of the main manuscript (item 422.1).

Occasionally, questions of pagination in the manuscript can be complicated. For instance, a chapter may contain two or more undeleted pages bearing the same page number. When one of these pages is not clearly marked as an insert but follows smoothly from the other and leads smoothly into the page that follows, this is indicated by the word *bis* (Latin for "twice"). Thus, *3.5.8bis* refers to a second page 8 in book 3, chapter 5; and *3.5.8bis2* refers to a third page 8 in book 3, chapter 5. Hemingway also often inserted pages in the manuscript at a later stage of revision. As a rule, the placement of these inserts is clearly marked in the manuscript, and these pages are signified by the letter *i*. Thus, *3.14.19ii* signifies the second page of the insert to book 3, chapter 14, page 19. In citing material from the manuscript, I have either paraphrased, cited passages previously published elsewhere, or confined myself to quoting short phrases.

MAPS

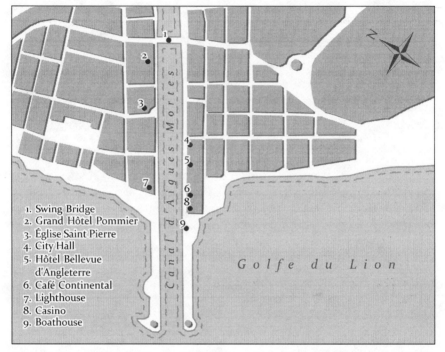

Map of Le Grau-du-Roi, by Harrison Brown. Based on a 1930 map produced for a regional government council.

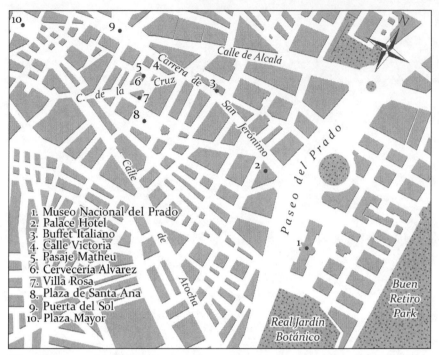

Map of downtown Madrid, by Harrison Brown, featuring places mentioned in the *Eden* manuscript. Based on a map from Bertaux's 1921 *Blue Guide* to Spain and Portugal.

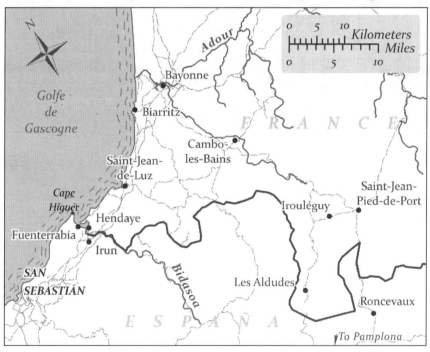

Map of the Basque Coast, by Harrison Brown, featuring locations mentioned in this book.

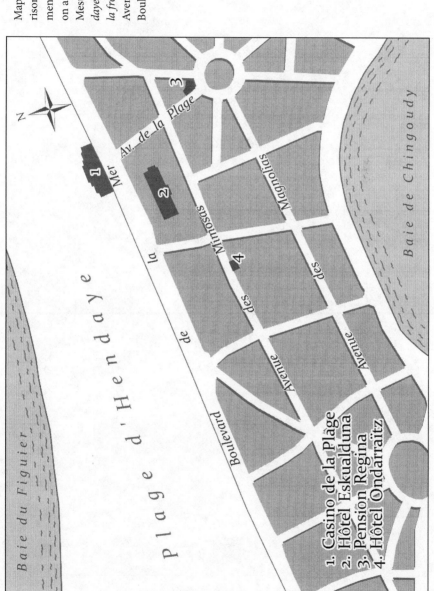

Map of Hendaye Plage, by Harrison Brown, featuring locations mentioned in this book. Based on a period map from Culot, Mesuret, and Delaunay's *Hendaye, Irún, Fontarabie: Villes de la frontière*. What was then the Avenue de la Plage is today the Boulevard du Général Leclerc.

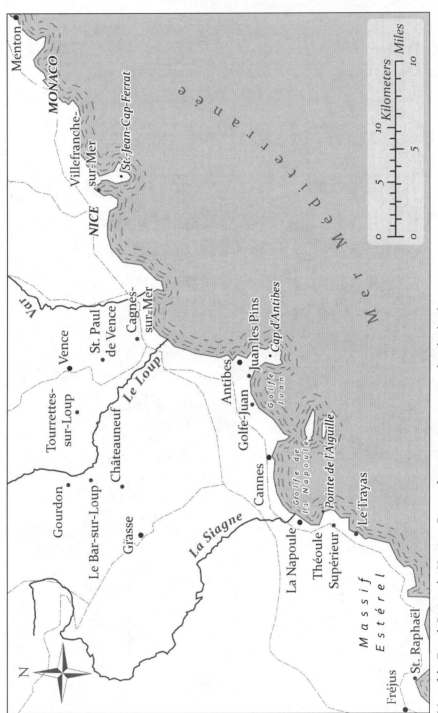

Map of the French Riviera, by Harrison Brown, featuring sites mentioned in this book.

Reading *The Garden of Eden*

FRONT MATTER

Title: Hemingway often came up with titles for his novels after making and sifting through long lists of possibilities late in the composition process. Such was not the case with *The Garden of Eden*. Hemingway seems to have settled on this theme, if not this precise title, by June 1948, and the myth of Eden is woven deeply into the fabric of the novel (Baker 460).

Given the novel's fascination with "innocence" and "wickedness," its temptress nicknamed "Devil," its fig-leaf-free sunbathing by a young couple whose life together begins as a cycle of eating, drinking, and making merry in bed—not to mention its forbidden fruit of sexual experimentation and David's locked suitcase—the action of the novel clearly invites comparison with the biblical story of Eden. Yet the degree to which the novel both invites and resists allegorizing readings can be seen in the range of critical response. Catherine has been read variously as Eve, serpent, and Satan—or "Eve and serpent rolled into one." She's been read as Lilith to Marita's Eve, and the manuscript's Barbara Sheldon has been read as another Eve, though she admits to "deviling" Andy. Even David, the obvious Adam, has been read (quite cleverly) as Eve.[1] Like Rodin's *Gates of Hell* set amid the Edenic gardens of the Hôtel Biron (see *[17:22] 1.1.21*), the novel suggests that "all things truly wicked start from an innocence" (*MF-RE* 217). Yet it's not simply that one can only "fall" from a comparative "innocence"—or that "innocence" is unknowable as such except from a postlapsarian position. Rather, as in Bosch's triptych *The Garden of Earthly Delights,* with its simultaneous depictions of Eden, earthly pleasure, and hell (see *[54:23] 3.10.4*), the novel sees innocence and sin as inextricably intertwined: "both narratologically sequential and oscillatingly simultaneous. . . . Hemingway and his characters are at odds with themselves—not so much *uncertain* as just profoundly *divided*—about what constitutes 'innocence' . . . and 'sin'" (Eby, "Gardens" 73–74). The Edenic condition can be "lost"; yet it is always already lost, and in a sort of felix culpa this very loss fuels David's creativity.

Wherever the Bournes turn, their world is an endangered Eden. Le Grau-du-Roi is a sleepy, undiscovered beach resort on the cusp of development (see 6:10 and 6:11). Places like Cannes-Eden (a neighborhood of Cannes) and Juan-les-Pins (with nearby Eden Roc)—indeed the entire Riviera—are on the verge of a tourism and

3

building boom that threatens to spoil the entire coast (see 6:9 and 86:30). As for Théoule, where the Bournes stay outside of La Napoule, the title of a 1927 editorial in *Comoedia* warned of its imminent overdevelopment: "An Eden to Be Saved: A Plea for Théoule" (see 75:2). David's Africa is an even more obvious Eden, defiled by the colonialists who slaughter both its native animals and people (see 197:14). His story of the "massacre in the crater" (223:3) gains meaning by its contrast with manuscript references to Ngorongoro Crater, famed for its teaming wildlife as "Africa's Eden." And nearby, within the Ngorongoro conservation area, lay the fossilized bones of a still older Eden: Olduvai Gorge, made famous by paleoanthropologist Louis Leakey and celebrated during Hemingway's lifetime as the "birthplace of the human race" (see *[210:16] 3.38.16;* see also *[244:25] 3.45.22*). As Andy says of the Sheldons in the manuscript: "The things they did were primitive. . . . It was all very primitive" *(422.2 3.10).*

Publisher's Note: With the posthumous publication of *A Moveable Feast* (1964), *Islands in the Stream* (1970), *The Dangerous Summer* (1985), *The Garden of Eden* (1986), *True at First Light* (1999), and *Under Kilimanjaro* (2005), Hemingway has been nearly as prolific from the grave as he was in life, and similar publisher's notes appear in the front matter to *A Moveable Feast* and *Islands in the Stream*. It might be argued, however, that this one adds an unintended prefatory note of comedy to *The Garden of Eden*. "Some cuts in the manuscript" somewhat understates the deletion of 65 percent of the full manuscript, slimming it from over 200,000 words to a little over 70,000. The scale of understatement is rendered only a little less comic if we take into account material Hemingway clearly deleted, or set aside, himself; then, only 59 percent of the manuscript was deleted by Scribner's editor, Tom Jenks. As Jenks himself has noted, "Some routine copy editing corrections" similarly fails to convey the deletion of an extensive subplot with Nick and Barbara Sheldon and their friend Andrew Murray, the deletion of entire chapters from the Bourne plot, and the deletion and occasional transposition of paragraphs, phrases, and words (10).

The claim, however, that "beyond a very small number of minor interpolations for clarity and consistency, nothing has been added" does, in fact, hold up. Where Jenks adds words—and this has been done very sparingly—it has almost always been done for clarity and consistency, and it is almost always well justified. (For notable exceptions, see 37:10, 67:18, 86:22, 140:19, and 244:17.) More important, even with the extensive editing, the claim that "in every significant respect the work is all the author's" is also accurate. We don't have the entirety of what Hemingway wrote, but what we *do* have Hemingway *did* write. It is, of course, impossible to edit a manuscript this radically without sacrificing and altering themes and subtle (and not so subtle) shades of meaning throughout the text, but with a few notable exceptions—the loss of the Sheldon and Andrew Murray subplot, the truly misleading editing of the novel's conclusion to manufacture a false reestablishment of heteronormativity, and the deletion of what Hemingway called the "provisional ending" of the novel—these losses are comparatively minor. For Tom Jenks, even these larger losses were the necessary and acceptable casualties demanded to complete his mission: to produce a coherent and compelling trade press novel from this sprawling and incomplete manuscript without adding new material.

In fact, the greatest injustice in the publisher's note may be to Tom Jenks, not Hemingway. The note fails to credit him in any way for a brilliant trade press edit. The job Jenks did hewing out and piecing together a lean and coherent novel from the *Eden* manuscript is nothing if not masterful. Even where he trimmed Hemingway's sentences—as he did often—the result is almost invariably an improvement. If Hemingway had edited his own manuscript into the trade press novel we now have, his editorial work would regularly be the subject of laudatory scholarly attention—though with pointed critique, undoubtedly, aimed at the novel's conclusion. When general readers have access to the entire manuscript Hemingway wrote, readers will gain a much richer understanding of Hemingway's ambitions and accomplishments and of this novel. Even then, however, the trade press edit produced by Tom Jenks will remain the more frequently read version of the novel.

NOTE

1. For Catherine as Eve, see Spilka 287. For Catherine as Satan, see Jones 7. For Catherine as serpent, see Silbergleid 107. For Catherine as both Eve and serpent, see Updike 88, Peters 19, and Eby, "Who Is" 99. For Catherine as both Eve and Satan, see Comley and Scholes 52. For Catherine as Lilith to Marita's Eve, see Powell 80 and Burwell 111. For David as Eve, see Putnam 129.

BOOK I (*MSS. BOOK I*)

CHAPTER 1 (MSS. CHAPTER 1)

3:1 **They ... then:** The novel begins, like so many Hemingway narratives, in a fragmentary fashion, with a *they* and a *then* without clear antecedents, drawing us immediately into the text and forcing us to ask who "they" are and when was "then." The *they* quickly becomes clear, but the *then* is more challenging.

The preponderance of evidence suggests that the action begins a few days after May 20, 1927. The fiestas of Seville and San Isidro in Madrid have recently finished (see 30:7)—the latter of which, San Isidro, ended on May 20 in 1927—and the manuscript indicates that David and Catherine attended the celebration of Saint Sarah (May 24) in Les Saintes-Maries-de-la-Mer, an easy bicycle ride from Le Grau-du-Roi (see *[53:31] 3.9.11*). It was in 1927 that Hemingway honeymooned with his second wife, Pauline, in Le Grau-du-Roi, and despite at least a dozen significant anachronisms (each noted in context), there are innumerable indications that *Eden* takes place in that year. The manuscript's most jarring anachronisms—such as a brief suggestion that the events recorded take place in 1923 or 1924 *(422.2 2.4)*—appear in material that Hemingway clearly deleted, though he occasionally takes poetic license to work in a reference to a favorite bullfighter, racehorse, or memorable incident from his life.[1]

While the historical accuracy of the novel is far more striking than its anachronisms, it is good to remember that it blends and reimagines Hemingway's memories of three different periods in his marriages to his first and second wives, Hadley Richardson and Pauline Pfeiffer. For the Sheldon subplot, deleted from the published novel, he drew heavily upon memories of his marriage to Hadley in Paris before 1926. The Sheldons sound very much like the Ernest and Hadley we know from the "Secret Pleasures" chapter of the "restored edition" of *A Moveable Feast*. For the Bourne plot and the love triangle with Marita, Hemingway blends memories of his May 1927 honeymoon with Pauline with memories of the summer of 1926 when Ernest, Hadley, and Pauline stayed together at Juan-les-Pins. "Here it was," Hadley recalled, "that the three breakfast trays, three wet bathing suits on the line, three bicycles were to be found. Pauline tried to teach me to dive, but I was not a success. ... We spent all morning on the beach sunning or swimming, lunched in our little garden. After siesta time there were long bicycle rides along the Golfe de Juan" (qtd. in Kert 181).

A still more important reason for some temporal ambiguity is Hemingway's desire to evoke a prelapsarian summer Riviera before the invasion of American tourists—a Riviera that was already starting to disappear in 1927. Hemingway was writing about a paradise on the verge of being lost.

3:1 **le Grau du Roi:** A small fishing village and nascent seaside resort, Le Grau-du-Roi in 1926 had a population of 1,348 (Berne 92).[2] Situated to the west of the Rhône delta, the village is neatly bisected by a straight canal, La Grande Roubine, which ends in two balanced jetties projecting out into the Gulf of Lions. The canal links Le Grau-du-Roi to the walled medieval city of Aigues-Mortes, four miles inland, and to the Canal du Rhône à Sète beyond.

Shortly after their 10 May 1927 wedding, Ernest and Pauline Hemingway, like the Bournes, honeymooned in Le Grau-du-Roi. Ernest wrote to Max Perkins on 27 May, "This is a fine place below Aigues-Mortes on the Camargue and the Mediterranean with a long beach and a fine fishing port. . . . Am healthy and working well and it ought to be a good summer" (*Letters 3* 241). While in Le Grau-du-Roi, Ernest finished two short stories: "Ten Indians" and "Hills Like White Elephants." He and Pauline were back in Paris by 7 June. Le Grau-du-Roi remained a special place for Hemingway, and he returned in 1949, probably in 1954, and again in 1959.[3]

Le Grau-du-Roi sometime between 1924 and 1928, after it became an official *station balnéaire et climatique* but before the expansion of its casino (first building on right). The Hôtel Bellevue d'Angleterre is the tall building to the left of center. (Photo by C. Denue. Image from the author's collection.)

Le Grau-du-Roi, taken sometime after 1948. A restaurant, which once stood on the bulge in the left jetty, has been demolished, and the casino, the building closest to the jetty on the right, has been expanded (see 6:11). Aigues-Mortes is visible in the distance in the upper left. (Photo by J. Cellard. Image from the author's collection.)

3:1 **hotel . . . canal:** The fact that the hotel faces the canal and the lighthouse (4:2) and that the view from the window of the Bournes' room looks toward the town and beach of Palavas in the west (4:6), establishes that the Bournes are staying at the Hôtel Bellevue d'Angleterre. In 1927, Hemingway and Pauline stayed at the more modest Grand Hôtel Pommier (in spite of its imposing title, just a small pension) on the opposite side of the canal, although he addressed letters from the more upscale Bellevue d'Angleterre (Simien 28, 35; *Letters 3* 239). During their 1949 visit to Le Grau-du-Roi, Ernest and Mary Hemingway stayed at the Bellevue d'Angleterre, which remains in business and is much closer than the Pommier was to the jetty. If the Bournes were staying at the Pommier, David wouldn't wonder if the fish he catches will take him "through the length of the town" (9:8); David would have already passed through the length of the town by the time he passed beneath his hotel window.

3:2 **walled city of Aigues Mortes:** Regarded by many as "the finest monument in existence of mediaeval military architecture," Aigues-Mortes in 1926 had a population of 3,959 (Muirhead and Monmarché 125, 126). Enclosed within a rectangular mile-long perimeter of twenty-five- to thirty-foot crenellated walls, with fifteen towers and the grand Tour de Constance beyond the city walls, Aigues-Mortes was begun in the 1240s by Louis IX to give the Capetian monarchy its first Mediterranean port. When the port silted up in the fourteenth century, upkeep proved too expensive and the town gradually became an untouched backwater. In a 1949 letter to Charles Scribner, Hemingway described the town as "a hell of a place."

> The only old fortified town that has ever remained intact without ever being restored. They never let [famous romantic nineteenth-century restoration architect] Viollette le Duc [sic] get his hands on it.[4] Where Saint Louis took off for the Seventh and Eighth Crusades that you must be familiar with from Froissard's Chronicles.[5] He picked up the old Rale on the first one and probably amoebic and died on the second; son finished building the town. St. Louis needed it for a port and supply base when the Dukes of Burgundy held Marseilles and le Grau du Roi was the only port he had. . . . I always love it down there. . . . (*SL* 683)

When Hemingway narrowly missed visiting Aigues-Mortes in 1953 because his boat from Marseille to Africa changed departure dates, he wrote to Bernard Berenson, "Christ I wish I could paint. I was painting that town in my head with the crusaders offloading their baggage and their piss pots to leave from le Grau du Roi. I remember that crusade so well that I always have to be careful not to say I made it" (*SL* 824). Hemingway's association of the town with the Crusades may also connect it with what he called "irregular sex lives." In *Death in the Afternoon,* Hemingway explains (incorrectly) that "syphilis was the disease of the crusaders in the middle ages. It was

The walled city of Aigues-Mortes. In the foreground, the Tour de Constance and the canal to le Grau-du-Roi. (Editions S. L., Lyon/Villeurbanne. Image from the author's collection.)

supposed to be brought to Europe by them, and it is a disease of all people who lead lives in which a disregard of consequences dominates. It is an industrial accident, to be expected by all those who lead irregular sexual lives . . ." (*DIA* 101).[6]

3:4 **across the low plain:** These "cities of the plain," Le Grau-du-Roi and Aigues-Mortes, may be the first of several allusions to Proust's *Remembrance of Things Past*. Hemingway owned Book IV, *Sodome et Gomorrhe,* in the original French as well as in Moncrieff's 1927 translation, *Cities of the Plain.* In the *Eden* manuscript, Catherine, who later wears a white sharkskin dress that David thinks of as her "pillar of salt suit" (see 65:26), is reading Proust. Although she promises David that she won't skip ahead in her reading, she "naturally" wants to read *Sodome et Gomorrhe* first (3.9.3). (She uses the French title.)

The allusion to *Remembrance of Things Past* is complex, but as with a later allusion to W. H. Hudson's *Far Away and Long Ago*—which Catherine and David both read (see [76:14] 3.16.11)—it suggests an autobiographical subtext to the novel, and suggests the importance in the present of a deep past that informs the African stories David will later write. As David works on these African stories, we see a Proustian interest in the reciprocal influence of memory on the present and of the present

CHAPTER 1 *(MSS. CHAPTER 1)* · 13

on memories of the past. The title *Sodome et Gomorrhe* and the sexual complexities of the world Proust chronicles foreshadow the sexual explorations of the Bournes, the Sheldons, and Marita.

3:13 **fishermen haul in the long net:** Now obsolete in the region, this style of fishing, *pêche au "bouillech,"* brought in mostly sardines. It was practiced in the summer, especially at night, with women and children often helping the men, pulling the nets by cables attached to canvas harnesses (Berne 77).

3:14 **café on the corner:** This may refer to the Café Continental—what is today the brasserie La Phare—two buildings down, closer to the sea, from the Hôtel Bellevue d'Angleterre. The building was not actually on a corner, but for reasons of poetic license Hemingway has erased the building along the canal closest to the sea (see 6:11).

3:15 **mackerel fishing boats:** Although the fishing fleet at Le Grau-du-Roi included several types of boats, by far the largest number, well over one hundred, were mackerel boats with lateen sail and jib (Berne 76).

3:16 **late in the spring:** The manuscript reads "too early in the spring" *(1.1.1)*, noting that the summer season had not begun, but the Scribner's edition changes this to "late in the spring." This editorial interpolation is justified. Textual details indicate that the novel begins soon after 20 May (see 3:1)—in late spring, but still too early for the summer influx of tourists, which was clearly Hemingway's point.

4:1 **restaurant and two billiard tables:** Given the direct reference to Van Gogh in the next sentence, Hemingway may have been thinking here of Van Gogh's painting *The Night Café,* which shows five customers at tables and a billiard table near the center of a room. Like *The Bedroom,* this was painted in Arles in 1888. The idea of living, more or less, in a Van Gogh painting may have spoken to Hemingway's idea of the Edenic, but Hemingway knew Van Gogh well enough to feel the darker undertones of this allusion. In letters to his brother, Theo, Van Gogh claimed that in *The Night Café* he tried to convey "the terrible passions of humanity": "I have tried to express the idea that the café is a place where one can ruin oneself, go mad or commit a crime. So I have tried to express, as it were, the powers of darkness. . . ." (31). If this is what Hemingway had in mind, it does not bode well for the Bournes.

4:3 **Van Gogh's room . . . Arles:** Hemingway here alludes to Van Gogh's famous painting *The Bedroom,* with its rustic wooden bed, table, and chair. Three versions of the painting exist. The first (1888) was painted in Arles, about twenty-five miles from Le Grau-du-Roi. Van Gogh painted two other versions during his time at the Saint-Paul asylum in Saint-Rémy.

Hemingway, who owned a dozen books on Van Gogh, boasts in a 1924 letter to Ezra Pound about making "a pilgrimage to Van Gogh's whorehouse in Arles and other shrines" (*Letters 2* 112). In his famous 1958 interview with George Plimpton, he lists Van Gogh as a literary forebear, and he routinely thought of the Rhône delta as "Cézanne and Van Gogh country" (*SL* 831). In her memoir, *How It Was,* Mary Hemingway calls the country near Aigues-Mortes "Van Gogh country" (290), and Valerie Hemingway remembers driving through this country with Ernest, talking about Van Gogh and comparing "reality to canvas, life to art" (72).

The simplicity of the bedroom represents the simplicity and innocence of the Bournes' lives at this point in the text. Yet the fact that two versions of *The Bedroom* were painted during Van Gogh's time in the asylum may foreshadow Catherine's eventual insanity. Kathy Willingham has suggested that Hemingway aligns Catherine with Van Gogh as a sort of "mad artist," and a scene later in the novel supports this assertion ("Hemingway's" 49). Returning from a drive along the coast, Catherine reports experiencing mild but disconcerting visual hallucinations. The colors, she explains, "were too bright" (162:11). The olive trees were "glittery" (162:12); even the greys were "extraordinary" and "brighter than El Greco yellows" (3.27.15). These lines might remind us of Van Gogh's hallucinations and passion for light and color, especially yellow.

Vincent Van Gogh, *Bedroom in Arles,* oil on canvas. (Van Gogh Museum, Amsterdam. Image from Wikimedia Commons.)

This passing reference to Van Gogh introduces the importance of the visual arts in this novel—a novel in which two of the major characters, Nick and Barbara Sheldon (omitted from the Scribner's text), are painters. At one point or another, the manuscript mentions Bosch, Braque, Bruegel, Cézanne, del Sarto, Derain, Dubois, Dufy, Dunoyer de Segonzac, Dürer, El Greco, Gauguin, Goya, Gris, Homer, Jongkind, Klee, Laurencin, Pascin, Patinir, Picasso, Peirce, Rodin, Teniers, and Tintoretto. In the manuscript, David Bourne also recommends the work of the famous art historian Bernard Berenson, who was a frequent Hemingway correspondent throughout the 1950s.

4:6 **white town and bright beach of Palavas:** Across the water, ten miles to the west of Le Grau-du-Roi, Palavas-les-Flots was a fishing village fast becoming a thriving seaside resort for the population of nearby Montpellier. The 1926 *Blue Guide* still describes it as a "small bathing resort with a casino" (Muirhead and Monmarché 257), but a 1926 article in *La Tribune de Marseille* describes the arrival of "thousands and thousands of bathers." "Cars and railways," it informs readers, "constantly unload the happy exodus of southern cities" (Brun). French papers described it alongside Deauville and Cannes as a Mecca for sunbathers and praised its thoroughly modern casino. In a novel deeply interested in the despoliation of Edenic places, Palavas, with its new villas, hotels, and casino, may serve as a contrast to what Hemingway suggests is a comparatively untouched Le Grau-du-Roi.

4:7 **They were always hungry but they ate very well:** As early reviewers noted, *The Garden of Eden* is obsessed with food and hunger—a hunger that is both literal and metaphorical. Even when the Bournes' "simple world" (14:2) grows complicated, the rhythm of the novel continues to be punctuated by cycles of swimming, eating, drinking, writing, and lovemaking.

David Bourne shares his creator's passion for good food and drink. He also shares his eating habits. In the best French tradition, he is a locavore, eating and drinking regional specialties wherever he travels. He is an expert with cocktails, aperitifs, and wines (and wine pairings); fond of caviar and vintage champagne, but happy to eat mackerel out of a tin. The food that the Bournes eat links them to the land and culture of France and Spain, it conveys their wealth and cultural capital, and it frequently carries other symbolic value.

As in *A Moveable Feast,* on which Hemingway worked while writing *The Garden of Eden* (a few manuscript pages contain notes for both books), hunger becomes a metaphor for desire—sexual and otherwise. As Hadley says in *Feast,* "There are so many sorts of hunger" (48). The Bournes' hunger early in the book—mirrored by the hunger of the Sheldons in the deleted subplot—suggests an insatiable desire for each other. In the manuscript, David tells Catherine that her erotic "inventions make people hungry" (3.18.4), and when Catherine and Marita aren't around, David feels a "hollowness that was like hunger" *(422.4 3.25.27)*. Catherine experiences her frustrated creativity as a sort of hunger: "Now it's just like being hungry all the time and there's nothing you can ever do about it" (53:20). And when young David awakens in the night and thinks of the old elephant he is tracking, he feels a hollowness that he mistakes for hunger *(3.29.7)*.

4:9 **eggs:** In an early review, Barbara Probst Solomon observed, "*The Garden of Eden* has got to be the 'eggiest' novel ever written—there is no end to egg references and egg jokes in the [manuscript]—but like the rest of Hemingway's wacky but meaningful humor, most of the eggs have been removed in the published book" (33). Solomon speculates that Hemingway's fascination with eggs might have been inspired by Hieronymus Bosch's *Garden of Earthly Delights*—an "eggy" triptych that figures prominently in the *Eden* manuscript (see *[54:23] 3.10.4)*. Robert Gajdusek reads eggs as symbols of David's artistic productivity, and H. R. Stoneback, in an essay largely devoted to the egg motif in *Eden,* links eggs to Wastelandish questions of fertility and infertility, and argues that the manner in which eggs are prepared and eaten serves as a gauge of David Bourne's moral and spiritual decline. He also associates Hemingway's egg symbolism with "the 'Philosophic Egg' or vase in which the Great Work of alchemy is completed" and with "the fundamental symbol of alchemy and this novel . . . : the hermetic androgyne" ("Memorable Eggs" 26).

(5:22) 1.1.3 **"think about lunch. . . ." "vice. . . . sin":** In the manuscript, when David suggests that they "think about lunch," Catherine is excited and suggests that they "give in to" the act of planning as if it were "a vice." That will make it more fun. After all, she thinks, they could use "some good vices." Together they plan a full and detailed Provençal meal with hors d'oeuvres, aperitifs, fresh grilled mackerel with a dry white wine and French fries, to be followed by artichoke hearts in a vinaigrette sauce with a bottle of Tavel, and finally a fruit or cheese course for desert.

This use of the word *vice* is playful, but Hemingway generally uses the word throughout his works to indicate addiction and compulsive repetition, whether that pertains to eating, drinking, gambling, drug-taking, writing, sex, or reading one's own obituaries.[7] As Barbara confides to David in the manuscript, "I didn't know things took possession of you." Now her desires "own" her. "And don't you try to tell me," she tells David, "when pleasure good lovely pleasure turns into vice because I know" *(3.5.8bis2)*.

Hemingway also associated the word *vice* with sin. Much as Catherine Barkley's pronouncement, in *A Farewell to Arms,* that "vice is a wonderful thing" soon leads her to say "I wish we could do something really sinful" (*FTA* 153),[8] Catherine Bourne's declaration that she and David could use "some good vices" soon leads her to suggest that "sin" gives her lovemaking with David "a certain quality" that makes it more than mere fun *(1.1.4)*. Later in the manuscript, in Madrid, Catherine wonders if David thinks it is a "sin" when she becomes a boy, no longer a girl and a boy both, and again the sense of sinning excites her *(3.12.10)*.

That a novel titled *The Garden of Eden*, with a heroine nicknamed "Devil," should play with the word "sin" is hardly surprising. Yet the novel seems less concerned with the religious meaning of sin than with the erotic charge that it carries for these characters. According to psychoanalyst Robert Stoller, fetishistic "excitement depends on one's feeling that one is sinning." While he acknowledges that the concept of sin is hardly scientific, he notes that it is equally unscientific to believe that people don't believe in sin, and for the fetishist, "the desire to sin is essential for being turned on" (7). Thus, when Barbara Sheldon first proposes her tonsorial plans to Nick, she urges him, "Let's think of something fun to do that we've never done that will be secret and wicked" *(2.1.1)*.

5:27 "I'm the inventive type." "I'm the destructive type": These lines introduce one of the novel's fundamental oppositions, tying David to the act of creation and Catherine to the process of destruction. On the face of it, this clearly makes sense: David writes stories; Catherine burns them. In the manuscript, Barbara calls Catherine "destructive" *(3.5.8)*, and the word *destroy* is so often associated with Catherine that David thinks the navy should name a destroyer after her (see *[204:23] 3.37.30*). But the dynamic between destruction and invention in the novel is governed by a complex counterpoint.[9] On some level, Catherine is a frustrated artist who "writes" with the body and by scripting the events of the Bournes' lives. David often speaks of her tonsorial and sexual games as her "inventions." On the other hand, in the manuscript, David destroys part of the honeymoon narrative he has written, long before Catherine ever destroys his African stories (see *[122:17] 422.4 3.21.42*). In other words, Catherine and David are both inventor/destroyers, although not in equal measure. Moreover, in the best Edenic tradition, destruction can facilitate creation. Discussing David's WWI novel, Catherine tells Marita, "It's a book you had to die to write and you had to be completely destroyed. Don't ever think I don't know about his books just because I don't think he's a writer when I kiss him" (112:15).

While Catherine's role as "destroyer" owes much to Hadley's famous 1922 loss of Ernest's manuscripts, what Hemingway considered Zelda's destruction of F. Scott Fitzgerald, and what he imagined to be his own mother's destruction of his father, it owes as much to Catherine Bourne's function on some level as a representative of the split-off, oppositionally gendered half of Hemingway's ego. As Stoller explains, in fetishistic and transvestic narratives,[10] the fetishist's female partner takes on the role of a "destroyer" who must ultimately be defeated to preserve the fetishist's masculinity. The fetishistic cross-dresser asks: "'When I am like a female, dressed in her clothes [i.e., wearing the fetish] and appearing to be like her, have I nonetheless escaped the danger? Am I still a male, or did the women succeed in *ruining* me?'" And his fantasy answers, "'No. You are still intact. You are a male. No matter how many feminine clothes [or hairstyles] you put on, you did not lose that ultimate insignia of your maleness, your penis.'" The result is excitement. "What can be more reassuringly penile than a full and hearty erection?" (30; my emphasis).

In a study of an individual with this sort of split-off, other-gendered half of the ego, D. W. Winnicott similarly notes that the female half was intensely jealous of the masculine half: "She [did] not want the man released.... What she want[ed] [was] full acknowledgment of herself and of her own rights over [his] body" (75). As Catherine explains to David in the manuscript, "Now you're me you're you so much better" *(3.31.44).* Thus, in *A Farewell to Arms,* when Catherine Barkley plans to cut her hair to become a "fine new and different girl" for Frederic, he asks her, "What do you want to do? Ruin me?" and she lovingly answers, "Yes, I want to ruin you" (305). And in *The Garden of Eden* manuscript, when Marita accuses Catherine of "ruining people" with her haircut, David admits, "She ruined me" *(3.25.12).* Nevertheless, near the end of the manuscript, after Catherine's departure, Marita gets an "African haircut" to become David's "boy and a girl both," and she is soon asking him, "Do you think I'll ruin you?" *(3.45.7).* It is, in part, this risk of being "ruined" that is so "dangerous" (5:34) about the surprise Catherine has in store for David.

6:3 **fisherman's shirts . . . shorts . . . very tan:** The Bournes don't just wear fashions. They set them. "People did not wear fishermen's shirts then and this girl that he was married to was the first girl he had ever seen wearing one" (6:13). The Bournes are also the first in this village to wear shorts (see 6:22), and later, after Catherine has tailored slacks made for herself, she confidently predicts that "everybody" will be wearing them next year. After all, "people are wearing our shirts now." She doesn't want to waste her new slacks on "Cannes in the off season" (79:10), but when she wears them into the much larger city of Nice, she's delighted by the scandal they create (see 110:7). Catherine and David are presented as pioneers of the summer season on the Riviera (see 6:9); they develop a passion for sunbathing before it becomes a fad (see 12:27); and Catherine imagines herself to be the inventor of several haircuts, including the Eton crop (see 46:19). When Marita enters the novel and joins them, she orders slacks like Catherine's and (in the manuscript) creates the woman's polo shirt—a man's shirt which she shortens to waist length, a style so new that she has to explain it to David (see *[140:29] 3.24.9).* Late in the manuscript, when Marita gets her hair cut as short as Falconetti in *La passion de Jeanne d'Arc* (see *[244:2] 3.45.2),* Madame Aurol remarks that it will probably soon be "the mode." For more formal occasions (again, in the manuscript), Catherine wears dresses and suits by some of the greatest Parisian designers of the day: Molyneux, O'Rossen, and Chanel (see *[88:16] 3.19.14).*

This fashion trendsetting has several inspirations, private and public, and it plays an important role in the novel. As Mary Louise Roberts argues in *Civilization without Sexes: Reconstructing Gender in Postwar France, 1917–1927,* "Fashion was a highly charged issue during the twenties," inspiring controversy that played out in novels, social commentaries, newspapers, and magazines (63). According to Roberts, "During the postwar period, fashion bore the symbolic weight of a whole set of social anxieties concerning the war's perceived effects on gender relations: the blurring or reversal of gender roles and the crisis of domesticity" (66). "Launching fashions" was also a genuine phenomenon associated with Americans on the Riviera in the second half of the 1920s (Guillet 5)—so much so that American *Vogue* devoted regular columns to the Côte d'Azur, a distinction otherwise enjoyed only by Paris, London, and Venice. Hemingway's second wife, Pauline, before her 1927 Le Grau-du-Roi honeymoon with Ernest, had worked as a writer and assistant to the managing editor at the Paris bureau of *Vogue,* and the novel gives her expert fashion sense to Catherine. In the *Eden* manuscript, David is devoted to Bettina Bedwell's fashion columns (see *[214:22] 3.39.9),* and both Catherine (88:26) and Marita *(3.35.12)* regularly read *Vogue*—as did Hemingway.[11] Hemingway also drew on his friends Gerald and Sara Murphy. As John Dos Passos later recalled, "Gerald had the knack of a Beau Nash for making discoveries that later proved fashionable" (*The Best* 149). The Bournes' fishermen's shirts were Gerald's innovation. According to Ellen Barry, Gerald "had discovered the French mariner shirt, the blue-and-white striped cotton shirt, when he had gone to Marseilles one day shopping. . . . He saw those wonderful cotton shirts that were designed for the French navy. And they were the absolutely perfect garment for the south of France . . . ; so he brought back dozens of them to Antibes and we all wore them. He gave them as gifts to friends and it was the uniform of the summer of 1923" (qtd. in Rothschild 82–83).[12] But if Murphy, who also popularized the espadrille, launched this fashion in 1923, the Bournes are still ahead of the times (in most respects) in 1927.

Although each of its contributing items has its own history, the Bournes' seaside style—deep suntans, espadrilles, shorts, slacks for women, polo shirts, and fishermen's shirts and sweaters—only truly became widely popular as a package in 1929. That summer, American *Vogue* declared,

> Nothing so amusing has ever been seen as the clothes of the people who now flock from all over the world to bathe off the famous rocks at the Cap d'Antibes. They have started a new fashion in dress that is both entertaining and intelligent, and that I think, largely accounts for the success of the place. And, mind you, the men's clothes are as amusing as those of the women; often they are the same.
>
> All of the women wear boyish bathing-suits, . . . and a woman in skirts is almost unheard of. . . . For the most part, both the men and the women wear trousers of every conceivable kind. . . . There are polo shirts dyed all colours of the rainbow. . . . A woman in a beautiful, expensive silk pyjama suit [an innovation of 1926, particularly associated with Juan-les-Pins] . . . will pass unnoticed, whereas the woman who has rigged herself out in sailor trousers and a sweater

that she has found in a shop . . . or hit upon some other amusing combination, is the center of all eyes." (McMullin 68, 126)

A July 1930 article in French *Vogue,* "Les costumes de plage," agrees, noting that in the previous year a new style had been born at Venice and Antibes and had now spread to Biarritz: "Taken by a sudden infatuation with the picturesque costume of the sailors, the elegant crowd invaded the modest native shops and supplied themselves with ticking and rough cloth. Sweaters, jerseys, espadrilles, shorts and fishermen's pants were a great substitute for the rich and elaborate wardrobes of Paris. A new fashion was born."

Yet Hemingway's interest in fashion reaches beyond his personal memories and his role as a cultural historian. Hemingway and his *Eden* protagonist David Bourne clearly find these styles fetishistically exciting. Fetishism is about, among other things, maintaining a divided attitude about sexual difference: acknowledging it, yet simultaneously disavowing its significance. The age of the *garçonne* (French for *flapper*), when haircuts and clothing traditionally coded as masculine became fashionable for women, was an erotic Eden for Hemingway. What better historical setting could be imagined for a boy-girl heroine and a husband who at night becomes her girl? While the changing fashions of the 1920s served as a symbolic battlefield for the changing status of newly empowered women, these fashions also facilitated more private fantasies for Hemingway. For instance, when Catherine and David get ready to drive into Cannes to see Monsieur Jean, Catherine changes out of her new flannel slacks, fisherman's shirt, and espadrilles (79:1) and into a "blue linen shirt" and a "heavy white linen skirt" (79:16). Meanwhile, David puts on his flannel slacks, "a fisherman's shirt," and his espadrilles (79:15). In other words, he put on precisely the outfit Catherine has just taken off. They then drive into town to get identical haircuts. The matching clothes and matching haircuts are all part of the same thing.

6:5 hair was streaked and faded by the sun and the sea: As a hair fetishist, Hemingway was excited by anything that could change hair: natural sun-bleaching, chemical dyeing, cutting, growing, shaving, waving, brushing, combing, or tousling, either by hand or wind. As Catherine explains, in the *Eden* manuscript, of her tanning fetish, "It's the *changing* that is as important as the dark" (1.4.3; my emphasis). Such changes seem to facilitate a "becoming other," a transformation into something "rich and strange" that, along with the effects of salt and sun on hair, inspired Hemingway's attachment to the Shakespearean expression "sea change" (see 12:11 and [31:20] 1.4.4). Hemingway's fascination with sun-streaked hair also appears in his short story "The Sea Change," and the novels *To Have and Have Not, For Whom the Bell Tolls,* and *Islands in the Stream.*

6:6 brother and sister . . . married: Sibling and pseudosibling romance is ubiquitous in Hemingway's work. Ad Francis in "The Battler" marries his sister, who "looks enough like him to be his own twin" (*CSS* 103); Harold Krebs's sister wants to be "Hare's" "beau" in "Soldier's Home" (*CSS* 114); in "The Last Good Country," Littless chops off her hair and wants to marry her brother, Nick (*CSS* 531, 537); Jordan and Maria, in *For Whom the Bell Tolls,* even before their fantasies of identical haircuts can come true, "could be brother and sister by the look" (67); Thomas Hudson and Jan, in the *Islands in the Stream* manuscript, cut their hair identically so they can "look like brother and sister," or "~~twins~~ brothers" (JFK item 113). Catherine and David fit comfortably into this pattern. Later in the manuscript, Catherine asks Monsieur Jean to cut their hair so they can "look like brothers," though Jean suggests that "brother and sister is better" (*3.31.4*).

It is no coincidence that such sibling and pseudosibling romance almost always entails twinning and haircuts. As has been abundantly documented, Hemingway's mother, Grace Hall Hemingway, wanted to have twins and raised Ernest and his older sister, Marcelline, as pseudotwins, often cutting their hair and dressing them alike.[13] As I explain at length in *Hemingway's Fetishism,* this pseudotwinning played a major role in Hemingway's psychosexuality—although his fetishism was far more complex than a mere repetition of, or simple compensation for, this early trauma. We see traces of this in Catherine's "ivory white hair" in *The Garden of Eden* (see 156:5). Hemingway's nickname for Marcelline was Ivory—a nickname he continued to use in letters to her at least until 1928. Catherine's "ivory white hair" clearly links her to the elephant in the story David writes, but it links her as well to Marcelline.

6:9 In those years only a very few people had ever come to the Mediterranean in the summer: Here Hemingway takes a little poetic license with history to establish the Bournes' credentials as pioneering trendsetters and to preserve a sense of the novel's setting as a prelapsarian Eden.

Although local boosters had been advocating for a summer "season" on the Riviera for decades,[14] credit for the creation of the summer season has traditionally gone to Hemingway's friends Gerald and Sara Murphy. In the summers of 1921 and 1922, Cole Porter rented the Château de la Garoupe on Cap d'Antibes from the American singer Mary Garden, and in 1922 he asked the Murphys to join him there. Until then, the Riviera season had lasted largely from January to the end of April, and it had been dominated by English as well as (before World War I) Germans and Russians, none of whom favored swimming or sunbathing. While Porter did not return to summer on the Riviera, the Murphys relished summer there so much that they returned in 1923—soon after the express, all-first-class Train Bleu first began running from Calais via Paris to Nice—and they persuaded Antoine Sella, manager of the Hôtel du Cap, to keep his establishment open with a skeleton staff all summer. There the Murphys enjoyed a quiet summer with their children and the Picassos, who were staying nearby.

When the Murphys returned to the Hôtel du Cap in 1924, they were joined by the likes of John Dos Passos, Don Ogden Stewart, Gilbert Seldes, Rudolph Valentino, the de Beaumonts, and again the Picassos, and they enjoyed periodic visits from Zelda and Scott Fitzgerald, who were staying forty kilometers to the west in Saint-Raphaël. Of that summer, Gerald remembered, "We saw what was happening down there—the crowd of people that was coming in—and realized that if we wanted to live simply we would have to hit out and get our own villa" (qtd. in Vaill 148).

Soon after the Murphys moved into their Villa America in the summer of 1925, Fitzgerald could report to John Peale Bishop, "There was no one at Antibes this summer except me, Zelda, the Valentino, the Murphy's, Mistinguet [sic], Rex Ingram, Dos Passos, Alice Terry, the Mclieshes [sic], Charlie Bracket [sic], Maude Kahn, Esther Murphy, Marguerite Namara, E. Phillips Openheim [sic], Mannes the violinist, Floyd Dell, Max and Chrystal Eastman, ex-Premier Orlando, Etienne de Beaumont [sic]—just a real place to rough it, an escape from all the world" (*Life* 126). Articles in the Paris edition of the *New York Herald* were already trumpeting, "The beaches from Saint-Raphaël to San Remo are attracting thousands of people, and the bathing is delightful. The summer season on the Riviera is becoming more and more popular with people from the large European cities, and Americans are seen in large numbers each summer. The new casino at Juan-les-Pins, almost at the center of the French Riviera, is enjoying a splendid season" ("Resorts").

By 1926, when Ernest, Hadley, and Pauline joined the Murphys at Cap d'Antibes and stayed in nearby Juan-les-Pins, the Riviera's summer season was international news, and a veritable boom was underway. The Paris edition of the *New York Herald* featured headlines like "Nice Is Becoming A Summer Resort," "Cannes Summer Season Popular," and "Boom Fortunes Made and Unmade as Casino Craze Sweeps Riviera." An article in the British periodical the *Graphic* noted that at "Cap d'Antibes and at Juan-les-Pins the joyous device '*Ouvert Toute l'Année*' is emblazoned on every hotel and restaurant, till the harassed *personnel* hardly knows what to do about the endless stream of cosmopolitan 'originals' who have had the bright idea of coming South for the summer" (Cloud). In September, papers reported a "gigantic increase in land values" along the Riviera and that "Juan-les-Pins, a minute hamlet a few miles from Cannes, has developed into a brilliant casino town since Christmas" ("Boom"). In December 1926, the Paris edition of the *New York Herald* could write,

> In the last few years a great change has come to the Riviera. Hundreds of smaller hotels and pensions have sprung up, and many of these, as well as a goodly number of the large hotels, never close their doors throughout the entire year. . . . By leaps and bounds the Riviera is becoming an all-the-year-round resort. The past summer has seen a tremendous gain in the number of visitors over the year before, in nearly all the towns on the Riviera, although Juan-les-Pins holds the banner in this respect. ("Building")

In February 1927, the *Graphic* complained of the "American literary settlement" at Juan-les-Pins and that "from Cannes to Nice is now very nearly one chain of houses" (Tuohy).

In other words, if the action of *The Garden of Eden* takes place in 1927, it is just a bit late to say "in those years very few people had ever come to the Mediterranean in the summer." Instead of being just ahead of the curve, the Bournes would be just behind it. Hemingway was sensitive to this problem and briefly experimented with a passage in which "the Cap d'Antibes" would be open "next summer" and in which David's friend Earl Ryan was planning to build there. (Among Hemingway's stray notes for *Eden,* one finds "G. Murphy / Alfred Ryan.") David is assured that the summer season is "going to be big" (see *[151:10] 422.4 3.25.20).* But this would have moved the action of the novel back to 1922, and it would have created so many other temporal problems that Hemingway discarded the passage. It was easier for Hemingway to fudge the history than it was for him to alter his timeline or abandon the Bournes' status as trendsetters. Nevertheless, if the novel's Mediterranean coast is an Eden, it is an endangered one.

6:10 **no one came to le Grau du Roi except a few people from Nîmes:** In 1909, Le Grau-du-Roi was linked by rail to Nîmes, twenty-eight miles to the north, and it quickly became a popular seaside destination for the people of that city. But visitors by 1927 were not all from Nîmes. What seemed to locals an "influx of foreigners," mostly British and American, began to arrive around 1920, fueling the development of a hotel industry.[15] In 1924 the national government named Le Grau-du-Roi an official *station climatique et balnéaire* (beach resort town), a designation the town had long been seeking (Berne 79; Mairie 36). Still, the presence of Americans in Le Grau-du-Roi in 1927 would have been negligible when compared with their presence on the Riviera, and Hemingway minimizes their presence to enhance the town's status as an innocent and Edenic locale "pioneered" by the Bournes.

6:11 **no casino:** By the mid-1920s nearly every fashionable French seaside resort sported a casino, so the absence of a casino marks the fictional Le Grau-du-Roi as comparatively "undiscovered," undeveloped, and unspoiled—in short, as an "Eden."

The real Le Grau-du-Roi did have a small municipal casino. Founded in 1880, a few doors down from the Hôtel Bellevue d'Angleterre, it had lost its authorization for games in 1909 but regained authorization in 1921.[16] With the exception of a small boathouse, it was the last building on the left bank before the jetty stretched into the sea. This modest casino, however, was nothing like the palatial casinos of the big resorts of the day. If Hemingway's erasure of this casino marks the fictional Le Grau-du-Roi as an Eden, Hemingway still must have thought of it as an endangered one. In 1927, the year Hemingway first visited, the town council of Le Grau-

Le Grau-du-Roi on a quiet day, perhaps in winter, circa 1921. *Left to right:* city hall; the Hôtel Bellevue d'Angleterre; and, a few buildings down, the municipal casino. (Editions Bazar du Progrès, photo by St.-Sernin. Image from the author's collection.)

du-Roi approved plans for a private casino—a "luxury establishment with gaming rooms, restaurants, terraces, and bars." These plans eventually fell through, but in 1927 and 1928 the municipal casino was remodeled and expanded into the Casino et Hôtel de la Jetée, with a large second-story terrace overlooking the sea. By 1935 the population of the town "doubled in June and September and tripled in July and August." Still, wrote one commentator, "despite the efforts of certain companies to turn le Grau-du-Roi into a substitute Deauville"—that is, a fashionable upscale seaside resort with a fancy casino—the beach seemed to "retain its character as a family beach and a popular resort for the citizens of Nîmes and Arles" (Berne 95–96).

6:13 **People did not wear fishermen's shirts then:** See 6:3.

6:22 **No one wore shorts either:** In wearing shorts, the Bournes are, indeed, fashion-forward. French *Vogue* first notes fashionable men wearing shorts in Biarritz in 1925 (Fernandez 4), but for women shorts were confined to swimwear and exercise clothing, and they were still uncommon ("From Trousers"). By 1927, the new fad for sunbathing made shorts more popular, but still strictly for beachwear ("Nous"). Women's shorts for wearing around town don't appear in newspapers or American or French *Vogue* until 1929, and the *New York Times* still speaks of them as "the new shorts" in 1931 ("The Mode").

6:24 **only the local priest disapproved:** Backlash against developments in women's fashions led Pope Pius XI in 1930 to issue "A Papal Decree Concerning Modesty." The decree forbade women to wear slacks in church and defined as "immodest" shorts which did not reach down at least to the knees.

6:25 **mass:** Hemingway converted to Catholicism to marry Pauline in May 1927, directly before their honeymoon in Le Grau-du-Roi.

6:26 **cashmere sweater . . . hair covered:** It is, of course, a traditional sign of modesty for women to cover their hair in church, but Hemingway's tendency to associate his fetish with "sin" gives it additional significance (see *[5:22] 1.1.3*). As I argue in *Hemingway's Fetishism,* Hemingway, via an association with hair, fetishized fur coats and fuzzy sweaters, so it would seem that in covering her hair Catherine has just displaced the fetish from one location to another (143–45).

7:7 **man, whose name was David Bourne:** In the manuscript, Hemingway initially names his protagonist John, then changes it to Phil, and doesn't settle on the name David until the beginning of the third chapter. As Robert Fleming has noted, Hemingway uses the name Philip for several writer protagonists, including the protagonist in "The Sea Change," a story closely linked to *The Garden of Eden* (*Face* 146). See *(31:20) 1.4.4*.

As for the Bournes' surname, Hemingway alludes twice in the manuscript to its origin in the famous metaphor for death in Hamlet's "to be or not to be" soliloquy. Mark Spilka suggests there is a further pun on *burn* (357). Late in the manuscript, bemoaning Catherine's destruction of his stories, David laments, "Who burned the Bournes out? Crazy woman burned out the Bournes." He then tells Marita, "I'll write in the sand. . . . That's my new medium. I'm going to be a sand writer. The David Bournes, sand writers, announce their unsuccessful peek into that undiscovered country from whose bourne no traveler returns . . ." (3.44.24).[17] In the manuscript ending of the Sheldon subplot, we also discover that Andrew Murray has written a story called "The Undiscovered Country" (see appendix A).

Spilka suggests that Bourne's surname may also allude to the World War I novel *Her Privates We* (1930), whose protagonist is named Private Bourne (358). Peppered with Shakespearean allusions, *Her Privates We* is the anonymously published and expurgated version of Frederic Manning's anonymously published and unexpurgated *The Middle Parts of Fortune* (1929). Hemingway owned both versions of the book and published excerpts from it in *Men at War*. In the preface to that volume, Hemingway writes: "It is the finest and noblest book of men in war that I have ever read. I read it over once each year to remember how things really were so that I will never lie to myself nor anyone else about them. . . . Each year in July, the anniversary of the month when I got the big wound, I read *The Middle Parts of Fortune* and it all comes back again as though it were not yesterday, nor long ago, but as though it were this morning before daylight and you were waiting there, dry-mouthed, for it to start" (xiv–xv). Given David Bourne's service in World War I, the allusion makes sense.

7:13 **sandworms:** David's fishing techniques are consistent with those found in Hemingway's 1922 copy of Lucien Jouenne's *Pendant vos vacances, pêchez au bord de la mer* (During Your Holidays, Fish by the Sea). Among several other techniques, Jouenne recommends sandworms, a black bamboo pole of four pieces, and fishing where a river or canal enters the sea between two jetties, noting that this way the "fish parade with the tide in front of the fisherman" (220). Jouenne also assures his readers that "powerful carnivorous marine fish," like the *loup de mer,* "give the fisherman emotions as strong as the salmonids of our rivers" (178).

10:1 **A *loup* . . . the biggest one . . . a little over fifteen pounds:** When André claims, "No one ever caught such a fish on such tackle," this is not hyperbole. David has caught a *loup de mer* ("wolf of the sea"), or European sea bass (*Dicentrarchus labrax*)—a fish "considered by many . . . sea anglers to be the best of all European game fish species"—and David's catch might well have been a world record (in the all tackle, saltwater line class) in its day—if such records had been kept in the 1920s (International 209).

While local clubs kept records, and *Field and Stream* in 1921 began annually publishing records for popular North American fresh- and saltwater fish caught on rod and reel, it wasn't until the formation of the International Game Fish Association (IGFA) in 1939 that rigorously accurate worldwide records by line class were kept for marine game fish. Hemingway, who served as a vice president of the IGFA from 1940 until his death, knew these records well, but records for the European sea bass weren't kept until 1983, long after his death. Hemingway's fishing books would have told him that European sea bass can weigh up to thirty pounds—and the current IGFA record (all tackle) is a little over twenty-two pounds—but as recently as 1986, the world record (all tackle) stood at a little over twelve pounds. That David catches a fifteen-pound specimen on light tackle, then, is not merely impressive. It would have almost certainly been a world-record-worthy achievement.[18]

The mythic size of this fish prefigures the equally mythic size of the elephant in the African story David later writes, much as the fish's eyes, which "still looked alive" (10:13), prefigure the eye of the dying elephant that was "the most alive thing David had ever seen" (199:20). But while there is a similar respect for a great animal, here the mood is different. The fish and the "mob" that follows David in a procession through the center of the town mark him as skillful and even heroic—a fisherman's fisherman in a village of fishermen. This catch is an example of the Bournes' prelapsarian "wonderful simple fun" (10:31), and it stands in contrast to the more complicated postlapsarian fun that will soon begin.

*(10:18) 1.1.9 **a lovely place. . . . what does Grau come from? . . . Ezra Pound:*** In the manuscript, Catherine and David congratulate themselves on having discovered Le

Grau-du-Roi and Aigues-Mortes. David had heard of St. Louis sailing from Aigues-Mortes for the Crusades but hadn't known anything else about the place when they found it on a map.[19] Catherine promises that they'll find all sorts of new places—introducing the motif of geographic exploration as a metaphor for self and erotic discovery. Catherine asks what *grau* means, and David explains that, since there's a Grau de Valencia, too, the word must be from the language along the coast, but he doesn't know if the language is Provençal or Languedoc. He says Ezra Pound would know—a detail which clearly places David in the orbit of expatriate American writers from Hemingway's circle. And given Pound's passion for the medieval Provençal troubadours, David is probably right. David promises to take Catherine sometime to the annual Feria Valencia (Valencia Fair).

The word *grau* in Le Grau-du-Roi is an Occitan (or *lenga d'oc*) word derived from the Latin *gradus,* meaning *passage.* The word was used specifically to denote natural passages that led from the region's marshy lakes to the sea. This particular *grau* belongs to the king (*roi*) since it linked the sea to the king's fort at Aigues-Mortes. There are several other *grau*'s along the coast between Le Grau-du-Roi and Marseille: the Grau de la Dent, the Grau de Vérau, the Grau de la Comtesse, and the Grau d'Orgon. Dialects of Occitan (which would include Provençal) and its close cousin Catalan have been spoken historically, and are still spoken today, along the Mediterranean coast from France's border with Italy to beyond Valencia in Spain. So David's assessment is correct.

10:30 **excited about the fish:** Here and throughout the meal that follows, Jenks substitutes "fish" and "bass" for what the Bournes actually eat in the manuscript: "mackerel" *(1.1.10).* While David does suggest that they eventually get a small *loup de mer* to eat (10:27), Catherine is still excited about the lunch plans they made earlier in the day (see *[5:22] 1.1.3*)—also deleted by Jenks—and this is precisely the meal they enjoy in the manuscript.

In the best tradition of wise travelers in France, David favors local cuisine, so it makes sense that he orders the mainstay of the local economy (see 3:15). Stoneback has suggested that Hemingway meant to play upon mackerel in "its familiar French and English sense of pimp or panderer, an agent administering to sexual debauchery.... Since the mackerel lunch is immediately followed by a lovemaking scene and Catherine's announcement of her dark sexual change," he considers the association "right on target" (27).

10:30 **Don't we have wonderful simple fun?:** In the manuscript, right after Catherine's question about "fun," David asks if Catherine wrote her letters. This leads to a conversation about writing and Catherine's observation that David hasn't been writing. Catherine wonders if David will write differently now that he is married to her. David isn't sure, but he tells Catherine that he doesn't yet want the temporary solitude required for writing. Catherine would like a written souvenir of their stay in Le Grau-du-Roi, but David promises her that she doesn't need it written to "have it" always.

(11:15) 1.1.12 **lovely golden freckles:** Over their meal in the manuscript, David and Catherine lovingly admire each other. David particularly admires Catherine's "lovely golden freckles," her tanned skin, and her hair, which is bleached and streaked by the sun and the sea. The freckles are more suggestive of Hadley than Pauline, but they are never mentioned in connection with Catherine again after the Grau-du-Roi chapters. Instead, Hemingway gives freckles and "red gold hair" to Barbara Sheldon in the manuscript *(2.1.7)*, making her a closer physical analogue to Hadley.

(11:15) 1.1.12 **artichokes . . . Tavel:** The Scribner's version of the text produces the impression that the Bournes are still drinking the restaurant's "good light, dry, cheerful unknown white wine" (11:6), but in the manuscript a waitress brings them artichokes and a bottle of Tavel. These details are not without meaning.

Celebrated as the "Rosé of Kings and the King of Rosés," Tavel remains the world's most famous rosé wine and was the first rosé to be designated Appellation d'Origine Contrôlée (1936). Tavel is grown across the Rhône from Avignon, a little over forty miles from Le Grau-du-Roi, in what remains "the only *terroir* in France reserved exclusively for rosé production" (Dominé 421).[20] As Hilary Justice has noted, Tavel stands up well to a great variety of foods and is always bone-dry—one reason why it pairs well with artichokes. A naturally occurring chemical in artichokes called cynarin tends to make most wines seem too sweet. Tavel is first mentioned in the manuscript when, planning this lunch, David proposes it to accompany artichokes hearts in vinaigrette, to be followed by fruit and cheese *(1.1.3)*. Catherine suggests that they drink it all through the meal, but David explains that it will be better after a white wine with the earlier part of the meal. Justice further suggests that the artichoke hearts are symbolic: "The Bournes are eating the hearts out." This makes Tavel and artichokes particularly appropriate for these lovers as they discuss Catherine's first big "surprise."[21]

11:16 I have a big surprise. . . . it's very simple but it's very complicated: The productive tension between a fused simplicity and complexity, and the resulting semantic compression, is a hallmark of both Hemingway's aesthetics and his fetishism. David Bourne shares these aesthetics, and we see this most plainly when he is writing about fetishized hair. Writing about the Sheldons in the manuscript, he asks himself why anyone should care about how a Latin Quarter couple wear their hair, but he quickly warns himself against such simplistic thinking: "Know how complicated it is and then state it simply" *(3.3.1)*. This aphoristic definition of Hemingway's aesthetics applies as easily to the fetish, since "a fetish is a story masquerading as an object" (Stoller 155). However simple it may appear, the fetish is radically overdetermined; it is the fetishist's all-purpose tool for negotiating the self, and it is linked to every aspect of the fetishist's psychosexuality (*HF* 10). Thus, it only makes sense that Catherine's fetishistic "surprise" is both simple and complex.

While this "big surprise" is Catherine's idea, Hemingway's wives and fictional heroines create fetishistically invested tonsorial "surprises" for their partners with such regularity that one must suppose their source is to be found in Hemingway's psychology and not in a quirk of their individual personalities. "Surprise" haircuts and hair dyeing occurs in *A Farewell to Arms*, the *Islands in the Stream* manuscript, "The Last Good Country," and *Under Kilimanjaro*.[22] In 1929, at Hendaye Plage, Pauline Hemingway dyed her hair blonde as a birthday surprise for Ernest, and more tellingly still, in 1947, shortly before Ernest dyed his own hair red, he asked Mary as a "surprise present" to become "a red-headed kitten" for him (*HF* 201). One might wonder why Hemingway always has his female characters, instead of male characters, initiate fetishistic experimentation, but this is almost always the case in fetishistic narratives (see 12:13).

11:26 **Van Gogh chairs:** Hemingway has already described the Bournes' room as looking like Van Gogh's painting of his bedroom at Arles (see 4.3), and two of these rustic wooden chairs with woven-rush seats appear in all three versions of that painting. But as Hemingway would have known, Van Gogh also painted what could almost be called a "portrait" of his chair (now in London's National Gallery)—a companion piece, or contrast to, his painting of Gauguin's less rustic chair (now in Amsterdam's Van Gogh Museum). Together, the two paintings symbolize both the companionship and the distance between the two painters. It is possible that the Van Gogh chairs here already foreshadow a similar tension in the Bournes' relationship.

12:11 **I'm going to be changed:** *Change* is a psychologically charged word in *The Garden of Eden*, and the metamorphoses signified by it are complex and far more profound than mere haircuts. It is unfortunate that Jenks edited out the vital role played by Rodin's *Metamorphoses of Ovid* in the gender transformations of both the Bournes and Sheldons, since it is in the Musée Rodin that "the changings" began for both couples (see *[17:22] 1.1.21* and *[32] 2.1.1*). When Catherine first becomes "Peter" and David first becomes "Catherine," Catherine wants David to "change" not only to be a "girl," but also to be "like he was" in Rodin's *Metamorphoses (1.1.20)*. These magical sea changes sometimes have an almost hallucinatory or supernatural power. Making love with Catherine, David *feels* "the change so that it hurt him all through" (20:17), and in the manuscript Nick Sheldon *feels* "strange and changed inside" after his tonsorially inspired lovemaking with Barbara *(2.1.12)*.[23] In what is either supernatural or a shared hallucination (or at least a tip-off that on some level Catherine and David represent split-off oppositionally gendered halves of the same authorial ego), Catherine's mouth "changes" when she goes through her metamorphoses (see 47:14), and she has a mystical ability to "change" David as if by decree: "Now you change. Please. Don't make me change you. Must I? All right I will. You're changed now. You are" (56:21). In the provisional ending of the manuscript (see appendix B), Catherine speaks with a God-like narcissism of her ability to make over everything in her own image. She could change herself, change David, even "change the seasons change everything" for her own "delight" *(422.2 1.7)*. Changing, in fact, is so important to fetishistic excitement in the novel that the act of changing is as exciting as the fetish object itself. As Catherine explains of her racially coded suntans, "It's the changing that is as important as the dark" *(1.4.3)*. See also 6:5.

12:13 **It's for you. It's for me too. . . . But it will do something to you:** Catherine's promise that her new haircut will "*do* something to" David raises interesting questions about the agency of desire in the novel. One could read Catherine's foreknowledge of David's response as merely an understanding of her husband's sexuality—an anticipation or recognition of his fetishistic response to hair before their tonsorial games officially begin—or as a fortuitous guess that his desires resemble her own, but many scenes in the novel force us to acknowledge that the symbiotic nature of the Bournes' erotic desires runs much deeper than this. In the psychosexual terrain of the text, Catherine and David often function like two halves of a single ego riven along a bigendered fissure. Catherine knows what David wants, because in many respects they are "the same person" *(3.31.4bis)*. (Such merging tendencies—lovers who feel they are versions of the "same person"—occur in *A Farewell to Arms, For Whom the Bell Tolls,* and *Across the River and into the Trees.* It was also a staple of Hemingway's relationships with his wives.[24])

The Garden of Eden is structured much like classic transvestic narrative. In such stories, fetishistic cross-dressers (i.e., fetishists in the psychological position of wearing their own fetish to facilitate a cross-gender identification) typically portray themselves (or their stand-ins) as compelled, or at least coerced, by a powerful female to wear the fetish and assume a cross-gender identification. As Stoller explains, this is accomplished "not by physical power but by the mysterious power inherent in femaleness and femininity" (24). *The Garden of Eden,* for the most part, conforms to this pattern, and David soon replies that Catherine can go ahead with her surprise "if it's something [she] really want[s]" (12:21). But in several scenes David will force himself to acknowledge that Catherine's desires are really his own (see 21:3 and *[168:3] 3.29.19)*.[25]

12:27 **tanned . . . without suits:** Nude sunbathing evokes a prelapsarian, pre-fig-leaf Edenic existence, but there is more to it than this. As with their engagement with other aspects of 1920s French fashion (see 6.3), the Bournes' passion for nude sunbathing and dark tans is at once profoundly personal and a matter of cultural history specific to the geographic and temporal setting of the novel.

The fashion for sunbathing in France has roots stretching back to the 1850s, when Arnold Rikli, a Swiss natural healer and the founder of the naturist movement, pioneered heliotherapy, a method of using sun and air baths to treat a variety of ailments. But sunbathing in France remained almost entirely medicinal, and pale skin remained the fashion until a small fad in Deauville in 1919, when Coco Chanel rebelled against her clients' "cadaverous skin" and convinced them to abandon their veils and parasols.[26] Yet the abandonment of parasols is a far cry from the Bournes' devotion to deeply bronzed skin and nude sunbathing. The action of *The Garden of Eden* takes place at a location and time when the naturist movement and a fashion craze for deeply tanned skin were both beginning to make international headlines. Nudist colonies, the direct descendants of Rikli's advocacy for medicinal sunbaths, had existed quietly in France since 1903, but the naturist movement burst into international prominence in the mid-1920s with headlines like "'Away with Clothing,' Cry the Back to Nature Crusaders: Europe Has 3,000,000 Sun Worshippers Who Even Invade the Restaurants without a Rag of Clothing." In France, journalist and former WWI pilot Marcel Kienné de Mongeot became a vocal advocate for nudism, in 1926 founding the naturist magazine *Vivre Intégralement* and a naturist club in Normandy. Meanwhile, brothers and physicians Gaston and André Durville had already in 1924 founded a naturist magazine, *La vie sage,* and they furthered the cause in 1927 by establishing the Société Naturiste and the community of Physiopolis, or the "Île des Naturistes," on an island in the Seine about forty minutes from Paris. Particularly gifted at promoting themselves and their cause, the Durvilles by 1929 had fifty thousand followers and sympathizers. According to Stephen Harp's *Au Naturel: Naturism, Nudism, and Tourism in Twentieth-Century France,* "Physiopolis alone was featured in more than seven hundred (overwhelmingly positive) articles in the mainstream, press between 1927 and 1929" (47).

On the secluded beaches of the Côte d'Azur, small groups of naturists had been practicing nude sunbathing for years,[27] and it's here that the fashion for deeply bronzed skin was born, along with a taste for nude sunbathing that, like that of the Bournes, had little to do with the strict health regimens prescribed by the naturists. A June 1925 report from Juan-les-Pins expresses admiration for the tans being cultivated by the women on the beach: "The sun-bathers are legion, and. . . . I have rarely seen a more becoming tint than the 'something between a peach and a café au lait' shade of tan that colours the very delightful feminine element on this plage" (Widower). By August 1926, a "modesty campaign" was underway at Juan-les-Pins, but in spite of this a contemporary report from Antibes describes almost precisely the sort of sunbathing practiced by the Bournes, and with aesthetic ambitions much like Catherine's:

We are really very well done all over, as the famous sun-bathing rocks [at] the villa of Lloyd Osbourne . . . are the happy and hospitable rendezvous of all true sun-worshippers, and there, 'in the altogether,' well coated with oil, we lie, gentlemen on one side of the old yacht sail, ladies the other, gently chatting and sweating till the pure marble tint of our skin is transmuted to bronze. Mrs. Lloyd Osbourne, the hostess of these unending beach picnics, sets ambition alight by the truly astounding sun-burn she has achieved." (Cloud)

By 1927, when Jean Patou began marketing the first suntan lotion, *L'huile de Chaldée,* French *Vogue* and *La Femme de France* were extolling the tanning craze, and *Femina* complained that every woman returning from the Riviera apparently wanted to look like a "blonde negress" or Josephine Baker.[28] In 1928, the fad went international and spread throughout the United States.[29]

Pauline Hemingway, a writer for *Vogue,* was not one to miss out on the fad. Hadley later recalled that during their summer on the Riviera in 1926, "Pauline wanted to get sunburned all over, so one day she and I went out on a very hot day and lay naked in the sun" (qtd. in Diliberto 225). For the Bournes, however, dark suntans are more than a passing fad. When in the manuscript David asks Catherine why she wants to be so dark, she replies, "I don't know why I want it so much. It's like I wanted to have my haircut. . . . It's to be a different person, I guess. Another me. Maybe that's part of it. It's like growing something. But it makes me excited too. Just good excited all the time" *(1.4.2).* And it excites David, too. In other words, suntanning is an erotic activity deeply woven into the fabric of the Bournes' fetishistic fantasies. This changing of skin tone *is* like changing the primary fetish object: hair. It helps Catherine somehow to be "a different person"—"another me"—to give expression to the split-off other-gendered half of the ego that is fundamental to the structure of fetishism.[30] This is why acts of *changing,* however abstract that may seem, are central to sexual excitement for the Bournes. They represent becoming "another me." (For the relation between suntanning and fantasies of racial transformation, see *[19:1] 1.2.1.)*

12:33 **mirror:** Mirrors play an important role in the Bournes' fetishism, and they are a major motif in the book. See entries for 43:17, 81:25, 84:16, and 102:29.

13:18 **married three weeks:** This would place the Bournes' wedding sometime around the twenty-fifth of April, give or take a few days.

13:19 **Avignon . . . bicycles. . . . Pont du Gard. . . . Nîmes:** Before they are blown off the beaten path by the mistral, the Bournes begin their honeymoon as fairly traditional tourists, visiting Avignon, the Pont du Gard, and Nîmes, sites renowned for their Roman and medieval architecture and long-popular tourist destinations.

The 1926 *Blue Guide* describes Avignon (then a city of 41,555 inhabitants) as "one of the most fascinating cities in the South of France" (Muirhead and Monmarché 102). Seat of seven popes during the Babylonian Captivity of the Papacy, from 1309 to 1376 when Saint Catherine of Siena persuaded Gregory XI to return to Rome, and seat of two antipopes during the Great Schism from 1378 to 1403, Avignon is famed for its Papal Palace, well-preserved ramparts, and ruined bridge reaching only partway across the Rhône. It was here that in 1327 Petrarch first saw his Laura, the muse of his sonnets. As a launching site for the Bournes' travels, then, Avignon might be associated with love, muses, schisms, and a beatified Catherine famed for her mystical marriage with Jesus.

Thirteen miles west of Avignon, the Pont du Gard is one of the finest surviving Roman aqueducts. Built in 19 BCE to carry water to Nîmes eleven miles to the southwest, it is an impressive example of Roman engineering and a major tourist attraction. With the strong tailwind, the bicycle ride to Pont du Gard and on to Nîmes would have been easy. (In a June 1927 letter, Hemingway bragged to his new mother-in-law that Pauline had cycled more than forty miles with him "without getting tired" [*Letters 3* 245].)

Known for such Roman remains as the Maison Carrée (one of the finest remaining Roman temples) and an amphitheater so well preserved that it is still used for bullfights and other events, Nîmes in 1926 was a city of roughly 78,000.

13:23 **mistral:** Winds are a minor motif in the book. To begin with, the mistral, a strong cold wind out of the northwest, is simply a fact of life in Provence. It is particularly common in the winter and spring, but it can occur in any season, blow up to gale force, and sometimes last for more than a week at a time. Usually dry, the wind contributes to the clear blue skies of Provence. Similarly, the sea breezes that punctuate the La Napoule section of the novel reflect a basic reality of weather along the Côte d'Azur. Yet the winds that blow through the book also have a broader significance.

A knowledge of winds was essential for early aviators, and David, an ex–WWI pilot, knows and notices the regional Mediterranean winds. When a cool Levant breeze blows later in the book, for instance, he tells Marita that it comes "all the way from Kurdistan" and that the "equinoctial storms will be coming soon" (183:24).

That Catherine and David don't initially intend to go to Le Grau-du-Roi but are driven there by the mistral suggests that they are driven in their actions by forces of nature beyond rational or intentional selection. Monsieur Aurol's later claim that the weather has been "insane" since the war makes it a symbol of how "everything was changed and what was not changed was changing fast" (94:13), even if David considers this a piece of "idiocy" (94:24). Shortly after this, David jestingly tells Marita that he and Catherine, like all members of America's "oldest families," "drink according to the wind," which can be "rugged in the blizzards and in hurricane months" (96:8). It's a playful joke, but it points again to the wind as a symbol of irrational forces that drive that Bournes.

Generally, in *Eden* a breeze is just a breeze . . . except when it isn't. We often see it blowing through Catherine's, Barbara's, or Marita's hair, and the way it dishevels hair seems to have an erotic import for Hemingway.[31] Any sort of change to hair—cutting, dyeing, mussing, shaving—seemed to carry a special charge for him. When Catherine and David go on a picnic that is partly spoiled by the wind, Catherine asks David to stand up and "let the wind comb" his hair; David then asks Catherine to do the same and admires how the wind flattens it against her head, suggesting that she'd make a fine figurehead for a ship *(3.19.12)*. In this respect the wind functions much like the natural bleaching of the hair by the sun—as a force of nature that changes hair in a way that carried erotic significance for Hemingway and his characters (see 6:5).

13:24 **the Imperator:** This is a minor anachronism. A luxury art deco hotel with a beautiful garden in the center of Nîmes, the Imperator didn't open its doors until 1929 (Paris). Bullfighters frequented the hotel when they came to fight in the Roman amphitheater at Nîmes, and such celebrities as Picasso, Ava Gardner, and Jean Cocteau stayed there. Valerie Hemingway remembers staying here with Ernest in 1959 (68).

13:33 **deadly clarity:** David finds what he calls this "sharp post-coital clarity" *(3.19.4)* necessary for his work (14:19). It comes up several times in the novel, and it is a theme throughout Hemingway's fiction. For Frederic Henry in *A Farewell to Arms*, after a night with a prostitute things are "hard and clear," and after making love to Catherine Barkley Frederic feels "very clear and cold" in his head (13, 154). The rich grain broker lounging on his yacht in *To Have and Have Not* thinks with "the same clear coldness" in his brain that had "always . . . been an after effect" of sex (234). After making the "earth move" with Maria in *For Whom the Bell Tolls*, Robert Jordan is able to use the "clear and hard and sharp" state of his mind to think through the problem of the bridge (160, 161). And in "The Summer People," after making love with Kate, Wemedge experiences this same clarity: "His mind was working very hard and clear. He saw everything very sharp and clear" (*CSS* 503). The ubiquity of this phenomenon in Hemingway's work suggests that it is, once again, a quirk of his own psychology, not simply a matter of individual characters and plots.

14:13 **It would be good to work again . . . enforced loneliness was regrettable:** David's need to write is presented as incompatible with the sort of Edenic symbiotic fusion that the Bournes have so far enjoyed, a state in which "they could not be held tighter together than they were now . . ." (14:22). As Robert Fleming argues in *The Face in the Mirror,* his book on Hemingway's fictional writers, *The Garden of*

Eden explores the emotional and marital costs of the writing life, with its enforced isolation. Fleming suggests that David almost sells his soul for his writing, retreating as the novel progresses into a world of his own, unshared by Catherine, that seems more important and real to him than the world he inhabits with his wife. As David leaves behind the honeymoon narrative to write the African stories that (she thinks) no longer concern herself, Catherine comes to feel more jealousy for his work than she does for the new woman she introduces into David's life and who aligns herself with David's work.

Catherine's and David's creativities work very differently, and this has a bearing on why for David writing entails a retreat from Catherine. To the degree that Catherine and David represent two halves of a single riven and bigendered ego (see 12:13), David seems to have access to the Lacanian symbolic in a way that Catherine does not. Whereas Catherine cannot write or paint but creates through imaginary identification, using her body and her life with her husband as a canvas (see 53:17), David has enough access to symbolization, displacement, condensation, and overdetermination to reimagine his situation with Catherine through the story of an elephant.[32] In this respect, David represents, in opposition to Catherine, the verbally creative side of Hemingway.

Unlike David, Hemingway wrote two short stories during his own 1927 honeymoon in Le Grau-du-Roi: "Ten Indians" and "Hills Like White Elephants."

14:23 **there was no badness afterwards:** This sentence takes for granted that it wouldn't be surprising if David *did* experience "badness" after making love with Catherine, although why this should be the case at this point in the novel is unclear. Why, we might wonder, would anyone experience "badness" after making love? Yet as the novel progresses, and particularly during the Madrid section of the novel, lovemaking sometimes leads to a sort of depressive response that David calls "remorse" (see 68:11).

This seems, in part, to be the result of the prominent role played in fetishistic sexuality by the desire to "sin" (see *[5:22] 1.1.3*). Remorse, after all, is a reasonable response if one feels one has sinned. The "badness" David later experiences after some of his lovemaking experiments with Catherine implies that these experiments are not entirely ego-syntonic. That is, they aren't entirely in harmony with his self-image and the needs and desires of his ego. To the degree that David represents, on some level, one half of a single ego riven along a bigendered line (see 12:13), ego-syntonic sexuality is hard to achieve. The riven ego is Hemingway's, and the split itself is a defensive response to irreconcilable desires.

14:31 **throaty voice:** Swollen throats are a common signifier of erotic excitement in Hemingway's fiction. For instance, watching Catherine Barkley getting her hair cut and waved near the end of *A Farewell to Arms,* Frederic Henry recalls, "My voice was a little thick from being excited" (292). The motif also appears clearly in "The Sea Change," *To Have and Have Not, For Whom the Bell Tolls, Across the River and into the Trees,* and *Islands in the Stream.*[33]

15:13 That's the surprise. I'm a girl. But now I'm a boy too and I can do anything and anything and anything: Catherine's tonsorial transformation demonstrates the power of the fetish to disavow sexual difference. Freud famously described the fetish as an imaginary "female phallus" that could be used by the fetishist to ward off castration anxiety ("Fetishism"); and Barbara Sheldon and Marita at various points in the *Eden* manuscript both describe having "erections" that seem for Hemingway to have carried a phallic significance in excess of clitoral corporeality (see *[45:6] 3.5.7, [242:15] 3.44.13,* and *[244:25] 3.45.22*; see also 17:4, 17:23, 47:14, and 175:28). The fetish's phallic properties, however, are less important than its more encompassing power to disavow sexual difference (Stoller 30). We see this, for instance, in the role played by haircuts in the gender transformations experienced by Catherine, David, Marita, Nick, and Barbara throughout the novel. Structured by a bigendered rift in the fetishist's ego, this disavowal—like all disavowals—is a half-measure, simultaneously acknowledging the very difference it would deny, according to Octave Mannoni's formula, "*je sais bien, mais quand même. . . .*"—"I know very well, but all the same" (68.).[34]

15:15 brother: See 6:6.

15:16 You see why it's dangerous, don't you? . . . Why do we have to go by everyone else's rules? We're us: Catherine's independence and willingness to flout needlessly constrictive social "rules" is admirable, but even a cursory survey of French *Vogue* for 1927 demonstrates that few would have been surprised by her boyish haircut—even if it did match her husband's (see 15:31 and 16:17). It is her accompanying gender transformation that would have been more socially taboo. Because fetishistic excitement depends upon confronting danger and breaking taboos, fetishism all too often inspires the creation of the very "rules" it must break (see *[5:22] 1.1.3*).

15:31 It's a true boy's haircut. . . . coiffeur at Aigues Mortes. The one who cut your hair: Catherine considers it exciting and transgressive that she had her hair cut by a true man's barber—and it is crucial for her that her hair be identical with David's and cut by the same barber. Yet Catherine's excitement and sense of transgression tell us more about her psyche (and, by extension, Hemingway's) than they tell us about any flouting of historical social norms. Remembering the 1920s in his 1931 classic, *Only Yesterday,* Frederick Lewis Allen noted that by 1924 in America there was "a lively battle between the professional hairdressers and the barbers" for the lucrative business in bobbing women's hair: "In the latter years of the decade bobbed hair became almost universal among girls in their twenties . . . and for a brief period the hair was not only bobbed, but in most cases cropped close to the head like a man's" (91). This battle between barbers and hairdressers was international and peaked in 1927, with coiffeurs from Australia forming the Master Ladies Hairdresser's Association to woo women away from barbers. In the same year, hairdressers' conventions in London, Vienna, and Paris declared the Eton crop (as the "true boy's haircut" for women was widely known) hopelessly *démodé*—despite the fact that nearly 40 percent of the illustrations and photos of women (at least those without hair-concealing hats) pictured in the May 1927 issue of French *Vogue* show women with some version of the Eton crop (see 46:19).[35]

Catherine's excitement and sense of transgression is rooted less in historical norms than in the structure of fetishistic desire: in the power of the fetish to disavow (that is, simultaneously acknowledge and deny) sexual difference; in the ability of the fetish to function like what D. W. Winnicott calls a "transitional object," facilitating merging, or "sameness," between the fetishist and his partner; in the ability of the fetish to produce the sense of transgression the fetishist depends upon for erotic excitement; and in the way the fetish helps the fetishist to triumph over a childhood trauma that threatened his core gender identity (namely, Grace Hemingway's pseudotwinning of Ernest and his sister, Marcelline, especially with identical haircuts) (see 6:6 and *[168:3] 3.29.19*).[36]

(16:3) 1.1.18i I was really really frightened: In the manuscript, directly before her question about what her haircut "does" to David, Catherine relates the dialogue between her and the barber with a play-by-play fidelity that sounds more like narration than conversation. She describes how "frightened" and "excited" she was when the barber began cutting and the hair kept hitting the floor.[37] She asks David if it is "exciting" to have his hair cut. He replies in the negative, but Catherine says it was "terribly" exciting for her.

Because a fetishist becomes most excited when an adult situation most resembles the childhood trauma at the root of his fetishism, anxiety plays a crucial role in fetishistic excitement. As Stoller has argued, "This anxiety—the anticipation of danger—. . . is experienced as excitement, a word used not to describe voluptuous sensations so much as a rapid vibration between fear of trauma and hope of triumph" (qtd. in *HF* 260). The childhood trauma in this instance, however, is not Catherine's or David's; it is Hemingway's.

16:3 **Doesn't it do anything to you:** See 12:13.

16:17 **No decent girls had ever had their hair cut short like that in this part of the country and even in Paris it was rare and strange:** Here Hemingway exercises broad poetic license and departs from historical reality. As Mary Louise Roberts explains in her aptly titled *Civilization without Sexes: Reconstructing Gender in Post-*

war France, 1917–1927, controversies over women's hairstyles constituted the front lines in a battle over women's fashions and gender presentations that rocked France in the years following WWI and that peaked between 1924 and 1926. As fashion historian Steve Zdatny notes of bobbed hair, "No other hairstyle in history provoked so much comment and controversy. Cultural conservatives hated it for its challenge to inherited gender verities. Stories abound of outraged men locking up, even murdering, their newly shorn wives and daughters" ("Hairstyles" 164). Yet if photos and illustrations in French fashion magazines like *Femina* and *Vogue* can be trusted, bobbed hair was nearly ubiquitous by 1927, and boyish bobs, often indistinguishable from men's haircuts, were immensely popular. In a 1926 article in the *Washington Post*, "Should Women Strive to Look Like Men? The Question of the *Garçonne*," the conservative Parisian couturiere Madame Cyber complained of flappers: "The *garçonne* style is a pathological craze, a nervous sign of world unrest among women. . . . After the armistice . . . women seemed to crave freedom, the kind that men enjoy in their relations with women, and the various *garçonne* styles were the consequence" (Hunt). British periodicals like *Gentlewoman and Modern Life* protested "that it would soon be hopelessly *démodé* to have any hair on our heads at all," and by 1927 professional hairdressers' organizations across Europe felt threatened enough to organize and lobby to end the fad ("Cult"). Coiffeurs in Vienna officially "frowned upon . . . the extreme boyish cut," declaring that "even the shortest shingle should retain something distinctly feminine" ("Bobbed"). And the International Hairdressing Exhibition in Paris decreed "the boyish bob and other exaggerated styles of close-cropped hair . . . officially *déclassé*" ("Boyish . . . Ruled Out"). Yet in spite of such decrees, the style remained popular until the end of the 1920s.

In other words, anywhere in France in 1927—and certainly in Paris—a haircut like Catherine's would hardly have been "rare and strange." Hemingway's willingness to bend history here suggests the depth of his investment in hair and in a heroine who invents new identities through novel manipulations of this fetish.

16:23: **flageolets:** *Flageolets* are a type of small, light green bean.

16:24 **Tavel. . . . great wine for people . . . in love:** See *(11:15) 1.1.12*.

16:25 **She had always looked . . . exactly her age . . . twenty-one:** In the manuscript, Hemingway initially writes that Catherine is twenty-four, but he revises this to twenty-one, no doubt calling attention to the traditional age of majority. It is important to remember this later in the novel when Catherine suddenly feels old, "older than [her] mother's old clothes" (162:30). This also means that Catherine is about nine years younger than David, since we later learn that David was "about eight years old" in 1905 (157:10).

17:1 **gone to the devil:** See *(5:22) 1.1.3*.

17:4 **"Where I'm holding you you are a girl. . . ." hard erect freshness:** The oppositions that structure this passage divide Catherine into what are known in psychoanalytic theory as part-objects: breasts representing girlishness; cropped hair representing boyishness. (Hemingway interestingly always uses the dichotomy boy/girl instead of man/woman.) Yet each part-object is, in the psychoanalytic perspective, a compromise formation embodying the fetishist's divided phallic position attitude towards "castration" and sexual difference. In Freudian terms, the fetishized hair represents a masculinizing "female phallus" (see 15:13), but the way it is cropped simultaneously represents "castration." The breasts represent girlishness, but their "hard erect freshness" simultaneously gives them phallic properties. Freud suggests that fetishes embodying such compromise formations are particularly durable since they appeal to both sides of a divided ego's disavowal of sexual difference ("Fetishism" 156).[38]

17:14 **He lay there and felt something and . . . felt the weight and the strangeness inside:** The physical lovemaking in this passage has been the subject of much critical perplexity and debate. Peter Messent observes that "it is difficult to know precisely what physically happens here. . . . [And] it . . . leads to a certain confusion and vagueness at a crucial moment in the text" (116). Comley and Scholes, likewise, note that Hemingway does not "provide readers graphic descriptions of the logistics of these sexual changings, leaving one befuddled critic to suggest that 'somehow, [Catherine] sodomizes [David]'" (60). This is precisely what Debra Moddelmog argues: "although reviewers of the novel criticized Hemingway (or Jenks) for being elliptical in this passage, . . . clearly Catherine has sodomized David. This is what is meant by 'the strangeness inside' and by Catherine's request to 'let me take you'" (69). Rose Marie Burwell suggests the mechanism: "digital anal penetration" (112).

As written, the lovemaking was cryptic enough for the editor at Scribner's, Tom Jenks, in violation of his general practice, to add two key words to the passage: "lower" and "inside." The manuscript passage—with Hemingway's deletions and insertions (indicated by strikethrough and ^) and Jenks's interpolations included and noted—appears as follows: "He lay there and he felt something and then ~~something that yielded and entered~~ ^her hand holding him and searching^ [Jenks adds: *lower*] and he helped with his hands and then lay back in the dark and did not think at all and only felt the weight and the strangeness [Jenks adds: *inside*] and she said, 'Now you can't tell who is who can you?'" (*1.1.20*). Jenks's interpolation of "inside" seems to be motivated by the deleted "~~something that yielded and entered~~," and his interpolation of "lower" answers an obvious but unasked question: where else *could* something enter that would even symbolically produce such a result? It is clear that David is penetrated.

Similar scenes of male protagonists penetrated by their female partners appear—heavily veiled—in the *Islands and the Stream* manuscript, *Across the River and into the Trees,* and *Under Kilimanjaro.* "In each passage, the male protagonist enters a state of 'not thinking' and then, aided by fetishistic/transvestic ritual and some form of anal penetration, hallucinates that he is physically transformed into a 'girl'" (Eby, "He Felt the Change" 79). In the *Islands in the Stream* manuscript, for instance, Thomas Hudson, after letting his first wife cut his hair so they can be "just the same" and he can be her "girl," lies beneath Jan as she swings her "silken hair" over him and tells him not to think. Then he feels something physical: "He felt weak through the base of his spine to his chest and back again. But the weakness was concentrated forward from the base of the spine. . . . He felt weak and destroyed inside himself" (JFK item 112). Similarly, in *Under Kilimanjaro,* Hemingway writes of shaving his head and of his pleasure in his wife's new "Kamba" haircut (410). Mary Hemingway's journal from these days reveals that Ernest bleached her hair himself. In Mary's journal, Ernest jokes about sodomy, calls her a "boy" and himself her "girl," and rechristens himself "Kathrin" and her "Peter" (JFK MHPP-014-016).[39] Hemingway remembers making love with Mary during these days, just feeling and "not think[ing] at all"; then he feels "the old splitting up his chest" (*UK* 410). Just so, in *Eden,* David Bourne's transformation is not simply imaginative: he *feels* "the change so that it hurt him all through" (20:16).

In an essay devoted to such moments in Hemingway's fiction ("He Felt the Change"), I suggest that the "not thinking," so crucial to them and usually urged by the female partner, may quiet the masculine half of a riven and bigendered ego so the feminine half can emerge with hallucinatory power. I also suggest that the masculine penetration in Hemingway's fetishistic erotic scenario may memorialize his traumatic wounding in WWI and the enema administered to him before the operation on his damaged legs. Such enemas, both administered by lovers who are nurses, appear in "A Very Short Story" and *A Farewell to Arms.*

17:21 **Will you change:** See 12:11.

(17:22) 1.1.21 **Will you be like you were in the statue? . . . that day in the Rodin:** Here the Scribner's editor, Jenks, makes an important and unfortunate deletion. In the manuscript, right after Catherine asks David, "Will you change and be my girl and let me take you" (17:21), she follows with another question: "Will you be like you were in the statue?" Strange and disorienting as the question may seem (how could David have been "in" a statue?), David immediately knows the statue Catherine has in mind: "The one there are no photographs of and of which no reproductions are sold." Their transformation, he thinks, *is* "like the statue."

We soon learn which statue they have in mind. When David asks Catherine how long she's been thinking about this sexual transformation, she tells him ever since they saw the *Metamorphoses of Ovid* in the Musée Rodin. And this is no mere quirk of Catherine's psychology. The excised Sheldon subplot begins with a memory of Nick and Barbara turning off the Rue de Varenne into the Hôtel Biron—the Musée Rodin—with its "beautiful gardens," where they, too, saw the bronze and their "changings" began (see *[32] 2.1.1*). So for both couples, their erotic transformations begin with a vision of Rodin's the *Metamorphoses of Ovid*. It isn't clear why Jenks decided to omit this from the Scribner's edition of the novel. It could be that the statue's power as a catalyst for both couples seemed unjustifiably strange and nonsensical—too supernatural for inclusion in a work by Ernest Hemingway, at least as Jenks understood the author. It does push far beyond the limits of mere coincidence. But if Jenks had known what Hemingway must have known about the statue, he never would have deleted it.

It's obviously significant that the bronze in question appears in the upper right-hand corner of Rodin's masterpiece, *The Gates of Hell*—a monumental, six-meter-tall sculpture set amid the Edenic gardens of the Hôtel Biron. As Hemingway wrote in *A Moveable Feast*, at a time when he was also working on *The Garden of Eden*, "all things truly wicked start from an innocence" (217). Rodin intended the *Gates of Hell*, his rendering of Dante's *Inferno*, to serve as a counterpoint to Ghiberti's Renaissance Florentine *Gates of Paradise*. And, much as Dante knew that the road to heaven can lead straight through hell, Hemingway implies that the path to hell can begin in an Edenic garden.

As he did for many of the figures on *The Gates of Hell*, Rodin also cast separate models of *The Metamorphoses of Ovid*, and the sculpture of two kissing women (one with a small faunal tail) is closely associated by Rodin scholars with another set of lesbian figures known by the Baudelairean title of *The Damned Women*. The allusion to Baudelaire's "Femmes Damnées," from *Fleurs du mal*, has been noted by Spilka and others, who have rightly suggested that the lesbian lovers prefigure Barbara Sheldon's attraction to Catherine and Catherine's later relationship with Marita. Rodin, indeed, described his models as "two priestesses of the isle of Lesbos" (Normand-Romain 74), but as I have argued elsewhere, Rodin had another, more important, literary inspiration for his sculpture ("Gardens" 78). When the important Danish collector Carl Jacobsen asked Rodin in 1907 to which Ovidian metamorphosis the sculpture's title alluded, Rodin replied that he had been thinking not of Daphnis and Chloe (subjects of another title often associated with the sculpture), but rather of the tale directly after that in Ovid's *Metamorphoses:* the tale of the water nymph Salmacis, who falls in love with the boy Hermaphroditus (Normand-Romain 74).

As Ovid tells the tale, one day as the beautiful water nymph Salmacis rearranges her hair, gazing into the mirror of her pool, she looks up and is stricken with love for the beautiful youth Hermaphroditus, son of Hermes and Aphrodite. She immediately longs to take him in her arms and tries to woo him, but Hermaphroditus rejects her. Yet when he strips to swim in the waters, the beauty of his body, "as if it were ivory," overwhelms Salmacis and she envelopes him in her embrace.

> The heir of Atlas struggled as he could
> Against the pleasure that the girl desired,
> But she clung to him as though their flesh were one.

As Hermaphroditus struggles to escape Salmacis's embrace, she prays to the gods to unite them forever.

> At which the gods agreed:
> They grew one body, one face, one pair of arms
> And legs, as one might graft branches upon
> A tree, so two became nor boy nor girl,
> Neither yet both within a single body.

When Hermaphroditus learns his fate, he curses the waters of Salmacis: "Make all who swim in these waters impotent, / Half men, half women" (Ovid 120–22). Hermaphroditus and Salmacis become one, with a new name: Hermaphrodite. This curse suggests a supernatural explanation for the mysterious transformative power Rodin's sculpture holds for the Bournes and the Sheldons.

Rodin's *The Metamorphoses of Ovid,* bronze. (Musée Rodin, Paris. Photo by author.)

Rodin's *The Gates of Hell*, bronze. Note *The Metamorphoses of Ovid* in the upper right-hand corner. (Musée Rodin, Paris, © agence photographique du musée Rodin—Jérome Manoukian.)

17:23 **"You're Catherine." "No, I'm Peter":** For those who doubt Freud's assertion that the fetish functions as an imaginary substitute female phallus, it is worth noting a sentence among the discarded fragments of the *Eden* manuscript: "I'd never known anyone named Peter that wasn't a prick" (see 15:13).

"Catherine" and "Peter" were the names Ernest and Mary Hemingway used for themselves in their own fetishistic love play. Fetishism and transvestism (or fetishistic cross-dressing) are two different logical moments, or positions, in the same psychology. In the fetishistic position, the female partner wears the fetish to become a "boyish" phallic woman; in the transvestic position, the male fetishist wears the fetish, often before a mirror, to identify himself as the phallic woman. Each position involves a disavowal—a simultaneous acknowledgment and denial—of sexual difference. This is organized along a bigendered rift in the ego, and named alter egos are a standard feature of the transvestic position, with fetishistic cross-dressers scoring differently on personality tests when dressed as males or females.[40]

By the time he wrote *The Sun Also Rises* (1926), Hemingway seems to have chosen the name "Catherine" for the split-off other-gendered half of his ego. At least, it is suggestive that Jake Barnes receives an invitation to the wedding of an unknown "Katherine" only moments before he stares at his penis-less body in front of a mirror (38). The *Sun* manuscript leaves a blank where the girl's name should be, but some deleted lines there suggest the emergence of the "Catherine" alter ego through a dissociative haze: "I could not remember who the girl was. It bothered me" (*SAR* Fac 120).[41] The name may have emerged in love play with his "feather kitty," Hadley, whom Ernest often called "Katherine Kat," and who regularly signed 1926 and 1927 letters to him with such variations as "Haddlecat," "Lovecat," "Cat," "Kittin," "Cithrin," "Katherine," and "Catherine." Whether Hemingway took the name to identify with Hadley or gave Hadley the nickname to identify her with his feminine alter ego, the shared nickname facilitated the sort of merger between lovers we see in this passage from *Eden:* "Now you can't tell who is who can you?" (17:17). Hemingway had clearly lost any dissociative distance from his feminine alter ego by the time he created Catherine Barkley and wrote *A Farewell to Arms* (1929), which could be read as a reimagining of the emergence of the alter ego in the wake of Hemingway's wounding in WWI.[42]

In a letter that seems to date to January 1946, Hemingway writes to his then fiancée, Mary, about what he calls their recent "hair adventures," a sort of experimental "holiday"—assuring her that he loves her as she is and doesn't mean to pressure her about hairstyles—and signing himself "E. (C.) H." If the parenthetical middle initial refers to his identity as "Catherine," it seems likely that Mary assumed her bedroom moniker, "Pete," at the same time. They had recently been visited by Hemingway's friend Colonel Buck Lanham and his wife, Pete. Mrs. Lanham's name, with its phallic associations, probably suggested itself for Mary's nighttime role-playing. By the spring of 1947, Ernest was writing to Mary, then in Chicago, urging her to dye her hair red as a "surprise present . . . for Papa (also for Pete and for Catherine)." A few days later, he enthuses, "My God it will be wonderful to have my blessed dearest wife and partner and friend and Pete home. Your girl hasn't been around at all except before daylight times, but know very well will turn up when you ask for her." Too excited to wait for Mary's return, he decided to dye his own hair, writing on 14 May to Mary:

> I thought, what the hell, I'll make really red for my kitten and did it carefully and good, same as yours, and left on 45 minutes and it came out as red as a French polished copper pot or a newly minted penny—not brassy—true bright coppery—and naturally in the morning I was spooked shitless—and then thought what the hell—with everything the way it is and we free people able to do anything we want that doesn't hurt other people, whose business is it but yours and mine. . . .
>
> So now I am just as red headed as you would like your girl Catherine to be and don't give a damn about it at all—(like very much). It's not deep red—but light, bright, coppery, like shiny copper pans—and I'll do it again before you come home—or do it again when you get here. . . . If a girl has a right to make her hair red I have—I've fought enough fights so no one can say anything to me. . . .
>
> Actually me and Catherine both would be better dark red than jolly new copper tinker's colour. But you can't do that at home. (qtd. in *HF* 201–3)

Nor was this a passing phase. On safari with Mary Hemingway in December 1953, Ernest wrote entries in Mary's journal about Mary being a "boy" and about "loving to be her girl." In an entry titled the "New Names Department," he writes:

Mary Peter Hemingway
Peter Mary Welsh-Hemingway
Pedro Maria Hemingway y Welsh (for social columns of the *Diario de la Marina*)
HRH Mary Peter Welsh-Hemingway
Lady Mary Welsh-Hemingway
Ernest Welsh-Hemingway
E. Kathrin Welsh
Kathrin Ernest Hemingway
E. K. Hemingway-Welsh
Ernest Cathrin Inez Hemingway y Welsh (for *Diario de la Marina*) (JFK MHPP-014-016)

Even more to the point, Hemingway briefly flirted with naming *both* Catherine Bourne *and* Barbara Sheldon "Catherine" and renaming *The Garden of Eden* "The Two Catherines" (see appendix A). On a page from the *Moveable Feast* manuscript blending notes and titles for both *Eden* and *Feast,* a deleted sentence reads, "I have called both of these women Catherine because I have the most pleasant name."

Needless to say, such passages demonstrate the degree to which the Bournes' sexuality mirrors Hemingway's.

18:8 his heart said goodbye Catherine goodbye my lovely girl goodbye and good luck and goodbye: This devastating conclusion of the first chapter does not, in fact, conclude the first chapter in the manuscript. Instead, in the manuscript, this line is almost immediately followed by lovemaking and post-lovemaking scenes that Jenks transposes in the Scribner's edition to 20:13–21:13. The post-lovemaking ruminations end with David beginning to come to terms with his own complicity with Catherine's desires. He admits that the statue moved him as it moved Catherine and as it must have moved Rodin (see *[17:22] 1.1.21*). He's lucky to have a "wild animal" for a wife, and he doesn't feel bad—so long as he has wine to mask his ambivalence. He kisses the sleeping Catherine and tells her, "I'm with you no matter what else you have in your head and I love you" (20:24).

(18:9) 1.1.24 ***In the morning she was still sleeping:*** In the manuscript, the chapter concludes with Catherine waking and dressing and the couple chatting and making plans for the day over breakfast. Catherine asks David not to worry, assuring him that she's "not dangerous anymore" *(1.1.25)*. David calls her "Peter," which Catherine thinks is "sweet," but this is deleted in the manuscript and replaced with her assurance to David, "I am your Catherine." David doesn't need to worry, she tells him, "until night." She promises that she won't let "the night things come into the day" *(1.1.25)*. The passage suggests how the name "Catherine" seems to be every bit as much a matter of role-playing as the name "Peter." The manuscript chapter concludes with her request for David to call her Catherine again. She tells him, "It's a name I love to hear."

Catherine's words here seem to play on Frederick Whitfield's nineteenth-century hymn "There Is a Name I Love to Hear":

There is a name I love to hear.
I love to sing its worth;
It sounds like music in my ear,
The sweetest name on earth.

NOTES

1. For a discussion of anachronism in the novel, see Rohy.
2. When French place names are composed of several words, the words are generally linked by hyphens. The Scribner's edition of *Eden* does not do this. When quoting text from the Scribner's edition, I follow its practice; when writing of the town itself, I follow the French practice.

3. Hotchner was with Hemingway for the 1954 trip, but he doesn't make it clear if they stopped in Aigues-Mortes or Le Grau-du-Roi. He mentions driving through Lunel, a mere thirteen miles away, and Hemingway telling stories about Aigues-Mortes (123), so it seems probable that Hemingway would have made the stop. This seems particularly likely when Peter Viertel, who was with Hemingway on the 1949 trip, recounts that visiting Aigues-Mortes and Le Grau-du-Roi demanded "a detour of sixty kilometers" (97). Hemingway had also wanted to go to Le Grau-du-Roi in 1953, but a changed departure date for his boat to Africa forced him to rush to Marseille without the detour (*SL* 824).

4. Correct spelling: Viollet-le-Duc.

5. Froissard wrote about the Hundred Years' War of the fourteenth century; in this passage Hemingway was clearly thinking of Jean de Joinville's chronicle of the Seventh and Eighth Crusades. Hemingway owned a copy, and he published a long excerpt from it in his edited volume, *Men at War*.

6. The first widely accepted European outbreak of syphilis was in 1494, and while the matter is still not conclusively settled, most medical historians have long believed the disease came back with Columbus from the New World. Hemingway may have confused syphilis with leprosy, which was indeed spread by the Crusaders.

7. See the *Eden* manuscript 6.10.11 (eating); *THHN* 222 (drinking); *UK* 145 (gambling); *CSS* 362 (opium); *EHWW* 223 or *GOE* 216 (writing); and *BL* 455 (reading one's own obituaries).

8. In the *FTA* manuscript, Hemingway initially wrote, "Sin is a wonderful thing," but he replaces "sin" with "vice" (JFK item 64).

9. For an extended consideration of this, see Eby, "Who Is."

10. For an extended consideration of the relation between *The Garden of Eden* and transvestic narrative, see *HF* 241–75.

11. Hemingway published a nonfiction piece, "The Clark's Fork Valley, Wyoming," in *Vogue* (American) in 1939 (*BL* 298–300). In *Across the River and into the Trees*, Colonel Cantwell reads *Vogue,* and a 31 January 1958 letter to Gianfranco Ivancich demonstrates that Hemingway remained a regular enough reader of the magazine to discuss who appeared in its pages "all the time" (JFK).

12. Credit for these elements of the Murphys' style is sometimes misattributed to Coco Chanel, but the evidence typically produced—the famous picture of Chanel in slacks and a striped sailor's jersey—is from 1930, though often misdated (Butchart 100). If anything, Chanel may have been influenced by the Murphys' style when she designed the costumes for Diaghilev and Cocteau's 1924 ballet, *Le Train Bleu,* about beachside athleticism and leisure on the Côte d'Azur. The ballet itself, with its beautiful opening curtain by Picasso, may have been inspired, at least in part, by the Murphys (Rothschild 49).

13. See Sanford, Lynn, and *HF*.

14. See, for instance, Hale 103 and Thierry de Ville d'Avray 192.

15. In renewing its request to become an official *station climatique et balnéaire* in 1920, the town council specifically requested the right to collect a tax on foreigners (Mairie 57).

16. See Simien 53 and Marie du Grau-du-Roi 35, 59, and 70.

17. Spilka also suggests there is a pun on *borne,* as in a burden carried (357).

18. In the manuscript, Hemingway first writes *fourteen* and then changes it to *fifteen* pounds *(1.1.8)*. It is a pleasant coincidence that, according to the IGFA database, the first European sea bass that would have broken David's record (all tackle, not light tackle) was a twenty-pound-and-eleven-ounces fish caught in May 1986 at Les Saintes-Maries-de-la-Mer, a mere fifteen miles from Le Grau-du-Roi. Today, of the eighty-four records in the IGFA database

for European sea bass, only ten would have surpassed David's catch—and of these ten, only three were caught on anything less than a robust twelve-pound test line. According to Rivkin, during the 1920s, "In granting recognition to outstanding catches, much credit was given to captures on light tackle," so the lightness of David's tackle is particularly important. Rivkin adds, "Fishing was religion to Hemingway, and he would deliberate with great care as to which element of tackle would create the most meaningful sporting experience" (22, 69). My thanks to Jack Vitek, the IGFA's World Records Coordinator, for his assistance.

19. The seeming random selection of the Bournes' honeymoon destination may have been inspired by Ernest and Pauline's 1927 honeymoon. In Hemingway's 1927 notebook detailing things he had to do before and after their marriage, one item on the list was to "decide where going" (JFK EHPP-OM14-007).

20. Remembering her travels with Ernest in the late 1950s, Valerie Hemingway recalls: "Once we were in Provence, Tavel became the mainstay of our journey, as the rioja had been on the other side of the Pyrenees" (73).

21. Hilary Justice, personal correspondence. For the ability of Tavel to pair well with difficult-to-marry foods like artichokes, see also Bichsel 141.

22. See *FTA* 304; JFK Item 112; *CCS* 531; *UK* 292.

23. For a more detailed discussion of hallucination in Hemingway's work, see Eby, "He Felt the Change."

24. As early as 1922, Hemingway wrote to Sherwood Anderson, "Bones [Hadley] is called Binney now. We both call each other Binney. I'm the male Binney and she's the female Binney" (*SL* 62). He likewise shared the nicknames "Feather Kitty" and "Kitten" with Hadley and Mary. He told Hadley that together they were the "same guy" (Diliberto 79), and he told Pauline that he and she were the "the same person" (*SL* 221). See also *HF* 24, 280.

25. For an extended consideration of the relationship between *Eden* and the structure of transvestic pornography, see *HF* 241–63.

26. The idea that Chanel originated the fad for suntanning has been dismissed in two histories of suntanning, by Kerry Segrave and Pascal Ory, due to the lack of supporting evidence, but both historians miss the 1919 fad at Deauville, then France's most prestigious seaside resort, where Chanel opened a boutique in 1913. A 1923 article in American *Vogue* recalls that summer after the armistice: "At Deauville, the charm of sunburned cheeks, necks, and arms had been discovered," and Parisiennes had taken to looking "like a race of quadroons"; by 1923, however, the fad had passed and "an interesting pallor" was newly popular (M. H. 126). More importantly, a 1919 article in *Le Cri de Paris* suggests that the fad was, indeed, initiated by Chanel: "A couturière known in the city, charming and ambitious, . . . trains her clients to become, as she has herself, burnished and gilded by healing sunburn: 'I will not dress you again,' she tells them gaily, 'as long as you have . . . a "cadaverous skin."'" Although the article does not mention Chanel by name, it describes the couturiere as wearing a *tunique grecque* (a "Greek tunic"), which seems to refer to the corsetless dresses Chanel was pioneering at the time ("Choses et Gens" 7). Other articles from 1919 make it clear, however, that the fad involved little more than the abandonment of veils, parasols, and excessive coverings (see, for instance, "Le quinze" and "Nos echos, 1920").

27. As early as the summer of 1923, a cartoon poking fun at nude sunbathing appeared in *Le journal amusant* with the telltale rocks of the Estérel in the background (Lorenzi). While the ever-prurient *Le journal amusant* needed little excuse to illustrate nudity, the punchline of the joke presumes a general familiarity with the satirized phenomenon.

28. See "Soleil, Soleil"; Dery; "Autumn Health Parades," and "La beauté á la mer."

29. See, for instance, "Smart Women Now Cultivate the Sun-Bronzed Complexion": "The Sun-Bronzed Complexion Latest Fad of the Smart"; "The Sun-Tan Vogue Makes Back and Arms Important"; and "Sun Tan Is So Smart!"

30. For an extended consideration of this, see *HF* 155–93, 208–16.

31. See, for instance, the "carelessness the wind [makes] with [Renata's] hair" when we first meet her in *Across the River and into the Trees* (80).

32. See Eby, "Who Is Destructive" 101.

33. For an extended discussion of this phenomenon, see *HF* 41–55.

34. For an extended consideration of these issues, see *HF*.

35. See "Hair Dresser's Exhibition," "Bobbed Hair and Curls to Be 1927 Style, Coiffeurs Declare at Vienna Exposition," and "Paris Frowns on Boyish Bob: Hairdressers Assert Feminizing Influence of Styles Has Doomed the Vogue of the Close Crop."

36. See *HF*.

37. The passage resembles one recalled by Marie Morgan late in *To Have and Have Not* (258–59) and another recalled by Thomas Hudson in the manuscript to *Islands in the Stream* (JFK Item 112).

38. For an extended exploration of this theme and such objects in Hemingway's work, see *HF* 72–82.

39. For a more complete treatment of this, see *HF* 173–79 and Eby, "He Felt the Change" 83–85.

40. For an extended consideration of these issues, see *HF*. For the different scores on personality tests, see Gosselin and Eysenck 172–73.

41. For a more developed version of this argument, see Eby, "Reading Hemingway Backwards."

42. "Though rooted in childhood, fetishism seldom becomes manifest until young adulthood when it is often triggered by a trauma constituting a severe castration threat, and Hemingway's wounding in World War I bears all the markings of such a trauma" (*HF* 60). Consider, for instance, Jake's wound in *The Sun Also Rises*.

CHAPTER 2 (MSS. CHAPTERS 2–3)

(19:1) 1.2.1 **brown as a Kanaka:** In some lines that Jenks deletes from the beginning of this chapter in the manuscript, David, as he spreads oil over Catherine, tells her that her skin is the color of black walnut meats or elks' antlers in September. Catherine replies that she wants to be "as brown as a Kanaka." A colonial term for Pacific islanders derived from the native Hawaiians' name for themselves, the word *Kanaka* was much in the press during World War II and when Hawaiʻi became a state in 1959. Today it is often considered offensive because of its historical use by British colonizers to describe island workers from across the Pacific. The word appears frequently in Robert Burnett's *The Life of Paul Gauguin* (1936), which Hemingway owned, and this suggests a link to several other references to Gauguin in the *Eden* manuscript (see *[154:7] 3.26.4* and *[163:31] 3.28.15*); these references, in turn, point to a more general romantic colonial fantasy of the island Pacific as an uncorrupted—or corrupted—Eden.

More importantly, this passage introduces one of the book's major themes, much muted by Jenks's editing: fetishistically invested fantasies of racial transformation. At various points in the manuscript, Catherine, Marita, David, and Nick try on, as if they were suits, a dizzying array of identities: American Indian, Asian Indian, Japanese, Javanese, Kanaka, Kamba, Mbulu, Somali, Tahitian, Wanderobo, and Watusi. For a time, Marita even becomes a "Bizerte street urchin." It's almost like traveling the world. What is at issue, then, is not cultural specificity but rather a fetishization of racial otherness writ large. The psychological and colonial significance of these fantasies is treated elsewhere (see 30:16 and *[31:7] 1.4.3*). Here, I want first to historicize the regularity with which French popular discourse in the 1920s portrayed the new fad for sunbathing (see 12:27) as either inviting or threatening racial transformation.

In a culture that had long built racial identity upon a valorization of pale skin, it was inevitable that the new fad for dark skin would be racialized. Articles about the brief 1919 fad for tanning in Deauville (see 12:27) already speak of Parisiennes looking "like a race of quadroons," and such racial fantasies came into full florescence in 1925 when the new fad on the Riviera was swiftly followed by the advent of Josephine Baker and the ensuing rage for Black music, dance, and art—the so-called *tumulte noir* that captivated Paris in the late 1920s. A typical article of the times opposing the new fad for suntanning accuses its readers, "You want to do like everyone else, you want your friends to exclaim when you come back from vacation on your resemblance to Josephine Baker or how you look like a spicy blonde negress" ("La beauté" 25–26). The invocation of Baker in articles on sunbathing became so cliché that she took to cleverly satirizing the Parisians at Juan-les-Pins in her signature tune "*Si j'étais blanche*" ("If I Were White"). Hemingway's fascination with racial transformations (like his own interest in Josephine Baker) was complex and deeply personal, but in *The Garden of Eden* it expresses itself through an exaggeration of this genuine feature of French discourse in the 1920s.[1]

19:6 **She ought not to stay too long in that position:** The care David takes overseeing Catherine's tanning may seem excessive—perhaps foreshadowing the way he will need to take care of her sanity—but it reflects attitudes of the times about the new fad (see 12:27). Articles on sunbathing often cautioned devotees to be careful. In a 1927 article in *Femina,* a physician counseled, "If women want to get brown, let them get ten minutes of sun on the first day, then half an hour for three days, then one hour during the last three days of the first week" ("La beauté" 27). Another 1927 article cautioned, "The sun stimulates the brain and the hot sand soothes the nerves; one is apt to forget the danger and overdo the joy. . . . Ten minutes' sunbath at a time is sufficient—spend the rest of the [day] under the shade of a sun umbrella" (Juta).

(20:12) 1.2.3 **Why does your wife want to seem to be of a different race and have a completely different pigmentation?** In the manuscript, as Catherine sleeps on the sand, David muses on his new "full-time occupation" as a tanner. But not of leather. No, he "makes copper skins." He "used to be a writer," he thinks, but this new business of tanning is "much more interesting." If he is "completely successful," Catherine "will look as though she belonged to a different race." And why does Catherine want this? Because she likes it: "She likes changes. . . ." (For "changes," see 12:11; for suntans and race, see *[19:1] 1.2.1;* for the fetishization of racial otherness, see 30:16).

20:13 **During the night . . . dark magic of the change:** Jenks has transposed this lovemaking scene and David's postcoital ruminations (20:13–21:13) from the place where they occur in the manuscript (see 18:8).

20:16 **asked the questions:** Note that these aren't just *some* questions, these are "*the* questions"—a set of ritual questions that seem to facilitate "the dark magic of the change." As Robert Stoller has demonstrated, fetishistic sexuality tends to be structured by highly ritualized erotic scenarios, with repeated actions and props (31). This set of ritual questions seems to have been as important for Hemingway's sexuality as it is for that of the Bournes.[2] We've already seen one such question: "Will you change and be my girl and let me take you?" (17:21), but the manuscript offers better examples than are available in the Scribner's text. When the Bournes visit Monsieur Jean to get their hair cut and dyed identically (79:20–82:14), it becomes clear that they are getting their hair dyed to be like a "Danish girl" they saw in Biarritz (see 77:13). That night in bed, as she admires David's hair and calls him "girl" (see 85:30), Catherine asks him if he's a Danish girl. She also asks who cut his hair, "Was it Jean?" *(3.18.16i).* Catherine already objectively knows the answer to these questions, so their function is not informational. It is ritual. As David relaxes and tries not to think, the questions and Catherine's pronouncements magically produce the effects they purport to describe.

20:16 **he felt the change so that it hurt him all through:** For an account of the physical hallucination that David *feels* at the moment of this change, see 17:14.

21:3 **But he was very worried now:** This is the first of several scenes in the novel in which David struggles with his impulse to pass judgment and with the nature and origins of his own desires. Although the novel most often presents Catherine as the primary agent of fetishistic desire in the text, David occasionally acknowledges, however reluctantly, that these desires are his own. He asks here, "Who participated and who accepted the change and lived it?" (21:7). In the manuscript, David also asks himself how he knows this wasn't his own desire. He admits that he was moved by Rodin's statue just as Rodin must have been (see *[17:22] 1.1.21).* (For further discussion of the agency of desire in the novel, see 12:13 and *[168:3] 3.29.19.)*

21:10 **a sin is what you feel bad after:** David's phrase is a variation on a familiar Hemingway formula. In *The Sun Also Rises,* Jake thinks that "morality" consists of those things that make one disgusted with oneself. "No," he corrects himself, "that must be immorality" (152). Hemingway refines the formula in *Death in the Afternoon:* "So far, about morals, I know only that what is moral is what you feel good after and what is immoral is what you feel bad after" (4). In *Eden,* Hemingway simply substitutes "sin" for "immorality."

David's suggestion that he isn't feeling bad because he's masking it with wine implies that he believes that what he is doing sexually with Catherine is, indeed, sinful. He struggles to free himself from self-judgment (see 21:3), but he is in an unwinnable bind because the sensation of sinning is essential to his fetishistic excitement (see *[5:22] 1.1.3).* A feeling of "badness" (see 14:23) or "remorse" (see 68:11) is something David and Catherine simply expect as a likely possible outcome after sex.

21:30 **It's nice to drink it for thirst. . . . brothers:** Following quickly on David's soliloquizing question to himself about using alcohol to mask his feelings—"Not with the wine you don't feel bad . . . and what will you drink when the wine won't cover for you?" (21:11)—it seems as if Catherine is reading his mind. The effect is enhanced, however, by Jenks's editing. Whereas these lines are separated by a little over 140 words in the Scribner's edition, they are in two separate chapters and separated by roughly 1,800 words in the manuscript. Nevertheless, Catherine's follow-up question—"You don't really mind being brothers do you?" (21:30)—indicates that she knows David has been using wine to mask his concerns. These concerns are a little clearer in the manuscript. With their wet hair plastered against their heads, they mirror one another (at least with respect to the all-important fetish), and this is when they each take a drink of the wine. Catherine then proposes that they get dressed and "be brothers." David asks if that is what she wants, and she tells him it isn't—implying that she'd rather have David as her girl—but it "might solve a lot of things" during daylight hours *(1.2.4)*.

The "brotherhood" of David and Catherine echoes the love banter of Hemingway and his wives. Early in his relationship with Hadley, Ernest wrote to her, "You're a very dear and much to be loved guy and I'm the guy to love you," and Hadley replied in kind, "Anything goes . . . between [us] honest men" (qtd. in Diliberto 79). Pauline and Ernest often referred to each other as "the same guy" (qtd. in Kert 186, 188, 219), and Ernest sometimes referred to Mary as his "kitten-brother" (*HIW* 373). For more on the sibling quality of Catherine and David's relationship, see 6:6.

22:17 You don't have to worry . . . until night. We won't let the night things come in the day: This brief paragraph reworks two disconnected sentences that Jenks moved here from the end of the first chapter of the manuscript *(1.1.25)*. The distinction between public "things of the day" and erotic "things of the night" is nearly ubiquitous in Hemingway's work, occurring more subtly in many stories and most of his novels, and it reflects a distinction that Hemingway made in his own life. In a subchapter in *Hemingway's Fetishism* devoted to this distinction, I note that Hemingway's split-off other-gendered alter ego Catherine seemed to emerge only at night. In a 5 May 1947 letter to Mary Hemingway, he tells his "blessed dearest wife and partner and friend and Pete" that her "girl hasn't been around at all except before daylight" (qtd. in *HF* 201). A few days later, remembering how Mary would "talk about Catherine in the night and how her hair was," he tells her that he dyed his own hair "as red as a French polished copper pot or a newly minted penny . . . and naturally in the morning I was spooked shitless. . . . So now I am just as red headed as you would like your girl Catherine to be . . ." (qtd. in *HF* 203). Similarly, in Africa in 1953, after waxing poetic about Mary's "naturally blonde to reddish golden blonde to sandy blonde" hair, Ernest wrote of her, in her journal, that Mary

> always wanted to be a boy and thinks as a boy without ever losing any femininity. . . . She loves me to be her girl, which I love to be, not being absolutely stupid, and also loving to be her girl since I have other jobs in the daytime. In return she makes me awards and at night we do every sort of thing which pleases her and

which pleases me. . . . On the night of December 19th we worked out these things and I have never been happier. (JFK MHPP-014-016)

Hemingway could work such things out in the night, but in the morning they "spooked him shitless." David shares these attitudes.

(22:18) 1.2.4 **Once we make up our mind:** In the manuscript, as they banter playfully, Catherine tells David that being "brothers" is fun "once we make up our *mind*" (my emphasis). David corrects Catherine's use of the singular *mind* to the plural, "our minds." Catherine responds with a joke: David can have the mind since he has to "do the writing."

This brief exchange is one of many revealing examples of the lovers' tendency to merge with each other. Later in the manuscript, Catherine will tell David she can no longer "tell who is who," adding with a terrifying narcissism, "Now you're me you're you so much better" (see *[178:7] 3.31.14*). Here Catherine intuits why she and David can merge so easily: together they represent, on some level, two halves of a single mind—a single riven and bigendered ego. In this case, that riven ego is not David's or Catherine's, but Hemingway's. Catherine's joke about David having the mind because he has to do the writing, moreover, reveals that the two halves of this divided ego have differential access to creativity (see 53:17).

22:22 **bank:** The contrast between Catherine's heavy envelope loaded with letters from her bank and the three letters forwarded from David's bank suggests the difference in wealth between them and introduces one of the novel's minor themes: the dangers of wealth and material comfort for young "innocent" writers. Hemingway came to associate this danger with his divorce from Hadley and his 1927 marriage to the much wealthier Pauline. It is a common theme in his work, occurring most famously in *A Moveable Feast* and "The Snows of Kilimanjaro," but the supposition behind it is most clearly expressed in *Green Hills of Africa*, where Hemingway fingers money as one of the ways American writers are "destroyed": "Our writers when they have made some money increase their standard of living and they are caught. They have to keep up their establishments, their wives, and so on, and they write slop" (23). Instead of financial statements, David's envelopes contain reviews, and David is soon thinking about his own earning power in implicit contrast to Catherine's wealth.

23:14 **five thousand copies . . . $2.50:** The numbers here align David with his creator. The first print run of David's second novel, *The Rift*, is 5,000 copies; the October 1926 first printing of *The Sun Also Rises* (Hemingway's second novel if we count *Torrents of Spring* as his first) was 5,090 copies (Grissom 58). David's novel has been priced, however, at $2.50, whereas *The Sun Also Rises* was priced at $2.00. The "sensational" reception of David's book, likewise, mirrors the reception of *The Sun Also Rises*.

24:14 **Is Madame also a writer?** In Catherine's jealousy of David's writing and in her own frustrated creativity many critics have rightly seen echoes of the tensions between Scott and Zelda Fitzgerald. By 1928, Hemingway was convinced that Zelda was undermining Scott as a writer (*Letters 3* 467), and in 1957 and 1958 he was exploring these memories in *A Moveable Feast,* writing that "Zelda was very jealous of Scott's work" (154). It is little wonder, then, that elements of Zelda's character seep into Catherine Bourne. To the degree that Catherine also represents the split-off other-gendered half of Hemingway's ego (see 17:23), her jealousy of David's writing and her frustrated creativity assume further complex dimensions which I explore elsewhere (see 5:27 and 53:17).

24:21 **How can we be us . . . and you be this that's in the clippings?** Despite his complicity in the creation of his own legend, the disparity between the writer's private self and public persona that so concerns Catherine similarly troubled Hemingway, both in 1927 and the mid-1950s.

What John Raeburn rightly calls Hemingway's "meteoric rise to literary eminence" with the publication of *In Our Time* (1925), *The Sun Also Rises* (1926), and *Men Without Women* (1927) fueled an insatiable public fascination with Hemingway, who soon discovered, to his great consternation, that his public persona was beyond his control (13). A few weeks before Hemingway honeymooned with Pauline at Le Grau-du-Roi in 1927, the *Hartford Courant* ran an article with the headline "Hemingway Legend Forming."

> Already the Hemingway legend is in the process of formation; having been credited with Italian decorations for distinguished service, a prep school record as a football star, and two children, Mr. Hemingway writes in protest to his publishers: "I was attached to the Italian infantry for a time as a very minor sort of camp follower—I was a long way from being a football star at school—and have only one child"—and he adds that he lately read that he earned his way through college as a boxing instructor. As Mr. Hemingway never went to college, and never told anyone that he did so, he finds this statement amusing . . .

In spite of Hemingway's protests, articles in newspapers and magazines often spoke of him as an occasional bullfighter, and one imaginative 1927 article described him breaking up an amateur village bullfight with the bulldogging skills he learned from his supposed "several years on the ranches in New Mexico":

> He vaulted the fence, dashed across the ring, and made a flying tackle through the air. A moment later the startled spectators, and the no less amazed performers beheld a sadly surprised bull prone in the dust, while a young Americano was ambling coolly back to his seat. The natives never did decide whether they should

honor Hemingway as a superman, or throw him in jail for busting up the fight. ("Christopher")

By the end of 1927, Hemingway had become "a fad and a fashion," and newspapers even spoke of a "Hemingway Cult."[3]

If Hemingway remembered 1927 as the year his public persona diverged from his private self and took on a bewildering life of its own, the problem had grown to truly ridiculous proportions by the 1950s when he was working on *The Garden of Eden*. In the aftermath of the two 1954 African plane crashes and the awarding of the Nobel Prize, "no private life was left" for him. As Michael Reynolds writes, "His life, no longer his own, had become a public sideshow open to anyone" (*Final* 279, 284). By then, as David Earle chronicles in *All Man! Hemingway, 1950s Men's Magazines, and the Masculine Persona,* Hemingway had also become a cultural icon for a sort of testosterone-crazed two-dimensional masculinity. Pulp magazines regularly featured cover images of a glowering Hemingway and articles with titles such as "Hemingway, Rogue Male," "Hemingway: War, Women, Wine, and Words," and "Hemingway: America's No 1 He-Man." As Hemingway wrote of the Bournes' gender-bending experiments—experiments rooted in his own erotic desires—this public image (however complicit he had been in its creation, and however much it spoke to the masculine half of his riven ego) must have felt like a thing apart. Given the rift in Hemingway's ego and his predisposition to dissociation, this must have been particularly self-alienating.

24:22 **"clippings...."** **"They're bad for you":** As Daniel Train has noted, the press clippings threaten Catherine, in part, because of their "potential to tell a competing narrative about David" and who he is (35). To Catherine, that competing narrative represents for David a sort of dangerous "false self"—the complex private man distilled, distorted, and oversimplified into the public writer. During an argument in the Hendaye section of the book, Catherine scolds David, "Do you think I married you because you're a writer? You and your clippings" (39:29). And when Catherine discovers that Marita has already read David's first novel before meeting him, she asks her, "Did you think of him as a writer when you kissed him . . . ?" Marita answers that she didn't think at all, to which Catherine replies, "I'm glad. . . . I was afraid it was going to be like the clippings" (112:2).

Whereas *Eden* links Catherine's fear that the clippings could "destroy" David to a Zelda-like jealousy of David's creativity, in 1927 Hemingway himself felt much like Catherine does about the destructive potential of press clippings. While after the 1925 publication of *In Our Time,* he had been enthusiastic about receiving them (*Letters* 2 417), and in August 1926 he had asked Max Perkins to renew his arrangement with "the original Romeike" (*Letters* 3 107), the same clipping service used by David Bourne (see 216:20), by February 1927 he had experienced a change of heart. Disturbed by the distortions about his life that marked the emergence of the Hemingway legend, he wrote to Perkins, "Of course the whole thing that is wrong is this damned clipping system. No living person should read as much stuff about themselves as they get through those cursed clippings" (*Letters 3* 213). Soon afterwards he stopped receiving them. A few months later, he explained to Barklie McKee Henry, "I stopped the bloody clippings last winter when they began to get too potent. . . . Hearing once in a while is useful and swell—but the clippings coming all the time are poisonous" (*Letters 3* 260).

In 1954, in the wake of his two African plane crashes, Hemingway's memory of this heady experience might have been jogged and colored by reading his own obituaries. In a piece for *Look* magazine, he records Mary admonishing him, "Darling. . . . I really wish you would not read so many of those obituaries. I think it is morbid probably. Anyway we are not dead and so it is rather an affectation. We never read other people's obituaries and I do not really see why we should read our own. Besides it could be bad for you." Ernest agrees but finds it an addictive "vice." He decides to preserve them in zebra hide– and lion skin–covered scrapbooks and "read them at least once a year in order to keep [his] morale up to par when the critics have recovered their aplomb and return to the assault" (*BL* 468–69).

(24:33) 1.2.8 **Bluebeard's closet . . . Look at Landru:** In the manuscript, the conversation about the clippings leads to a conversation about self-destructive impulses. Catherine claims that anybody who is any good inevitably destroys themselves, but she'd rather she and David do that in their own way instead of by "eating a mess of dried clippings." She then compares her own desire to read the clippings to the impulse to open "Bluebeard's closet. They always do it. Look at Landru even."

The obvious reference is to Perrault's classic folktale. A wealthy man seeks a bride from among the two daughters of his wellborn neighbor, but both girls are initially reluctant to marry him because of his frightening blue beard—and because he has already married several wives and no one knows what has become of them. Won over by Bluebeard's wealth, the younger sister marries him. A month later, Bluebeard goes on a journey, first giving his keys to his wife and telling her that during his absence she may go into any of his splendor-filled rooms, save one. Her curiosity, of course, gets the best of her, and she opens the door to the forbidden room to find a floor clotted with blood and the bodies of Bluebeard's previous wives hung along the walls. When Bluebeard returns, he is ready to cut her throat as well.

The reference to "Landru" will be less obvious for readers today, but in the 1920s Henri Désiré Landru—popularly known as the "Bluebeard of Gambais"—was the young century's most famous serial killer. Eventually found guilty of killing ten women and the teenage son of one of the women, Landru advertised in the papers as a widower seeking a widow for matrimony. After seducing the women who replied to his ad and securing their assets, he then killed them, dismembered them, and burned their bodies in a stove that featured prominently at his trial. Because these women simply disappeared, and because Landru used multiple aliases, it took the police several years to make an arrest. When he was finally arrested in April 1919, the evidence was all circumstantial: a notebook with his victims' names, "locks of hair from his victims in envelopes bearing their names," and an enormous heap of cinders outside of his villa in Gambais (Mitchell). These cinders were found to contain bits of women's garments and fragments of human teeth and bones. The search for evidence and the eventual trial, which devolved into a media circus, riveted the world for the better part of three years—during which time Landru's wit and courtroom persona turned him into "a kind of musical comedy character": "The revue writers and the Montmartre chansonniers soon got busy, and vaudevilles and cabarets resounded with Landru jokes and songs" ("All France Agog"). Landru was guillotined on 25 February 1922, two months after Hemingway moved to France. (For more on the guillotine, see *[106:8] 3.20.31*).

The folktale's theme of forbidden fruit has Edenic overtones, and Bluebeard's locked room sounds suspiciously like David's writing room and locked suitcase. Later in the novel, after reading the story set in the year of the Maji Maji Rebellion, David's "new wife," Marita, tells him, "I like going in the room when the door is locked" (154:5). Catherine's burning of David's manuscripts may resonate with Landru's incineration of his victims, and the oft-bearded Hemingway—a man of four wives—may even have seen a bit of Bluebeard in himself. He was well aware of the dangers of being married to a writer.

In an important early article on *Eden,* Steven Roe explores the novel's Bluebeard allusions, arguing that Hemingway portrays David from "an ironic distance" as a figure whose "'Bluebeardism' lies primarily in his creative vanity, in the self-absorption, detachment, and pride that inform his compulsion to write" ("Opening" 53). For Roe, "the clippings . . . embody a murderous secret. For Catherine, as for Hemingway, they reveal the monstrous vanity of David's writerly quest for self-validation" (55). In this reading, Catherine's "attempt to overthrow the imperialistic ego of her writer-husband" is "a necessary countermeasure to male tyranny" (60, 53). This attempt, however, inevitably turns Catherine herself, "to a lesser degree," into a sort of monster, "a vindictive savior who re-enacts the murderous egoism she detests" (54).

(26:2) 1.3.3 **Cat:** In dialogue cut from the manuscript, David calls Catherine "Cat"— much as Frederic Henry calls Catherine Barkley "Cat" in *A Farewell to Arms,* and much as Hemingway called Hadley "Katherine Kat" and Mary Hemingway "Kitten" (see 17:23). In a bedroom scene later in the *Eden* manuscript, David strokes one of Catherine's new haircuts "as she move[s] under his hand like a cat" *(3.6.2),* and in yet another scene from the manuscript, Marita asks him to stroke *her* new haircut "so [*she*] can purr." She's been purring, she tells him, ever since she got her hair cut *(3.45.3).* Catherine describes herself as "lion color" (30:23), Barbara thinks

Catherine has "lioness eyes" *(3.5.7)*, and David even calls her a "lioness" *(3.11.9)*. Nick Sheldon meanwhile, describes his long hair as getting heavy like the "mane" of a lion *(2.1.14)*, and Hemingway briefly toyed with Nick using "Cat" as a pet name for Barbara (see appendix A).

In *Hemingway's Fetishism,* I argue that Hemingway's famous affinity for cats was colored by a degree of fetishist investment. As a fetish word, "cat" functions as a variation on "Catherine," the name for the split-off other-gendered half of his ego (see 17:23). Cats recall memories of Ernest's "Feather Kitty," Hadley, but his hair-stroking games harken back to much earlier memories of Ernest recorded by Grace Hemingway in her scrapbooks: "He loves to play kitty and be the baby kitty, and Mama be the mama kitty and stroke him and purr" (qtd. in Spilka 57). The cat motif clearly plays into a theme of "miscegenation across species lines" noted by several critics (see 62:28).

26:4 It's because I'm married: The checks Catherine receives liberate the Bournes from more than financial concerns. The money seems to liberate them from social "rules" and expectations of all sorts, even if such liberation is ironically obtained through Catherine's assumption of her socially sanctioned role as wife. "Why," Catherine asks David, "do we have to do other things like everyone does?" (27:7). The "travels and voyages" financed by these checks are less geographical than they are personal, spiritual, and psychological (see *[78:3] 3.16.29)*. And as Kathy Willingham notes, Catherine's suggestion that they use her money "to perpetuate the honeymoon" is driven, in part, by her recognition that "its end will halt the narrative which she is creating" through her experiments with David (*Ernest* 55).

Hemingway is again drawing on biography in this passage. When he married Pauline in 1927, they began their marriage with thousand-dollar checks from Pauline's parents, her Uncle Henry, and her Uncle Gus, not to mention additional financial gifts from other members of Pauline's extended family. As Ruth Hawkins notes, "The total could have supported Pauline and Ernest for another year in Europe without other income" (75). On top of this, Pauline had a well-endowed trust fund, and her father and Uncle Gus regularly paid her expenses.

26:8 if I live to be twenty-five or if I ever live to be thirty: These words sound ominous coming from a twenty-one-year-old. Yet they provoke no direct response from David.

(26:14) 1.3.4 *if I were a negro:* In the manuscript, Catherine apologizes to David for her reaction to the clippings, but she wants him to understand. She isn't "being crazy," she just "hates the clippings," explaining nonsensically that she "can't help it any more than if [she] were a negro." "Or a Kanaka," David adds. We might wonder why on earth Catherine would associate negritude with compulsivity. It may be that Catherine's fetishization of racial otherness (see 30:16) leads her to associate the compulsivity of fetishistic desire with the fetishized object.

26:19 **What is there that's real?** In the manuscript, Catherine's question is provoked by David's suggestion that they have a pastis, which he says is "almost as good as absinthe." Catherine, however, doesn't want "something that's *almost* as good as something else" (my emphasis, *1.3.1*).

This is not an anachronistic reference to the product commercialized by Paul Ricard under the name Pastis in 1932, but rather to the local Provençal product that inspired Ricard. Having banned absinthe and similar anise-based alcohols in 1915, the French government in 1922 revisited the regulations to define what it meant by "similar" (Domenichino et al. 15). In the process, they legalized very sweet anise-flavored liqueurs with an alcohol content below 40 proof. "The people of Provence had long appreciated the refreshing flavor of anise," but they favored a stronger, less sweet drink that, like absinthe, clouded with the careful addition of ice-cold water, and they did not pay much attention to the regulations. The result was pastis:

> Every winemaker and bartender could conjure up a recipe of his own. The forbidden drinks were poured "under the counter" in bistros and cafés. The ingredients were common knowledge: alcohol and water, anise, licorice, and a little sugar, with various herbs and spices added according to taste and whim. The *pastis* tasted different from one place to the next, some better, some not so good. (Dominé 404)

By 1924, articles in the French press warned that "Pastis is king. It is made everywhere, even in families," so that distillers who complied with the laws were losing out to unfair competition ("Danger"). When in 1932, after much controversy, laws changed enough for Paul Ricard to market his Pastis, it soon became the most popular aperitif in France.

26:23 **Perrier water:** Even in their choice of waters, the Bournes are upscale locavores. Perrier's naturally carbonated water is bottled at its source in Vergèze, a mere fifteen miles from Le Grau-du-Roi. David later remembers having passed the place on the way to Aigues-Mortes (222:29). Although there is no connection between Perrier and the Perrier-Jouët that the Bournes also drink, Perrier advertised itself in the 1920s as "the champagne of table waters."

27:1 **For heroes:** In the *Eden* manuscript, David and Catherine drink this "hero drink" (28:6) several times. An important clue as to what makes Armagnac and soda "heroic" can be found in *A Farewell to Arms*. There, Catherine Barkley admonishes a Cognac-drinking Frederic, "I know brandy is for heroes. But you shouldn't exaggerate" (140). Like Cognac, Armagnac is a type of brandy, and Boswell records Dr. Johnson famously opining to Edmund Burke, "Claret for boys, port for men, brandy for heroes"—to which Burke replied, "Then let me have claret: I love to be a boy; to have the careless gaiety of boyish days" (372). Even if she does drink Armagnac, Catherine, like Burke, "loves to be a boy."

Although Hemingway read Boswell, he may also have been thinking of the same phrase where Lord Byron uses it in "The Island," his poetic account of the mutiny on the Bounty. There, Fletcher Christian encourages his fellow mutineers to keep reason at bay by remaining drunk:

> And now the self-elected chief finds time
> To stun the first sensation of his crime,
> And raise it in his followers—"Ho! the bowl!"
> Lest passion should return to reason's shoal.
> "Brandy for heroes!" (417)[4]

This passage echoes the way David attempts to use the "hero drink" to mask his misgivings. The mutineers' escape with native women to a deserted South Pacific island would also resonate with *The Garden of Eden*'s other Pacific island fantasies and allusions to Gauguin (see *[154:7] 3.26.4* and *[163:31] 3.28.15*).

27:16 That way we can have the fun before I have a baby: The prospect of having a baby, a minor theme in the novel, first appears here, as part of a larger conversation that includes Catherine's objection to the clippings and her proposal for an extended honeymoon that would defer David's return to writing until "afterwards." In other words, the prospect of a baby occurs as part of a conversation about creativity—a conversation driven by Catherine's jealousy of David's work. For Catherine, this work threatens their dyadic union ("I don't have to leave you when you write do I?" 27:26). Instead, she wants to prolong the honeymoon through which she scripts a narrative, using as her medium—instead of text, stage, or canvas—her own body and the bodies and lives of other real people. (See also 14:13.) In conversation with David later in the manuscript, Catherine spells this out even more clearly:

> I can't write nor draw nor even paint in water colors. I can't even draw a map to show how to get anywhere. Do you know if I couldn't talk, I'd have no means of communication? I mean any real communication. So try not to mind if I talk. . . . You're the only person I ever could communicate with or wanted to. Don't say it's the same with you because you know it isn't. If we'd had the damned baby I wouldn't want to have it around any more than my parents wanted me around. They were honest enough about it. (3.16.11)

The baby appears here as the last item in a list of potential creative media. David even suggests in the manuscript that procreation may be the only moral form of creation *(3.23.9bis)*. On this level, childbirth functions as yet another potential vehicle for Catherine to "write" with her body (see 53:17). (For a further consideration of this theme, as it relates to David's desire to "make a baby" with Marita and Hemingway's desire to do the same with his "African fiancée," Debba, on his 1953–54 safari, see *[204:8] 3.37.25.)*

27:22 **Then write, stupid. You didn't say you wouldn't write**: In the manuscript, Catherine adds, "You haven't sold your soul to the devil" *(1.3.7)*. The implication, however, is that somehow this is precisely what David has done. His brain is too clouded to clearly remember that Catherine *had* said something about deferring writing until after their travels (27:16).

27:26 **I don't have to leave you when you write do I?** See 14:13 and 27:16.

NOTES

1. For Hemingway's interest in Josephine Baker, see *HF* 155–57, 180–83. For Hemingway's interest in racial transformations, see *HF*; Moddelmog, *Reading Desire*; Morrison; Comley and Scholes; del Gizzo; Strong, *Race*; and Dudley.

2. For an exploration of how such questions function in *The Garden of Eden, Islands in the Stream, Across the River and into the Trees,* and *Under Kilimanjaro,* see Eby, "He Felt the Change."

3. See, for instance, "He Drank with Them," "Ernest Hemingway Shown at His Best," and "The Hemingway Cult."

4. The poem that appears directly before "The Island" in Hemingway's edition of Byron, "Mazeppa," is alluded to later in the novel (see *[140:29] 3.24.9).*

CHAPTER 3 (MSS. CHAPTER 4)

29:6 I'm how you want but I'm how I want too and it isn't as though it wasn't for us both: See 12:13 and 21:3.

29:10 when we go to Africa I'll be your African girl too: In the manuscript, Catherine and Marita—both together and separately—aspire through fetishized suntans and haircuts to become David's "African girls" (see *[161:8] 3.27.3*). With their own "tribal taboos and tribal pleasures" *(3.29.20)*, they can become David's "Somali wives" to escape Western sexual prohibitions—including the ban on polygamy (see *[136:13] 3.23.25bis*). Late in the manuscript (after Catherine's departure), Marita even uses her new "African haircut" to become a boyish "Bizerte street urchin," so she and David can play with a colonial fantasy of pederasty (see *[244:2] 3.45.1*). Such changes perform a vital psychological function by helping Catherine to imagine herself as "a different person . . . another me" (see 30:16), and they allow Catherine and Marita to stand in for something lost in David's distant past: his first love, his boyhood African "fiancée" (see *[163:24] 3.27.27*).

Hemingway's own fantasies of racial transformation were remarkably intense (see 129:1), and Catherine and Marita's "African girl" fantasies draw upon several sources: the Trudy/Prudy Boulton of the Nick Adams stories (see 202:28), Hemingway's own African "fiancée" from his 1953–54 safari (see *[163:24] 3.27.27*), and the "African haircuts" he talked Mary Hemingway into getting in 1953 and 1954 (see *[161:8] 3.27.3*).

After returning from Africa in 1954—the trip during which he and Mary were injured in two plane crashes (an important inspiration for David Bourne's history as a WWI pilot [see 168:2])—Hemingway began work on the long, unfinished book that was eventually published posthumously as *Under Kilimanjaro*. Though his work on this book was interrupted, notes in his letters throughout the summer and late fall of 1956 indicate that he intended to return to and finish the African book—indeed, he intended to return to Africa itself to conduct further research for the book while visiting his two youngest sons, both living in what was then Tanganyika. His return was prevented, however, by Mary Hemingway's bout with anemia in late 1956, and he never resumed work on what he called the African book. The book is generally regarded by scholars as an abandoned text, but it might be fairer to say that Hemingway decided to reimagine and repurpose the material from the African book in *The Garden of Eden,* which began to occupy his writing energies in 1958. As he worked on *Eden,* he still longed, and planned, to return to Africa,[1] and the African stories David will later write are full of details drawn from Hemingway's 1953–54 safari.

29:11 **"Are we going to Africa?" "Aren't we? Don't you remember?":** In the manuscript, Catherine is not asking David to remember their conversation from that morning; rather, she is asking him to remember a conversation "downstairs at the Crillon" *(1.4.1).* We later learn that this is where they first met (237:28). This implies that "Africa," and everything it represents in this novel, has been on Catherine's and David's minds since the inception of their relationship.

Housed in what was once a neoclassical palace on the Place de la Concorde, the famous Hôtel Crillon opened in 1909 and boasted the longest bar in Europe. In 1919, the American delegation responsible for negotiating the League of Nations stayed at this ultra luxury hotel. It appears often in Hemingway's fiction, most famously in *The Sun Also Rises.* In *A Moveable Feast,* Hemingway remembers, "When I had money I went to the Crillon" (164). This passage in *Feast*—written about the same time he was writing *Eden*—leads in turn to memories of Baron von Blixen and the beautiful book, *Out of Africa,* written by his first wife, who wrote under the name Isak Dinesen.

30:7 **Sevilla is over and so is San Isidro:** The Feria de Abril de Sevilla is an annual weeklong fair that in 1927 opened on 18 April ("Comienza"). "San Isidro" refers to Madrid's weeklong festival in honor of its patron saint, San Isidro Labrador. The festival is held each year around 15 May, and in 1927 it ended on 20 May. Both festivals traditionally book top-ranked matadors for their bullfights. Hemingway may also have been thinking of a central feature of Seville's feria: an amusement park popularly known (due to its noise) as the Calle del infierno (Hell's road).

30:8 **Basque coast:** Book II of the Scribner's edition begins with the next chapter set in Hendaye, on the Basque coast, but the Bournes do not go there immediately because it is too early, cold, and rainy. Instead, David and Catherine explore the area around the Estérel (30:30) and discover La Napoule, to which they will return in book III of the Scribner's edition. This time, lasting for probably a little over a month (see 57:10), is alluded to in several places (see 36:2), but it is not described in the manuscript.

30:16 **"Why do you want to be so dark? . . . blonde. . . ." "lion color . . . away from other people. . . . changed":** David asks a vital question: Why *does* Catherine want to be so dark, and what is at stake in this for her? Her answer is more fully developed in the manuscript, but it must have seemed so strange to Jenks that he edited out much of what is most revealing in it. Her seemingly flippant counter-question "Why do you want anything?" points to the very nature and origins of desire. Catherine wants it "very much," but she struggles to say why: "I don't know why I want it so much. It's like I wanted to have my hair cut. But this takes so long. ~~It's to be a different person I guess. another me~~ Maybe that's part of it. It's like growing something. But it makes me excited too. Just good excited all the time." Doesn't it excite David? she asks. It does, he admits. Catherine supposes it represents one of the ways they're now "changed." She declares that she doesn't "want to be a white girl anymore." She's "half-caste already and [she] think[s] [she] can be darker and it still be good." She asks David if he thought she "could ever be this dark" (clearly a moral or spiritual double entendre), and he is surprised that she could because she's "blonde." To this, Catherine answers,

> "I can because I'm lion color and they can go dark. . . . But I want every part of me dark and it's getting that way and you'll be darker than an Indian and that takes us further away from other people. You see why it's important. . . . I wish I had some Kanaka blood or some Indian blood but then it probably wouldn't mean anything. It's the changing that is as important as the dark. But I'm going to be so dark you won't be able to stand it and you'll be helpless. White women will always bore you." *(1.4.2–3)*

David can only reply that they already do.

In what way, we might wonder, is Catherine's desire to "have a completely different pigmentation" and look as if she belonged to "a different race" (see *[20:12] 1.2.3*) like her desire to have her hair cut? It isn't that both desires are mere whimsical larks. Quite the opposite. As I have argued in *Hemingway's Fetishism*, Hemingway not only fetishized hair, he also fetishized racial otherness—and, for him, the two fetishes were linked. Thus, later in the *Eden* manuscript, when Marita decides to become David's "African girl" or his "Bizerte street urchin," she accomplishes this through haircuts (see *[161:8] 3.27.3* and *[244:2] 3.45.1*). This is why, in the manuscript, when the Bournes and Marita want to play at being Tahitian (see *[163:31] 3.28.15*) or Danish (see 77:13 and 85:30), they imagine doing so by changing their hair; and this is why Hemingway asked his wife Mary to get "African haircuts" in 1953 and 1954 (see *[161:8] 3.27.3*). Thus, when Hemingway assumed a cross-racial identification in Africa in 1953 (see 129:1)—flirting with the Kamba girl Debba, dyeing his clothes the rusty pink ochre worn by the Masai, taking up spear hunting, and fantasizing about having black skin, pierced ears, and tribal marks—he also shaved his head "to the scalp, like a Masai girl" (*HIW* 367). As he wrote to Harvey Breit in January 1954: "Have my head shaved because that is how my fiancée likes it. . . . My girl [Debba] is completely impudent . . . but absolutely loving and delicate rough. I better quit writing about it because I want to write it really and I mustn't spoil it. Anyway it gives me too bad a hardon" (*SL* 827). In other words, the sort of "excitement" Catherine and David feel about racial otherness is *erotic* excitement.

It is telling that Catherine describes her racialized tanning as part of an attempt to become "a different person . . . another me." To the extent that her ego, like David's, like Hemingway's, is riven—after all, she later calls herself "two persons" (see *[66:11] 3.14.4*), and she has two names: Catherine/Peter (see 17:23)—she can communicate with her *other me* by wearing the fetish. (Catherine later tells the Colonel that she "wears" her suntan [64:14].) The mechanism is essentially the same one we see when David later inspects his recently bleached hair before the mirror and sees himself as a Danish girl, or Catherine's mirror image (see 84:16). Thus, when Hemingway assumed his cross-racial identification during his 1953–54 safari—that is, when he engaged in an act of fetishistic cross-dressing, *wearing* fetishized racial otherness—he shaved his head like a Masai *girl*, desired pierced ears, and wrote in his wife's journal: Mary "always wanted to be a boy and thinks as a boy without ever losing any femininity. . . . *She loves me to be her girl, which I love to be,* not being absolutely stupid, and also loving to be her girl since I have other jobs in the daytime. In return she makes me awards and at night we do every sort of thing which pleases her and which pleases me" (qtd. in *HF* 176; my emphasis). He became, in short, his *other me,* rechristening himself in his wife's journal: "Kathrin Ernest Hemingway." Catherine Bourne's "lion color" in this passage aligns her with the feline permutations of the name that Hemingway gave to this split-off other-gendered half of his ego (see 17:23).

These racialized suntans, like the fetish more generally, recall something lost in David's (and Hemingway's) youth (see 29:10) and mark the way the Bournes are now "changed" (see 6:5 and 12:11). Because it "takes [them] further away from other people," the fetish facilitates their dyadic union—a codependent imaginary world in which they stand apart from everyone, like Adam and Eve in the garden (see 27:16 and *[178:7] 3.31.14*).

30:30 **"Estérel. . . ." "wild places . . . nobody is there in the summer":** Noted for its beautiful and rugged landscape of unspoiled forests, jagged red porphyry mountains, deep ravines, innumerable coves, and cliffs plunging into a cobalt Mediterranean, the Massif de l'Estérel, between Saint-Raphaël and La Napoule, remains the wildest part of the Riviera. Today, much of it is protected national forest. With a rocky volcanic soil and topography unsuited to agriculture, the name Estérel is derived from the Latin for *sterile.* The old Estérel route between France and Italy was once so teeming with highwaymen that "the phrase 'to pass the Estérel pass' was used to describe any action involving a high degree of risk" (Marsh 216). See also 30:8 and 6:9.

30:33 **could get a car:** We later learn that the Bournes purchase a Bugatti (see *[54:23] 3.11.2*), the "small low car" we see them driving when they arrive in Hendaye (35:1). We should remember that they took the train from Paris to Avignon and rode their bicycles from there to Nîmes and then Le Grau-du-Roi (13:19). Given the novel's interest in historical accuracy, we might surmise that they purchase the Bugatti, before going to Spain, at the only dealership then in the South of France, the one opened in July 1924 by race car driver Ernest Friderich at 40 Rue de la Buffa in Nice.[2]

(31:7) 1.4.3 so dark that they won't let us into places. . . . So dark they'll make us sit at a separate table going out to Africa: In the manuscript, as they get ready to sleep, Catherine tells David, "I'm going to dream that we're so dark that they won't let us into places. . . . So dark they'll make us sit at a separate table going out to Africa." Lines such as these, as I have argued elsewhere, reveal how the critique of colonialism that emerges as a minor theme in *Eden* is hopelessly entangled with and compromised by Hemingway's psychosexual concerns—including his fetishization of racial otherness (see 59:31, 60:21, 111:11, 147:13, and *[214:22] 3.39.9*).[3]

(31:20) 1.4.4 we must have the sun to make this sea change: In the manuscript, the passage beginning "She changes from a girl into a boy and back carelessly and happily" continues as follows:

> and she enjoys corrupting me and I enjoy being corrupted. But she's not corrupt ~~and maybe it is not corruption~~ and who says it is corruption? I withdraw the word. Now we are going to be a special dark race of our own with our own pigmentation ~~and we already have our own tribal customs.~~ growing that way each day as some people would garden or plant and raise a crop. The trouble with that is that it will not grow at night too. It can only be made in the sun, in the strong sun against the reflection of the sand and the sea. So we must have the sun to make this sea change. The sea change was made in the night and it grows in the night and the darkness that she wants and needs now grows in the sun.

Hemingway briefly toyed with the idea of using "The Sea Change" as the title for the third book of the *Eden* manuscript (the other two books would have been "The Huntress" and "The Sand Castle"[4]), and he had already used the Shakespearean phrase as the title of a 1931 short story that reads almost like a capsule version of *The Garden of Eden*. The story

> packs into a very tight space a hint of the plot and many of the erotic symbols and obsessions that preoccupy Hemingway in [*Eden*]: love triangles, lesbian affairs, sun-bleached closely cropped hair, deep suntans, erotic throat swelling, twin-like lovers, the experience of dissociation in front of the mirror, and mysterious sea changes. And if we consider "The Sea Change" manuscript, to this constellation we can add sibling romance and anxiety about male homosexuality. (Eby, "Sea" 83).

Perhaps more importantly, the short story and novel share an internal tension—a set of divided, opposing yet simultaneously held, attitudes—over what is "corruption," "vice," or "perversion." Hemingway probably began the story in the autumn of 1929, not long after his wife Pauline dyed her hair blonde for him as a surprise during their vacation at Hendaye beach, making it clear that the themes and concerns that drive *The Garden of Eden* had preoccupied Hemingway for decades.

Hemingway associated the phrase "sea change" with the bleaching effect of sun and salt water on the hair (see 6:5), but its source in Ariel's song to Ferdinand from Shakespeare's *The Tempest* also implies a link with "corruption":

> Full fathom five thy father lies.
> Of his bones are coral made;
> Those are pearls that were his eyes;
> Nothing of him that doth fade
> But doth suffer a sea-change
> Into something rich and strange,
> Sea-nymphs hourly ring his knell:
> Ding dong.
> Hark, now I hear them
> Ding-dong bell. (1.2.397–405)

However beautiful these lines may be, the song is after all about decomposition: corruption. The question of whether or not erotic experiments are "sinful" or "wicked" (see 5:22)—whether Catherine (see 150:21) or Marita (see 245:31) "corrupt" David or their sexual innovations are "innocent"—remains an unresolved tension throughout the *Eden* manuscript. (The Scribner's edition implies a resolution of this tension that the manuscript does not support.) Using the logic of disavowal (see 15:13), the novel's characters seem to entertain opposing positions simultaneously, or in oscillation. David will soon discover, to his surprise, that as he "corrupt[s] or change[s]," his ability to write improves; yet I would suggest that his creativity is fueled precisely by the tension between his conflicting beliefs (see 132:11).

31:24 Everything was free for a time: In the manuscript, this line comes at the end of an extended simile:

> He was like those drunken stragglers who when a town is hurriedly evacuated and the defending troops are gone sit quietly in a great café toasting each other solemnly, enjoying the unaccustomed luxury and the quietness of the city and everything being free, as happy in the clarity and euphoria of their rummyhood, they realize the insanity of fighting and marching and the beauty of this day and

confidently open another bottle as the first enemy patrol is moving into the outskirts of the city *(1.4.5)*.

Needless to say, this colors David's judgment that "everything was free for a time." In the manuscript, David thinks that what Catherine said about money was "true," just as the "drinks were all free in the great café in the town that was no longer defended."

31:25 What was it that she had said about destruction? Catherine has said several things about destruction. Most recently she's said that the clippings "could destroy you if you thought about them or believed them" (24:25). In the manuscript, she adds that "everybody that is any good destroys themselves," demanding that she and David do it in their own way instead of by "eating a mess of dried clippings" (see *[24:33] 1.2.8)*. Still more ominously, in the opening pages of the novel, Catherine announces, "I'm the destructive type. . . . And I'm going to destroy you" (see 5:27). It would seem that destruction looms in David's future, but he has been too distracted to fully recognize this (see 31:24).

NOTES

1. In a letter dated 8 Aug. 1957, Mary Hemingway told Kyungu (the Chungo of *Under Kilimanjaro*) that she and Ernest hoped to return to Africa in September 1958 (JFK). That trip never happened, but in a 24 Nov. 1958 letter to his son Patrick, Hemingway wrote that he still hoped to return to Africa in 1959 (*SL* 888).
2. See "La Quatrième." See also Dick 241.
3. See Eby, "'In the Year of the Maji Maji'" 31.
4. These possible subtitles appear on a page of jottings from the *Moveable Feast* manuscript that contains passages written on different parts of the page, at different angles, from both *Eden* and *Feast* (JFK Item 123).

(MSS. BOOK II)

(MSS. CHAPTER 1)

(32) 2.1.1 **With the other two. . . . Hôtel Biron . . . beautiful gardens:** Here Scribner's editor Tom Jenks deletes a long chapter that in the manuscript Hemingway calls book II. This chapter gives readers the backstory of two new characters, Nick and Barbara Sheldon, both painters. Set in Paris, this chapter seems to have been an afterthought inserted into the manuscript after Hemingway had already introduced readers to Nick and Barbara in the Hendaye chapters of the novel. In fact, Hemingway may have completed the Madrid section of the novel and begun the La Napoule chapters before he wrote and inserted this chapter.

Nick and Barbara's erotic experiments had begun in late February (although a narratorial aside suggests they had "really started long before"), after they, too, had seen "the bronze" in the Musée Rodin, housed in Rodin's former residence, the Hôtel Biron (see *[17:22] 1.1.21*). As they lie in bed together one night, huddled against the cold, Barbara proposes that they do something fun that will be "secret and wicked." As they make love, Barbara tells Nick to close his eyes and not think at all, and together they inhabit a "strange country." Barbara touches him and strokes his hair, "doing something purposefully" with her hands *(2.1.2)*. Eyes closed, she swings her hair over Nick "like a silken curtain."

Afterwards, Nick isn't surprised at anything that they've done. It all seems familiar. But Barbara tells him she's only given him a clue. She knows Nick has been growing his hair out, and she asks him if they can get their hair trimmed identically. She suspects this might be a "bad wickedness," but she thinks it will be wonderful in bed at night. Nick says he is willing, although Barbara suspects this is just "night talk." She has asked him to do this before, but he hasn't done it yet. If he'll do it, she promises, they'll be "just the same, only you'll be a boy and I'll be a girl" *(2.1.6)*.

(32) 2.1.7 **skiing trousers and boots:** When Nick wakes in the cold morning, he is careful not to wake Barbara. He puts water on the stove and goes out to buy bread, eggs, and ham for breakfast, and brioche for a present. Living together in a poverty that distinguishes them from the Bournes, Nick and Barbara must give each other "things that don't cost money." When Nick returns with the food and a newspaper, Barbara is up and wearing a sweater with a sheepskin vest and "skiing trousers."

Nick wears a sweater and "ski jacket," too, and his face, like Barbara's, is "still dark from the sun on the snow." It is so cold in their apartment they can see their breath.

With Barbara's "red gold hair" and "delicately freckled skin," and with the Sheldons' ski clothes and fantasies of growing their hair out identically, the lovers sound remarkably like the Ernest and Hadley we meet in the "Secret Pleasures" chapter published in the restored edition of *A Moveable Feast*: "When we lived in Austria in the winter we would cut each other's hair and let it grow to the same length. One was dark and the other dark red gold and in the dark in the night one would wake the other swinging the heavy dark or the heavy silken gold across the others lips in the cold dark in the warmth of the bed. You could see your breath if there was moonlight" (186).[1]

With her "skiing trousers," Barbara, in spite of her bohemian poverty, is, like Catherine Bourne, on the cutting edge of a masculinizing trend in women's fashion. In April 1927, Lucile Buchanan, fashion editor at *Harper's Bazaar,* speculated about a possible future for women's trousers. Noting the recent popularity of the divided skirt as "the first shy trousers to appear" for any purpose beyond active sportswear, she noted, "Already, among smart people, actual trousers for women have been accepted without a murmur for winter sports and for country riding." Building on celebrated designer Paul Poiret's then-recent prediction that women would someday wear slacks for non-sporting purposes (see 110:7), Buchanan suggested how that future might play out:

> The development of the wearing of trousers by women sums up like this: First the smartest woman cut her hair and wore it exactly like a man's. She also wore, in extreme cases, a 'smoking' [jacket] in the evening.... cut on the lines of a man's Tuxedo. In the daytime this lady took to sports clothes, which became more and more severe in their cut.... With this as a start, the next move was the wearing of pajamas on the beach at the Lido, where all the world could see that the lady was, after all, a mere biped. Then followed ski trousers (not knickers) at St. Moritz, and now the stage is perfectly and completely set for any further drama of trousers the designers care to plot.

For more on trousers for women, see 6:3 and 110:7.

(32) 2.1.9 **"*You're a funny boy....*" "*So are you*":** As they banter lovingly, admire each other's snow-tanned faces, and hungrily devour their breakfast, Barbara asks Nick if he wants to be released from his nighttime promise. Nick, however, has no intention of backing out. When Barbara says he's a "funny boy," he replies that she's one, too. This has special meaning for Barbara, and she asks him to repeat it. He won't, but Barbara is content that he said it in the first place. The Sheldons' erotic games with suntanning and matching haircuts, then, clearly involve Barbara being a "boy," much as the erotic games played by the Bournes do the same for Catherine.

(32) 2.1.10 **He felt the scissors cutting:** Nick and Barbara decide to get started with their plan. Barbara (whose name may have been inspired by her role as barber) places a towel around Nick's neck and begins cutting his hair. As she snips away, she explains that soon his thick, heavy hair will cover his ears, whether he wants it to or not. Barbara asks how his hair feels, and Nick's reply points to a Bourne-like fetishization of racial otherness: "Like any Indian's" (see 30:16). When Barbara stops cutting, they are both frightened and suspect that they've done something "wicked." Barbara wants to comb it under so it will be just like hers, but Nick is frightened and needs a drink first to screw up his courage. After they each have a whiskey, Nick allows her to comb his hair and is relieved to discover that it is too thick to stay curled under properly. Nonetheless, he still doesn't have the courage to look at it in the mirror. They immediately decide to make love, and Nick feels "very strange and empty but very excited" *(2.1.12)*. As they lie together in bed afterwards, Barbara wonders how "something so simple" could be "so exciting." Nick, however, isn't sure it's simple at all. They both agree that it must be wicked. (See *[5:22] 1.1.3.*)

(32) 2.1.13 **The same barber that cut yours:** As they lie in bed, Barbara asks Nick how long it had taken to let his hair grow so long. It had taken five months, he explains, and it had required great patience. He'd done it for her, trying his best to hide its length all the time, as a "surprise and for a present." She'd asked him to do it so often before, and he'd gone to the same barber she used, who trimmed it so it wouldn't show too badly while it was growing out. He'd been afraid the whole time that Barbara would suspect what he was doing. She tells him she had suspected at night when they played together in bed but then thought she might just be "making it up." Nick had been planning to go this morning to get it cut just like hers so he could then surprise her at the bistro, but Barbara is glad it has turned out as it has. After all, she adds, they couldn't make love at the bistro. Feeling fortunate to be in bed, they make love again, but no amount of lovemaking can quell their excitement, and Nick feels "hollow and strange and changed."

Needless to say, the Sheldons' experiments with hair sound remarkably like those practiced by the Bournes. Both couples are inspired by the same statue; the lovers' haircuts must be identical; both partners must use the same barber; the haircuts are coded as "sinful" or "wicked"; and the haircut must be a "surprise."

(32) 2.1.15 **Lipp's . . . pomme à huile, cervelas,** *and* **choucroute garnie:** To celebrate, the Sheldons splurge on a visit to Brasserie Lipp to drink beer and eat "*pomme à huile, cervelas,* and *choucroute garnie.*" At 151 Boulevard Saint-Germain, across the street from the Café les Deux Magots, Brasserie Lipp was Hemingway's favorite place in Paris for beer, and his standing side order was potato salad (*pomme à huile*), with sausage (*cervelas*) and a sort of Alsatian sauerkraut cooked in wine (*choucroute garnie*). He famously pays tribute to Lipp's several times in *A Moveable Feast,* and

he mentions it as well in *Green Hills of Africa, Islands in the Stream,* and many of his letters. See also *(51:2) 3.9.3.*

As they enjoy their beer and food, Nick and Barbara admire themselves in the mirror across the room and discuss how excited they are to make their hair exactly the same. Nick thinks his hair looks just like the hair of the "Indian kids" he knew in his youth. Barbara is thrilled by how it will be in the night. They plan to go to their barber that afternoon to get it touched up, but they are so excited that they first have to return home to make love again.

(32) 2.1.17 **the Spaniard's:** Later that night, in bed, Nick and Barbara look back joyfully on their expensive day, with the trip to Lipp's and the hairdressers. They refer to their coiffeur's establishment—a place for both men and women—as "the Spaniard's." In two deleted sentences from the manuscript, we later learn that the "Spaniard's place" was on the Boulevard Saint-Germain, "just past where Payot's used to be," and past the Café de Flore (see appendix A). It is likely, however, that Hemingway first wrote and deleted the reference to Payot's, and then wrote and deleted the reference to the Flore. At 106 Boulevard Saint-Germain, Payot's was a bookstore and publisher, no longer at this location but still active today. At 172 Boulevard Saint-Germain (across the street from Lipp's), the Café de Flore, one of Paris's great literary cafes, was several blocks distant. Given this distance, it is unlikely that Hemingway was thinking of a single location. Hemingway probably just wanted to place Nick and Barbara in an area of Saint-Germain-des Prés that he associated with a vibrant queer community. This also explains why Andy later encounters the Sheldons at the Café les Deux Magots, a stone's throw from the Café de Flore, at 170 Boulevard Saint-Germain (see *[44:33] 3.5.6).*

Thinking back on their day, Nick and Barbara remember how the Spaniard's hands shook and how excited he had been as he cut their hair. Their hair is still not exactly the same length, but Barbara is thrilled that the Spaniard will be able to make it so when they visit him next. Exhausted by the day's excitement, Nick goes to sleep while Barbara watches him and drifts into a long internal monologue about their hair and how best to take care of him. She thinks how fortunate it is that their desires are the same—she'd only needed to pressure him a little to get him to do this. (For a consideration of consent and coercion in these dynamics, see 12:13 and 79:21.) In summer they will tan at the beach and wear "Basque shirts." That will be beautiful, she thinks. Inspired by these thoughts, which she calls "crazy," she wakes Nick so they can make love again. But even after making love and after Nick drifts off to sleep again, Barbara still cannot sleep. Nothing can satiate her desire. In a long unpunctuated stream-of-consciousness passage, she thinks about how she'll get Nick to wear his hair, how fortunate it is that they are just the same, how she could cut his hair herself, how surprised she was that Nick went "so far," how she will help him to go still further, and how wonderful it will be in three months when their hair is finally just the same.

(32) 2.1.26 **It's funny not to say the name:** In the midst of Barbara's stream-of-consciousness reverie about how she and Nick will wear their hair, she thinks, "it's funny not to say the name." In three months, though, when their hair is truly identical, they'll be able to say it: "He'll not mind then." The passage is oblique, but the implication is clear: just as David and Catherine Bourne have special names for their alter egos in fetishistic love play—with David becoming "Catherine" and Catherine becoming "Peter" (see 17:23)—Nick and Barbara have at least one special semi-taboo name for their fetishistic love play. This, however, is the last time we see the Sheldons together in bed, so we never do learn the name. Barbara's monologue grows erratic as she tires, and soon she is asleep.

NOTE

1. Hemingway also drew on these experiences for some deleted chapters of *Islands in the Stream*. For an extended consideration of these chapters, see HF 263–68.

BOOK II (*MSS. BOOK III*)

CHAPTER 4 (MSS. CHAPTERS 1–4)

35:4 **at Hendaye:** The words "at Hendaye" have been added to this sentence by Scribner's editor Tom Jenks. In the manuscript, this chapter is, indeed, set in Hendaye, but Hemingway does not mention the town by name until Catherine and David are leaving it seven manuscript chapters later. These chapters are largely concerned with the Bournes' encounter with Nick and Barbara Sheldon, and Jenks has condensed the seven chapters into two, deleting or repurposing all of the Sheldon material.

David and Catherine drive in from the north along the then-new Route de la Corniche, past the rolling green headland of Pointe Sainte-Anne, and onto the Boulevard de la Mer. This puts them in the recently developed resort of Hendaye Plage, not the old town of Hendaye proper, the latter of which then had a population of about 5,600 (Monmarché 120).

35:5 **ocean side . . . big hotel . . . casino:** Hemingway takes a little poetic license with the layout of the town. The neo-Moorish Casino de la Plage was actually the only building on the ocean side of the Boulevard de la Mer. The large, neo-Basque-style Grand Hôtel Eskualduna stood across the street from it, set aside just enough for an unobstructed view of the ocean. Hemingway may place the hotel on the ocean side to emphasize the quality of its view.

A line in the manuscript reveals that the Bournes stay at the luxurious, three-hundred-room Eskualduna, then "center of Hendaye's elegant social life" ("La Saison à Hendaye"). Where the Scribner's edition says that the Bournes' room is "high up in the big hotel" (36:13), the manuscript is clear that they are "on the sixth floor" (3.2.1). The only hotel in Hendaye with six floors was the big Hôtel Eskualduna, where Hemingway stayed in 1953, and rooms on the sixth (top) floor were the grandest in the hotel. By contrast, the Ondarraïtz Hotel, which Hemingway favored for his stays in Hendaye in the 1920s, was family-run, very small, and on the Avenue des Mimosas, one street back from the ocean.[1] Some lines from the manuscript's ending of the Sheldon subplot suggest that Nick and Barbara stay at a pension much like the Ondarraïtz (see appendix A).

Hendaye Plage, Casino, and Hôtel Eskualduna. (Photo by Marcel Delboy. Image from the author's collection.)

35:6 **Basque villas:** Architect Henry Martinet, who designed the Eskualduna and oversaw the development of Hendaye Plage, developed city planning regulations that required new villas to be built in the Basque style. In the late 1920s, Hendaye Plage was still a relatively young resort in the process of development, and these villas were being built at a rate of fifty per year (Culot et al. 82–83). This is why David can later dismiss them as "phony Basque villas" (44:31), and this is why David and Catherine notice the immature landscaping.

35:12 **river . . . Spanish town . . . lighthouse:** The town, across the River Bidasoa, has three names: Hondarribia (Basque), Fontarrabie (French), and Fuenterrabía (Spanish). Today it more often goes by Hondarribia, but in the 1920s it was more widely known as Fuenterrabía, and this is the name Hemingway uses in the manuscript. The Cape Higuer lighthouse, similarly, has Spanish, French, and Basque versions of its name.

36:2 **mimosas. . . . To compete with where we've come from:** When David and Catherine drive into Hendaye, Catherine notes the "new planting" and wonders why they planted mimosas. "To compete," David replies, "with where we've come from." These mimosas serve as a reminder that where they've come from is not Le Grau-du-Roi but rather the place where they spent the month of June: "not far from la Napoule" (64:8). At the end of book I, when Catherine and David discuss where to go next, David points out that it's still "too early for the Basque coast,"

82 · READING HEMINGWAY'S *THE GARDEN OF EDEN*

where Hendaye is located (30:8). David suggests that instead they "go over by the Estérel" and discover a new place, the way they discovered Le Grau-du-Roi (30:30). Thus, when the Bournes return to France after their stay in Spain and arrive in La Napoule at the edge of the Estérel, they stay in the same hotel "where they had stayed before" (75:3). The mimosas serve as a subtle reminder of this missing time in the narrative.

Advertised as "Le Paradis du Mimosa" and "La Capitale du Mimosa," La Napoule was particularly noted for the culture and trade in yellow mimosa flowers, which were used in perfumes and shipped in bouquets all over Europe. A flowering tree native to Australia and New Zealand, the mimosa was brought to the Côte d'Azur by the English in the mid-nineteenth century. By 1920, there was an "extraordinary vogue" for mimosa flowers (Marande 233), and contemporary sources describe "thousands of baskets of mimosa waiting every day on the platform of la Napoule station," from which eight thousand kilograms of mimosa were sent daily (Pickard). In 1928, La Napoule inaugurated an annual mimosa festival, which the city still celebrates each February.

In Hendaye Plage, the Rue de la Guadeloupe, one street back from the beach, had only recently been rechristened the Avenue des Mimosas. Catherine and David must be driving back down this avenue, past the back of the "big hotel" Eskualduna, when they see their café (35:17), probably the Bar Americain beneath the Pension Regina, near the corner of the Avenue des Mimosas and the Avenue de la Plage (now the Boulevard du Général Leclerc). Here they would have found some of the last "old trees" (35:18) in Hendaye Plage. As Henry Martinet planned the town's development, he did, indeed, claim that Hendaye should compete with other seaside resorts and should model itself on Cannes, which is a mere five miles from La Napoule. According to Martinet, Hendaye should be to Biarritz what Cannes was to Nice: a quiet, calm, elegant, and flowery alternative (Culot et al. 83). Although Martinet favored a semi-indigenous neo-Basque style in architecture for Hendaye, as a landscape architect he favored exotic species (Culot et al. 181). Recognizing the incongruity and artificiality of this, David dislikes the "newly planted magnolias and bloody mimosas" (44:30).[2]

36:4 **it's a wonderful beach:** Hendaye Plage boasts the longest beach on the Basque Coast.

36:6 **Biarritz is a horror:** "The most frequented seaside resort on the Atlantic coast of France" (Muirhead and Monmarché 347), Biarritz in 1927 had grown tenfold in the previous seventy years and was a town of twenty thousand inhabitants visited by half a million travelers each year (Monmarché 75, 79). Given the novel's concerns about the threats posed to Edenic spaces by overdevelopment, Biarritz may be a cautionary tale.

Once a simple fishing village, Biarritz in 1838 became popular with Spanish aristocrats barred by the Carlist Wars from access to their traditional seaside resort, San Sebastian. After Napoleon III's Spanish wife, the Empress Eugénie, built a splendid villa there in 1855, royalty from across Europe began to arrive, and Biarritz became known as "the beach of kings." King Alfonso XIII of Spain, Princess Ena of Battenberg, Empress Elisabeth of Austria, Empress Maria Feodorovna of Russia, King Oscar II of Sweden, King Leopold II of Belgium, and King Alexander of Serbia all vacationed there with their aristocratic hangers-on, but it was the arrival in 1889 of Queen Victoria and the subsequent regular visits by King Edward VII of England that made Biarritz especially popular with British high society. (We might remember Hemingway's mockery of the "awful" "Biarritz English" in *The Sun Also Rises* [184, 209].) This is why Barbara Sheldon in the *Eden* manuscript later refers to Biarritz as an "outpost of Empire" *(3.5.8)*.

In the 1920s, Biarritz competed with Cannes, Nice, Monte Carlo, and Deauville as a seat of high fashion, and such designers as Coco Chanel, Jean Patou, and Paul Poiret kept boutiques there. It is natural that Catherine would drive the seventeen miles from Hendaye to shop there and get her hair cut (44:6).

36:10 **by themselves:** This sentence about the pleasures of eating by themselves has been transposed and is four manuscript chapters out of place *(3.4.1, not at 3.1.1)*. In fact, this solitude contrasts directly with the company they meet at this moment in the manuscript: Nick and Barbara Sheldon.

As they drive past the café, Catherine is stunned, and "frightened," by the beauty of Nick and Barbara Sheldon sitting there at a table, and she asks David to stop the car *(3.1.1)*. It turns out that David knows the Sheldons, and he tells Catherine that Nick is an impressive painter. Together, they walk over to the café, and David introduces Catherine to the couple, who are drinking Pernod and eating crayfish. Barbara invites them to sit down and join them for a drink. Catherine admires Barbara's tanned face, red-gold hair, and Basque shirt, but it is Nick's long black hair, cut almost identically with Barbara's, that "upset[s] her" and makes her "feel so strangely" *(3.1.2)*. Barbara invites Catherine to look at Nick, announcing, "We're a scandal." But Catherine calls them "the two most beautiful people [she's] ever seen"—though she corrects herself adding, "except David" *(3.1.3)*. Barbara immediately likes Catherine and asks how she and David got so dark. She is moved by Catherine's insistence that she's "that dark all over."

(36:12) 3.1.3 **Pernod. . . . Don't let the bottle fool you. It comes from Spain:** In the manuscript, Nick encourages Catherine and David to join them for a Pernod, assuring them that it's the "real" thing and that they'll be served. To understand why Nick insists that the Pernod is "real," that it's from Spain, and that the waiter is willing to serve it, one has to understand a little of the history of absinthe.

Pernod Fils (est. 1797) had dominated the thriving French market for anise-flavored absinthe throughout the belle époque—a time when "the Green Fairy" was so ubiquitous in Parisian cafes that the traditional cocktail hour became known as *l'heure verte* (the green hour). The drink had been particularly associated with the Bohemian artists of Paris—figures such as Baudelaire, Rimbaud, Verlaine, Manet, Toulouse-Lautrec, Degas, and Wilde—but as it became ever more popular, adulterated—even toxic—cheap imitations flooded the largely unregulated market, and absinthe became a lightning rod for public outrage, blamed not only for public drunkenness but for a vast array of neurological disorders and even blindness: "By 1880, rather than asking for *un Pernod,* a Parisian could order absinthe by the term *une correspondance,* meaning 'a ticket.' The term referred to a ticket to Charenton, a well-known insane asylum on the outskirts of the city" (Wittels 30). Under the influence of French temperance activists and a hostile French wine industry, absinthe's reputed psychoactive properties (though entirely mythical) fueled a belief that the drink produced madness, and by 1915 the drink was declared illegal, not only in France but throughout much of the world.[3]

Following the First World War, Pernod Fils introduced as a replacement a *liqueur d'anise* that removed wormwood from the recipe, added sugar, and greatly decreased the alcohol content—from the whopping 136 proof of prewar years to 90 proof. But in 1918 Pernod also licensed production of its original product to a distiller in Tarragona, since Spain had never outlawed absinthe. In the novel, the café in Hendaye is serving this 136-proof Spanish absinthe in the bottles for the 90-proof French *liqueur d'anise*—and since they are doing so on the French side of the River Bidasoa, they need to do so carefully. Nick thoughtfully allows the nervous waiter to return inside and pours his own ice water into the drink, one drop at a time so the absinthe clouds.

As habitués of the art world, Nick, Barbara, and David are familiar with absinthe, but they have to explain it to Catherine, who has never tried it before. Nick tells her that merely serving it is a "plenty" serious offense. They warn her to drink it slowly—a warning well justified by its high alcohol content but reinforced by their (mistaken) conviction that absinthe has psychoactive properties. Repeating a line from *The Sun Also Rises,* Nick tells Catherine that absinthe isn't "good for girls."[4] When Catherine asks why, Nick tells her that it will make her "think things" that otherwise she wouldn't. It will also, he adds, lower her inhibitions. They hardly need a drink for that, Catherine assures Nick. She and David already do whatever they want.

(36:12) 3.1.4 **"wonderful haircut. . . ." "like a boy. . . . But I don't like girls":** In the manuscript, it quickly becomes clear that the Bournes and Sheldons speak the same erotic language. Nick compliments Catherine on her "wonderful haircut." Catherine wants to know if he thinks it makes her look "like a boy," and she's glad to hear that it does, at least around her face. That's what she'd been aiming for. She assures

Barbara, though, that she doesn't go in for girls, so Barbara "doesn't have to worry about that." Barbara promises she won't worry and with a somewhat disconcerted humor tells David that this must be a relief. With their tans, Catherine and David "look like brothers," Barbara thinks. Catherine doesn't mind sharing the "secret" that she and David are, indeed, "brothers."

(36:12) 3.1.7 **frightened because it did something to me:** Under the influence of her first sips of absinthe, Catherine confesses to Barbara that she'd initially been "frightened" by the sight of her and Nick—because it "did something to" her. When Barbara asks why, Catherine replies that it was because she thought their matching haircuts were "abnormal," and that it meant she liked something abnormal. She knows better now, though: it was just two people being brave enough to do what they wanted.

David and Nick, meanwhile, talk about their work, catch up, and admire the two women. Nick offers to paint a portrait of Catherine for David as a wedding present. David wants to buy it, but Nick won't hear of it. He can write something in a copy of his last book, Nick suggests, instead. As they watch the two women become better friends under the influence of absinthe, Nick suggests that David and Catherine stay in town for a while, telling David that, if he stays, he might even want to start working. David thinks the same thing. With this thought the chapter in the manuscript ends.

(36:19) 3.2.2 **sort of the way I am except in a different way:** In the manuscript, as Catherine and David talk in bed, they chat about Nick and Barbara. Catherine likes Barbara and says she understands her. According to Catherine, Barbara is "sort of the way I am except in a different way." Catherine even offers to grow her hair out identically with David. When David says that he couldn't do for Catherine what Nick does for Barbara—presumably referring to wearing his hair long—Catherine is perceptive enough to realize that Nick must like it. "It must do something to him," she says. David agrees. Catherine praises the Sheldons' beauty and remembers how hollow she felt when she first saw them: "It was like a fright and a great joy." David warns her to be careful with Barbara, but Catherine makes no promises.

37:8 **we're us against all the others:** Variations on Catherine's phrase appear elsewhere in Hemingway's fiction and private writing. In *A Farewell to Arms,* Frederic and Catherine feel "alone against the others" (249), and in his 1926 letters to Pauline, Hemingway described their relationship as being a matter of "us against the others" or "us against the world" (*Letters 3* 173, 138). In the *Eden* manuscript, Catherine makes it clear that "the others" even include Barbara "with all her inventions." Besides, Catherine adds, everybody looked like the Sheldons in the Middle Ages.

Catherine asserts that she is the real inventor. "Everybody" will follow her style, she claims, "and nobody will do [Barbara's] but queers" *(3.2.4)*. David reminds her that Nick and Barbara aren't "queer." Catherine knows this but thinks Barbara's invention isn't "practical."

(37:8) 3.2.4 **what are you going to write about?** Catherine asks David what he's going to write about, but he isn't sure. Catherine then suggests that he "write about us and the others." David isn't sure how that plot works out. Catherine isn't either, and the undertones are ominous. She asks him to make love to her as she was in Avignon the night before they rode their bicycles to Le Grau-du-Roi. When David assures her that she's still "the same girl," Catherine tells him that he doesn't have to lie. They may love each other more now, but they don't love each other the same.

37:10 **You know I haven't done anything bad to us:** Here, Jenks has changed what Hemingway wrote in the manuscript: there, Catherine "hopes" she hasn't done anything bad to their relationship. This difference is significant.

37:23 **Know how complicated it is and then state it simply:** In this and all other respects, David shares Hemingway's aesthetics. This is a lovely way to rephrase Hemingway's famous "iceberg principle" (see 42:15).

37:26 **Do you suppose the Grau du Roi time was all simple:** This reveals that David has begun writing the honeymoon narrative—essentially the novel we are reading—but in the manuscript, the story that is going "so simply and easily" (37:20) is not the honeymoon narrative but rather the story of Nick and Barbara Sheldon that David is trying to write *(3.3.1)*. David remembers seeing them together, happy and excited, at a Paris bistro the previous February. He had seen them earlier in the day at the coiffeur's, and now in the bistro Barbara smiles at him as a "co-conspirator." It is when David wonders why he's writing about the length of the Sheldons' hair that he warns himself against thinking too simply. He could write about what happened at Le Grau-du-Roi simply, too, but did that make it simple?

37:27 ***cahier:*** David's writing practices mirror Hemingway's in the mid-1920s. The holograph of *The Sun Also Rises* is written in precisely such cahiers. In 1958, as he worked on the *Eden* manuscript, such details would have been fresh in Hemingway's mind. At the Ritz Hotel in November 1956, he recovered two boxes full of "penciled notebooks and sheaves of typed papers, ancient newspaper cuttings" that he had packed away before leaving for Key West in 1927 (M. Hemingway, "Making" 26). These papers served as an inspiration for *A Moveable Feast,* and they must have also brought back memories that Hemingway used in *The Garden of Eden.*

38:8 ***boina:*** Although popular throughout Europe and much of the world, the *boina*, or beret, is a traditional element of Basque costume. David's is from Tolosa, a Basque town noted for their manufacture *(3.19.6)*. It is noteworthy that David wears one while he is staying on the Basque Coast.

38:11 **cloudy yellow-tinged drink.... She was very far ahead of him:** In spite of the "ordinary Pernod bottle" (38:23), Catherine is drinking the real absinthe (see *[36:12]* 3.1.3). In the manuscript, Catherine is with Nick and Barbara, and they are all soaking wet from the rain and "far ahead" of David *(3.3.2)*. There is drunken banter about David looking like a "*sinistre individu*" or "renegade Kanaka" and Nick looking like a "Lascar" (an East Indian sailor) or "wet reservation Indian."

39:11 **G.N.'s.... Whatyoumacallits nationals:** Catherine is referring to the Gendarmerie Nationale, a branch of the French military responsible for policing small towns and rural areas.

39:22 **you clipping reader:** In the manuscript, the quarrel does not develop so quickly after Catherine's "I didn't say it." Nick and David talk about their work, and Barbara remembers that the last time Nick's normal outdoor painting routine was spoiled by rain, he had painted her nude except for a Basque shirt (an echo of the Bournes' fisherman's shirts—see 6:3). Catherine has seen this painting before and asks Nick if she can buy it. It's Barbara's, though, and Barbara won't sell it. David then condescendingly explains to Catherine the way professional painters, like Nick, sell their work through dealers—and the tension between David and Catherine grows. Nick credits David with finding him his dealer, but David credits their mutual friend Andy. They did it working together, Barbara says. David then asks Catherine if she'd like Nick and Barbara to ask her about her "finances." It is this bit of nastiness that provokes Catherine to protest that they'd all been enjoying themselves before he arrived: "Just because you wrote this morning and feel so damned self-righteous" *(3.3.5)*. Why, she demands, are writers always so self-righteous about writing? This is what leads to her question, "Do you think I married you because you're a writer? You and your clippings" (39:29).

39:32 **Can you tell me the rest of it when we're by ourselves?** The presence of the Sheldons in the manuscript clarifies what David means by "by ourselves."

(40:4) 3.3.6 ***It was the clippings:*** In the manuscript, after David walks out, Catherine explains to Nick and Barbara that what set things off had been her remark about the clippings. She shouldn't have mentioned them. Trying to understand, Barbara asks if David reads them all the time. No, Catherine replies, he'd only read them once, at Le Grau-du-Roi, and she'd reacted badly. She doesn't know what led her to mention

them. Nick suggests it was the absinthe, but Catherine considers that a poor excuse. David was rude enough, Barbara offers. But Catherine thinks it was her comment about the clippings that started things.

40:13 **Don't be stupid. . . . you being the only one who had worked:** In the manuscript these words are not spoken by Catherine but by Barbara, who like Nick is a painter. In other words, Catherine is not, as the Scribner's edition suggests, concerned with not having worked herself. Nick, Barbara, and Catherine all cajole David to rejoin them, in spite of his protest, "the hell with women drinking absinthe." "Without you," Barbara smiles *(3.3.7).* David and Catherine encourage the Sheldons to join them for lunch, but Nick and Barbara find an excuse to leave.

(41:19) 3.4.1 ***It was a big dining room:*** An entire manuscript chapter has been deleted here and is summarized in the following entries. David and Catherine lunch at their hotel as the rains beat against the windows outside. Catherine has changed into a cashmere sweater and pearls, and David admires her hair and tanned skin. Catherine wants to know if the contrast with the linen tablecloth and silver makes her look "dark enough not to be white." David thinks so.

(41:19) 3.4.2 **Rosé de Béarn. . . . Irouléguy:** As the Bournes drank Provençal wine in Provence, they now drink Basque wine in the Basque country. With their hors d'oeuvres and mushroom omelet, they drink a carafe of Rosé de Béarn, an unpretentious dry rosé from the foothills of the Pyrenees, about fifty miles from Hendaye. With their steak au poivre, they drink Irouléguy.

A little more than twenty-five miles as the crow flies from Hendaye, the village of Irouléguy owes its viticultural tradition to the famous monastery of Roncevaux, established at the pass in the Pyrenees where the legendary French paladin Roland died in 778 (see *[44:28]* 3.5.6). Unable to grow vines successfully at three thousand feet, the monks established two sites in the foothills, at Irouléguy and Anhaux. Here they produced wine for themselves and for pilgrims on the Camino de Santiago, for whom they set up a hostel in Saint-Jean-Pied-de-Port. (For Hemingway's career-long fascination with Roncevaux and the Camino de Santiago, see the work of Stoneback.[5]) The Cabernet Franc, Cabernet Sauvignon, and Tannat vines used to produce Rosé de Béarn and Irouléguy were damaged by phylloxera in the nineteenth century, and the region's wines were almost forgotten until revived in the 1950s (Dominé 287).

(41:19) 3.4.2 **Chateau Yquem . . . Romany Stain:** The Bournes don't just drink wines: as a deleted line from the manuscript makes clear, they "really learn about" them. They find the Irouléguy a bit stronger than a Beaujolais but (struck through in the manuscript) lighter than "a moderate red Burgundy." Catherine agrees that it's stronger than they need, but she's glad they don't drink heavy wines just because they're famous or "literary." She couldn't imagine having to drink "that syrupy Chateau Yquem or that awful Romany Stain."

Famed as the greatest and most expensive of all Sauternes—as concentrated sunshine in a glass—Chateau Yquem was in 1927, and perhaps still is, "the most celebrated white wine in the world" (F. Butler 82). The wine is celebrated for its sweetness, complexity, and ability to mature for more than a century. It is often described as sheer perfection. In Proust's *Remembrance of Things Past,* the narrator sips Yquem in the Guermantes' cellar as a liquid symbol of aristocratic wealth and privilege (1082). It is, however, a wine far too sweet to drink with most dishes.

When it comes to "Romany Stain," Catherine's complaint against "literary wines" is quite literary. While "Romany Stain" might sound like a name for the berry juice with which Hemingway and Pauline supposedly disguised themselves as "Gypsies" at Les Saintes-Maries-de-la-Mer in 1927 (see *[53:31] 3.9.11),* it is in fact an elaborate pun. It refers to the famous Premier and Grand Cru wines from Vosne-Romanée (pronounced *Romanay*)—some of Burgundy's most sought-after and prestigious wines. More specifically, Catherine is punning on La Tâche, a Grand Cru appellation in Vosne-Romanée. In French, *la tâche* means "work," but *la tache,* without the circumflex, means "stain." Hence, Romany Stain. To make the allusion still more complex, 1926 saw the publication of a book of essays by Christopher Morley titled *The Romany Stain.* In this book about an American traveling in France (including the Latin Quarter), Morley attributes the title phrase to John Mistletoe's *Uncollected Writings*. John Mistletoe, however, is a fictional alter ego appearing throughout Morley's works. In his regular column for the *Saturday Review of Literature,* Morley had written of Hemingway, "*The Sun Also Rises* is a clever bit of work. . . . Boy, that boy can write; if he'll just learn not to shove in little topical jokes about individuals that have nothing to do with the story" ("Bowling").[6] It would seem that this devilishly complicated allusion in the *Eden* manuscript, written thirty years later, is Hemingway's riposte to Morley.

(41:19) 3.4.2 **the damned absinthe:** In the manuscript, after they discuss how much they enjoy discovering new wines, David warns Catherine about absinthe. Yet absinthe does something to Catherine that she likes. She feels that she has to discover it for herself. The prohibition itself is an attraction, she admits, but she also feels it helps her to deal with other people. David understands but knows it can suddenly make him "completely and dangerously reckless." They agree that if Catherine becomes reckless, David will give her a signal by placing his hand on hers. They both acknowledge that their experimentation with absinthe is dangerous, and David reminds her that "they don't write insurance on what we have" *(3.4.4).*

NOTES

1. For Hemingway's 1953 stay at the Eskualduna, see Reynolds, *Final Years* 264. For Hemingway's 1927 and 1929 stays at the Ondarraïtz, now at 33 Ave. des Mimosas, see *Letters* 3 102. Hemingway often called the Ondarraïtz the Hotel Barron because the Barron family owned the hotel.

2. It's no coincidence that David pairs magnolias and mimosas. In Hendaye Plage, the Avenue des Magnolias parallels the Avenue des Mimosas, one street further back from the beach.

3. Though traditional prewar absinthe recipes contain traces of thujone, a toxic chemical compound found in wormwood, these are at entirely safe trace levels, and thujone does not have any known psychoactive properties.

4. See *SAR* 22.

5. See Stoneback's *Reading Hemingway's* The Sun Also Rises and his essay "From the Rue Saint-Jacques."

6. Morley had also used "Romany Stains" as the title of his "Bowling Green" column on 9 Oct. 1926.

CHAPTER 5 *(MSS. CHAPTERS 5–8)*

42:15 **sinister part . . . reef:** This is a lovely rephrasing of Hemingway's famous "iceberg principle" or "theory of omission": "If a writer of prose knows enough about what he is writing about he may omit things that he knows and the reader, if the writer is writing truly enough, will have a feeling of those things as strongly as though the writer had stated them. The dignity of the movement of an ice-berg is due to only one eighth of it being above water" (*DIA* 192). This is one of many instances where we see that David Bourne is not only a writer like Hemingway, he shares Hemingway's aesthetics.

The use of the word *sinister* here in the Scribner's edition suggests that David finds a "sinister" undercurrent in the sexual experiments Catherine initiated at Le Grau-du-Roi. In the manuscript, however, it is clear that David is not writing about Le Grau-du-Roi. Rather, David initially writes about running into Nick Sheldon in Paris one spring afternoon at the Café les Deux Magots (see *[44:33] 3.5.6*), and he remembers the "strange" things Barbara had said when she joined them. These lines, however, are deleted, and a note in the margin from Hemingway reminds him to "redo" them because this is now in the "Andy part" of the manuscript (see appendix A). Nevertheless, as the manuscript passage continues beyond the deletion, it becomes clear that the "sinister part" of the story mentioned in the Scribner's text refers not to the Bournes' honeymoon narrative but rather to what David has been writing about Nick and Barbara. It is this that brings the action in what he is writing "up to now."

(42:17) 3.5.1 **Winslow Homer. . . . Jongkind:** In the manuscript, David wants to be sure that his narrative conveys how well Nick paints. He paints the sea, David thinks, "as well as Winslow Homer" painted the Bahamas. David clarifies that he is thinking of the watercolors, not Homer's famous oil canvas *The Gulf Stream*. In a section of the manuscript where Andy tells the story of Nick and Barbara, Andy thinks that Nick paints even *better* than Homer did in the watercolors (see appendix A). His unnamed interlocutor can't believe it, but Andy backs up his own judgment by claiming that lots of French painters agree with him. The interlocutor is surprised that any French painters know Homer's work. Andy assures her, however, that an "American exhibition" had come over "before [her] time," and Hemingway

is being historically accurate. The exhibition took place in the spring of 1923 at the Hôtel de la Chambre Syndicale de la Curiosité et des Beaux Arts. It was well covered in the press and earned Homer, then "little known in France," high praise for his watercolors, several of which were devoted to Bahamian themes (Raynal).[1] It is instructive to note Hemingway's care about such details.

Hemingway was deeply moved by the work of Winslow Homer. After seeing twenty-two Homer watercolors at the Art Institute of Chicago in 1928, Hemingway wrote to his close friend, the Maine painter and fellow fisherman, Waldo Peirce, that some of the Homers gave him "the same feeling" he got from catching "monsters" deep-sea fishing or from watching a faena by the great matador Belmonte (*Letters 3* 471). When Mary Hemingway went to Chicago in 1948, Hemingway reminded her to see the Winslow Homers for him (*HIW* 221), and the paintings of Thomas Hudson, in *Islands in the Stream,* have more than a touch of Homer about them: "Pictures of Negroes in the water. Negroes on land. Negroes in boats. Turtle boats. Sponge boats. Squalls making up. Waterspouts. Schooners that got wrecked. Schooners building" (22).

David thinks that Nick also paints as well as Dutch pre-impressionist marine painter and watercolorist Johan Barthold Jongkind (1819–1891)—who can be seen as a sort of European analog and contemporary to the American Homer. Hemingway was probably first exposed to Jongkind when his work was exhibited along with Homer's at the Chicago Art Institute's 1921 *First Annual Exhibition of Watercolors.* The Louvre held a good collection of Jongkind's watercolors, and Hemingway probably saw the exhibit of sixty Jongkind watercolors at Paris's Galerie L. Dru in 1924. Long before Hemingway's time, Jongkind had been a patron of the Closerie des Lilas, and he was regarded as a master by such impressionists as Monet. In Andy's narration of the Sheldon subplot, Nick tells Andy that he's just been developing the ability to capture in paint the changing currents and the bulge in the water of feeding mullet on the sandbar at Hendaye. It's terribly difficult, Nick reports, but sometimes he "does some Jongkind" to cheer himself up. That's impressive enough for Andy, and he's sure it will cheer Nick's dealer *(422.2 3.19ii).*

(43:4) 3.5.2 **We have money. . . . Why not reproduce the pictures:** In the manuscript, after trying to describe the work Nick produced in winter in the high Alps, David gives up. Rereading his narrative, he finds that he is "describing and qualifying" Nick's painting instead of really "making it." It's better, he decides, to leave it to Nick to "say it." As he watches Catherine sleeping, he realizes that, instead of describing the pictures, they now have enough money to "reproduce" them when he publishes the story, and he thinks their money could be put to no better purpose. Paintings, David thinks, should be "looked at, not . . . written about."[2]

This passage should color our understanding of Catherine's later plans to have the honeymoon narrative illustrated by Picasso and other famous painters (see

189:2), among whom in the manuscript Nick is foremost *(3.35.5)*. The Scribner's text produces the impression that this plan is simply another manifestation of Catherine's growing insanity. Indeed, the entitlement Catherine feels to take over this aspect of the narrative David is writing may be a little crazy—but it is important to recognize how much Catherine has "scripted" the events of the honeymoon narrative, so much so that it functions as a sort of coproduction. Similarly, Catherine's disconcerting assertion that she has "only tried to make it economically possible" for David to do his best work (156:2) should be colored by David's recognition that he can use the money Catherine has brought into the marriage to produce a new sort of illustrated text.

Nevertheless, we also need to distinguish between David's plan to replace descriptions of paintings with reproductions of those paintings and Catherine's plan to supplement David's text with illustrations. Whereas David resists an ekphrastic mutation of painting into text; Catherine's plan relies on transforming text into visual art, as if the text were insufficient in its own right. This distinction was vital for Hemingway, a writer who "felt almost holy" about his mission to truly make landscape as Cézanne had *seen, broken down,* and *made* landscape—but not by actually imitating Cézanne's paintings (*NAS* 218). When Charles Scribner asked Hemingway how he felt about having his work illustrated, Hemingway replied:

> Unless the artist is as good or better a painter or draftsman than the writer is a writer, there can be no more disappointing thing than for the writer to see the things and the places and the people that he remembers making drawn and put on paper by someone else who was not there.
>
> If I could write a book that took place in the Bahamas I would like it to be illustrated by Winslow Homer, provided he did no illustrating but simply painted the Bahamas and what he saw there. If I were Guy de Maupassant, a good job to have dead or alive, I would like my work to be illustrated by the drawings and paintings of Toulouse Lautrec, some outdoor scenes of the middle time of Renoir and have them leave my Norman landscapes alone, because no painter ever did them better. (*HMF* 97)

It should be noted that Hemingway's response to Scribner comes from Hemingway's preface to a 1948 edition of *A Farewell to Arms* illustrated by Daniel Rasmusson—a preface in which Hemingway never praises, nor even mentions, Rasmusson's illustrations.[3] Yet, in the spring of 1947 when this edition was being planned, Hemingway suggested to Max Perkins that he might be able to talk Picasso into doing the illustrations: "He can illustrate beautifully you know and is a good friend of mine" (*SL* 617).[4] Nor is this the first time Hemingway hoped to have Picasso illustrate his work. In fact, at Hemingway's request, Picasso did provide a line drawing for *Der Querschnitt*'s 1925 translation of "The Undefeated"—a printing which also featured two drawings by Jules Pascin (see 189:2)—and in 1958 a German edition of "The Undefeated" was printed with twenty-eight black-and-white images by Picasso.[5] In accordance with Hemingway's preferences, however, these images were not really illustrations of "The Undefeated." In fact, twenty-one of the twenty-eight images are from a famous series of twenty-six aquatints Picasso completed in 1957 to illustrate Pepe-Hillo's eighteenth-century manual on bullfighting, the *Tauromaquia*. The other seven images are lithograph illustrations Picasso had recently completed for what would eventually become his book *Toros y Toreros* (1961). There are no images of "characters" or specific "scenes" in Hemingway's story. These illustrations were surely on Hemingway's mind when he wrote this theme into *The Garden of Eden*.

43:9 **lazy naked wife:** In the manuscript this sentence reads, "I'm your lazy naked octoroon half-caste wife" *(3.5.5)*. This illustrates a more general tendency in the Scribner's edition to mute the racial dynamics of Hemingway's manuscript.

43:16 **Weren't you wonderful to after yesterday and everything:** In the manuscript, this is "after *last night* and everything" (*3.5.2;* my emphasis). In other words, where the Scribner's edition suggests that the previous day's argument could have interfered with David's work, the manuscript makes it clear that what is at issue is the previous night's sexual explorations. Hemingway initially has David respond that these explorations are "good for" him, but he then deletes this. Instead, he has David ask what it was that they did the previous night. Catherine plays along and pretends not to remember. It is after this that Catherine and David admire themselves in the mirror on the bathroom door (43:19).

43:17 **look at us in the mirror:** Self-inspection in the mirror is a ubiquitous motif in Hemingway's fiction, occurring in almost all of his novels and many of his short stories. A convenient device to invite a moment of introspection, it is also much more. Hemingway's characters don't merely recognize themselves in the mirror, they often *misrecognize* themselves in it, experiencing a curious dissociation from the image they find there.[6] (See for instance 81:25 and 84:16.) As I explain in *Hemingway's Fetishism,* mirror fantasies and misrecognition are central to fetishism and fetishistic cross-dressing, because the mirror is where the divided ego confronts its own alterity, where the self becomes other and the other becomes self (208–16). Rather than taking the illusory phallic woman as an object (see 15:13 and *[45:6] 3.5.7)*, in a different logical moment within the same psychology, the fetishist-become-fetishistic-cross-dresser wears the fetish to produce the illusion of *becoming* the phallic woman in a moment of cross-gender identification. (The defining act of transvestism is not wearing female *clothing,* it is wearing the *fetish*—which can be clothing, but in Hemingway's case was hair—to negotiate a cross-gender identification.) When Hemingway's male protagonists look in the mirror, they frequently see women reflected there. Frederic Henry, in *A Farewell to Arms,* excitedly watches the reflection of Catherine Barkley in three mirrors as she gets her hair done (292). In *Across the River and into the Trees,* Cantwell talks to the reflection of Renata's raven-haired portrait in the mirror of his armoire (164). And when Robert Jordan, in *For Whom the Bell Tolls,* tells Maria how she can grow her hair out like his own, she answers "I would look like thee. . . . And then I never would want to change it" (345); they can go to a hotel then, Jordan tells her, "and we will sit in the famous bed together and look into the mirror of the *armoire* and there will be thee and there will be me in the glass . . ." (346). Catherine and David standing naked in front of the mirror is just such a moment. To the extent that Catherine and David represent, on some level, two oppositionally gendered halves of a single riven ego, both halves appear here in the mirror. This will become even clearer when David inspects himself in the mirror after he and Catherine have bleached their hair (see 84:16).

44:11 **And you'll like it:** In the manuscript, Catherine explains that she has been thinking about this surprise for about a week, and it will be their first surprise since Le Grau-du-Roi. She asks him, "Now are you frightened?" To which, David replies, "My God" (3.5.5). The Scribner's edition mutes the significance of anxiety in this scene.

44:24 **Biscay was Vizcaya. . . . Guipúzcoa:** David's rumination on French, Spanish, and Basque place names calls attention to the cultural complexity of this frontier region of the Basque Country, where all places seem to have names in each of these languages. (See 35:12.)

(44:28) 3.5.6 ***Ah, que ce cor a longue haleine:*** In the manuscript, as soon as he thinks of Navarra, this line from *The Song of Roland* pops into David's head. In fact, this is the first of two times this line surfaces in the *Eden* manuscript (see [194:4] 3.36.3i). David is thinking of the Navarrese pass between France and Spain at Roncevaux (in Spanish, Roncesvalles, and in Basque, Orreaga) where in 778 Charlemagne's rear guard, returning from a siege of Zaragoza and the destruction of Pamplona, was destroyed by Basque tribes. The twelfth-century Old French epic poem about the fight—in which the Basques are replaced by Muslims—was first published in a modern edition in 1837, under the title *La Chanson de Roland, ou de Roncevaux,* and the line David remembers recounts a crucial moment when Roland, after first refusing to do so, blows his hunting horn, the oliphant, with skull-bursting force to summon the main body of Charlemagne's army back to fight the Muslim army swarming the failing rear guard. The line, spoken by Charlemagne, translates loosely as "Ah, this horn has a long breathe."

Stoneback has written extensively about the presence of *The Song of Roland* in Hemingway's work and about Hemingway's lifelong passion for Roncevaux, which figures importantly in *The Sun Also Rises* (see [41:19] 3.4.2). Whereas Carlos Baker, coming across a version of this same phrase in a 1956 letter from Hemingway to Harvey Breit, wonders in a footnote "how this handsome line came into Hemingway's possession" (*SL* 870), Stoneback argues at length that in 1926 it was simply a matter of cultural literacy (*Reading* 188–96). No doubt, some familiarity with *The Song of Roland* was a matter of cultural literacy at the time, but this particular line was not quoted in print with any great frequency. It is almost certain, and it is of some consequence for *The Garden of Eden,* that in using this line Hemingway also meant to allude to a more contemporary source: Archibald MacLeish's poem "The Too-Late Born" from his 1926 book *Streets in the Moon:*

> We too, we too descending once again
> The hills of our own land, we too have heard
> Far off—*Ah que ce cor a longue halaine*—
> The horn of Roland in the passages of Spain,
> The first, the second blast, the failing third,
> And with the third turned back and climbed once more
> The steep road southward, and heard the faint sounds
> Of swords, of horses, the disastrous war,
> And crossed the dark defile at last, and found
> At Roncevaux, upon the darkening plain
> The dead against the dead and on the silent ground
> The silent slain.[7]

MacLeish and Hemingway were very close during the mid-twenties (another poem in *Streets in the Moon* is dedicated to Hemingway), and MacLeish may have been indebted to Hemingway for this line in his poem. Hemingway's love for *The Song of Roland* probably influenced his choice of Burguete—a mere stone's throw from the monastery at Roncevaux—as the location for his post-Pamplona fishing trip in 1924. At least during his stay there, he mentioned the old epic in letters and discussed it with his friend Chink Dorman-Smith (*Letters* 2 133).[8] *Streets in the Moon* was in press, however, by the time MacLeish and Hemingway drove together from Bayonne—probably over the pass at Roncevaux—to Zaragoza in 1926.[9] Whoever inspired the other, Hemingway uses the version of the line that appears in MacLeish's poem, which differs slightly from that found in other editions of *The Song of Roland.* (Of the many available translations of the line from Old to modern French, only MacLeish uses the "que.") More to the point, MacLeish's poem, an elegy for the dead of the First World War, was dedicated to his brother, Kenneth, who died flying on the western front on 14 October 1918, a month before the war ended. David Bourne, himself a former WWI aviator, remembers Kenny MacLeish by name later in the *Eden* manuscript (see *[204:23] 3.37.30),* and MacLeish's poem links the death of Roland and his troops to the recent war that still haunts David.

MacLeish was on Hemingway's mind as he worked on *The Garden of Eden*. After a twenty-year lull in their correspondence, in December 1956 they began to correspond regularly again as MacLeish led the effort to get Ezra Pound released from Saint Elizabeths Hospital, where he had been committed for what amounts to political insanity. This led them both to reflect on the early days in Paris. On 15 October 1958, Hemingway wrote from Ketchum (a few miles from Pound's birthplace) to MacLeish: "You dope. Did you think I had forgotten rue du Bac, Juan-les-Pins, Zaragoza, Chartres, . . . our bicycles, Ada and the Six Jours, rue Froidevaux, and a million things, Gstaad,—don't ask me to name them all" (*SL* 885). And when Hemingway wrote this, his inscribed 1926 copy of *Streets in the Moon*—copy sixty of sixty printed—may have been at his side. The book remains in the collection at his Ketchum house to this day.[10]

44:31 **newly planted magnolias and bloody mimosas and . . . phony Basque villas:** See 35:6 and 36:2.

(44:33) 3.5.6 **Let someone else write it. . . . Deux Magots:** David questions the value of his morning's work, and he wonders if he really "gives a damn" about the story of Nick and Barbara. He decides he doesn't, and he thinks his friend Andy knows their story better and is in a better position to write it. Andy has always been in love with Barbara, and it was Andy who told David about the conversation with Nick and Barbara at Deux Magots (see 42:15). Andy told the story so well that David felt the story had happened to him, but he realizes he ought to be writing about his "own damned girl." He feels like a crook stealing someone else's story and thinks he had better write about Catherine "soon because it is going too fast," and he can feel himself deteriorating with it. "Full of . . . righteous self-denunciation and good resolution," he tells himself to start anew and "bite on the nail" tomorrow morning.

In this mood he finds himself standing under the trees of the café looking at Barbara. Nick has taken his bicycle into the hills to paint, and Barbara had accompanied him partway before returning.

Close to major French publishing houses and associated with such figures as Mallarmé, Verlaine, Rimbaud, Wilde, Breton, and Barnes, Les Deux Magots is one of the most famous literary cafés in Paris. At the corner of the Boulevard Saint-Germain and the Place Saint-Germain-des-Prés, close to the Café de Flore and across the street from Brasserie Lipp, Les Deux Magots became Hemingway's "café of choice" between late 1926 and early 1928, during the period of his divorce from Hadley when he stopped frequenting the Closerie des Lilas (M. Reynolds, *American* 164). In *A Moveable Feast,* Hemingway remembers drinking dry sherry there with James Joyce.

It is significant that, in the manuscript, Andy finds the Sheldons here. Deux Magots is close to "the Spaniard's," where Nick and Barbara have had their hair cut identically (see *[32] 2.1.17),* and in conversation with Andy at Deux Magots, Nick asks if his haircut makes him look like a "bloody sodomite" (see appendix A). In spite of his own patronage of the café, Hemingway clearly associated Deux Magots with homosexuality. It was close to Natalie Barney's home on the Rue Jacob, and Djuna Barnes, who also lived nearby, was a regular. In a September 1928 letter to Waldo Peirce, Hemingway writes of sitting at Deux Magots and watching the "fairies and lesbians" (*Letters 3* 459), and in a 1930 letter to Peirce he writes, "The Deux Magots must be a good cafe if 100,000 lesbians can't be wrong" (*Letters 4* 286). The café is the setting of the final scene in Hemingway's story in *Death in the Afternoon* of a young man's traumatic homosexual initiation (182).

*(45:6) 3.5.7 **get her out of here. . . . mouth. . . . Like a Laurencin:*** In the manuscript, Barbara warns David that if he loves Catherine he should take her away. David stops her monologue while he gets a drink. When the absinthe arrives, Barbara resumes, with a plea instead of a warning that David take Catherine away. The shape of Catherine's head, her ears, her nose, the cheekbones, the "lioness eyes," and her tan are simply too much for Barbara. She's forgetting the mouth, David adds, but Barbara isn't; she says Catherine's mouth is "indecent" and "ought to be forbidden."

Barbara claims that Catherine's mouth belongs on a woman painted by Marie Laurencin. The observation is astute and rich with possibility. Described by the chic magazine *Vu* in 1930 as "one of the three most famous women in France" (Hyland and McPherson 72), Laurencin was a painter, set designer, and poet celebrated throughout the 1920s for images that were "quintessentially" or "excessively feminine"—so feminine that some critics regarded them as "subtley naughty" or even "perverse" (Elliott 93).[11] These critics hint at a sort of self-conscious "female female impersonation," or feminine masquerade, structured by a self-alienating split in the ego such as one might find in fetishism.[12] Barbara calls attention to this when she claims, with obvious sarcasm, that Catherine's mouth is "absolutely innocent. Sure." Such a presentation of gender would have an obvious appeal for Hemingway in representing a character who on some level represents the split-off other-gendered half of his own ego. Laurencin had affairs with both men and women, and Hemingway would have known her both as Apollinaire's former lover and as the illustrator of Natalie Barney's translation of Sappho. Laurencin worked alongside such figures as Picasso, Cocteau, and Diaghilev, who figure elsewhere in the *Eden* manuscript. There is a strong family resemblance between all of Laurencin's female figures, including her self-portraits, and her work has been described as "supremely narcissistic" (Elliott 109). Again, this is only appropriate for an analog with a character who can say, "Now you're me you're you so much better" *(3.31.35).*

*(45:6) 3.5.7 **You know no man ever looked at her that didn't have an erection. I don't know what women have but whatever it is I have it:*** In the manuscript, Barbara describes her attraction to Catherine with these remarkable words, which

seem to illustrate Freud's assertion that the fetishist uses the fetish, among other things, to ward off castration anxiety by endowing women with an illusory female phallus. It is one of several times women in the novel speak of having "erections" (see 15:13). For an extensive exploration of this, see Eby's *Hemingway's Fetishism*.[13]

David tells Barbara that Catherine doesn't like girls, but Barbara already knows about Catherine's plans for the surprise, and "if it comes off," she tells him, he'd better get her out of town.

(45:6) 3.5.8 I'm not a queer or I never was: Barbara praises how good Nick and Andy have been to her. She admits that she may be a bit "crazy," but she protests that she's isn't "queer"—at least hasn't been until now. She just had a "special thing," "a simple delight or ecstasy" that her haircuts with Nick made public. "It was private," she tells David, but she had to make it public. This was a "necessary danger." But she hadn't realized it would "take possession" of her. David tries to reassure her that there's nothing wrong with doing whatever she and Nick like, but she isn't reassured. "Now it owns me," she tells him. When David replies that she can't blame Catherine for that, Barbara agrees, but she finds Catherine "destructive," and Barbara is defenseless "destroy material." She knows all too well when "good lovely pleasure turns into vice."

David asks Barbara if she is painting. No, she replies. Talking of herself dismissively, she thinks she "painted well enough for a woman," but she sees no point in painting when Nick is painting so much better. When David says that he and Andy like her work, she tells him that Andy doesn't count because he's in love with her. Since David is waiting for Catherine to return from Biarritz, and Barbara is waiting for Nick to return from painting, they decide to have lunch together. This ends a chapter in the manuscript.

45:12 **for an instant he did not know her. . . . breasts . . . sweater. . . . pushing her head against him. . . . "new girl":** Catherine's return from Biarritz with the haircut "surprise" that makes her a "new girl" for David recalls a scene near the end of *A Farewell to Arms* when Catherine Barkley promises to cut her hair after the baby is born: "We'll go together and get it cut, or I'll go alone and come and surprise you." Then, she promises, "I'll be a fine new and different girl for you" (304). The point isn't so much the similarity between the two novels as it is the continuity in Hemingway's erotic fantasies.

This passage in *Eden* features a constellation of Hemingway's fetishistic associations: the cropped hair, the breasts beneath the cashmere sweater, the contrast between the pearls and Catherine's "dark face." Catherine pushes her hair against David "again and again," and the manuscript makes it a little clearer that Catherine's "thank you" to David (46:4) is for his vote of confidence: an erection. David's initial misrecognition of Catherine doesn't seem to be a register of the difference in

Catherine's appearance so much as it is a register of the reality of her transformation into a "new girl." This feels like a moment of dissociated misrecognition of the split-off other-gendered half of the ego, not unlike those moments experienced in mirrors by so many of Hemingway's male protagonists (see 84:16).

45:23 Devil: The biblical significance of this nickname in a book titled *The Garden of Eden* is obvious. This is the first time David uses "Devil" as a nickname for Catherine, but it has long been percolating on the back burner. When Catherine first becomes a boy in bed and David becomes her girl, Catherine asks him if he minds that they've "gone to the devil" (17:1). Another evening in bed, Catherine assures David that they "don't always have to do the devil things" (29:2). In the manuscript, when Barbara warns Catherine that drinking absinthe will soon make her life "even less dull," Catherine asks to hear what she and David will start doing that they "wouldn't do ordinarily," and David calls her "a devil" *(3.1.6)*. Now "Devil" has become another name for Catherine.

46:3 sculptured tawny head: The association of haircuts with sculpture recalls the effects of Rodin's *Metamorphoses of Ovid* on the Bournes and Sheldons. (See [17:22] 1.1.21.) It also may allude to Monsieur Antoine (Antoine Cierplikowski), the man Hemingway recommended in a 1928 letter to his sister Marcelline as the "only decent coiffure in Paris" (*Letters 3* 395). The first modern celebrity hairdresser, Monsieur Antoine claimed to have invented modern coiffure, including such innovations as the short bob, and by 1927 he advertised himself as "the most famous hairdresser in the world" (Saks). He commuted between his shops in Deauville, Biarritz, Cannes, Nice, New York, and Paris, where he was located on the Rue Cambon, directly behind the Ritz Hotel, close to the headquarters of Coco Chanel. Friends with Modigliani, Cocteau, and Kissling, Antoine was also a sculptor, and he particularly admired the work of his early mentor Xavier Dunikowski, whom he called "the Polish Rodin." Antoine famously thought of his work as "hair sculpture," writing in his memoir, "I have always tried to bend to my desire whatever material I am working with. So it seemed to me quite natural to consider the hair as though it were a sculptor's medium" (69, 52). Antoine's sculptural aspirations were famous enough to be featured in headlines when he opened his New York salon in 1927: "Makes Art of Bobbing Hair: Antoine, Who Wanted to Be a Sculptor, Here from Paris to Open Shop."[14] Monsieur Antoine may even be a model for *The Garden of Eden*'s Monsieur Jean (see 79:21).

46:16 I went to the best place: In the manuscript, Catherine doesn't know what the best place is, so she asks at Sonny's Bar *(3.6.2)*. At the corner of the Avenues Edouard VII and Reine-Victoria, opposite the Hôtel du Palais, Sonny's Bar was a famous gathering place for aristocrats, celebrities, and Spanish exiles. The bar, presided over by a barman named Harry (who else to consult about a haircut?), was one of Hemingway's old favorites in Biarritz, and he used it as a sort of home base to handle his mail when he was in town.[15]

Owned by socialite Sonny Robinson, whose mother was the American-born Marquise de las Claras, the bar occupied part of a new wing of the Carlton Hotel building that was added in 1926 after the demolition of an adjacent hotel, the Pavillon Henri IV. This location was occupied by a couturier, however, until Sonny's Bar opened in April 1935.[16] Hemingway's knowledge of this anachronism may have inspired an association eight pages later in the manuscript, when Catherine recalls first making love with David, at a different "Pavillon Henri Quatre"—this one outside of Paris at St.-Germain-en-Laye (see 47:14). During the late 1920s, the prestige bar in Biarritz was the Bar Basque, but Hemingway may have anachronistically used Sonny's Bar instead to avoid confusion with a different Bar Basque in Saint-Jean-de-Luz, which he will soon mention (see 49:15).

46:19 I wanted it cut like a boy . . . *not* an Eton crop: As the coiffeur makes clear, Catherine does *not* get an Eton crop. Though she begins with the idea of an Eton crop, she then gets something even shorter. But Catherine tells the story of her haircut in a way that makes it sound like, on the way to her new haircut, she *invents* the idea of the Eton crop as a haircut for women, choosing among British boys' public school haircuts from Eton, Winchester, and Rugby. And this is not the first time Hemingway imagined one of his heroines as the inventor of this style. In *The Sun Also Rises*, Brett Ashley enters the novel with "her hair . . . brushed back like a boy's. She started all that" (30). Such an act of invention—although an anachronism in 1927—would be no small feat, since the Eton crop was generally considered the most radical and notorious of the boyish bobs popularized for women in the 1920s.

If debates surrounding bobbed hair functioned as a symbolic battleground in the gender wars of the 1920s, the scandalized newspaper articles devoted to the Eton crop constituted the front lines. The style appears in *Vogue* as early as 1923 in "A Parisienne's Philosophy of Coiffures," with the author complaining that "to be chic," women must now have their "hair cut like that of an Eton student" (Foster). By December 1924 a headline in the *Washington Post* announced, "Exaggerated Bob Is London Rage":

> The Eton crop has appeared among London's ultra-fashionable women and bids fair to become rapidly popular in modish Mayfair. As the name indicates, it is a style which has been traditionally popular in England's public schools. It is essentially masculine in appearance. The hair is cut short and shaved from the nape of the neck, the ears are entirely exposed. . . . The cut is considerably shorter than is usual for a boy, with the hair widely parted on the left and brushed back severely.

(*Left*) The Duchesse de Gramont with an Eton Crop, *Vogue* (French), May 1928. (Source gallica.bnf.fr / Bibliothèque nationale de France.) (*Right*) Newlyweds Ernest and Pauline Hemingway, 1927. Pauline sports an Eton crop. (Ernest Hemingway Collection. Photographs. John F. Kennedy Presidential Library and Museum.)

Described in the press as "the closest, shortest coiffure there is"—"the absolute minimum"—the Eton crop played upon all kinds of cultural anxieties about the changing status of women ("Eton Crop Is Latest"; "Ordeal"). Articles complained of Eton-cropped women that "but for their skirts it would often be difficult to determine their sex" ("That Eton Crop"). Employers soon banned the cut, and articles with headlines like "The Eton Crop Peril" warned women that the style had been found to "induce baldness."[17] Still other articles claimed that "it will soon be hopelessly *demode* to have any hair on our heads at all . . ." ("Cult"). By 1927, hairdressers in Paris, London, and throughout Europe had organized campaigns against the hairstyle that threatened to cost them clients who could now get their hair trimmed by barbers.[18] Inspired by pronouncements from the Hairdressing and Allied Trades Exhibition in London and the president of the Paris Hairdressers' Association, fashion experts began predicting the demise of the Eton crop—with even more certainty than they'd been predicting it for the previous two years.[19] Yet despite what the arbiters of taste declared in the papers, the style dominated the pages of French *Vogue* throughout 1927 (see 15:31).

If Catherine Bourne can, however anachronistically, claim to be the inventor of the women's Eton crop, she is a major trendsetter (see 6:3). Given the uproar provoked by the Eton crop, the fact that she gets her hair cut *even shorter* than this is a measure of her daring.

47:14 **new girl . . . her mouth was changed too:** As part of Catherine's transformation into a "new girl," David notes that her mouth changes. We might wonder *how*. Is she pouting her lips? Is this just a change of expression? Elsewhere in the manuscript, he thinks of it as "a tumescence and a firming like her breasts"—one might call it a sort of a lip erection *(3.13.6)*. Whatever it is, the change isn't just in David's imagination; Catherine sees it too. It is something *physical*, perhaps even quasi-supernatural, that happens when she becomes a "boy," or transitions back to being a "girl."

The gap in the text on this page of the Scribner's edition indicates deleted material from the *Eden* manuscript. As they lie in bed after making love, David coos, "My lovely Catherine," to which Catherine replies, "Yes. I'm a girl again. For whatever that's worth" *(3.6.4)*. And she wants to know if David saw her mouth change. The haircut has just "brought it out more," David suggests, but Catherine corrects him: no, her mouth has been "changing ever since I thought of changing back." That's just her imagination, David protests, but Catherine insists it isn't, and that David knows it. David feels her lips and then wants to make love again. "What about work?" Catherine asks. "The hell with work," says David. "No," says Catherine, but the day is "special." (For more about Catherine's mouth, see *[47:18] 3.7.6*.)

As they make love, Catherine tells David that she loves to be a girl, and she's proud that she could change back when David didn't think she could. Unlike the Sheldons, she and David aren't "prisoners." This ends a chapter in the manuscript *(3.6.5)*.

(47:18) 3.7.1 **the two others:** Later that evening, in the manuscript, while out for a walk along the sea wall, Catherine and David see Nick and Barbara at the café. Catherine disdainfully thinks that they look "so Montparnasse" and is reluctant to join them. Surprised, David reminds her of the effect the Sheldons had on her only two days before, but Catherine doesn't want to be reminded. David suggests that they can go instead to the bar at the Eskualduna, but Barbara sees them and they feel obliged to join the Sheldons.

As Catherine walks over with her new haircut she is almost unrecognizable to Barbara, and she carries herself artificially and with a great sense of her own superiority, looking "distant and contemptuous." In response to Barbara's glance, she asks if she should model the haircut for her, but Barbara declines.

(47:18) 3.7.2 **"Chanel uniforms. . . ." "not number five. . . ." "Gardenia. . . ." "not Cuir de Russie":** Noting Catherine's stiff posture, Barbara assures her that she can see her breasts through her sweater quite clearly if that was her concern. This leads to a quip about Catherine wearing "Chanel uniforms." Barbara wonders "what number" Catherine's sweater is. Catherine retorts that it isn't number five. Noting its short sleeves and "slashed" neckline, Barbara suggests that it's probably *Gardénia*. It isn't *Cuir de Russie*, Catherine parries.

Catherine and Barbara here bandy about the names of three famous Chanel perfumes. Chanel's debut and signature perfume, *No. 5,* was launched in 1921 and derived its name from the fact that it was the fifth scent perfumer Ernest Beaux offered as a sample to Chanel. (Five was also reputed to be Chanel's lucky number.) At a time when perfumes were generally representational and tried to capture the essence of single flowers, *No. 5* was immediately recognized as revolutionary, modern, and abstract. The first perfume "deeply and inherently" structured by synthetic aldehydes—as well as floral contributions from lemon, bergamot, rose, ylang-ylang, jasmine, musk, vetiver, and sandalwood—*No. 5* was designed to make a woman smell like a woman, not a flower (Stamelman 246). Describing this revolution in scent, an article in the December 1925 issue of French *Vogue* declared, "Today our perfumes, like our books, must correspond to the modern age as acutely as possible: we repeat every five minutes that we are modern, as if all eras had not been in turn.... Our perfume has become mystifying: it is a point it has in common with our literature" ("Les Parfums" 29). Yet *No. 5* is what Catherine says her sweater is *not*.

Barbara's association of Catherine's sweater with *Gardénia* is suggestive. Hemingway was fond of the fragrance, counseling his sister Marcelline in 1928 about her upcoming trip to France, "If you want the best perfume there is, get Chanel's *Gardénia*..." (*Letters 3* 395). If *No. 5* is as abstract as a Cubist painting, *Gardénia* is a sort of olefactory trompe l'oeil, since the natural scent of the flower cannot be successfully extracted and has to be synthesized artificially.[20] Launched by Chanel in 1925, the scent was well timed to take advantage of a small fad for gardenias and gardenia fragrances: "Its bloom being short-lived, the flower became a poignant metaphor for young women in the prime of their beauty" (Ostrom 94). And its associations make it a particularly appropriate perfume for Catherine: "Gardenia perfumes were often marketed to the ... sophisticated newlywed, though their swoon-inducing qualities made the flower a neat literary leitmotif for a darker taste in sexual infatuation" (Ostrom 95).

Catherine's reply that her sweater isn't *Cuir de Russie* is both biting and ironic. Created by Ernest Beaux in 1924, but not launched by Chanel until 1927, *Cuir de Russie* ("Russian Leather"), with its overtones of leather, birch, and tobacco, was self-consciously marketed as "masculine," "unisex," and "androgynous" (Aveline 12). It was a perfume for "women who dared to smoke in public," and a Chanel advertisement claimed that "well-bred ladies" would find its scent "improper" (Stamelman 234). In other words, it was the quintessential perfume for flappers, and Catherine clearly associates it with the Montparnassian qualities she currently finds objectionable in Barbara.

Given these knowing references to perfumes, it should be noted that the 1920s and '30s are often considered "the golden age of modern perfumery" (Mazzeo 33), and the capital of the French perfume industry was the "earthly Paradise" of Grasse (Le Gallienne 40), a hill town a mere ten miles from La Napoule and visible beyond the valley of the Siagne to someone staying, as the Bournes later do, in Théoule-Supérieur (see 75:2).[21] In 1926, Pauline Pfeiffer stayed with Kay Boyle and Ernest Walsh in Grasse, and Hemingway, then sleeping with Pauline but still married to Hadley, wrote to her there daily, using as a subterfuge the excuse that he was telling Pauline what perfumes and lingerie to bring back for Hadley.

(47:18) 3.7.2 *it makes you like a girl and not like a boy . . . jailbait:* In the manuscript, Barbara wants to know why Catherine is being so rude and why she feels like the world's most beautiful haircut empowers her to "trample on people," but Catherine sips away at her absinthe and tells Barbara not to be "boring." Barbara knows, she tells Catherine, that the haircut—in spite of its extreme shortness—makes her "like a girl and not like a boy." It also makes her look like "jail-bait." Catherine doesn't understand (perhaps because the expression would have been very new in 1927),[22] so Barbara explains that Catherine looks like she's about "fourteen"—under the age of consent. This is noteworthy because Catherine, who in fact is twenty-one, later quite suddenly feels terribly, terribly old (see 16:25 and 162:30).

(47:18) 3.7.3 *what you are going to do to people:* In the manuscript, Barbara wants to know if Catherine understands the effect she will have on people. Catherine claims that she only wants to have this effect on David, but Barbara promises her that she'll have the same effect on others—and that she already has on her. Catherine and David will leave, then, Catherine offers. She doesn't want to have a bad effect on Barbara—but would it be bad for her if Catherine and David stay "just two days on the beach," since they haven't had a chance to swim? (49:33). At this, Barbara throws up her hands and asks David to do something. It must have been easier for Nick, she says, when he only had "one un-certified crazy to handle." Catherine promises not to have any bad effect on Nick if she stays. At this point, Catherine feels David's hand on hers—their agreed-upon warning signal if she is becoming unreasonable under the influence of absinthe. Catherine sips her absinthe and tells everyone that she's glad they all understand one another and that David made her come over to join them. David grips her hand more tightly, and she smiles with pride that she remembers the signal. Barbara notes that it was nice of her to join them if she hadn't felt like it. When Barbara shifts the conversation to where the Bournes will go next, Catherine asks for her suggestion. "Anywhere would be fine," Barbara tells her, and David's hand closes on Catherine's again. "Well maybe that's where we'll go," Catherine replies. "Truly [she doesn't] want to do anything to [Barbara] or have any bad effect on [her]" (see 50:12). They will leave tomorrow, Catherine says, but Barbara assures her that Nick can help her to hold out for a day or two. In spite of David's warning hand, Catherine agrees that Nick is kind and will help her. But why, she asks, does Barbara make Nick wear his hair in a way that embarrasses him, like "someone out of Montparnasse"? At this, the Sheldons decide to leave.

(47:18) 3.7.5 **But I was so cruel and awful:** In the manuscript, Catherine immediately apologizes to David and begins to cry. It's as if a detached part of herself could hear how cruel and awful she was being, but she'd been powerless to stop it. Nick will understand, David reassures her, and he'll help Barbara to understand. She had meant what she said, though, "even the awful stupid part." David understands this as a reference to what Catherine said about Nick's haircut. "Everybody has strange things that mean things to them," he tells her, "and we have to understand them." He gently defends Barbara as a fine and strange girl. Catherine replies that "two days ago," when she first saw Nick and Barbara, she "understood everything, but then [she] turned on it" (49:19). David knows that she couldn't help herself, but he wants to be careful so they don't hurt other people. Thinking of the absinthe-fueled argument from the day before, Catherine feels awful for trying to hurt David, but in lines that have been transposed to later in the Scribner's edition (49:22–32) David tells her that he wasn't hurt and that she's beautiful when she cries.

(47:18) 3.7.6 **You made my mouth change. . . . Pavillon Henri Quatre at St. Germain:** David tells Catherine that crying has made her lips "even more the way they are." He is the one who made her mouth change, she tells him (see 47:14). The change began the first time they made love at the Pavillon Henri Quatre. "It changed back at le Grau du Roi." "I know," David admits.

Famous for its fine restaurant and the commanding view from its terrace over the valley of the Seine toward Paris, the Pavillon Henri IV is a luxury hotel housed in the remains of the late-sixteenth-century "new" chateau completed by Henry IV in Saint-Germain-en-Laye, on the outskirts of Paris. (The "old" chateau, mostly early-sixteenth-century but with elements dating back to the twelfth century, remains intact nearby.) The Sun King, Louis XIV, was born there and used the new chateau as his residence of preference until moving to Versailles in 1682, after which most of the new chateau was allowed to fall into disrepair and decay. The hotel opened in 1836, and it hosted many celebrities, including Alexandre Dumas, who wrote *The Three Musketeers* and *The Count of Monte Cristo* there (Gruyer 108). Like the Hôtel Crillon, where David and Catherine first meet (237:28), the Pavillon Henri IV housed diplomats and served as an important setting for the treaties between the victors and vanquished that settled the First World War. The hotel is a suitably romantic and expensive location for the Bournes to first make love, but given the haunting presence of the war in the background of the novel, the hotel's role in the postwar settlement may also have symbolic value. (See also 46:16.)

47:28 **a wild girl:** Where the Scribner's text reads "I'll be *a* wild girl," the manuscript reads "I'll be wild girl" (3.7.6). In other words, "wild girl" is not a *thing* she will be, it is a *who* she will be. It is a sort of persona or alter ego. In the same passage in the manuscript, Catherine says she'll also "be thief girl." She'll be *all* of David's girls.

She likes to be "thief girl," but for the moment she'll be wild girl, who stays awake and keeps thief girl at bay. When the next morning David asks why she was thief girl, Catherine answers that she couldn't help it and asks with a hint of dissociation, "Was she nice?" (For more on "wild girl," see *[50:18] 3.8.1.*)

48:30 can we have champagne if it's not wicked? In the brut they have Lanson and Perrier-Jouët of the good: Champagne for breakfast symbolizes the Bournes' taste for luxury and sensual indulgence—a taste coded as potentially corrupting and wicked. The morning alcohol also represents a threat to David's work. Two of the most prestigious champagne houses, Lanson (est. 1760) and Perrier-Jouët (est. 1811) both specialized in dry sec and brut wines and were known for their strong ties to the British export market. Perrier-Jouët offered several qualities of wine, which is presumably what Catherine has in mind when she specifies "of the good." (See 122:4.)

49:8 I can cut it shorter. . . . Or you can: Although David never cuts Catherine's hair in the novel, the suggestion here that he could is noteworthy. Hair fetishists often find it erotic to cut their partners' hair—in his seminal essay on fetishism, Freud even writes about the phenomenon (157)—and Hemingway enjoyed playing the barber and hairstylist for his wives. (For more extensive notes on Hemingway's barbering, see 77:13 and 79:21.)

49:15 St. Jean. . . . Bar Basque: About eight miles up the coast from Hendaye Plage, Saint-Jean-de-Luz in 1927 was a seaside resort town of roughly five thousand inhabitants at the mouth of the Nivelle River. The town was "quieter than Biarritz" but of "growing popularity" and more developed than Hendaye Plage (Muirhead and Monmarché 350). It may represent yet another of the novel's endangered Edens. A contemporary guide book warned, "Only a little while ago this was a very charming little town. . . . Alas! it, too, is becoming rather too modern and has had its head turned by the luxury of Biarritz, which it is inclined to copy" (Praviel 49–50). In the novel, Catherine describes Biarritz as a "horror" (36:6)

The Bar Basque, at 22 Boulevard Thiers in Saint-Jean-de-Luz (not to be confused with the Bar Basque at the Grand Hotel et Bellevue Palace in Biarritz), was opened in 1920 by the Cerutti family and remains in business today. Baron George Wrangel wrote in 1931 that Saint-Jean-de-Luz drew "together in crowded intimacy the fashionables of international society. . . . For cocktails, dinner and dancing, the Bar Basque is quite likely to be so bursting with cheerful, brightly dressed humanity that it is difficult to move about. . . ." In 1959, Hemingway claimed it was at the Bar Basque that he overheard the conversation that inspired his 1931 story, "The Sea Change" ("Art" 88). There are good reasons to doubt this claim (he had already offered several other conflicting accounts for the origin of that story),[23] but it suggests something of the position occupied by the Bar Basque in Hemingway's imagination during the time when he was working on *The Garden of Eden*.

49:19 **Two days ago I understood everything:** In the manuscript, this sentence is about Nick and Barbara, not the clippings. See *(47:18) 3.7.5*.

49:25 **Everybody has strange things that mean things to them:** In the manuscript, "strange things" refers to Nick's haircut (see *[47:18] 3.7.5*).

49:33 **will it be bad for you:** This sentence has been transposed from where it occurs in the manuscript. There, the question is directed to Barbara, not David (see *[47:18] 3.7.3*).

50:7 **Well maybe that's where we'll go:** In the manuscript, this conversation is between Catherine and Barbara (see *[47:18] 3.7.3*).

50:12 **Truly I don't want to do anything to you or have any bad effect on you:** In the manuscript, this line is directed at Barbara, not David (see *[47:18] 3.7.3*).

(50:18) 3.8.1 **Before they left Hendaye:** The Scribner's editor, Tom Jenks, deletes an entire short chapter from the manuscript here. Before leaving Hendaye, Catherine, who has already apologized to Nick, wants to apologize to Barbara. David thinks a note might be best, but Catherine wants to do it in person. When she finds Barbara at the café, Barbara greets her as "wild girl" *(3.8.2)*. How, Catherine asks, did Barbara know she was "wild girl"? "It was just a name I thought up for you," Barbara replies. Barbara's lucky guess implies a fundamental psychological affinity between the two women (see 47:28). When Catherine says she came to apologize, Barbara is gracious and won't hear of it and asks her to have a Pernod instead. Catherine tells Barbara that she tried very hard to get this apology right, but Barbara assures her that she doesn't like apologies, even beautiful ones. She wishes Catherine luck. She thinks Catherine will need it, and she thinks she will need it as well. They drink as friends and wish each other luck.

NOTES

1. For a record of Bahamian watercolors at the exhibit, see Goodrich.
2. This echoes a line from Hemingway's 1938 introduction to the Luis Quintanilla exhibit at New York's Museum of Modern Art. Of Quintanilla's drawings, Hemingway writes, "They are to be looked at; not written about in a catalogue" (*HMF* 64).
3. In a 7 Sept. 1947 letter, Hemingway expressed lukewarm enthusiasm for Rasmusson's work, but still asked Scribner to pass along his thanks to the artist (*SL* 627).

4. After the Second World War, Picasso was quite devoted to producing illustrations. Between 1945 and 1963 Picasso illustrated more than eighty-five books (Curtis and Holo 76).

5. For *Der Querschnitt*'s 1925 translation of "The Undefeated," see *Letters 2* 324. For the 1958 edition, see Hemingway's *Der Unbesiegte*. This 1958 edition with illustrations by Picasso should not be confused with another German edition of *Der Unbesiegte* from the same time with illustrations by Wilhelm M. Busch.

6. For such moments of misrecognition, see *THHN* 259; *FTA* 311; *CSS* 89, 305; *FWBT* 351.

7. This poem was republished in *The Best Poems of 1926* as "Toward a Romantic Revival" and was later republished again as "The Silent Slain."

8. See also M. Reynolds, *Paris Years* 218.

9. MacLeish had submitted the collection to Houghton Mifflin in December 1925, and it was published in November 1926 (MacLeish, *Letters* 177–78).

10. Many thanks to Jenny Emery-Davidson, Executive Director of Ketchum's Community Library, for calling this to my attention.

11. For contemporary accusations of perversity, see Cogniat and Courthion.

12. My formulation of female masquerade here stems from Joan Riviere's famous essay "Womanliness as a Masquerade" and is aware of Judith Butler's critique of Riviere in *Gender Trouble,* but in calling attention to ego splitting and in distinguishing between performativity and a degree of self-conscious and self-alienating theatricality it is more influenced by Louise Kaplan's book *Female Perversions*.

13. Given the repetition of this theme in *Eden,* one wonders about Catherine's claim that her fetishized suntans are "like growing something" (see 30:16). Outlandish as it may seem, could this be the female phallus that Freud associates with fetishism?

14. A measure of Antoine's success in 1927 would be the opening of his ultramodern "glass house" that year in Paris. Nearly fifteen hundred guests—including many from the rich, famous, and royal—attended the opening of this all-glass home, beauty school, and sculpture studio (Cierplikowski 132).

15. See Hotchner 127–28 and Ernest's letters to Mary Hemingway dated 26 and 28 April 1954 (JFK). For the name of the barman, see "Au Bar du Carlton."

16. For the opening of the new wing of the Carlton and the famous couturier, Worth, at the location eventually occupied by Sonny's Bar, see "English and American News: Biarritz Notes." For the opening of Sonny's Bar, see "Au Bar du Carlton"; see also "Septembre sur la Côte d'Argent." For information on Sonny, see Gwynne.

17. See, for instance, "Eton Crop Ban," "Cropped Waitresses Banned," "Eton Crop Scare."

18. See "Boyish Bob Is Banned by Paris Hairdressers," "The Eton Crop Goes," "Eton Crop Doomed," and "Eton Crop Banned."

19. See "Deserting Eton Crop," "Eton Crop Going," "The Eton Crop Will Die," and "Death of the Eton Crop."

20. See Stamelman 35. In her book devoted to *Chanel No. 5,* Mazzeo compares *No. 5* in its abstraction to the work of Picasso (45).

21. Hemingway owned Richard Le Gallienne's history of perfume, and he knew the author. He attended an exhibition of paintings by Le Gallienne's daughter Gwen on the Rue Jacob in June 1927, and Richard was present ("Social World"). This event and the 1928 publication date of Le Gallienne's book suggest that Hemingway may have associated perfume with this era of his life. For the view of Grasse from Théoule Supérieur, see Gibbons 3.

22. The earliest occurrence in the *Oxford English Dictionary* and several slang dictionaries is 1934.

23. For a consideration of these reasons, see Eby, "Sea Change" 84–85.

CHAPTER 6 (MSS. CHAPTERS 9–12)

51.1 They had spent the morning at the Prado: For Hemingway, the Prado—one of the world's greatest art museums—represented the symbolic heart of Madrid and of Spain. As he writes in *Death in the Afternoon,* it is only in Madrid that one can find "the essence" of the country, and if the city "had nothing else than the Prado it would be worth spending a month in every spring" (51). The museum was an essential component of what made pre–Civil War Spain a sort of Eden for Hemingway: "A man could live a week on [a hundred pesetas] in a bullfighters' boarding house in Madrid, go to the Prado four times a week, buy good seats in the sun for two bullfights, buy the papers afterwards and drink beer and eat shrimp in the Pasaje Alvarez off the Calle de Vitoria, and still have something left to get his shoes shined with" (33). (With the exception of attending a bullfight and staying in a bullfighter's hotel, this sentence from *Death in the Afternoon* describes precisely what the Bournes are doing in the opening pages of this chapter.) When in 1953 Hemingway returned to Spain for the first time after the Civil War, it was above all to show Mary Hemingway the Prado (*UK* 265)— not only to show her the Goyas, El Grecos, and works by Velázquez, but to share with her as well works by Bosch, Bruegel, Rubens, and Andrea del Sarto (*HIW* 313). Mary remembered of that trip, "Whatever else we did on that first visit to Madrid, we went each morning to the Prado for an hour" (*HIW* 335). In the novel, the Bournes' trips to the Prado seem to be inspired by these memories and these same passions.

(51:2) 3.9.1 shade outside the Cervezería Alvarez in the Pasaje Alvarez. . . . Andrew Murray: This chapter in the manuscript begins with Catherine and David sitting outside of the Cervezería Alvarez, not in the "building with the thick stone walls" (see 51:2), which is where they go to lunch after their drinks at the cervecería.

The Cervecería Alvarez first opened for business at 4 Pasaje de Mathéu, at the corner of the Calle de la Victoria, in April 1927. Today the Taberna La Carmela stands on the site. David and Catherine sit in "the passageway" of the little alley, the Pasaje de Mathéu. One of Hemingway's favorite places in Madrid, this cervecería appears often in his writing, most notably in the entry for *cerveza* in the glossary to *Death in the Afternoon:* "There is good draft beer almost anywhere in Madrid, but the best is found at the Cervezería Alvarez in the Calle Victoria."[1]

As he sits with Catherine, sipping beer and eating shrimp in the shade, David sees Andrew Murray coming down the narrow passageway towards them, observing all of the details around him with writerly attention. David hails him, introduces him to Catherine, and they all sit down together. This is our first introduction to the Andy who is in a better position than David to write the story of the Sheldons, who is in love with Barbara, and who with David's assistance helped Nick to find his dealer (see *[44:33]* 3.5.6 and 39:22). In an interesting shift of narrative focalization, Catherine sizes up Andy. He needs a haircut, but otherwise, she finds him almost too clean and nice-looking to be a writer. She wonders if he's as good a writer as David. In another narrative shift to external focalization, we're told that David and Andy are each about as good as the other.

(51:2) 3.9.2 **"Primo . . . roads. . . ." "The king drove it to San Sebastian in eight hours":** In the manuscript, David, Andy, and Catherine make small talk. When David mentions that he and Catherine had driven down from Hendaye, Andy asks how the Spanish dictator, Primo de Rivera, is doing with the roads. David notes some "torn up" parts but gives a largely favorable report. Andy's question is doubtless prompted by Primo de Rivera's initiation in 1926 of the *Circuito Nacional de Firmes Especiales* (National Circuit of Roads with Special Surfaces), "the greatest public works program ever seen in Spain, [and the] beginning [of] the country's modern highway system" (Payne 20). David adds that the king drove the road from Madrid to San Sebastian in eight hours—perhaps less. To understand this, it helps to know that "King Alfonso XIII was fond of turning his annual move from Madrid to San Sebastian into a kind of one-man race on a road that was closed to traffic for the occasion. The king used to clock himself to make sure that he beat his record of the previous year in his latest Hispano Suiza or whatever he was driving" (Hofmann). In September 1926, when the king had to dash back from San Sebastian to Madrid to help quell a mutiny among the armed forces, newspapers reported that he managed the drive in a little over six hours ("King").

(51:2) 3.9.2 **gypsy. . . . princess:** In the manuscript, as Andy and the Bournes chat, the bootblack who had been working on Andy's shoes asks Andy if Catherine is a gypsy. Andy tells him yes, and that she's a princess in her country. When the bootblack replies that he could tell she was a princess, Catherine rewards him with a peseta. This incident reinforces Catherine's fantasy that her suntan can effect a racial transformation (see *[19:1]* 1.2.1).

(51:2) 3.9.3 **"Lipp's. . . ." "Weber's . . . Prunier's. . . ." "Proust":** In the manuscript, David and Andy wonder whether the beer at the Cervezería Alvarez (see *[51:2]* 3.9.1) is better than at Lipp's (see *[32]* 2.1.15). Soon after leaving Paris in 1928, Hemingway wrote to Guy Hickok that he was "cockeyed nostalgique for Paris . . . and Lipp's

beer," and he assured his sister Marcelline, who was preparing for a trip to France that year, that Lipp's had the "best beer in Paris" (*Letters 3* 448, 395). In the *Eden* manuscript, however, Catherine doesn't remember Lipp's, though David assures her that she's been there.

Catherine does remember drinking beer at Weber's, on the Rue Royale, and she specifically remembers David being disappointed that she didn't like it. Café Weber, 21 Rue Royale, was founded in 1865 and closed in 1961. It doesn't appear anywhere else in Hemingway's published fiction. He probably mentions it here in the *Eden* manuscript because the brasserie, popular with writers and artists, was particularly favored by Marcel Proust and appears in *Remembrance of Things Past* (Tadié 314). After Catherine proceeds from her memory of Weber's to a particularly sharp memory of eating at the legendary seafood restaurant Maison Prunier, David asks her when she started "talking like Proust." Catherine supposes that it's because she's been reading him since Hendaye. She promised David she wouldn't skip ahead, but "naturally" she was curious about book four, *Sodome et Gomorrhe* (*Cities of the Plain*), and read a bit of that first (see 3.4). She's disappointed that she didn't find it very "instructive"—perhaps because she already knew "examples of that sort of person" from her schooling in Switzerland. Now she is halfway through *Swann's Way*. (Much like Catherine Bourne, Mary Hemingway was reading Proust during her 1953 stay with Ernest in Madrid [*HIW* 324].)

Catherine's vivid memory of eating *crabe Mexicaine* and drinking Sancerre, and wanting but not ordering oysters, at Prunier's closely resembles a scene with Ernest and Hadley in *A Moveable Feast*. Catherine hadn't ordered the large *marennes* oysters, which were quite expensive, because she'd been afraid David wouldn't have the money. (*Crabe Mexicaine* is crab meat sautéed in butter and herbs on a bed of grilled mushrooms covered with an aromatic creamy wine-fish sauce. Sancerre is a lovely crisp, dry Sauvignon blanc wine from the eastern Loire Valley, about sixty miles southeast of Orléans.) According to a 1925 article in the Paris edition of the *New York Herald*, "Few Americans visiting the Continent have failed to visit the Prunier establishment . . ." ("Emile"). (For more on Prunier's, see 122:4.)

(51:2) 3.9.4 **Henry James:** In the manuscript, Andy asks Catherine what she thinks of Henry James. She likes him but finds his work less well written than Proust's, and she always pities him because "he is so poor." "He wasn't poor," David objects, and Catherine clarifies: her point isn't that James suffered from poverty, but in what may be an indirect nod to *The Portrait of a Lady*, she suggests that James didn't have enough money to meet the requirements of his imagination. Andy doesn't think money was the issue, but Catherine thinks it would have made him happier. At least it worked for her uncle. Catherine suspects herself of talking too much, but she says she's doing it to avoid talking of the Prado.

(51:2) 3.9.5 **Santiago de Compostela. . . . Teresa of Avila and San Juan de la Cruz:** Catherine asks Andy if he plans to stay in Madrid. He does, for a little while before traveling to Santiago de Compostela. David and Catherine tell him that Nick and Barbara are in Hendaye and have asked about him. They decide to lunch together, and while Catherine steps inside to freshen up, Andy asks David about Nick and Barbara. Barbara isn't painting, David reports. Nick is a great painter but somehow unknowable.

As he sees Catherine returning to their table, Andy notes admiringly that Catherine looks unshaken by the restrooms. David explains that she's used to such places. "I see," Andy replies, she's being introduced to Spain "the hard way. Teresa of Avila and San Juan de la Cruz." The reference to the sainted Spanish mystics alludes to their austerity. Together, under Saint Teresa's leadership, Teresa and Juan de la Cruz reformed the Carmelite Order in the sixteenth century. They advocated a return to the original "primitive rule": continual prayer, abstinence from meat, lengthy periods of fasting and silence, courser habits, a life of poverty, and sandals instead of shoes. In 1580, their Discalced, or "barefoot," Carmelites split from the rest of the Carmelite Order.

As Stoneback has argued, Hemingway was deeply interested in the famous pilgrimage to Santiago de Compostela. He links this to a fascination with sacred landscapes that spanned Hemingway's career and, more specifically, to the pilgrimage to Les Saintes-Maries-de-la-Mer in *Eden* ("Pilgrimage"). See also *(53:31) 3.9.11*.

51:2 **building with thick stone walls:** If we follow the clues to determine where the Bournes eat lunch, we can uncover a subtle and ominous literary allusion. The manuscript notes that the restaurant with the thick stone walls is a brief shady walk from the Cervezería Alvarez, where Catherine, David, and Andy have been drinking. Inside the restaurant, "only small windows with bars high up . . . gave onto a narrow street where the sun did not shine. The doorway, though, gave onto an arcade and the bright sunlight on the worn stones of the square" (54:8). The "arcade" tells us that the Bournes are dining at a restaurant on the Plaza Mayor, which in the 1920s featured amid its worn stones a few flowerbeds, trees, and fountains. The "narrow street where the sun did not shine" and the Andalusian food and drink they enjoy suggest that Andy and the Bournes are dining at Cancionera (est. 1925), an Andalusian bar which changed its name in 1932 to La Torre del Oro, and which remains in business today. One side of the bar runs along the narrow alley of the Arco del Triunfo, which runs beneath the famous Casa de la Panadería on the north side of the plaza—hence the absence of sunlight.[2] As Hemingway would have known from his copy of Pio Baroja's *Memorias de un hombre de acción*, this alley formerly went by the name of the Callejón del Infierno (Hell's Alley). According to Madrid lore, during a fire in the plaza, from the outside, this dark passage looked like the gates of hell. In the *Aprendiz de Conspirador* volume of *Memorias*, Baroja tells how the alley had been widened to create a more regal passage to town hall for royal carriages and how at the time a satirical poet, who was also a cleric, had written:

*¡A qué estado habrán llegado
las costumbres de este pueblo,
que es necesario ensanchar
el callejón del Infierno!* (215)

("At what state will the ways of this town have arrived when it is necessary to widen the path to hell!"; my trans.) Hemingway, who was profoundly influenced by Baroja, and who visited his deathbed and attended his funeral in 1956, knew this tale.[3] It is ominous, then, that the Bournes dine on their first day in Madrid at a place where the path to hell widens.

51:6 **manzanilla from the lowland near Cádiz called the Marismas:** *Manzanilla* is a light, straw-colored, very dry type of *fino* sherry from Sanlúcar de Barrameda, at the mouth of the Guadalquivir River. The distinction between a typical fino from Jerez (sixteen miles to the east) and a manzanilla from Sanlúcar is based less on where the grapes are grown than where the wine is aged. Grapes from Jerez aged in a bodega in Sanlúcar will develop into a manzanilla, while grapes from near Sanlúcar aged in Jerez will develop into a more traditional fino: "The sea air in Sanlúcar has a decisive effect on the wine, making it even lighter than Jerez fino and endowing it with a delicate and highly individual aroma. It is completely dry, and leaves a clean but faintly bitter aftertaste on the tongue, without being 'full' like the Jerez fino" (González Gordon 108). In the glossary to *Death in the Afternoon,* Hemingway writes of manzanilla, "One *chato* [short glass] lightens the spirits, three or four makes you feel rather good, but if you eat tapas as you drink, a dozen of them will not make you drunk."

The Marismas ("Marshes") are extensive marshlands in the area around Sanlúcar, which in several ways resemble the Camargue region around Le Grau-du-Roi. For sherry, when David isn't drinking Tio Pepe (see 230:8), he favors *marismeño* (59:12), by which he seems to mean a sherry from the Marismas. In a 28 September 1955 letter, Mary Hemingway advised a friend traveling to Spain, "For an aparatif [sic], don't fail to ask for Maresmaña [sic], iced. It is a sherry, or one of that family, and so light and flowery and dry and just heavenly, you'll want to keep a couple of bottles on ice in your room constantly" (JFK). The word *marismeño,* however, is not frequently used to designate a type of sherry; it does not appear as a term of general use in Spanish, French, or English books or journalism about sherry or manzanilla, and it more frequently appears in the popular Spanish press as an adjective to describe horses, bulls, or rice from the Marismas. There is one wine, however, which has long marketed itself as a marismeño: Sanchez Romate Hermanos Fino Marismeño. To be strictly correct, however, it is aged in Jerez and is a fino, not a true manzanilla.

51:9 **spicier dark sausage from a town called Vich:** David is describing Salchichón de Vich, a dark reddish sausage similar to salami and containing whole pepper corns. Popular in tapas, it is often described as "the king of Catalan pork sausages" (Luján 10).

52:7 **They drank Valdepeñas now from a big pitcher:** A bold, full-bodied red wine, made primarily from Tempranillo grapes, Valdepeñas has long been a popular bargain wine in Spain. The inexpensive price explains why it is served here in pitchers. In the manuscript, David calls it a "tough wine," and Catherine memorably describes it as tasting the way "the circus smells," though she means the feeling you get from the odor, not the odor itself *(3.9.7)*. The village of Valdepeñas and its *denominación de origen protegida* (which also produces a white wine in smaller quantities) is situated not far from Ciudad Real, in southern Spain, where the central plains meet the mountains of Andalusia. It is this proximity to the South that inspires David's assertion that Valdepeñas is an "African wine."

52:13 **Africa begins at the Pyrenees:** This French proverb is frequently attributed to Alexandre Dumas père, but Domingos António de Sousa Coutinho, Count of Funchal, had already written "*fait commencer l'Afrique aux Pyrenées*" in 1816, when Dumas was a teen, and the Count in turn credited Dominique Dufour de Pradt with the authorship of this idea, if not the phrase itself (Funchal xxiv). Others have credited Napoleon with the line, or its inverse: "Europe ends at the Pyrenees." In any case, the expression was in wide circulation, both in English and French, by the end of the nineteenth century, and Hemingway would have encountered it in his copy of Richard Ford's *Gatherings from Spain* (1846).

52:20 **You can tell:** In the manuscript, David adds that Catherine couldn't be "that color" (i.e., tanned so dark) and not be able to tell "where Africa begins" *(3.9.7)*. In other words, we are reminded again that Catherine is coded as a sort of symbolic African.

52:31 **Except Greco's Toledo:** Catherine is almost certainly thinking of El Greco's *View of Toledo,* at the Metropolitan Museum of Art in New York, not the *View and Plan of Toledo* now in the Museo del Greco in Toledo. Anticipating a trip to New York in 1945, Ernest wrote to his soon-to-be wife, Mary Welsh, how wonderful it would be to see "Greco's Toledo at the Metropolitan" (*HIW* 175), and visiting the Met with Lillian Ross in 1950, Hemingway described Greco's *Toledo* as "the best picture in the Museum" (Ross 58).

Catherine is correct about the relative neglect of landscape painting in Spain. Because the Council of Trent in 1563 enjoined painters to treat religious themes and discouraged landscape painting, landscapes are rare in Renaissance and Baroque

Spanish painting. El Greco's *View of Toledo* (circa 1600) is the earliest and most famous major Spanish landscape painting of its time (Liedtke 13).

53:17 The whole way here I saw wonderful things to paint and I can't paint: In the manuscript *(3.9.8),* these sentences about Catherine's inability to paint and write follow directly after the observation about El Greco above. As Willingham, Burwell, and others have noted, Catherine's frustrated creativity, expressed through her inability to write or paint, belies other outlets for her highly creative nature. Yet the differences in creativity for Catherine and David are rooted in their function, on some level, as two halves of a single riven ego. Whereas David, the writer, has access to the Lacanian register of the symbolic, Catherine's imagination seems largely confined to the register of the Lacanian imaginary. She complains that she can't write or paint, but she expresses herself through her body: "sculpting" her own head through her haircuts, cultivating deep suntans, and adopting all sorts of daring fashions. She also "writes" with human lives—her own and others'—scripting the honeymoon narrative that David commits to the page for herself, David, and Marita. In the manuscript, she even tells David and Marita: "I feel as though I invented you. . . . You really are something that I made. . . . It's better than a painting if anyone knew" *(3.35.14).*

> On some level, Catherine doesn't really think symbolically—rather she *identifies.* Think of her obsession with buying a mirror for the bar in La Napoule, her need for David to mirror her with identical haircuts, her assertion that "I'm you and her. . . . I'm everybody" (196:27). Whereas Catherine insists upon the importance of the honeymoon narrative as a direct *reflection* of her life with David, David is able to engage with and negotiate his present dilemmas by displacing them into the symbolized realm of the African stories. Whereas Catherine engages in a sort of imaginary thinking . . . whereby a haircut "makes her" a boy, David can rethink his situation with Catherine through the story of an elephant. His imagination makes use of a degree of symbolization, displacement, condensation, and over-determination that doesn't seem to be available to Catherine. (Eby, "Who Is Destructive" 100–101)

(53:19) 3.9.8 **Borrow . . . Ford . . . now there's Andy:** In the manuscript, conversation about what first brought Andy to Spain at the end of the First World War leads to a discussion about Andy's memoir about living in a village in the Sierra de Gredos mountains. Andy is a travel writer now trying to write about Madrid. David puts Andy in illustrious company, with Borrow and Ford, as a foreigner who writes of Spain with true love and understanding. David here alludes to two masterpieces of travel literature: George Henry Borrow's *The Bible in Spain* (1843) and Richard Ford's *A Handbook for Travellers in Spain* (1845).[4] Both of these books were published in London by John Murray—the same John Murray who in 1836 established

the *Murray's Handbooks for Travellers* series that eventually developed into the *Blue Guides*. When Hemingway named his travel writer Andrew Murray, he may well have been thinking of John Murray. In creating Andrew Murray, Hemingway may also have drawn on the British writer and Hispanist Gerald Brenan, author of, among other things, *The Spanish Labyrinth* (1943) and *South from Granada: Seven Years in an Andalusian Village* (1957). Although Hemingway wrote this page in the *Eden* manuscript a year before he met Brenan, he was already a great admirer of his work and considered *South from Granada* "excellent."[5] Brenan, like Andy, came to Spain directly after WWI and wrote a book about living in a Spanish village.

(53:30) 3.9.10 **hoopoes in a cage:** In the manuscript, directly after reassuring Catherine that she doesn't need to be a painter to "have" the country, that it will always be there for her, David asks her, "you don't want to put the hoopoes in a cage do you?" Although hoopoe birds can be found across Africa, Asia, and Europe, Ernest, according to Mary Hemingway, always associated them particularly with Spain. In *How It Was,* Mary remembers that at the Prado in 1953, "Ernest found a hoopoe bird in Hieronymus Bosch's *Garden of Eden* painting [*The Garden of Earthly Delights*]. No discovery in Madrid pleased him more" (383, 388). This association of hoopoes with the Garden of Eden and Bosch's masterpiece, which figures so prominently in this novel (see *[54:23] 3.10.4),* lends added significance to David's question.

(53:31) 3.9.11 **Camargue horses . . . gypsy wagons:** In the manuscript, after the memory of riding through the Camargue on bikes, David reminds Catherine of the Camargue horses riding across the marshes from the sea. He then reminds her of the "gypsy wagons" and crowded church—a clear reference to the Roma pilgrimage held annually to honor Saint Sarah on her feast day, May 24, in the seaside village of Les Saintes-Maries-de-la-Mer. The Bournes would probably have cycled the two-hour ride from Le Grau-du-Roi, as Ernest and Pauline did on their honeymoon in 1927. According to Hemingway family lore, Ernest and Pauline stained their faces with berry juice to blend in with the Roma pilgrims—a story that resonates with the fantasies of racial transformation in *The Garden of Eden* (Reynolds, *American* 125).

(54:23) 3.9.14 **women for breeding, boys for pleasure, and melons for delight. . . . everything that Kipling left out:** The section break in the Scribner's text on this page represents a large cut from the manuscript. Jenks deletes the end of chapter 9 and all of chapters 10 and 11 from the manuscript. The cut from chapter 9 represents only two pages of holograph text, completing the lunchtime conversation between Catherine, David, and Andy.

As Andy and the Bournes continue their lunch, Catherine asks if they can get some melon. She then asks Andy, "do you believe it about women for breeding, boys for pleasure, and melons for delight?" Andy replies that he only *eats* melons. Catherine thinks it's a "lovely proverb" and it's "everything that Kipling left out." She senses that Kipling sometimes understood it (by "it," she seems to mean same-sex passion and the full complex range of human sexuality), but then felt "ashamed of it" and retreated. She doesn't want David to do the same. Although Richard Francis Burton is sometimes credited with introducing the English-speaking world to the Pashtun proverb about women, boys, and melons (Khan 276), Hemingway almost certainly knew it from Havelock Ellis's *Studies in the Psychology of Sex* (312). Hemingway had read the British sexologist avidly in the early 1920s and had recommended the *Psychology of Sex* to "all of his friends," including Hadley (Reynolds, *Young* 184).

The link between Kipling and these lines in Havelock Ellis for Hemingway was probably the famous *Well of Loneliness* trial in 1928 (see also *[244:25] 3.45.22*). Ellis wrote a preface for Radclyffe Hall's novel of lesbian desire, but in the British obscenity trial that followed the book's publication, Kipling, who had come to believe that same-sex desire posed a threat to society, argued for banning the book and offered to testify for the prosecution, although he was not used. Howard Booth has argued that a complaint from Kipling to the home secretary about *The Well of Loneliness* may have even helped to instigate the trial (231). When in 1929 the novel went on trial for obscenity in the United States, Hemingway supplied a statement for the defense. Meanwhile, Owen Wister had told Hemingway that Kipling considered *The Sun Also Rises* "smut" (*Letters 3* 540).

Long before the *Well of Loneliness* trial, lauding the learned and open-minded Havelock Ellis in contrast to the chest-thumping virile blustering of Kipling, H. L. Mencken had described Ellis as an "anti-Kipling" (191). Yet John Addington Symonds—who collaborated with Ellis on the first (German) edition of *Sexual Inversion* (1896), contributing a treatise on "Soldier Love and Related Matter"—was enthusiastic about Kipling's *Soldiers Three* (1888) and initially thought he had found in him an understanding ally, if not a kindred spirit. As Booth notes, "Early proponents of society's acceptance of same-sex passion alighted upon [Kipling's early] depictions of soldiers, misrecognizing it as a homophile political strategy" (236). Perhaps sensing and recoiling from this, "Kipling retreated from the representational spaces he had used to depict and indeed celebrate masculinity and close relationships between men. A sense of constriction and loss resulted" (226). As Kipling told Hugh Walpole at the time of the *Well of Loneliness* trial—a time when Walpole was also corresponding with Hemingway—there was "too much of the abnormal in all of us to play about with it" (qtd. in Booth 232). It was best left alone and unsaid. Catherine feels the resulting loss and wants David to avoid a similar fate. This drives her advocacy for the honeymoon narrative. It also feels like a sort of mission statement for Hemingway's project in *The Garden of Eden*.

(54:23) 3.10.1 **big room in the Palace:** Deleted manuscript chapter 10 begins with David and Catherine bathing in the cool waters of their long, luxurious bathtub in their

The Palace Hotel in Madrid, early 1920s. (Photo by Blass S. A. Image from the author's collection.)

room at the famous Palace Hotel, on the Plaza Canovas del Castillo, across the street from the Prado. Built in 1912 to rival luxury hotels like the Ritz in Paris and the Savoy in London, the Palace boasted lavish facilities and, with eight hundred rooms, was the largest hotel in Europe. It was one of the first hotels in the world to provide each room with a bathroom, and it was the first in Spain to install a telephone in each room. At the time of its opening, an article in the Spanish newspaper *ABC* called it "the most comfortable hotel in the world," and it prided itself on being "the epicenter of Madrid's social life" (Bettonica and Bosch 26, 54). Once again, the Bournes' choice of hotels indicates their discriminating consumerism and taste for luxury.[6]

David and Catherine drift into love banter, now in bed, about what their money can and cannot buy. Catherine is feeling proud, and she knows that David is proud too. She wonders if when David is feeling "proud or pleased or moved"—that is, experiencing an erection—it isn't too uncomfortable in public. This makes her glad that she isn't a boy, though she admits that she's sometimes "jealous about it." But for now she is his girl, his "thief girl" who will take whatever she wants, day or night. Understood within a dynamic where Catherine and David represent two halves of the same riven and bigendered ego, each half envies the properties of the other. For Catherine, this can take the form of penis envy—not simply in the Lacanian sense in which both men and women lack the phallus, but in what looks like a more traditional Freudian sense.

(54:23) 3.10.3 **that Andrea del Sarto girl:** In the manuscript, Catherine continues her love banter with David, asking him if he loves her more than he loves "that

Andrea del Sarto girl." Speaking of the painting as though it were alive, she playfully tells David that it looked that morning like the portrait in the Prado had been hoping for a visit from him.

The painting in question, Andrea del Sarto's *Portrait of a Woman,* is traditionally thought to be a portrait of the painter's wife, and David's taste in art mirrors Hemingway's. According to Mary Hemingway, del Sarto was Ernest's "favorite portrait painter" (*HIW* 313). On his birthday in 1925, Ernest sent a postcard of this painting from the Prado to his friend Bill Smith (*Letters 2* 364).

(54:23) 3.10.4 **Maja Desnuda:** When in the manuscript David assures Catherine that he loves her much more than he loves the del Sarto girl, Catherine teasingly asks if he loves her more than the *Maja Desnuda.* David protests that he doesn't love the *Maja;* he "just knew a girl who was built like her." Catherine knows "she's no rival," just "a tramp in uncle's clothing."

The reference, of course, is to Goya's *Nude Maja*—a painting of his mistress, the Duchess of Alba, famously paired at the Prado with a clothed copy hurriedly painted, according to legend, when the Duke of Alba asked to view the picture for which his wife had been posing. Like David and Catherine, Hemingway enjoyed playfully thinking about old master painters and their subjects as if they were still alive. In a 21 June 1952 letter to Harvey Breit, Hemingway includes a mock journal entry that alludes specifically to Goya and the Duchess:

> Friday.—Attended the Crucifixion of our Lord. Tintoretto was there. He took copious notes and appeared to be very moved. Dined with Goya. He asserted the entire spectacle was a fraud. He was his usual irascible self but sound company. He says Joyce drinks too much and confirmed several new anecdotes of Gide. The unfortunate Gide it seemed was refused admission to the Crucifixion as they had decided (officially) to call it. Goya offered me La Alba for the evening. Really charming of him. A well spent evening. (*SL* 768)

(54:23) 3.10.4 **Hieronymus Bosch:** In the manuscript, directly after the quip about the Nude Maja as "a tramp in uncle's clothing," the playful tone ends abruptly. Catherine asks David if he loves her enough to keep her "from dying and going to hell like in the Hieronymus Bosch." "I'll try," David promises. "Please try very hard," urges Catherine. Concerned, David suggests that they leave that picture for a while, but Catherine wants "four more days" with it. That's all she thinks she can take—unless David wants to stay in Madrid for "two or three months," so she can "go an hour each morning."

Although he doesn't name the painting, Hemingway is clearly referring to the hell panel on the right side of Bosch's famous triptych *The Garden of Earthly Delights.* (Hemingway may leave the painting unnamed because it was not housed in the Prado in 1927 but thirty miles away at El Escorial and did not come to the Prado until the Spanish Civil War. He may also have left it unnamed because he—or, at least, his wife—was in the habit of calling it Bosch's "Garden of Eden painting.") In an article devoted to Hemingway's engagement with Bosch, I have suggested that the three panels of the triptych—on the left, Adam, Eve, and God in Eden; in the middle, a wildly imaginative carnival of polymorphous eroticism; on the right,

Hieronymus Bosch, *The Garden of Earthly Delights,* oil on oak panels. (Museo del Prado, Madrid. Image from Wikimedia Commons.)

a terrifying and equally imaginative depiction of hell—constitute the single best illustration of Hemingway's novel. Although the novel could be seen as a design consisting of an early Eden "panel," a vast "panel" of polymorphous eroticism, and a smaller fiery "panel" with the hellish incineration of David's manuscript, like Rodin's *Gates of Hell* and the lovers of the *Metamorphoses of Ovid* set amid the beautiful gardens of the Hôtel Biron (see *[17:22] 1.1.21*), Bosch's *Garden of Earthly Delights*

presents viewers less with a linear narrative of innocence, sin, and damnation than an oscillating simultaneity of all three. It is this oscillating simultaneity that reflects the divided attitudes of Hemingway's characters—attitudes structured by the disavowal central to fetishistic thought (Eby, "Gardens of *Eden* and *Earthly*" 71–74).

(54:23) 3.10.4 **black Goyas . . . basement room:** David and Catherine talk about the possibility of a longer stay in Madrid in the autumn. Catherine says that the light of the day had been so fine that she "could really see the black Goyas even in that basement room." The Black Paintings are the fourteen chilling murals Goya painted late in life for the walls of his own two-story house outside of Madrid. Haunting images, such as *Saturn Devouring His Son, The Witches' Sabbath, The Three Fates,* and the *Pilgrimage to San Isidro,* they are uniformly dark both in palette and mood, and they are considered by many to be Goya's greatest works. The paintings were later hacked from the walls, transferred to canvas, and in 1889 donated to the Prado, where they are housed together in a single basement room. David suggests that these works ought to be displayed more effectively.

(54:23) 3.10.7 **percebes. . . . cigalas . . . langostinos:** In the manuscript, David and Catherine decide to go to a café for seafood, certain they can find *percebes, cigalas,* or *langostinos*. Catherine sends David down to read the papers and promises to join him soon. She wants to see first if she has time to "make a surprise." At the café on the Paseo del Prado, next to the Palace Hotel, where the Bournes are staying, David finds Andrew Murry waiting for them, drinking beer and eating *percebes*. David orders a Pernod and a plate of *percebes*.

A Spanish delicacy, *percebes* (gooseneck barnacles) are harvested at great risk amid waves crashing off the rocky coast of northwest Spain and Portugal. For this reason, they are expensive. Like vintage champagne and caviar, they are yet another luxury indulged in by the Bournes. A Spanish cookbook describes them as follows:

> Shaped like small fingers, sheathed in a dark-gray sea leather that is like elephant skin, and topped with pointed, triangular, shingled black shells for mouths, the *percebes* grow in clusters in pools among the sharply cut inlets of the Galician coastline. . . . Tinged with salt and iodine, cleaned by soaring waves, sweet and juicy as they are tender, *percebes* are another of those foods that you cannot stop eating . . . (Feibleman 137)

David thinks they taste "as the clean sea swells at high tide on a rocky coast" *(3.10.8),* and Catherine (after she joins Andy and David) finds them so addictive that she thinks eating them should be made a "vice" *(3.10.12).* Given this association with vice (see *[5:22] 1.1.3),* they may carry symbolic value. Catherine thinks they look like "the devil's thumb nails on the tubing of a bicycle pump" *(3.10.13)*. They are also hermaphroditic—"each barnacle is male and female at once"—and they have a reputation (later mentioned by Catherine) as an aphrodisiac (Cruz 45). *Cigalas* are Norway lobsters; *langostinos* are large prawns.

(54:23) 3.10.9 **Litri:** In the manuscript, at a nearby table, Andrew and David notice a young bullfighter dressed in a traditional Andalusian gray *traje corto* (short suit) and wide-brimmed hat sitting with an older man, a middle-aged woman, and a very pretty girl. David notes the boy's brown face, "buck rabbit teeth," receding chin, and dark eyes. Andy tells David that the boy is Litri, sitting with his fiancée and his father. Andy has seen him fight, but David has not. Andy says that Litri is bowlegged, lacks technical knowledge of bullfighting, and "wink[s] when the bull charges," but he's very brave. "No one passes a bull closer. Everyone knows he's going to be killed except him." A few pages later, Catherine says he looks like a "very nice friendly desperate carnivorous rabbit" in danger of going mad *(3.10.14)*.

If the novel is set in 1927, this is one of the book's anachronisms. Manuel Báez, called Litri, was mortally wounded in the ring in Málaga on 11 February 1926, and he died a week later, at twenty-one years of age, a day after the amputation of his leg ("Estadistica"). It could be that Hemingway brings him into the novel, in spite of the anachronism, because Andy and the Bournes are sitting at the same café where Hemingway remembers seeing Litri. In the final pages of *Death in the Afternoon*, in the famous long passage about what Hemingway wishes he could have included in the book, he describes him almost precisely as we see him in *Eden:* "like a little rabbit, his eyes winking nervously as the bull came; . . . very bow-legged and brave . . . [at] the beer place on the cool side of the street underneath the Palace [Hotel] where he sat with his father . . ." (272). The sight of Litri at a table with his *novia* (fiancée) and his father, however, has a further and more complex resonance: as Miriam Mandel notes, after Litri's death, his *novia* married his father, a former bullfighter who also fought as "El Litri" (*Hemingway's* 70). Their son, Miguel Báez Espuny, carried on the family tradition, fighting under the name Litri, and became one of the great matadors of the 1950s.

(54:23) 3.10.15 **Villa Rosa:** In the manuscript, after joining them, Catherine asks Andy where the three of them should go that night, and Andy suggests the *tablao,* or traditional flamenco bar, Villa Rosa. Located at 17 Calle de Nuñez de Arce, at one corner of the Plaza de Santa Ana, the Villa Rosa was "the center of Madrid's nightlife" during the 1920s. According to flamenco historian José Blas Vega, this was the final decade of a golden age of flamenco, and the Villa Rosa was Madrid's "Sistine Chapel of Flamenco," with the singer Don Antonio Chacón as its pope (120). Chacón drew to the Villa Rosa his large fan base of writers, artists, politicians, and

aristocrats, including the king and Primo de Rivera. Hemingway frequented the *tablao,* and Vincent Sheean mentions it in his *Personal History* (62), a book that Hemingway drew on for several passages in *Eden.*

(54:23) 3.11.1 ***volunteer ambulance service. . . . Mangin's army. . . . Verdun . . . Avocourt Wood . . . Chemin des Dames in Nivelle's offensive . . . mutinies:*** Manuscript chapter 11, deleted in the Scribner's edition, begins with Andy's backstory. The details Hemingway provides of Andy's WWI military service—that he served with a field section of a volunteer ambulance service attached to Mangin's army, that he served at Verdun and was "wounded near Avocourt Wood," that "he had seen the butchery of the Chemin des Dames in Nivelle's offensive in the spring of 1917 and the mutinies" that followed—are enough for us to determine that Andy served in Section One of the American Ambulance Field Service (AFS). This helps to explain why Andy hates the war and refuses to speak of it.

Organized in January 1915, Section One of the AFS was comprised primarily of young, idealistic American college boys from prestigious schools who happened to be in Europe when the war began. The volunteers enlisted for sixth-month terms, with optional three-month extensions, so they were not compelled to serve for the duration—but as the oldest of the thirty-four sections of the AFS, Section One saw more of the war than any other unit.[7] Andy's wounding at Avocourt Wood suggests that he saw some of the bloodiest fighting—the fighting for nearby Dead Man's Hill and Hill 304—at Verdun, the longest and one of the bloodiest battles of the war. Section One served for six months at this ten-month battle of attrition, and as the Germans tried to take the Meuse Heights in the spring of 1916, Dead Man's Hill and Hill 304 were under constant bombardment and then "a continuous series of sledgehammer blows" (D. Johnson 396). The denuded, muddy no-man's-land here was a legendary waste of barbed-wire, water-filled craters, and rotting corpses. What Andy would have seen later serving with Section One and General Charles Mangin's Sixth Army in April 1917 as part of the disastrous Nivelle Offensive would have been even more demoralizing. In an attempt to dislodge the Germans from the heights of the Chemin des Dames plateau in the Second Battle of the Aisne, "Under a terrific fire the magnificent armies of France were hurled up the slopes, against some of the most formidable positions which ever defied armed force" (D. Johnson 300). For three weeks, the men tried to ascend the slopes, with Mangin's men assaulting the front of the escarpment under withering machine-gun fire. By the end of that period, the French had suffered 20 percent casualties, with some divisions suffering 60 percent losses. Mutinies followed, and "and the morale of the French army was for the moment shaken to its foundations" (D. Johnson 300). No wonder Andy passionately hates the war.

As an American volunteer, Andy was free to leave when the three-month extension on his term of enlistment was up, and it was not unusual that he did so in 1917.

In September 1917, with the United States joining the war, AFS sections were folded into the United States Army Ambulance Service. At this time about half the men in the AFS left to join other units. Andy managed to secure an intelligence job in Madrid, and this is how he got to know Spain. He inherited some money when his father died, and he still has enough money to live off of for a few more years if he lives modestly. He hopes to be able to support himself by writing.

(54:23) 3.11.1 **David Bourne I had been . . . poorer than Andy:** In the manuscript, for a paragraph, Hemingway experiments with writing David in the first person, though he edits it into the third person. David had been poorer than Andy, but as a novelist instead of a nonfiction writer like Andy, he stands, if successful, to make more money. He is self-conscious and embarrassed to be staying in the Palace Hotel (see *[54:23] 3.10.1*), but Andy talks him out of this attitude. He should be enjoying his money. Besides, once you get used to luxury, it's hard to go back to the way things were before. When Andy waves away the topic of money, David asks if he needs any. "Don't act so bloody newly rich," Andy tells him. No, he does not need to borrow money; he'll ask when he needs it. David reminds him that he's loaned David money, and Andy replies that David has already paid it back. Being wealthy is still a new experience for David.

(54:23) 3.11.2 **Who picked out the Bugatti?** In the manuscript, Andy thinks David has been "fairly adult" with his newfound wealth, but he asks who picked out the Bournes' new Bugatti. David and Catherine both did, David replies. A deleted passage notes that Catherine wanted only two seats *(3.11.2bis)*—a symbol of her dyadic union with David that also conveys information about the model. The fact that this is a two-seater, a "small blue car" (99:21), and that it is new (see 30:33), suggests that the Bournes are driving an iconic Type 35. A car sold to wealthy consumers for regular use, the T35 was also Bugatti's most successful racing car, with over two thousand victories, including the Targa Florio (every year between 1925 and 1929) and the French Grand Prix (1926, 1928, 1929, and 1930). The T35 was renowned as "nothing short of an aesthetic masterpiece. There was a simplicity and functional beauty about every detail, and a balance of line and proportion about the whole that were immensely satisfying . . ." (Barker 72). It fits naturally into the Bournes' world of luxury and consumer chic. Although Bugattis came in all colors, their race cars were so closely associated with the racing blue of France that many car enthusiasts believe "Bugatti blue" is an actual hue, although the shade of blue in fact could vary.

Bugatti was also associated with a special feminine chic celebrating speed, danger, and the sexual energy of the new woman. A 1927 French *Vogue* article, "Une Formule Nouvelle de l'Élégance Féminine," features two socialites in their Bugattis, enthusing, "Nothing is more impressive than to see these young women boldly facing the dangerous turns." The T35 was the car of the celebrity Grand Prix drivers Elizabeth Junek

Bugatti Type 35 adorned with plaques to mark racing victories, Paris Motor Show, 1926. (Source gallica.bnf.fr / Bibliothèque nationale de France.)

("Queen of the Steering Wheel") and former nude model and dancer Hellé Nice ("The Bugatti Queen"). In popular lore it was also the car in which Isadora Duncan died in Nice in September 1927 when her long, flowing red scarf tangled in a wheel, flinging her from the car, breaking her neck, and nearly decapitating her. In this case, however, the lore is mistaken: Duncan died in an Amilcar Grand Sport, which looked so much like a Bugatti T35 that it was often called "the poor man's Bugatti."[8] (In fact, according to Peter Kurth's biography of Duncan, the great dancer mistook the car for a Bugatti, and used "Bugatti" as a nickname for its dashing young French-Italian driver.) The special feminine appeal of the Bugatti is perhaps best captured in Tamara de Lempicka's iconic art deco image *Autoportrait* (*Tamara in a Green Bugatti*) (1929).

(54:23) 3.11.4 ***How does Catherine drive?. . . . Duesenberg:*** In the manuscript, Andy warns David to be careful on the roads, and he wonders how Catherine is as a driver. She has "beautiful reflexes," David replies, but Andy wants to know if she is "sound." David can't answer that in the affirmative. Andy urges him to take care of Catherine. Since Andy is so worried about her driving (clearly a metaphor for her "soundness" in other respects), David suggests that Andy give her some driving lessons. "I'll tell her you used to race," he adds. Andy tells him to go to hell, adding, "And don't say Duesenberg to me."

Working on the conclusion of the novel during the summer of 1959, Hemingway thought he might kill off his characters and end the story with a car crash. Valerie Hemingway remembers Ernest scouting Provençal roads, pacing out distances, and considering speeds (70).[9] He did not, however, have this in mind yet when he wrote this chapter in May 1958. This is the same month that he wrote a very different "provisional ending" for the novel (see appendix B). Nonetheless, beginning with this passage, the theme of dangerous driving becomes prominent enough to prepare fertile ground for such an ending, and this is how Nick Sheldon eventually dies (see appendix A).

In May 1927, George Souders won the Indianapolis 500 in a Duesenberg. This marked the final year of a Duesenberg dynasty in the race that had included wins in 1922, 1924, and 1925. In the American market, the Duesenberg occupied a position not unlike Bugatti. When production of the Model J began in 1929, Duesenberg realized their "dream of producing the biggest, fastest, and most powerful stock automobile the world had ever seen—and on a 'no-expense-is-to-be-spared' basis. . . . The car quickly became the darling of the moneyed and the mighty, and to everyone the vision of owning a Duesenberg became the *ne plus ultra* of status symbols" (Automobile).

(54:23) 3.11.4 **Being new married is so new:** In the manuscript, David says if Andy doesn't want to teach Catherine to drive, he can at least stop worrying. Andy had forgotten David was an adult, he says, because David had been so childish about money. David thinks that's an effect of being newly married. It's made everything— "eating, drinking, country, every day, every place, every night, everything"—utterly new. David sounds a little like the biblical Adam getting ready to name the animals.

(54:23) 3.11.4 **Prado. . . . Bosch and Patinir . . . Tintoretto:** In the manuscript, after some more vivid banter about the dangers of driving on Spanish roads, Andy wonders where Catherine is. She's coming from the Prado, David explains. She's been so absorbed in the paintings there that she twice didn't even notice when David passed her in the gallery earlier in the day. One time she was with Bosch and Patinir; the other time she was with Tintoretto.

In his 1958 *Paris Review* interview with George Plimpton, when asked about his "literary forebears . . . those [he had] learned the most from," along with many writers Hemingway listed the painters Bosch, Patinir, and Tintoretto (as well as other painters important to *Eden:* Goya, Cézanne, Van Gogh, and Gauguin). As he explained to Plimpton, "I learn as much from painters about how to write as from writers" (*EHWW* 227–28).

The first time David passes Catherine, she would have been in Hall XLIII of the Prado, which in 1927 housed such Hieronymus Bosch paintings as *The Haywain,*

The Temptation of Saint Anthony (two versions), the *Adoration of the Magi,* and the *Extraction of the Stone of Madness,* along with such paintings by Joachim Patinir as *Charon Crossing the Styx, The Rest on the Flight to Egypt, Landscape with Saint Jerome,* and *The Temptation of Saint Anthony.* The same room also housed Pieter Bruegel the Elder's terrifying and Bosch-like *Triumph of Death* (see *[204:8] 3.37.28).* (Hemingway also, no doubt, expects readers to think of Bosch's *Garden of Earthly Delights,* although in 1927 that was still housed at the royal palace–monastery of El Escorial, thirty miles from the Prado. See *[54:23] 3.10.4.)* The paintings in this room have more in common than their early sixteenth-century Low Country origins, and their imagery resonates with the themes of Hemingway's novel. The *Extraction of the Stone of Madness* plays upon a folk tradition that madness was caused by a stone lodged in the brain, and the symbolism of Bosch's painting associates this madness with lust (Maroto, "*Extracting*" 358). Similarly, the room's three different version of *Temptations of Saint Anthony* collectively warn against temptations of the flesh. Nightmarish demons and hell scenes appear not only in these paintings but also in Bruegel's *Triumph of Death,* Patinir's *Charon Crossing the Styx,* and the right panel of Bosch's *Haywain* triptych.

Much like *The Garden of Earthly Delights, The Haywain*'s three panels depict (on the left) the Garden of Eden, (in the large central panel) a warning against worldly desire, and (on the right) a terrifying and wildly inventive vision of Hell. The three panels are each devoted to sin. The panel on the left depicts the rebel angels being cast out of heaven above three Eden scenes with Adam and Eve: (1) God's creation of Eve from Adam's side, (2) Adam and Eve tempted by the serpent, and (3) the expulsion from Paradise. Much less explicitly erotic than the central panel of *The Garden of Earthly Delights,* the central panel of *The Haywain* is more concerned with the desire for worldly goods—another theme in Hemingway's novel. The figures grabbing at the hay play upon the Flemish proverb, "The world is like a Haywain and each man takes what he can." The dangers of lust are also alluded to by such figures as the lovers on top of the hay, oblivious to the presence of the demon beside them. The ultimate destination for those following the Haywain is indicated by the Hell panel on the right (Maroto, "*Haywain*" 287).

Hemingway greatly admired the sixteenth-century Venetian painter Jacopo Robusti Tintoretto (in *Across the River and into the Trees,* Cantwell's portrait of Renata looks "the way you would want your girl painted if Tintoretto were still around" [45], and Cantwell thinks that he ought to live in Venice and "go every day to see the Tintorettos at the Accademia" [146]), but what captures Catherine's attention in the Prado's Tintoretto room may be three paintings of biblical femmes fatales. In *Joseph and the Wife of Potiphar,* Potiphar's sexually aggressive wife, Catherine-like, lies naked in bed except for her pearls. Joseph, who will be falsely accused of rape but who will retain his virtue, recoils from her reach. The other two paintings are both of the Jewish widow Judith, who uses her beauty to charm the Assyrian general Holofernes before getting him drunk and beheading him. A later allusion in the *Eden* manuscript to the biblical story of Samson and Delilah (see *[152:29] 3.25.29*) suggests a similar fetishistic interest in powerful phallic women who symbolically castrate their men.

Detail, Hieronymus Bosch, *Extraction of the Stone of Madness*, oil on oak panels. (Museo del Prado, Madrid. Image from Wikimedia Commons.)

Hieronymus Bosch, *The Haywain*, oil on oak panels. (Museo del Prado, Madrid. Image from Wikimedia Commons.)

Jacopo Tintoretto, *Joseph and the Wife of Potiphar,* oil on canvas. (Museo del Prado, Madrid. Image from Wikimedia Commons.)

(54:23) 3.11.8 **un-roped glacier skiing. . . . chasse pilots are crazy:** In the manuscript, when Andy returns yet again to the dangers of driving on Spanish roads, David urges him to relax. He's doing his best to take care of Catherine, and just because they are driving a Bugatti doesn't mean they are driving it like a race car. David implies that having been "spooked in the war" has made Andy spooked about everything else, but Andy sees David as an irresponsible risk-taker, addicted to pastimes like unroped glacier skiing (which Hemingway also enjoyed in the 1920s [*Letters 2* 259]). Andy thinks David, like all *chasse* pilots, is crazy. David disagrees: "The crazies are dead." This is the first time in the novel we learn that David is a former WWI fighter pilot.

David presses Andy further: What would Andy suggest? Does he want David to "domesticate" Catherine or put her in a cage? Andy protests that David shouldn't "corrupt her." David admires Andy's seriousness as a writer, but he asks if women are really his "field." Andy admits that they are not. At this point, they see Catherine approaching.

(54:23) 3.11.11 **Larousse . . . Rowland Ward's Records of Big Game:** In the manuscript, having admired Catherine's walk as she approaches, Andy asks her how she learned to walk that way. She replies that she did by balancing on her head "Larousse" or *"Rowland Ward's Records of Big Game."*

This reveals that Catherine, like David, grew up in an affluent environment with someone devoted to big-game hunting. In the late nineteenth century, renowned taxidermist James Rowland Ward founded a London firm devoted to taxidermy, big-game hunting, and books about big-game hunting. In 1892, Ward began publishing its *Records of Big Game* series, which eventually became a who's who of big-game

CHAPTER 6 *(MSS. CHAPTERS 9–12)* · 133

hunting, listing trophies by the likes of Theodore Roosevelt, King George V, Queen Elizabeth II, Baron de Rothschild, the Maharaja of Cooch Behar, Lord Curzon, Winston Churchill, Richard Meinertzhagen, and Ernest Hemingway. Hemingway owned the ninth (1928) edition of the book—which weighs about four pounds.[10]

Éditions Larousse, a publishing firm founded by Pierre Larousse, specializes in large, handsome reference books. Catherine is probably thinking of the firm's most famous work, the encyclopedic dictionary, *Le Petit Larousse Illustré* (1905), which Hemingway owned in a later edition.

(54:23) 3.11.11 **"Flamenco didn't move me. . . . Stravinsky or Juan Gris or Klee. . . ."** **"Teniers":** In the manuscript, as Catherine talks with Andy, she thinks he's trying to "classify" and "account for" her. She asks him to stop and to behave naturally. She thinks he's hurt because she wasn't moved by the flamenco dancing the night before at the Villa Rosa (see *[54:23] 3.10.15*). Perhaps she will like flamenco more when she knows more about it, but she won't "simulate" enjoyment for him just because Barbara liked it. She can't be Barbara for him. Besides, people aren't born liking such things any more than they're born liking oysters, Stravinsky, Juan Gris, or Paul Klee. In other words, flamenco, like high-modernist music and painting, is an acquired taste. Gris and Klee, however, were tastes that Hemingway did acquire; he owned two paintings by Gris (*The Bullfighter*, 1913, and *The Guitarist*, 1926) and one by Klee (*Erection of the Monument*, 1929). Hemingway used Gris's *The Bullfighter* as the frontispiece for *Death in the Afternoon*.

When Catherine protests that "only live oysters were born liking oysters," David shifts the subject by asking how she liked the "live Teniers" at the Prado. They were "wonderful," but she wants to let them become "part of [her]" before she talks about them. The Prado owned thirty-nine works by Teniers the Younger (1610–1690), mostly lively scenes of Flemish village life, but there are also two *Temptations of Saint Anthony* that resonate with what Catherine was viewing in the Bosch and Patinir room earlier in morning (see *[54:23] 3.11.4*).

(54:23) 3.11.14 **impermanent arts . . . Berenson:** In the manuscript, when David suggests that we need criticism only for the impermanent arts, Andy disagrees. If Catherine is trying to learn about paintings, how is she to do that without criticism? By looking at them, David replies, just as you learn about oysters by eating them. He does concede to Andy that "one book by someone you trust" could be helpful—for instance, Berenson in his specialization.

Hemingway could sometimes sound a bit like David on this topic. In the introduction to a 1938 catalog for a showing of drawings by Luis Quintanilla, he suggested that art is "to be looked at; not written about in a catalogue" (*HMF* 64). Yet his own library on the visual arts was immense. This passage is really an homage to his much-admired pen pal Bernard Berenson, generally regarded in Hemingway's day as the preeminent art historian specializing in the Italian Renaissance. Hemingway's gossipy and voluminous correspondence with Berenson extended from 1949 to 1957. In 1952, when Hemingway was awarded the Nobel Prize, Berenson was one of three writers he called more deserving of the award (*HIW* 412). See also *(210:16) 3.38.16.*

(54:23) 3.11.15 **"Prado. . . . Proust. . . ." "Cézanne. . . . Flaubert. . . ." "Picasso. . . ." "Braque. . . . Rosenberg":** In the manuscript, the richness and emotional intensity of experiencing the Prado has made Catherine thirsty. She is moved by the way "the world could be so much in one place" and finds that by comparison Proust feels "thin and syrupy." They chat about the way Spain makes you want to paint, and Catherine asks if "great painting" will "come back again." David replies that it hasn't been gone very long. Catherine agrees and loves great contemporary painting, which moves her in a way that flamenco did not.

When Catherine asks if great painting is only possible "in a shitty time like now," David replies that everybody probably thinks their time is shitty. What does she imagine Cézanne thought of 1870, when the Prussians besieged and captured Paris? Catherine thinks Cézanne "never even noticed his time." When David answers that Flaubert noticed his time, Catherine replies that she's "sick of Flaubert." She thinks Picasso "never noticed the war." Braque certainly noticed it, Andy replies. Badly wounded while leading his platoon against German trenches at Carency in 1915, Picasso's friend and fellow Cubist pioneer Georges Braque had been left for dead for several hours in no-man's-land, suffered temporary blindness, and was afterwards trepanned to relieve pressure on his skull. He was awarded the Croix de Guerre and made a Chevalier of the Legion of Honor. It was because he was trepanned, Andy says, that he "could hit Rosenberg at the sale."

The incident Andy alludes to (also recounted in Stein's *Autobiography of Alice B. Toklas*) occurred in 1921. At the outbreak of WWI, Braque's dealer, the pioneering supporter of Cubism Daniel-Henry Kahnweiler, a German national, had been forced to flee France and his stock had been sequestered. For a while, Léonce Rosenberg, owner of the Galerie de l'Effort Moderne, became Braque's dealer, but after the war Braque returned to Kahnweiler, dissatisfied with what he considered Rosenberg's "sharp" business practices. When in 1921 the French government sold Kahnweiler's sequestered collection at several auctions, the sales were presided over by none other than Rosenberg, who savaged Braque's reputation, failed to advertise to his interested buyers, and discounted his prices, flooding the market with 135 works. It was for this act of sabotage that Braque hit him. One result of this fire sale was that "*Le tout Paris* bought a Braque in the early 1920s" (Danchev 149); it was during this time that Hemingway purchased his own, *Still Life with Wine Jug*. This painting was stolen from Hemingway's Cuban home after his death (*HIW* 505).

(54:23) 3.11.17 ***war . . . politics:*** In the manuscript, Catherine declares that she "hate[s] people who were affected by the war. That's why [she] loves David." In response to this stunning misinterpretation of David, Andy simply stares at her. But Catherine assumes David was not affected by the war because he never speaks of it. Nick doesn't talk about it either, she notes approvingly, and he was in the war. We should, however, remember the beginning of this chapter, where we learn that Andy never speaks of the war precisely because what he saw was so horrible (see *[54:23] 3.11.1*). The depth of the silence is a measure of the severity of the trauma.

They don't hear Andy discuss politics either, David notes, for which Catherine is doubly glad. She hates politics—though she admits that she doesn't know anything about them. But then, Andy asks, how does she know this is a "shitty time"? She has some sense that things are bad in Germany and Austria, but she isn't aware of how difficult things are in Primo de Rivera's Spain. That is all censored. What she sees is picturesque. Catherine apologizes for being "didactic" and admits that she doesn't really understand the times. They're "shitty enough," Andy says, but the point is to enjoy life. Catherine agrees and suggests Andy should do the same. Andy agrees but observes that he doesn't "bring as much to it" as Catherine and David. "As much of what," Catherine wonders. "Innocence," Andy replies.

54:25 **The Palace:** See *(54:23) 3.10.1*.

56:15 **Nobody can tell which way I am but us:** In the manuscript, Catherine returns with her new haircut, which looks just the same as the one she got in Biarritz (see 46:19)—yet somehow it isn't. "Now it's either," she tells David *(3.12.9)*. This is when she tells him, "Nobody can tell which way I am but us." For the moment, she's a boy. Before, she was "a girl and a boy," David reminds her. Yes, but "this time it's changed," she tells him. She asks him to please not be sad. After all, they had "no voice in making the rules." What they experience is the same as it was at Le Grau-du-Roi, yet somehow it has "gone further" *(3.12.13)*. David can feel her mouth changing (see 47:14).

56:18 **I lied when I said I didn't have to:** In other words, there is a compulsive, even "desperate" (56:20), quality to the oscillations between Catherine's gender identities. They are not merely playful experiments. In the manuscript, when David accedes to her request, Catherine announces that she will immediately run out to get her hair cut. As at Le Grau-du-Roi, it is the manipulation of the fetish that enables the ensuing gender transformation.

(56:29) 3.12.14 ***mirror of the armoire. . . . "No remorse? . . ." "Thank you very much for letting me be Catherine":*** In the manuscript, when Catherine gets up and goes to the bathroom, David looks at himself in the mirror of the armoire, raising a glass

of marismeño to his image. He brings a cold glass of wine to Catherine in the bathroom, where he finds her in the bath. She asks how he's doing and wants to know if he feels any remorse (see 14:23 and 68:11). Not only does he feel none, he thanks her for letting him be Catherine. Since he has just "been Catherine," it is no surprise that he experiences a mild form of dissociation in the mirror, toasting his image as if it were an other (see 43:17).

NOTES

1. For the 1927 grand opening of the Cervecería Alvarez (which, as is more common, spelled *cervecería* with a *c*, not a *z*), see "¿Donde?" and "La Nueva Cervecería." In several places, Hemingway writes that the "beer place" was on the "Pasaje Alvarez," but contemporary advertisements and maps give the name of the alley as the Pasaje Mathéu, which remains its name today. The cervecería derived its name from its owner, José Alvarez, not from the little alley. A "Cervecería del Pasaje" existed on the Pasaje Mathéu in 1924 and may have been a precursor of the Cervecería Alvarez ("Cervecería del Pasaje"). This is significant because Hemingway told George Plimpton in 1958 that he had worked on *The Sun Also Rises* at the "beer place in the Pasaje Alvarez" (*EHWW* 231); this would have predated the opening of the Cervecería Alvarez.

2. See Río López 277 and Ortega Rubio 227. It may also be worth noting that in 1940, La Torre del Oro redecorated with the bullfighting theme it preserves to this day. It was once a favorite bar of Luis Miguel Dominguín, whose 1959 mano a mano with Antonio Ordóñez is chronicled by Hemingway in *The Dangerous Summer*.

3. Luis Quintanilla remembered that Hemingway was "an assiduous reader of Baroja" (qtd. in Vega 67), and Vega rates Baroja's influence on Hemingway as comparable to Cézanne's (64).

4. Hemingway owned *The Bible in Spain*, along with Borrow's novel *Lavengro: The Scholar, the Gypsy, the Priest* (1851) and his Romany-English dictionary (1874). He owned Ford's *Gatherings from Spain*, which reprinted material from the *Handbook for Travellers* along with new material. In *Death in the Afternoon*, Hemingway holds Ford up as an exemplar of good writing about Spain, in contrast to Waldo Frank (53).

5. For Hemingway's admiration by 1952, see *SL* 766 and 794; for his response to *South from Granada*, see his letter to Rupert Belville, 7 Dec. 1957 (UT).

6. The hotel today has a "Hemingway room."

7. For a history of Section One of the AFS, see Seymour, particularly 21, 120, 178, 198.

8. In 1927, some newspapers reported that Duncan died in a Bugatti, while others reported correctly, and in much more detail (even with the car's Nice license plate number), that she died in an Amilcar. Nonetheless, the legend that she died in a more prestigious and romantic Bugatti is so strong that several of her biographers (for instance, Blair, Daly, Kozodov, and Lever) repeat this as fact. See Kurth's biography of Duncan and the automotive detective work of Lerner and Stone.

9. Even if these roads were in Provence, Hemingway may have been thinking of the Basque Country. In a 15 October 1959 letter to Mary Hemingway, Ernest recounts taking notes on all of the roads the Bournes drove, including around Hendaye, paying particular attention to the "fast car stuff" (JFK). Perhaps he was scouting the location and circumstances for the death of Nick Sheldon (see appendix A).

10. In November 1958, as he prepared to revise the elephant story, Hemingway wrote to Scribner's to request somewhere between four and ten books from Rowland Ward that he needed "badly" for his work. One of these works seems to have been Neumann's *Elephant-Hunting in East Equatorial Africa* (see 164:9). This indicates how carefully he researched the elephant story.

CHAPTER 7 (MSS. CHAPTERS 13–14)

(57:4) 3.13.1 **Andrew at the Villa Rosa:** In the manuscript, we learn that the previous night they had been out late with Andy at the Villa Rosa. (See *[54:23] 3.10.15.*) Catherine had heard better music and seen better dancers than she had on her first night there, but Andy still found her insufficiently moved by cante jondo (deep song). Catherine feels like she's been besieged by a missionary trying to make a convert. She sees why Andy is in love with Barbara. She thinks Barbara "is a prisoner" of what she has to do and that she likes to convert people, too. Now, Catherine's tired of Andy and all of his worries about driving safely. She supposes he'll try to talk David out of flying.

(57:4) 3.13.4 **Evan Dudleys at Antibes:** In the manuscript, when Catherine says that she only liked Andy because she and David hadn't seen anyone else in so long, David reminds her about Nick and Barbara, and also about the Evan Dudleys at Antibes. Catherine thinks Nick is "too good to be true," but she isn't fond of the Dudleys. She knows they like David, but they treat her as if she were a "specimen." The Dudleys are clearly based on Gerald and Sara Murphy, who pioneered the summer season at Antibes (see 6:3). When Hemingway, Hadley, and Pauline spent time on the Riviera with the Murphys in the summer of 1926, Hadley had felt that the Murphys liked Ernest but not her. In *A Moveable Feast*, Ernest portrays them as the rich "pilot fish" who contribute to the demise of his marriage to Hadley.

(57:10) 3.13.8 **What can I write that's better than this?** In the manuscript, the way Catherine's head reminds him of the head on a coin (57:8) leads David to a long reverie about how she might cut her hair. He envies that she is the one who "makes all the surprises," and he sees how creating with hair is like "drawing ... or painting using a person" *(3.13.6)*. He imagines her hair as if it were "cut with a chisel," with him as "the sculptor" *(3.13.7)*, envying her creativity just as she envies his (see 27:16 and 53:17). He wonders what he can write "that's better than this" yet knows he'll write again soon. In the meanwhile, he tells himself, he has been learning something from his erotic experiences with Catherine, even if he doesn't understand them: "Maybe it's how people always were and never admitted and they made rules against it as stupid as many of the others ..." *(3.13.7)*. Nobody understands such things.

He and Catherine have come a long way, he thinks, from their first meeting at the Crillon bar (see 29:11), from the Pavillon Henri IV at St.-Germain-en-Laye, where they first made love (see *[47:18] 3.7.6*), and from Le Grau-du-Roi. What seems different to him this time—even "dangerous"—is the absence of any feeling of "remorse." "After the wrench and the breaking" at Le Grau-du-Roi, he thinks there is no more remorse. He thinks he has "embraced" Catherine's changes, but he still has to fight his urge to resist. "Don't deny any of it now," he tells himself *(3.13.9)*. He doesn't need to "apologize nor explain," only to recognize the danger.

(57:10) 422.4 3.13.10 **the seed of our cure and our destruction:** In a discarded fragment that originated here in the manuscript, David rejects the categorization of people, insisting on individual uniqueness. He then (anachronistically) reworks a line from the first page of Thomas Wolfe's *Look Homeward Angel* (1929), perhaps alluding to the novel's subtitle: *A Story of a Buried Life*. Where Wolfe writes, "The seed of our destruction will blossom in the desert, the alexin of our cure grows by a mountain rock . . ." (3), David thinks, "In each of us is the seed of our cure and our destruction." Central to Hemingway's erotic vision is the idea that the seed of our cure and our destruction is a single seed. The cure and destruction are two sides of a single coin—or the two side panels of a Bosch triptych.

(57:10) 3.13.10 **all new countries are forbidden. . . . The bones of the others:** David compares his sexual experiments with Catherine to a new and uncharted country, which he doesn't understand and for which his head remains the only "compass." He knows that no countries are truly new: "They are new to everyone who comes to them for the first time. And all new countries are forbidden by something." What will he find there? He isn't sure, but a phrase suggests itself to him: "The bones of the others." In an important study of Hemingway's creative process, Hilary Justice argues that this phrase marks the inception of the elephant story David will later write (59). The undertones of settler colonialism in the passage (the faux-Edenic "discovery" of an old country as "new") further suggest another set of bones: the remains of "the massacre in the crater" from David's earlier African story (see 111:11 and 223:3).

57:10 **It lasted a month:** The timeline David gives us in this and the next four sentences has been transposed a few pages from where it occurs in the manuscript *(3.12.8)*. There, reclining in the bathtub drinking marismeño, David waits for Catherine to return from getting her hair cut. His calculation of the periodicity of Catherine's experiments suggests that he thinks her behavior might be cyclical. It can also be used to roughly date the action of the text. Since the Bournes have been married for "three weeks" when the novel opens (13:18), and since the novel opens a few days after May 20 (see 3:1), the Bournes must have been married sometime around April 30, 1927. Since we are told now that the Bournes have been married for three months and two weeks, it must now be the second week of August.

58:10 **Bullfight weeklies ... English language papers:** That David wraps his English-language papers in Spanish bullfight weeklies implies that David wants to mask his status as a foreigner. Like many Hemingway protagonists, he constructs an expatriate identity that blends in well with the locals and distinguishes him from American tourists, yet he never tries to go entirely native. He is cosmopolitan—part "insider," part "outsider"—wherever he goes. But his bullfight weeklies aren't merely for show. He does read them, and he also regularly reads Spanish and French newspapers in addition to English and American ones.

In fact, journalism is a constant presence in *The Garden of Eden*, and David is a serious news junkie. We see him with a "stack of the morning papers" (51:13), and then reading the "evening papers" *(3.10.8)*, and his days are punctuated by trips to pick up the latest news. More interestingly, we get the names of the newspapers he reads. In this passage, Hemingway initially has David reading *El Debate*, then Spain's leading Catholic newspaper—conservative, but noted for its innovative journalism and sports reporting. This, however, is crossed out in the manuscript, and there's a note in the margin to check *El Liberal*, a popular liberal paper *(3.13.11)*. David then picks up a copy of *ABC*, one of Spain's leading conservative papers *(3.13.13)*, before buying the Paris editions of the *New York Herald*, the *Chicago Tribune*, and the *London Daily Mail* (59:7). In La Napoule, David reads local papers like *l'Éclaireur de Nice et du Sud-Est* (83:3), and in Cannes, David and Catherine buy French *Vogue*, the hunting magazine *Chasseur Français*, and the sporting weekly *Le Miroir des Sports* (88:26).[1] Much later in the manuscript, Catherine complains that since Marita arrived no one reads the papers anymore. According to Catherine, before the advent of Marita, David "couldn't live without" newspapers. Journalists, like sports reporter Sparrow Robertson, fashion reporter Bettina Bedwell, and political reporter Vincent Sheean, so filled David's life that Catherine used to "imagine he was unfaithful" to her with them (see *[214:22] 3.39.9*). It was fun, she thinks, when they used to "live so much in the papers" as well as "in each other" *(3.39.11)*. Back then, she tells Marita, David's real life had been as interesting as Vincent Sheean's seemed to be in the papers. She wants David to introduce her to Sheean and thinks Sheean might even be a good partner for Marita as an alternative to David. The importance of journalism in *Eden* forces readers to acknowledge that this is a novel deeply engaged with the history of its times.

Writing of Hemingway's stay at the Palace Hotel in Madrid in 1954, Hotchner remembers,

> To approach a magazine stand with [Hemingway] was a unique experience. He would carefully go down the lines of magazines on display and choose just about

one of everything, except what he called the ladies'-aid magazines.... He would cart off twenty or more magazines, but the amazing part of it was that he actually read them through and would discuss their contents. Spanish, French, and Italian kiosks were treated with equal patronage. (137)

58:13 **Buffet Italianos ... "isn't a beer place":** The Buffet Italiano (correct name) was a popular Italian restaurant and bar at 37 Carrera de San Jerónimo, a short walk up from the Palace Hotel where the Bournes stay, and just beneath the Pensión Aguilar, where Hemingway frequently stayed during the 1920s when he was in Madrid. The bar advertised that it served "all sorts of drinks," but cocktails were the "specialty of the house" ("El 'Buffet'"). It really wasn't a beer place.[2]

It is significant that David finds "no one in the place yet" (58:13), because the Buffet Italiano was a gathering spot for intellectuals and artists—a group including Juan Negrín López (professor of physiology and, later, last prime minister of the Second Spanish Republic), Ramón del Valle-Inclán (dramatist and novelist), Luis Araquistáin Quevedo (journalist, member of the Spanish Socialist Workers' Party, and ambassador to France during the Spanish Civil War), Julio Álvarez del Vayo (journalist, writer, and minister of foreign affairs during the Spanish Civil War), Léon Rollin (French journalist), Juan de la Encina (historian and, later, director of Madrid's Museum of Modern Art), Alberto Lozano (sculptor and poet), and Hemingway's good friend, the revolutionist and painter Luis Quintanilla. Quintanilla's son, Paul, writes of the group that regularly gathered here:

> Few people would have predicted that one of the regulars at this lively *tertulia del café* would become Prime Minister of the Spanish Republic during its war for survival, and that another would be its Foreign Minister. Or that this group would include some of Spain's leading artists, thinkers, and left activists and that eventually some of them would be instrumental in overturning the monarchy and bringing in the Republic in 1931. (38)

Hemingway knew this group well. In *Death in the Afternoon,* "the author" invites his interlocutor, the "Old Lady," to dine at an Italian restaurant "full of politicians who are becoming statesmen while one watches them" (93), and according to a 1941 article in *Life* magazine, Hemingway "had sat with Republican leaders in the little Buffet Italiano on the Carrera de San Jerónimo in Madrid when ... a constitution for the Spanish Republic was penned (1931)" ("The Hemingways").[3]

The mention of the Buffet Italiano, however, is more than an opportunity for Hemingway to memorialize his friendship with this group. David will soon run into Colonel Boyle at the bar of the Palace Hotel (60:6), and the Colonel will offer David, an ex-WWI pilot, a job flying against Abd el-Krim in the Moroccan Rif War *(3.13.24)*. David not only rejects this offer, he implies that he would rather fly *for* Abd el-Krim—

a dangerous sentiment to express in Primo de Rivera's Spain, as the Colonel quickly points out. If David, like Hemingway, knows and seeks out the liberal artists and intellectuals of the Buffet Italiano, this implies that his response to the Colonel represents a deeper political interest and is not merely a passing flippant remark.

58:22 **Cervezería Alvarez:** Hemingway often came to this cervecería (see *[51:2] 3.9.1)* with Luis Quintanilla (*HMF* 66), which implies an association with the Buffet Italiano (see 58:13) that extends beyond their close proximity.

59:31 **Coolidge fishing for trout in a high stiff collar in a fish hatchery in the Black Hills we stole from the Sioux:** Calvin Coolidge vacationed in the Black Hills of South Dakota from June to August 1927. After the novice angler landed large trout day after day—fishing, to the consternation of more serious anglers, with a worm—headlines in American newspapers gushed over the president's natural ability as a fisherman. Coolidge, who indeed fished in a business suit with a "high stiff collar," proudly boasted about his catches. Meanwhile, unbeknownst to him, the section of Squaw Creek reserved for his private use was being regularly stocked with tired old hatchery fish raised on ground liver and horse meat. During the three

Calvin Coolidge fishing in a "high stiff collar," Plymouth, Vermont, undated. (Image from the Yankee Publishing Photograph Collection, 1890–1950. Courtesy of Historic New England.)

months of the president's stay, over two thousand unfinicky old breeding fish from the hatchery were gradually and stealthily dumped into the river near the president's lodge (Smith 145).

More important is the reference to "the Black Hills we stole from the Sioux." This advances a critique of settler colonialism that becomes a minor theme in the novel.[4] It is no coincidence that it appears shortly before the introduction of the Colonel (see 60:21).

60:1 **wondering if their baby does the Charleston:** The line "I wonder does my baby do the Charleston" comes from "I Wonder Where My Baby Is Tonight," by Walter Donaldson and Gus Kahn. It was recorded by several bands in 1925 but became a bigger hit when recorded in French by both Josephine Baker and Maurice Chevalier in 1926. The Charleston dance craze hit its peak in 1926 and 1927.

60:3 *The Dial . . . The Bookman . . . The New Republic:* Hemingway held grudges against these periodicals, dating back to the 1920s and early 1930s. Although Edmund Wilson published important early praise of Hemingway's work in *The Dial,* Hemingway could not forgive the review for rejecting his early poems, *in our time* sketches, and "The Undefeated." *The Bookman,* in 1929, irked Hemingway by publishing Robert Herrick's "What Is Dirt?," which accused *A Farewell to Arms* of being gratuitously prurient and obscene. *The New Republic* annoyed him by, in 1933, printing Max Eastman's "Bull in the Afternoon," which accused Hemingway of inventing a literary style of wearing "false hair on the chest"—a claim which four years later still rankled Hemingway enough to inspire an infamous altercation between Hemingway and Eastman. Coming upon Eastman during a visit to his editor, Max Perkins, Hemingway had at first behaved well enough. As Perkins watched,

> the two men shook hands and exchanged minor pleasantries. Perkins, relieved, had just settled back in his chair when Ernest, grinning broadly, ripped open his own shirt to expose a chest which, as Perkins said, was "hairy enough for anybody." Eastman laughed and Ernest, still grinning, opened Eastman's shirt to reveal a chest "as bare as a bald man's head." The contrast led to further laughter, and Perkins was just preparing for a possible unveiling of his own when Ernest suddenly flushed with anger.
> "What do you mean," he roared at Eastman, "accusing me of impotence?" (Baker 317)

When Eastman, taking a handy copy of his volume *Art and the Life of Action* from Perkins's desk, tried to show Hemingway what he actually wrote, Hemingway pushed the book in his face, and the two ended up in a ridiculous wresting match on Perkins's floor. The story made national headlines.

60:21 **Colonel John Boyle:** The manuscript provides a few more details about the Colonel. "*Across* his left lapel"—importantly, not *on* his left lapel—is "the unusual combination of narrow yellow and green of the Médaille Militaire and the rosette of an officer of the Legion of Honor" (*3.13.21;* my emphasis). A discarded fragment from the novel also indicates that the man David meets in the bar is "C. S." These details, and others to be considered below, reveal that the Colonel is transparently based on Hemingway's friend Colonel Charles Sweeny—but the Sweeny of legend even more than the real man Hemingway met as a fellow correspondent during the 1922 Greco-Turkish War and who served as an honorary pallbearer at Hemingway's funeral.

Son of millionaire parents, soldier of fortune, sometime journalist, world traveler, and passionate Francophile, Charles Sweeny—having been twice expelled from West Point and having already served in three Latin American revolutions—was the first American to volunteer for the French Foreign Legion in August 1914 to serve France at the outbreak of the First World War. Wounded several times during the war, he was made a chevalier of the Legion of Honor (in 1926 raised to commander) and awarded the Croix de Guerre with palms ("Une Decoration"). In 1916, he was recovering from a machine-gun bullet through his lungs when his friends formed the Lafayette Escadrille, the squadron of American volunteer fighter pilots that won fame on the western front.

> It has often been suggested that Sweeny himself was one of the crack pilots of the Lafayette Escadrille. . . . This is incorrect, despite many statements made in the press and in obituaries to this effect. Sweeny was closely associated with the Escadrille, mainly because his friends helped to form the unit and he maintained this association with them after the squadron was formed. Out of this—and out of the fact that Sweeny was always talking about the Escadrille—grew the legend that he became as famous as an air fighter as a soldier. It has even been stated that he shot down more than fifty enemy aircraft. (McCormick 76)

In Colonel Boyle, Hemingway gives us the Sweeny of legend. The "unusual combination of narrow yellow and green of the Médaille Militaire" that *crosses* his left lapel is not the medal itself but a fourragère with ribbon colors of the Médaille Militaire. A fourragère is a braided cord distinguishing not an individual soldier but an entire military unit—and the Lafayette Escadrille had been awarded a fourragère with ribbon colors of the Médaille Militaire. Since David Bourne is a former WWI fighter pilot, we might imagine that he served with Colonel Boyle in the Lafayette Escadrille, but this is not correct. We later learn that David, from British East Africa, served with the Royal Air Force (RAF) (see *[209:16] 3.38.3* and *[244:23] 3.45.17*).[5]

61:5 **What was the job?:** In the manuscript, David asks this question a second time and gets a one-word answer: "Morocco." For which side? David asks. "The French of course," answers the Colonel. David doesn't see why the French need help. The one who needs help, he says, is Abd el-Krim. David should "know better than to talk that way in a bar in Madrid," the Colonel warns, but David is sure they haven't been overheard.

One of the novel's more notable anachronisms, the implication is that Colonel Boyle is offering David, a former WWI fighter pilot, a job flying for a reconstituted Lafayette Escadrille in the Rif War between the colonial French and Spanish and the Riffian Berber resistance led by Abd el-Krim. With much coverage by the press and much resistance from the US government, Colonel Charles Sweeny (see 60:21) was recruiting precisely such a squadron of American volunteer pilots in July 1925, although he was eventually forced to abandon use of the Lafayette Escadrille name. As Hemingway wrote at the time to Gertrude Stein,

> Charley Sweeney [sic] and collection of former Capts, Majors, Lieut. Cols. Off to fight the Riffs. Awfully sweet thing to do. But if you've got the Legion of Honor already what's it all about?
>
> Can understand fighting for Abd-el-Krimmy against French although not attractive but to deliberately go and fight for Caillaux in Morocco—not for the adventure or what's in it—oh no—for high moral purposes. You have to admit it's touching. (*Letters 2* 381)

To Ezra Pound he wrote, "Would join Abdelkrim tomorrow if chance of Riffian invasion of Sunny France. Jesus how I hate the bastards" (*Letters 2* 378). In September of 1925, Hemingway even flirted briefly with the idea of accompanying John Dos Passos to Morocco (*Letters 2* 392).

The Spanish had been fighting the Riffians since 1911, and it was fallout from their disastrous defeat at the Battle of Annual in 1921 that polarized Spain and helped bring the dictator Primo de Rivera to power in 1923. This is why the Colonel warns David to watch what he says about Abd el-Krim in Madrid. When Abd el-Krim's forces attacked French outposts in disputed tribal territory north of the Spanish protectorate in the spring of 1925, the French entered the war in partnership with Spain, and their combined manpower and superior technology soon turned the tide of the war. Much later in *The Garden of Eden,* Catherine reads in the papers about the Colonel and his men in Morocco "bombing all the native villages." It was precisely such bombing by Charles Sweeny's squadron in September and October 1925 that brought outraged denunciations from around the world (see [214:22] 3.39.9).

Though Hemingway remained friends with Sweeny (who even served as one of the models for Colonel Cantwell in *Across the River and into the Trees*), it is no mistake that the same page in the *Eden* manuscript that mentions the bombing of Moroccan villages also mentions David Bourne's fondness for the journalist Vincent Sheean. Sheean, another good friend of Hemingway's, covered and denounced the war in Morocco for American newspapers. In his *Personal History*, which Hemingway owned in two copies and indirectly references in *Eden* (see *[66:11] 3.14.7*), Sheean writes:

> That Imperialism was murderous and hypocritical was no discovery. The Imperialists themselves recognized the character of the undertaking by the vociferation of their denials—denying, always, before they were accused. . . . But until these journeys to the Riff I had not realized its awful stupidity—the ghastly wrongheadedness with which it sacrificed the time and the lives of its best men for the enrichment of its worst. A few Frenchmen were richer for the possession of Morocco, and many were dead. Those who died in such disreputable enterprises were for the most part the young, the honest, the unsuspicious—men who had been fed on patriotic lies until they thought they were accomplishing something for their native country by murdering the inhabitants of another. Populations that had shown, in their own defense, the very qualities Europeans called heroic under other circumstances, were rewarded by economic enslavement. (160)

Interviewed by American journalists, Sweeny claimed that the Rif War was "a battle for white man's civilization," but as the interviewer added archly, "Of course, what the white man's civilization needs and wants in Africa is less political rule over the native tribes than access to the raw materials there" ("American"). Apparently Hemingway thought the same thing. When David, in the *Eden* manuscript, asks the Colonel what he's fighting for, the Colonel answers: "Isn't the iron enough." Does David "want a list of all the other minerals? What do you think people fight for?" (*3.13.24*). This sort of mineral-based extractive colonialism mirrors the ivory-based extractive colonialism practiced by David's father in the story of the elephant hunt.

For a consideration of how *Eden*'s critique of colonialism coexists with entrenched colonial attitudes, see my essay "'In the Year of the Maji Maji': Settler Colonialism, the Nandi Resistance, and Race in *The Garden of Eden*."

61:9 **Knew her father . . . Killed himself in a car. His wife too:** This passage advances the novel's symbolic motifs of dangerous driving (see *[54:23] 3.11.4*) and self-destruction (see *[24:33] 1.2.8*). Catherine and David are both the children of self-destructive parents. In the manuscript, the Colonel adds that Catherine's father was also a "damned good flyer" (*3.13.22*). This would seem to align David, an ex-pilot, with Catherine's father, although the Colonel later tells Catherine that David doesn't resemble her father in the least (*3.13.30*).

62:27 **young chief of a warrior tribe . . . gotten loose from his councilors:** The Colonel's reply is perceptive, picking up on Catherine's wildness and her cross-gender and cross-racial identifications. Catherine takes this as his recognition that she "was a boy" when he saw her in the Prado (63:27). It is interesting that the Colonel should have this insight and that Catherine should reveal herself to him. It might be significant that Colonel Charles Sweeny, who served as a model for Colonel Boyle, was known for letting his hair grow long. At West Point he received demerits for his long hair (Roberts and Hess 47), soldiers he served with in the First World War wondered "why the [then] major never bothered to get a haircut," and as late as the Spanish Civil War he was noted for "his preference . . . for long hair" (McCormick 110, 159). Perhaps this meant nothing to Sweeny, but it may still have signified something to Hemingway.

62:28 looking at that marble of Leda and the Swan: The statue in question is not in the Prado. In the manuscript, the Colonel's "young chief of a warrior tribe," has, in a more extended simile, "gone *into the Luxembourg* by himself and is looking at the marble of Leda and the Swan" (3.13.28; my emphasis). In the Luxembourg Gardens in Paris, there is a bas-relief of Leda and the Swan by Achille Valois (sculpted in 1807) on the back side of the Medici Fountain, where it has been since 1864. But this is not the work the Colonel has in mind. The 1927 catalog of the Musée du Luxembourg lists a single marble titled *Leda and the Swan* (1894) by Rodin's friend and protégé Jules Desbois (Masson 61).[6] The Colonel is surely thinking of this far more erotic work, and his perception is once again acute. Desbois worked in Rodin's shadow as his collaborator from 1884 to 1914—one can seldom find his name uncoupled from that of Rodin—and Hemingway must have associated his sculpture with Rodin's *Metamorphoses of Ovid* (1886), the work that serves as a catalyst for the metamorphoses of both the Bournes and the Sheldons (see *[17:22]* 1.1.21). In the Colonel's simile, Comley and Scholes have seen an erotic interest in "miscegenation across species lines" as "a metaphor for racial miscegenation" (96).[7] One might also note that, as a result of this union, Leda gives birth to two eggs—one containing Castor and Clytemnestra, the other containing Helen and Pollux; thus, we might link this allusion to Hemingway's fascination with twinning and the novel's pervasive egg symbolism (see 6:6 and 4:9).

When Hemingway changed his Paris address to 6 Rue Férou, after his 1927 marriage to Pauline, he lived a minute's walk from the Musée du Luxembourg. It is not surprising that in a novel set in 1927 memories of the Luxembourg surface more than once (see also *[163:31]* 3.28.15).

64:9 not far from la Napoule: This reminds us that between their time in Le Grau-du-Roi and Hendaye, the Bournes spend a little over a month near La Napoule that is never described. They will return to this same location and stay there throughout the second half of the novel. Note that while it is close to La Napoule, it is not in La Napoule proper (see 30:8 and 75:2).

Jules Desbois, *Leda and the Swan,* marble. In 1927, this was in the Musée du Luxembourg, Paris. Today it is in the Musée Jules Desbois, Parçay-les-Pins. (Image from the author's collection.)

64:16 **I don't really wear it. It's me:** Catherine's quip about "wearing" her fetishized tan because it's "becoming in bed" reveals how the fetish functions as a dissociable part-object—something that can be worn or discarded at will to negotiate different identifications.

65:9 **How fast will it go?:** David's question implies that he, like Catherine, assumes the Colonel intuitively understands the inner workings of Catherine's mind and the dynamics of their relationship.

65:19: **The get's no good. . . . It's kinder to shoot the get:** In the manuscript, David asks the Colonel to clarify these enigmatic lines, but he cannot. David takes "get" as a reference to progeny.[8] Hence, "there isn't any get yet." But the conversation leads to vague and broad claims about the random nature of chance in the universe. "Then why be so dogmatic," David asks. But the Colonel claims he isn't "theorizing": "*J'ai constaté*"—"I have seen," or "I have discovered" (3.13.36). The Colonel advises David to take care of Catherine and assures him that he'll continue to write.

(65:24) 3.13.36 **Rimbaud:** To the Colonel's assertion that writers will always write, David has an answer: Rimbaud. The precocious French poet and sometime lover of Paul Verlaine, Arthur Rimbaud famously abandoned writing at age twenty-one to serve briefly in the Dutch Colonial Army in Java, live for a time in Cyprus, and pursue life as a merchant and gunrunner in Africa. He was thirty-seven when he died.

65:26 white sharkskin outfit: Jenks has muted some heavy-handed symbolism here. In the manuscript, David suggests that the Colonel's advice could be boiled down to a simple formula: just keep going, and check back periodically to make sure you haven't become a "pillar of salt." The Colonel replies that David and Catherine don't look like "pillar of salt material." Moments later Catherine enters the bar wearing a "white sharkskin outfit," and David silently wonders if this is her "pillar of salt suit" *(3.13.37).* (Later, Marita also wears a "white sharkskin dress," although it isn't clear if this is the same dress or a different one. See 134:6.)

The obvious reference is to the biblical story of God's punishment of the sexually iniquitous Sodom and Gomorrah and the transformation of Lot's fleeing wife into a pillar of salt for looking back upon the destruction. The allusion to Proust's *Sodome and Gomorrhe,* which Catherine has been reading, is also transparent (see 3:4 and *[51:2] 3.9.3).* The allusion, however, is also linked more subtly to the African stories David begins writing when he returns to La Napoule. In "Safari," a January 1954 article for *Look* magazine, Ernest records Mary—who was also reading Proust at the time—saying that the drought-stricken, parched African landscape where they hunted reminds her of the "Bible in the part where Lot's wife looked back and they turned her into a pillar of salt" (20). The article includes a picture of a tall "extinct soda cone" in the "desert west of Lake Magadi" (22).[9] This is the same landscape crossed by David Bourne's father in the story of the massacre in the crater (see 128:9).

In the manuscript, we later learn that this dress is a creation of the famous designer Molyneux (see *[88:16] 3.19.14).* Given the novel's interest in fashion history, it is worth noting that true sharkskin—thanks to a new industrial process for preparing skins—only began to be used for fashion accessories such as shoes, purses, hats, belts, luggage, and umbrella handles in the 1920s.[10] By 1926, one can find articles like "Paris Has New Fad: Sharkskin on Hats, Shoes" praising the new, expensive material as "beautiful beyond words."[11] Catherine's sharkskin outfit, however, would probably be an anachronism. "Natural sharkskin"—an expensive and lustrous woven blend of mohair, wool, and silk (not the actual skin of a shark)—first became available as a fabric for suits only in 1929,[12] and a lighter, less expensive, sharkskin fabric containing rayon made sharkskin dresses popular after 1935 and throughout the 1940s. This newer material had a reputation for producing a "very white white" ("Sharkskin"), and it is this dazzling white that Hemingway wants for its contrast with Catherine's dark, fetishized tan.

(66:11) 3.14.4 ***Anyway I'm two persons:*** When in the manuscript David declares that he loves only "one person," Catherine replies that she is "two persons." Much as the

split in Hemingway's ego finds expression through the twin characters David and Catherine, Catherine is herself split: blonde/dark, boy/girl, Catherine/Peter. Similarly, David later describes himself as "riven" (see 183:14), and in some extraordinary lines from the ending of the Sheldon subplot, Barbara tells Andy: "There's two of me and there are two of you. You and Nicky. Nicky makes three because I made him two. . . . At first I thought it would be nicer if you could be two like Nicky. But now I know better" (422.2 4.19vi; see appendix A).

(66:11) 3.14.4 **He's in love with France. . . . He's pimping for her now:** In the manuscript, Catherine asks for more information about the Colonel. David calls him a "romantic" who loves France. He's learned all about France now and knows "she's a whore," but he still loves her and now, in his recruiting efforts for the Rif War (see 61:5), he is "pimp[ing] for her." The Colonel is articulate, educated, civilized, sensitive, loving, and tolerant, but he has a temper that can approach the "edge of insanity." "France is his only illusion," David says. Catherine suggests they order champagne to celebrate the Colonel loving France.

(66:11) 3.14.7 ***Vive la France et les Pommes de terres frites:*** In the manuscript, when the wine arrives and Catherine toasts the Colonel's "true love," David responds with a toast of his own: "*Vive la France et les pommes de terres frites.*" Hemingway also uses this silly expression ("Long live France and French fries") in *Across the River and into the Trees* (26) and in the "Education of Mr. Bumby" chapter of the restored edition of *A Moveable Feast* (204), but it takes on a different significance in this context in the *Eden* manuscript.

The phrase ridiculing a peculiarly French brand of patriotic jingoism dates back to at least the nineteenth century, but David's use of it alludes more specifically to the patriotic idiocies of France and Spain during the Rif War. In 1924, Vincent Sheean, Hemingway's friend and the most important journalist covering and critiquing the Rif War for American papers (see 58:10 and 61:5), was detained in Madrid by Primo de Rivera's secret police and accused of trying to depress the "exchange value of the peseta"—a story he recounts hilariously in his *Personal History* (64). Incredulous, Sheean asked to see the evidence against him. He was shown one of his recent dispatches, flagged by the Censor, "a vague and mild account of the new disaster that had overcome the Spanish army in Morocco" (65), and then, as if it were the coup de grâce, he was shown a comic telegram he had recently sent: "*Vivent la France et les patates frites!*" (66). After he stopped laughing, Sheean explained that it was just a joke sent in congratulations to his friend and fellow noted journalist Louise Bryant, who had just given birth. The censor's office, however, somehow considered it more menacing. The interrogating officer released Sheean to the American embassy to await military trial, warning him that he would be under constant surveillance by the secret police. Much later in the *Eden* manuscript, when asked about Sheean's whereabouts, David replies that he is in some sort of "trouble in Spain" (see *[214:22] 3.39.9*). This seems to be a direct reference to this incident.

After Sheean exposed atrocities committed by American fliers in Morocco (see *[214:22] 3.39.9*), he interviewed the pilots who had been duped by the French into bombing unarmed Berber villages and published an article headlined "Love of French Spurs Aviators: Case for American Flyers in Morocco Given." In his toast, David's subtle inclusion of the Rif War's most vocal American critic quietly resists celebrating the sort of love for France that leads the Colonel to participate in what David considers an unjustified colonial war. It can be no mistake that this is the second time the novel employs Sheean as a foil for the Colonel.

In *Personal History,* Sheean writes about running into Ernest and Pauline on their 1927 honeymoon:

> Here was a highly conscious, deliberate artist, more conscious and deliberate than any American I knew about in our time, who apparently felt no relationship between individual and mass—no necessity to discover a relationship. Why couldn't I (allowing for the general inferiority of my equipment as a writer) do what he did—shut out the whole world and live, both as a writer and as a human being, in the restricted company of my own kind?. . . . He wrote prose with the precision and power of poetry, upon subjects of the narrowest individual significance—the very special quarrel of a girl and her lover at a railway station; the tragedy of a man who had had his testicles shot away in the war; the mind of a prize-fighter, or a bull-fighter; the loyalty of a jockey to his worthless father. . . . He was, of all the writers or artists of this approximate age, the one who had most amply developed and exactly applied the gifts he possessed. You got the impression of finality from even his slightest story—that this was *it;* that it could not be done otherwise, and that if he lived a thousand years he could never improve upon it. (280–81)

With its devotion to erotic explorations, *The Garden of Eden* would seem to be nothing if not a work of the sort of "narrowest individual significance" of which Sheean gently complains, but there *is* a political dimension to the book—both in the politics of gender and sexuality and in the politics of colonialism. This dimension of the novel may be Hemingway's long overdue response to Sheean.

(66:11) 3.14.8 **going up the stair and in through the turnstile. . . . too exciting:** In the manuscript, now that Catherine and David are alone in bed, Catherine tells him how exciting it was to go that morning to the Prado as a boy. At first too excited to understand if her transformation has changed the paintings in any way, she eventually finds that she, too, loves the "Del Sarto girl" that David loves so much (see *[54:23] 3.10.3*), and she has a new understanding of the *Maja Desnuda,* reclining

"so self-consciously unselfconscious. . . . like a whore" (see *[54:23] 3.10.4*). David wonders where she learned about whores, but she says it was just the experience of being a boy this morning. She can't talk about the other paintings, though, because she was too excited—too involved in feeling instead of thinking.

66:14 **We'll go there whenever you want:** The manuscript is clear: they will be in La Napoule the "day after tomorrow" *(3.14.9).*

67:1 **Not if you're a boy and I'm a boy:** In a dynamic where Catherine and David can each be a "girl" or a "boy," male-male desire has until now been a taboo combination. In some discarded pages from the manuscript that were originally written for this spot, David and Catherine do kiss when they are both boys, but they have to talk around what they are doing. It has to remain unspoken. Catherine says it feels wonderful and promises she can do this for David and be "better than any boy." She teasingly asks if David will like it better and leave her. "No," David replies. Catherine then declares herself a girl again, and promises to postpone further experiments until after dark (*422.4 3.14.11*).

In the pages Hemingway wrote to replace the discarded pages, David not only refuses to kiss Catherine if they are both boys, he goes into a brief state of psychological withdrawal—"going away"—that disturbs Catherine. She doesn't see what he has to lose if he explores intimacy with her as both a girl and a boy. She thinks he needs to try this too, so he can know about it. But if Catherine "*has* to try," David at least wants to wait until it's dark. She thinks it's dark enough now, but David disagrees. Sensing his discomfort, Catherine offers to be David's girl. When he responds by saying her name, she answers, "Yes, I'm Catherine. . . . Why didn't you say you wanted Catherine." It is implied that they then make love.

(67:10) 3.14.16 **In the night . . . her head ~~pushing~~ stroking against him like a cat. . . . "I'm a boy. . . . and you are":** In the manuscript, David wakes later that night to the feeling of Catherine stroking her fetishized hair against him as if she were a cat. She is now the boy she was when she entered the Prado that morning. She tells David he is a boy too, and she doesn't care "how wrong it is." She asks him not to be "ashamed or sad" and wants him to try not to "think." She just wants him to "feel." As they make love, she asks him to say "the name," which David says, although "the name"—presumably "Peter"—does not appear in the text.

67:14 **You call me Catherine always when you want. I am your Catherine too:** The manuscript makes it clearer that she is Catherine "*too*" because she has just been "Peter" as they made love. Catherine's dissociation from her own name—her sense that it is one role among others she can play—speaks to a split in her ego that mirrors a split in Hemingway's ego.

67:18 **Let's first lie very quiet in the dark:** The final paragraph of this chapter in the Scribner's edition is highly misleading. Jenks stitches the first part of this long sentence together from three different places: "Light . . . dark" *(3.14.18);* "lowered the latticed shade . . . side by side on the bed" *(3.14.7);* and "the big room in the Palace" *(3.10.1).* Even more problematically, Jenks invents from whole cloth the final forty words of this sentence: " . . . Catherine had walked in the Museo del Prado in the light of day as a boy and now she would show the dark things in the light and there would, it seemed to him, be no end to the change." These words simply do not appear in the manuscript. What's more, the ending of this chapter in the manuscript is utterly different.

(67:18) 3.14.19 *"Can I . . . try to invent?" . . .* ~~He had never thought that he could do what he did now happily and completely~~: In the manuscript, Catherine and David, in bed, begin trying to "invent" again, at first with only their thighs touching. Presumably they are "inventing" a way of making love in which they are both boys. Something about this invention clicks, and it is suddenly "all changed" for David, as it had been for Catherine that morning as boy at the Prado. A deleted line in the manuscript here suggests what happens for David: "~~He had never thought that he could do what he did now happily and completely and he did without thinking and with delight what he could never do and would never do~~." Nor, in the morning, does David immediately suffer from remorse. The manuscript chapter ends with David and Catherine waking, both feeling happy and proud.

In the manuscript, where Catherine and David begin to invent, Hemingway left a note in the margin, reminding himself to check his discarded pages for deleted material. He notes that two pages are missing. Pages that would fit here, however, do not appear among the discarded manuscript pages in the Hemingway Collection at the Kennedy Library.

NOTES

1. In this passage, Hemingway originally wrote the name of a different sporting paper, *l'Echo des Sports,* but replaced it with the *Miroir des Sports (3.19.18).*
2. The restaurant, established in 1870 at 32 Carrera de San Jerónimo, had moved temporarily to Calle del Príncipe due to building renovations and reopened at 37 Carrera de San Jerónimo in 1923. (The street number 37 of 1923 corresponds to today's street number 17.) The restaurant occupied the whole floor of its building and also had an entrance in back at 8 Calle Arlabán.
3. In "The Republic of Honest Men" (1933), John Dos Passos refers to the leaders of the new Spanish Republic as "the liberal group of wellintentioned gentlemen, who moved the witty conversations of the Buffet Italiano" (352). Hemingway expressed interest in a republican alternative to the dictatorship of Primo de Rivera as early as 1924. See his letter of 10 November 1924 to Ezra Pound, where he reports dining with the exiled Miguel de Unamuno,

describes efforts to smuggle items over the border, and writes, "I am going to release the Republican propaganda for the states. Am inserting it in the press services here etc. Keep this under your hat" (*Letters* 2 179–80). For a measure of Hemingway's interest in the political commitment of the Buffet Italiano group, see his 1934 introduction to *Quintanilla*, an exhibition of Luis Quntanilla's engravings at New York's Pierre Matisse Gallery, shortly after Quintanilla was jailed for revolutionary activities (*HMF* 31–35).

4. For an extended consideration of this theme, see Eby, "In the Year of the Maji Maji."

5. During WWII, Hemingway flew as an observer on several RAF missions, and when he worked on his unpublished manuscript the Land, Sea, and Air Book (much of which evolved into *IIS*) after the war, he wrote a few chapters with Thomas Hudson in the RAF (Scribner's Archive, Hemingway VI, Box 10, Folder 4, PUL).

6. The marble is now in the Musée Jules Desbois, which opened in Parçay-les-Pins in 2000 (Huard and Maillot 13).

7. Cary Wolfe suggests the same thing (239).

8. In a 9 Jan. 1958 letter to Buck Lanham, Hemingway disparagingly refers to "all the get in Pauline's family" (qtd. in Christian 245). He clearly means progeny.

9. Pillar-of-salt jokes also appear in *Under Kilimanjaro* (201) and Mary Hemingway's East Africa Journal (9 Sept. 1953, 56). It looks like pillar-of-salt jokes were an ongoing motif during Hemingway's 1953–54 safari. It should also be noted that, during their 1926 affair, Hemingway's code name for Pauline, later made famous as the name of his boat, was "Pilar" (Spanish for *pillar*); thus, Catherine's "pillar of salt suit" aligns her with memories of Pauline.

10. See, for instance, "New Process on Sharkskin" and "Nouvelles Inventions."

11. For a contemporaneous French perspective on the fad, see Trévières.

12. A representative advertisement boasts, "Sharkskins are the latest development of the woolen science! Here is truly a fabric for every wear . . . dress or business! A close woven texture that is both shape-retaining and wear resisting . . . a rich mixture in a duo-tone color effect" ("And Now Tilton's").

CHAPTER 8 (MSS. CHAPTER 15)

68:1 **In the Buen Retiro. . . . The lake:** A 353-acre park in central Madrid, just two blocks from the Prado, the Retiro is known for its shaded walkways, riding paths, ponds, fountains, and statuary. Near the center of the park is a rectangular artificial lake adorned with a monument to Alfonso XII, which was completed in 1922.

68:3 **the distances were all new:** David is disturbed profoundly enough to experience a mild form of hallucination. (In "The Snows of Kilimanjaro," Hemingway used the same language—"all the distances seemed wrong"—to describe the sensation after riding all day through fields of opium poppies [CSS 48].) David's deep "remorse" and his conviction that the lake (only a few feet away) is "too far to ever walk to" suggest a feeling of helplessness indicative of depression. Yet mild forms of hallucination in the novel—David's ability to physically feel his sex-change in bed (see 17:14), Catherine's perception after her lesbian experience with Marita that "all the colors were too bright" (see 162:11), and David and Catherine's shared conviction that Catherine's mouth changes with her sea changes (see 47:14)—are always linked to the Bournes' sexual activity. This suggests that something more than depression (though not exclusive of it) is at work. In the manuscript version of this scene at the Retiro, Catherine seems to know what David is experiencing, although we don't hear them discuss it, and she claims to be able to control David's experience. "The distances don't matter," she tells him. She "can change them all back." "It never happened," she tells him *(3.15.2)*. This, the manuscript tells us, is when David would "usually . . . [come] awake" and find himself in a real, non-dreamlike, space—implying that such episodes have happened before. At such moments, Catherine and David seem less like two real people and more like two halves of a single riven ego.[1]

68:11 **remorse:** David's remorse has been read as homophobic anxiety and old-fashioned heterosexist moralizing. It is both of these, but it also speaks to the double bind of fetishistic desire: since this form of excitement depends upon a sensation of transgression (see *[5:22]* 1.1.3), there's a tendency to reify—or even invent—the very rules that must then be transgressed. The power of David's remorse this morning in the Retiro is precisely commensurate with the power of his breakthrough the night before when he did "~~happily and completely and~~ . . . ~~without thinking and with delight what he could never do and would never do~~" (see *[67:18] 3.14.19i*). This divided attitude, like so much else about fetishism, is structured by ego-splitting and the logic of disavowal (see 14:23 and 15:13).

(69:7) 3.15.5 **"They have the worst words for the loveliest things. . . ." "Ecstasy is a name for a cat":** In the manuscript, as Catherine tries to describe how happy their lovemaking has made her, she complains that "they have the worst words for the loveliest things. Like Ecstasy." David answers that "Ecstasy is the name for a cat." (Hemingway did, in fact, have a cat named Ecstasy.) Catherine picks up this phrase, and it becomes a sort of refrain for her, appearing several more times throughout the course of the *Eden* manuscript. This association of cats with orgasmic pleasure plays into a larger pattern in the novel (see 17:23 and *[26:2] 1.3.3*).

69:19 There aren't many more moves to make. . . . we can always go back to where we started: In the manuscript, Catherine assures David that "nothing's ever gone." They "can't lose anything" *(3.15.7)*. Given the novel's interest in the Edenic, such a claim resonates with tragic irony. Catherine then asks her fellow "inventor" if he remembers when he "found our friend" the night before. Jokes about "her" (apparently David found his feminine self at some point during their lovemaking) get mixed up with what David calls his "friend . . . from Couvet Switzerland," absinthe. (In 1797, Henri Louis Pernod had opened the world's first absinthe distillery in Couvet.) This leads to further banter about Switzerland, where Catherine attended school.

69:26 This drink tastes exactly like remorse: The most notorious ingredient in the original absinthe was wormwood, a plant proverbial for bitterness and synonymous with grief and regret.

69:33 Look at me and watch it happen. . . . The lips are your girl again: The substantiality of Catherine's transformation back into a girl—a transformation both psychological and physical (her lips visibly change)—must not be underestimated (see 47:14). This truly is "wrenching" and not something casually or breezily accomplished. Catherine asks David to look at her. She knows he can see that her transformation is real, and in the manuscript she wants to know if this makes him happy. Not if she isn't happy, he impossibly replies. "Why shouldn't [she] be happy," she asks in exasperation. They're handsome and rich. David is talented and "will be famous." And "I'm a noted what?" Catherine asks: "Not horsewoman, not tennis player, not painter, not writer. What? Clubwoman, patroness of the arts, salon bitch? Member of the Paris Colony?" "Bon vivant," David offers. When she stops, David encourages her to keep going, and Catherine can see him "storing it away."

"Do I help you as a writer," she asks him. "Fuck my career," he responds, to which Catherine answers, "I hope we haven't" *(3.15.11).*

As Hilary Justice notes, Catherine's complaint about her "lack of identity (outside of being the sexual partner who brings David ecstasy or remorse)" leads tellingly into a discussion of David's writing and then into a discussion of her own biological infertility (80). (For more on this dynamic, see 27:16.) In many ways, Catherine creates her identity through scripting the action of what will become, in David's hands, the honeymoon narrative.

70:18 You wanted a girl didn't you? Don't you want everything that goes with it?: As Nancy Comley notes, in this scene, Catherine, who is menstruating (71:2), "performs feminine hysteria, thus becoming the stereotype she so despises" (216). Catherine's performance, Debra Moddelmog suggests, demonstrates that, in spite of her menstruation, "there's nothing natural about being a woman. In fact, being female requires a performance that is unnatural for some women and often belittling to women in general" ("Who's Normal" 147).

71:3 I thought if I'd be a girl and stay a girl I'd have a baby at least. Not even that: The novel's concerns about childbearing (see 27:16) should also be historicized. In *Civilization without Sexes,* Mary Louise Roberts has shown that following the First World War, debates about fertility raged in the popular press of a depopulated France. In these debates, short hairstyles and flapper clothes were associated with sterility. Monique, the quintessential flapper and heroine of Victor Margueritte's *La Garçonne* (1922), is literally sterile.

71:11 Aix . . . Cézanne country: Paul Cézanne was born in Aix-en-Provence and painted in its environs many of his greatest works, including his many pictures of nearby Mont Sainte-Victoire. The literature on Hemingway's stylistic debt to Cézanne is extensive.

NOTE

1. For a more thorough consideration of hallucination in the novel, see my essay "He Felt the Change."

BOOK III *(NOT A NEW BOOK IN MSS.)*

CHAPTER 9 (MSS. CHAPTERS 16–17)

75:1 The new plan lasted a little more than a month: Given earlier hints about the calendar and the action of the novel (see 57:10), it should now be mid-September.

75:2 long . . . house. . . . in the pines on the Estérel side of la Napoule. . . . delta of the small river: The Scribner's edition has already told us that this location is "not far from la Napoule" (64:9), not in La Napoule proper. The manuscript offers further hints about this location. The Bournes stay at a site four kilometers outside of La Napoule *(3.43.10)*, at a hotel elevated on a headland above the sea *(3.28.48)*. This would put them in Théoule-Supérieur, close to the Pointe de l'Aiguille, on the edge of the Massif de l'Estérel, the rocky wild country between La Napoule and Saint-Raphaël. From here, they would have the view Hemingway describes of the "empty beaches" and "the high papyrus grass at the delta of the small river" (the Siagne) with the "white curve of Cannes" across the bay.

When the novel's action takes place, Théoule was still part of the commune of Mandelieu-la-Napoule, but in 1927 local business owners began agitating to split from Mandelieu-la-Napoule and to join with two other tiny hamlets to become Théoule-sur-Mer. In "An Eden to Be Saved: A Plea for Théoule," a 1927 editorial in the important arts newspaper *Comoedia*, poet and novelist Gaston Picard warned of incipient overdevelopment and a coming colonization by Americans. And when the French Chamber of Deputies approved the split in 1929, the language of the bill called attention to the location as "one of the most beautiful on the Côte d'Azur," noting that it was "destined to become an important winter resort," the site of many villas and hotels (Sénat 2). The fact that Théoule was still comparatively undeveloped in 1927 probably explains why Hemingway chose it as a setting instead of the rapidly developing Juan-les-Pins, where he had stayed with Hadley and Pauline in 1926. Nonetheless, Théoule is yet another of the novel's endangered Edens.

Locating the precise hotel where the Bournes stay is more difficult here than it was in Le Grau-du-Roi, Hendaye, and Madrid—but this is because Hemingway never came to a final decision about it. In his early manuscript references to it, he repeatedly calls it a "long house" (75:9), and this is intentional. Reckoning the time he's spent with Catherine since their marriage, David thinks about the time they've spent together at Le Grau-du-Roi "and at the *Casa Longa*" (*3.13.9;* my emphasis). Here Hemingway must have been thinking of what was then La Napoule's best-known hotel, the thirty-two-bed Maïon Longa (which regularly advertised in the Paris edition of the *New York Herald* as the Maison Longa). A 1927 advertorial in

1930 advertisement for La Maïon Longa in La Napoule. (Archives photographiques du Touring Club de France. Image from the author's collection.)

162 · READING HEMINGWAY'S *THE GARDEN OF EDEN*

Le Figaro describes it as "the most charming getaway that can be imagined. Nestled in the pine trees with its terrace and splendid palm grove, facing the incomparable scenery of the gulf, the Maïon Longa offers a delightful stay to its visitors, who are assured they will always find the friendliest welcome from its owners and the gentle intimacy of the home with its neat kitchen" ("La Saison"). With the exception of the palm grove, this sounds much like the Bournes' hotel—but it would have been right above the harbor of La Napoule, directly above a railway track, and not in the more dramatic location in Théoule-Supérieur that Hemingway desired. (La Maïon Longa apparently had similar misgivings about its location and featured more rugged parts of the Estérel in advertisements.) Thirty chapters later in the manuscript, Hemingway intended to pin down the exact hotel, but he was never able to complete the passage. As Marita and Madame console David after the loss of his manuscripts, calling him "*metaphysique*" and "*mystique*," he replies that the gallant craft *SS Mystique* was lost "in latitude ——— longitude ——— in the back yard of the Hotel ——— 4 kilometers from la Napoule, Dept. of the Var, France at ———" (3.43.10). These gaps are simply blank spaces in the manuscript that Hemingway meant to eventually fill in. (The impression that the passage is unrevised is bolstered by its inclusion of a rare geographical mistake: the hotel would, in fact, have been in the department of Alpes-Maritimes, about five kilometers away from the border with the department of the Var.[1])

75:16 **a cove in the rocks where there was a sand beach:** Such coves, often accessible by steep paths or stairways, abound along the entire twenty-mile coastline of the Estérel.

76:2 **pastis:** See 26:19.

(76:14) 3.16.9 **I've worked hard for a month. . . . And I did promise. . . . And I took money:** In the manuscript, David watches Catherine drive up to the hotel in the Bugatti, speeding along the flat by the ocean, then getting quieter as she climbs the hill. When she arrives with a "treasure trove" of goodies from her shopping, they chat over martinis about how well David has been working for the past month and how well everything has been going. Catherine has been good, too, but she misses "ecstasy" (see *[69:7] 3.15.5*). Without further prompting, David acknowledges that he has worked well for a month, and he did promise Catherine this time for their honeymoon. To himself he also thinks, "And I took money." So he feels purchased when he asks Catherine, "What do you want to do?" She isn't sure yet, but she will let him know when she's figured it out.

(76:14) 3.16.11 **Proust. . . . Buddenbrooks. . . . Far Away and Long Ago:** In the manuscript, David apologizes for how boring it must have been for her while he was writing, but Catherine has been busy consuming literature. She has "finished the Proust" (see 3.4 and *[51:2] 3.9.3)* and read Thomas Mann's *Buddenbrooks* and W. H. Hudson's *Far Away and Long Ago.*

Hemingway read *Buddenbrooks* in late 1925 and wrote to MacLeish: "½ of it's a pretty good novel" (*Letters 2* 451). In the spring of 1926 he read *Far Away and Long Ago* and "loved it very much" (*Letters 3* 91). Hemingway listed both books in a short 1935 list of required reading for aspiring writers (*BL* 218), and in his own copy of *Far Away and Long Ago,* he wrote, "Hudson writes the best of anyone" (*Letters 4* 79). Hudson is mentioned briefly in *The Sun Also Rises* and "A Natural History of the Dead," and he may have inspired the name of Hemingway's protagonist Thomas Hudson in *Islands in the Stream.*

While this passage is the only mention of *Buddenbrooks* in *The Garden of Eden,* both Catherine and David read Hudson's natural history and memoir of growing up on the pampas of Argentina; the book is mentioned several times, and David reads other works by Hudson (see 194:26). As with the title of Proust's *A Remembrance of Things Past,* the title *Far Away and Long Ago* hints both at Hemingway's relationship to the autobiographical material in *Eden* and to the importance of childhood memories, soon to be explored in the African stories, in shaping the adult David Bourne. In particular, Hudson shares Hemingway's interest in the dual directionality of memory: how the past shapes our present and how our present inescapably shapes our memories of the past. In *Far Away and Long Ago,* Hudson writes, "It is difficult, impossible I am told, for anyone to recall his boyhood exactly as it was. It could not have been what it seems to the adult mind, since we cannot escape from what we are, however great our detachment may be; and in going back we must take our present selves with us: the mind has taken a different colour, and this is thrown back upon our past" (225–26). Hudson's memories of his childhood in the grasslands of Argentina may, in fact, help to inspire David to write his African stories. In *Under Kilimanjaro,* Hemingway suggests to a game warden friend that he write his boyhood memoirs and call them "*Far Away and Long Ago in Abyssinia*" (256).

(76:14) 3.16.11 **I can't write nor draw nor even paint in water colors:** Directly after the talk about David's successful work and her own prodigious reading, Catherine complains of her own limited means of creative expression. This important passage is discussed elsewhere (see 27:16).

(76:14) 3.16.14 **What's the book about?:** When in the manuscript Catherine asks David what his book is about, he replies that he doesn't know. He's discovering "a little more about this one each day." Catherine knows that it is a sort of honeymoon narrative. She asks how far he is in the story. He is well past Hendaye.

(76:14) 3.16.14 **I saw a writer last week in St. Raphael:** In the manuscript, as Catherine and David chat, Catherine remembers to tell David that she recently saw a writer in Saint-Raphaël. Identified as a writer by the proprietor of a vegetable shop, the blond man "wore plus fours and golf shoes," "looked sort of college," and "had a face like a collar ad." The portrait of F. Scott Fitzgerald, often photographed in the long knickers known as "plus fours" and who stayed during the summer of 1924 in Saint-Raphaël (a seventeen-mile drive southwest down the coast from David and Catherine), is transparent. In some discarded manuscript pages, David runs into a friend who tells him that Scott is staying in Saint-Raphaël. David knows. "My wife saw him," he replies *(422.4 3.16.22)*. Catherine remembers the writer watching her as if she were "some sort of wild animal." He "didn't look happy." He just regarded Catherine with an expression that looked "hurt and puzzled and very curious" *(3.16.16)*. She wonders if she shocked him. See also *(151:10) 422.4 3.25.20*.

76:29 **What sort of plans?:** In the manuscript, Catherine offers David a choice of two plans, one of which involves growing her hair out. But that would take a year, and David likes her hair the way it is *(3.16.19)*. She would be happy to do it, but her other plan would be more fun. This is the plan she will show David.

77:11 **Bugatti:** See *(54:23) 3.11.2*.

77:7 **try to get you to have yours cut the same way. . . . Are you afraid?:** In the manuscript, Catherine promises that with their identical haircuts, nobody will be able to tell them apart "except for how we're built" *(3.16.23)*. For the psychological dynamics and significance of such moments in the novel, see 6:6, 15:31, and *(16:3) 1.1.18i*.

77:13 **He wants to lighten it. . . . as fair as a Scandinavian:** In the manuscript, Monsieur Jean has already given Catherine a chamomile rinse to lighten her hair a little, but now she wants to lighten it intensely. She wants to make it like a beautiful Danish girl David saw in Biarritz. She promises David that Monsieur Jean is the magician behind such results for "everybody that's as fair as you like, the ones you always think are so wonderful" *(3.16.24)*.

As a hair fetishist, Hemingway could wax poetic over golden, red, or raven-black hair (in this manuscript passage, Catherine briefly toys with being "dark as a Japanese"), but as Mary Hemingway wrote about Ernest after he talked her into first bleaching her hair in 1945, "Deeply rooted in his field of esthetics was some mystical devotion to blondness, the blonder the lovelier, I never learned why" (*HIW* 170). Wife number two, Pauline, may have surprised Ernest when she first dyed her hair blonde for him in 1929 (see 11:16), but by 1934 Ernest was expert enough that when

Pauline dyed her hair "pale gold" for him while he was away in Havana, she wished he was there with her "to watch it and advise" her.[2] Hemingway's letters to wife number three, Martha Gellhorn, are full of reminders for her to use lime juice on her hair, try peroxide, or buy special hairdressings.[3] As he later assured Nita Houk, then working as a sort of secretary for him, before cutting and dyeing *her* hair, "he'd had personal training in hair-blonding from folks at Alberto-Culver V05 in Los Angeles," which he visited with Martha en route to China in 1941 (Hendrickson 362).[4] In an 18 October 1942 letter to Gellhorn, he reminds her how he had worked "to get the red out" of her hair and speaks at such length and with such detail about the dangers to hair texture that comes with combining ammonia and peroxide that one imagines he must, indeed, have received some formal training in the art (JFK). As he told wife number four, Mary, in 1949: "We know how to bleach from the best people that ever did it," adding that "Clairol Silver-Blonde," or red with "Roux oil shampoo," would be "very exciting" (qtd. in *HF* 126). The very thought of having her "really platinum," he told her in a 1954 letter, gave him an erection (15 July, 1954, JFK).

But Hemingway not only dyed his wives' hair; he also dyed his own in 1947 to facilitate his transformation into his alter ego, Catherine (see 17:23).

77:29 Can you publish it or would it be bad to?: In the manuscript, Catherine suggests that they publish the honeymoon narrative in a very limited edition: five copies *(3.16.27)*. Two copies for themselves and one each for Nick, Barbara, and the Colonel. She thinks the book would be too shocking for Andy; David isn't so sure of that, so she decides to include him as well. Catherine launches into the idea, suggesting Nick illustrate the book. David thinks they'd need to sell a copy to have the book copyrighted, and Catherine promises to get a lawyer to look into it. David warns Catherine that she might not like the book, but she assures him she'll like it as long as it's true.

It is difficult not to see this discussion as metatextual. Did Hemingway intend to publish *The Garden of Eden*? A true answer might be far from simple, since Hemingway's attitude may have evolved and oscillated over the years. Mary Hemingway remembers that, as he worked "intermittently" on the novel between 1946 and 1958, he "did not invite me to read this new work each evening, as I had done with other books" (*HIW* 452). This suggests an intensely private text—an interpretation bolstered by David Bourne's metatextual suggestion that he is his own real audience (see *[247:24] 3.46.17*). Yet, as he worked feverishly on *Eden* throughout 1958 and early 1959, Hemingway reported to his friends on the steady progress of the novel—albeit without mentioning its subject matter—and he seemed intent on publishing it. (For a fuller consideration of this topic, see appendix C.) It was a brave novel to write; and—given Hemingway's hypermasculine public image and the pervasive sexual prejudices of late 1950s America—it would have been even braver to publish.

(78:3) 3.16.29 *"travels and voyages. . . ." "donkey":* In the manuscript, David tells Catherine that what he's writing isn't a novel; it's "an account," or "travels and voyages." Catherine doesn't know why it *should* be a novel. (The novel, of course, was the most prestigious and lucrative of literary genres in the 1920s, and Hemingway's departure from it in the early 1930s to write the nonfiction works *Death in the Afternoon* and *Green Hills of Africa* did not entirely please his publishers.) She just hopes these travels won't be with a "donkey" or in "Arabian deserts." "Travels and voyages" is a stock phrase common in travel writing since the seventeenth century, but Catherine's quip alludes to two classics of travel writing: Robert Louis Stevenson's *Travels with a Donkey in the Cévennes* (1879) and Charles Montagu Doughty's *Travels in Arabia Deserta* (1888).[5]

More important than the specific allusions, however, is Hemingway's use of travel as a metaphor for personal and sexual exploration, or what Mark Spilka calls an "inner journey" (285). Le Grau-du-Roi, Hendaye, Madrid, La Napoule, and Africa aren't merely geographical locations; they are intimately woven into a network of memory, association, and fantasy. These places metonymically represent stations of a psychosexual journey, and Hemingway is pioneering a new sort of travel writing. In the manuscript, for instance, after the burning of David's stories and Catherine's departure, Marita plans to console him by getting an "African haircut." David promises that they'll go to Africa, but Marita says they'll "*have Africa*" that very night (*3.44.29;* my emphasis). And when Marita tells David that she "knows about Madrid" (185:4), she isn't talking about a place; she is talking about the sexual experiments with Catherine that took place there. Similarly, when David tells Catherine that they can always go back to "where [they] started" (69:21), he means not a place but a psychosexual state. Catherine is an intrepid traveler in this inner terrain—the Bugatti representing her attraction to the speed and danger of the journey—always wanting to go forward, wherever that may lead. Sometimes the road leaves the physical world entirely behind: "'When you start to live outside yourself,' Catherine [says], 'it's all dangerous. Maybe I'd better go back into our world, your and my world that I made up; we made up I mean. I was a great success in that world'" (54:12).

78:11 road from Madrid to Zaragossa . . . red buttes . . . dusty road picked up the Express train: The old road from Madrid to Zaragoza ran roughly parallel to today's A-2, but it hugged the Río Henares to Sigüenza and then the river Jalón until it joined the valley of the Ebro near Las Casetas, a few miles upriver from Zaragoza. The "country of the red buttes" is the valley of the Jalón from Lodares to Arcos de Jalón. The manuscript notes that it is just beyond Calatayud that the road turns left to follow the Jalón (near Huérmeda), while the train disappears through the tunnel. David is interrupted in his writing close to where the valley of the Jalón widens, its edges lined with white hills all the way to the valley of the Ebro and the train junction at Casetas.

This junction is the setting for "Hills Like White Elephants," which Hemingway wrote while on honeymoon with Pauline in 1927.[6]

(78:26) 3.17.3 **heard her voice in the garden. . . . You're excited about the day too:** In the manuscript, hearing Catherine's voice in the garden, David decides that his writing is at a convenient stopping place for the day. As he puts his papers away, he reflects that, ever since he woke up, he's been excited about the day and the trip to Monsieur Jean's. A little surprised by this, he wonders if he has "forgotten Madrid" already, or did writing about that "exorcise it"? Perhaps it did. He isn't sure. A little later, as they leave for Monsieur Jean's, both Catherine and David are quite excited *(3.17.6)*.

79:6 **slacks. . . . Everybody will next year:** See 6:3 and 110:7.

79:21 **Monsieur Jean . . . was about David's age. . . . "I don't belong to the syndicate":** In the manuscript, to help Jean understand what they want, David and Catherine show him pictures of themselves from Spain. Jean suggests they begin with the cut from Madrid and then proceed from there, asking first for David's approval. David's reply—that he doesn't belong to the syndicate—implies an awareness that there were, in fact, several French trade unions for coiffeurs during the 1920s, including the socialist-leaning Fédération des Syndicats d'Ouvriers Coiffeurs Confédéré, the communist-leaning Fédération Nationale des Syndicats d'Ouvriers Coiffeurs, and the anarchist-leaning Fédération Autonome des Syndicats d'Ouvriers Coiffeurs. These unions, with a good measure of success, agitated and organized strikes to secure better wages and hours for workers in the hairdressing industry (Zdatny, *Fashion* 88).

David's quip is meant to suggest that the fascination with exciting new haircuts is entirely Catherine's, not his own. He is merely the somewhat reluctant and indulgent husband. Although David woke up this morning excited about the haircut and struggles at several points in the novel to admit to himself that Catherine's desires are his own, Catherine is generally presented as the desiring agent behind these haircuts and sexual experiments who compels a reluctant David to go along with her plans. Insofar as we read Catherine and David as autonomous desiring agents, each with their own individual psyches, this is a reasonably fair description of what happens in the novel. It should be borne in mind, however, that this is the familiar narrative structure of transvestic fantasy. In the erotic stories told by fetishistic cross-dressers, the male who wears the fetish to facilitate a cross-gender identification (see 5:27, 12:13, and 17:23) is almost always compelled to do so by a mysteriously powerful female (see 12:13). In this respect, the dynamics of sexuality in the novel can be better understood by regarding Hemingway, not his characters, as the desiring agent.[7]

Though "not a member of the syndicate," Hemingway almost could have been. He not only claimed to be an Alberto-Culver-V05-trained hair colorist (see 77:13), he also spent a good deal of time cutting women's hair. As early as 1922, Gertrude Stein wrote to Sherwood Anderson about teaching Hemingway to cut Hadley's hair (Reynolds, *Paris* 36); in one of his hair-obsessed letters to Martha Gellhorn, he describes himself as her "coiffeur" (15 Oct. 1942 JFK); in 1949, a few days after bleaching the hair of his part-time secretary Nita Houk, he cropped it for her, "severely short" (Hendrickson 307); he often cut Mary Hemingway's hair—and when he didn't do the cutting himself, he sometimes substituted tediously detailed letters that Mary could share with her coiffeurs:

> Tell him you have decided . . . to wear your hair sleek and long instead of short and curly. But you are keeping the same style of hair-cut. You don't want to lose any of the length and you want the very front, that was so short, to grow into the sweep of the back. You would like the bottom of the hair neatened; trimmed in the same style as it is when you go in. This will take about five minutes.)
>
> Doing this in a week it will look chic-er than any dame in *Vogue* and as it grows (*and does it grow*) it will keep the same fine shape. . . .
>
> Ask Gustavo if there is anything he can recommend and *guaranty* to be absolutely harmless to the hair . . . to keep it straight and sleek. You don't want to lose the curl because you will be wearing it curly again (as no one else can). But you want something which will do it no harm but keep it sleek and flat as you comb it.

The letter goes on for two more paragraphs about the haircut—promising that it will make Mary "look about 18," that Mary will probably "set another hair style just as [she] did with her last one," that it was a style "nobody without naturally curly hair" could pull off, and so forth. Hemingway eventually writes that he "ought to be a fashion writer," promising, "the girl in my book will have her hair the way you are fixing yours . . . and some 500-000 [500,000] up people will have d'erections about it" (qtd. in *HF* 245). If all this is too much to remember, he suggests that Mary can just give the letter to the coiffeur.

The hair-bleaching passage in the manuscript is significantly longer than in the Scribner's edition, with more details of the bleaching process, and with more excitement and anxiety from Catherine about how it will turn out. This sort of excitement in cutting or changing hair is a regular feature of hair fetishism (see 49:8). That Monsieur Jean is about David's age, that he is a fellow artist "working like a sculptor" (see 46:3), that his métier is as important to him as David's is to him, these things all suggest that he is on some level David's double.

80:19 **As fair as my pearls:** After this in the manuscript, Monsieur Jean promises to make Catherine's hair "as fair as the Danish girl," explaining to David that Catherine has told him about the Danish girl in Biarritz he was so crazy about *(3.17.11)*.

81:25 She looked in the mirror as though she had never seen the girl she was looking at: Catherine's dissociative misrecognition of herself in the mirror resembles Marie Morgan's response, in *To Have and Have Not,* to seeing her image in the mirror after getting her hair bleached: "I looked strange to myself.... I couldn't believe it was me and I was so excited I was choked with it" (259). It also resembles how David will soon respond to the sight of his own bleached hair in the mirror (84:27). Such moments of misrecognition in the mirror—almost always involving the fetish—are common in Hemingway's work.⁸ For more on the phenomenon, see 43:17.

81:29 The cut: In the manuscript, David requests "The Madrid cut," noting that he "neglected to get it in Madrid" *(3.17.16).* Jean encourages him by calling the cut "conservative" and "*sportif.*"

82:9 David looked at Catherine and then at his own face in the mirror. His was as brown as hers and it was her haircut: With the same tan, same haircut, same bleached hair, David becomes a mirror image of Catherine (see 43:17). The structure of fetishistic excitement depends upon turning trauma into triumph. The same pseudotwinning that Hemingway experienced as an extended childhood trauma is now a tool for producing erotic excitement (see *[16:3] 1.1.18i*).

NOTES

1. Before 1860, Théoule, La Napoule, Cannes, and Nice were all in the department of the Var, but this changed with the creation of the department of Alpes-Maritimes in 1860.
2. See letters from Pauline to Ernest, 22 Sept. and 15 Sept. 1934 (JFK).
3. See letters from Ernest to Martha, 23 Sept. 1940, 12 May 1941, and 13 Oct. 1942 (JFK).
4. For Hemingway's two-day stay in Los Angeles, see Moreira 20. After reading *Hemingway's Fetishism,* Walter Houk, Nita's husband, wrote to me: "Realizing there would be no hairdressers in China, Ernest took time out for lessons in haircutting and the chemistry of bleaching by someone at Alberto Culver cosmetics, which had just originated V05 products." According to Houk, "the hairdressing session was an hour or two long.... That is what [Ernest] told my late wife, Juanita Jensen [maiden name], in 1949.... She later recorded the anecdote on tape...." (personal correspondence, 4 Aug. and 6 Aug., 2006).
5. According to his sister Marcelline, Hemingway "devoured Stevenson" as a child (Brasch and Sigman 10). In his library at the Finca Vigía, he owned a ten-volume set of Stevenson's works in addition to separate copies of many of his most famous books. Hemingway owned two copies of Doughty's *Travels in Arabia Deserta:* an abridged 1908 version edited by Edward Garnett (*Passages from Arabia Deserta*), and a complete edition with an introduction by T. E. Lawrence. An important book in the history of travel writing, Doughty's *Travels* was "rediscovered" and popularized by Lawrence in his 1921 edition. In an April 1925 letter to Perkins, Hemingway mentions *Arabia Deserta* as a model for what would eventually become *Death in the Afternoon* (*Letters* 2 318).

6. The junction is mentioned by name in the earliest draft of what would become the story (JFK Item 472).

7. See also *HF* 241–59.

8. For similar scenes, see *FTA* 311; *CSS* 89, 305; and *FWBT* 351.

CHAPTER 10 (MSS. CHAPTERS 18–19)

(83:1) 3.18.1 **lunch in the restaurant at the outdoor table:** In the manuscript, the new chapter begins with David and Catherine lunching outdoors under the shade of "great plane trees," with a view of the harbor (see 88:28). After glasses of the "old giant killer drink," Armagnac and Perrier (see 148:21), they savor regional specialties: cold lobster in Provençal mayonnaise with a bottle of Tavel, and then rouget (red mullet) grilled in butter, capers, and herbs. Catherine is glad they had a drink with Jean after all the barbering. Now they both look like Scandinavians. As they admire each other, they both feel wonderful. David doesn't care what people think, and he wishes they could see themselves. "Just look at me," Catherine answers. "We're the same." In other words, looking at Catherine for David is just like looking in a mirror (see 43:17). Catherine feels changed, but more than ever she's David's "girl."

83:9 **ont fait décolorer les cheveux:** When Monsieur Aurol observes that they have bleached their hair, they answer that they always do this in August. The quip is at odds (probably unintentionally) with other hints in the text that suggest it should be mid-September by now (75:1).

(84:15) 3.18.9 **It was so fast.... I tell you so when you're my girl:** In the manuscript, this is part of a postcoital conversation between Catherine and David. David apparently achieved orgasm so quickly that Catherine wonders if the wait before they made love caused him physical pain. David wishes "all hurts were like that." Catherine, whom David calls an "inventor," says she'll understand when she is a boy, but for now she's still a girl. Yet at this moment, David is a girl, too—or, as Catherine corrects herself, David is her boy and her girl both. (Lines 86:6–11 in the Scribner's edition have been moved from this position in the manuscript.) Tonight they'll really do it, she promises. It would be "wicked" to do it, she says, in the daytime.

(84:15) 3.18.4bis **Do you like your new girl? ... I don't care about being a boy ... now:** In the manuscript (on a page whose numbering reveals it to be from an earlier draft), Catherine asks David if he likes his "new girl." Is she "dark enough ... light enough ... silky enough?" When he replies that he loves her, Catherine tells him

that she loves her "new girl too." In other words, David is this new girl, and they have made love when they are both "girls." This becomes even clearer when they make love later that evening. See 85:30.

84:16 After she was asleep David... looked at himself in the bathroom mirror.... it was someone else he saw but it was less strange now: This is a curious moment of both identification and dissociation for David. On the one hand, he confirms his sameness with Catherine. He looks at the mirror, then at napping Catherine, then back at the mirror, and finds his hair is just like hers. In the manuscript, we're also told that he is "as blonde as that girl in Biarritz," and the idea of it gives him an erection *(3.18.11i)*. Yet, if he sees himself as the mirror image of Catherine, or the mirror image of the Danish girl he saw in Biarritz (see 77:13), he is also dissociated from the image he sees in the mirror. In the manuscript, he greets the mirror, "I don't think I know you," and we're told that the image he sees "was not himself." What David finds in the mirror is the split in his own ego—his own otherness, and the representative of the split-off other-gendered half of Hemingway's ego that is walking around in the form of Catherine. For more on this phenomenon, see 43:17.

84:26 You like it.... You like it.... You like it. Remember that. Keep it straight: In the manuscript, the voice of the narrator reinforces what David is trying to tell himself. After the first "You like it," the voice of the narrator adds, "and it was true." In the manuscript, as he smiles in the mirror, David doesn't say "you like it" three times; he says it *six* times, and three times the *narrator* adds some version of "That's what was true" *(3.18.12)*. In other words, David is not trying, as has sometimes been suggested, to convince himself of something that isn't true; as he smiles at the mirror, he is trying to admit to himself a vital truth that he finds strangely difficult to admit, surprisingly difficult to "keep straight." And his admission has an effect: the image in the mirror "no longer looked strange to him at all" (85:1). David no longer sees, in the dissociation-inducing split in his ego, the emptiness of the gulf itself; he now sees the split-off other-gendered half of his ego and recognizes it as himself. He owns the part of himself from which he is usually defensively shielded by dissociation.

That David must struggle to recognize and take possession of his own desires may strike some readers as anything but courageous, but there is something deeply courageous in this scene, and others in the manuscript, where David struggles to acknowledge his own desires. In these moments, Hemingway transcends the traditional narrative structure of transvestic fantasy, where the unwitting male is always compelled to wear the fetish and assume a cross-gender identification by a mysteriously powerful female. In rejecting a version of his self-narrative in which he is "bitched" by Catherine, David is specifically rejecting the classic cop-out of transvestic fantasy (see 12:13, 21:3, and 79:21). Although David struggles, often unsuccessfully, to "keep this straight," the effort itself involves courage, not so much from

David as from Hemingway. Here, on paper, Hemingway tries to honestly come to terms with his own desires—desires that are wildly at odds with his public image in the sexually censorious 1950s.

85:4 **Of course he did not know exactly how he was. But he made an effort aided by what he had seen in the mirror:** In the manuscript, the line "Of course he did not know exactly how he was" continues: "... and no one does" (3.18.13). The point being made is not just about David. It is about the human condition.

85:30 **How are you girl?:** Catherine here addresses David as her "girl." She knows the answers to the questions she asks—"Who cut it? Was it Jean?"—but they are involved in a sort of erotic role-playing in which Catherine's calling David "girl" is essential to his transformation into one (see 20:16). In the manuscript, Catherine asks him if he is "a Danish girl" (3.18.16i). She tells him that she'd been uncertain if his haircut was a boy's or a girl's, but "it's a girl's now." Not only is David a "girl" in this lovemaking; as a brief postcoital conversation in the manuscript reveals, Catherine is "still a girl" as well. "I never changed at all," she tells him, which is why "it's so complicated" (3.18.19). Catherine is a little troubled that she feels "so good." It can be no coincidence that this same-sex female lovemaking—like that from earlier in the afternoon (see *[84:15] 3.18.4bis*)—directly precedes the introduction of a new character: Marita.

(86:14) 3.19.1 **In the morning ... wind was blowing a gale:** The break in the Scribner's text on this page marks a new chapter in the manuscript, and the first three manuscript pages of that chapter have been deleted. As a fierce symbolic wind blows outside (see 13:23), David awakes to the sound of Catherine in the shower and finds himself "suddenly happy," and with "no remorse at all." Returning to bed to snuggle, Catherine tells David that he's slept in so late because he hasn't "changed" since the previous night. That is, he is still a girl. She suggests that he work while she prepares a picnic for later in the day. As David shaves and gets ready to shower, he talks to himself in the mirror. Regarding the previous night, he thinks that "things are really confused now," and yet he is himself "a little less confused." In his previous self-reflection he "straightened out" something. Now he wants to see if he can write.

86:19 **David found the bottle:** The manuscript indicates that this is a bottle of Tio Pepe, Spain's most famous sherry. Best known for its fino, a very light, pale, dry wine, the brand became internationally famous in the 1930s with a marketing campaign featuring a Cordobes-hat-wearing, guitar-brandishing bottle.

86:22 **He had not worked this morning:** Hemingway did not write this sentence. Jenks adds this misleading sentence to fill in the gap left by his deletion of the description of David's work that morning. It is important that, in the manuscript, David wakes without "remorse" and writes "easily and with sharp post-coital clarity" (see 13:33). In fact, David has the most productive morning he has had in a month (3.19.3).

86:28 **passed Golfe-Juan:** This refers to the village between Cannes and Juan-les-Pins, not the eponymous body of water on which it sits. The 1926 Blue Guide calls it "a lively little bathing resort" (Muirhead and Monmarché 152). Contemporaneous pictures of the waterfront suggest that the "good bistro" and "small open bar" was the Reserve du Golfe associated with the Hôtel de la Mer (the Chez Marcel later favored by Picasso).

86:30 **Juan-les-Pins:** In the manuscript, as they drive through Juan-les-Pins, Catherine tells David that she has read in the paper that a big hotel will be built there. The town will then be spoiled. David says he never liked it much anyway. Catherine agrees (3.19.5).

Hemingway bends his chronology a little here to mark Juan-les-Pins as yet another endangered landscape, if not quite an Eden (see 3:1). As recently as 1924, Juan-les-Pins was still a small fishing village with a lovely beach and a few hotels, but in early 1925 a new casino opened there and a New York Times article, "Riviera Developers Plan a Palm Beach at Juan-les-Pins to Rival Deauville," announced plans for a new "mammoth hotel." The article predicted that "within the next few years," Juan-les-Pins might "become the center of Riviera life and Europe's Palm Beach," but change came more quickly than anyone could imagine. By August 1926, an article in Le Temps described Juan-les-Pins as a noisy, fashionable beach, defined by casinos, dancing parties, and swarms of bathers "all devoted to the cult of bronzed skin" ("Entre le ciel"). There one could see "*l'aristocratie du monde entire*" ("La Saison de Juan-les-Pins"). In November 1926, British newspapers were reporting "a land boom on a large scale" overtaking the Riviera.

> Now every pretty stretch of shore with a few trees and a site whereon may be built a casino is selling at forty times the price at which the same land could have been bought about a year ago. . . . Mr. [Frank Jay] Gould found a quiet little village not far from bustling Cannes, which had escaped notice. This place, Juan-les-Pins, was known to comparatively few people. Two years ago there was an hotel with a reputation for hors d'ouvres, a few cottages, and about twenty yards of sandy beach shaded by a handful of pines. Today the places boasts a casino, five large hotels, and as many more under construction—all Gould built. Cottages are springing up overnight. In another few years the place may rival Cannes, Nice, and Monte Carlo in size and importance. ("Fortunes")

By the time Catherine and David drive through the town in 1927, Juan-les-Pins was "the recognized sunbath of the Riviera summer" (Juta).

Hemingway, Hadley, and Pauline were staying in Juan-les-Pins, visiting with Gerald and Sarah Murphy at nearby Cap d'Antibes, when on 19 June 1926, with great fanfare, the cornerstone was laid for Frank Gould's Le Provençal. This is the "big hotel" Catherine has read about in the papers (in *Tender Is the Night*, Fitzgerald describes its frame going up), and it opened its doors for business in June 1927—a few months before Catherine and David arrive back on the Riviera.[1] The fact that Hemingway never knew the Juan-les-Pins in its "unspoiled" state may explain why David and Catherine never liked it much anyway.

87:1 **Antibes:** See 6:9 and *(57:4)* 3.13.4.

87:8 **clear stream that came out of the mountains:** The manuscript indicates that this stream is the River Loup. The stream flows out of the mountains through a spectacular gorge and into the plains and then the sea close to Cagnes-sur-Mer, between Antibes and Nice. This is a special place for Catherine, and David thinks it's the "best wild country left" on this part of the coast *(3.19.5)*. Following closely, as it does, on their remarks about the new hotel going up in Juan-les-Pins, it reminds us again of the rapid development on the Riviera. The Bournes inhabit a fragile Eden, and they know it is disappearing before their very eyes.

87:21 **hanging villages:** The road up the Loup valley and along a smaller stream, the Malvan, would take Catherine and David to the spectacular *villages-perchés* of Saint-Paul-de-Vence, Vence, Tourettes-sur-Loup, Gourdon, Le Bar-sur-Loup, and Châteauneuf. Catherine has done the famous drive recommended by Baedeker and the *Blue Guides*, but she reacts against its very picturesqueness. This resistance positions Catherine and David as travelers, not tourists.

87:27 **stuffed eggs . . . Savora mustard:** About 40 percent by volume ground mustard seed, Savora blends eleven spices and aromatics into a complex condiment that balances vinegary-ness with a touch of sweetness. Along with roast chicken and a light rosé wine, the Bournes picnic on deviled eggs (see 4:9), a symbolically significant snack Catherine has prepared with Grey Poupon mustard and truffles. Her lavish use of the truffles she bought in town had shocked the proprietress at the hotel. In the manuscript, they also have melon, and Catherine repeats the phrase, "Melons for delight" (see *[54:23]* 3.9.14).

87:33 **And you haven't felt bad. . . . about anything I said:** In the manuscript, it is "*everything* I said," not *anything*. As Catherine notes, she "said an awful lot and . . .

loved saying it" *(3.19.11)*. (For the importance of such pillow talk, see 20:16.) David hasn't had remorse, and he tells Catherine that he woke that morning feeling happy.

88:5 **wind . . . blew her sweater against her breasts and whipped her hair:** In the manuscript, the Bournes take turns standing in the wind and admiring the effect it produces on each other (see 13:23).

(88:16) 3.19.14 **clothes are awful now. . . . French Vogue. . . . Chanel uniforms. . . . O'Rossen suits. . . . Molyneux:** In the manuscript, David's admiration of Catherine's sweater (see 6:26) leads to a discussion of current fashions, which Catherine considers "awful." She promises to show him what she means in French *Vogue*. David tells her that she always looks lovely. He likes what Barbara calls Catherine's "Chanel uniforms," and he likes her O'Rossen suits and Molyneux dresses.

Reimagining a time when Hemingway had just married a writer for *Vogue, The Garden of Eden* is deeply concerned with fashion (see 6:3), and Catherine regularly wears clothes by three of the era's greatest designers. By far the most famous of these designers, Gabrielle "Coco" Chanel did more than anyone else to define women's fashions of the era. Having pioneered during the First World War the use in women's wear of comfortable jersey fabrics, Chanel's uncluttered designs helped to liberate women from the corset and paved the way for the ascendency of the slim "boyish silhouette." Her dresses and suits dominated the pages of French *Vogue* throughout the 1920s. (See also 12:27 and *[47:18] 3.7.2*.)

Far less well known today, Louis O'Rossen began as a man's tailor but became famous for making tailored suits for women. He was considered "the prince of Paris tailors," and the "O'Rossen suit" became for women of the 1920s synonymous with a "woman's man-tailored suit" ("Tailleur"). A "boyish ensemble" that "out flappers the flapper," it was one component of a much broader turn towards "masculine" or "boyish" modes for women in the 1920s, and Hemingway was a fan (Finamore 155). In a 1928 letter to his sister Marcelline, who was preparing a trip to Paris, he wrote, "If you want a tailored suit go to O'Rossen in the Place Vendome" (*Letters 3* 395).

Edward Henry Molyneux, who maintained shops in Paris, London, Monte Carlo, and Cannes, was "a modernist designer of consummate good taste, walking a fine line between the refinements of couture style and a modernist aesthetic and the ambition to be socially and culturally advanced in the age of Anita Loos and Gatsby" (Martin and Koda 24). He was particularly noted for elegant evening wear with simple flowing lines. He is the designer of the white dress that David considers Catherine's "pillar of salt suit" (see 65:26).

(88:16) 3.19.15 **We'll go in November. . . . safari clothes:** In the manuscript, the conversation about appropriate clothes leads Catherine to ask David if he knows where

they will go next and when. David plans on a safari in November. He explains that their safari clothes will be made in Africa. To Catherine, "it sounds grim," but David assures her it will be "luxurious." (For Hemingway's own hopes of returning to Africa while working on *Eden,* see 29:10.)

88:18 I want to do what you want. I can't be more compliant than that can I? In the manuscript, Catherine's promise to be compliant is about a trip to Africa, not a trip to the local café. The difference is significant. Only after the quarrel begins about Africa (a quarrel preceded by much loving and mutually admiring conversation) does it end with a final exchange about the café.

88:26 French *Vogue* . . . *Chasseur Français* . . . *Miroir des Sports:* See 58:10.

88:28 café: Clues in the manuscript reveal that this is the famous Café des Allées in Cannes, although it is never named. Sitting at the café, David looks at the boats in the harbor through a double row of plane trees *(3.46.15).* This was precisely the view from the Café des Allées, which also appears several times (under two different misspellings) in Fitzgerald's *Tender Is the Night.*

88:29 Haig pinch bottle: David's choice in whisky is yet another sign of his luxurious tastes and discriminating consumerism. Haig advertised itself as having the oldest family tradition in Scotch whisky, dating back to 1627. Haig & Haig Pinch was the American name for Haig & Haig Dimple, the upmarket version of Haig & Haig Five Star blended scotch that derived its name from its distinctive three-sided pinched decanter bottle, first introduced in 1893. Advertised as "The Aristocrat of Whiskies," on the eve of prohibition Haig Pinch was the most expensive blended Scotch whisky on the American market, and Hemingway was a fan. In letters from 1924 and 1925 he praises "real good whiskey. Haig and Haig in the pinch bottle" (*Letters* 2 216). By 1931, however, something had changed. In a letter to Karl Pfeiffer, he complained, "Haig in a pinch bottle is no longer reliable" (*Letters* 4 447).

John Haig & Company was taken over by the Distillers Company conglomerate in 1919, and its sister company, Haig & Haig, was acquired by the Distillers Company in 1923 and made a subsidiary of John Haig & Company in 1925. Between 1924 and 1928, Field Marshall Earl Haig, commander of the British Expeditionary Force in WWI, was chairman of the company. Given its predominance in the American market, Haig & Haig was hit particularly hard by prohibition, and the company "remained practically dormant" until the lifting of prohibition in 1933 (Laver 60). Advertisements for Haig & Haig in the early 1920s noted that wartime restrictions on production had created a shortage of aged and matured whiskys, so "there is not enough Haig & Haig Whisky to meet the demand." This, they explained, is why their whisky was more expensive than that produced by their competitors ("Haig").

89:18 **old Isotta:** What David calls Marita's "big old Isotta convertible" (98:12) is a very expensive car. The fact that the brakes are bad, the engine needs work, and that David actually calls the car "that miserable Isotta" has led some critics to describe it as if it were a jalopy (3.24.11bis), but Isotta Fraschini was "Italy's finest marque" (Duffield), and it "appealed to that section of the plutocracy whose tastes extended beyond the portentous dignity of a Rolls Royce" (Nicholson, *Noble* 65). In fact, due to the exchange rate, by 1927 Isotta Fraschini cars had become "prohibitively expensive in France" (Anselmi 66). Other owners of Isottas included King Feisal of Iraq, King Victor Emmanuel of Italy, Pope Pius XI, William Randolph Hearst, Clara Bow, Peggy Joyce, Rudolph Valentino, and the fictional Divers in Fitzgerald's *Tender Is the Night*. Moreover, Marita's car, with its Swiss plates further signifying wealth, can't be too old. The size of the car suggests that it is a Tipo 8 or 8A, the first production car with a straight-eight engine, which "only began to appear in quantity in the early part of 1921" (the 8A replacing the Tipo 8 in 1924), and which reached peak popularity in 1927, right as the company began to focus on airplane engines (Nicholson, *Noble* 68). Since Isotta Fraschini had a one-model policy throughout the 1920s, and the difference between the Tipo 8 and 8A was confined to the engine, and because every Isotta Fraschini had a unique custom-built body, there's only one small way David could identify this Isotta as "old": a square blue and white radiator badge on the Tipo 8A distinguished it from the round insignia on the Tipo 8 (Nicholson, *Tipo 8*). But this could only tell David that the car was pre- or post-1924.

Yet if the Tipo 8 was the incarnation of unadulterated prestige, it was nonetheless not known for good performance, and this doubtless explains David's attitude toward it. In 1923, "a client who paid $8,500 for his chassis, plus at least $6,000 for a custom body worthy of Italy's best, was entitled to expect something pretty good—after all he could get ten Buicks for the same money." And yet owners—or their chauffeurs—were often disappointed: "'A beast of a car—about as big as a hotel' . . . and 'a very bad car in the Grand Manner' are two assessments of it by well-known drivers, and almost every modern critic has stressed the fussiness of the engine, the awkwardness of the driving position, and the degree of physical effort demanded to do anything" (Nicholson, *Noble* 63). In other words, David's concerns are justified, but the car was probably a masterpiece of luxurious coachwork. David later calls it "a fine car"; he simply thinks it is "too much car" for Marita (136:10).

The fact that David can speak so slightingly of what must have been a visually stunning automobile speaks to his comfort with luxury and his discrimination as a consumer of luxury goods, whether that be the Bugatti, the champagne and caviar, or the services of luxurious establishments like Maison Prunier or the Palace Hotel.

90:19 **the—:** Jenks has edited this so it looks like Nina interrupts Marita, introducing herself informally to avoid being introduced by her aristocratic title. In the manuscript, however, Nina is the one to come over and ask about the haircut, not Marita, who is too shy. And Marita is the one who was intended to have the aristocratic title. Nina introduces her as "my friend the ——— of ———" *(3.19.22)*. Hemingway apparently intended to fill in these blanks, but he never did. (In the manuscript, blanks that Hemingway intended to fill in later are formatted differently—with a longer, thinner straight line—than blanks that were supposed to remain blank.) While he repeatedly makes it clear that Marita is rich, he leaves her title a mystery. A hint later in the manuscript, however, suggests that her cousin is Comte Étienne de Beaumont, which would link her to the aristocratic Bonnin de la Bonninière de Beaumont family (see *[162:4] 3.27.9*).

Like Fitzgerald in *Tender Is the Night*, Hemingway may have intended to allude to the Riviera's role as a postwar epicenter of disintegration for the old social order—a feature of Paris he certainly explores in *The Sun Also Rises*. As a rather snobby and antisemitic 1925 article complained, "The new-rich are to-day undisputed monarchs of the Riviera":

> The dislocation of values, which has flooded the South of France with a deluge of moneyed nobodies and a torrent of tourists of restricted means, has played havoc with the outward distinction of the Riviera. In the first place, the survivors of the old order have compounded with the new. Class barriers have been brushed aside in a measure which would stagger anybody with Victorian or even Edwardian ideas. Crowned heads hobnobbing with shady individuals, a lady of royal blood perched at an American bar alongside a Parisian demimondaine and her court of admirers, a duchess sharing a bank with a Levantine moneylender— these are incidents out of many that linger in my memory in evidence of the extraordinary social chaos of the Riviera of today. (Williams)

Yet, in *The Garden of Eden*, while he displays a keen interest in consumer culture, the temptations of wealth, and the commodification of art, Hemingway shows little interest in exploring class relations (see *[205:11] 3.37.52*)—at least outside of the financial disparity between David and Catherine. It seems more likely that Marita's aristocratic title appeals to a snobbish taste for titled company that is visible in *Across the River and into the Trees* and that appealed to Hemingway throughout the 1950s.

90:24 She blushed: Blushing is a defining feature for Marita. David will later nickname her Haya, which he explains means "the one who blushes" (142:6). Hemingway's Swahili dictionary defines the term as "shame, modesty, bashfulness" (F. Johnson 131).

91:13 She's in love with you. . . . Well I can't help it if she is with me: Marita enters the novel in love with a haircut and already in love with both David and Catherine—

which is to say, she sounds more like a product of Hemingway's fetishistic fantasy than a real person who bends herself to fit the fantasies of the couple she would seduce.

92:9 **In the night he woke:** In the manuscript, when David wakes up, Catherine is already awake, and they briefly talk. David asks if she's a girl. She is, she replies, but when David asks if she's sure about it, she admits she isn't. She wants to know if David will let her "find out." He will, and whatever she has to do to find out is "all right" *(3.19.28)*. They then fall asleep.

NOTE

1. A story in *L'Èclaireur du Dimanche* (the Sunday edition of the local Nice paper David Bourne reads) dated 20 June 1926 describes the laying of the cornerstone for the hotel ("La pose de la première pierre de l'Hôtel Provençal à Juan-les-Pins"). For the opening of the hotel, see "L'Ouverture de l'Hôtel Provençal à Juan-les-Pins."

CHAPTER 11 (MSS. CHAPTER 20)

93:2 He left the ongoing narrative of their journey . . . to write a story: Here David puts aside the honeymoon narrative and begins the first of several African stories. These stories, and the surrounding story of their creation, offer us Hemingway's most remarkable portrait of the creative artist at work. Since David's stories are portrayed as being semi-autobiographical, they also help Hemingway to explore his Proustian interest in memory and the complex reciprocal relationship between the past and the present. David's past has clearly shaped his present, yet something in David's present prompts him to revisit, write, and, later, rewrite his past. It is not simply that the story comes to David in a dream, "It was *the necessity to write it* that had come to him" (93:17; my emphasis). Catherine and David's tonsorial twinning, their girl-girl lovemaking, and the arrival of Marita all seem to work together to drive David away from the honeymoon narrative and towards the African stories in which he explores, reimagines, and rewrites his damaged relationship with his father. Seen in this light, the African stories seem like a defensive attempt to shore up a threatened masculinity—and, no doubt, they do function this way. These same stories, however, simultaneously explore types of primal loss essential to the novel's Edenic theme, and they imply a critique of patriarchy and the very masculinity embodied by David's father.

93:18 He knew how the story ended now: David's African stories all seem to end with images of loss: a locust plague followed by wind and sand-scoured bones (see *[118:10] 3.21.25)*; the remains of a massacre (see 223:3); the corpse of a magnificent elephant (see 199:20).

94:4 the evil in the shamba: The "evil in the shamba" is here unnamed, but a later allusion to David's father and Juma "drunk with their *bibis* at the beer shamba" (181:18) hints at the nature of the evil. *Shamba* is the Swahili word for farm, or cultivated land. Hemingway's copy of Frederick Johnson's *A Standard Swahili-English Dictionary* defines *bibi* as follows: "A term of respectful reference and address to women, now fallen into evil days in some places because of its use to refer to concubines of Europeans" (34). In his *Kenya Diary, 1902–1906,* Richard Meinertzhagen—

anything but a paragon of virtue himself—remembers his first impression of his brother officers in the King's African Rifles: "I was amazed and shocked to find that they all brought their native women into the mess; the talk centers round sex and money and is always connected with some type of pornography" (10). (A constant motif in *Under Kilimanjaro* is Hemingway's temptation to visit the shamba to see his African "fiancée," Debba. See 30:16.)

94:19 weather was insane now. . . . since the war. . . . everything was changed: David may dismiss Aurol's comments as banalities and idiocies, but they are introduced here because they have some symbolic validity. Weather is symbolic in the novel (see 13:23), and the Eden that David and Catherine inhabit is changing fast. The Riviera is undergoing a land boom and flood of new visitors, cars are revolutionizing mobility, the old aristocracy has been shaken to its core, class relations have been transformed, social mores and fashions have been transfigured, and then there is the advent of the *femme moderne,* a phenomenon many considered "above all a creation of the war" (Jacques Boulenger, qtd. in Mary Louise Roberts 19). See also *(196:25) 3.36.11.*

94:28 *Far Away and Long Ago:* See *(76:14) 3.16.11.*

94:30 Galignani's: The Galignani family has run an English-language bookstore in Paris since 1801, and Galignani's has long prided itself on being the oldest and most elegant foreign-language bookstore in continental Europe. In 1856 the store moved to its present location, Rue de Rivoli 224, across the street from the Tuileries. The store is famed for its vast holdings, which are particularly rich in the arts. Hemingway was a famous patron.

Later in the manuscript, Marita tells David that she had tried to get his "flying book" at Brentano's, at Smith's, and at Galignani's, but they had all sold out of it *(3.27.8).* Galignani's, Brentano's, and Smith's were "the famous trio" of English-language bookshops on the right bank of the Seine (Maris).[1] This suggests that the wealthy Marita is a creature of the right bank. Unfamiliar with the left bank, she does not mention trying Sylvia Beach's Shakespeare and Co.

96:10 Only the oldest families. . . . Us, the Morgans, the Woolworths, the Jelkses, the Jukeses: The progression of names here is comic. Unlike many of the legendary Americans who made fortunes during the Gilded Age, financial titan J. P. Morgan came from a prosperous and distinguished family that proudly traced its lineage back to prerevolutionary New England. The story of F. W. Woolworth, who founded the first five-and-dime in 1879, however, was a classic tale of "rags to riches." When the action of *The Garden of Eden* takes place, the Woolworth Building in New York, built in 1913, was the tallest building in the world. During the

1930s, the troubled Woolworth heiress, Barbara Hutton, became popularly known as the "poor little rich girl," and this implicit but anachronistic allusion functions as a segue to the next name on the list.

The inclusion of "the Jelkses" (misspelled) on this list is legitimate within the 1920s setting of the novel but gets its comic twist from a couple of anachronisms that would have been all too clear to an American audience in the 1950s. John F. Jelke made the family's fortune during the Gilded Age in oleomargarine, particularly with the Jelke Good Luck Margarine brand. John Jelke's eldest son, Ferdinand Frazier Jelke, was a successful businessman and socialite, who used his portion of the family's margarine wealth to establish a highly successful Wall Street investment house. Frazier and his younger brother, Jack, who took over the family margarine business, bought mansions in Newport and hobnobbed with the likes of the Vanderbilts and Rockefellers. In 1947, Frazier, who had gone through two highly public and nasty divorces and a custody trial, published a memoir, *An American at Large,* which according to a contemporary reviewer read "like a vacuous society column," though it contained a "wealth of material for students of the society of the '20s and '30s."[2]

But the real anachronistic punch line of Catherine's joke has to do with the arrest of Mickey Jelke, son of Jack Jelke and an heir of the margarine fortune, on 15 August 1952, for coercing women into prostitution and serving as their pimp. A full-time playboy and habitué of the Stork Club, where he could have met Hemingway, Mickey Jelke had become involved with the seamier side of New York's celebrity-obsessed café society. Needing money to support his lavish lifestyle until he turned twenty-five and received his inheritance, he had taken to pandering for the elite before being arrested in a wide-ranging vice raid. The story, featuring sex, money, and celebrity culture, was splashed across newspapers around the globe, with Jelke being described by his own defense counsel as a "poor little rich boy" ("Jelke to Take Stand"). The story stayed in the papers through the 1953 trial and conviction, the unsuccessful 1955 retrial, and Jelke's eventual 1957 release from prison. A story of the arrest appeared in the same 1 September 1952 issue of *Life* magazine that first published Hemingway's *Old Man and the Sea,* and separate items about Hemingway and Jelke appeared often in the same Walter Winchell columns. Jelke jokes were so ubiquitous that in her syndicated Broadway column, Dorothy Kilgallen wrote, "The newest Broadway fairy tale begins, 'Once upon a time there was a night club comic who didn't tell a Mickey Jelke joke.'" This sentence in *The Garden of Eden* is Hemingway's Mickey Jelke joke.

By the time we reach the final name on Catherine's list, we have traveled from the sublime to the ridiculous. A supposed family of "convicts, imbeciles, and undesirables . . . immortalized in college textbooks on sociology" (Harmon), the pseudonymous Jukeses were the ignominious field on which participants in the American eugenics debate battled during the late nineteenth century and into first half of the twentieth century. While conducting prison research in upstate New York in 1874, R. L. Dugdale found six members of the same family, using four different family names, in jail. After further investigation, he found widespread criminality, indolence, and "feeble-mindedness" within the extended family—a family with roots dating back to the Puritan settlement of New England—and published his findings in *The Jukes: A Study in Crime, Pauperism, Disease and Heredity* (1877). Dugdale thought that environment probably played a larger role than heredity in shaping the Jukes family, but this judgment was reversed by Arthur H. Estabrook in his pro-eugenics study *The Jukes in 1915* (1916), and this argument was used to advocate the forced sterilization of supposed "undesirables." Clarence Darrow published an amusing and devastating rebuttal of Estabrook's argument in the October 1925 issue of *The American Mercury*, but the Jukeses remained a fixture in eugenicist arguments until World War II.

96:13 **autumnal equinox:** With the exception of the Bournes' quip to Aurol that they always dye their hair in August (83:9), hints about the novel's timeline would place the action of this scene within a few days of the autumnal equinox, which in 1927 fell on 23 September.

97:1 **Nina:** In the manuscript, David is thinking of Barbara Sheldon as his example of a nonbitch. Catherine guesses this, and Marita, who of course does not know Barbara, wishes her happiness, something that she thinks comes all too rarely to intelligent people. Catherine does not ask about Nina's happiness.

99:11 **junction with the N.7:** This detail tells us that David has taken the Boulevard Jean Hibert (today the Blvd. du Midi Louise Moreau) along the coast from La Napoule to Cannes, and he has now arrived at the harbor. Marita's car is parked along the harbor in front of the Café des Allées.

100:11 **I haven't examined her papers:** In the manuscript, Catherine has a little more information about Marita. She is wealthy, with "her own money," and she is about Catherine's age. Her parents are divorced. Her father is now dead, and her mother has remarried. More interestingly, Marita has been married, "but it didn't take" (3.20.15).

(100:12) 3.20.16 **Jean cut her hair:** The manuscript reveals that Monsieur Jean cut Marita's hair at Catherine's direction. It is cut the way Catherine had her hair cut at Biarritz (see 46:19), "only much longer." Marita, however, "thinks it's terribly short because she doesn't know any better."

100:31 **Estérel road . . . brakes:** The 1926 *Blue Guide* notes that the Corniche d'Or along the coast of the Estérel is "picturesque . . . but with numerous sharp curves

CHAPTER 11 *(MSS. CHAPTER 20)* · 185

requiring caution" (Muirhead and Monmarché 164). This is precisely the sort of road to challenge the big old Isotta with its "too sudden brakes."

101:2 coves where we swim without suits: The coast here abounds in innumerable hidden coves where the red volcanic rock of the Massif de l'Estérel plunges down to the sea. (For nude sun bathing, see 12:27.)

101:32 you'd like one of your girls lighter than the other: Given the novel's association of tanning with fantasies of racial transformation (see *[19:1] 1.2.1*), the fantasy of book-end "girls," one light and one dark, may harken back to Hemingway's 1953–54 safari when his sexual fantasies were preoccupied with both Mary and the Kamba girl Debba (see *[161:8] 3.27.3*). Psychoanalyst Phyllis Greenacre has written about the importance of color contrast for many fetishists (321). We see something like this in David's fascination with the effect of Catherine's white dress or bleached blonde hair against her tanned skin.

102:7 cashmere sweater. . . . Catherine said we'd both wear them: Although Marita actively seduces David, Catherine often seems to have written the script. For the significance of cashmere sweaters, see 6:26.

102:29 We'll get a mirror. . . . A bar's no good without a mirror: See 43:17, (56:29) *3.12.14*, 81:25, and 84:16.

105:9 having two girls . . . I am yours and I'm going to be Catherine's too: As is so often the case in Hemingway's fiction, Catherine's desires are betrayed not by her words—"I don't go in for girls"—but by what happens to her voice when she speaks these words. We might wonder what has changed since she assured Barbara, with whom she clearly shared a mutual attraction, "I don't like girls" (see *[36:12] 3.1.4*). Is it that Marita is that much more attractive, more her type, than Barbara? Has Catherine's journey progressed to a point where what wasn't possible before now is? Marita's response, "That's why I came here"—that is, to be both David's and Catherine's girl—implies an answer that is somehow determined less by Catherine's fantasies than by a field of fantasy that Catherine shares with David and Hemingway. With Catherine and David making love from a psychological position in which they are both "girls" (see 85:30), it seems like they are now ready to share lovemaking with the same girl. Like a genie from a rubbed lamp, Marita appears in answer to their fantasy. As she tells Catherine in the manuscript, she wants to do "everything that [Catherine] and David want" (*3.20.27*).

(106:8) *3.20.31* guillotine on the Boulevard Arago: In the manuscript, Catherine thinks even the guillotine wouldn't hurt as long as you weren't solemn. David replies that he's been there on the Boulevard Arago at 5:00 A.M. and has "heard the thud." This spot behind La Santé Prison, across the street from where Hemingway regularly played tennis, was where the final thirty-seven public executions in France were carried out between 1909 and 1939. In 1927, probably in response to Sacco and Vanzetti, there was an active movement to abolish capital punishment in France.

NOTES

1. To get an appreciation for Hemingway's shopping habits at Galignani's and Brentano's, see the impressive itemized bills reproduced in Elder et al. 148–49.
2. See "American At Large." In a 1933 letter to the editors of the *New Republic,* Hemingway jokes about one of Jelke's divorces (*Letters 5* 405).

CHAPTER 12 (MSS. CHAPTER 21)

107:17 **beer:** If the beer and "*pomme a l'huile* with course black paper corns on it" sounds suspiciously like the description of Hemingway's meal at the Brasserie Lipp in *A Moveable Feast* (68), the *Eden* manuscript confirms these suspicions. The manuscript makes it clear that David is, indeed, thinking of Lipp's (see *[32] 2.1.15*).

108:10 **everything he had locked out by the work:** When David works, he "lives in" his stories "and nowhere else" (107:4) and thereby seems to "lock out" his present circumstances. The way he turns to write another story to escape his present worry (108:19)—and as an alternative to the honeymoon narrative (108:7)—suggests that the African stories are somehow escapist. But it might be more accurate to describe them as defensive, and as an attempt to work through his present circumstances by revisiting and rewriting his past. See 93:2 and *(140:3) 3.24.5*.

108:20 **write the hardest one . . . you know. . . . the new story that he had always put off writing:** Here begins David's second African story. Set in the year of the Maji Maji Rebellion—the 1905 native revolt against colonial rule in German East Africa—the story is about a desert crossing and a trek above the eastern escarpment of Kenya's Great Rift Valley. Only much later do we learn why the story is so hard for David to write: the end of the trek reveals a massacre and the "heartlessness" of David's father (223:3).

109:6 **Maquereau Vin Blanc Capitaine Cook:** Building on his claim that Hemingway plays upon mackerel in "its familiar French and English sense of pimp or panderer, an agent administering to sexual debauchery" (see 10:30), Stoneback associates David's consumption of mackerel here with the arrival of Marita in the novel: "Like Captain Cook, David Bourne is an explorer, a sexual adventurer in an undiscovered country. . . ." For Stoneback, David, like Captain Cook, "slays and is slain by the Kanakas"—his dark lovers, who, like David himself, are occasionally coded as Polynesian ("Memorable" 28). (See *[19:1] 1.2.1*, 154:29, and *[163:31] 3.28.15*.)

A more prosaic link to this scene can be found in Hotchner's *Papa Hemingway*. While Hemingway was driving along the Riviera in 1954 after stopping in Cannes, his eye was caught by the window of a charcuterie: "'If I'm not mistaken,'" he told Hotchner, "'they're showing tins of Capitaine Cook's mackerel in white wine. Haven't seen Capitaine Cook since 1939.' Ernest invested all his Monte Carlo winnings in tins of the Capitaine's mackerel, containers of *pâté de fois gras,* bottles of Cordon Rouge champagne, and jars of pickled mushrooms and pickled walnuts. We could barely fit all of it into the Lancia" (112).

109:31 **That's being a good wife:** Having lived with the Bournes for one day, Marita has already become a symbolic second wife for David. This can hardly be because of anything that she has done. Rather, it represents one more way in which she has walked into a pre-scripted role already mapped out by fantasy. See 91:13.

110:7 **"we . . . made scandal. . . ." "Someone said something about her slacks":** Just how scandalous would a woman in slacks be in France in 1927? More than we might easily imagine today. Yet Catherine's exciting transgression of societal norms is not wildly fashion-forward, and her prediction that "everybody" will be wear slacks "next year" (79:6) is prescient.

Whereas the mere sight of women wearing trousers in Paris in 1925 was by itself enough to warrant a brief story in the newspapers ("Nos echos" 1925), broad beach pajamas began to appear in Juan-les-Pins in 1926 and became such a rage that the town was soon dubbed "Pyjamapolis" (Duménil 80). Yet these beach pajamas, very wide and flared at the bottom, were not true slacks. We might take a measure of Catherine's sartorial daring by noting the breathless response to French designer Paul Poiret's January 1927 "prophecy"—picked up by newspapers around the world—that in thirty years women would be wearing slacks. According to Poiret, in women's fashions, in the wake of the First World War, "a perfect tempest of masculine ideas blew across the ocean" (32). Finding the French "at the present moment . . . slaves to American influence," Poiret considers "the tendency which our young ladies manifest when they affect a masculine appearance . . . , the vogue of cigarettes and pajamas," to be American as well (32). "It is safe to predict that this thirst for emancipation is not yet quenched and that women will reach out for even greater liberties, which means that for several years more they will be striving to come nearer and nearer the boyish, bachelor type. . . . Already we have been treated to women in dinner jackets," he notes, "and we shall soon witness a revival of trouser skirts under various guises. . . ." his, he confidently predicts, will eventually lead to true trousers for women: "And trousers for women will not be a mere short-lived fad; they will become as inevitable as bobbed hair, which is here to stay" (32–35).

Rather more quickly than predicted by Poiret's "prophecy," true slacks for women first became popular on the French Riviera in the summer of 1929 (see 6:3). From there the fashion spread to the rest of the world. See also *(32) 2.1.7.*

110:16 **Do I look any different?** In the manuscript, David calls Catherine's belief that sexual experience or desire can transform her physical appearance "crazy" *(3.21.11)*, but David himself expresses the same belief elsewhere—for instance with Catherine's mouth (see 47:14)—and the same belief is shared by other characters in Hemingway's fiction—notably by Phil at the end of "The Sea Change." A few pages later in the manuscript, Catherine is disappointed that the mirror they've bought for the bar hasn't arrived. She's afraid her transformation won't be visible by the time it does. Later, while brushing her hair in the bedroom mirror, she asserts that she *does* look different, "more experienced." David tells her that she looks as if she were sixteen. (See also 68:3 and *[47:18] 3.7.2.*)

(111:3) 3.21.10 **good honest kiss:** In the manuscript, while Catherine goes to check on lunch, David and Marita discuss their kiss. David knows that it shouldn't make him happy, but it does. They also discuss Marita's kiss with Catherine. Marita claims she would have left Catherine alone if Catherine hadn't wanted it so much. She hadn't known that Catherine was inexperienced in such things. She promises not to try to take Catherine from David, but she tells David she would try to take him from Catherine if she could, though she knows she can't. Marita also makes it clear how much she cares about David's writing, and David senses a mysterious sincerity that puzzles him. After all, they've only really known each other for a day. It is soon revealed that she has already read David's first novel (111:19).

111:9 **She spends money like a drunken oil lease Indian:** Thanks to the discovery in 1897 of oil on land to which they controlled mineral rights, members of Oklahoma's Osage tribe were already described by 1900 "as the wealthiest people in the world," and the true boom times didn't even begin for them until the first half of the 1920s (Burns 433). Between 1906 and 1926, oil from Osage lands "produced more money than all the combined gold rushes in American history," and stories of wild spending by Native Americans were commonplace in the newspapers (Burns 419). A 1920 *New York Times* article, "Indians Lavish Spenders," sums up the stereotype: "The extravagance . . . is almost appalling. They buy everything in the way of merchandise which looks bright and gaudy, without any consideration for utility." Later in the manuscript, David describes "Oklahoma oil Indians" cutting the mudguards off of Cadillacs instead of washing them *(3.23.23)*. Describing this era, the distinguished Osage historian Louis Burns writes: "Stories of the Osage fantasies are endless. Here were a fun loving people of limited means who had acquired the economic means to fulfill their sense of humor and fantasies" (435).

111:10 **are they like Maharajas?:** The obvious joke is that Marita is uncertain about the difference between millionaire American Indians and millionaire Asian Indians; but in 1927 on the Riviera, it's no surprise that Marita is familiar with maharajas, and it speaks to her wealth and the social circles in which she has traveled. A September 1928 item in *La Vie Parisienne* claimed that between the months of July and September, "the French discover the Indies"—not by going there, but by importing rajas. The item goes on to complain that the Aga Khan, the Maharaja of Kapurthala, the Maharaja of Pudukkottai, and the Maharaja of Kashmir have become so familiar as to entirely cease to seem exotic. Several maharajas were regulars at the casino in Juan-les-Pins, and a February 1927 "La Riviera Mondaine" column asks, "What would the Riviera be without the rajahs? Every year they return like the Three Magi, only having traded their camel caravans for the more practical comfort of the blue train." The article goes on to describe "the long row of rajahs" along Nice's Promenade des Anglais and asks, "But what grand hotel on the Riviera today does not have its little rajah to offer as a bonus to its customers . . . even to double the price of the rooms, as it should, of course?" ("Choses et autres").[1]

111:11 **He comes from Oklahoma. . . . East Africa:** This rift at David's point of origin, where he "comes from," is reflected in the title of his first book (see 111:16), and it mirrors a geographical division in Hemingway's childhood between his suburban Oak Park home, memorialized in the pun "Oak-la-home-a," and his summers spent in the "wilds" of northern Michigan. As I argue in *Hemingway's Fetishism*, it also points to a more fundamental bigendered splitting of Hemingway's ego that is one of the signature structural features of fetishism. (For David's feelings of being riven, see 183:14.)

David's twin boyhood homes also mark him—or at least his father—as a settler colonial. We're later told that David was "about eight years old" in 1905 (157:10). This means that he was born in Oklahoma in 1897, which implies that David's father came to the Indian Territory during one of the land rushes of the 1890s, well before Oklahoma became a state in 1907. That David and his father were in East Africa by 1905 is also significant. As a 1905 article in the *Southern Reporter* explains, "Two years ago there were not more than six European farmers in East Africa, whereas now there are as many hundreds. . . . Lands granted to settlers in 1903 amounted to about 445,000 acres, and in 1904 to 638,000 acres" ("Prospects"). In other words, David and his father came in on the ground floor of the colonialist project—a project much on Hemingway's mind throughout the 1950s, with the Mau Mau crisis underway, which would eventually lead to a free Kenya, and with Hemingway's two youngest sons living as settler colonials in what was then Tanganyika. For an extended discussion of Hemingway's response to settler colonialism in the novel, see my essay "'In the Year of the Maji Maji.'"

111:16 **novel about . . . East Africa when he was a boy:** The title of David's first novel, *The Rift*, appears to allude not only to Kenya's Great Rift Valley, but also to the rift between David and his father, and the rift in David's self at its very point of origin (see 111:11). Marita's response—"It made me cry.... Was that your father in it?"—and her understanding of the love between David and his father that survived whatever divided them stands in contrast to Catherine's response. As Catherine sometimes misunderstands his silence about the war (see *[54:23] 3.11.17*), she seems to misunderstand his relationship with his father. Like so many Hemingway heroes, David is haunted by traumas about which he remains profoundly reticent. Marita seems to have an understanding for this buried part of David's identity, a part that Catherine understands in David's second book (112:15) but not the first. This may be because Catherine, more clearly than Marita or David, functions on some level as half of a riven ego, and this aspect of her identity hinders her from seeing across the rift when it comes to David's relationship with his father. (See 12:13, 14:13, 17:23, and *[22:18] 1.2.4.*)

111:31 **Don't overreach:** In the manuscript, Catherine's caution to Marita is not about saying she loved David's book. When Catherine responds to David's reticence about his father by saying that this is "what being married to a writer is like," Marita promptly replies that she'll be happy to take it if Catherine doesn't want it (*3.21.14*). This is what Catherine calls the "overreach."

112:2 **did you think of him as a writer when you kissed him:** Catherine's comment, "I was afraid it was going to be like the clippings," links her fear that Marita might be a sort of writer groupie to her ongoing concerns about the distance between David's public and private personas (see 24:21).

112:11 **The Rift:** See 111:16.

112:12 **The second one is about flying in the war:** In a war in which men were so often ground into emasculating and dehumanizing insignificance—forced to huddle endlessly in pestilent muddy trenches, dwarfed by the vast armies at play and the terrifying effects of shelling, machine-gun fire, and gas—fighter pilots like David, alone among the clouds, were the public heroes, celebrated in the press and popular imagination as chivalric "knights of the sky." (Jake Barnes, in *The Sun Also Rises,* is also a former WWI pilot.) The period after the war, when barnstorming by ex–war pilots thrilled crowds and the promise of prize money and fame inspired one trailblazing flight after another, has come to be known as the Golden Age of Flight. *The Garden of Eden* is set in the year of Lindbergh's celebrated solo flight across the Atlantic, when the enthusiasm for flight reached its peak. That year, the public's thirst for aviation stories was unslakable, and many newspapers, such as the *L'Éclaireur de Nice* and *Le Miroir des Sports,* both of which David reads (133:13 and 88:26), featured aviation stories in nearly every issue.[2]

112:15 **It's a book you had to die to write and you had to be completely destroyed:** This insight is more striking when we remember that Catherine has told Andy she loves David because (as she misunderstands him) he *wasn't* affected by the war (*[54:23] 3.11.17*). See also 5:27.

(112:18) 3.21.16 *"crime. . . ." "punishment. . . ." "sin. . . . evil":* In the manuscript, Catherine describes David as her "partner in crime and everything else." David adds "punishment," but Hemingway deletes this. When Marita questions Catherine's use of the word "crime," Catherine clarifies: she means "sin. . . . or good and evil." Catherine adds, however, that she hates evil, something David finds "cheering." (See *[5:22] 1.1.3.*)

113:8 **Cannes:** This is an editorial mistake. The manuscript is clear that Catherine sees Cagnes ahead on the hill, not Cannes. Cagnes was then a hill town of about 7,500 inhabitants, crowned by a fourteenth-century Grimaldi castle, about twelve miles further along the coast in the direction of Nice. (Cannes, by contrast, had 26,500 inhabitants.) This is, more or less, the same "wild place" along the Loup where Catherine had stopped with David for their picnic only two days before (see 87:8). Catherine and Marita have a sort of seclusion here that they wouldn't have found close to Cannes, but the return to this location marks the act as a betrayal of David.

113:17 **better if I was her girl:** In the manuscript, Catherine first asks Marita to be her girl *(3.21.18)*, so when Marita suggests that it is "better" if Catherine is "*her* girl," she is proposing a sort of role reversal. The exact nature of the reversal isn't entirely clear, but since neither of them claims to be a "boy," it seems to be something akin to which dancing partner leads.

113:24 **I only kissed her but I know it happened with me:** In *The Garden of Eden*, sexual acts aren't merely sexual acts. They are portals to psychological—even physical—transformation. Catherine wonders whether the aftereffects of the kiss and gentle fingering she has shared with Marita might be visible to people on the streets in Nice. "It happened with me" implies a moment of psychological transformation. As she says, she "didn't know [she'd] ever *be* like this" (114:4; my emphasis).

114:20 **Not this part:** In the manuscript, when David tells Catherine that he can't understand this part, she admits that she started their experiments, but she reminds David that they weren't just in her mind. Yes, she changed David, but his transformation at Le Grau-du-Roi was "true." He truly "changed in the night." They "*both* changed" and they "were each other." David doesn't dispute this, but it was different because it was *them* and "in the dark."

(114:25) 3.21.18bis2 **it had hit you already:** In the manuscript, David tries to understand Catherine's needs, though he hates the idea of what she's about to do. Catherine says that she'd been "trying to be . . . good," too—an allusion to the month during which she muted her erotic experiments and let David work (see *[76:14] 3.16.9*). David agrees, but he says, "it had hit [her] *already*" (my emphasis). This *already,* and the fact that Catherine "remembers" it, implies that Catherine's desire for a lesbian experience "hit her" *before* Marita walked into their lives. This seems to allude to their own version of same-sex female desire from the night before they first meet Marita (see 85:30). Catherine tells David that the whole experience has made her feel like a schoolgirl, but once she "gets it over with" she'll be "grown up."

115:6 I've told her too much about you but that's all she likes to talk about: Catherine seems oblivious to clear warning signs that Marita intends to take David away from her. This echoes a motif in *A Moveable Feast*. Here, Hemingway shifts blame from himself to Pauline for the demise of his marriage to Hadley. Pauline is portrayed as "infiltrating" his marriage to Hadley by "using the oldest trick . . . there is."

> This is when an unmarried young woman becomes the temporary best friend of another young woman who is married, comes to live with the husband and wife and then unknowingly, innocently and unrelentingly sets out to marry the husband. When the husband is a writer and doing difficult work . . . so that he is occupied much of the time and is not a good companion or partner to his wife for a big part of the day, the arrangement has advantages until you know how it works out. The husband has two attractive girls around when he has finished work. One is new and strange and if he has bad luck he gets to love them both. The one who is relentless wins. (215–16)

NOTES

1. See also Richter. When Hemingway was writing *The Garden of Eden,* he was friends with a couple of maharajas, including the maharajas of Cooch Behar and Jaipur, both of whom attended his sixtieth birthday party in Spain in 1959.

2. In a French example from 1933 of the Hemingway legend (see 24:21), hagiographer Jean Lasserre describes Hemingway as a boxer, bullfighter, lion killer, champion of the winter sports ("he's won all the cups"), *and* aviator. It is worth noting that Hemingway read Lindbergh's memoir *The Spirit of St. Louis* (1953) soon after its publication (*UK* 197) and saw the film of the same name, produced by his friend Leland Hayward, soon after its release in 1957, so Lindbergh may have been on his mind as he returned to work on the *Eden* manuscript in early 1958.

CHAPTER 13 (MSS. CHAPTER 21)

117:19 **It might:** In the manuscript, David adds that once when he "had true remorse" a drink helped. Catherine protests, "But that was us" *(3.21.22)*. This is when David adds, "We're still us."

117:27 **There isn't any us. . . . Not anymore:** In the manuscript, David claims that he felt this bad in Madrid when he had remorse, but Catherine doesn't believe it because he had never been unfaithful to her. She says that what happened in Madrid was just something they did together that disturbed David, it wasn't like unfaithfulness *(3.21.23)*.

117:30 **It's all shit:** The manuscript is clearer about what specifically is "shit." David reminds Catherine about the guillotine and not being solemn (see *[106:8] 3.20.31*). *This* is what she calls shit.

118.8 **Semi-precious stone . . . pocket:** Kathy Willingham reads this moment with the garlic olive as "a symbolic castration scene, reflecting Catherine's sense that she has emasculated her husband" (*Ernest* 170).
  Given the sense of loss Catherine feels due to what she considers her "unfaithfulness to David" and the damage done to their dyadic union (see 27:16), it is noteworthy that she gives David the stone as a sort of talisman. Valerie Hemingway remembers Ernest telling her in 1959 that "he always hedged his bets by keeping a lucky stone close to him. To prove it, he . . . reached into his pocket and pulled out a handful of objects: a grubby white linen handkerchief, a rusting pen knife, a piece of string, an old chestnut, and a smooth, flat black pebble . . ." (59). At different moments, Ernest gave Valerie a rabbit's foot and an elk's tooth as lucky charms (67).[1]

(118:10) 3.21.25 **awfully proud you could work . . . father . . . locusts:** In the manuscript, as Catherine starts to feel a little better, she asks David if he worked well this morning. He replies that he finished a story. Catherine tells him she is proud that he could work when he was so worried about his father and the locusts. She has a vision of them "in great clouds" over the distant hills, "and it's like that shivering in a very old cinema film" *(3.21.26)*. That's the way it is, David agrees.

This is how we learn that the story David finished this morning was about his father and a locust plague (see 93:18 and 94:4). The passage, with its allusion to punishment on a biblical scale, also reveals that Catherine has been reading David's work without his permission, and she is unsettled enough, and experiencing a degree of mental dissociation so strong, that part of her is unaware that she has read the very story that she is asking about.

(118:10) 422.4 3.21.26 **odd she should have been in Kenya:** In a brief discarded fragment that fits here in the manuscript (literally like a piece of a puzzle—there are two half-sheets of paper sliced with a pair of scissors, one kept, one discarded), Catherine suggests that David find Marita and bring her back to join them for a drink. Marita knew David's father, didn't she? Catherine asks—although she thinks that Marita looks much too young for that. She finds it strange that Marita would have been in Kenya then.

It could be that, in her distraught state, Catherine confuses Marita's familiarity with David's first novel with her literally having been in Africa—after all, David soon tells Marita that Catherine has been "out of her head"—but a later undeleted passage in the manuscript reveals that Marita has, indeed, been to Kenya (see *[205:11] 3.37.34*). This latter passage, however, does not mention David's father, and a still later passage in the manuscript makes it clear that Marita has never been to Africa (see *[247:24] 3.46.20vi*). Hemingway was apparently torn between his desire for Marita to share David's African experience and his recognition of its unlikelihood and incongruity.

118:15 **All we lose was all that we had. . . . I wish I could remember what it was we lost:** Suffering from obvious emotional distress, Catherine here expresses a profound existential loss—a loss so deep that she has even lost track of (or, more accurately, psychically split off or foreclosed) what she has lost. This not only speaks to her immediate fears on waking up to find David gone and her fears that she has irrevocably damaged her relationship to David, it speaks to an almost primal loss, like the loss of Eden—not unlike the sense of loss David has begun exploring in his African stories (see 93:18).

118:31 **But I wasn't unfaithful. . . . How could you say I was? . . . When I knew I was unfaithful:** Catherine's disoriented dialogue on this and the next page, her attribution to David of lines that he did not speak and which obviously are the dissociated words of another part of herself—a psychotic response in which what is foreclosed within returns from without (i.e., supposedly out of the mouth of David)—points to a rift in her identity—not unlike the rifts in David's identity (see 183:14) and

Hemingway's ego (see 17:23). That she projects these words onto David also speaks to the degree to which she identifies this split-off part of herself with him.[2]

120:13 what I wanted to do all my life ... grown up: This seems to privilege Catherine's experience with Marita as tapping finally into her "real" desire, yet it's important to consider this declaration in the context of the self-division evident in Catherine's dialogue in the past few pages (see 118:31). I don't mean to suggest that Catherine's same-sex desire isn't "real," but I do mean to question whether it is her "core," "true," or "essential" desire. Catherine tells David not long before that she's had such opportunities throughout her life (114:27), but they hadn't been attractive enough until then. And not long after this, Catherine seems to lose any special proclivity for same-sex female desire. It seems more accurate to say that Catherine's desires vacillate and wander throughout the possible permutations available between a self-conception and partners oscillating between "boyish" and "girlish" identities.

120:19 Apprentice allowance claimed: An "apprentice allowance" is a weight concession given to an apprentice jockey. In the manuscript, this turn of phrase sends the conversation off onto a brief detour about horse racing, a minor theme in *Eden*. (Marita often thinks of David as a racehorse and herself as his trainer. See *[140:29] 3.24.9* and *[247:24] 3.46.5*.) Catherine tells us that her uncle races. Coincidentally, so does Marita's. Apparently "everybody's uncle races," quips David, suggesting that he'll try to get his to start. Marita asks where his uncle is. David isn't sure, but he thinks he's currently "Consul General in Hong Kong" *(3.21.32)*. Hemingway is here drawing on a memory of his friend Addison Southard, who was US Consul General when Hemingway visited Hong Kong in 1941. Hemingway had first met Southard on his way to Africa in 1933, when Southard was serving as a US representative in Addis Ababa.

Marita remarks that there's horse racing in Hong Kong, "but not thoroughbreds," and in 1927 she would have been correct. In fact, David compliments her on her "encyclopedic knowledge"—and the fact that David can recognize the encyclopedic nature of this knowledge indirectly indicates the encyclopedic nature of his own knowledge. Hong Kong's Happy Valley Racecourse was established in 1846, only five years after the British took possession of the island, and in early years the "equine mix was as cosmopolitan as the racegoers," with a mixture of Arabians, Manila ponies, and cavalry mounts from Australia and South Africa. Soon "China ponies," bred in the grasslands of Mongolia, came to dominate the races, which they continued to dominate until after the Japanese invasion of Manchuria in 1931 (Moss 34). Hemingway attended races at Happy Valley several times during his 1941 visit to Hong Kong (Moreira 38).

120:21 Perversion's dull and old fashioned: Extending the horse racing motif, after this comment in the manuscript Marita squeezes David's hand and smiles with pride as the owner of a horse would in seeing the horse "start to make his move at the three-quarter pole" *(3.21.33)*.

David's use of the word *perversion* here—like Marita's ridiculous and dishonest dismissal of lesbian sexuality as "only something girls do because they have nothing better" (120:32)—seems to single out and pathologize same-sex female desire, yet it reveals more about David than it does about Catherine. This scene recalls Phil's use of the same word in Hemingway's closely related short story "The Sea Change," again to describe lesbian sexuality. There, Phil's partner replies, "I'd like it better if you didn't use words like that. . . . There's no necessity to use words like that." When Phil asks, "What do you want me to call it?" his partner replies, "You don't have to call it. You don't have to put any name on it," wisely adding, "We're made up of all sorts of things. You've known that. You've used it well enough." To help Phil understand, she asks him, "You don't think things we've had and done should make any difference in understanding?" (*CSS* 304). This conversation, which Hemingway first published in 1931, could be inserted almost seamlessly into this moment in *The Garden of Eden*, except that at this moment Catherine is much less sure of herself than is Phil's partner in "The Sea Change." What David has had and done with Catherine—specifically playing the role of her "girl" in bed while Catherine was also a "girl" (see 85:30)—does help him to understand, but it also contributes to a jealousy and sense of betrayal that makes Catherine's report all too difficult for him to hear. The word *perversion* is used to shut down a conversation about Catherine doing with Marita what she has already done with him. Understandably, he doesn't want to hear about it.

In the manuscript, Marita will later claim that her lovemaking with David, in which she is his "boy and a girl both at the same time" *(3.45.5)*, is "not perversion. It's variety." But such pronouncements reveal through negation that Hemingway does associate fetishistic desire with "perversion." Otherwise, there would be no need to deny it. Similarly, in a chapter deleted from the *Islands in the Stream* manuscript, Thomas Hudson thinks he is "a long way past any thought of what were perversions and what were not," but the word triggers an extended memory of his tonsorial and gender-swapping adventures with his first wife in Switzerland that mirrors the experiments of the Bournes and the Sheldons (JFK Item 112). It helps to see such moments of censoriousness as part of a larger pattern, structured and maintained by disavowal, of conflicting attitudes toward social taboos. The Bournes' need for sexual desire to be transgressive leads to a fundamental tension and contradiction: social taboos are both broken—and in more progressive moments dissolved—yet, in order to be broken they are more often reified and associated with terms like *vice* and *sin* (see [5:22] 1.1.3).

120:27 Heiress: Heiress is a prophetic nickname for David to give Marita, since Catherine later plans for Marita to "inherit" David (145:1). The pet name plays upon Marita's wealth and recalls Pauline Hemingway's status as an heiress to the Pfeiffer fortune. But Hemingway also occasionally used this pet name for Mary Hemingway, and he used it as well for his African "fiancée" from his 1953–54 safari, Debba.[3] Given the linguistic nature of fetishistic associations, it is probably significant that it chimes with "hair."[4]

120:29 **Highness:** See 90:19 and *(162:4) 3.27.9*.

121:2 **Steeplechase Park:** Following fast on a number of horse racing references (see 120:19 and 120:21), the allusion to Steeplechase Park is a good joke. Steeplechase Park was an amusement park at Coney Island that included a mechanical horse race which gave the park its name. In 1927, Hemingway counted among his friends Eddy Tilyou, owner of Steeplechase Park (*Letters 3* 337).

121:3 **in a plane:** David is here drawing less upon his own experience of flight than he is satirizing Golden Age of Flight rhetoric about flying.

121:34 **Would you like me to go away?:** In the manuscript, Marita goes a bit further. She thinks she *should* go away. David asks her to stay *(3.21.37)*. Marita's sleeping with Catherine oddly brings David closer to Marita.

122:4 **caviar. . . . "Bollinger Brut 1915":** Champagne and caviar, of course, signify Marita's and Catherine's wealth and indulgence in sensual pleasures, but perhaps more so than might immediately be obvious. As Hemingway knew, before 1926 caviar was not considered a summer food on the Riviera because it would spoil too quickly on the long train ride from the Caspian Sea. In 1926, however, a savvy importer hit upon the idea of flying in caviar, and thanks to Gerald Murphy, Hemingway was among the first beneficiaries. Determined to be among the first to enjoy summer caviar on the Riviera, Murphy welcomed Ernest to the Côte d'Azur that summer by throwing the Hemingways a "caviar and champagne party" at the casino in Juan-les-Pins (Vaill 4). In the *Eden* manuscript, however, the caviar comes not by air but directly by wagon-lit from the celebrated Parisian seafood restaurant Maison Prunier, which distributed seafood to many of the finest hotels in Europe *(3.21.38)*. In 1927, Prunier's was famous for being the only restaurant in western Europe to receive their caviar within twenty-four hours of production. The proprietor, Émile Alfred Prunier, was famed as "the world's greatest expert on sea-food" and as "the Caviar King" (Prunier 157).[5] The fact that the caviar is "large" and "gray" (122:8) suggests that it is beluga, the most expensive kind, and probably from the Caspian Sea. It of course also fits into the novel's egg symbolism (see 4:9).

The case of Bollinger Brut 1915 is quite a luxury as well. A good vintage champagne will continue to improve with age for twenty years or more, and Bollinger Brut 1915 continued to appear on the menu at Prunier's at least as late as 1939 and may well have still been available when Hemingway visited Prunier's upon the liberation of Paris in 1944. The 1915 vintage is particularly noteworthy because, while the weather had been good, the working-age men of Champagne were busy fighting WWI, and the harvesting, winemaking, and bottling all had to be done, often at night to avoid enemy fire, by women, children, and old men. During the war, champagne became "a symbol of France's determination to survive" (Kladstrup 188).

(122:17) 3.21.39 **young writers . . . dejection slips . . . She's a certified book reader:** In the manuscript, Catherine and Marita promise to take care of David, and Marita plans to "study his needs." Catherine is bored by stories of "poor young writers" locked in their garrets moping over their "dejection slips." Catherine says Marita is a "certified book reader," so David ought to write all the better now. But it could hardly be said that Catherine is anything other than a "certified book reader" herself. During the summer she has read Proust's *Remembrance of Things Past,* Mann's *Buddenbrooks,* and Hudson's *Far Away and Long Ago* (see *[76:14] 3.16.11);* it's a wonder we don't see her more often curled up with a good book.

(122:17) 422.4 3.21.42 **In the night she woke once:** Page 42 in chapter 21 of book 3 in the manuscript is sliced in half with scissors, and the other half appears, along with a following page, among the discards from the manuscript. In the discarded portion, Catherine wakes during the night and runs her fingers through David's hair. Catherine first wants David to "teach" her; then she wants to "teach" him something. Whatever David does is unclear, but Catherine wants him to do it to Marita too. Afterwards, David "said nothing and was more alone than he had ever been." He finds it difficult to get back to sleep. This is why he has only slept "about two hours" when daylight awakens him at the beginning of the next chapter (123:1).

In the manuscript, directly after the part of the text he discarded, Hemingway writes, "Later when he wrote the narrative, [David] destroyed the part about what happened and what was said when Catherine woke" during the night *(3.21.43).* Hemingway tells us that David later destroys many other things, but this was the first. And this destruction only brings momentary relief; on the following day, the words she had used and the request she had made are still etched in his mind.

As I have argued in an essay devoted to the novel's contrast between creativity and destruction, it is noteworthy that David destroys part of the honeymoon narrative long before Catherine destroys David's clippings and African stories. This is not to suggest an equivalency, moral or otherwise, between the two acts, "but David's own act of destruction—the last moment in the manuscript that mentions him working on the honeymoon narrative—prefigures and colors Catherine's act" ("Who Is" 102). Within the novel's dialectic between creation and destruction (see 5:27), Catherine can too easily be equated with the destroyer and David with the creator, when in fact both in different measures partake of each. Moreover, this attempt to erase a memory is a tangible and unsettling moment of denial for a writer who struggles to tell the truth and who tells himself, "you must never leave out anything because you are ashamed of it or because no one would understand" *(3.29.10)*, and who later berates himself, "you cheap denier. . . . How do you expect to write the way you must write now if you deny like that. . . . You have to think truly how things were and not change them and not deny nor even ameliorate and above all you must not forget. Forgetting is the worst denial" [see *(168:3) 3.29.19]*. Perhaps the second worst form of denial is self-conscious expurgation in an attempt to forget. (102)

That Hemingway himself sliced this page of his manuscript in half and discarded material here makes David's act all the more poignant.

NOTES

1. For a consideration of Hemingway's lifelong penchant for carrying such talismans to ward off anxiety, depression, and loss, see *HF* 146.

2. For a consideration of Catherine's relation to psychosis, see *HF* 205–7.

3. See *HIW* 218, 220; *SL* 826; and letter from Hemingway to Harvey Breit 11 Mar. 1955 (JFK). See also an undated 1954 letter to Marlene Dietrich (JFK).

4. For the linguistic nature of fetishistic associations, see Lacan and Granoff. See also *HF* 110–18.

5. See also "Emile Prunier, of Restaurant Fame, Is Dead." This article notes that Prunier's was "one of the largest exporters of Russian caviar to all parts of the world." Prunier was famed for his expertise in transportation and refrigeration, and his methods were recommended in such refrigeration trade journals as the *Revue générale du froid*. Prunier's is mentioned several times in the *Eden* manuscript, and it is where Hemingway dined with F. Scott Fitzgerald before the infamous 1929 boxing match between Ernest and Morley Callaghan.

CHAPTER 14 (MSS. CHAPTER 22)

123:10 **attacking each thing that for years he had put off facing:** In the manuscript, the previous chapter ends with David destroying part of the honeymoon narrative that he does not want to face. Now in his Africa story, David attacks "each thing that for years he had put off facing." This can be no coincidence; confronting, exploring, and rewriting his past becomes a way of dealing with his present.

123:13 **playing chess . . . in the garden:** Marita is beating Catherine, and not only at chess, for she is playing winning moves in a competition for David. In the manuscript, Marita asks if Catherine minds that she's truly in love with David. Catherine does not. She doesn't know why, but she does not *(3.22.6)*. See 115:6.

124:7 **wife of the day:** We can too easily overlook the speed with which relationships are developing. David and Catherine have known Marita for only three days, and Marita is already David's "wife of the day."

126:3 **Wouldn't you like to take a nap?** In the manuscript, David initially resists the idea of sleeping with Marita. He would like to, but he thinks that there was "enough remorse around yesterday to last for a long time," and he isn't sure that he can ever make love with Marita without remorse *(3.22.11)*. Marita thinks Catherine wouldn't mind, but David discounts what Catherine has said to them both because he thinks she isn't in her right mind. He teases Marita about her blushing, and she tells him that all that morning, while he was working, she was pretending she was his wife.

David goes to check on Catherine, taking her temperature and pulse again. She tells him not to worry and to "do what I asked you to" *(3.22.14)*. After watching Catherine drift back to sleep again, David returns to Marita and proposes that they take a nap together.

126:12 **But I can't do the other:** In the manuscript, Marita tells David that she's never made love with a man before, and this, in addition to the trouble it could cause, is part of why she "can't do the other." But she's been married, David objects (see 100:11). Yes, Marita admits, but the marriage "could have been annulled" *(3.22.21)*. She has been with girls, but not men.

One wonders why Hemingway bothered to give Marita a past marriage if he wants to insist on her virginity—which may explain Jenks's omission of both details. Later, in three passages from the manuscript (two of which were deleted), we are told that she has only loved one man before David—not her husband but her brother, and he had loved her (see *[162:4] 422.4 3.27.8, [232:2] 422 3.42.22,* and *[247:24] 3.46.21*). This not only plays into Hemingway's fascination with sibling romance (see 6:6), it suggests that Marita may have entered into a celibate marriage as a sort of replacement for her relationship with her dead brother, with whom sex would have been taboo. That Marita's brother was a WWI pilot who died in the war (see *[162:4] 422.4 3.27.8*) further suggests that David, a former war pilot, is a replacement of another sort for the same long-lost object.

127:6 **Things will turn out or they won't:** In the manuscript, David is the first to say this *(3.22.25)*. He then dismisses it as a "moronic" banality. When Marita says it here, she is gently teasing David. Once Marita leaves, David wishes the bar mirror had arrived so he could see his "bloody stupid face." He thinks he couldn't say such stupid things if he could see himself.

127:30 **And I love you:** This sentence has been added by the Scribner's editor, Tom Jenks. It is consistent with what David has just experienced, since David now loves "Catherine *too*" (127:23; my emphasis), but the sentence does not appear here in the manuscript. Instead the chapter in the manuscript ends with Catherine returning, refreshed from her sleep and promising to see about the mirror in the morning. David tells her that in the morning he'll be at work. In adding this sentence, Jenks highlights David's growing love for Marita as the end of the chapter's truly significant development.

CHAPTER 15 (MSS. CHAPTER 23)

128:9 **broken volcanic desert . . . dry gray lakes . . . distant blue of the escarpment:** Scattered as they are across several pages, the landscape details of the trek David's father makes across the "broken volcanic desert" (128:9) and dry gray lakes (128:10), to the crusted slime along an alkali lake (138:14), and on to where a stream dissipates into a thinning grayish-pinkish fan in the desert beneath a tongue of land reaching out from the escarpment *(422.4 3.24.2)* are neither imaginary nor haphazard. They are precise, and they "sketch an almost straight line across southern Kenya from near Machakos, southwest to the southern tip of Lake Magadi, and on to the Ewaso Ng'iro River and what today is the Shompole Conservancy beneath the Nguruman escarpment" (Eby, "In the Year" 12).[1]

This line mirrors the route described by Edgar Beecher Bronson in his account of his 1908 safari, *In Closed Territory*. Bronson, a West Texas rancher and big game hunter. . . . whom Hemingway (inveterate reader of Africana) surely read, claims that "most of the country [he] traversed"—this "lava-strewn plain . . . absolutely molten with heat"—"still remain[ed] unmapped" (x). With a very few exceptions, "it had never before been entered by white men save by the Anglo-German Boundary Commission, whose work of locating and marking the boundary line between British and German East Africa had been finished roughly four years earlier . . ." (6). In fact, whites were forbidden to enter this "Closed Territory" except by rare special permit (ix). So David's father, traveling in 1905, would have been among the very first whites to cross this hellscape Edenically untouched by Western hands.

Of course, Hemingway, who hunted near Kenya's alkali Lake Magadi, would have been relying far less on Bronson than on his own intimate knowledge of the land. In September and October 1953, Ernest and Mary Hemingway stayed at Denis Zaphiro's "Fig Tree camp beyond Magadi," high on a bank above where the clear Oleibortoto stream joins the muddy Ewaso Ngiro River (*UK* 206), and this is where David Bourne's father . . . rests beneath the fig trees (139:6).[2] The novel describes air foul with the smell of baboon feces and rotting figs, and Hemingway recalls having observed near the camp "the tops of the fig trees along the creek loaded as though these trees bore fruit of baboons rather than figs" (*BL* 466).

Mary Hemingway found the spot lovely and described it as "heaven on earth."[3] On January 21, 1954, two days before the first of their two famous African plane crashes, Ernest and Mary Hemingway flew at low altitude in a Cessna over much of the route taken in the novel by David Bourne's father.[4] This would have given Hemingway a God's eye view of the story's terrain. (Eby, "In the Year" 12)

The details of this landscape matter because they place David's father in Kenya's Great Rift Valley, three hundred miles away from the nearest action of the Maji Maji Rebellion in what was then southern German East Africa. This and other details of the story David writes suggest that his father is participating not in the Maji Maji conflict but in a "punitive raid" in response to the Nandi Resistance of 1905, which was in British East Africa (see 147:13 and 157:5).[5]

128:11 **weight of the heavy double-barreled rifle:** In the later story of the elephant hunt, David's father carries a double-barreled .450 (198:23), and this is probably the same gun. The .450 Nitro Express was the classic big-game "stopper" for dangerous charging animals. Legendary elephant hunters Arthur Neumann, Walter Bell, Chauncey H. Stigand, and Pondoro Taylor all carried .450s at various times, as did Hemingway's friends, the "white hunters" Bror von Blixen-Finecke and Philip Percival.[6] For a story set in 1905 (157:6), the choice of a .450 is important for understanding the weight of the gun.

The invention of the smokeless cordite .450 Nitro Express cartridge in 1898 (and the .450 No. 2 Nitro Express in 1903) revolutionized the double-barrel rifle, generating as much muzzle energy as older, mammoth breach-loading black-powder elephant guns, but in a much lighter rifle. As a double-barreled rifle, the gun carried by David's father would have been heavy—probably in the range of eleven to thirteen pounds—but as a .450, it would have been significantly lighter than the double-barreled black-powder guns of the early 1890s (Caswell 18). (On his 1953–54 safari, Hemingway carried a .577 Westley Richards Double that weighed a hefty sixteen pounds.[7] The weight of this heavier gun may have been on his mind as he wrote these lines.)

128:12 **pebble in his mouth:** An old trick to produce saliva and stave off thirst.

128:16 **three hours too late:** A deleted line in the manuscript tells us that the crossing should have been accomplished in the darkness (3.23.2).

129:1 **Kamba servant and brother:** The manuscript adds that the porters are also Kamba (3.23.2bis). Since the trek begins near Machakos (see 128:9), in western Ukambani, the traditional home of the Kamba people, this is unsurprising. Yet Hemingway's interest in Kamba identity goes much deeper.

Like David's father, Hemingway during his 1953–54 safari referred to his Kamba gunbearer, Ngui, as his "blood brother," and he considered himself an honorary member of the tribe. While on safari, his desire for a cross-racial identification was so strong that he dyed his clothes rusty Maasai ochre, shaved his head like a Masai girl, engaged in an elaborate flirtation with his Kamba "fiancée," Debba, and fantasized about having a "black skin like any other Kamba" (*UK* 349, 320). In *Under Kilimanjaro,* he writes: "For a long time I had identified myself with the Wakamba and now had passed over the last important barrier so that the identification was complete" (130). In her memoir, *How It Was,* Mary Hemingway remembers, "For days he had been talking about becoming 'blood brothers' with his Wakamba friends among our servants." Returning to camp one evening, she was greeted by a surprise: 'We got home before six. Papa had started ceremonies for face-cutting and ear-piercing'" (391). More than eighteen months after leaving Africa, as he worked on what would eventually be published, posthumously, as *Under Kilimanjaro,* Hemingway's urge to identify with the Kamba remained so strong that Mary had to dissuade him from piercing his ears with a rather remarkable note:

Honey Papa—

For the well-being of both of us, I ask you please to reconsider having your ears pierced. The only good that can come from it would be the momentary sensation you get at the time of the pricking, a sensation you've already had from the taking of blood for tests. But it could cause a variety of trouble, primarily because it would be flouting the mores of western civilization. I do not defend the modern idea that men, except for a few sailors, rakish fellows, do not wear earrings—but I think we should recognize that it exists.

Everything you do sooner or later gets into print, and I feel truly that your wearing earrings or having your ears pierced will have a deleterious effect on your reputation both as a writer and as a man. If you were a chorus boy, it wouldn't make any difference. But you are an important man with a reputation for seeing reality and the truth more clearly than any other writer of your time. The fiction that having your ears pierced will make you a Kamba is an evasion of the reality, which is that you are not and never can be anything but an honorary Kamba, and it is out of harmony with your best character which is that of a wise, thoughtful, realistic adult white American male.

I know that you are impassioned about Africa and the Africans, writing about them, and allured by the mystery and excitement of becoming one of them. And you know that I love the fun of make-believe as much as you do. But the attempt to convert fantasy into actuality can only result, I think, in distortion and failure. There are other ways of proving brotherhood between you and the Kamba. I do hope you will find them, my Big Sweetheart—

Mary

(qtd in *HF* 178–9)[8]

129:2 **guilt and knowledge of the delay:** See 94:4.

129:9 **It was not him, but as he wrote it was:** In other words, David's story is not autobiographical, in the sense that he himself had not been with his father on this trek; yet in his writing process, David enters so deeply into the story that it becomes a complex sort of autobiographical experience. As David writes, he has to "think what his father would have thought" (146:10), and knowing "what his father did and how he felt . . . he *became* his father" (147:2; my emphasis). As David enters the story, the story enters David (as it will enter the reader). He can explore, write, and rewrite his relationship with his father, and in doing so, he can change *himself* (see 93:2, 111:16, and *[140:3] 3.24.5*).

129:11 **what they found when they should reach the escarpment:** This is ominous, but the phrasing is a bit misleading. David's father and the porters don't find anything at the base of the escarpment. Rather, they climb nearly four thousand feet up the Nguruman Escarpment to the "high wooded and parklike country" above (147:14); they then travel two days through this new high country and still have another day and a night to trek before reaching their destination (147:13). "What they find there" is initially unclear, but it is so "horrible," so "bestial" (157:25), that when Catherine reads the story, she calls David "a monster" (158:4) for writing it and rips the cahier almost in two. It is only many chapters later that we learn, and then only in passing, that the story involves a "massacre in [a] crater" and what Catherine calls the "heartlessness" of David's father (223:3). (For more on the massacre, see 147:13, 157:5, and 157:23.)

130:5 **Yesterday you ate it with champagne. Today with beer:** After "living" in his African story, David craves beer, and having it with caviar speaks to his position between worlds. It also suggests a split in his identity between the luxurious world of the Riviera and his roots in the unforgiving wilderness.

130:7 **bicyclette:** This is Jenks's substitution. In the manuscript, Hemingway uses the more common French word *velo* (3.23.4). In the same way, Jenks substitutes *tires* (131:2) for the French word used in the manuscript, *pneus* (3.23.6). Jenks also corrects the manuscript's franglais "*ne blaguer pas*" (3.23.6) to the proper phrase for "you're joking!": "*Sans blague*" (131:8).

130:18 **Do you feel any good effect?:** David is playfully flirting with Madame, alluding to caviar's supposed effects as an aphrodisiac. See 4:9.

131:20 **red-topped kilometer marker:** The fact that the kilometer marker has a red top means that David is on a national (red) road, as opposed to a departmental

CHAPTER 15 *(MSS. CHAPTER 23)* · 207

(yellow) road or a municipal (white) road. This tells us that David is on the N7, which between 1904 and 1937 hugged the coast of the Estérel, along the Corniche d'Or, between La Napoule and Saint-Raphaël. (After 1937, the N7 returned to an older interior route over the Estérel Massif.) The 1931 Baedeker describes the Corniche d'Or as rivaling the Grande Corniche, between Nice and Menton, in scenic beauty, "affording glorious and ever-changing views of the deep-blue sea and the red porphyry cliffs of the Estérel" (271). If David begins at the hotel (see 75:2), his climb along the N7, around the headland, past two kilometer markers, and down to the sea suggests that he goes to one of several coves between the Pointe des Deux Frères and the Pointe de l'Esquillon.

131:33 **dark red rocks:** In these red rocks, Peters and Stoneback find an allusion to T. S. Eliot's *Waste Land* ("Come in under the shadow of this red rock") and the poem's concerns with fertility and Dantean imagery.[9] It should, however, be noted that the entire length of the Massif de l'Estérel, between Saint-Raphaël and La Napoule, is famously composed of red porphyry rock. The volcanic origin of this rock accounts for the innumerable coves along this rugged coast.

132:11 **Nothing with either of those two can end well and neither can you now. . . . But do not start blaming:** Critics have had much to say about the passage that follows this in the manuscript:

> If you live by the senses you will die by them and if you live by your invention and your head you will die by that too. All that is left entire in you is your ability to write and that gets better. You would think it would be destroyed. By everything you have been taught it should. But so far, as you corrupt or change that grows and strengthens. It should not but it has. Is it possible that the only creation that is a moral act is pro-creation and that is why all other kinds are suspect. It could be but it seems too simple and too much like a justifying. All you know is that you have written better, clearer and *plus net,* he used the French phrase in thinking, as you have deteriorated morally. But that could be temporary or it could be a building up and strengthening by what good there is trying to build up against the destruction. *(3.23.9)*

Mark Spilka reads this passage as a "self-revelation from Hemingway: that his emotional dependency on his wives and mistresses, his androgynous complicity with their several obsessions with hair, skin, dress, gender, and lesbian attachments . . . makes for his strength as a creative writer" (156). Comley and Scholes similarly read it to suggest that David's "sexual transgressions" lead to his creative breakthroughs (283). Rose Marie Burwell, building on the passage's link between creation and procreation (see 27:16), sees in the passage David's "recognition that his [literary] progeny needs both masculine and feminine origins" (113). And in an essay on the novel's dialectic between creation and destruction, I have argued that the passage suggests that "the relation between creation and destruction is clearly not a zero-sum game." As with the felix culpa in Eden, creation and destruction are mutually dependent: "In different ways and to very different degrees, Catherine and David are both creators and destroyers, and in this—as in so many other respects—they are mirror images of one another" ("Who Is Destructive" 104).

For both Hemingway and David, it is worth asking whether it is the courageous self-exploration and bold honesty of the honeymoon narrative or the defensive displacement and (comparatively) masculine re-entrenchment of the African stories that drives creativity. An answer, I would argue, is baked into the very form of the novel, in which the honeymoon narrative continues metatextually (it is, after all, the story we are reading) long after it is abandoned by David so he can devote himself to his African stories. While it is more satisfying to believe that sexual exploration and self-honesty alone liberate creativity, the novel and this passage seem to suggest that it is the productive/destructive tension between liberatory exploration and defensive re-entrenchment that drives creativity for both David and Hemingway.

133:11 **looked into the mirror . . . I do not know if I'd have a drink with you or not:** See 43:17.

133:13 **Éclaireur de Nice:** *L'Éclaireur de Nice et du Sud-Est* (1888–1944) was the major regional newspaper for the Riviera. In the manuscript, David reads this paper on at least three occasions. See 58:10 and *(183:19) 3.32.17.*

(134:5) 3.23.13 **Suze:** In the manuscript, David asks Catherine what she drank at the café when she was with Jean. She can't remember its name, but it tasted "quite awful," like gall and wormwood, and it had "something called Suze on it." An aperitif made with gentian roots macerated in alcohol, Suze "is the best known of the gentian liqueurs; it stimulates the appetite, and is served as a long drink with ice cubes and soda" (Dominé 405). Gall and wormwood is, of course, the biblical flavor of grief, regret, and God's punishment (see 69:26).

134:6 **white sharkskin dress:** Earlier in the novel, Catherine wears a "white sharkskin outfit" that David, in the manuscript, thinks of as her "pillar of salt suit" (see 65:26). It is not clear if this is the same outfit, now on Marita, or a different dress. Following directly the reference to gall and wormwood (see note above), it again carries an allusion to divine punishment.

134:31 **Now be a good girl:** In the manuscript, Catherine answers that's she's "sick of being a girl." It's trying to be a girl that got her into all this "terrible changing back and forth" *(3.23.18)*. David encourages her to decide what she is so they can move on to lunch. She repeats her desire for Marita to be both David's girl and her girl.

136:4 how dangerously the brakes were working. . . . "Had I ought to get a new one?" In the novel's frequent references to the bad brakes of the Isotta, Hemingway may have been laying the groundwork for a conclusion that he never wrote (see *[54:23] 3.11.4*). The bad brakes also function as a metaphor for the runaway developments in the lives of the Bournes.

Marita's ridiculous response, "Had I ought to get a new one?" recalls the mythic spending of Oklahoma oil Indians (see 111:9), which explains why in the manuscript, David tells Catherine and Marita how Oklahoma oil Indians would cut mudflaps off Cadillacs instead of washing them *(3.23.23)*. It should be remembered that Marita's Isotta Fraschini is an extremely expensive car (see 89:18).

(136:13) 3.23.23 **beautiful Oklahoma oil Indian. . . . Kanaka. . . . Somali:** In the manuscript, in response to David's comment about Oklahoma oil Indians (see note above), Catherine claims that David once almost married a "beautiful Oklahoma oil Indian." She was lighter-skinned than Catherine, too, David adds. For many Hemingway readers, the beautiful Native American lover will recall Nick Adams's boyhood love, Prudy or Trudy Boulton (or the Prudence Boulton in Hemingway's life), but as the passage proceeds it becomes obvious that the significance of Native Americanness here has little to do with any individual and much more to do with a sort of exoticized and fetishized racial otherness that is oddly and endlessly interchangeable (see *[19:1] 1.2.1*). David and Catherine urge Marita to get as dark as them, and Catherine brags that she herself used to be Kanaka but is now "working to be Somali."

Catherine wants to know if what she's heard is true, "that Somali women have ways of holding a man so he can never leave them." And does it work on white men as well as Somali men? David says that "it's happened that way." Did it ever happen to David? "A little," he admits. Catherine asks how they do it. "They treat them like they know Somali men really like to be treated," David says, "and the men think they're the first person this ever happened to." He then clarifies: they treat the Somali men not how the men are supposed to be, "but how they are." Catherine asks, are the Somali men like you? "Yes, maybe," answers David.

(136:13) 3.23.25bis **Lutherans and Calvinists and St. Paul:** In the manuscript, Catherine asks if there's anything wrong with the men in Somalia (see note above), and David replies, "No more than anywhere else." Well, Catherine asks, if David is like Somali men, and there's nothing wrong with Somali men, why doesn't he "quit worrying and thinking in terms of Lutherans and Calvinists and St. Paul"—traditions which aren't his own, anyway? It's an important question with broad implications. If David comes from an Africa that is imagined as outside of the Judeo-Christian tradition

that underwrites the central Edenic metaphor of the novel—with all of its attendant submetaphors: devils, hell, *Sodome et Gomorrhe,* pillars of salt, and so on—what does he have to do with a tradition that reads any deviation from an imaginary idealized heteronormativity as a sin against God? And why on earth would any nonharmful exchange of pleasure between consenting adults be construed as a sin?

David sees Catherine's point and promises to mend his ways. Yet as the novel progresses, he finds it difficult to remain true to his word—in fact, Catherine and Marita both realize now that David's worrying has only stopped for the moment—and it's worth considering why. The matter for David is not simply, or even primarily, one of faith, justice, or the intellect. It is too heavily swayed by the structure, for David, of unconscious pleasure. As we have seen (see *[5:22] 1.1.3),* the sense of transgression, of sin (however unjustified), is essential to fetishistic pleasure. It can be dismissed rationally, but it wells up again from the unconscious.

(136:13) 3.23.26bis: **just ran into Somali women. . . . you aren't ruined:** Continuing the conversation in the manuscript, Catherine tells David that in herself and Marita he's just run into some Somali women. One Somali woman is enough to "ruin" a man, David says. Well, he's run into two, Catherine replies, and he isn't "ruined."

This passage recalls an exchange between Hemingway and the Informer in *Under Kilimanjaro.* The Masai Informer complains to Hemingway that he has been "ruined" by his Somali wife. When asked how a Somali woman ruins a man, he answers, "She takes away everything. She even takes away your manhood. She is not happy until she has taken that." Do Somali women always do this? Hemingway asks. "Always, brother," replies the Informer. "And men are enslaved by it. . . . Brother, never take a Somali woman as a wife" (145). The Informer, of course, is a ridiculous and unreliable character, but what he says plays directly into Hemingway's psychosexual fantasies about women who "ruin" their men (see 5:27).

136:28 **head that was sleek as a seal:** The "wet seal," a slicked-down Eton crop, was a popular hairstyle of the mid-1920s (Turudich 173). Josephine Baker, who popularized the style, marketed her own product, Bakerfix, for slicking down the hair. But by November 1927, newspapers were announcing that the vogue for "the coiffure resembling that of a sleek wet seal is past" ("Curls and Waves").

137:14 **Wouldn't it be wonderful if I wasn't crazy?:** We might wonder why Hemingway presents Catherine as "crazy." After all, it might be argued, her liberation from a Pauline tradition that condemns as immoral the nonharmful exchange of pleasure between consenting adults is far more rational than David's remorse (see *[136:13] 3.23.25bis).* Critics have suggested that, in the creation of Catherine, Hemingway drew on the instability of Zelda Fitzgerald (see 24:12), but while this may be so, the "craziness" of Catherine Bourne, like the "craziness" of Catherine Barkley in *A Farewell*

CHAPTER 15 *(MSS. CHAPTER 23)* · 211

to Arms, owes more to her ties to the split-off other-gendered half of Hemingway's ego, which he also called "Catherine" (see 17:23). As I have argued elsewhere, it is not simply that Hemingway considered this alter ego to be a "crazy" symptom, but rather that this half of his riven ego—considered in isolation—entertains a different relation to reality than the two halves of the ego considered together. Whereas the fetishist "disavows reality, balancing two contrary attitudes about sexual difference in a riven ego, this single split-off feminine half of the . . . ego holds an attitude that *in isolation* is psychotic. Instead of arriving at an illusory compromise to the contrary demands of delusion and reality, it merely repudiates reality in deference to the delusion" (*HF* 205). This, in part, accounts for the role of hallucination in the novel (see 17:14 and 68:3).

137:18 We're pretty well out, Devil: Catherine's drive to swim out, or swim straight down until she and David "can just make it up," speaks to her passion for dangerous extremes and risky self-exploration. It may also have been meant as foreshadowing. In the provisional ending Hemingway wrote for the novel in May 1958—written probably a month-and-a-half before he wrote the present chapter—death by water is the implied fate for his characters (see appendix B).

NOTES

1. In 1953, Hemingway stayed at Philip Percival's Kitanga Farm in the Machakos District, on the edge of the broken desert, and the place mattered enough in his imaginary universe for him to name one of his dogs Machakos (*SL* 890).
2. In "The Christmas Gift," Hemingway describes the camp as being "on a small stream of clear water which comes down out of the escarpment," close to Lake Magadi (*BL* 427). Mary Hemingway, however, gives us a more precise location of the camp in her East Africa Journal.
3. See Mary Hemingway's East Africa Journal for 24 September 1953, 94 (JFK).
4. See Ernest Hemingway's "The Christmas Gift" (*BL* 427–28) and Mary Hemingway's East Africa Journal (248).
5. For an extended consideration of this and its implications for the novel's treatment of race and settler colonialism, see Eby, "In the Year of the Maji Maji."
6. Before 1898, Neumann carried a single-barreled .450 Black Powder Express—although he preferred his lighter .303; he later acquired a .450 Nitro Express. Bell shot a double-barreled .450/.400. See Bell 6. For Percival and Blixen, see Hemingway's "Notes on Dangerous Game: The Third Tanganyika Letter," *BL* 168. Hemingway owned a .577 Nitro Express Double and rented a .470 Nitro Express Double for his 1933–34 safari, but he did not own a .450. See Calabi et al. 105.
7. See Mary Hemingway's East Africa Journal, 5 and 9 Oct. 1953 (JFK).
8. For a further consideration of this theme in *Eden*, see Eby, "In the Year of the Maji Maji."
9. See Peters 27 and Stoneback, "Memorable" 24.

CHAPTER 16 (MSS. CHAPTER 24)

138:14 **white with crusted alkalis:** A passage much later in the manuscript tells us that David's father is crossing Kenya's "Magadi desert" *(3.42.7)*. His path from the "dry grey lakes" to a tongue of land reaching out from the escarpment (see 128:9)—today the site of the Shompole Conservancy—would take him along the salt-encrusted southern shore of Lake Magadi. In Swahili the word *magadi* means "soda." For many years there has been a salt factory on the lake.

139:8 **Baboons had been eating the wild figs:** See 128:9.

139:16 **kongoni:** The word *kongoni* usually refers specifically to Coke's hartebeest, an antelope whose range is confined to southern Kenya and northern Tanzania. This is consistent with the route David's father takes across the Magadi desert (see 128:9).

139:20 **locked the suitcase:** The locked suitcase suggests that David, Bluebeard-like, means to keep these stories, and the parts of himself that they represent, sequestered from Catherine. Yet from Catherine's knowledge of David's story of the locust plague, we should already suspect that she has a key to this suitcase (see *[118:10] 3.21.25*). Indeed, we later learn that this Louis Vuitton case is a present from Catherine and came with two keys, one of which she still has *(3.33.13ii)*. It might be fair to say that Catherine has access to parts of David's psyche that he thinks he has walled off from her.

Hemingway considered Vuitton the "best and most . . . steal proof and smash proof luggage in the world" (*SL* 597–98), and when he discovered two old suitcases full of his thirty-year-old manuscripts at the Ritz Hotel in November 1956 (see 37:27), he promptly went to Louis Vuitton's shop in Paris and splurged on fine new luggage to better protect his treasures (*HIW* 444). Recovering these suitcases full of long-lost manuscripts must have felt for Hemingway like cosmic repayment for the suitcase full of his juvenilia that Hadley famously lost on her way to meet him in Lausanne in December 1922. That such a suitcase contains the manuscripts Catherine will burn and that David will rewrite seems to reimagine the loss Hemingway experienced in 1922 and the restoration he experienced both in the discovery of the Ritz papers and in the subsequent composition of *A Moveable Feast*.

(140:3) 3.24.5 baboon shit . . . eyes ached . . . swelling in his right groin: In the manuscript, as he talks to Marita, David is still partially inhabiting his story. He can still smell baboon shit and rotting figs, his eyes ache, and he feels a swelling in his right groin. As he eats his eggs, he feels dehydrated and misses the sensations of the camp. In very similar terms, Mary Hemingway described Ernest "living in" *The Garden of Eden* as he worked on it. In a July 1958 letter to Bill Horne, she writes: "Papa lives from early morning to lunchtime in a far-away country, in another time, with people who are doing, naturally splendid/exciting/dangerous/compelling living. If unexpected guests who are friends appear suddenly, he makes the journey back to the Finca and now, quickly, but it is a wrench."[1] See also 183:32 and 216:19.

140:19 Can we stop being so polite? . . . Everything was so simple and fine until now: In the manuscript, the line reads, "Can we stop this?" not "Can we stop being so polite?" And Marita adds, "Everything was so simple and fine *last night*," not "until now" (3.24.7; my emphasis). These distinctions are important because, in the manuscript, David interprets her comments to be about "the Somali nonsense" (see [136:13] 3.23.23), not about "I can't David nonsense." The latter phrase is Jenks's addition to the text. Marita wants to know why David is behaving this way, and he gives her a single-word answer: "Working." It must be "terrible," Marita says, to which David answers, "It is. And it's the only thing I give a damn about." This is when Marita says she'll be in her room.

140:28 Poor David. What women do to you: Between the previous line and this line in the manuscript, Marita goes to her room to change her shirt (3.24.9). Part of Marita and David's bickering in the previous lines had involved David's comment that Marita's shirt was too large. Now she returns wearing a "shirt that was very much not too large" (see note below). It is David's excited reaction to seeing her in this shirt, not their bickering, that inspires her comment about what women "do to" David. They discuss the new fashion for a while before she strokes David's head. While the passage in the Scribner's edition produces a David who is the infantilized victim of difficult women, the manuscript produces a very different effect.

(140:29) 3.24.9 It's a polo shirt: In the manuscript, the tight shirt Marita returns wearing (see previous note) is novel enough that it needs to be explained to David. Indeed, Marita seems to be the inventor of the modern women's polo shirt (anticipating the equestrian allusion in the next entry), having cut a shirt down to waist length and shrunk it. Catherine later calls it "one of those shirts heiress invented" (3.30.13). And here Marita, indeed, seems to be fashion-forward.

The original men's polo shirt, with origins at the end of the nineteenth century, was what we would today call an Oxford-cloth button-up shirt with a button-down collar—which is why Brooks Brothers, who pioneered the marketing of these shirts, still calls them "the original polo shirt." It was tennis great René Lacoste, tired of the uncomfortable starched, long-sleeve button-up shirts then worn for tennis, who invented the modern short-sleeved, soft-collared polo shirt of breathable loose-knit piqué cotton and wore it in public for the first time at the US Open championship in 1926. It first appears as a fashion item for women in the summer of 1928 and is first touted for women in *Vogue* in 1929 reports from the Riviera (see 6:3).[2]

(140:29) 3.24.9 **Mazeppa:** In the manuscript, Marita asks David if he has cooled down now from work, saying she should have "walked [him] like a horse instead of being bitchy." This is when she strokes his head (140:29). She supposes the writing process must be "like being horse and rider both.... Or like Mazeppa." Once again, we see Marita thinking of herself as a sort of horse trainer, with David as her horse (see 120:19 and *[247:24] 3.46.5*).

The allusion to Mazeppa is complex. A legend about the youth of the Ukrainian military leader Ivan Mazepa (1639–1709) inspired Lord Byron to write his famous narrative poem "Mazeppa" (1819). In the poem, Mazeppa, is caught in flagrante with a married Polish countess. Taken before the count, he is punished by being strapped naked to a wild horse which is then provoked and set loose. Much of the poem recounts his frenzied ride. For artists in the age of Victor Hugo, the hero was taken to be a symbol of the romantic artist; "the wild horse symbolized his genius" (O'Rourke, "Grace" 21). For Hemingway—who had been working throughout 1958 "like a fiend," as in a "fever," "enslaved" by *The Garden of Eden* (see 216:19)—the analogy must have seemed apt. Byron's poem inspired musical compositions by Liszt and others, romantic paintings by the likes of Géricault, Vernet, and Delacroix, even ballets and stage shows. (Marita also briefly compares David to Prometheus, bound to the rock, waiting for the vultures who would daily eat his liver—an analogy that seems to be governed by the visual similarity between these paintings of the bound Mazeppa and Rubens's famous painting of the bound Prometheus.) In a popular nineteenth-century melodrama, the actress Adah Isaacs Menken, with her "outrageously short-cropped" hair, thrilled and scandalized America and Europe by dressing in flesh-colored tights to portray Mazeppa (Mankowitz 21). In 1863, a reviewer in the *New York Clipper* wrote, "Male actors have no business to play Mazeppa anymore. It is decidedly out of their line since Adah Menken donned the tights, and showed what an actress could do with the part" (Ed James). Many other actresses followed, making productions popular up through the turn of the twentieth century. For the relationship between Marita and David, these aspects of the allusion are richly suggestive.

While Marita is undoubtedly referring to Byron's poem and its artistic progeny, this is not the work that would have been foremost in Hemingway's mind: Evan

Shipman's long poem "Mazeppa." Begun as a surrealist collaboration between two of Hemingway's good friends, Shipman and André Masson (who planned to supply illustrations), the poem took more than a decade for Shipman to complete. In *A Moveable Feast,* Hemingway remembers the horse enthusiast Shipman working on the poem in 1920s Paris (104); in 1932, Shipman sent Hemingway a typescript of the poem (*Letters 5* 275); and in 1936 Shipman finally published the poem in *The New Caravan.* Aside from a half-dozen lines scattered throughout the dream-like poem that align the artist-speaker with Mazeppa, Shipman's work appears to have little to do with Byron's poem and sheds little light on the relationship between Marita and David. It is, however, a tribute to a dear and recently deceased friend. In

Peter Paul Rubens, *Prometheus Bound,* circa 1611, oil and canvas. (Philadelphia Museum of Art. Image from Wikimedia Commons.)

Horace Vernet, *Mazeppa and the Wolves*, 1826, oil on canvas. (Musée Calvet, Avignon. Image from Wikimedia Commons.)

1927, Hemingway had dedicated *Men without Women* to Shipman; Shipman died 24 June 1957.

141:22 **anchors . . . cables:** In the manuscript, the mention of anchors and cables leads Marita to propose that they buy a boat *(3.24.11)*. David jokes that they'll buy a dhow—but first they need to fix the brakes on the Isotta.

141:27 **Names go to the bone:** If "names go to the bone," to the core of identity, we should bear this in mind when we consider Catherine's named alter ego, "Peter," and David's named alter ego, "Catherine." Such names are not a matter of casual role-playing in freewheeling love play; they acknowledge the reality and individuality of the split-off other-gendered half of the ego that is a vital component of fetishistic identity (see 17:23).

In the manuscript, this discussion about names develops from Marita's observation that Isotta is a lovely name for a girl *(3.24.11)*. David suggests that this could be a "private name" between them, something Marita can share only with David so she won't be jealous of Catherine. David then gives her the Swahili nickname Haya, "one who blushes" (142:6). Yet thinking in Swahili leads him to realize that he can't shorten Isotta to Sota, which he tells Marita is "bad." (According to Hemingway's copy of Johnson's *Standard Swahili-English Dictionary, sota* is a verb meaning "to move along on the buttocks, as a person who has lost the use of his legs.") Marita truly wants to change her name to Isotta, but David has misgivings, realizing the name might be the same as Isolde, and he is correct. Isotta is, indeed, a variant of Isolde, along with such variants as Iseult, Yeseult, Isode, Isoude, and Izolda. In the Arthurian legends there are several Isoldes, most importantly Iseult of Ireland, wife of Mark of Cornwall and adulterous lover of Sir Tristan, and Iseult of the White Hands, daughter of Hoel of Brittany, who eventually becomes the wife of Tristan.

Iseult of Ireland heals Tristan of the wounds he received fighting, unbeknownst to her, either her uncle or her fiancé (depending upon the version), which makes her in the grand Hemingway tradition—like Brett Ashley and Catherine Barkley—a nurse figure. (One thinks of Marita's ministrations later to David after Catherine burns his manuscripts.) After having first fled back to Cornwall, Tristan returns to Ireland to seek Iseult's hand for his uncle, Mark of Cornwall. On the ship back to Cornwall, they drink a love potion that Iseult thinks is poison and begin the affair that causes Mark to banish Tristan.

In the most famous version of the story, when Tristan is banished, he marries Iseult of Brittany, daughter of his new host, Hoel of Brittany, because she shares the name of his love, Iseult of Ireland. The marriage, however, is not consummated. Tristan is then wounded and sends for Iseult of Ireland, the world's greatest healer, to cure him; the ship will fly white sails if she comes and black if she will not. On his deathbed, Tristan sends his wife, Iseult of Brittany, to the window to ask if she sees sails, and though she sees white sails, in a fit of jealousy she tells him that she sees black, and Tristan dies. The legend, then, features doubling, splitting, adultery, love triangles, and jealousy. Wagner's opera *Tristan und Isolde* also plays up a vital contrast between a quotidian daylight and a nighttime that enables an illicit love that is more fundamentally real. In other words, there are powerful resonances with the story of the Bournes and Marita.

142:17 **It's *cendre:*** *Cendre* means "ashen," or as Catherine translates it in the manuscript, "*ash blonde*" (3.24.14). The effect on her hair is from "a rinse," so swimming would wash it out, but she'd like to wear it into town first.

142:20 **strange and exalting:** This is a mistranscription. This should be "strange and *exciting*" (3.24.15; my emphasis). In the manuscript, Catherine predicts that Jean will be a "very great hairdresser," and Marita wonders if he can patent his formulas. When Catherine asks David if he worked well that morning, he replies, "Nothing spectacular like Jean." Catherine hopes he isn't "jealous of Jean," which she thinks would be "silly," but given Hemingway's passion for cutting hair (see 77:13), there may indeed be an element of jealousy here.

(143:7) 3.24.21 **splits him in two:** In the manuscript, Catherine is exhausted from the excitement of getting her hair done and goes to sleep after lunch. David goes to Marita's room to ask her if she wants to swim. She wants to stay in her room with David, but she is still sore from making love for the first time with him, so they agree to nap. While David naps beside her, in a long and interesting detour in focalization, Marita thinks about how David is being split in two by his relationship with two women; she thinks about how lovely Catherine is, how crazy Catherine is, how she must replace Catherine, and how they are all beyond the threat of scandal now. She also thinks about how jealous she is of Catherine. She admits to herself that she is still "moved by" Catherine, especially with her latest haircut, even "vain and stupid" and crazy as she was today. She suspects it's like war—"a war without even an enemy.... Just destruction": something "impossible" that you do nonetheless and eventually get used to. She remembers how she first saw Catherine and fell for *her*, and then saw Catherine with David and fell for *them*, but she loved David alone when she first saw him. She couldn't help herself, and now she knows David loves both her and Catherine. She mustn't try to take David from Catherine; she'd lose David if she tried, and David is losing Catherine anyway. Marita realizes she must try to help David through this loss.

(143:19) 3.24.25bis **Does it do anything to you?** In the manuscript, Catherine not only wants to know if David likes her hair this way—he does—she wants to know if it *does anything* to him. In other words, is it the fetishistic trigger that she intends it to be (see 12:13)?

144:4 We could in Africa if I was registered Mohammedan: In the manuscript, Catherine and Marita have already toyed with calling themselves David's "two Somali wives" (see *[136:13] 3.23.23* and *[136:13] 3.23.26bis*). Under the British colonial system in East Africa, marriage was regulated by a patchwork of customary law, Islamic law, Hindu law, and statutory Acts of Parliament, and one could be married under any one of these systems. Polygamy was allowed under both customary and Islamic law, but David is mistaken about the number of wives allowed. Under Sharia law, as practiced by Muslim communities in both Kenya and Somalia, one could marry up to four wives (Philips and Morris 131).

The fantasy of multiple wives could harken back to a time in the early twenties when Ernest and Hadley were visited in Paris by their friends Isabelle Simmons and Janet Phelan. According to Diliberto, "the three women started referring to themselves as 'the harem' and to Ernest as 'the Moslem'" (142). The more immediate inspiration, though, would have been Hemingway's 1953–54 safari, when he entertained fantasies of having two wives, one light and one dark: Mary and Debba. In her African journal, Mary records Ernest's complaint that she "was depriving him of his new wife," though she was, in fact, surprisingly accommodating (1 Dec. 1953).

145:1 **Why does she have to inherit?** Catherine's sense of her fragile mortality is not merely a sign of her deteriorating mental state. In the early pages of the novel, this twenty-one-year-old woman is already uncertain she will live to see her twenty-fifth or thirtieth birthday (see 26:8).

(145:16) 3.24.33 **normal school:** In the manuscript, the chapter continues later that evening with David and Catherine talking in bed. Catherine wants David to know that she was serious about the three-way marriage. David tells her that he understood her, "but women aren't like that. . . . It isn't normal for any woman to want to share with anyone." "Who's normal?" Catherine asks. "What's normal? I never went to normal school to be a teacher and teach normal." The pun behind these lines is fairly obvious, but Hemingway may have been playing upon a passage in a best-selling self-help book that he owned, Louis Bisch's *Be Glad You're Neurotic* (1936). In his chapter "To Be Normal Is Nothing to Brag About," Bisch writes, "There is something almost sinister in the fact that the institutions that train teachers are called Normal Schools. Here the word normal is used with a vengeance!" (29). Doubtlessly, Bisch's book—which contains chapters with titles like "I'm Neurotic Myself and Delighted," "You Hate Yourself. No Wonder!," and "Of Course Your Sex Life Is Far from Satisfactory"—was less the source of Hemingway's critique of the coercive power of sexual ideology than his ownership of it testifies to his prior distaste for this coercive power.[3]

Catherine's critique of the concept of "normalcy," like her critique of "Lutherans and Calvinists and St. Paul," is important and liberatory but difficult for the novel to sustain. Because the sensation of transgression is central to the structure of desire in the novel (see *[5:22] 1.1.3*), the characters repeatedly turn to ways of thinking that depend upon codes—religious, moral, or normative—that can be transgressed (see *[136:13] 3.23.25bis*).

Debra Moddelmog has published an important pedagogical essay on *Eden* that approaches the novel from the perspective of normality studies.

(145:16) 3.24.34 **my credits from Vevey:** In Catherine's manuscript monologue about "normal schools" (see above) she mentions transferring credits from Vevey. Her Swiss education indicates her wealth and privileged upbringing. The association with Vevey, however, may also align Catherine with the young heroines in two tales of failed American romances in Europe: Hemingway's "A Canary for One" and Henry James's *Daisy Miller*. It is also noteworthy that F. Scott Fitzgerald stayed in Vevey in 1930 during Zelda's treatment for schizophrenia at the Prangins Clinic.

(145:16) 3.24.35 **mixed up with other people:** In the manuscript, Catherine insists to David that she means what she says about being co-wives with Marita, but she asks him not to press her further about it "because it gets sad." David protests that he

hates to have their dyadic union "mixed up with other people." He wants to know why they can't be the way they were. He loved "all the ways" Catherine was. (In a discarded fragment that fits here in the manuscript, Catherine says that of all her experiments, making love the way they did at Le Grau-du-Roi is best and always makes her "as excited as the first time" *[422.4 3.24.38]*.) She asks him to love her this way too. David says he does, but, he protests, "there's too many people." In ominous reply, Catherine answers, "There won't always be." Why? David wonders. "Because I turned out wrong," she answers. "Just like a story." See 145:1.

NOTES

1. Mary Hemingway, letter to Bill Horne, 1 July 1958 (JFK).
2. See, for instance, "From Dawn to Dinner Paris Says—" and "A Forecast of the Bathing Mode for Palm Beach." An item called a "polo shirt" was marketed for women's sportswear as early as 1925, but it was a long-waisted, long-sleeved, turtleneck angora sweater, not what we would today call a polo shirt.
3. One should not overstate the progressive spirit of Bisch's book. Bisch argues that for men and women who can't be heterosexual "despite scientific knowledge—the truth—... psychoanalysis is necessary" (139).

CHAPTER 17 (MSS. CHAPTER 25)

(146:1) 422.4 3.25.2 **Your boy as well as your girl:** Among the discarded fragments from the *Eden* manuscript, there are four false starts to this chapter, each several pages long. In the earliest version, David and Marita are lying on the beach, talking. Marita promises to invent "new things" to "hold" David. She can anticipate his needs, she says, because she and David are "just the same." Marita, who has an exciting new haircut that shocks her every time she looks at herself in the mirror, wants to know if David finds it dull having her as both his boy and his girl. He does not. She knew he'd like her haircut, just like she knew he'd like her polo shirts. She asks him if the next time he goes to Jean's he'll go with her to get his hair cut just like hers. "Sure," David says. Marita wants to find out if the sea will bleach her hair as light as Catherine's.

While it must be remembered that this is a discarded passage that must be read as if under erasure, its implications are important. The fetishistic accoutrements of Marita's desire—a boy/girl identity, periodic self-reinvention, dissociation in the mirror, exciting shirts and haircuts, hair bleaching, identical haircuts with David, and a twin-like "sameness" between lovers—are virtually identical with those we already associate with Catherine. In other words, these are not merely the wild desires of "crazy" Catherine. These are also David's (and Hemingway's) desires. For even if Marita's behavior is dismissed as mere copycatting (instead of being recognized as yet another manifestation of Hemingway's fantasies), we must acknowledge that she is copying Catherine *to win David*. She's known David for a little less than a week, but she already knows what he likes.

(146:1) 422.4 3.25.1ii **by the time the remorse had come he was in the high country:** In the second false start to the chapter among the *Eden* discards (see note above), David works on his African story, and the remorse he feels over what transpired the previous evening becomes "part of what happened before the story started and what he knew was coming." This line points to the complex interrelationship between David's honeymoon present and fictionalized African past.

146:13 **His father had dealt so lightly with evil . . . denying its importance:** K. J. Peters has suggested that, "Since the first corruption at le Grau-du-Roi, David, like his father, has denied the importance, and more specifically the significance, of sin and yet never denied the sin itself. And, like his father, who defrauded himself [210:8], David allows his own betrayal." Writing of David's ability at the end of the novel to rewrite the works Catherine has burned, Peters argues, "It is David's sin which improves his literary insight and gives him a clearer, not so flattering perception of himself. David's father has more dimensions now than before because David recognizes his own guilt—the guilt of betrayal which he and his father share, and, in doing so, he has a clearer perception of himself and his father" (25–26).

146:15 old entrusted friend: This is a mistranscription. The phrase in the manuscript is "old *untrusted* friend" (3.25.3; my emphasis) The difference is significant.

147:3 he became his father: See 129:9.

147:11 Ndiyo: Swahili for "yes, it is so."

147:13 high wooded and park-like country above the escarpment: David's father and the porters have ascended more than four thousand feet up the Nguruman Escarpment on the west side of the Great Rift Valley and are now traveling at an altitude in the vicinity of 6,500 feet above sea level. The fact that this is a "wooded and park-like country" tells us that David's father is traveling not west toward the Masai Mara and Serengeti Plain, but north, toward the Nandi Hills, site in 1905 of the last major native revolt and the "largest punitive [action] ever employed in British East Africa before the Mau Mau operations" of the 1950s (Matson 158). In other words, David's story takes place "*in the time of* the Maji-Maji War. . . . in Tanganyika" (157:5; my emphasis), but it is actually *about* the Nandi Resistance in Kenya, over three hundred miles away from the nearest Maji Maji fighting.

The Nandi Massacre that brought an end to the Nandi Resistance has long symbolized for Kenyans a sort of founding act of violence that solidified British settler colonialism in Kenya. That Hemingway would write about this massacre at a time when the Mau Mau Rebellion of the 1950s was bringing an end to British colonial rule in Kenya implies a critique of British colonialism. Yet Hemingway's conflicting settler-colonial sympathies lead him to disavow and mask this critique. For an extended version of this argument, see my essay "'In the Year of the Maji Maji.'"

147:32 He had intended to ask his father about two things. . . . marvelous advice: If it weren't already clear that David is revisiting his relationship with his father to work through his present difficulties with Catherine and Marita, these lines should make it so. In the manuscript, David's father gives advice with "a Tyburn Hill accuracy and precision" (3.25.7). A traditional site of London executions, Tyburn Hill was synonymous with capital punishment, a minor theme in the novel (see [24:33] 1.2.8 and [106:8] 3.20.31).

CHAPTER 17 (MSS. CHAPTER 25) · 223

148:20 **rather awful story really:** See 129:11, 147:13, 157:5, and 157:23.

148:21 **giant killer:** In his slang dictionary, Partridge lists this as army officer's slang for whiskey, with examples as early as 1890 and 1910. In the *Eden* manuscript, Marita picks it up from reading David's WWI novel, and David notes how "dated" the phrase "spot of the giant killer" now sounds *(3.32.14)*. Nevertheless, David uses the expression throughout the manuscript—sometimes for Armagnac and Perrier, sometimes for whiskey and Perrier. In his letters and such works as "The Short Happy Life of Francis Macomber," "The Gambler, the Nun, and the Radio," *For Whom the Bell Tolls,* and *Under Kilimanjaro,* Hemingway uses "giant killer" variously for whiskey, gin, and absinthe. The phrase almost always carries connotations of self-medication, with alcohol being used to ward off anxiety or depression. Like his biblical namesake, or Christian in Bunyan's *Pilgrim's Progress,* David must kill off the "giant Despair" after the destruction of his stories, a connection Marita makes explicit late in the manuscript (see *[240:2] 3.44.4*).

150:1 **fuck her good for me:** This sentence calls attention to the role of a sort of proxy sexuality with the Bournes, insofar as they represent as two halves of a single riven ego. David's bedroom ability to become "Catherine" implies that his wife's sexual experiments with Marita can serve as a proxy lesbian experience for David, while David's sex with Marita can serve as a sort of proxy heterosexual intercourse with Marita for Catherine.

150:11 **Kiss me goodbye:** Another contribution to a series of foreboding lines from Catherine. See 26:8 and *(145:16) 3.24.35*.

150:21 **You aren't very hard to corrupt. . . . There isn't any corruption:** Although the novel often implies that Catherine "corrupts" poor "innocent" David (see *[31] 1.4.4*), he is so easily "corrupted" precisely because Catherine's transgressive inventions speak for his own unspoken desires (see 12:13).

151:7 **he felt her body against his:** The implication in the Scribner's text is that David and Marita are about to make love. The passage continues in the manuscript, however, and David and Marita do not have intercourse. Marita tells David that she wants to have intercourse but cannot "yet" because "it's happened already." This seems to imply that she is menstruating. "Let me," she tells David, and it seems that she stimulates him either orally or manually *(3.25.17)*. Afterwards, they talk, and Marita explains to David that she loves both him and Catherine. Catherine, in turn, loves both Marita and David. And David loves both Catherine and Marita. It is a perfect love triangle.

In a passage from this point in the manuscript that Hemingway discarded, Marita explains that if she wasn't the way she was, David wouldn't love her. How she is? David asks. She doesn't explain, but the passage develops from a discussion of her bisexuality, and she remarks that David, who has known her for less than a week, already knows her well; it seems like he's known her forever *(422.4 3.25.21)*.

(151:10) 422.4 3.25.20 **Dick Blake.... "Scott's down here.... Cap d'Antibes.... Earl Ryan...." "Hemingstein.... Mike Strater":** Among the *Eden* discards, there is a gossipy, strangely self-referential, and chronologically tortured fragment that was written and rejected for this position in the manuscript. Angered by the complications of the love triangle, David leaves Marita and goes to check on Catherine. Finding her asleep, he leaves her a note and takes the Isotta into Cannes to get it repaired. As he reads the papers and waits with a drink at the Café des Allées, he runs into his old friend Dick Blake. David tells Dick about seeing Andy and the Colonel in Spain, and it turns out that the Colonel had also tried to recruit Dick for his Moroccan adventure (see 61:5). (This implies that Dick, like David, is a former fighter pilot. Marita later calls him David's "old war friend.") Dick mentions that Scott (i.e., F. Scott Fitzgerald) is at Saint-Raphaël. Yes, David replies, Catherine saw him there (see *[76:14] 3.16.14*). Scott's wife had gotten into "a jam with a French Naval flyer," but things are better now and Scott is working well. Dick tells David that the Cap d'Antibes will be open next summer and that the summer season on the Riviera is going to be a big thing (see 6:9). This leads to talk of Earl Ryan (a transparent portrait of Gerald Murphy), whom Dick dismisses as a "phony," although he likes his wife. They talk of Paris, and David asks Dick if he's seen "Hemingstein." They talk of his going to Canada, coming back to live on the Rue Notre-Dame-des-Champs, his travels in Austria and Spain. David hadn't seen him in Spain, and the talk drifts to Waldo (Peirce) and the Brasserie Lipp. The details of the passage would suggest that the action takes place simultaneously in 1922, 1924, and 1925. No wonder Hemingway deleted it.

It is at this point that Catherine and Marita drive up in the Bugatti. Seeing them, David realizes that he has been missing them and that his anger has been gone for a long time. The fragment then switches from the third to first person, with David narrating. Marita's hair has been cut shorter than Catherine's has ever been, so her hair is now "black and smooth and sleek as a sea otter" (see 136:28). Catherine had first cut Marita's hair, but the results had been unsatisfactory, so they had gone to Jean's (for the second time in two days) to get it done right. Marita explains that she had to do "something to compete" with Catherine. Catherine thinks Marita now looks "like a real street boy" (see *[244:2] 3.45.1)*, "very young but steeped in sin." David tells them he had missed them both, badly. Catherine suggests they eat dinner and then "all go to bed." "Can we?" Marita asks. David assents without resistance, although he admits he will probably afterwards suffer remorse. The implication is clearly that all three will sleep together. It must be remembered, though, that this entire fifteen-page section was discarded; it should be read in brackets, as it were.

151:17 The girls were talking but he did not listen to them: In the manuscript, while David goes out for a swim, we hear the conversation between Catherine and Marita. This shift in focalization, however odd, reveals that both Catherine and Marita find David depressed. Catherine urges Marita to make him happy. She explains that David always really desired her various sex changes. All "except one," Marita interjects, thinking of what she's heard about their adventures in Madrid. But Catherine disagrees. David wanted that, too, she says, although afterwards he suffered from "terrible remorse" *(3.25.22)*. Marita tells Catherine how much she loves David, and Catherine again urges her to make David happy.

151:20 What are you thinking?: In the manuscript, Marita goes out to swim with David. When they return to the beach, David thinks about the word *soul,* deciding that it became obsolete about the same time that cavalry did. But "good writers," David thinks, "had always lost it." This has obvious implications in a book concerned with the Edenic always-already-lost. David mourns a postlapsarian state that he simultaneously recognizes as a prerequisite for a writer. To be a writer, David thinks, requires the honesty of a priest of God and the guts of a thief. This is what is on David's mind when he turns to Marita and asks her what she is thinking *(3.25.24)*.

151:24 Prado: Although Catherine loves the Prado deeply, her inspiration to return to Madrid probably has as much to do with her sexual experiments with David there, of which Marita (in the manuscript) has just reminded her (see 151:17).

(152:29) 3.25.29 pull down the pillars of the temple: In the manuscript, the chapter continues for a few more lines. As David and Marita talk out of Catherine's earshot, David explains that, until he'd remembered that Catherine was "crazy," he'd been "angry enough" with her "to pull down the pillars of the temple." This allusion to the story of Samson and Delilah is particularly interesting in a book so heavily influenced by Hemingway's hair fetishism. It metaphorically places Catherine in the role of Delilah, who betrays her lover, Samson, into revealing the source of his strength in his unshorn locks. Delilah then cuts his hair and delivers him to the Philistines, who gouge out his eyes and put him on display. David's metaphor suggests that Catherine's tonsorial experiments have unmanned, even castrated him, but he feels his strength returning.

CHAPTER 18 (MSS. CHAPTER 26)

154:1 **Was this when you stopped loving him?** Marita's question and Catherine's later comment about the "heartlessness" of David's father (223:3) tell us that David's father does something in this story so brutal, so horrible, that it has the potential to end the love between father and son—hinting at the title of David's first novel, *The Rift* (see 111:16). Yet David never stopped loving his father. Their relationship is not so much irrevocably broken as it is profoundly damaged. In the manuscript, when David says, "This was when I got to know him," Marita objects that David himself wasn't there. David answers, "That isn't the way it works in stories" (3.26.3).

David "gets to know" his father imaginatively—not through anything he ever experienced himself firsthand—but by thinking through what he knows and has heard about his father, imagining himself in his father's alkali-crusted shoes. It's a sort of retroactive knowledge, for surely David didn't get to know his father at the time of the story; rather, he got to know him through writing the story. In fact, this is a knowledge David had long put off facing but needs now. In the face of "all the pressure that had built up while he was writing" the story (153:1), David needs to revisit, reimagine, and repair his damaged relationship with his father. The present reimagines the past so the reimagined past can be used to reimagine the present. It is not that David wants to rehabilitate the kind of toxic masculinity embodied by his father so much as he needs to interrogate it, to decide what is to be rejected and what is of value; only then can he understand and embrace his own style of masculinity, shaken by his experiments with Catherine and Marita.

154:5 **I like going in the room when the door is locked:** See *(24:33)* 1.2.8.

(154:7) 3.26.4 **Where did Catherine go?** In the manuscript, after putting away David's story, Marita returns and talks to David. Catherine has gone into Cannes, and she's not entirely well. Marita thinks that they can't go to Madrid with Catherine in this condition, and David thinks he probably shouldn't even have let her go into town. Yet David is in a "*belle epoque*" as a writer. Marita urges him to begin a new difficult story tomorrow morning and compares him to an unbeatable "weight carrying horse" *(3.26.5)*. Tired of being a horse (see 120:21 and *[140:29] 3.24.9)*, David wants to go for a swim.

(154:7) 3.26.4 **Gauguin . . . riding . . . horses out into the sea:** In the manuscript, the transition from talk about horses to talk of swimming inspires Marita to think of Gauguin's *Riders on the Beach* (1902). David thanks her for thinking of this.

Gauguin painted two distinct versions of this scene from late in his life when he was living in the Marquesas. *Cavaliers sur la plage* (I) has been owned by the Museum Folkwang in Essen, Germany, since 1904; *Cavaliers sur la plage* (II) has been in private hands since 1904 and is currently in the private Niarchos Collection. Hemingway knew the Niarchos version, since it was reproduced in the same 1930 issue of *Cahiers d'art* that reproduced Paul Klee's *L'érection du Monument* (1929), which Hemingway owned.[1] More importantly, in April 1959, when he thought he was within three chapters of completing *The Garden of Eden*, Hemingway saw the Niarchos version at the Museum of Modern Art (MoMA) in New York. Hemingway had just loaned Miró's *The Farm* to the MoMA for an exhibit, and both paintings were on display at the same time (Wildenstein 263). Hemingway was in New York, and he surely visited.[2]

This reference to Gauguin fits into a thread—including references to Captain Cook (109:7), Kanakas *([19:1] 1.2.1)*, "half-assed Tahitians" (154:29), and Gauguin's *Femmes de Tahiti ([163:31] 3.28.15)*—that points to the Pacific islands as yet another lost Eden. Hemingway, who owned Burnett's biography of Gauguin, knew that Gauguin had hoped to find a new Eden in Tahiti and the Marquesas, and he knew that Gauguin blamed the colonial French for decimating the islanders and destroying their culture. This resonates with Hemingway's critique of colonialism throughout *Eden*.

154:27 **You're very British today:** David often uses Briticisms, such as "spot of the giant killer" (see 148:21), and given his boyhood in East Africa, this makes sense. Hemingway owned Mencken's *The American Language*, with its extensive comparative lists of Americanisms and Briticisms, and he was sensitive to these differences. Earlier in the manuscript, when David says to Andy, "Sorry old boy," Andy replies, "Don't try to British me off" *(3.11.2bis)*.

154:29 **Half-assed Tahitian:** David's remark about feeling "half-assed Tahitian" plays into the fantasies of racial transformation that attend the Bournes' experiments with tanning (see *[19:1] 1.2.1.)* It also follows naturally from the reference to Gauguin that precedes it by two pages in the manuscript. Within the novel's ongoing interest in colonialism, David claims here that he feels less like a colonizer and more like a "half-assed" version of the colonized.

155:21 **dusky paramour:** A cliché by the mid-nineteenth century, the phrase dates back at least to Henry Hart Milman's poem, *Samor, Lord of the Bright City* (1818).

155:24 **Do you want to try to be decent?** Directly after Catherine's negative reply to David's question, Jenks has deleted a devastating line from the manuscript. Catherine greets Marita by announcing that her room has a "much nicer bidet" than Marita's, but that Marita is "always welcome to use anything" of hers *(3.26.11)*. In other words, she has just compared her husband to a bidet. Marita merely thanks her and asks if she had fun in Cannes. It is then that Catherine follows up with her question about David's drinking.

156:3 **I've only tried to make it economically possible:** Catherine's claim that she doesn't read David's work, that she only tries to make it economically possible for him to do it, tragically alienates her from the inner world symbolized by his locked suitcase (although we must remember that she secretly holds a twin key to that world). An indicator of Catherine's growing instability, her claim that she "put up the money for" for this story (156:18) will soon justify her claim that she has a right to burn David's stories because she "paid for them" (220:13) and that she can compensate David for their loss by having "their value determined" and putting twice that dollar amount into David's bank (226:21). In the face of such a brutal and absolute reduction of life and art to dollars and cents, David can only ask, "Who appraises these things?" (226:27).

Working through the lens of Gilbert and Gubar's *Madwoman in the Attic,* Mintler has argued that Catherine's assertion of economic authority over David's art—like her scripting of the actions David recounts in the honeymoon narrative, or her self-expression through haircuts and fashions—is a reflection of her own frustrated creativity (see 24:12 and 53:17). While this is persuasive, Hemingway harbored long-standing anxieties about male artists being "bought" or "owned" by rich women (see 22:22). Nevertheless, a glance at the tools used by Hélène Bradley in *To Have and Have Not* to "collect writers," or the leashes used by Cornelia in "Mr. and Mrs. Eliot" or Frances in *The Sun Also Rises* to tether Hubert or Robert, suggests that such fetters need not be forged out of gold. Hemingway's anxiety seems to be less about the commodification of art than it is about female power of any sort over the male artist.

156:5 **ivory white hair . . . like a scar:** David here associates Catherine with "ivory" *before* he begins writing the story of the elephant hunt. This implies that the story that comes to David in a dream later this evening is, on some level, an attempt to work through his present situation with Catherine. As Marita notes a little later in the manuscript, he is writing "in [his] own defense" *(3.27.12)*. It is no mistake that this story comes to him on the same evening that Catherine has ripped his other story in two, after she said horrible things to him, after she revealed the split in her ego (see *[158:8]* 3.26.20), and after he has failed to talk her into seeking psychiatric help. Nor is it a coincidence that David associates the word *ivory* specifically with Catherine's hair. Ivory was Ernest's nickname for his older sister, Marcelline—the sister with whom he was pseudotwinned, with matching haircuts, until he was six years old. In his letters to Marcelline, Ernest addresses her variously as "Dear Ivory," "Dear Antique Ivory," "Dear Old Ivory," "Dearest of Ivories," Dearest Carved Ivory," and "Dear Ivory Tower."[3] That David sees the line of Catherine's white hair across her dark forehead as a "scar" should remind us that, thanks to the logic of disavowal, the fetish simultaneously represents both an imaginary phallus and castration. (Similarly, in *For Whom the Bell Tolls*, when Maria's braids are hacked off by the fascists who rape her, she receives a scar on her ear that she asks Jordan to feel—a scar that mirrors the scar on her genitals that Jordan speculates about only a few pages earlier [*FWBT* 351, 343]).[4]

(156:16) 3.26.13 **"study it in school...." "maybe your children ... sterile ... clap.... Maupassant ... syphilis":** In the manuscript, Marita tells Catherine that she would have been moved by the story even if she'd had to study it in school. Unless she's more careful, Catherine warns, she just might have children who do have to study it in school—unless David "really is sterile." Catherine isn't sure if David is sterile, but according to his first book, she reminds him, at age fourteen he'd had the clap. Perhaps that's why they haven't been able to have a baby.

David escapes to take a shower, but when he returns Catherine's mood is unchanged, and their previous conversation continues as if without interruption. Catherine greets David by telling him that she has just been telling Marita all about a book she's been reading about "what was wrong" with various writers. The book argues that Maupassant's writing was "mediocre ... until he contracted syphilis." When David asks if Catherine really believes such stuff, she protests that it was "in the book." Doesn't David agree, she asks, that "The Horla" was Maupassant's "best story"? David replies with an emphatic *no*. Catherine's implication—soon stated explicitly—is that David's creative energy, much like Maupassant's, comes from his having had "the clap."

Catherine's imputation is clearly intended to be understood as absurd and insulting, yet, according to Michael Reynolds, "In Paris and later, [Hemingway] would, on the slightest provocation, trot out the old cliché that a good dose of syphilis or the clap improved the creative mind, implying he had contracted his share of venereal disease" (*Paris Years* 63). A few medical treatises of the times did speculate about a supposed "expansive" form of thought, lasting about two years, that could precede syphilitic general paresis of the insane (GPI). As Claude Quétel explains in his social history of syphilis, there was a widespread epidemic of the disease in the aftermath of the First World War, and there was a deep fear in France that mass infertility would be the result: "Contemporaries were struck by the comparison between the dreadful war which had killed millions of men, the 'Spanish' flu of 1918 which had killed as many or more, and syphilis (hereditary syphilis in particular) which would supposedly finish off those who remained" (176). To combat the disease, the French launched a major propaganda campaign and enlisted the press. In 1926 alone, there were over 15,000 articles about syphilis in the popular French press, not to mention articles published in medical journals (Quétel 183). It is against this backdrop that Catherine both aligns and contrasts biological and artistic fertility. This plays into one of the major themes of the novel: the question of whether sexual experimentation and honesty serves as an aid or threat to artistic creativity.

By 1927, Hemingway had read of Maupassant's syphilis in the second volume of Frank Harris's *My Life and Loves*. Harris's prime exhibit was Maupassant's tale of insanity and psychological terror, "The Horla" (449).[5] As for Catherine's book about "what was wrong" with various writers, this could be an anachronistic reference to Philip Marshall Dale's *Medical Biographies: The Ailments of Thirty-Three Famous Persons* (1952). Dale devotes a chapter to Maupassant's syphilitic insanity, and the only story he discusses is "The Horla."

157:5 **In the time of the Maji Maji War . . . 1905:** David says that the story takes place "*in the time of* the Maji Maji War" (my emphasis)—not that it is *about* that war. Again, much later, when he rewrites the story after it is burned, he thinks of it as happening "*in the year of* the Maji Maji rebellion" (246:17; my emphasis). The landscape details of the story place its action in what was then British East Africa, over three hundred miles away from the nearest Maji Maji fighting in German East Africa, suggesting that it is in fact about the Nandi Resistance and Nandi Massacre of 1905 in Kenya (see 128:9, 129:11, and 147:13). In my essay "In the Year of the Maji Maji," I explore Hemingway's complex reasons for seeming to conflate the two wars, which indeed had much in common (see 158:5). While the reduplicative name of the Maji Maji War echoes that of the Mau Mau conflict that rocked Kenya throughout the 1950s, the extreme subtlety of Hemingway's treatment of the Nandi Massacre simultaneously acknowledges, masks, and symptomatically displaces the founding violence of British colonialism in East Africa.

In the manuscript, Hemingway describes the Maji Maji War as "the native rebellion of 1904 in Tanganyika" (3.26.16). The war, in fact, began in July 1905, and Jenks makes the correction.

157:10 **when I was about eight years old:** This means that David was born in 1897, which would make him thirty years old in 1927—two years older than Hemingway.

157:16 **passage:** Jenks substitutes *passage* for the French word in the manuscript, *paysage*, but it is not a felicitous translation. *Paysage* means "landscape," in a painterly sense.

157:23 tore the cahier in two. . . . "horrible. . . . bestial": Only much later do we learn that the story is about a "massacre in [a] crater" and what Catherine calls the "heartlessness" of David's father. In my essay "In the Year of the Maji Maji," I suggest that Catherine's visceral response to the story may allude to the 1957 publication of *Kenya Diary, 1902–1906*, by Richard Meinertzhagen, perpetrator of the 1905 Nandi Massacre (see 129:11, 147:13, and 157:5). Of the *Diary*, one early reviewer wrote: "It would be possible to dismiss the book as mainly a chronicle of slaughter, the successful killing of Africans and game animals being described at equal length and with equal zest. . . . This is emphatically not a book for the squeamish, and includes some grim and revolting details . . ." (F. A. M.). According to his biographer, Brian Garfield, Meinertzhagen and his KAR soldiers, by Meinertzhagen's own admission,

> brought order and punishment to rebellious East African tribes time after time by shooting and clubbing Africans to death in large numbers. In *Kenya Diary* he writes of one such incident: 'I gave orders that every living thing except children should be killed without mercy.' He describes how, with bullet and bayonet, he and his *askari* [see 173:6] annihilated entire villages. From a reading of his diaries one can estimate his body count at 1,500 Africans. No prisoners. No survivors. (59)

In 1956, writing in what would become *Under Kilimanjaro* of his safari during the time of the Mau Mau uprising, Hemingway wonders about how "rough" things may have been in the early days of British East Africa (114, 260). If the 1957 publication of Meinertzhagen's *Kenya Diary* provided him with his answer, that may help to explain the strength of Catherine's reaction to the story.

158:5 It was a very odd rebellion: While this would seem to suggest that the story was, in fact, about the Maji Maji Rebellion, I have argued that David here conflates the Nandi Resistance with the Maji Maji. Both uprisings took inspiration from versions of "the Yakan or Allah Water Cult, whereby warriors sprinkled with sacred water would be impervious to European bullets, or the bullets themselves would turn to water" (Eby, "In the Year" 15). It was this belief that gave the Maji Maji (*water water*) Rebellion its name.[6]

(158:8) 3.26.20 I can hear myself say them like another person: In the manuscript, directly after the break in the text on the Scribner's page, Catherine bemoans having said "such horrible things" to David. David assures her that somehow it really isn't her who says such things, but Catherine is torn. She knows that she *is* the one who says them, yet sometimes she can hear herself "say them like another person." It's almost as if she's possessed. In other words, Catherine has a rift in her ego, just like David has a rift in his ego and just as Catherine and David, together, represent on some level the two halves of Hemingway's riven ego (see 17:23 and 111:11). As I write in *Hemingway's Fetishism*, "fetishism not only perpetuates and reinforces a split in the ego, it is itself largely a response to . . . an unstable ego already deeply riven and prone to merger and fragmentation" (191).

158:12 **Switzerland:** In the provisional ending Hemingway wrote for the manuscript, Catherine, who was educated in Switzerland, says that sanatoriums are really all Switzerland has to offer "except cows and time pieces and goiters" (422.2 1.8, see appendix B). Needless to say, her judgment is far from fair (though goiter was, indeed, endemic in Switzerland).[7] A glance at the 1922 edition of Baedeker's guide to Switzerland, however, suggests where one might get such an idea. In addition to a section devoted to health resorts, listing seventy-seven towns with such facilities, the guide lists at least forty specific sanatoriums by name or presiding doctor. The attention devoted to medical tourism in Baedeker guides of the same period for other European countries cannot compare. In addition to its long tradition as a refuge for those suffering from tuberculosis, Switzerland was particularly distinguished in psychiatry, with numerous famous clinicians like Eugen Bleuler, Carl Jung, Karl Abraham, Ludwig Binswanger, and Hermann Rorschach practicing in Zurich alone. In making Switzerland synonymous with mental health clinics, Hemingway was also no doubt drawing upon Zelda Fitzgerald's Swiss treatment for schizophrenia, and Scott Fitzgerald's treatment of Switzerland in his fiction, most notably *Tender Is the Night*.[8] See also (242:26) 3.44.17.

159:3 **went direct from that dream to work:** See 156:5.

159:16 **left tusk was so long it seemed to reach the ground:** The big tusker of David's story draws on an experience from Hemingway's 1953–54 safari. In *Under Kilimanjaro*, Hemingway recalls flying at low altitude over a huge old bull elephant. His later reflections on that vision contain many of the themes picked up in the elephant story that David writes:

> In the night I thought about the elephant . . . and about the long time he had lived with so many people against him and seeking to kill him for his two wonderful teeth that were now only a great disadvantage to him and a deadly load for him to carry. I loved ivory [see 156:5] which is one of the truly satisfying things to touch it being even smoother than the skin of a Chinese girl which is the smoothest and loveliest thing to touch that I know. It had many other strange and satisfying things about it too or it would never have been sought as it has been nor the crimes committed. The sight of the old bull elephant and his unbelievably long and heavy tusks had excited the three of us . . . as though we had been hunting dogs unleashed on a fresh scent. . . . Lying in the cot, unable to sleep . . . I tried to remember what it was that had brought me into such close connection with the

tusks so that if I never saw them again I would always possess them and I knew finally in the night that it was the rain on them and the slow terrible effort the elephant made to lift them high into the air and against the aircraft.

In the night I thought where the elephant would be now and what he had said to his friend or askari as the Africans always called the younger companion of an old bull. . . . They would have traveled a long way after we were gone. I wondered, in the sharp coldness of the night listening to the talking of the animals, how great a trouble the huge weight of his tusks was to him and whether he was impotent and what sort of comradeship he had with his askari. (312)

For the size of the tusks, see 173:13.

159:18 no other elephant came by: As legendary ivory hunter W. D. M. "Karamojo" Bell writes on the first page of his 1923 book *The Wanderings of an Elephant Hunter* (which Hemingway owned), "The most interesting and exciting form of elephant-hunting is the pursuit of the solitary bull. These fine old patriarchs stand close on twelve feet high at the shoulder and weigh from twelve thousand to fourteen thousand pounds or more, and carry tusks from eighty to one hundred pounds each. They are of great age, probably a hundred or a hundred and fifty years old." Such old bulls are wise and silent and "will play hide-and-seek with you all day long and day after day" (3). They are liable to eventually charge out of dense foliage giving a hunter only a moment's notice to make a difficult killing shot. This is, of course, what happens in David's story.

159:22 He was traveling toward the mountain: Details of the story suggest this is Kilimanjaro (see 173:13).

160:12 two hunting spears: On safari in 1953, Hemingway took to hunting by moonlight with a spear. As he writes in *Under Kilimanjaro*: "Now the moon was up over the shoulder of the mountain and I wished I had a good big dog. . . . But . . . I checked the spears and put on my moccasins. . . . and I left [our] lights behind and left the moon over my right shoulder and started off on the long walk" (360). This seems to be part of the inspiration for the elephant story in *Eden*.

NOTES

1. See Tériade 81 and "La Peinture" 157.
2. Although Hemingway wrote this chapter in late July or early August 1958, these sentences about Gauguin's painting were a later addition.
3. For a consideration of the linguistic nature of fetishistic associations, see *HF* 111–18.
4. See *HF* 79–82.

5. Hemingway's 1927 satirical piece "My Own Life" carried the explanatory subtitle: "After reading the second volume of Frank Harris's 'My Life.'" By 1927, Hemingway had also read Robert Harborough Sherard's *The Life, Work and Evil Fate of Guy de Maupassant,* which also discusses Maupassant's syphilis, but with less emphasis on "La Horla" (Michael Reynolds, *American* 68). Hemingway also writes of Maupassant's syphilis in *Death in the Afternoon* (102).

6. For an extended consideration of this, see Eby, "In the Year."

7. As Hemingway wrote in a 15 December 1923 article for the *Toronto Star Weekly,* "Goiter and Iodine": "People who live in high mountain countries, where . . . iodine . . . [is scarce], are the most gravely affected with goiter. In Switzerland the disease is almost universal among the men and women of the mountains" (*DLT* 411). Indeed, before the 1922 introduction of iodized salt, in some regions of Switzerland "100% of schoolchildren had large goiters and up to 30% of young men were unfit for military service owing to a large goiter" (Bürgi et al. 577).

8. See Bouzonviller.

CHAPTER 19 (MSS. CHAPTERS 27–28)

161:3 **She won't go to Switzerland:** In the manuscript, Marita first announces that Catherine "won't go to Africa" *(3.27.1)*. David doesn't think she should, in any case. Marita adds that Catherine never truly wanted to go to Africa. After this, she announces that Catherine "won't go to Switzerland" either, although "that's what she should do" (see 158:12).

161:6 **I feel as though we'd been married all our lives:** They have, in fact, known each other for twelve days.

(161:8) 3.27.3 **get my hair cut short like the young African girl:** As David and Marita worry about Catherine's deteriorating condition, Marita announces that she has a "surprise" plan to "cheer up" David. She wants to cut her hair "short like the young African girl" in David's second story. She can't possibly get it cut that short, David protests, and she isn't African. Marita thinks it will be fun. Once, in Madrid, Catherine had cut hers very short, David remembers. Marita knows about this but says with her it will be different and David will like it. She plans to get it cut the next time she goes into town, but David tells her she doesn't have to do things like that, and she can't be "like an African girl." She thinks it will help him to relax, but David is skeptical. When Marita asks if David liked it when Catherine did it, he admits that he did: "Too much." He asks her to wait until they go to Africa, but she says she knows he is "homesick" for it. She sees it in the terrible, almost frightening, nostalgia in his writing. "Don't you be crazy," he tells her. They already have enough craziness with Catherine. But Marita says she wants to do it for herself too. "That's different," David admits, but he cautions her against trying for a Mbulu or Kamba look since "That's impossible."

How this passage further exemplifies Hemingway's fetishization of racial otherness needs no elucidation (see 30:16). Such passages—and there are several in the *Eden* manuscript (see also [243:31] 3.44.21)—belie critical readings that see Marita as a compliant figure of heteronormativity meant to undo or counterbalance Catherine's experiments with gender and sexuality. By deleting these passages, the Scribner's edition does produce this impression, but as Debra Moddelmog has noted, such deletions tell us more about Tom Jenks's impression of Hemingway than they tell us about Hemingway the man, Hemingway the writer, or the novel that he actually wrote (*Reading* 58–63).

A 1928 article in *The New York Times* reported, "New styles of bobbing the hair have reached civilization from the heart of Africa, where hairdressing is an ancient and complex art" ("African"). The inspiration for Marita's planned African haircut, however, was clearly less historical than it was personal. In a 3 January 1954 entry in her safari journal, Mary Hemingway noted: "We've had a big business about my hair which we've bleached again and Papa cut very short then I cut across the front in idiot imitation of the local Kamba girls." (This was quickly followed by a "big love.") Hemingway mixes his memories of Mary's "African haircut" with some silly but revealing tribal generalizations in *Under Kilimanjaro*:

> The Wakamba are not homosexual. I do not know about the Lumbwa because Arap Meina was the only Lumbwa I have ever known intimately but I would say that Arap Meina was strongly attracted by both sexes and that the fact that Miss Mary with the shortest of African haircuts provided the pure Hamitic face of a boy with a body that was as womanly as a good Masai young wife was one of the factors that channeled Arap Meina's devotion until it became worship. (290)

Any doubt we might have about such devotion being more Hemingway's than Arap Meina's should be dispelled by a 15 July 1954 letter Ernest wrote in which he urged Mary to "get a good boy safari hair-cut the way you had in Nairobi and on the boat *and to please me in Madrid* [my emphasis]. I love it that way and you never look prettier and when we get really brown on the boat it will look so wonderful really platinum.... Mr. S. ["Mr. Scrooby" was Ernest's pet name for his penis] cannot wait until we are together again in the biggest and widest and loveliest of all beds. Mr. S. is at present arms as I write and I cannot wait to see my kitten" (qtd. in *HF* 318). See also *(244:2) 3.45.1*.

161:9 dive from the high rock. The really high one: David and Marita seem to be at the smallest and most secluded of the three coves (161:1) at Pointe de l'Aiguille, beneath Théoule-Supérieur. Diving from the rocks into the sea became popular at Cap d'Antibes in the 1920s, and during the summer of 1926 Pauline tried to teach Hadley to dive from them (Kert 181). At Pointe de l'Aiguille, diving from the cliffs into the sea remains popular today, and the "really high" cliff for diving is more than sixty feet tall. A particularly popular diving platform there is the natural arch known as the Pont de Gardanne.

(162:4) 422.4 3.27.8 **He was in the Cigognes. He flew a Spad:** In a discarded fragment that fits here in the manuscript, as they discuss David's book about flying in WWI, Marita tells David that her brother had also been a pursuit pilot. He flew a Spad in

the famous French squadron the Cigognes (the storks) and died in the war. (The Cigognes did, indeed, fly Spads.) That David resembles Marita's brother—a brother who loved her with something more than brotherly love—links David's relationship with Marita to the sort of fascination with sibling romance that we also see between David and Catherine (see 6:6 and 126:12).

(162:4) 3.27.8 **book plate. . . . get Picasso to make us one:** In the manuscript, Marita tells David she had tried to buy his WWI book in Paris, but it had been sold out (see 94:30). She considers it strange that Catherine doesn't have a copy with her, but David assures her that she wouldn't like the sort of writers who keep their own books always at hand. When Marita says she would have it specially bound with "our bookplate in it," David tells her that he and Catherine don't have a bookplate. Marita answers that she'll get Picasso to design one for them.

Marita is clearly feeling rich. Within a page she's offering to replace what David calls "the damned Isotta"—a fabulously expensive vehicle (see 89:18)—with a "really good car." David mocks her, suggesting that "the second footman" can place the plates in the books *(3.27.9)*, and Marita's plan is nearly as outlandish as Catherine's project to get Picasso and other famous artists to illustrate the honeymoon narrative David is writing (see 189:2). David asks Marita what makes her think Picasso would design the bookplate. Marita doesn't know why he wouldn't, since he designed the "décor for a ballet" for her cousin.

The false equivalence is comic. It might also seem to imply—incorrectly, as it turns out (see *[162:4] 3.27.9*)—that Marita's cousin is none other than Serge Diaghilev, founder of the Ballets Russes. Picasso famously designed the décor for several of Diaghilev's ballets, including *Parade* (1917), *Le tricorne* (1919), *Pulcinella* (1920), and *Cuadro flamenco* (1921), and he designed the curtain for *Le train bleu* (1924), which is about sporty vacationers frolicking on the French Riviera. The pattern of associations in this passage suggests that Hemingway—who had his own custom bookplate (*not* by Picasso)—knew that Diaghilev had once asked Picasso to design a bookplate, which Picasso had agreed to do but had never completed (Richardson 277–78). Later in the manuscript, David remembers Picasso telling him to "always accept invitations from the rich" because it so clearly pleases them, but don't worry about following through, because a suitable excuse could always be found (3.38.6). (Hemingway repeats the anecdote almost verbatim in *A Moveable Feast*.) Bookplates were very popular between 1890 and 1930, and Picasso did produce bookplates for friends and wealthy patrons, including Apollinaire, Max Pellequer, Joyce Cary, Paul Rosenberg, and Nelson Rockefeller. Given David's attitude about bookplates, it may be significant that Hemingway apparently did not use his own.[1]

(162:4) 3.27.9 **Picasso . . . ballet for my cousin:** As noted above, Marita's claim in the manuscript that Picasso designed the décor for a ballet for her cousin, and the

associations surrounding her claim, might seem to imply that her cousin is the Russian-born ballet impresario Serge Diaghilev; yet Marita's tone of frivolous aristocratic privilege doesn't fit with the consummate artistry of the Ballets Russes, and other hints in the manuscript soon reveal that Marita's family is not Russian but French (see *[163:31] 3.28.4*). Hemingway is alluding here not to Diaghilev but to his sometime patron, sometime competitor, and the only other impresario for whom Picasso designed ballet décor: Comte Étienne de Beaumont.

The model for Comte d'Orgel in Raymond Radiguet's posthumous 1924 roman à clef, *Le bal du comte d'Orgel*—and known as "the Maecenas of Paris" for his patronage of the arts and as "the Diaghilev of costume balls" for his lavish entertainments—Comte Étienne Jacques Alexandre Marie Joseph Bonnin de la Bonninière de Beaumont actually commissioned Picasso to design the décor for two ballets (Laporte 48, Gold and Fizdale 238). Beaumont first commissioned Picasso to design the scenery and costumes for *La statue retrouvée*, a four-minute micro-ballet with music by Erik Satie, scenario by Jean Cocteau, and choreography by Léonide Massine (the same team who collaborated on the groundbreaking 1917 Cubist ballet *Parade* for Diaghilev and the Ballets Russes). This brief but costly entertainment—the balletic equivalent of a bookplate by Picasso—welcomed guests to Beaumont's *Bal de l'antiquité* in 1923.[2] Beaumont's homosexuality was an open secret, and the milieu of his parties has been described as "a world somewhere between *Guermantes' Way* and *Sodom*" (Vaill 103). Yet along with Proust and his models from the upper aristocracy (Beaumont actually hosted a ball in 1927 at which guests dressed as characters from Proust[3]), one might encounter here such figures as André Gide, Valentine Hugo, Coco Chanel, Misia Sert, Igor Stravinsky, Marie Laurencin, André Derain, Man Ray, Francis Poulenc, Darius Milhaud, and Gerald and Sara Murphy.

Encouraged by his success assembling talent for *La statue retrouvée*, Beaumont decided in 1924 to stage an ambitious season of ten productions, dubbed *Les soirées de Paris* and held at the Cigale music hall, to compete with the Ballets Russes and coincide with the Eighth Olympiad, held that year in Paris. As part of this project, he commissioned Satie, Massine, and Picasso—this time without Cocteau—to work together again on what became the ballet *Mercure*. The exclusion of Cocteau, who produced his own version of *Romeo and Juliet* (with himself playing Mercutio) for the *Soirées*, was not accidental. Picasso, Satie, and Massine used *Mercure* to poke fun at Cocteau, who was fond of dressing as the god Mercury, with winged hat and shoes, for costume parties and similar events. The three felt that Cocteau had been taking far too much credit for their collective work on *Parade*, and *Mercure* was their revenge. Without a Cocteau scenario, Beaumont asked for a ballet based on a series of *tableaux vivants*, which naturally showcased Picasso's skill. The result, according to John Richardson, was "the most provocative of Picasso's works for the theater" (261). Diaghilev fumed that it was "a Ballet Russes performance from which only my name is missing" and actively tried to sabotage everything to do with *Les soirées de Paris*

(Epstein 92). Though not part of Diaghilev's plan, the opening night of *Mercure,* 14 June 1924, was famously interrupted by André Breton and the surrealists shouting insults at Satie and Tristan Tzara and praising Picasso. While Beaumont recruited artists, commissioned works, wrote scenarios, and did choreography for *Les soirées de Paris,* his exalted "social status required him to maintain a purely disinterested façade. In 1924 Paris, Beaumont had little recourse for preempting the eventual reputation of the *Soirées* as the trivial plaything of a wealthy dilettante . . ." (Epstein 109). This explains the tone of frivolity in Marita's allusion to it in *Eden.*

Hemingway knew this history well. Soon after *Les soirées de Paris,* in the pages of the *Transatlantic Review* Hemingway ridiculed Cocteau's production of *Romeo and Juliet,* and in a letter from Pamplona to Gertrude Stein, he joked that Don Ogden Stewart's Riau-Riau dancing featured "a lot of Massine's stuff" (*Letters 2* 129). What's more, the social orbits of Hemingway and Beaumont soon began to cross. Hemingway's new friends Gerald and Sara Murphy had gotten to know Beaumont and the figures surrounding Diaghilev and the Ballets Russes soon after they first arrived in Paris in 1921. When Gerald decided to study painting seriously, he selected as a teacher Natalia Goncharova, who often designed sets for Diaghilev. Becoming part of the wider circle of artists and hangers-on around the Ballets Russes, the Murphys attended rehearsals, helped to paint sets, and threw a legendary party on a barge on the Seine for the company after the première of *Les noces* (1923). Guests included such figures as Diaghilev, Beaumont, Picasso, Stravinsky, Cocteau, Misia Sert, the Princesse de Polignac, Darius Milhaud, Tristan Tzara, and Blaise Cendrars. It has been suggested that when Diaghilev and Cocteau began planning a ballet about the summer beach lifestyle made possible by the new express train to the Riviera, *Le train bleu* (1924)—a ballet with music by Milhaud, costumes by Chanel, and a curtain by Picasso (and perhaps launched as part of Diaghilev's attempt to sabotage Beaumont's *Soirées de Paris*[4])—the Murphys and their life at Cap d'Antibes, where they were sometimes visited by Beaumont, served as an inspiration (Rothschild 82–3). In a September 1928 letter to Fitzgerald, Hemingway described the Murphys as "figures in a ballet. A very attractive ballet" (*Letters 3* 454), and Fitzgerald used a version of this line to describe the Divers in *Tender Is the Night* (43).

As he worked on *The Garden of Eden,* Hemingway's memories of this history would have been jogged by more recent events. When Adriana Ivancich, the inspiration for Renata in *Across the River and into the Trees,* visited Hemingway in Paris in 1950, she stayed with a good friend from her Swiss boarding school, Monique Bonnin de la Bonninière de Beaumont. Like *Eden*'s Marita, Monique was a cousin of Étienne de Beaumont but was a daughter of a different Comte de Beaumont. In *How It Was,* Mary Hemingway remembers her as "marvelously beautiful . . . with . . . masses of sparkling auburn hair," and recalls Monique accompanying Adriana everywhere (298). In an 18 April 1950 letter to Adriana, Hemingway suggests Monique's mother, Paule, as a potential translator for *Across the River* (UT), and Paule did eventually translate Hemingway's preface to François Sommer's book about big-game hunting in Africa, *Pourquoi ces bêtes sont-elles sauvages* (1951). Hemingway's letters to Adriana from this year often inquire about the "gentle and lovely Monique" (21 Aug. 1950, UT), and surprisingly enough, these letters are importantly concerned with questions of ballet.[5] Earlier that year in Venice, before he came to Paris, Ernest had made an agreement with another aristocratic dabbler in ballet. Adriana's friend Anne-Marie Lacloche, stepdaughter of the First Count of Misurata, had written a scenario to transform Hemingway's story "The Capital of the World" into a ballet, and Hemingway had promised to split proceeds with her fifty-fifty. Hemingway put Hotchner in charge of realizing the vision, and Hotchner's treatment of the ballet eventually replaced the one by Lacloche. Hemingway and Hotchner initially tried to place the ballet with a revived Ballet Russes de Monte-Carlo (*DPDH* 98), but when this proved unsuccessful the ballet was ultimately produced by the American Ballet Theatre, with music by George Antheil and a televised première at New York's Metropolitan Opera House on 27 December 1953. The production toured America in 1954 and was widely covered in the press.

(162:4) 3.27.10 **prejudiced against everyone with money?** In the manuscript, as David teases her about the bookplates and her casual confidence that Picasso will do her bidding, Marita asks David if he is "prejudiced against everyone with money." She imagines his father must have been wealthy. His grandfather was, David corrects her. Marita wants to know if his father lost it all. No, David answers, "some of it he spent." He should have found a wealthy wife, then, Marita suggests. He did, answers David: his mother. David never knew her. His father didn't spend her money, but he lost it anyway. Marita says from the way Catherine had talked to David of money—even making the allowance that she wasn't herself when she said such things—she could tell that David's people had more money than hers. David doesn't buy the logic of this but confesses he isn't really interested in money—an attitude Marita considers "chic." (A deleted line calls this a "defect in a novelist.") David is delighted that Catherine and Marita are both rich, he says, but "banal" as it may seem, he would have loved them just the same if they hadn't been.

162:7 **little Corniche:** Three spectacular cliff roads run from Nice to Menton. High above the coast and perched villages runs the Grande Corniche (or Corniche Supérieure); between the Grande Corniche and the coast runs the Moyenne Corniche, affording views of both the cliffs and the sea; along the coast runs the Corniche Inférieure, also known as the Basse Corniche, the Corniche du Littoral, or the Petite Corniche. Catherine has been driving the road along the coast, which is still elevated enough to look down on Villefranche.

162:11 **All the colors were too bright:** See 4:3.

(162:19) 3.27.16 **you and Marita should buy a place. . . . Spain:** In the manuscript, Catherine's disorientation is even clearer. She suggests that Marita and David buy a house on the Riviera, though she herself wouldn't want one. Then she suggests they all go to Spain—which David promises to do as soon as he finishes his story. She wants to take the Bugatti, forgetting that they wouldn't have room for Marita. Marita offers to take the train, but Catherine is afraid she'd leave them. No, they can take the Isotta.

(162:19) 3.27.17 **Barbara. . . . Nick . . . illustrations:** In the manuscript, David recommends that they drive to Madrid by way of Perpignan and Le Perthus—that is, by the most direct route, along the Mediterranean—but Catherine wants to go by way of Hendaye. She wants to see Barbara and ask Nick about the illustrations for the book. She's feeling an urgency to get this done now. She's afraid she's put things off "until too late." She'd like Marita to meet Nick and Barbara, or for them to meet her.

(162:19) 3.27.20 **David ski:** In the manuscript, the mood lightens as Catherine and Marita trade what David considers silly generalizations about nationalities and languages. This leads to a conversation about skiing, and Catherine is relieved to hear that Marita loves skiing. Before Catherine ever met David, she first saw him skiing—which comes as news to David. One gets the distinct impression that Catherine is "getting her things in order" and is glad to hear David shares something else with Marita before she hands him off to her. She wants to make sure David is "taken care of" (162:32).

162:28 **It's just speeded up so much lately:** From its early pages (21:4), the novel has been haunted by a sense that Catherine's mental state and sexual experiments constitute a course of action with an implied end point, and that things have been moving towards this end point very quickly. As he worked feverishly on the novel throughout the summer of 1958, Hemingway seems to have felt something similar (see 216:19). Explaining his writing frenzy to Harvey Breit on 21 September 1958, Hemingway wrote that he had been laboring under a sense that "time was short," that there wasn't any to waste (JFK).

162:30 **All of a sudden I was old:** We should remember that Catherine is, in fact, only twenty-one (16:25). Her dysphoria about age seems to be part of a broader dysphoria that includes her misperception of color and brightness. More importantly, her sudden sensation of being terribly old, "older than [her] mother's old clothes"—her feeling that she won't outlive the dog in David's story—aligns her with that story's old bull elephant (see 173:13).

Catherine's experience of sudden aging may also reflect Hemingway's experience. As many biographers and critics have noted, after years of hard living, and particularly after his two African plane crashes, Hemingway aged with frightening speed in the final decade of his life. This was something he confronted in the mirror every morning.

163:22 **Kibo. He had a lovely name:** As David notes, "It's the name of a mountain. The other part is Mawenzi." Kibo and Mawenzi are the primary and secondary peaks of Mount Kilimanjaro. Hemingway was also drawing on his 1953–54 safari, where the local game warden, Denis Zaphiro, had a puppy named Kibo.[6]

(163:23) 3.27.26 **Did your father have to kill everything?** In the manuscript, as part of her reaction to the elephant story, Catherine asks, "Did your father have to kill everything?" "I guess so," David answers. Catherine is glad David didn't grow up to be like his father. The sense of existential loss in these lines resonates with the loss David feels for Catherine's mental deterioration.

(163:24) 3.27.27 **story about your fiancée . . . jealous:** In the manuscript, Catherine says that Marita's favorite story is the one David wrote (which we don't get to see him writing) about his African fiancée, but Catherine is too jealous to feel the same way about it. Catherine isn't jealous of Marita because she feels like she "practically invented her" for David, but she is jealous of his boyhood fiancée because she had David first (see 30:16, 129:1, 202:28, and *[204:8]* 3.37.25).

(163:31) 3.27.30 **understudy. . . . When you catch the show in Tulsa . . . original company at the Music Box:** The chapter in the manuscript ends with David consoling Catherine and convincing her to take a nap. She asks him to pass the time while she naps by cheering up Marita, her "understudy." The theatrical metaphor inspires her to add, "When you catch the show in Tulsa . . . don't think too much about who played her in the original company at The Music Box." David asks where she learned a phrase like that. From his father, she replies. Presumably she means David's father as she knows him from his stories, but her answer is enigmatic enough to sound a little otherworldly.

The Music Box is a glitzy theatre on Times Square in New York City. In 1921, Irving Berlin left the Ziegfeld Follies to manage the new theatre and open it with a new show, the *Music Box Revue*. The show was a big hit, lasting for 440 performances, and Hemingway wrote an October 1923 article for the *Toronto Daily Star* covering Lloyd George's attendance at a performance. After the show's success in New York, rights to duplicate the scenery, costumes, and songs—and to add new material—were sold separately to outfits in different regional territories, leading to headlines like this 1927 one from the *New York Times*: "Arrests Stop Show at Jackson, Miss.: Manager, 16 Men and 41 Girls in a 'Music Box Revue' Accused of Improper Performance." In other words, David shouldn't be disappointed if the understudy in Tulsa (Marita) fails to live up to the original star from Le Grau-du-Roi (Catherine).

(163:31) 3.28.1 **Chapter Twenty-Eight:** An entire chapter of the manuscript has been deleted here. With Catherine napping, David asks Marita if she'd like to drive into Cannes, but Marita is too upset about the idea of their going to Madrid. It isn't right for Catherine or for David's writing, and he shouldn't feel obliged by promises made to "crazy people." David and Marita, both in bad moods, squabble but agree to drive into town to be alone together. David is so upset that he unthinkingly drives in the direction of Saint-Raphaël—the direction they would normally take to go swimming—instead of driving towards Cannes.

(163:31) 3.28.4 **cursing my family:** In the manuscript, as they drive, Marita invites David to curse her family. This is the proper way, she explains, for a row to begin. In a discarded fragment that fits here in the manuscript, she offers him fodder to get started: her mother was "a tiresome whore" and her uncle failed to get "elected to the Jockey Club" *(422.4 3.28.34)*. She then repeats a French joke about this failure that Hemingway also used to describe the horse-besotted Pablo in *For Whom the Bell Tolls:* "Il a manqué son Jockey." Like someone who has "missed the boat," or a rogue horse in a steeplechase, he's missed his jockey.

Marita's comment about her uncle refers not to the celebrated eponymous Parisian nightclub, but to the bastion of wealth and power after which the nightclub was named: the Jockey-Club de Paris. In the 1920s, jockey clubs in the United States, England, and France were among the world's most exclusive organizations, and the Jockey-Club de Paris was "the hardest club in France to get into" (Carroll). Although the club was large enough in 1927 to boast over a thousand members, more than 90 percent of these members came from the aristocratic peerage with a rank of baron or higher (*Annuaire*). Nevertheless, in the period following WWI, men who were considered mere "idle aristocrats" were often blackballed ("Paris Clubs Exclude Idle Aristocrats"). That Marita's uncle hoped to be elected to the club suggests that he belonged to the upper aristocracy—an indirect allusion to Marita's own aristocratic title (see 90:19).

The role of the jockey club as a symbol of social standing and tool for social climbing is important in Proust's *Remembrance of Things Past,* where it is frequently mentioned. Swann takes "endless pains to get himself elected to the Jockey Club"— a special challenge for him given his Jewish heritage—and the Duc de Guermantes is deeply upset when, as senior vice-president of the jockey club, he is twice passed over for the presidency (Proust 360).

(163:31) 3.28.4 **Then there's money. . . . Comité des forges . . . tenebrous affaires . . . canal:** In the manuscript, continuing her advice about how David can best attack her family, Marita suggests he can make insinuations about how her family came by its wealth: the canal scandals of the late nineteenth century, profiteering by leaders of the iron and steel industry in the First World War (the *Comité des forges*), and

other shady deals (*tenebrous affairs*). Whenever a canal was built, Marita offers, her family "robbed France."

While David has been polite and careful to avoid using "certain terms," Marita suggests he can always attack her for her lesbian relationships. David considers all of that already "explained." Marita adds that he'd never be attracted to any woman who didn't have such a history, or near future. David disagrees and suggests they end the "row game." He then turns the car around so they can head back towards home with the sun behind and a cool breeze facing them.

(163:31) 3.28.10 **pair of freaks:** In the manuscript, as they head back toward La Napoule, Marita tells David that she no longer wants to go to the coiffeur's in Cannes. Catherine, with her impossibly light hair, she thinks, already looks "conspicuous" enough. Marita doesn't want David to suffer embarrassment in Madrid with a "pair of freaks." Catherine can pull off her bleached hair, but Marita is afraid of looking like an "exhibitionist" or a bohemian from the Latin Quarter. Marita is jealous of the love that made David agree to take Catherine to Madrid (in some deleted lines she also tells him that she's jealous of Catherine for having bleached his hair), but they agree to just love one another and not argue. Marita suggests they drive into Cannes and bury David's depression and read the papers, but David first wants to stop at the hotel to see if Catherine will join them.

(163:31) 3.28.15 **Tahitian girl in that Gauguin at the Luxembourg:** In the manuscript, Marita had been playing with the idea of cutting her hair in some dramatic new way untried by Catherine, but she now toys with the idea of growing her hair "really long," like the "Tahitian girl in that Gauguin at the Luxembourg." Marita is thinking of *Femmes de Tahiti* (1891), one of two Gauguin paintings owned by the Luxembourg in 1927 (now at the Musée d'Orsay), and yet another of the novel's several allusions to the Pacific islands as a lost or endangered Eden (Masson 28). See *(154:7) 3.26.4*.

After a moment's reflection, Marita decides that her plans for long hair can wait until after they return from Africa. David notes that Swahili lacks words meaning "love" and "sorry"—although Hemingway corrects himself in the margin of the manuscript. (*Penda* means "love," and *samahani* means "I'm sorry.") The theme of foreign words leads David to apologize for his *cafard,* or despair. Marita acknowledges that *cafard* "kills people," but she knows David isn't a "*cafard* man."

The way talk of Tahiti slides easily into talk of Africa in this passage points once again to fetishistic fantasies of racial transformation writ large. The particular race or ethnicity does not matter to Hemingway and his characters; the fantasy is more essentially about becoming a "dark other" (see *[19:1] 1.2.1* and 30:16).

(163:31) 3.28.18 **I'm always going to see you have your men friends:** Marita asks David to drop her off at the hotel and to go off into town to get a drink and read the

papers by himself. He's been overrun with women, she thinks, and she wishes he had "a club or a real café" where he could see his male friends. "I'm always going to see you have your men friends," she promises. Jenks prints this line in the Scribner's edition of the text (244:23), but he moves it to a position twenty-seven manuscript chapters later. Needless to say, this changes its context entirely, and it contributes importantly to a misplaced sense of masculine retrenchment and restored heteronormativity that colors the conclusion of the Scribner's edition. This misrepresents what Hemingway wrote.

NOTES

1. For Hemingway's bookplate, see Elder et al. 147. The imagery of the bookplate—a cabin with a bear skin nailed to it above another image of a *rejoneador* (a mounted bullfighter)—suggests that it dates to 1932 or soon thereafter. Hemingway would publish his book about bullfighting, *Death in the Afternoon,* in 1932, and that year he shot a large black bear near Cooke City, Montana. A 1932 photo in the collection of the JFK shows Hemingway standing in front of a bear skin nailed to a cabin—a clear model for the image on the bookplate. Elder's book claims that the bookplate appears in "many" of the volumes from Hemingway's library at the Finca Vigía, but this does not seem to be accurate. Of more than eighty books from Hemingway's personal collection now in the JFK—including many from the '30s, '40s, and '50s—not one carries Hemingway's bookplate. Conservators working with Hemingway's books at the Finca Vigía also don't remember seeing Hemingway's bookplate (private correspondence, Mary Patrick Bogan). This doesn't mean that he never used it, but he certainly was not in the habit of doing so.

2. See Epstein 97.

3. See Faucigny-Lucinge 109.

4. For this suggestion of sabotage, see Epstein 108.

5. For letters about the ballet, see for instance, letter to Adriana 18 Apr. 1950 (UT) and letters to Hotchner (*DPDH* 98, 146). In *Hemingway at Auction 1930–1973,* Matthew Bruccoli suggests that letters from Hemingway to Monique de Beaumont exist from 1959 and 1960, but he was mistaken. These letters were misattributed by Carlos Baker, and are addressed to Monique Lange, not Monique de Beaumont.

6. See *UK* 288 and *HIW* 349. A good friend, Zaphiro stayed with the Hemingways at the Finca in July 1957.

CHAPTER 20 (MSS. CHAPTER 29)

164:9 **Juma:** As Johnson notes in his *Standard Swahili-English Dictionary*, "Juma is a very common personal male name" (160). Yet Hemingway's choice of the name may be an homage to Arthur Neumann, considered by many to be "the greatest elephant hunter of all time" (Blunt 166). In Neumann's *Elephant-Hunting in East Equatorial Africa* (1898), Juma is the name of Neumann's favorite gunbearer. Hemingway owned this book and may have mined it for other details of the elephant hunt, such as the guns—a .303 and a .450—that Juma and David's father carry and the wounding of Juma, which recalls the way Neumann's face was similarly barked by an elephant. In *African Game Trails* (1910), Theodore Roosevelt, who knew Neumann only by reputation, describes him as a "strange moody man who died by his own hand" and a "mighty hunter": "With whites he was unsocial, living in this far-off region exactly like a native, and all alone among the natives; living in some respects too much like a native" (244). Neumann died two years before Roosevelt's safari, so it is conceivable that Kermit Roosevelt's gunbearer, Juma, was the same man who served Neumann, but it must be borne in mind that the name was common.

Gunbearers like Juma were absolutely essential partners for the early white elephant hunters, and they did far more than carry firearms. Hemingway would have read the following in his copy of Stigand's *Hunting the Elephant in Africa* (1913): "As it seldom falls to the lot of the white man in Africa to find an instructor of his own colour, he generally has to pick up his knowledge of bushcraft through long, and sometimes bitter, experience, with the help of the natives he is amongst. As the latter are seldom able to impart the information they possess, he must needs learn from them by observation and deduction" (18). Hemingway knew well the value of gunbearers from his own experience on safari in Africa, and the relationship between David's father and Juma owes much to the close relationship between Hemingway and his gunbearer, Ngui, in *Under Kilimanjaro* (see 129:1).

164:17 **the mountain:** The mountain is Kilimanjaro (see 173:13), and the "broken country" (165:15) they will soon cross is to the northwest, near today's Amboseli National Park. This is country Hemingway knew well from his hunting near Kimana Swamp in 1953–54.

165:21 dry camp . . . in the forest: The camp lacks running water yet is in a forest. This suggests that they have made it either to Mount Longido or Ol Doinyo Orok Mountain, each about twenty miles northwest of the forests on the lower slopes of Kilimanjaro. This is why David's father can say, "Plenty of creeks come off the mountain" (166:2).

166:18 come alive again . . . Maybe I can: In the manuscript, right after he thinks about bringing the elephant to life through his story, David thinks that maybe he "can make Catherine whole again and happy too" *(3.29.7)*. But he knows he can't. Just as there had been nothing he could do for the elephant, there's now nothing he can do for Catherine except to bring her to life in the honeymoon narrative as she had once been. He can also do his best to do what she wants. He can do "many things" for Marita, and she can do the same for him. He misses both "girls."

166:22 The elephant was old: See 173:13.

166:26 use the sorrow that you have now to make you know how the early sorrow came: In the manuscript, David tells himself to write the African stories "as well as he can" and then return to the honeymoon narrative *(3.29.9)*. This is part of his effort to make Catherine live in the narrative, just as he is trying to bring the elephant back to life. The sorrow of each loss clearly informs the sorrow of the other, and this is central to Hemingway's message about writing and memory: just as memories shape our present, our present leads us to reimagine and rewrite our past. The process is reciprocal.

(166:27) 3.29.10 **highlands on the equator:** In the manuscript, David thinks that others have written well about South Africa, but not yet about where he grew up, in Kenya's "highlands on the equator." As a writer, he's exploring uncharted geographical (and psychological) terrain, and he has no guide.

The Crown Lands Ordinance of 1902 established a vast expanse of southern Kenya, almost entirely above five thousand feet, cool even at the equator, where land grants would be awarded exclusively to Europeans. Failing to acknowledge the pastoralists who used much of this land but whose populations had been decimated in the late nineteenth century by smallpox and whose herds had recently been devastated by epidemics and droughts, the British pronounced this territory "empty" and a "white man's country." This and the dispossession of land from Kikuyu agriculturalists laid the groundwork for the Mau Mau Rebellion that would later shake the Kenya colony throughout the 1950s, eventually leading to Kenya's independence in 1963. Although David's use of the term *highlands* cannot be divorced from its political implications, he uses the term in a geological, rather than a strictly political, sense. The action of his stories largely takes place to the south of the officially designated "White Highlands."

166:27 **You must always remember the things you believed:** In the manuscript, this line directly follows David telling himself that he must never omit anything because he is "ashamed of it or because no one would ever understand," and he mustn't deny the things that he's not supposed to say because he is white *(3.29.11)*. In a variation on Hemingway's famous iceberg principle, David reflects that the "tribal things" can remain unstated so long as he truly knows them; they will still find their way into his work (see 42:15). He simply must not "betray" them. That David is thinking here about sexuality as much as he is thinking about colonialism and race is made clear when he next supposes that he might have "Catherine and her disasters" to thank, just as much as Marita's support, for his recent burst of creativity. Soon he has to remind himself not to mix up his African story with the honeymoon narrative—precisely because the two stories are so deeply entwined in his mind.

(166:27) 3.29.12 **Menton or St. Tropez; Charenton or Malmaison:** In the manuscript, Catherine has left David a note to tell him that she and Marita won't join him for lunch. They have driven to "Menton or St. Tropez" and will return late in the afternoon or evening. Since the two destinations are at opposite ends of the Riviera, in two different directions and ninety miles apart, David finds the note erratic and worrisome. Soon, as he wonders what Madame thinks of his situation with Catherine (167:24), David imagines that the "beautiful young wife who goes mad" must be a stock figure in France, much like "the ex-Premier or President of the Republic who ends up at Malmaison." Much as one might end up at Saint-Tropez or Menton, one might end up at "Charenton or Malmaison" *(3.29.16)*.

A famous lunatic asylum, Charenton is most noted for having housed the Marquis de Sade. The sanatorium at Malmaison, former residence of the Empress Pauline Bonaparte, housed President of the French Republic Paul Deschanel after his breakdown in office in September 1920. In September 1925, former premier of France René Viviani died at the sanatorium there. But where David thinks of politicians, Hemingway was surely also thinking of Zelda Fitzgerald, who stayed at Malmaison after her breakdown in April 1930. Among the symptoms listed in her admittance report appears her chief "obsessive idea": "her fear of becoming a homosexual. She thinks she is in love with her dance teacher" (qtd. in Bruccoli, *Some* 289). That Hemingway knew something of this seems clear from the "Hawks Do Not Share" chapter of *A Moveable Feast*. There he remembers the change when Zelda pivoted from making Scott jealous with other men to "making him jealous with other women" (155).

167:28 **so long as it pays and isn't violent:** The manuscript clarifies that the "it" here refers to "madness."

167:29 **Russians are gone:** If the French and English formed the "backbone" of Riviera society before the First World War, Russians constituted "its gaudy head"

(Blume 63). A 1914 article, "On the Riviera," claims, "There are so many Russian Grand Dukes at one's elbow, figuratively speaking, that one feels quite familiar at the end of a week with the royal family that surrounds the Czar." Yet by 1925, in the wake of the Russian Revolution, it was all too easy to find articles with titles like "Russian Princess, Reduced to Poverty, Drinks Poison on Promenade at Nice."

167:32 **pioneers in opening up the summer season:** See 6:9.

168:2 **critical distaste . . . silvery whiteness of his hair:** In the manuscript, David's self-critical inspection in the mirror continues. Thin white scars, like an "old road map" or "aerial photograph," cross his brown cheeks and forehead *(3.29.18)*. He playfully thinks of them as "tribal marks" and remembers how proud the surgeon had been of the reconstruction. He needs a haircut, he thinks, if he's going to go to Spain. He can't go looking like "a white-headed Cherokee."[1] He wonders how "crazy" he must have been to allow Catherine to do this to him. Experiencing dissociation again, he sees himself "as though he had never seen himself before" (see 43:17 and 84:16).

David's "tribal marks," even if they are the result of a wartime plane crash, align him with figures from the universe of his African stories and play upon the fetishization of racial otherness that he shares with Catherine and Marita (see 30:16). In this respect, David also shares a symbolic universe with his creator. As early as *Green Hills of Africa* (1935), Hemingway admired African "tribal marks" and "regretted not having any of [his] own. [His] own scars were all informal, some irregular and sprawling, others simply puffy welts" (53). After Mary Hemingway's 1945 car crash, Ernest thought of the "very fine delicately cut scars across one cheek and [the] horizontal light traces of cuts on the forehead"—marks which mirror David Bourne's—as "her tribal scars" (*UK* 45). That David received his scars from a plane crash recalls the two plane crashes that ended Hemingway's 1953–54 safari, but months before these crashes, in a September 1953 safari letter to Slim Hayward, he described himself as "burned black by the sun" and enthused, "Hope you won't mind me with head shaved. . . . Let me know how you feel about piercing of ears and tribal marks" (*HF* 174). His desire for tribal marks that year was strong enough that Mary surprised Ernest one evening in the midst of "ceremonies for face-cutting and ear-piercing" (*HIW* 391). See 129:1.

David's scars—like his white hair—function as a sort of "wearing of the fetish" that is essentially transvestic. That is, by giving his fictional proxy, David, these scars, Hemingway could identify with Mary, with her "tribal scars," and thereby identify with the split-off other-gendered half of his own ego. In a discarded passage that fits here in the manuscript, as David views himself scarred and white-haired in the mirror, he sees "something . . . happening that he did not understand" *(422.4 3.29.20)*. This seems to be the "transvestic moment," when the fetishist, wearing the fetish in front of the mirror, sees the dissociated split-off other-gendered half of his own ego.

(168:3) 3.29.19 You cheap denier . . . tribal taboos and tribal pleasures: In the manuscript, after casting blame on Catherine for his white-haired transformation, David castigates himself as a "cheap denier" and wonders how he can write well if he can't be honest with himself about something this simple. He has to remember how things truly were, without changing them—or forgetting, which is the worst form of "denial." Yes, he had initially been "reluctant and spooked" to let Catherine dye his hair but, once done, he had liked it just as much as she had. His hair had been exactly the same as Catherine's, and it was fun, and he had loved Catherine and everything they did together, including what they did in Le Grau-du-Roi and Madrid. He had suffered "remorse," though, after Madrid, and anything that made him feel like that must, he thinks, have been wrong for him. Perhaps it was. He isn't sure. But everyone has their "tribal taboos and tribal pleasures," and he needs to be honest about how he and Catherine felt, and he needs to get it right in the narrative. It is, he thinks, all they have left. Getting it completely right, though, is difficult, because "no one is completely sane. Certainly no writer is."

David's struggle to acknowledge and take possession of his own desires is admirable and brave. As I argue in *Hemingway's Fetishism,* the story of David Bourne conforms in several ways to the narrative structure of transvestic pornography. As Robert Stoller explains, "In all samples . . . of transvestite pornography the fundamentals are the same: the heterosexual young man, unquestionably totally male, innocent, is captured by females who do so not by physical power but by the mysterious power inherent in femaleness and femininity" (24). He is then forced, against his will, to wear the fetish to negotiate a feminine identification. The element of compulsion repeats the childhood trauma reenacted in the fetishistic scenario—being feminized by a more powerful woman—and is essential to the excitement. The old danger is reapproached, but this time trauma is transformed into triumph: masculinity is reconfirmed through the production of a hearty erection.[2] David still portrays himself as strangely compelled by Catherine to get his hair cut and dyed, but at least he acknowledges his own pleasure in the act.

168:18 **I don't see any good reason why I should give that up. . . . prematurely:** In the manuscript, having finished her shower (168:12), Catherine announces that she has abandoned her plans for them to go to Madrid (3.29.22). When David asks why, she tells him she just doesn't want to go anymore, and Marita agrees. In other words, she has just "given up" something; this clarifies why she says she won't "give up" her love and desire for David. The word "prematurely," however, is ominous.

168:23 **Get dressed and come on out:** In the manuscript, David goes out to the bar after this line and finds Marita there wearing a white linen dress. As David mixes a martini, Marita tells him that the trip to Madrid is off, though she'll leave the explanation to Catherine. She reports that she and Catherine picked up a tin of caviar sent down from Prunier's (see *[51:2]* 3.9.3 and 122:4), and her copy of David's WWI book has finally arrived from Galignani's (see 94:30). Catherine enters also wearing a white linen dress, "a different shade of ivory" than her hair. David wonders what changed her mind about Spain. Catherine says she just woke up knowing that she wouldn't be "going crazy for a while," and she is no longer in such a hurry. It is now that she says she just wants "to have fun" with David "like in the old days" (168:24), and she is no longer in such a hurry to relinquish David entirely to Marita.

(168:25) 3.29.27 **We take turns:** In the manuscript, it is now that Catherine proposes her plan for taking turns with Marita, swapping David in two-day shifts (see 170:4). David thinks both women are "crazy," and he is "very skeptical," but he doesn't put up much of a protest. He is too delighted that Catherine is feeling so much better, and when Marita encourages him to get on board with the plan, he agrees, feeling his voice thicken with excitement (see 14:31). After this, there is a temporal break, followed by the lovemaking scene that begins at 168:32.

169:8 **Are you—:** If Catherine and David are just as they were at Le Grau-du-Roi, Catherine is now "Peter," and she must be asking David if he is now "Catherine" (see 17:23). Her talk about having returned after having "gone away" (169:5) is echoed by David: "You did come back" (169:21). These lines recall Catherine Barkley's "crazy" request to Frederic in *A Farewell to Arms*: "Say, 'I've come back to Catherine in the night'" (30). What is returning is not a physical person; it is a figure of fantasy, a character in the psychodrama that is the fetishistic scenario.

169:26 **darkest white girl in the world. / And the blondest. You're just like ivory:** See 30:16 and 156:5.

NOTES

1. In a 2 Aug. 1950 letter to Adriana Ivancich, Hemingway describes a suntanned Mary as looking like "a very blonde Indian" (UT).
2. For an extended consideration of this, see *HF* 241–60.

CHAPTER 21 (MSS. CHAPTERS 30–31)

171:4 **.303 rifle:** The standard British military rifle of the time, the .303 Lee-Metford and Lee-Enfield was popular with such legendary elephant hunters as Arthur Neumann, Karamojo Bell, Frederick Courteney Selous, and Denis Lyell. The introduction in 1891 of smokeless cordite ammunition allowed comparatively small-bore rifles to deliver an impact of terrific velocity and force, and hunters like Neumann and Bell came to prefer the .303 for its greater accuracy over larger-bore rifles. Citing Neumann's success with elephants, Horace Hutchinson's *Big Game Shooting* (1905), which Hemingway owned, recommends hunters in Africa carry, first, a .303 and, second, a .450 double rifle (Bryden 9). This is what Neumann carried (see 128:11 and 164:9), and it is precisely the arsenal carried by David's father and Juma (198:23).

171:19 **past the broken country . . . climbing again . . . distant stony island . . . three far blue hills:** Having crossed the "broken country" from Ol Doinyo Orok Mountain or Mount Longido (see 165:21), the hunters have arrived at the Nguruman Escarpment west of Lake Magadi, not far from where David's father ascends in the story of the massacre. Looking down from the ridge of the escarpment here, at 6,500 feet above sea level, they would see a "far distant stony island of hills in the dry country" near Shompole (the Fig Tree Camp of Hemingway's 1953–54 safari, where in the story of the massacre David's father rests [see 128:9]), and on a clear day they would see "three far blue hills on the horizon": Mount Kenya (17,057'), Mount Kilimanjaro (19,341'), and Mount Meru (14,977').

172:13 **two spur fowl with his slingshot . . . Francolin quite so high:** Davey's slingshot aligns him with his biblical namesake (see 148:21), and the details of his kill are significant. Hemingway's knowledge of birds was vast. He owned over seventy books on birds, and at least nine books specifically devoted to African birds—including Mackworth-Praed and Grant's massive two-volume *African Handbook of Birds*. It would seem that David's father shares a similar expertise.

Hemingway knew from his copy of B. G. Lynn-Allen's *Shot-Gun and Sunlight* that "there are well over a hundred recognized species and sub-species of francolin," and "that in Kenya and Uganda alone there are about twenty full species"

(103). Hemingway's books contained hundreds of pages devoted to francolin, with color plates and charts articulating their distinguishing features, favored habitats, and range, including altitude limits. Indeed, making such fine distinctions in flora and fauna—a sort of Edenic naming of species by strangers in a strange land—was a common hobby for gentlemen naturalists among the early European settlers in Kenya; thus, it should come as no surprise that David's father, a big-game hunter, has such knowledge.

Lynn-Allen writes that early morning and evening are the time to hunt francolin, "because in these cooler periods the birds are naturally in more open ground on their way to feed, water, and dust," so the circumstances of Davey's kill make sense (118). Lynn-Allen also notes that these birds "are thought to be monogamous," which suggests that the second bird that pecks the first and that is shot in turn may well be a grieving mate—ironically echoing the theme of "friend killers" that emerges during the elephant hunt (108). While most francolin (members of the pheasant family) have spurs, David's designation of the birds as "spur fowl" tells us that the birds Davey shoots belong within a particular genus (*Pternistis*) of francolin known "to most East African sportsmen . . . as 'spur-fowl.'" Judged by the standards of English partridge, spur fowl are "very large (cocks being nearly twice as bulky as . . . English birds)," so Davey has supplied his father and Juma with a good meal (Lynn-Allen 171). This information, together with information about the part of Kenya where David grew up and the fact that his father is surprised to find these birds at this altitude, suggests that Davey has killed yellow-throated Francolin, "the great standby of sportsmen in East Africa," particularly in "Kenya and the northern half of Tanganyika" (Lynn-Allen 102). This species is found "from sea-level to about 6,500 feet," so the fact that they are near the edge of this bird's altitude range indicates that the hunting party is probably on top of the Nguruman Escarpment, at 6,500 feet, directly west of Lake Magadi (see 171:19). If so, they have crossed some of the same territory that David's father crossed in the earlier African story.

A common love of natural history unites David with his father, much as it united Hemingway with his father. David not only admires his father's skills as a naturalist, he continues to identify with him through his adult reading of natural history. David reads fellow bird-lover W. H. Hudson's *Nature in Downland* and *Far Away and Long Ago* (see [76:14] 3.16.11 and 194:26)—both classics of natural history writing with many pages devoted to birds. (Hudson was also the author of several other volumes on birds in Hemingway's library.)

173:6 **askari:** Swahili word for soldier, guard, or armed attendant. The word was commonly used to describe native African soldiers in the colonial forces, but it is also used to describe the younger companion of an old bull elephant (*UK* 312).

173:9 **toto:** Variant of *mtoto*, Swahili for child.

173:13 **Close to two hundred ... only one greater elephant ... near here:** Hemingway's 1928 edition of *Rowland Ward's Records of Big Game* (see *[54:23] 3.11.11*) lists only one elephant with a tusk greater than two hundred pounds, an elephant killed near Kilimanjaro in 1898 with a 226.5 pound tusk, then on display in the British Museum. This tusk was reunited with its partner in 1933, and the pair remains to this day at the British Museum, where they are described as the world's biggest elephant tusks. Tusks lose some weight in drying, and the British Museum now records their weight as 207 and 196 pounds respectively.

The size of these tusks is not merely a measure of market value; it is a measure of the elephant's great age and wisdom. In his copy of David Enderby Blunt's *Elephant*, Hemingway would have read the following:

> Nobody knows exactly to what age an African elephant actually lives, but it is supposed to be from 120 to 150 years. I should not be surprised to learn that he may live to considerably more than that age. . . . The older [the elephant] grows the more elusive he becomes to the human hunter, so wise is he and full of experience.

The "Kilimanjaro tusks," the largest pair ever recorded, photographed outside Arnold, Cheney & Company's Ivory House in Zanzibar by Ernst D. Moore, 22 December, 1908. This "one greater elephant" was killed on the lower slopes of Kilimanjaro in 1898. Hemingway knew this image as the frontispiece to Moore's *Ivory: Scourge of Africa* (1931). (Pratt, Read Co. Records, Smithsonian, National Museum of American History.)

> ... Even when an elephant has attained his full size, his tusks continue to grow, and for this reason some say that the age of an elephant is in proportion to the weight of his tusks, every pound weight of ivory in one tusk being equivalent to a year of his life. (65–66)

If this were true (it is not), then the elephant in David's story would be nearly two hundred years old—older than America, practically out of Eden.

174:8 he had been trying to remember truly how he felt and what had happened: Once again, David shares Hemingway's aesthetics. Here he echoes the formula that Hemingway provides for his writing in *Death in the Afternoon:* "I was trying to write then and I found the greatest difficulty, aside from knowing truly what you really felt, rather than what you were supposed to feel, and had been taught to feel, was to put down what really happened in action; what the actual things were which produced the emotion that you experienced" (2).

175:17 when you climb ... Six kilometers ... *côtes:* If Catherine cycled six kilometers along the Estérel from Théoule-Supérieur, that would take her to Le Trayas. Catherine uses the word *côtes* in the sense of hills, not coast.

175:28 They looked at each other ... in the long mirror: As they stare at each other with their identical haircuts in the mirror, David gets an erection ("Oh you like us" 175:30), but Catherine has a "breast erection" as well. This is especially clear in the manuscript version of this passage, where Catherine's breasts are described as "firm" and "erect" *(3.30.12),* or later in the manuscript when Marita, touching a sleeping David with her breasts, thinks with pride that "they do the same thing he does" *(3.34.5).*[1]

176:3 combed her hair straight back so it looked as though she had just come out of the sea: Mary Hemingway wore her hair this way in Torcello, Italy, in 1948.

177:22 I wish you could see yourself: The break on this page in the Scribner's edition represents a new chapter in the manuscript and a deletion of more than eight manuscript pages describing the action at Chez Jean. Monsieur Jean, Catherine, and David discuss at length the difficulty of getting the Bournes' hair exactly the same. Jean admires the great "compliment" David is paying to Catherine by agreeing to this cut. He is sure that afterwards there are "great rewards." Catherine insists that Jean get "the same ivory color" for both of them (see 156.5). When David hears that Catherine has brought along Perrier-Jouët champagne to toast their haircuts, he exclaims, "I'll be damned." Oh, he is, Catherine assures him *(3.31.3).* The haircut is "the same old Madrid haircut," but David talks Catherine into leaving her bangs just a little bit longer. Jean urges Catherine to keep her hair just a little bit longer so David's can grow in, and then in a few weeks he can shorten hers so they'll be identical. She must be patient. So long as she and David look "like brothers," Catherine is satisfied—though Jean thinks "brother and sister" (see 6:6) would be more appropriate. (In some lines deleted from this passage, David "~~disassociates~~" himself from the haircutting so he won't spoil Catherine's fun, and in an erased but still legible line, Catherine declares she is a "~~boy~~" *[3.31.4].*) As the haircutting continues, Jean declares that Catherine and David look as if they were "the same person."

Pretending to be tired of the two "dedicated artists" and avoiding the mirror, David pays Jean twice his usual fee and asks Catherine where she wants to get lunch. When she asks to return to the restaurant on the harbor where they ate after their last hair-dyeing session, David recognizes a "pattern that had to be repeated" *(3.31.5)*. (Such is the nature of fetishistic fantasy.) As they dine at the same table where they sat before, David remarks that a single bottle of champagne was hardly adequate for a "*shauri*" like they'd had at Jean's. Catherine wants to know what *shauri* means, and David explains that it is the Swahili equivalent of the British "show." Sensing (correctly) that David is retreating defensively into the world of his African stories, Catherine asks him not to worry or think about his writing. She's elated by their latest adventure, but David admits being "frightened." She praises his bravery and asks him if he feels "damned." Yes, "a little," he confesses. This pleases her. That's the way she wants it to be. As they eat artichokes and drink Tavel (see *[11:15] 1.1.12*), Catherine explains that she wanted their desires "to be public." She knows this is something they couldn't have done in Madrid. Feeling conspicuous, David would like to have some "non-damned fun." Catherine replies that that kind of fun no longer exists. As they eat *loup,* Catherine reminds David of the one he caught at Le Grau-du-Roi.

177:26 **Just look at me. . . . That's how you look:** In other words, Catherine *is* David's mirror image. See 43:17, 81:25, 84:16, and 102:29.

178:5 **incredibly flat ivory color of her hair:** See 156.5.

(178:7) 3.31.10 **really spooked:** The chapter continues in the manuscript, and David confesses that this time he is "really spooked." This phrase recalls Hemingway's 1947 letter to Mary after he dyed his hair bright red so he could become Catherine. The next morning, he tells her, he was "spooked shitless" (see 17:23). In the *Eden* manuscript, Catherine tells David that to be fun, things need to be "dangerous enough to scare you," and he soon gathers enough courage to look at himself in her hand mirror. He decides he's through with being "spooked" and wonders if people will think his new look is "tribal." Catherine suggests they take a "siesta."

(178:7) 3.31.14 **Now everything is like I really wanted it. I can't tell who is who:** In the manuscript, the chapter ends with a loving bedroom scene later that evening.

Catherine is delighted that when they make love she can no longer "tell who is who." When David replies "I'm me," she admits as much but answers disconcertingly, "Now you're me you're you so much better."

Lovers who fantasize about merging identities are common in Hemingway's work—think of Catherine Barkley's plea to Frederic in *A Farewell to Arms*, "There isn't any me. I'm you. Don't make up a separate me" (115)—and if we are to judge from a 1926 letter from Pauline to Ernest, the fantasy was hardly confined to his fiction: "We are one, we are the same guy, I am you" (qtd. in Kert 186). In *Hemingway's Fetishism*, I argue that such merging tendencies reproduce the childhood trauma of Ernest's pseudotwinship with his sister Marcelline (See 6:6), and they rely on the power of the fetish, inherited from what Winnicott calls the transitional object, to deny distinctions between the self and the other. Perhaps more importantly, such moments are experienced by the fetishist as revelations of a vital truth: insofar as the lover represents the split-off other-gendered half of the ego (see 17:23, 22:17, and 43:17), she *is* himself—or at least a mirror image of that self.

NOTE

1. For a consideration of Hemingway's work and what Otto Fenichel calls the "breast = penis equation," see *HF* 143–45, 312.

CHAPTER 22 (MSS. CHAPTERS 32–34)

180:11 It was a skull as high as David's chest: Stigand, in his *Hunting the Elephant in Africa* (which Hemingway owned), notes how often the spoor of a hunted elephant "leads you past an old skull or the spot at which one has been killed. This happens so often that I think it must be more than coincidence" (52). Elephant mourning—revisiting and circling the remains of a dead companion, often gently feeling the bones with the trunk—is well documented. As Ryan Hediger and Cary Wolfe have noted, young Davey's empathy for the elephant's loss involves a "cross-species and cross-gender identification" that also unites David with Catherine, who is clearly aligned with the elephant (Hediger 79–95; C. Wolfe 239). Much as the elephant has returned to the site of an earlier trauma, David has done the same to negotiate the pain he feels at the prospect of losing Catherine. He touches and explores the bones of an older primal loss. And what does he find? A weathered skull, where gaping holes mark the ivory that has been hacked away. The old bull elephant associated with Catherine, with its overstated ivory, leads David back to a primal loss that is not so much his as it is Hemingway's: the traumatic castrating absence of the identically coiffed pseudotwin sister Ernest nicknamed Ivory (see 156:5).

181:18 drunk with their *bibis* at the beer shamba: See 94:4.

181:19 I'm going to keep everything a secret always: David's traumatic primal loss leads directly to a primal repression—a truth he will always keep "secret." But while this secret detaches and isolates David from his father and Juma, it is inseparable from the shared secrets that bind him so closely to Catherine and Marita (see 180:11).[1]

181:31 Fuck elephant hunting: As Burwell and Hediger note, David here rejects not only elephant hunting, but his father. In this light, it is worth noting that these father-son dynamics in some ways reverse those that preoccupied Hemingway during the 1950s. Although famed as a big-game hunter who shot rhinoceros, buffalo, lion, leopard, kudu, and zebra, Hemingway pointedly never shot an elephant. The possibility that during his 1953–54 safari, as an honorary game warden, he might have to shoot an elephant to protect human life or property troubles him throughout *Under*

Kilimanjaro. Yet when Ernest's youngest son, Gregory, moved to what was then Tanganyika in 1955 to buy a farm and become a "white hunter," his target became elephants—though he admits in his memoir, "The thing I was hunting was huge, but blacker in my mind" (10). Gregory was driven, he implies, by his deep-rooted love-hate relationship with his father—a relationship whose tensions were brought to a fever pitch following the death of his mother, Pauline, in 1951. Gregory had been arrested in Los Angeles for cross-dressing, and when Pauline called Ernest that night to discuss it, they argued bitterly. Later that night, Pauline woke in pain and was brought to the hospital, where she died at 4:00 A.M. from complications related to a tumor of the adrenal gland. Instead of sharing his conflicted feelings about his own fetishistic desires—desires intimately linked to "ivory" (see 156:5 and 180:11)—Ernest frankly accused Gregory of killing his own mother, devastating his son. In 1960, Gregory, then a physician, learned that it was more likely Ernest's argument with Pauline that released a flood of adrenaline, spiking her blood pressure and killing her, but since Gregory was hunting in Africa in 1955 he did not know this, and he was profoundly damaged. In his memoir, he remorsefully remembers shooting eighteen elephants in a single month.

183:14 he could feel himself start to be whole again. . . . all the rest of him could be riven: This rift in David's identity, memorialized in his Oklahoman/African point of origin and the title of his first novel (see 111:11 and 111:16), is further manifested in his competing identifications with Catherine and his father and the way his writing is torn between the honeymoon narrative and his African stories. In the manuscript, David compares it to a "splitting . . . of green, not dry wood . . . [that] was alive and growing" *(3.32.11bis)*. As I note in *Hemingway's Fetishism,* it is no mistake that Freud's late essay "Splitting of the Ego in the Defensive Process" grew specifically out of his work on fetishism. Here, Freud argues that the fetishist's irreconcilable but tenaciously held phallic-position attitudes toward feminine "castration"—his recognition that women don't have the phallus and his simultaneous disavowal of this same intolerable fact, which seems to threaten the possibility of his own castration—creates nothing less than a "rift in the ego which never heals but which increases as time goes on" (276). The phenomenon is seen most clearly in the two names and two identities adopted by the fetishistic cross-dresser to represent the two halves of the ego: in Hemingway's case, Ernest and Catherine (see 17:23). Phyllis Greenacre and other post-Freudian analysts have suggested that the rift in the ego is not so much the *result* of disavowal as the adoption of disavowal as a primary defense is the result of an ego *already* riven by bigendered identifications and already prone to merger and fragmentation: "The rift in the fetishist's ego is a bisexual one dating back to the time when the ego was in the very process of formation" (*HF* 191).

(183:19) 3.32.11bis2 **You were awfully good to do what she wanted. . . . twin brother:** In the manuscript, as they sit at the bar and drink whiskey, Marita praises David for having dyed his hair again to match Catherine's. It made Catherine so happy. David compares the experience to waking up after a "drunken debacle" to find himself "tattooed." Marita tells him he looks like Catherine's "twin brother," but he's still too "spooked" to look at himself in the mirror. David wants to please Marita now, but she tells him he has, just by working.

(183:19) 3.32.13 **wouldn't mind being myself . . . my own name . . . not be confused with anyone else:** In the manuscript, while Marita admires David's hair, he tells her that he wouldn't mind being himself, with his own name, instead of "being confused with anyone else." David is clearly referring to his experience the night before playing the role of "Catherine" in bed (see *[178:7] 3.31.14*). Smiling at his image in the bar mirror, he says his hair is "a hell of a color . . . for a man." He is "enough man," Marita assures him.

(183 :19) 3.32.15 **Donnez-moi un peu de trop. C'est juste assez pour moi:** In the manuscript, Marita wonders if "making much too much love" might be bad for David's writing. How do you know what's "too much"? David asks. Marita isn't sure. Without naming his source, David replies with the words of Jean Cocteau: "*Donnez-moi un peu de trop. C'est juste assez pour moi,*" ("Give me a little too much. That's just enough for me."). Cocteau's motto—which appears variously as "*Trop est tout juste assez pour moi,*" "*C'est trop et c'est juste assez pour moi,*" and "*Un peu trop c'est juste assez pour moi*"—appears first in his 1921 essay "Visites à Maurice Barrès" and again on one of the self-portraits he published in *Le mystère de Jean l'Oiseleur* (1925). According to his biographer Claude Arnaud, a version of the phrase was pinned to the wall above Cocteau's work table.

The phrase is witty and appropriate, but given the gender anxiety David is experiencing at this moment, it is also worth noting that Hemingway seldom missed a chance to mock Cocteau's homosexuality. Hemingway, of course, knew Cocteau, a central figure in the French artistic world both in Paris and on the Riviera. In the July 1924 issue of the *Transatlantic Review,* Hemingway took an entirely unnecessary and patronizing swipe at Cocteau (see *[162:4] 3.27.9),* but Cocteau's feelings could not have been deeply bruised, for when Hemingway published "The Undefeated" in a 1925 issue of *Der Querschnitt,* Cocteau supplied a photograph of the wounded El Gallo to accompany bullfight photographs by Hemingway and others. When Hemingway's "Today Is Friday" was printed in 1926 in a special edition, it was accompanied by a Cocteau drawing; and in a doubly cruel gesture, Hemingway sent a copy to their mutual friends, Gerald and Sara Murphy, writing "fairy" next to Cocteau's name. In *Death in the Afternoon,* Hemingway recounts a story of Cocteau and Raymond Radiguet, again emphasizing Cocteau's homosexuality.

Hemingway owned a copy of *The Journals of Jean Cocteau*, published in 1956, and he probably read them while working on *A Moveable Feast* and *The Garden of Eden*. These essays—not a true journal—recount Cocteau's dealings with such figures as Proust, Gide, Picasso, and Diaghilev—all figures alluded to in the *Eden* manuscript. From this volume, Hemingway would also have known that at one time Cocteau rented a wing of the Hôtel Biron, where Rodin lived. The Hôtel Biron—since 1919 the Musée Rodin—is of course where the Bournes and the Sheldons see Rodin's *Metamorphoses of Ovid* and the *Gates of Hell,* the sculptures that inspire their sexual adventures (see *[17:22] 1.1.21*).

(183:19) 3.32.17 the Éclaireur. . . . quite a good murder: In the manuscript, before going to get David some food and a beer, Marita hands him a copy of the newspaper *L'Éclaireur de Nice et du Sud-Est* and recommends a story about "quite a good murder" from "up in the hills." This is how the manuscript chapter ends. For readers who wonder what constitutes "quite a good murder," Hemingway is almost certainly alluding to the 19 October 1927 murder of Marcelle Lord-Vernet, the estranged French wife of the American writer Horace Wilfred Lord, by Wlatchylas de Klupfell, her lover and a former officer in the Russian imperial guard. Lord-Vernet was killed in Nice with a "bejeweled dagger" through the heart during what Klupfell claimed was an attempt to prevent him from suicide, but what *L'Éclaireur* and other French newspapers speculated was a jealous fit of rage in a love triangle.[2] *L'Éclaireur,* which seldom devoted much space to stories of crime, splashed the story across its front page for two days and reported it in sensational detail.

The love triangle and attempted suicide resonate with the plot of *The Garden of Eden,* but the story made international news for reasons still more relevant to the novel, as is made clear by sensational headlines such as "French Murder Reveals Unclad Mountain Colony" and "Love Cult Colony Cultivates Cabbages in Its Modern Eden; Inmates 'Wear' Nature's Garb." As *L'Éclaireur* and other papers reported, Klupfell and Lord-Vernet first met at a nudist free-love colony at Courmettes, up in the hills above Cannes. As a leader of this "modern Eden" explained for the papers, "We have no money, no property, nothing individually, everything belongs to the community. We have no marriages and the children no names, except sons and daughters of the Zarathustra colony." The same article adds that "public opinion on the Riviera is greatly agitated over the disclosures, and it is reported that several villas at the seaside owned by Americans and English have been used as meeting places for groups more or less affiliated with similar cults" ("Nude"). The story speaks to the cultural atmosphere on the Riviera in 1927, and Hemingway would have been interested in the Zarathustra colony's Edenic aspirations.

(183:19) 3.33.1 side by side on the beach: In the manuscript, a new chapter begins with Marita and David still talking, but now on the beach. David is happy with the new arrangement alternating between Catherine and Marita, and he has had no remorse. This, Marita says, is because he has a clean conscience. He's done everything he could to make Catherine happy. She promises to do the same for Catherine, although David cautions her not to endanger what they also share together.

Soon they are back at the bar in the hotel. Marita asks if she can read David's story after lunch, but he says it is in a "bad place" right now. Marita tells him that she "care[s] about the writing as much" as she does about him. "Naturally," David replies. "The writing is much better." Hungry from having made love, they decide to eat.

183:24 **cool breeze . . . from Kurdistan:** See 13:23.

183:30 **Can you still remember that long ago:** When David notes that there hasn't been "a blow of any kind" since the day they met, Marita asks if he can "still remember" events from "that long ago." David agrees that that day seems "further away than the war." They have, in fact, known each other for exactly two weeks.

183:32 **I had the war the last three days:** Having spent the past three days reading David's WWI book, Marita has been living in that book, much as David has been living in the elephant story he's been writing. In very similar terms, Mary Hemingway described Ernest "living in" *The Garden of Eden* as he worked on it (see *[140:3] 3.24.5* and 216:19).

184:14 **nobody knows about himself:** In the manuscript, Marita tells David she loves his stories of self-discovery, and in a deleted line, he admits that he has only begun to learn about himself *(3.33.8)*. When Marita warns that Catherine is "jealous" of his work, David defends her, but Marita insists Catherine is jealous, just as she herself is jealous of everything about him—especially, in a protective way, of his work, since it is "the best part" of him.

184:19 **Can I read the narrative?** In the manuscript, in making her request, Marita tells David that Catherine said the narrative was "written to be read" *(33.3.11),* and David admits that it was. Marita doesn't see why she shouldn't read it, then, if others will be able to. David, however, would still prefer she didn't. When Marita tells him that Catherine has already told her "everything," David replies that Catherine "doesn't know everything." In other words, he doesn't know that Catherine has also already read the narrative. When Marita confesses having already read the manuscript, David asks her how Catherine got her hands on it. Marita explains that his Vuitton luggage came with two keys, and Catherine has one (see 139:20).

185:4 **"Madrid. . . ." "I'm just the way you are":** In the manuscript, Marita tells David that Madrid was "the least clear" part of the narrative, but she "understand[s] it the best" because she is "just the way" he is *(3.33.13iii)*. Does she mean, he asks, that she suffers from "remorse"? No, she replies. She means that she is exactly like him, and she is "however you want me." Since "Madrid" is a code word for a sexual combination in which both partners are "boys" (see 67:1 and *[67:10] 3.14.16*), it should be clear that Marita is not the simple heteronormative counterbalance to Catherine frequently imagined by critics familiar only with the Scribner's edition. It should also be clear that whatever remorse David may have suffered in Madrid, this is a sexual combination he still desires. The chapter promptly ends in the manuscript with David's suggestion that they "make a siesta."

185:19 **No one has to but we are—:** In the manuscript, beginning to climax, Marita follows David's "but we are" with ecstatic affirmations that they really are. As she reaches climax, repeatedly oscillating between "I want to" and "I don't" and "Yes I do," she seems to undergo "the change" (see 12:11).

(185:31) 3.34.3 **lovely dream . . . his Somali girl:** In the manuscript, before the final paragraph of the chapter, we are privy to a long internal monologue from Marita's point of view. As she plays "softly and searchingly" with the sleeping David, she wonders if he will have lovely dreams of Africa and his "Somali girl." She knows what the Somali girl did, and she decides to do it herself now so gently that she won't wake David. She wishes she'd known him when he was a boy but feels, in some respects, thanks to his writing, as if she knows the boy David better than the adult. She admits to herself how jealous she has been of Catherine but tells herself she can do anything Catherine can. She could undergo the change and make David change too "if that's what he wanted ever." She could do Madrid better than Catherine, she knows, if that's what David wants. She can, she tells herself, because she "really know[s] about it." But she could also "release him and not hold him to it." In fact, she thinks she'll do it tomorrow—but to help him, not unsettle him. She gently touches the sleeping David with her breasts and feels "so proud they do the same thing he does" (see 175:28). As she thinks about how much she enjoys David's erotic touch, she hopes she is "as good as Catherine" and not just a novelty. She continues to play gently with him as he sleeps.

NOTES

1. For the use of secret-sharing as a mechanism to bind together Hemingway's lovers, see *HF* 22–24.
2. For the original article in *L'Éclaireur de Nice et du Sud-Est,* see "À Nice, hier matin." See also "L'Ancien capitaine Russe qui a tué Mme. Lord-Vernet aurait frappé par jalousie." For the "bejeweled dagger," see "Russian Captain Admits."

CHAPTER 23 (MSS. CHAPTERS 35–36)

187:13 **She looks about sixteen:** In the manuscript, reminded that Barbara had once called her jailbait (see *[47:18]* 3.7.2), Catherine misses Barbara. Yet Marita notes that Catherine hadn't wanted Barbara when she could have had her.

187:16 **I started to read it:** The manuscript makes it clear that Catherine initially began reading the narrative to investigate the need for illustrations. See *(43:4)* 3.5.2 and 189:2.

188:1 **if he ever says no . . . just keep right on:** Catherine's assertion is unsettling, yet David truly does struggle to acknowledge his own desires, and he must be compelled to do what he actually wants (see *[168:3]* 3.29.19). As Catherine will soon tell him, "You always do everything I want because you really want to do it too" (196:24).

188:10 **it will be so much better when you have a dark girl too:** In the manuscript, Catherine actually says that "the *illustrations* will be much better when you have a dark girl too" (3.35.3; my emphasis).

188:33 **Don't you want it brought out? I do:** See 77:29.

189:2 **Laurencin, Pascen, Derain, Dufy and Picasso:** Catherine's ideas for illustrations here are presented as a manifestation of insanity—in the manuscript, she plans to have passages of the honeymoon narrative translated into French for the illustrators and imagines she can have this effectively done by her lawyers or bankers (3.35.6)—but we should remember that David, in the manuscript, has already considered adding illustrations to his story of the Sheldons—and as is the case with Catherine in the manuscript, his first choice for an illustrator is Nick. (For this and a broader consideration of illustration as a theme, see *[43:4]* 3.5.2.) Moreover, in the manuscript, Barbara Sheldon imagines an illustrated version of "The Undiscovered Country," the book Andy is writing about her and Nick. Barbara enthusiastically describes it for Nick and Andy with "colour plates" or "snap shots" of them in the café or at the beach in Hendaye—perhaps painting together far out on the sand or posing in an enormous sandcastle *(422.2 3.12,* see appendix A). (In fact, some notes in the *Moveable Feast* manuscript, on a page blending text from *Eden* and *Feast,* suggest that Hemingway briefly contemplated using "The Sand Castle" as a possible title for the first book of *Eden.* See *[31:20] 1.4.4.)* Barbara looks forward to a time when the book has made them all famous and people will admire Nick's nude portraits of her on the walls of the great museums.

For Catherine's—and Hemingway's—interest in commissioning illustrations by Picasso, see *(43:4) 3.5.2.* For Marie Laurencin, see *(45:6) 3.5.7.*

Pascen is a misspelling for Bulgarian-American-French artist Jules Pascin. Born Julius Pincas and celebrated as one of the "most astonishing draughtsmen" of his time, Pascin was an artist of the flesh, so devoted to the female nude that he was sometimes called an erotomaniac or pornographer (Dupouy 216, 84). A fixture of Montparnasse café life, he was famed for his ninety-five lovers (i.e., sleeping with his models), the two "wives" he simultaneously juggled (one of whom was actually married to the Norwegian painter Per Krohg), and his eventual suicide. Hemingway knew him well and in 1925 was planning "a book of . . . dirty poems to be illustrated by Pascin." The book never materialized, but that year two drawings by Pascin (and a line drawing by Picasso) did accompany a German publication of "The Undefeated" (*Letters* 2 323, 324). In *Islands in the Stream,* Thomas Hudson fondly remembers Pascin as someone with a Joycean knowledge of female sexuality and as someone who "could paint more beautifully than anybody then" (76). In *A Moveable Feast,* Hemingway remembers joining Pascin at the Dôme one evening in the company of two models, the sisters Bronia and Tylia Perlmutter (unnamed in the text), the younger of whom Pascin invites Hemingway to "bang." Today, the dark sister, Bronia, is best remembered for her affair with Raymond Radiguet, memorialized both in Djuna Barnes's 1925 story "Le Grande Malade" and, more briefly, in Hemingway's *Death in the Afternoon* (71).[1] The blonde sister, Tylia, "was a member of the lesbian circle that included Berenice Abbott, Natalie Barney, Djuna Barnes, and Alice Toklas" (O'Rourke, "Who" 162), but in the *Feast* manuscript Hemingway mistakenly writes that Bronia was "a lesbian who also liked men" (84). Given Pascin's skill as an artist, his obsession with sexuality, his two "wives" (even if one wasn't truly his wife), and his association in Hemingway's mind with bisexual sisters, one dark and one blonde, his credentials to illustrate the honeymoon narrative seem unimpeachable.

The French painters André Derain and Raoul Dufy are less obvious choices. In the manuscript, David can't understand why Catherine would want Derain, who, though celebrated by some in the mid-1920s as "the greatest living French painter" (Kospoth), is dismissed by David as without talent *(3.35.10).* When Catherine tells him she is thinking of the vineyards outside the walls of Aigues-Mortes, David replies that she probably meant to say the French painter André Dunoyer de Segonzac, who indeed painted such scenes. Catherine admits he's right, though David also dismisses him as a painter. Nonetheless, he can see how she'd use him and Dufy, who was known during the 1920s for bright, colorful, decorative paintings of the French Riviera. Catherine thinks the painters would never understand the honeymoon narrative, but she's sure the project would inspire their best work.

190:28 **Vogue:** See 6:3.

190:34 **She may decide to have an affair with another woman:** In the manuscript, the "other woman" is named. It is Barbara Sheldon: "There's quite a bit about Barbara" *(3.35.12)*.

191:7 **I feel as though I invented you:** In the manuscript, Catherine adds, "You really are something that I made. . . . It's better than painting if anyone knew" *(3.35.14)*. Catherine's "creation" of David and Marita may recall the way in which young Ernest and his pseudotwin sister, Marcelline, were treated as almost doll-like "creations" by Grace Hemingway (see 6:6 and *[168:3] 3.29.19*). For more on Catherine's creativity and her use of real people as her medium, see 14:13, 27:16, and 53:17.

191:14 **like acrobats:** see 204:20.

192:8 **gamin type:** The boyish "gamin type" was a recognizable fashion for young women in the 1920s. In the summer of 1927, one could find in the pages of the *New York Times* and French *Vogue* advertisements for "gamin" hats and sweaters. Throughout the 1920s, actresses such as Mary Pickford, Lillian Gish, Alla Nazimova, Colleen Moore, Elissa Landi, and Louise Brooks all played "gamin" roles, and in 1926 Norma Talmadge was a box office sensation in *Kiki* as a "French street gamin with the soul of a 'great lady'" ("Delightful 'Kiki'"). A 1921 fashion article declared, "Today is the day of the gamin. The flapper is the gamin in society" (Rittenhouse), and in his book *The French Riviera in the 1920s*, Xavier Girard writes, "close-fitting swimsuits, shorts, espadrilles, . . . the gamin look, . . . and tanning were all basic ingredients of a new intermingling of the sexes" (20). This captures the style of the Bournes.

192:25 **You're a girl and a boy both and you really are:** In the manuscript, instead of "You're a girl and a boy both and you really are. You don't have to change and it doesn't kill you and *I'm not*," Hemingway wrote, "You're a girl and a boy both and you really are. *And I'm not*. You don't have to change and it doesn't kill you" *(3.35.18; my emphasis)*. The difference is subtle, but Jenks's transposition of "and I am not" obscures the point Catherine is trying to make. As much as one might wish otherwise, Catherine's use of "you" is particular, not universal. In other words, her point is not the Freudian understanding that "every human being is endowed constitutionally with both masculine and feminine dispositions" (Laplanche and Pontalis 52); she means, rather, that whereas she herself oscillates, sometimes wrenchingly, between girlishness and boyishness, Marita is both girl and boy simultaneously, without any need to change. Marita makes this point herself late in the manuscript: "I'm better than she is because I really am both. I'm a better boy because I really am. I don't have to change back and forth and I'm a better girl I hope. She isn't really a girl at all . . ." (3.45.34). This tension between oscillating and simultaneous bigendered identities exemplifies the sort of divided attitude towards sexual difference that characterizes fetishistic disavowal (see 15:13).

193:15 **So they were friends:** In the manuscript, this sentence begins a new chapter. Lines in this paragraph deleted from the manuscript speak of Marita's belief in the "preposterous arrangement" proposed by Catherine to share David. Catherine now speaks more calmly—"sensibly, intelligently, and wittily"—about her plans for publishing the honeymoon narrative, yet underlying her talk is always the same "basic insanity." She plans illustrations for unwritten scenes—scenes that may never be written—with no sense of how the manuscript will end, "nor whether she would be alive or dead in it" (3.36.2).

193:25 **He had been happy in the country of the story:** The Scribner's editor, Tom Jenks, here changes a line. In the manuscript, David has been happy "to be intact all day with Marita," not to be in the country of his story (3.36.2). Marita, we are told, is the only woman with whom he had ever been able to truly discuss his writing.

193:29 **Catherine was not his enemy except as she was himself:** This points once again to the way Catherine and David function on some level as if they are two halves of a single riven ego (see 12:13, [22:18] 1.2.4, and 43:17).

(194:4) 3.36.3i **the pass of Roncevaux. . . . Ah, que ce cor a longue haleine:** In the manuscript, David reflects that Catherine and Marita can be both friends and enemies. They "respect and like each other," but they are wary of rivals and dislike other women, except for Barbara, who is too far removed to be a threat. David supposes that, for Catherine, Barbara must remain frozen in time, always as she was before Catherine rode through the pass of Roncevaux and into Navarre. At the thought of Roncevaux, David remembers, for the second time in the *Eden* manuscript, a line from the *Song of Roland*, "Ah, que ce cor a longue haleine" (see [44:28] 3.5.6). In his mind's eye, he sees the Irati River and the walls and towers of Pamplona rising in the distance.

(194:4) 3.36.4 **"I'll ask Braque. . . ." sand castle:** In the manuscript, as David thinks about how lovely Marita had been that day and how quickly Catherine had smashed their pact, he overhears the two women discussing plans to illustrate the honeymoon narrative. What he hears implies that Marita knows Georges Braque and other painters, although she is sure Braque would decline the commission. An important painter among the Fauves, Braque became, along with Picasso, one of the founders of Cubism. (For more on Braque, see *[54:23] 3.11.15.*) David thinks of these plans for illustrations as a "house of cards" or "sand castle"—alluding to a possible subtitle Hemingway considered for the first book of *Eden* (see 189:2).

(194:4) 3.36.5 **crazy pigeon:** In the manuscript, David compares Catherine to a "crazy pigeon" who keeps building and destroying her own nests, abandoning them and rebuilding them again in new places.

This unusual metaphor may be grounded in a passage from a book that Hemingway owned: Carl Naether's *The Book of the Pigeon*. The book's first chapter, "Till Death Do Part?," debunks the myth of pigeon fidelity and raises the topic of "crazy" nest-building as part of a larger conversation about gender fluidity among pigeons as well as their female-female and male-male nesting pairs:

> Pairing of males or of females is not at all uncommon among pigeons. It happens frequently among females which are kept by themselves. . . . Almost invariably there will be some females consorting with others, building nests, each pair laying four eggs, which of course do not hatch. As time goes on, the behavior of one of them will become somewhat more masculine, though she will continue to lay eggs.

"Somewhat less common," Naether further explains, "is pairing among male pigeons," but it is far from rare (3–4). He goes on to describe a devoted pair of males who nested together only to abandon their nest when eggs failed to appear, but who rebuilt a nest in a new place and tried again. When the new attempt again failed to produce eggs, they fell to fighting one another.

In an influential reading of *The Garden of Eden*, Cary Wolfe has suggested that, for Hemingway, "the discourse of species . . . serve[s] as a crucial 'off-site'—an/other site—where problems of race or gender may be either 'solved' or reopened by being coded as problems of species" (226). This "crazy pigeon" metaphor seems to be a case in point. If eggs are a symbol of creative fertility in the novel (see 4.9), then Catherine's crazy nests symbolize a sort of disordered creativity.

194:26 **Nature in Downland:** In the manuscript, Hemingway initially had David pick up *Hampshire Days*, one of Hudson's books of natural history, and find it boring, but he deletes this and replaces it with another by Hudson: *Nature in Downland*. Yet the initial choice of *Hampshire Days* is not without meaning. It is a natural segue from the metaphor of Catherine as a crazy nest-builder, since the bulk of the first chapter of *Hampshire Days* is devoted to the process by which a baby cuckoo ejects eggs and chicks from the nest in which it has been parasitically laid by its mother. Perhaps the metaphor of Marita as the cuckoo in Catherine's crazy nest, ready to replace Catherine and take over David, seemed to Hemingway unfair or too obvious. Perhaps it absolved David too much of responsibility. For whatever reason, he deleted *Hampshire Days* and replaced it with *Nature in Downland*. The passage David reads, a memory of Hudson's youth in Argentina, speaks to the unreality of David's situation and to his psychological state. After a big wind, Hudson and his brother would find "immense masses" of thistle down piled high in sheltered hollows:

> These masses gleamed with a strange whiteness in the dark, and it would please us to gallop our horses through them. Horses are nervous, unintelligent creatures, liable to take fright at the most unfamiliar objects, and our animals would sometimes be in terror at finding themselves plunged breast-deep into this unsubstantial whiteness, that moved with them and covered them as with a cloud. (3)

Putting down his book and returning to his own world from this unsubstantial world of thistle down, David finds the girls' voices "real again."

(196:25) 3.36.11 **world is changed. . . . Crazy things aren't crazy now:** In the manuscript, Catherine briefly tries to historicize and universalize her mental state. The world, she claims, has changed, and "crazy things aren't crazy now." What *is* crazy is trying to act "sensibly." Silly as such generalizations may be, she has a point. Public attitudes about gender, sexuality, race, class, and proper public deportment—particularly in France—had changed more rapidly and dramatically in the decade after World War I than they had in any decade in the previous century. The French, after all, have their reasons for calling the 1920s *les années folles* ("the crazy years"). See also 94:19.

196:27 **Anyway I am you and her. . . . I'm everybody:** See *(22:18) 1.2.4* and *(178:7) 3.31.14*.

NOTE

1. I give the title of Barnes's story as it appeared, revised, in *Selected Works of Djuna Barnes* (Farrar, Straus and Giroux, 1962). It was originally published in *This Quarter* (1925) as "The Little Girl Continues."

CHAPTER 24 (MSS. CHAPTER 37)

197:14 **Nothing would ever be as good as that again. . . . They would kill me and . . . Kibo too if we had ivory:** In other words, David's betrayal of the elephant marks a fall from an Edenic state, after which nothing would ever be as good again. And the cause of this fall is human rapacity. To understand this, it is crucial to recognize that David's father is hunting at the very end of the heyday of elephant hunting in East Africa, when this enormous tusker is essentially the last of its kind.

As Hemingway knew well from his collection of Africana, the conception of Africa as a natural Eden destroyed by a rapacious European desire for ivory was common even before the turn of the twentieth century. In his copy of Clive Phillipps-Wolley's *Big Game Shooting* (1894), he would have read that, in the mid-nineteenth century, South Africa had been so full of game that it reminded the author of "children's pictures of Adam naming the beasts in the Garden of Eden," but by the final decade of the century it had been overhunted (49). Complaining in 1913 that he had been born "fifty years too late," C. H. Stigand, in *Hunting the Elephant in Africa*, wrote that "in the early days in the East African Highlands, things must have been much the same as in the old days in South Africa . . . ," but the days of unlimited elephant shooting were long gone (2). Carl Schillings's *In Wildest Africa* (1907) registered an even stronger note of primal loss: before the arrival of white hunters, Africa "must have been a veritable Garden of Eden" (32). Yet, "now in its last refuge this most wonderful wave of life [was] rapidly ebbing away. . . . Through the trifling fact that we have ivory balls for billiards, the African elephant goes to destruction" (129). Schillings hoped that scientists would study "the last elephants" while they still could. In his copy of Ernst Moore's *Ivory: Scourge of Africa* (1931), Hemingway would have read that even in the 1880s, "[i]vory-hunting was not a sport . . . but a cruel, bloody business, as terrible a vocation as the world has ever seen. . . . The bloodshed and cruelty, the inhumanity and suffering the precious ivory caused, never can be fully known." The lust for ivory fueled the slave trade and "turned thousands of square miles of fertile country into a wilderness of rapine, plunder, and fire-blackened ruin. Hundreds of thousands of mighty elephants were slain; but for every elephant that perished for its ivory a dozen human lives were wrecked or snuffed out" (xv–xvi). Moore, once one of Zanzibar's great ivory traders, con-

Ivory warehouse, London docks, 1895. (London Metropolitan Archives.)

cludes, "Never has there been a more bitter example of the 'curse of civilization'" than the arrival of European ivory traders in East Africa (12).

198:23 **the .303 then . . . his father's .450:** See 128:11 and 171:4.

199:20 **his eye was the most alive thing David had ever seen:** In *Death in the Afternoon,* remembering his apprenticeship as a writer, Hemingway describes his struggle to isolate the "actual things" that, like T. S. Eliot's objective correlatives, "produced the emotion that you experienced" (2). This sad and marvelous eye that so powerfully registers the death of the elephant and all that it signifies is precisely such a thing. Young Davey, seen through the eyes of the older David, is already thinking like a writer. Noting the difference in color between the blood on the elephant's flanks and the blood now coming from its ear, Davey thinks, "I must remember that," though "it had never been any use to him" (199:32). Now that the time has come to write the story, it is finally "of use."

Cary Wolfe has argued that in "focusing on the privileged sensory apparatus of the human"—the eye—Davey experiences cross-species identification, and the death of the elephant becomes "literally an act of murder." The long eyelashes, moreover, link the elephant "via stereotype to the category of the feminine" and Catherine (239). Building on this, Robin Silbergleid has suggested that whereas Davey had once seen his father through the elephant's eyes, "with its long feminine eyelashes . . . , he now identifies with his father, symbolically killing Catherine as well as his 'feminine' self." This, for Silbergleid, is part of David's attempt to "write himself into white, heteronormative, patriarchal masculinity and out of the wonderfully 'perverse' narrative of Catherine's racial, gender, and sexual play" (107). Silbergleid's interpretation, however, is shaped powerfully by Jenks's misleading editing of the novel's conclusion.

200:5 **Humpty Dumpty:** Linking this passage to a pattern of egg imagery in the novel (see 4.9), Stoneback has suggested that the vision of Juma as Humpty Dumpty alludes to David's own spiritual fall through his betrayal of the elephant and "complicity in Catherine's dark changes." Stoneback views him now as a "broken man" who can no longer be put together again, even by Marita ("Memorable" 26). The final chapters of the manuscript, however, do not support a moralizing reading of this sort. See also *(230:16) 3.42.4.*

200:7 **bringing the tail of the elephant that had no hairs on it at all:** After a successful hunt, the tail of an elephant is always cut and presented to the hunter, as proof of possession in case anyone else should come across the carcass (Blunt 45). The lack of hair on this tail is a sign of the elephant's great age. Blunt tells us that "in very old elephants the hairs of the tail are generally worn down to mere bristles" (45), and when Neumann sees an elephant without hair on its tail, he immediately recognizes it as a "patriarch" (362).[1]

202:17 **No one, not even his father, could reach the top of the bend where they curved in for the points to meet:** See 173:13.

202:28 **wall of the hut:** In the manuscript, this is the "wall of the hero's father-in-law's hut," and the cups are brought by Davey's "semi-fiancée, now a hero's promised bride" *(3.37.19).*

Jenks, no doubt, edited Davey's "promised bride" out of the passage because he couldn't square her with the "very young boy" (201:16) of the tale, but early sexual initiation is a recurrent theme in Hemingway's work, particularly in the Nick Adams stories. The *Eden* manuscript makes clear that David had been initiated into sexuality at an early age and had already had "the clap" by the time he was fourteen (see *[156:16] 3.26.13*). Though based in part on Debba, the young woman Hemingway nicknamed "fiancée" during his 1953–54 safari, this fiancée has roots in such figures as the Trudy or Prudy Boulton of "Ten Indians," "Fathers and Sons," and "The Last Good Country."

202:34 *Ngoma:* A Swahili word for drum, it has come to signify any sort of music or dancing that accompanies a celebration or ceremony.

(203:12) 3.37.21 **went to see Picasso:** In the manuscript, Marita says that Catherine has gone to Antibes or Cap d'Antibes to see Picasso about illustrations for the honeymoon narrative. David wonders what Picasso is doing there, but Catherine apparently read about it in the papers.

In the summer of 1926, after first spending some time at the Hotel Majestic in Cannes, Picasso rented a villa in Juan-les-Pins, on the neck of Cap d'Antibes. When the Murphys and Hemingways returned from their trip to Pamplona, Picasso visited with them, but as the summer wore on, he found Hemingway's post-Pamplona "appropriation of Andalusian machismo offensive" and the antics of Scott and Zelda Fitzgerald off-putting and began to distance himself from the crowd around the Murphys (Richardson 316). In the summer of 1927, Picasso was again on the Riviera, first at the Hotel Majestic, and then at a different villa on the outskirts of Cannes, but he saw little of the Murphys' circle at Cap d'Antibes.

(204:8) 3.37.25 **"fiancée. . . ." "make a baby. . . . Wanderobo":** In the manuscript, after asking what happened to the blood in his pocket, Marita asks David what he did on the night of his return to the shamba. David tells her that he made love with his fiancée. Using a curiously infantile phrase, Marita asks him if they "[made] a baby." David answers that, young as he had been, he had been experienced and careful enough not to.

Marita's question echoes the pidgin English of Nick Adams's boyhood Native American girlfriend, Trudy Boulton, in Hemingway's story "Fathers and Sons": "You think we make a baby?" (*CSS* 374). And the idea of David having a baby by his African fiancée echoes a fantasy of Hemingway's from his 1953–54 safari, when he shaved his head "to the bone," stained his scalp brown in a sort of tonsorial blackface (so it wouldn't "shine"), and wrote to Slim Hayward of his flirtation with the African girl he nicknamed "fiancée": "I bought two good wives here. One is rough but fine. One loves me which is bad. . . . I say I will send the boy to . . . the best school available, and if it is a girl will buy her a good dowry" (qtd. in Eby, "Hemingway's Truth" 25).

Marita wants to make love with David right then, and she doesn't want to worry about whether or not they "make a baby." After a break in the manuscript that stands in for their lovemaking, Marita thinks they have "made the baby," and she doesn't mind. If they are kicked "out of the tribe," they can be "Wanderobo"—a derogatory Masai term (meaning "poor people") for several unrelated hunter-gatherer groups in Kenya that have no cattle. The quest to "make a baby" points to Hemingway's easy fetishizing equation of Native Americans and Africans as all-purpose racial others (See *[19:1]* 1.2.1 and 30:16), and it calls attention to the way Marita tries to emulate and replace David's boyhood African fiancée.

(204:8) 3.37.28 **"go to see Picasso too. . . ." "go and see Breughel and Hieronymus Bosch":** After some playful postcoital love banter, Marita mockingly suggests that

they go to see Picasso, too. David counters by suggesting that they go instead to "see Breughel and Hieronymus Bosch." He isn't proposing a trip to the museum; he is lightheartedly speaking of Bruegel and Bosch as if they were still alive. Hemingway was fond of doing this (see *[54:23] 3.10.4*). The pairing of Bruegel with Bosch suggests that David may be thinking of Bruegel's apocalyptic and Bosch-like *Triumph of Death,* which in the Prado in the 1950s hung in the same room as Bosch's *Garden of Earthly Delights* (see *[54:23] 3.10.4*).

(204:20) **It was a day for flying:** In the manuscript, David's reverie about a day for flying, and his desire to take Marita up in the air, is more fully developed. Exhilarated after finishing the elephant story, David wants to show Marita "what Ernst or Michel or I can do." She might understand what it means, he thinks, just as she understands his writing.

This passage not only reminds us that David flew in WWI, it puts him into very exalted company as a pilot. The manuscript makes it clear that the "Ernst" in this passage is none other than Ernst Udet, Germany's second greatest WWI ace, with sixty-two kills. "A virtuoso of aerial acrobatics," Udet survived the war and during the interwar years worked as a stunt pilot and aerial photographer ("Le Cinema"). He also appeared in several films, hunted big game in Africa (David knows Udet is "going out to Africa"), and was something of a playboy before in 1934 joining the newly formed Luftwaffe. He committed suicide in 1941. In *Across the River and into the Trees,* Hemingway's protagonist, Colonel Cantwell, claims to have liked him and imagines feasting with the ace in Valhalla. Hemingway apparently knew Udet, for he expresses this same fondness for him in a 19 June 1950 letter to their mutual friend Marlene Dietrich, whose aunt flew around Africa with the German ace. (Udet was also friends with Hemingway pals Bror von Blixen-Finecke and Dick Cooper.) In 1927, Udet belonged to one of several European and American teams preparing transatlantic flights to compete for the $25,000 Orteig Prize before Lindbergh secured it. He was much in the papers, both before and after Lindbergh's flight (see 112:12).

The "Michel" of this passage probably refers to Michel Détroyat, who first became friends with Udet at an aerial acrobatics competition in 1928. (A pun on his last name, as well as a shift to naval aviators, explains David's musings about "destroyers" on this same page in the *Eden* manuscript.) Détroyat, who joined the French air force in 1923 and soon thereafter helped found an aerial acrobatics school, first came to public attention on 21 May 1927 when he welcomed Lindbergh and helped save him from crushing crowds upon his arrival at Le Bourget Field. A few days later, on May 27, Lindbergh and Détroyat, in two planes, thrilled Paris by flying a stunt tour over the capital, followed by a simulated dogfight and "exhibition of air acrobatics seldom excelled" over Le Bourget Field (Edwin James). In June 1927, Détroyat left the military to become a test and stunt pilot. Little known in the United States before he won the Thompson Trophy air race in 1936, he was celebrated in

France throughout the 1920s and 30s. As early as July 1927, the *Revue Aéronautique de France* was calling Détroyat "the most gifted pilot of his generation" (Weiss), and French newspapers were soon writing regularly about his "legendary" or "incomparable" virtuosity in aerial acrobatics.[2] David thinks that Michel is "the most beautiful" flyer. During WWII, Détroyat served as Marshal Pétain's personal pilot and after the war was convicted of being a collaborator. He died in 1956.

(204:23) 3.37.30 **destroyers. . . . Kenny MacLeish. . . . Marita's brother:** In the manuscript, David remembers Catherine's remarks about aerial acrobatics from the night before (191:14) and thinks she acted very "snotty" for someone whose only talent is for "destruction." The navy "ought to name a destroyer after her," he thinks. (For the opposition between destruction and invention in the novel, see 5:27.) Reflecting that destroyers are named to honor "dead naval heroes," he supposes they'll probably name one after Kenny MacLeish. The brother of Hemingway's close friend, the poet Archibald MacLeish, Kenneth MacLeish was a naval aviator shot down while flying his Sopwith Camel on the western front on 14 October 1918. The US Navy had, in fact, already commissioned a Clemson-class destroyer, the *USS MacLeish* (DD-220), in his honor in August 1920. (The *MacLeish* helped evacuate refugees from Smyrna during the Greco-Turkish War of 1922, an event recalled in Hemingway's story "On the Quai at Smyrna.") Hemingway began writing a story about Kenneth MacLeish in 1926, but he never finished it (Reynolds, *American* 93–95), and the line from *The Song of Roland* that David twice recalls in the manuscript (see *[44:28] 3.5.6* and *[194:4] 3.36.31*) comes from Archibald MacLeish's elegy for his brother, "The Too-Late Born."

David wonders if Marita's brother had been a good pilot (see *[162:4] 422.4 3.27.8*). The odds are that he was killed before he ever had a chance to get good. They had died so fast then.

(204:23) 3.37.30 **Chante pour Lydia Pinkham. . . . Vive le cast iron steel the pilot's best friend:** After remembering an alliterative series of expressions for getting one's testicles shot off flying different WWI fighters (e.g., "spayed in a Spad")—an injury that recalls the one suffered by Jake Barnes in *The Sun Also Rises,* wounded "flying on a joke front" (38)—David remembers two bawdy WWI songs on the same theme. First he remembers a French version of the opening lines of a ballad popular (in English) with English and American troops: "*Chante, chante, chante pour Lydia Pinkham et sa grand amour pour l'humanité.*" (David meant to add the tune to which the ballad was sung, but Hemingway couldn't remember it and left blanks in the manuscript. Comically enough, it was sung to the tune of the hymn "I Will Sing of My Redeemer.") The creator of Lydia Pinkham's Vegetable Compound, an herbal tonic sold as a remedy for "all female complaints," Pinkham was a savvy marketer, given to taking out full-page ads in major newspapers. Her picture ap-

peared on the bottle and on the front page of such papers as the *Boston Herald*, where the vegetable compound was described as the "Greatest Medical Discovery Since the Dawn of History" (Mulligan 8K). Thus the ballad's chorus:

> Then we'll sing, we'll sing,
> We'll sing of Lydia Pinkham,
>   Savior of the human race,
> How she makes, she bottles,
> She sells her vegetable compound,
>   And the papers publish her face.

Pinkham's efforts to distribute frank information about female physiology in a sexually inhibited age, her claims for her nostrum's ability to enhance fertility, and her promise of "unbelievable results" made the compound the butt of many bawdy jokes. Carl Sandburg published two innocuous verses of the much longer "Ballad of Lydia Pinkham" in his *American Songbag* (1927), but given the chain of associations that brings David to this memory, he is clearly thinking of the following verse, printed in *Immortalia* (1927), an anonymous anthology of American ballads:

> Arthur White had been castrated,
>   And had not a single nut,
> So he took, he swallowed, he gargled,
>   Some Vegetable Compound,
> And now they hang all 'round his butt. (Anonymous 19–20)

Robert Gajdusek has argued persuasively that the second bit of doggerel David remembers—which would obviously apply as well to the lines above—is linked thematically to the novel's broader concerns with biological and creative fertility:

> Vive le cast iron steel the pilot's best friend,
> for who would have his cock or balls shot free
> so that he could no proper part of England be,
> nor progeny and wealth acquire,
> some Fokker having blasted his desire.
> Come celebrate with me the thin steel sheet
> where languidly we park our meat,
> thus shielding England's tools and seed
> against our country's future need.

David attributes these lines (whose actual source I have been unable to locate) to "the *Unplucked Nettle* in the *Complete Unpublished Works*" (3.37.30i), an apt allusion to a line from Shakespeare's *Henry IV, Part One:* "Out of this nettle, danger, we pluck the flower, safety." The source, however, is probably apocryphal. Hemingway was fond of the Shakespearean line and parodies it in a 1927 letter to Ezra Pound that is much about Archibald MacLeish (*Letters 3* 187).[3] In a 1943 letter to MacLeish, Hemingway also remembers the lines, "*Chante, chante, chante pour Lydia Pinkham et sa grand amour pour l'humanité*" (*SL* 546). It seems, then, that working in 1958 with MacLeish to get Pound released from Saint Elizabeths (see *[44:28] 3.5.6*) jogged Hemingway's memory as he was working on *Eden*—suggesting how David's thoughts flow from his musings about the death of Kenneth MacLeish to Lydia Pinkham to the *Unplucked Nettle.*

204:30 **faithful to you, Perrier, in my fucking fashion:** Coming as it does after David's admission to himself that he truly loves Marita, this allusion to the refrain that ends each stanza of Ernest Dowson's famous poem "Non sum qualis eram bonae sub regno Cynarae"—"I have been faithful to thee, Cynara! in my fashion"—acknowledges that he nonetheless still loves Catherine. Like the nighttime ghostly presence of the "old passion" that comes between the speaker of Dowson's poem and his new love, David's love for Catherine remains between him and Marita. Like the speaker of Dowson's poem, David remains "desolate and sick of an old passion."

(205:11) 3.37.32 **by the old port.... ketch sloop.... "Red Sea...." "P and O ship.... Mombasa":** The chapter continues in the manuscript for another twenty-four holograph pages. David and Marita drive into Cannes and stroll along the Quai Saint-Pierre, admiring the yachts in the old port. They begin to think about buying a boat and stop to admire one. In the manuscript, this is initially a ketch, but Hemingway strikes this out and replaces it with *sloop*. The revision from a two-masted craft with three sails (ketch) to a one-masted ship with two sails (sloop) may symbolize a shift in the relationship between David, Catherine, and Marita.

After David and Marita discuss sailing in bad weather, David asks Marita if she would like to sail to the Red Sea, where there are "wonderful reefs," fish in great abundance, and ideal places to sun themselves. Marita has been there before on a P&O (Peninsular and Oriental Steam Navigation Company) ship and thinks it might be too hot. David, however, assures her that they can go when it is cool, noting that there are two monsoon seasons, one hot and one cool. Marita suggests it would make more sense to ship their boat out to Mombasa. She's been to Kenya before and remembers "mountain seas," much too rough for a small boat, between the horn of Africa and Mombasa. This makes David think that a ketch or a yawl, on which sails can be trimmed quickly, would make more sense than a sloop. Marita would like something with a centerboard they can pull up, so they can explore the reefs without running aground. She thinks they should see a broker about the boat and explore shipping costs and offers to take care of that so David can remain focused on his writing.

Although David registers no surprise, it is a bit jarring for readers to discover this late in the manuscript that Marita has already been to Kenya—and to see this introduced for such a flimsy reason. Hemingway is drawing on his own experience passing through the Red Sea with Mary in August 1953 on their way to Kenya, when "the heat closed in with a vengeance, accompanied by heavy monsoon winds that raised twenty-foot waves" (Baker 513), but his decision to give this experience to Marita is one sign among others that we are entering a less polished part of the manuscript. In a discarded passage from earlier in the manuscript, Hemingway briefly toyed with the idea of an African past for Marita (see *[118:10] 422.4 3.21.26*), yet later in the manuscript Hemingway reconsiders and has Marita say she has never been to Africa (see *[247:24] 3.46.20vi*). Beyond discarding the one earlier passage, he never revised and reconciled these contradictions. Hemingway noted in the manuscript, chapter by chapter, that he had "rewritten" chapters 20 to 32 of book III in November 1958. Pagination indicates, however, that manuscript chapters 32 through 36 of book III were originally a single long chapter, written in September 1958 and probably divided in the November rewrite. With manuscript chapter 37—which carries composition dates from early December—we begin the section of the manuscript Hemingway wrote after the major rewrites of November 1958. Conversations between David and Marita from this point on are often chatty and more loosely connected to the plot of the novel.

(205:11) 3.37.38 **went to the café:** In the manuscript, David and Marita sit down at the Café des Allées (see 88:28) and enjoy the view of the yachts through the plane trees. As they admire them appraisingly, Marita suggests they could collect pictures, too. "To hang in the boat?" David teases. For the "fleet," Marita teases back, but the mood has soured a little. Marita strangely salves David's wound by telling him, "All women are pigs" *(3.37.39)*. David assures her, however, that she is his partner in writing in a way that Catherine has never been. Marita answers that she is his "mistress" and she "ought to have a flat." They can buy paintings for that: a Picasso and a Cézanne landscape. She'll be his "Somali wife," and Catherine can have all the Barbaras and projects she wants *(3.37.41)*.

They decide to lunch at the café. As they enjoy cold lobster and Provençal mayonnaise with a bottle of Sancerre, and grilled entrecôte with a carafe of Beaujolais, they discuss Catherine's "crazy" plans to illustrate the honeymoon narrative, which may include trips to Paris, Saint-Jean-de-Luz, or Hendaye; Catherine's "fairy godmotherly" advice about how Marita should take care of David *(3.37.44)*; David's prior experience with prostitutes and other women *(3.37.46)*; whether or not other women were attracted to his wounds *(3.37.47)*; and their love for each other.

(205:11) 3.37.48 **changed my allegiance:** In the manuscript, David tells Marita that today is the day he "changed [his] allegiance" from Catherine to her *(3.37.48)*. When

Marita asks if he still loves Catherine, he answers, "Not today" (3.37.49). This changing of allegiance, however temporary, mirrors (in the sense that a mirror image is a reverse image) what happens in the elephant story he finished that very morning. Whereas Davey changes his allegiance from Juma and his father to the doomed elephant, the adult David abandons Catherine, long associated with ivory and the elephant (see 156:5 and 162:30), for Marita. However insane, narcissistic, and destructive Catherine may be, this could be read, in fact, as a betrayal, not unlike his first betrayal of the elephant. We should remember, however, the recent allusion to the lingering, haunting presence of Cynara in Dowson's poem (see 204:30). Catherine's presence lingers between David and Marita, perhaps not unlike the way Davey's love for his father must have remained, albeit wounded and submerged, after his rejection of him. The changing of allegiance from Catherine to Marita is aligned with David's ability to reconnect with his father and certain aspects of his masculinity—yet the impression created by the Scribner's edition that this is one and the same with a change of allegiance from Catherine's experiments with gender and sexuality to some sort of heteronormativity is not supported by the course of events in the manuscript.

(205:11) 3.37.50 **It's a mystère:** In the manuscript, David tells Marita he has long resisted "letting people in," although he admits that he once did as a boy in Africa and did again during the war. The experience of learning together with others made those experiences "tribal," he explains. He let people in a little in Paris, too, after the war, but not when it came to writing. Never "all the way." That is, until her. When she asks why her, he explains that it was because she understood the essential "*mystère.*" Marita says she only began to understand it when she read his stories. To her, that felt like being initiated into a religious "mystery." That's a secret, David tells her, that they must share together.

(205:11) 3.37.52 **shoot with shits, nor lose the common touch:** The conversation in the manuscript drifts onto the subject of David's distaste for "society." Marita thinks David could study and satirize society, but David would rather stick to writing what he knows. He tells her that others have already written about society better than he ever could. Marita has society friends "who have really fine shooting," and she thinks David would enjoy that. Alluding to Kipling's poem "If—," David answers, "Shoot with shits nor lose the common touch."

The substitution of "shits" for "kings" in Kipling's "walk with Kings—nor lose the common touch" is a common refrain in Hemingway's letters from the 1940s and '50s.[4] The modified phrase functioned as an easy all-purpose tool for expressing his (far from consistent) aversion to high society. Yet, in *Eden,* the allusion to Kipling's poem, and the significance of its if-then structure, is something more than this. In the back of David's mind, he might easily be applying the opening lines of Kipling's poem to his situation with Catherine:

> If you can keep your head when all about you
> Are losing theirs and blaming it on you,
> If you can trust yourself when all men doubt you,
> But make allowance for their doubting too;

The poem's second stanza speaks suggestively to his erotic "dreams," his lost and found loves, his completed and burned manuscripts, and his ability to ultimately rewrite what Catherine destroys:

> If you can dream—and not make dreams your master;
> If you can think—and not make thoughts your aim;
> If you can meet with Triumph and Disaster
> And treat those two impostors just the same;
> If you can bear to hear the truth you've spoken
> Twisted by knaves to make a trap for fools,
> Or watch the things you gave your life to, broken,
> And stoop and build 'em up with worn-out tools:

Like a classic Hemingway protagonist and young Davey at the end of the elephant story, David seems to endorse a vision of himself in which he must "lose, and start again at [his] beginnings / And never breathe a word about [his] loss." Yet he also knows better. As the central consciousness of the novel—as a sort of implied author—forcing his "heart and nerve . . . / To serve [his] turn long after they are gone," he tells precisely the story of his vulnerability and loss, saying on the page what he would never say out loud. The final stanza of Kipling's poem promises that "If neither foes nor loving friends can hurt you"—or, in David's understanding, if you can bottle up and *use* that hurt and transform it into art—*then*

> Yours is the Earth and everything that's in it,
> And—which is more—you'll be a Man, my son!

The Scribner's edition of *Eden* ends with precisely this promise—and with the vision of masculinity and father-son relations that it implies. It must be remembered, however, that the ending of the Scribner's edition is quite misleading. The edits misrepresent what Hemingway wrote, and this is not the ending he envisioned for his book.

(205:11) 3.37.53 *"good wing shot. . . . Tolstoi . . . Turgenieff. . . . the Sologne. . . .* bécasse *and* bécassinne": In the manuscript, Marita asks David if he's "a good wing shot." He considers himself "fair," but when it comes to shooting, there are only three classes: "worthless, fair, and one of the ten finest shots in Britain." Of the latter, he tells her, there are hundreds.[5] (When Hemingway wrote these lines in December 1958, he had been in Ketchum, Idaho, since October, hunting duck, pheasant, partridge, quail, and snipe almost daily.) Marita wants to know if David will ever write anything about wing shooting. He hopes to. She is glad he'll join the likes of Turgenev (whose *Sportsman's Sketches* Hemingway loved) and Tolstoy (who wrote beautifully of wing shooting in *Anna Karenina*). She hopes he'll write about "shooting in the Sologne," the great marshy forest and aristocratic hunting grounds near Orléans that she loves. (In *Green Hills of Africa* and *The Fifth Column*, Hemingway writes of shooting pheasants there.)

Marita tells David she has always doubted the translation in Tolstoy, where she thinks they may have confused woodcock (*bécasse*) with snipe (*bécassine*). Given the night flying and bird size, David suspects she may be right and says he'll have to ask a Russian who can set them straight. A comparison of translations of *Anna Karenina* available to Hemingway (who owned three copies of the novel) justifies Marita's suspicion:

- Nathan Haskell Dole (1886): "I doubt if we find any woodcock, but snipe are plenty" (562).
- Constance Garnett (1901): "I can't answer for our finding grouse, but there are plenty of snipe" (528).
- Louise and Aylmer Maude (1918): "I don't know whether we shall get any snipe, but there are plenty of woodcock . . ." (673).
- Rosemary Edmonds (1954): "I doubt if we shall find any snipe, but there are plenty of woodcock" (600).

A more recent (2000) translation by Richard Pevear and Larissa Volokhonsky is more accurate, though less felicitous in English: "I don't know if we'll find any great snipe. But there are plenty of snipe" (570).[6]

(205:11) 3.37.53 **happiest I've ever been:** In the manuscript, Marita tells David that today has been the happiest day of her life. It was as if the joy of David finishing the story radiated other forms of happiness outwards in "ripples." The *mystère* is powerful, David answers, and it can't be accomplished without love.

NOTES

1. Elephant tail hair was reputed to bring luck, and there was a small fad in the early 1920s for the use of elephant hair in such items as hats, rings, bracelets, and lorgnette chains.
2. For example, see Torres's article "Michel Detroyat, virtuose de l'air."
3. Hemingway also parodied the line in a 1946 letter to Buck Lanham (Baker 457).
4. See *SL* 624, 782, 850.
5. In the margin here, Hemingway wrote "check." This suggests this is a quotation, but I have been unable to locate the source.
6. In Tolstoy's Russian, the distinction is between дупелей (great snipe, *Gallinago media*) and бекас (common snipe, *Gallinago gallinago*).

BOOK IV *(NOT A NEW BOOK IN MSS.)*

CHAPTER 25 (MSS. CHAPTERS 38–39)

209:12 **Paris Herald:** Founded in 1887 as the *Paris Herald,* the paper was rechristened the *Paris Herald Tribune* in 1924 when its parent company, the *New York Herald,* was purchased and became the *New York Herald Tribune.* A mainstay of Paris's expatriate community, the paper featured a column titled "With Latin Quarter Folk" that, like the Paris *Chicago Tribune*'s "Latin Quarter Notes," and the *Paris Times*'s "In the Quarter," regularly covered Hemingway's doings and travels.

(209:16) 3.38.2 **"Picasso? . . ." "Eddy Cantor's":** In the manuscript, David asks Catherine if she saw "her man." Yes, she answers. She saw Picasso and found him "utterly charming." David inquires after him, Catherine doubts his sincerity, and they immediately find themselves in a verbal duel. Catherine holds up Picasso as an ideal to belittle David, calling Picasso "kind, human, understanding, vital, [and] manly as a little

Eddie Cantor in *The Kid from Spain,* 1932. (Courtesy Everett Collection.)

Spanish bull." By contrast, she calls David a "conceited poseur of a writer," a "slob," a "degenerate," a "pervert," and a "scribbler." David gleefully retorts, "You publisher."

Catherine says that Picasso's eyes "have more sex appeal than—" but hangs fire. In one of the funniest, but now sadly dated, lines in the novel, David completes the sentence for her: "Eddy [sic] Cantor's." Born Edward Israel Iskowitz, Cantor was an American comedian, actor, and song and dance man who first made his name in the Ziegfeld Follies and then onscreen with Clara Bow in *Kid Boots* (1926). Thanks to his wide-eyed, eye-rolling antics, Cantor was famous by 1927 as a "comedian with the eyes," eventually earning the nickname "Banjo Eyes" ("Eddie"). In 1932, Cantor starred as a matador in *The Kid from Spain,* a film that also featured Hemingway's bullfighter friend Sidney Franklin in a minor part.

(209:16) 3.38.3 **"*savage friend. . . . Russian princess. . . .*" "*colonel's daughter*":** In the manuscript, Catherine claims that David doesn't even belong "in the same room" with Picasso, yet she was surprised to find that Picasso likes David and called him "his savage friend." I can find no record of Picasso calling Hemingway his "savage friend," but it sounds like the sort of thing he might have said. In David Douglas Duncan's *The Private World of Pablo Picasso* (which Hemingway owned), Picasso recalls the Americans he knew in the twenties, a group that included "wild ones like Hemingway" (122). Since the mid-nineteenth century, the phrase "savage friend" was a racist cliché for any racial other. This may simply be another example of *Eden*'s fascination with racial otherness.

Catherine reports being charmed by Picasso's beautiful child and his wife, whom she thinks is a "Russian princess." David corrects her: "a colonel's daughter." (Picasso's wife, Olga, a former dancer with the Ballets Russes, was given to claiming that her father was a general, though he was, in fact, a colonel [Richardson 5].) Calling David a "phony bogus hero," Catherine demands to know *his* former rank. "Temporary captain," he answers, and he had later been a "flight lieutenant" (making it clear that he served in the RAF, where a flight lieutenant ranked above a flying officer but below a squadron leader [see *(244:23) 3.45.17]*). Catherine praises Olga's "grace and formality." (Richardson writes that in 1927 Olga still "took the role of Madame Picasso—elegant consort, zealous mother, impeccable *maîtresse de maison*—very much to heart.") She was a bit "stuffy," Catherine admits, but Catherine claims to prefer this version of domesticity to the "half-baked Bohemian existence" from which she has tried to rescue David. What she fails to realize is that in the summer of 1927, despite the pretense of bourgeois respectability, Picasso had come to see Olga as "tyrannical," and their marriage was falling apart (Richardson 294, 333). Olga was mentally and physically ill, and Picasso was already obsessed with the new mistress who would inspire him for most of the next decade: Marie-Thérèse Walter. The marriage of the Picassos, in other words, in some ways mirrors the situation with the Bournes.

(209:16) 3.38.4 **wonderful man and a great painter:** In the manuscript, David is glad Picasso agreed to do the illustrations; now all David needs to do is the writing. Catherine demands that David write it *now,* to which he replies, "in the pig's asshole." They trade insults until Catherine, suddenly tired, begins to cry. David gently calms her and assures her that Picasso must have been happy to meet her. Catherine admits she hadn't really liked Olga or the boy, but she'd admired Picasso as she admired no other man except David and Nick. She wonders if Picasso will really do the illustrations. David explains that Picasso always accepts "invitations from the rich" because he knows it pleases them, and he can always find an excuse not to follow through (see *[162:4] 3.27.8*). Disappointed, Catherine wonders why David "hates" her now. David assures her that he doesn't hate her, they're "friends." And Picasso is as good as he seems—even better. She tells David that Picasso admired him, too, and told her, "Nick was the only good American painter" *(3.38.8)*. Picasso had asked about Spain and had really listened to her and joked with her, and it made her happy, but that was all spoiled now. It's spoiled because David has "gone away" from her, emotionally. David lies and tells her that this isn't true, but she knows better. She asks for a truce because when they call each other names, David's are so much more accurate and hurtful. The unjust names she calls David make him angry, but the accurate names hurled at Catherine "destroy" her. They agree to enjoy a drink and the beauty of the day and be friends.

(209:16) 3.38.9 **Gambled ... all my estates. ... Tolstoi:** In the manuscript, after wondering if Marita will join them for a drink, Catherine decides Marita can wait. She's already "getting everything so fast." Catherine feels as if she were in Tolstoy's old Russia and had gambled away her estates. She could be thinking of Nikolai Rostov in *War and Peace* or Yashvin in *Anna Karenina,* both ruined at cards, but she's probably thinking of Tolstoy himself, who had to sell properties—and the serfs attached to those properties—as a young man to pay his gambling debts (Troyat 61). Or she may be thinking of Tolstoy's wife's grandfather. Hemingway would have read of him in *Tolstoy as I Knew Him* (which he owned) that "one estate after another went in payment for his card debts" until the family was ruined (Kuzminskaya 15).

(209:16) 3.38.10 **"here's to ... the spoiled of war. ... Picasso. ..." "Braque. ... trepanned":** In the manuscript, they open a bottle of Perrier-Jouët, and Catherine proposes a toast to all "the spoiled of war." As they drink to those damaged by the war, Catherine suggests that having the good sense to avoid it altogether made Picasso superior—"stronger and better." Rather than replying directly, David suggests that they "drink to Braque," who was trepanned (see *[54:23] 3.11.15*). Surprisingly, Catherine now adds, "So were you." While we have long known that David was damaged and scarred by the war, it seems a little late to be learning that he was trepanned. As with the late discovery that Marita has already been to East Africa, this is a sign of

the comparatively loose and less edited state of these late chapters in the manuscript (see *[205:11] 3.37.34)*. David compares being trepanned to being circumcised and adds Lydia Pinkham to their toast (see *[204:23] 3.37.30)*. Catherine accuses him of being a fraud for mentioning the war, and they fall to quarrelling again. Catherine drinks to his "damnation." This is when Catherine asks about David's "whore" (209:17).

210:9 **sketches or vignettes:** Catherine's response to David's stories mirrors that of some of Hemingway's less perceptive early critics, unsure of what to do with stories in which key elements of plot were often implied instead of shown. In the manuscript, Catherine finds the stories full of "juvenile sadism and bathos" *(3.38.14)*. "Bathos is my pal," David answers. "There were three of us," he explains, punning on Athos from *The Three Musketeers*.

(210:16) 3.38.15 **Dilatory Domicile:** In the manuscript, after a few more of David's jokes, Catherine demands to know if "Picasso would clown like this." Of course he would, answers David. When Catherine talks about writing, she's simply out of her league, he says. She sounds "like a Dilatory Domicile." A section first added to the *Social Register* in 1898, the "Dilatory Domicile" is a listing of members who either changed their addresses since the publication of the main directory or were late announcing to the *Register* where they would be staying for a given season (Higley 63). In other words, Catherine sounds like the ignorant, entitled rich. She appreciates the jab, nonetheless, and is glad to be married to David if for no other reason than to hear him say that.

(210:16) 3.38.16 **"I wish I'd known your father. . . ." "Ngorongoro Crater. . . . Mrs. Jack Gardner":** In the manuscript, Catherine says she wishes she'd known David's father and wonders if he'd have liked her. David says he would have sold her the "Ngorongoro Crater and poxed [her] twice" before the check cleared. When she asks if *she* would have liked *him,* David says she would have "fought Mrs. Jack Gardner" for the privilege of paying his overdraft. She wonders why David doesn't write more about his father's charm, but David says he leaves those stories to his pal "Bathos."

David's choice of Tanzania's famous Ngorongoro Crater as a stand-in for the proverbial Brooklyn Bridge is richly suggestive. An extinct volcanic caldera, two hundred miles south of the equator, with 102 square miles of grassland floor at six thousand feet above sea level and a rim towering two thousand feet above that, the crater so teems with wildlife, including the world's densest population of lions, that it has long been known as "Africa's Eden." In 1922, newspapers around the world reported that arms merchant and big-game hunter Sir Charles Ross had purchased this "Eden in the heart of the African wilderness" (actually only a large part of it) and turned it into a game reserve ("Buys a Volcano").[1] To this day, the invocation of Eden remains part of the Ngorongoro Conservation Area's marketing strategy. These associations with Eden were undoubtedly deepened for Hemingway by Richard Leakey's discoveries at Olduvai Gorge, a mere eighteen miles to the west of the crater. (Hemingway, who visited the crater during his 1933–34 safari, had passed within four miles of the gorge, and he flew at low altitude over them both in 1954 [Cushman 468, *BL* 425].) As early as 1929, the *New York Times* was reporting that Leakey had dug up "the earliest specimen of modern man" ("Skeleton"), and a 1933 article about Leakey in the *New York Times* reported, "A remote spot in East Africa, somewhere in the vicinity of the Rift valley, is the most likely site of the original Garden of Eden, birthplace of the human race . . ." ("Birthplace").[2] In offering to sell Ngorongoro Crater, then, David's father is precisely the man who would commit the original sin of betraying and bogusly commodifying Eden. (For another allusion to a paleontological Eden, see *[244:25] 3.45.22.*)

The suggestion that Catherine would fight "Mrs. Jack Gardner," of all people, for the privilege of paying Bourne père's overdraft is rooted in such personal associations for Hemingway that it would have been entirely incomprehensible to any general audience. This is yet another sign that Hemingway's writing in these final chapters of the manuscript is looser, comparatively unrevised, and deeply personal. The "Mrs. Jack Gardner" in question is Isabella Stewart Gardner, "Boston Society's greatest grande dame," the "millionaire Bohamienne" art collector and founder of the Isabella Stewart Gardner Museum. As Hemingway would have read in his copy of Cleveland Amory's *The Proper Bostonians*, "All Boston knew her as 'Mrs. Jack' but nobody called her anything but Mrs. Gardner" (132). And the overdraft that inspired Hemingway's association would have belonged to one of Hemingway's favorite correspondents in the 1950s, famous art historian Bernard Berenson (see *[54:23] 3.11.14*), who more than anyone else, other than Mrs. Gardner herself, had helped her to acquire her astounding collection of old masters. According to Douglass Shand Tucci, "On at least one occasion it is known that only a three-thousand-dollar check of Gardner's saved Berenson from an overdraft of over two-thousand dollars"—and this at a time when Berenson was suspected (probably correctly) by Jack Gardner of swindling his otherwise shrewd wife (189). Fully understanding Hemingway's allusion, however, relies on more than the inside baseball of art history. One has to understand that Hemingway also regarded Berenson as a father figure, writing to him from Africa, soon after his twin plane crashes, on 2 February 1954, "In some ways I am your pup from being educated, a little, by you. . . . You never have to acknowledge me and can always denounce me with impunity. / But B. B. (my brother and father) if you ever wanted to father a really bad repeat bad . . . boy then you have this worthless object . . ." (*SL* 828).[3] In other words, to create David's swindling African father with his imaginary overdraft, Hemingway drew on his own African letter to a swindling and fatherly Berenson, informed by the story of the latter's overdraft.

As if this allusion were not complicated and convoluted enough, it must be noted that one of Hemingway's own sisters, Carol, was *also* "Mrs. Jack Gardner." In *How It*

Was, Mary Hemingway recalls Ernest explaining that Carol "married Jack Gardner. I was absolutely nuts about her. She looked as a girl exactly as I looked as a boy. No compromise, no change" (261). Hemingway had opposed his sister's marriage to Gardner so violently and irrationally that she complained to a friend: "You'd think Ernie wanted to marry me himself" (qtd. in Sinclair 44). After the marriage, Ernest and Carol never communicated again. Given the importance of sibling romance and cross-gender twinning to the novel (see 6:6), it is noteworthy that Hemingway imagines Catherine Bourne in competition with Mrs. Jack Gardner.

(210:33) 3.39.2 **mess of Roger's brother's regiment:** In the manuscript, after finishing the champagne, David remembers a rule from "the mess of Roger's brother's regiment" that allowed men dining alone to order a bottle of champagne with the bill going to the regiment. This is the only time in the novel we hear about Roger, or his brother. Roger had intended to go to Africa with David after the war, but he and his brother were both killed. In his war book, David had written well about Roger, and while he considers it "presumptuous" to write about the dead, this at least had given him some measure of "immortality," though David is uncomfortable with the word. He is repulsed by clichés like "grave responsibility" and "chivalry of the air." After his plane went down, instead of looking like a knight in armor, Roger had looked like a "roast pig," without the pig's head or apple. He knows he could have written his WWI book better now with the skills he has acquired writing his recent stories, and this is what brings him to the reflection at 211:1 in the Scribner's edition.[4]

(211:8) 3.39.2ii **It was fortunate just now that his father was not a simple man:** This sentence, which Jenks moves to the final page of the Scribner's edition (247:15), occurs here in the manuscript. David feels the newfound ability to understand and represent his father is a measure of his growth as a writer. It is in this context that David is "fortunate . . . that his father was not a simple man."

211:9 **What Catherine had said about the stories:** In the manuscript, it is Catherine's "chance remark" about flying *(3.39.3i)*—not about the stories—that has hurt David and set him to thinking, not about his father, but about the war again. Catherine doesn't understand his flying, David thinks, and she understands his writing "even less."

213:5 **three French destroyers:** The 1926 *Blue Guide* for Southern France notes that "the French Mediterranean squadron," based out of nearby Toulon (213:26), was "frequently to be seen" in the Golfe-Juan (Muirhead and Monmarché 152). Nonetheless, however realistic this symbolism, the three destroyers with their confusing "smoke screen" (213:29) and the warplanes passing in "three echelons of three" (214:14) clearly represent the destructive potential of the Bournes' three-way relationship. After all, Catherine refers to herself as "a destroyer" *(3.19.10),* and David even thinks that they ought to name a destroyer after her (see *[204:23] 3.37.30).*

213:21 **flank speed:** *Flank speed* is a term that emerged during WWI naval warfare with destroyers to signify maximum speed. (This is faster than *full speed.*) It is generally reserved for outflanking maneuvers or for situations when a ship finds itself in imminent danger. Both uses have possible symbolic implications for the Bournes. Are they in imminent danger? Are Catherine and Marita trying to outflank each other?

214:1 **gunnery practice off the Porquerolles:** The largest and most westerly of the Îles d'Hyères, the Île de Porquerolles lies just off the coast of Hyères. During the 1920s, the French navy, stationed at nearby Toulon, regularly used these waters for gunnery practice.

(214:22) *3.39.9* **"Abd el-Krim. . . ." "Morocco with the Colonel. . . . bombing all the native villages":** In the manuscript, Catherine wonders if the navy is training for Mussolini. No, David answers. They're training to fight the Moroccan Riffian resistance leader, Abd el-Krim, who doesn't have a navy. She wonders why they aren't already in Morocco, then, with the Colonel, "bombing all the native villages." Where, David demands, did she hear that? From the papers, she answers, adding that perhaps she forgot to bring that paper home. (For the Colonel and his involvement with the Sharifian squadron of American volunteers in the Rif War, see 61:5.)

The historical atrocity that inspires Catherine's observation may follow (via Hemingway's association) from David's recent dismissal of the cliché "chivalry of the air" (see *[210:33] 3.39.2),* since it profoundly shook Americans' belief in any such chivalry. Instead of engaging in daring dogfights with enemy fighters, Colonel Charles Sweeny's Sharifian squadron found themselves, under French orders and unaware of the true situation, bombing and strafing unarmed villages of noncombatants. On 24 September 1925, Norman Thomas denounced the squadron's actions in the *New York Times:* "In some five days they have dropped nine tons of bombs upon the villages of the Riffs, who themselves have neither airplanes nor anti-aircraft guns. . . . This is not war between equals. It is not adventure as the American aviators in Morocco seek it and adventure as it might be sought in fighting . . . imperialism" (qtd. in "Krim"). In his article "Yankee Air Unit . . . Part in Rif War Denounced: Bombing Unarmed Villages Condemned as Crime . . . ," Vincent Sheean cited the following denunciation from an American reserve pilot, "America's reputation for sportsmanship and fair play has been handed a jolt by Col. Sweeney [sic] and his opera bouffe flyers. . . . It is inconceivable that any aviator with a proper pride in his profession and thought of its honor should engage in such an enterprise. Flying heretofore has been that activity of the true sportsman and gentleman—there is no room for men like those."[5]

Just as the mineral-based extractive colonialism of the Rif War mirrors the ivory-based extractive colonialism practiced by David's father (see 61:5), the atrocity of bombing these unarmed villages mirrors the "massacre in the crater" (223:3) in David's other African story. This suggests that the Colonel functions as a sort of loved and disavowed father-figure for David—with all of the complexities and problems that entails.

(214:22) 3.39.9 **Sparrow Robertson . . . Vincent Sheean . . . Betina Bedwell:** That David hadn't seen news of the Colonel in the papers makes Catherine, in the manuscript, reflect on how they used to consume so much more journalism before Marita arrived. David used to be so devoted to the papers that she feared he was "unfaithful to [her] with Sparrow Robertson and Vincent Sheean and Bettina Bedwell." For David's devotion to journalism and a consideration of this scene in the manuscript with particular attention to what is says about Sheean, see 58:10. For additional background on Sheean, see 61:5, *(66:11) 3.14.7,* and the previous entry.

Bettina Bedwell was the regular fashion columnist for the Paris edition of the *Chicago Tribune*. She collaborated with Kay Boyle on the novel *Yellow Dusk* (1937), which appeared under Bedwell's name. Sparrow Robertson wrote the "Sports Gossip" column for the Paris edition of the *New York Herald*, and he was one of its most colorful characters. His columns were often less about sports than they were about drinking with his "old pals"—and *everybody* was his "old pal." Other journalists claimed readers began their mornings with his column primarily "to savor the mayhem it inflicted on the English language" (Weber 157). As John Lardner remembered, "Technically, he wrote in English, but actually his prose was a unique and unparalleled emulsion of English and pure Robertson, and few American readers in Paris, or in all France, for that matter, could get along without it." Robertson printed a paragraph by "boxing enthusiast" Ernest Hemingway in his 21 February 1923 column.

(214:25) 3.39.10 **Tour de France:** In the manuscript, thinking of how much she used to enjoy living through the newspapers with David, Catherine remembers how much the Tour de France meant to him—as much as Wall Street means to those whose lives depend upon it. She'd been fond of it, too, David reminds her. Yes, Catherine tells Marita, the Tour had taught her "geography and how to suffer."

In his memoir *The Best Times,* Dos Passos remembers that "Hem was mad about bicycle racing" (142), and though Hemingway wrote more often about the six-day velodrome races, he also shared David's passion for the Tour de France. Like Jake Barnes in *The Sun Also Rises,* who follows the Tour by reading the papers, Hemingway regularly followed it by reading the French sporting paper *L'Auto,* which served as one of the Tour's sponsors. Even after he moved to Key West in 1928, he continued to ask his friends to send him *L'Auto* so he could follow the race.

215:14 **"the same pictures"**: The reproduction of the same image in article after article powerfully represents the dangerous and disconcerting oversimplification of David in his public image. See 24:21 and 24:22.

215:23 **he never puts anything he writes in the wastebasket:** In a 1931 letter to Archibald MacLeish, Hemingway called his "faithful old wastebasket" his "~~best~~ only other friend" (*Letters 4* 629), and in 1934 he told Fitzgerald, "I write one page of masterpiece to ninety one pages of shit. I try to put the shit in the wastebasket" (*Letters 5* 615). His actual writing practices, however, closely resembled David's. According to Mary Hemingway, Ernest "never threw away anything. Once in a while I could get him to throw away the wrappers in which magazines arrived, otherwise absolutely nothing, not a scratch pad, not a laundry list, nothing" (qtd. in Brasch and Sigman 126).

Yet David has "destroyed" parts of the honeymoon narrative (see *[122:17] 422.4 3.21.42*)—much as Hemingway seems to have destroyed portions of the *Eden* manuscript. There are no rough holograph pages for the comparatively polished early typescript pages of the *Eden* manuscript; pages of the manuscript have been sliced in two with scissors, with the missing halves not always appearing among the discards; and during the long hairdressing scene in the manuscript with Monsieur Jean, Hemingway left a note in the margin: "After page 18 there is a big empty part—maybe you threw it away . . ." *(3.24.19)*. It can be no coincidence that Catherine, unwittingly and indirectly, reminds us of David's destruction of portions of the honeymoon narrative (and Hemingway's destruction of portions of the *Eden* manuscript) right before we learn that she has destroyed David's African stories.[6] It is not that there is a moral equivalence in the two destructive acts, but they do inform one another.

215:25 **child's notebooks:** See 37:27.

215:31 **his French. . . . try to write it:** David's difficulty writing French mirrors Hemingway's in the 1920s.

216:5 ***Ta queule:*** This is a mistranscription of what appears in the manuscript: "*Ta gueule.*" A common slang abbreviation for *ferme ta gueule*—something like *shut your gob*, or *shut your trap*—the expression is an example of how David is "amusing with his slang" (215:33). Although David says it "cheerfully," the word *gueule* signifies the mouth of a carnivorous animal, and the expression *ta gueule* is considered aggressive and rude and generally implies that an argument will follow.

216:19 **solitary vice:** The ingredients of this argument have been brewing since the opening pages of the novel (see 14:13), and this image of writing as masturbatory and isolating for the writer has inspired much commentary. Burwell argues that David uses his African writing "as a barrier against the feminine," rendering it essentially masturbatory (119), and Silbergleid suggests that Catherine punishes him for such masturbatory unfaithfulness by burning his stories, giving "him the opportunity to do better work, both in marriage and on the page" (109). According to Fleming, Hemingway suggests that the writer's necessary isolation from others is a "major sin" (145), and Hediger agrees that it certainly "contributes to the death of David's relationship with Catherine" (90).

As he worked on *The Garden of Eden,* Hemingway had good reason to explore this theme. In a 1 July 1958 letter to Bill Horne, Mary Hemingway wrote that for months work had been "driving Ernest like a fiend": "He takes one day off about every two weeks and we go out fishing . . . but otherwise he's busy without breakfast about 6 o'clock, doesn't knock off until time to swim a minute before lunch at 2, and all too often I keep findin[g] him silently back at work at 4. . . . We have kept delaying decisions, even discussions, of holidays until the dragon lets him loose" (JFK). On 22 August to Bill Seward, Mary reported that Ernest was still "enslaved" by the project (JFK), and by late September Ernest admitted that he'd been working as if in "a fever" (letter to Harvey Breit, 21 Sept. 1958, JFK). In other words, isolated by his writing from even his wife, Hemingway explored the dangers of how writing isolates David Bourne from Catherine.

216:20 The Original Romeike: Henry Romeike founded the first newspaper-clipping service in London in 1881, providing clients with articles mentioning their names or products, and opened a New York branch in 1884. When, after Henry's death in 1903, his son George came of age in 1916 and assumed the reins of the company, Henry's brother Albert split to found his own rival clipping service. After a failed 1917 lawsuit to deny Albert the corporate use of the name "Romeike," the "Henry Romeike" company, under George's direction, began asserting itself as the "original Romeike," warning in advertisements "Be Sure It's Henry. Other Romeikes May Disappoint." In a 1926 letter to Max Perkins, Hemingway jokes about his own dealings with "Mr. the original Romeike" (*Letters 3* 107, 108).

NOTES

1. In 1956, Hemingway may also have read about the crater in one of Robert Ruark's syndicated columns: "Stupidity Is Dooming African Garden of Eden."

2. Hemingway owned two of Leakey's books, but not his 1934 suggestively titled *Adam's Ancestors.* Mary Hemingway, however, writes about Leakey's discoveries at Olduvai Gorge in the drafts of *HIW* (JFK).

3. For more on Hemingway's regard for Berenson as a father figure, see Brasch, "Christ, I wish I Could Paint."

4. Burwell has suggested that this very brief mention of a character named Roger links *Eden* to *Islands in the Stream* and the figure of Roger Davis. I do not find this persuasive. This Roger in *Eden,* after all, shares nothing beyond his first name and died in the First World War.

5. See also Sheean's "Yankee Flyers Regret Bombs: Americans in Morocco Slay Women and Children: Discover Truth Only after Several Bombardments" and "Love of French Spurs Aviators: Case for American Flyers in Morocco Given."

6. See Eby, "Who Is Destructive."

CHAPTER 26 (MSS. CHAPTERS 40–41)

218:16 **Vuitton suitcase:** See 139:20.

219:32 **they were worthless:** As Daniel Train has noted, Catherine now ironically sounds like the kind of critic whose authority, when considering the clippings, she earlier wanted to dismiss: "If the reviewers had said it was worthless . . . I would have been just as proud and just as happy" (25:9). When David soon "begs her repeatedly to just not talk about the burnt stories, . . . Catherine, like a pedantic critic, insists, 'I like to, [. . .]. When it's constructive and has some valid purpose. . . . I want you to realize why it was so necessary to burn them'" (Train 39).

220:13 **I paid for them:** See 226:27.

220:30 **In the iron drum:** While notes in the *Eden* manuscript indicate that Hemingway wrote these pages in late December 1958 or early January 1959, it is nonetheless noteworthy that in the spring of 1960, when Ernest's brother, Leicester, sent him a draft of his memoir, an enraged Ernest carried it outside and "deposited it in the burn barrel." In *Running with the Bulls,* Valerie Hemingway remembers Ernest dousing the manuscript with lighter fluid and striking a match: "The flames curled upward to the sullen sky." Leicester never did learn what happened to his manuscript (6).

Since Hemingway had written this passage in *Eden* before he burned Leicester's manuscript, he clearly couldn't have been influenced by his actions at the time of composition. Nevertheless, his actions reveal a part of himself that was capable of disturbingly Catherine-like behavior—suggesting how the conflict between David and Catherine on some level represents a battle for control between two oppositionally gendered halves of a single riven ego. One wonders what happened to the missing pages of the *Eden* manuscript (see 215:23). Is it possible that they ended up in a burn barrel?

222:29 **where they bottled Perrier:** See 26:23.

223:3 **massacre in the crater:** See 129:11, 147:13, 157:5, and 157:23.

225:7 **To Hendaye and then to Paris to see about artists for the book:** Readers of the Scribner's edition might wonder why Catherine wants to go to Hendaye, which is hardly on a direct route from the Riviera to Paris. (It adds more than 450 miles to her trip.) The manuscript, however, makes it clear that she is going to there to see Nick about illustrations for the Hendaye section of the honeymoon narrative (3.41.3). In the manuscript, she's less certain about going to Paris, but she'd like to go there to recruit Marie Laurencin, André Dunoyer de Segonzac, and Raoul Dufy to the project (see 189:2). When David makes fun of Dufy, Catherine insists that her project is "reasoned" and carefully planned, not "tossed off" (3.41.5).

226:15 **Weren't the stories worth a lot? It's bothered me terribly:** Jenks condenses dialogue here. In the manuscript, between these two sentences appears the passage that Jenks transposes to 227:4–228:2. This transposition more clearly juxtaposes Catherine's offer of monetary support (226:13) with her purely monetary valuation of David's work (see below). This, in turn, more clearly raises concerns about Catherine's mental state before she and David discuss her drive.

226:27 **Who appraises these things?** David's question, of course, exposes Catherine's brutal commodification of experience and art. Such a commodification, as Daniel Train notes, reveals Catherine's "inability to really understand the 'value' of art and the 'cost' for the artist" (39). Yet the burden of this passage seems to be less about Catherine's core identity than it is about how far she has fallen into mental illness. The distance between Catherine's words now and her words earlier in the novel, when she explicitly distinguishes between the value of David's work and the money and critical praise it earns, is a key measure of her mental deterioration. Moreover, it is important to note that David has never been able to make such a clear distinction himself. When the earlier Catherine tells him she would have known the value of his second novel and would have been just as proud of it "if the reviews had said it was worthless and if it never made a cent" (25:9), David, a professional author, privately thinks that he wouldn't have been. It can be no coincidence that the list of potential appraisers that Catherine soon names (see below) points to the moment when Hemingway's own publishing began to leave the confines of "art publishing" in such modernist "little magazines" as the *Little Review,* the *Transatlantic Review, transition,* and *This Quarter* and broke into the popular magazine market—in other words, to the moment when Hemingway's stories became commodified in a new way. As Hemingway worked feverishly on *The Garden of Eden,* a novel he may not have always intended to publish (see 77:29), he may well have contemplated what the commodification of his art had cost him in the form of self-expression and truth.

226:32 ***Atlantic Monthly, Harper's, La Nouvelle Revue Française:*** Like so much of the novel, Catherine's list of potential "appraisers" is rooted in the events of

Hemingway's life in 1927. This was the year that Hemingway's short stories—until then published only in modernist little magazines—finally broke through into the popular magazine market. Though he had for several years unsuccessfully submitted stories to the likes of *Cosmopolitan, Scribner's Magazine,* and *Harper's,* it wasn't until the *Atlantic Monthly* accepted "Fifty Grand" for its July 1927 issue (after the story had first been rejected by *Colliers,* the *Saturday Evening Post, Cosmopolitan,* and *Scribner's Magazine*) that one of his stories reached a wide magazine audience. The $365 Hemingway received in payment from *The Atlantic* was the most he had received for a story to that point, and a translation of the story appeared a month later in *La Nouvelle Revue Française.* Enjoying the recent success of *The Sun Also Rises,* he could report to Max Perkins that his work was now being solicited by the *New Yorker, Vanity Fair,* and *Harper's Bazaar,* and before the year was out he could boast three stories in *Scribner's Magazine* and another in the *New Republic.*

In the manuscript, after hearing Catherine's list, David asks, "Not *Blackwood's?*" to which Catherine replies, "If you like" *(3.41.10).* David's mocking inclusion of the once-great-but-then-musty conservative British magazine seems to imply that Catherine's list is unduly staid, but even if *La Nouvelle Revue Française* was slow to pay Hemingway what it owed him, the magazines on Catherine's list paid well, which is why Hemingway aspired to publish in them.

227:4 **I was going to Paris:** See 226:15.

CHAPTER 27 (MSS. CHAPTER 42)

229:12 **the N.6 to Cannes:** In the manuscript, Hemingway left himself a note to check the road number. The road then running along the coast to Cannes was actually the N7 (see 131:20).

229:15 **the trees:** In the manuscript, Hemingway is careful to note that these are "plane trees." This detail reminds us that we are at the Café des Allées (see 88:28).

230:8 **Tio Pepe:** Tio Pepe is far more prominent in the manuscript than in the Scribner's edition. In the *Eden* manuscript, there is even a magazine advertisement for Tio Pepe with Hemingway's notes scrawled on it. This advertisement, from the 22 August 1959 issue of *Blanco y Negro*, the Saturday supplement of the Spanish newspaper *ABC*, tells us that Hemingway continued to work on *Eden* during the "dangerous summer" of 1959. See appendix C.

230:13 **except the narrative. The stuff about her:** K. J. Peters has argued that Catherine, in burning all of David's writing that isn't about her, is trying "eliminate the competition" represented by his African stories and take control of his authorship: "Unable to create her own fiction by manipulating the lives of Marita and David, Catherine eliminates David's fiction. In this way Catherine can create her own story, and David can concentrate on recording it in the narrative" (24). Her choice of fuel for her bonfire is, of course, also a testimony to her narcissism—to the Catherine who can declare, "now you're me you're you so much better" *(3.31.35)*, or "I am you and her. . . . I'm everybody" *(3.36.12)*. If we look at Catherine and David as two oppositionally gendered halves of a single riven ego (see 12:13 and 17:23), Catherine's decision to burn the African stories in which David explores and rewrites his relationship with his father can be seen as part of an internalized battle between the sexes in which the feminine half tries to assert itself over the masculine half to commandeer the body (see 5:27 and 93:2). Thus, Marita's observation: "I didn't know it was a battle when I came" (231:28).

(230:16) 3.42.4 **all the King's horses nor all the King's men:** In the manuscript, in the novel's second allusion to Humpty Dumpty (see 200:5), David laments that his African stories are gone and there's no use summoning "all the King's horses nor all the King's men." The allusion suggests that the African stories are David's creative "eggs," his progeny. In a further extension of the novel's egg motif (see 4.9), we also soon learn that one of David's African stories concerned an incident where his father ate thirteen bad eggs (3.42.11), and this becomes a metaphor for David's current condition. In the story, David's father had responded by resuming a daylong march, but David is unable to be as stoic.

231:6 **Rube Goldberg:** Reuben "Rube" Goldberg was an American cartoonist most famous for his drawings of whimsical, fanciful, and excessively complicated mechanisms to complete comparatively simple tasks. Trained as an engineer, Goldberg began drawing such machines in 1914, and by 1927 his name had become synonymous with them. David's metaphor calls attention to the almost comic insanity of Catherine's plan to somehow transform money into adequate compensation for what David has lost.

In the *Eden* manuscript, a blank appears after Goldberg's name, and Hemingway has written a note above the blank: "British caricaturist contemporary of Bairnsfather" (3.42.10). Hemingway, whose attempt to finish *The Garden of Eden* would soon be interrupted,[1] was never able to fill in this blank, but he was clearly thinking of W. Heath Robinson, the Rube Goldberg of the United Kingdom and a contemporary of British cartoonist Bruce Bairnsfather. The term "Heath Robinson contraption" had entered the English lexicon by 1912, and during the First World War, Robinson became famous for his cartoons of complicated, jury-rigged, and unlikely mechanized weapons. In 1927 France, Goldberg and Robinson were both well known, but Robinson was the more famous.

(231:28) 3.42.16 **mosaics at Torcello and Ravenna:** In the manuscript, trying to console David, Marita suggests that he might have to begin his stories all over again and build them anew, "like the mosaics at Torcello and Ravenna." She wonders if David knows them, but he does not. She assures him that he'll be able to re-create the stories "like a new civilization" built on the ruins of the previous one, strengthened by an understanding of what came before.

The story of the Venetian island of Torcello, which Hemingway tells in *Across the River and into the Trees,* involves cycles of destruction and rebuilding. Driven by the barbarian invasions of Italy in the fifth and sixth centuries from their mainland home in Aquileia, one of the late Roman Empire's great cities, the founders of what would become Venice first settled on the island of Torcello. There, as Hemingway tells it, they built a cathedral and a flourishing new home for thirty thousand people before some centuries later the mouth of the Sile River silted up and mosquito-borne malaria forced the people to pick up their homes stone by stone and move to what is now the center of Venice, five miles to the southwest. Today Torcello is sparsely populated, but the Cathedral of Santa Maria Assunta, founded in 639, remains, with its magnificent mosaics. These mosaics, however, postdate a rebuilding of the cathedral in 1008. When Marita refers, then, to David's need to rebuild his stories as the mosaics of Torcello were rebuilt, it isn't clear if she is referring to the initial move from Aquileia to Torcello, the transition from Torcello to Venice, or the need to rebuild the mosaics of Santa Maria Assunta in 1008. Hemingway was almost certainly thinking, though, of the mosaic of the *Last Judgment* that covers the interior west wall of Santa Maria Assunta, a mosaic he associated with spiritual doubt and which recalls, in its imaginative depiction of hell, Bosch's *Garden of Earthly Delights* (Hemingway, "Torcello" xi). (See *[54:23]* 3.10.4.) He was doubtless also remembering his 1948 stay in Torcello, which Mary Hemingway describes as follows: "We had joyous late mornings in bed. . . . Small loving jokes, speculations on girl and boy love, with which Ernest was brimming in those days. The Kinsey people would not have believed us, I noted. Ernest taught me many new delights and I taught him some" (*HIW* 237).

Why in 1927 Marita would mention the resplendent mosaics of Ravenna is less clear. Those that adorn Ravenna's eight surviving monuments from the fifth and sixth centuries are the finest early Christian mosaics in western Europe and served as inspirations for those in Torcello, but they had never been destroyed and reconstructed in any wholesale manner. During WWI, an Austrian bomb had damaged the Basilica of Sant'Apollinare Nuovo, but not its mosaics. Hemingway must have been thinking, however anachronistically, of the extensive damage done to Ravenna by fifty-two Allied bombings during WWII. Most notably, "Bombs intended for the railway station . . . pulverized" the mid-fifth-century Basilica of San Giovanni Evangelista and its mosaics. But as Judith Herrin writes, "The Italians are among the finest art restorers in the world. Immediately after the war they set about repairing their unique heritage in Ravenna. To raise the funds for this and re-establish tourism, an exhibition was mounted that reproduced some of the most glorious mosaic images, which toured Paris, London and New York in the 1950s" (xxix). There is nothing anachronistic, however, in Marita's point about the cycle of destroyed and succeeding civilizations in Ravenna. Between the fifth and eighth centuries, the city served as a capital for Roman, Ostrogoth, and Byzantine rulers in Italy.

231:28 I didn't know it was a battle: see 230:13.

(232:2) 422 3.42.22 I hated everybody when my brother died: In a discarded fragment that originally fit here in the manuscript, Marita tells David that she "hated everybody when [her] brother died" flying in WWI. She understands loss and the resulting loneliness. She thinks David would have liked her brother: "He was in love with me." David thinks this was "intelligent," adding that he "never minded incest if it was in the same family." It is important, of course, to remember that this is discarded material. See 6:6, 126:12, and *(162:4)* 422.4 3.27.8.

(232:2) 3.42.21 **Richthofen:** In the manuscript, after more encouragement from Marita, David tells her he still feels "like something brought in on a platter." This, and the discarded memory of the flying death of Marita's brother (see above), prompts David to recall the death of the Red Baron, Manfred von Richthofen, who was shot down behind Allied lines near the Somme on 21 April 1918. The unstated association behind David's memory seems to be the piece of corrugated metal—a sort of "platter"—used as a stretcher by members of the No. 3 Squadron of the Australian Flying Corps to carry Richthofen's dead body into their hanger at Poulainville. David remembers, with historical accuracy, Richthofen's "deadstick landing"[2]—when Richthofen was "deader than a stick"—and Richthofen's burial by the Allies (struck through in the *Eden* manuscript) "with full military honors." What appears to be pure fiction, however, is David's memory of Richthofen's dead body propped up in a chair at the head of a table, with somebody's lit cigarette stuck in his mouth. In *The Day the Red Baron Died,* Dale Titler writes that Richthofen's body, still tied to the galvanized sheet, was propped up at a sixty-degree angle against a tent pole (195).[3] Allied pilots came to the hangar that evening to pay their respects, but the Allies were quite sensitive to the body's propaganda value, and all available records suggest that the body was treated with respect. In lines struck through in the manuscript, Marita asks David why these memories weren't in his flying book. David replies that he "wasn't there." These lines may have been deleted because they are inconsistent with the vividness of a memory that recalls such details as prying Richthofen's fingers off of the flying stick.

NOTES

1. This page in the manuscript is dated January 14. In a 10 April 1959 letter to Alfred Rice, Hemingway explains that Taylor Williams's death (18 February 1959) "upset things entirely" and upended his attempt to complete the novel (JFK).
2. A "deadstick landing" is a forced landing when an airplane's propeller ceases to function and is of no more use than a dead stick.
3. The respectful nature of the burial is emphasized in Quentin Reynolds's *They Fought for the Sky* (1958), which Hemingway owned.

CHAPTER 28 (MSS. CHAPTER 43)

233:14 **looked at Madame Aurol:** In the manuscript, Madame Aurol responds to David's pain by kissing him on the mouth. She begs Marita's pardon, but she knows what Catherine has done and she wants to apologize to David "for all the women of this world" (3.43.3). In the manuscript, instead of asking if Catherine seemed like herself, David states that she had not been herself, and Madame Aurol's reply is far less circumspect. To her "Perhaps not, Monsieur" (233:16), she adds that perhaps Catherine had simply been "more herself" than ever.

In the manuscript, Madame Aurol encourages David and Marita to speak French "like honest people," though she has to admit that "*la brûleuse*" (the one who burns things) spoke French without an accent. When David smiles at the epithet, Madame Aurol blurts out, "*La putaint brûleuse sadique et pervertie*" ("the sadistic and perverted burning whore"). David asks her not to "speak ill of the dead." Madame Aurol declares that what Catherine has done is "monstrous," a crime against nature and the literature of David's country. David simply repeats that Catherine "wasn't herself." It was an "illness." Crying, Madame Aurol apologizes for speaking about "things that are not [her] business," but she cannot reconcile herself to his loss.

234:5 **belote:** Invented around 1920, the card game belote quickly became a fad in France, where it remains to this day the most popular card game. In 1924 the French chanteuse Mistinguett had a hit song with "La Belote," and by 1925 the *Paris Times* was calling belote "the most French of all French games" ("In the Margin"). Played with thirty-two cards (the aces, kings, queens, jacks, tens, nines, eights, and sevens) and two, three, or four players, the game often involves gambling. Within the game, the term *belote* designates a trump-suit pair of king and queen.

234:21 **the omelette:** As if the implications for the novel's egg motif (see 4.9) were not clear enough, David makes them explicit in the manuscript by inverting the famous French aphorism "*on ne saurait faire d'omelette sans casser des œufs*": "You can't break an omelette without making eggs" (3.43.9). Marita attributes the saying to Napoleon, whom David calls "a famous egg maker," yet though the phrase is often popularly attributed to Napoleon, the *Oxford English Dictionary* traces it back to 1742 (before Napoleon's birth) and suggests it may be older.

Marita remarks that it's nice to eat in the kitchen for a change, and Madame Aurol agrees that it is the only place for some meals. A soufflé would never survive the trip to the terrace. As the cracked-egg reference called attention to David's status as a sort of Humpty Dumpty (see 200:5 and *[230:16] 3.42.4),* the reference to soufflé further hints at his general fragility.

(234:18) 3.43.10 **SS Mystique . . . latitude —— longitude ——. . . . Hotel —— 4 kilometers from La Napoule:** See 75:2.

(234:18) 3.43.10 **K. A. R. or the Oklahoma National Guard:** After misunderstanding David's joke about the loss of the "gallant craft" "*SS Mystique*" (see 75:2), Madame Aurol asks David if he had been drafted into the navy. No, he answers. If he had been drafted, it would have been into the King's African Rifles or the Oklahoma National Guard (see 111:11). Without understanding his joke, Madame Aurol then understands that he was "*volontaire.*" Yes, David answers.

235:25 **it's so sure now:** The Scribner's edition implies that the thing Marita is "sure" of is her love, but what Marita wants to be sure of in the manuscript is that they "make the baby tonight," if they didn't already in the morning (see *[204:8] 3.37.25).* She can feel it growing inside her as if it were an entire tree planted there, but to make "sure, sure, sure" they make love again. It is after Marita's climax that David thinks "nothing is sure."

(235:31) 3.43.17i **"death's little brother. . . ." "Thy rod and thy staff shall comfort me":** In the manuscript, after Marita tells David how excited she is to sleep with him "tonight and always," David replies that "always" can be found only in death. Tweaking a line from the *Aeneid,* he calls sleep "Death's little brother." Marita responds by quoting Psalm 23: "Thy rod and thy staff shall comfort me." In this context, the sexual double entendre is comic, but when David asks for clarification, Marita explains that she will be comforted "when we go with his brother." Whether by "his brother" she means sleep or death is unclear, and this is purposeful. This is why, when David wakes in the morning, he notes that "he could see her spirit had not gone from her body when she slept" (236:12). This passage aligns sleep, death, and sex (*la petite mort*) in a way that gives the simple act of going to sleep together oddly cheerful overtones of David's and Catherine's suicide pact in the provisional ending of the novel. It should be borne in mind, however, that the provisional ending was written nine months before this passage in the manuscript was composed (see appendix B).

237:4 **hitting . . . a child . . . with a car:** This metaphor was almost certainly inspired by an incident in August 1959 when Hemingway saw a young girl hit by a car in Aranjuez, Spain. As Lisa Twomey has noted, "The swift and caring way Hemingway tended to the girl" was deeply appreciated in the Spanish press (38). A full-page article in the Madrid daily *ABC* included a photograph of Hemingway with the girl in his arms, and the article's author considered it a great and telling portrait: "Looking closely at the face, you can see that the injured animal is, in fact, him" (Sueiro).

237:7 *écrasseuse:* The word should be *écraseuse,* a colloquialism for a clumsy and dangerous driver, particularly one who hits a pedestrian. It is derived from the verb *écraser,* to crush.

(237:14) 3.43.22 **blown the Bosch room in the Prado. . . . not blame it on women. . . . love what I didn't understand:** In the manuscript, Catherine's letter assures David that she's feeling "all right in [her] head," except for her "shame." She feels as if she'd "blown the Bosch room in the Prado," which she says is the only thing she ever loved besides David. By comparing the destruction of David's stories to the destruction of the Bosch room in the Prado, Catherine implicitly aligns David's writing with the painting of Bosch. By extension, *The Garden of Eden* is aligned with Bosch's masterpiece *The Garden of Earthly Delights.* (For an extended consideration of this, see Eby, "Gardens of *Eden* and *Earthly Delights*"; see also *[54:23] 3.10.4* and *[54:23] 3.11.4*.) Catherine urges David to be good to Marita and not to blame all women for what has happened. She says she never hated Marita and hated David only when she was "crazy." She blames herself for failing to "love what [she] didn't understand."

237:14 **I had to burn the other things:** In the manuscript, Catherine is not justifying her actions, she is denouncing them. Her point is that she not only "threw away" what she had with David, she "had to burn it." She is not only referring to his stories, she is referring to their relationship.

237:28 **Crillon bar in Paris:** See 29:11.

237:29 **American Church at Avenue Hoche:** The Scribner's edition obscures an important point of French law by deleting the phrase "*mairie* of the —— arrondissement," which appears in the manuscript before "and the American Church at —— Avenue Hoche." Legal marriage in France is only possible through a civil ceremony performed at a town hall, or *mairie* (each arrondissement of Paris has its own *mairie*), which then, if so desired, may be followed by a religious ceremony.

Next to each blank in the manuscript, Hemingway has written "check," so he intended to fill in these blanks. The easier one to fill in is the address number for Paris's Catholic church for English-speaking parishioners, St. Joseph's, at 50 Avenue

Hoche. While Hemingway drew heavily on his marriage to Pauline in constructing the story of the Bournes' honeymoon, Ernest and Pauline were not married at St. Joseph's but instead in the church of St. Honoré d'Eylau on Place Victor Hugo. Pauline was friends with the rector of St. Joseph's, Father Gabriel MacDarby, but she and Ernest could not wed there because the Church required parishioners to have lived for at least three months in the parish where they married (Hawkins 69). As for identifying Hemingway's intended *mairie,* he may have meant to insert the number for the arrondissement where he and Pauline were married (the fourteenth), or perhaps he intended to insert the number for the arrondissement of the American church, St. Joseph's on Avenue Hoche (the eighth).

238:7 **a grave and violent thing:** In the manuscript, the words *grave* and *gravity* get David ruminating, and he considers permutations of the root word in Spanish and French. There is then an interesting, but deleted, slip, a French translation of Italian: Le grave de Papadopoli *(3.43.26).* "Grave di Papadopoli" is a large island in the Piave River—about twenty kilometers from Fossalta, where Hemingway was wounded in WWI. *Grave* here refers to gravel, the rocky nature of the place. After the Italian retreat from Caporetto, the island was part of a no-man's-land between the Italian and Austrian lines. On 15 June 1918, the Austrians attacked and took it. The island was then recaptured in fall 1918 (Raab 83).

David Bourne fought on the western, not the Italian, front in WWI, so this is an interesting slip. It is yet another measure of the degree of identification between Hemingway and his protagonist—an identification stronger even than that between David and his father in the African stories that he writes. Valerie Hemingway's declaration that "David Bourne *was* Ernest Hemingway" (69) is obviously hyperbole, but there is also much truth in it. Perhaps the embedded *Papa* in Papadopoli carried special significance for Hemingway. He no doubt realized the inappropriateness of the association, which explains his deletion of the line.

(238:22) 3.43.28 **If she's awake:** In the manuscript, the chapter continues. Knowing that Marita wakes early, David decides to brush his teeth and check on her before he goes to work. It will be a long wait for her otherwise. When he enters the room, Marita is brushing her hair before the mirror, wearing only her tight polo shirt. David kisses her and they chat, and then David explains that he is going to go to work. She wonders if he can, but he tells her he is going to try. In the meantime, she plans to go into town to pick up the Isotta. She plans to put Catherine's car in the garage, and then she wants to buy David a new car and put it in his name. David suggests that they discuss it over lunch, once he's done with work. Marita announces, somewhat mysteriously, that she's planning to do "some other things too" (see *[243:31] 3.44.21).* She can't just "stand by like a spectator" as David works. She wants to "take action" to help him. David kisses her as they get ready to part for the morning.

CHAPTER 29 (MSS. CHAPTERS 44–45)

239:6 **simple declarative sentence:** David's writing practices, once again, reflect those of his creator. This sounds much like the famous cure for writer's block Hemingway describes in *A Moveable Feast:* "Do not worry. You have always written before and you will write now. All you have to do is write one true sentence" (22). Once started, he could go on from there. Only here, even that strategy no longer works. In the manuscript, however, David knows that his "impotence" is "a passing thing" (3.44.1).

(240:2) 3.44.4 *"your name's David. . . ." "Harold or Roland":* In the manuscript, after Marita suggests they get a drink (240:1), David asks if she wants a "spot of the giant killer" before changing his mind in favor of a "really dry martini." "Fuck the giants," he declares. He *is* named after a famous giant killer, Marita notes—a thought which has never occurred to David. (For David's need to kill the "giant" Despair, see 148:21.) He has always just been glad he hadn't been named Harold or Roland. The name Roland clearly plays on the novel's several allusions to *The Song of Roland* (see [44:28] 3.5.6 and [194:4] 3.36.3i). Harold is, of course, a permutation of the name Harry, which for Hemingway was not just a fetish object but a fetish word. Harrys abound in Hemingway's fictional universe: Harry Morgan in *To Have and Have Not;* Harry Walden in "Snows of Kilimanjaro"; Harold Krebs, whose sister calls him Hare, in "Soldier's Home"; Frederic Henry in *A Farewell to Arms;* Harry's Bar in *Across the River and into the Trees;* and Herr Hudson in the Swiss portions of the *Islands in the Stream* manuscript; not to mention characters named Harris in *The Sun Also Rises*, "Homage to Switzerland," and *Under Kilimanjaro*. Marita's nickname, Heiress, no doubt also belongs to this family (see 120:27).[1]

240:6 **not waste it, David thought:** In the manuscript, Marita, not David, thinks this (3.44.4). Throughout much of his career (with several notable exceptions), Hemingway favored narrative strategies focalized through a single central consciousness. Jenks's decision to focalize this passage through David is clearly influenced by this, but Hemingway intentionally shifts focalization several times throughout the *Eden* manuscript (see *[51:2] 3.9.1; [143:7] 3.24.21;* and 151:17), and this shift lasts for sixteen manuscript pages. The glimpse we receive into Marita's consciousness helps us to see that she is authentically driven to support David, which is why she stayed nearby all day instead of going into town. David compares his morning's writing experience to walking past a familiar stream only to find it dry. Marita assures him that this was just a "bad dream," but David resists anything that feels like false encouragement. Marita hopes that David doesn't think she's trying to "manage" him *(3.44.8).*

(242:15) 3.44.13 **white headed seal . . . ~~an erection? I had one when he kissed my breasts~~ . . . "The Naulahka by Kipling":** In the manuscript, as David comes out of the water, Marita thinks to herself that he looks like a "white headed seal" (see 136:28). The strange simile makes her glad she isn't a writer. In a deleted line, she adds that at least she didn't think he looked like a "~~sea lion or walrus~~." This attention to sea mammals leads her to wonder if David can swim "~~when he has an erection~~." After all, whales must do it, and she herself had an erection when he kissed her breasts. This fits into a larger pattern of women in the novel who describe themselves as having erections (see 15:13).

David now tells Marita that, with her wet head, *she* looks like a seal (242:16), and she wonders to herself if she might have talent as a writer after all. She asks David if seals are "nice," and he asks her if she's read Kipling's *The Naulahka*. In the margin, Hemingway left himself a note to check this—and with good reason. Naulakha is the name of the house Kipling built in 1893 in Vermont, and, misspelled as *Naulahka*, it is the name of an 1892 East-meets-West novel that he cowrote with Wolcott Balestier—but there are no seals in it, black or white. Hemingway was probably confusing *Naulahka* with Novastoshnah, the setting for Kipling's *Jungle Book* story "The White Seal" (written while Kipling was living at Naulakha). The story of a one-of-a-kind white-seal savior who leads his brethren to what seems to be the world's lone beach safe from the depredations of human hunters, "The White Seal" speaks to Hemingway's concern with the despoliation of Edenic spaces. David says that he's only seen seals in circuses and zoos, and Marita then wishes they could go to a zoo. The world's greatest zoo, David answers, is Ngorongoro Crater—another place associated with Eden (see *[210:16] 3.38.16).*

(242:26) 3.44.17 **Africa . . . Switzerland:** In the manuscript, as they sit on the beach eating chicken and wearing only their shirts, Marita asks David if they are going to Africa. "Sure," he answers. Thinking of the cold in Africa's high country, Marita notes that it will be cold, too, in Switzerland if they have to go there to take care of Catherine. Marita suggests she can take care of David while he takes care of Catherine. It is discussion of this that leads Marita to say, "There isn't anything we can do about her today so let's not think about it" (242:27).

(243:31) 3.44.21 **The North Africa thing?** In the manuscript, Marita suggests that she and David go into town that afternoon to "do the other thing [she] wanted to do." "The ~~North~~ Africa thing?" David asks (see *[161:8] 3.27.3*). "Please," pleads Marita. Does she really want it? David asks. Wouldn't it be inconvenient if they have to travel? And is now the right time? Marita thinks it will be fun. David warns her not try to make herself "like a Wakamba or Mbulu girl," but Marita promises to be even better. Then they can "have Africa tonight" *(3.44.29)*. In other words, on the morning after Catherine's departure, Marita is already planning to get an ultrashort African haircut that "mixe[s] up the genders" *(3.45.2)* and that will transform their bedroom into a fetishized "Africa."

This passage alone (and there is more to come) should undo the impression created by the Scribner's edition and endorsed by many critics that the ending of Hemingway's novel reestablishes heteronormativity and traditional gender roles after they have been troubled by Catherine. The novel Hemingway wrote does no such thing, and it is unfortunate that the Scribner's edition produces this mistaken impression. In Hemingway's text, the broader contrast that Jenks draws between Catherine and Marita is confined largely to two areas: the question of sanity and support for the full range of David's writing.

(244:2) 3.44.25 **"Shakespeare. . . . Duff Cooper. . . . Harsh harsh the lark who screamed when Kosciusko fell. . . ." "Poniatowski":** In the manuscript, after David announces his new career as a "sand writer," he rewrites a line from *Hamlet* to pun on his own name: "The David Bournes, sand writers, announce their unsuccessful peak into that undiscovered country from whose bourne no traveler returns . . ." (see 7:7). David explains that he cowrote this with Shakespeare, who was "extremely talented" and whom "Duff Cooper believes was a sergeant." First Viscount of Norwich, British Conservative Party politician, diplomat, historian, and philanderer, Duff Cooper wrote a 1949 book called *Sergeant Shakespeare* that Hemingway enjoyed and also recommended in *Under Kilimanjaro* (255). (Either this is an anachronism or David has heard this theory firsthand from Cooper, whom Hemingway knew and liked.) Inspired by his experience in the First World War and the death of a Sergeant Shakespeare in his own battalion, Cooper argues that William Shakespeare must have been a soldier.

It is this combination of Shakespeare and war that leads to David's next ridiculously complex allusion. When Marita asks why Catherine was "so strange about the war," David suggests that it was mere jealousy. Marita finds this "harsh," which inspires David to say, "Harsh harsh the lark who screamed when Kosciusko fell." David's line is a mash-up of Shakespeare's "Hark, hark! The lark at heaven's gate sings," from *Cymbeline,* and "Freedom shriek'd—as Kosciusko fell" from Thomas Campbell's 1799 prorevolutionary poem *The Pleasures of Hope.*[2] There is probably also a hint of T. S. Eliot's "Sweeney among the Nightingales," where nightingales sing through the murder of Agamemnon—but the "Sweeney" Hemingway had in mind is Charles Sweeny, the model for *Eden*'s Colonel Boyle (see 60:21). As a former pilot, David alludes to the well-known military hero of both Poland and the American Revolutionary War, Andrzej Tadeusz Bonawentura Kościuszko, less because he is thinking of Enlightenment struggles for freedom than because he is thinking of the Polish 7th Air Escadrille, better known as the Kościuszko Squadron. Formed in 1919 by American volunteers, including many former members of the Lafayette Escadrille (see 60:21 and 61:5), to fight in the Polish-Soviet War of 1919–21—a war in which Sweeny recruited volunteer pilots and served as a brigadier general—the unit served as a model for the reconstituted Lafayette Escadrille (renamed the Sharifian Squadron) that Sweeny recruited to fly in the Moroccan Rif War in 1925 (see 61:5). David's allusion to Campbell's poem calls ironic attention to the less-than-revolutionary service being performed by Sweeny in Morocco (see *[214:22] 3.39.9*).

Marita wonders, where *did* Kościuszko fall? In Poland, of course, David answers, adding that the repeated partitioning of the country with "indefensible frontiers" gave the lark plenty to shriek about. (The foremost beneficiary of the three partitions of Poland at the end of the eighteenth century was Catherine the Great of Russia—so David may be, consciously or unconsciously, alluding to the divisive power of his wife. Or Hemingway may be associating Catherine, in her manifestation as the split-off other-gendered half of his ego, with self-division.)[3] Upon reflection, though, David thinks Kościuszko may have died in Switzerland—which is in fact where he died, in 1817 at age seventy-one. Playing on "shriek," David punningly thinks that "the day of the *hoarse* cavalryman is over" (my emphasis), and his judgment, however comically expressed, echoes what Lieutenant Colonel Cedric E. Fauntleroy, leader of the Kościuszko Squadron, was saying to the press in 1921: "Poland has demonstrated that peace on the eastern fringes of Europe can be enforced most effectively by opposing the fleet Cossack horseman with the fleeter airplane" ("Fleet").

David tells Marita he had just enough sense not to go to the Polish-Soviet War himself. Marita tells him that she has "a cousin who married a Poniatowski." Józef Poniatowski, nephew of Stanislaus Poniatowski, the last king of Poland, and close associate of Kościuszko, served as a Polish general and resigned at the prospect of the second and third partitioning of the country. (So, is Marita related to a lineage that resists the self-division represented by Catherine?) He led the defense of Warsaw during the 1794 Kościuszko Uprising against Prussia and Russia, and he was exiled by Russian authorities in 1798. Napoleon later made him a marshal of the French Empire and in 1807 minister of war for the Duchy of Warsaw. Poniatowski took part in the 1812 invasion of Russia and died in 1813. When Marita, a member of the Bonnin de la Bonninière de Beaumont family (see *[162:4] 3.27.9*), says her cousin married a Poniatowski, she seems to be referring (anachronistically) to a real marriage. In 1948, Prince Phillippe Edmond Marie Joseph Stanislaus Poniatowski married Irène Marguerite Marie Thérèse Bonnin de la Bonninière de Beaumont. Such connections further underscore her aristocratic credentials (see 90:19).

(244:2) 3.44.31 **It isn't a Catherine thing. It's us. . . . your fiancée . . . Madrid. . . . remorse:** In the manuscript, after Marita talks some more about her plans for an African haircut and once more shows David how alluring her hair looks when it's wet, David tells her that she doesn't need to do "Catherine things." Marita assures him this isn't a "Catherine thing." This will be different. Besides, her hair is the "only thing" about herself she can "change." David tells her she doesn't need to change, but Marita knows better. She knows this from reading the story about David's boyhood fiancée, and she knows from having read the honeymoon narrative—even the part about Madrid. David doesn't want to hear about "Madrid" (meaning a psychosexual position, not a geographical location), but Marita knows she can do what David and Catherine tried without David suffering from remorse. When David asks how she could know that, Marita explains that she knows because she is "the same" as David. Whereas Catherine had forced David to change because she had to change herself, Marita won't make David change, because she truly understands him. Knowing this, they are both ready to go into Cannes to run errands.

(244:2) 3.45.1 **"What kind of a boy are you supposed to be? . . ." "Bizerte street urchin":** As a new chapter begins in the manuscript, David meets Marita at the café in Cannes and is shocked by her hair, which is "cropped as close as a sheared beaver." (The word *beaver* has been used as slang for the female genitals since at least the 1920s.) He wants to know "what kind of boy" she is supposed to be. She had been aiming to look like his boyhood "African girl," but she thinks she must now look like a "Bizerte street urchin." It's "wonderful," David tells her, but a "shock." The hairstyle looks North African, like a "waterfront Arab's," and it "mixe[s] up the genders."

Marita's new haircut crystalizes the novel's tonsorial, sexual, gender, racial, and colonial dynamics. As promised (see above), Marita's new haircut is like "Madrid," insofar as Marita and David are both occupying "boyish" positions (see 67:1)—but this now takes on overtones of pederasty and colonial sex-tourism. Marita is soon playfully calling David "Effendi" and "Sahib" *(3.45.15),* while he calls her "Ali" *(3.45.17).* This sort of association of Middle Eastern and North African "sensuality with male pederasty" is a staple of Western fantasy (Boone 54), but Hemingway is probably playing on the version of it he encountered in his extensive reading of Gide. Earlier in the manuscript, Marita tells David that she once hoped to "keep a journal like Gide" *(3.37.36).*

For more on the North African ("Hamitic"), homoerotic, and gender-mixing characteristics of Marita's African haircut, and for its connection to Mary Hemingway's 1954 African haircut in Madrid, see *(161:8) 3.27.3.*

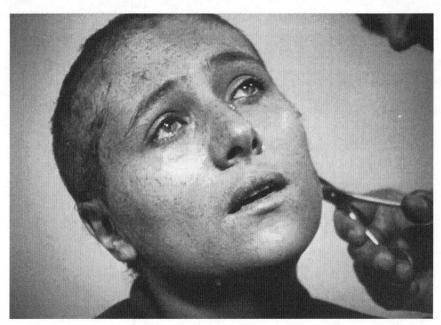

Renée Jeanne Falconetti. Still from Carl Theodor Dreyer's 1928 film *La Passion de Jeanne d'Arc*.

(244:2) 3.45.2 **Falconetti in Jeanne d'Arc:** In the manuscript, Marita wonders if her new haircut makes her look like Renée Jeanne Falconetti about to be burned at the stake in Carl Theodor Dreyer's 1928 silent film masterpiece, *La Passion de Jeanne d'Arc*.[4] In her legendary portrayal of the cross-dressing saint, partly shot in Aigues-Mortes, as she is readied for the flames Falconetti's hair is cropped to the scalp. (The violence of the scene recalls the rape of Maria and the cutting of her braids in *For Whom the Bell Tolls*. For Hemingway's erotic excitement in cutting, and watching the cutting of, hair, see 79:21.) David has described himself and Marita as "burned" by what Catherine has done (243:29), which aligns them both with Joan of Arc. It may also be significant that the original master negative of Dreyer's film was destroyed in a fire in December 1928—much like David's manuscripts.

(244:2) 3.45.4 **Back at the hotel. . . . "go to bed very quickly. . . . I want to be your boy. . . . It's not perversion. It's variety":** In the manuscript, back at the hotel, excited by Marita's new haircut, David and Marita immediately go to bed. Afterwards, as they talk, Marita revels in being "scandalous" and wishes she could have really been like David's African girl. When David tells her she was "better," she replies that she wants to be "worse" and she wants to be his "boy." David demurs, but she presses forward. Yes, she will be his boy and he'll "love it," and he'll "never have remorse." She tells him she "won't ask permission either." In fact, she thinks she'll make the change now, and when David says "no," she loves the sound of his voice. There's something so "non-

definite" about the way he says "no." "It's better than anybody's 'yes.'" She loves his "weaknesses" as much as his "strengths," because the weaknesses are "what make the strengths." In a textbook example of fetishistic disavowal—the simultaneous entertainment of two irreconcilable positions (see 15:13)—she promises she can "be a boy and a girl both at the same time," and David will never have remorse, because she'll wait until dark, telling him that she's really his girl and going so far as to say, "and it never happened. It's not perversion. It's variety." David loves her "infinite variety."

(244:2) 3.45.7 **Do you think I'll ruin you?** In the manuscript, Marita asks David if he thinks she'll "ruin" him. See 5:27.

244:3 They slept well: In the manuscript, this passage and the next twenty manuscript pages are focalized through Marita, and we once again have access to her thoughts. As she watches David sleep, she compares him to a marble "warrior on a tomb" and admires his scars *(3.45.8)*. She must try to "heal" him, she thinks, and satisfy his needs. She looks at herself in the mirror and thinks that her haircut and their lovemaking have been good for David. She and David are "so alike" that it would be "frightening" if it weren't "so wonderful." She wonders if anyone else is "like us." Or perhaps everyone is. No, that can't be true, "but many must be." And it can't be a "sin" if it feels so wonderful. She "owe[s] Catherine so much for what she did to him"—before she did such awful things *(3.45.11)*. Marita never would have been able to accomplish this on her own, but she reminds herself that she can't love Catherine, too, because David "mustn't be split in his heart nor his head" (see 183:14). She hopes for a "miracle" so that David's ability to write returns quickly.

After a conversation with Madame Aurol about what David will eat for dinner, Marita returns to the bedroom where David is still sleeping. Looking at his "whitish" hair against his "dark face," Marita thinks, "I wish I'd done that to him . . ." *(3.45.14)*. She couldn't help being jealous of Catherine for that—and for "everything" Catherine did with David. And she thinks Catherine knowingly fueled her jealousy by showing her the honeymoon narrative. Remembering the Grau-du-Roi section of the narrative, Marita knows David must have liked what he did with Catherine; otherwise, he couldn't have written it so well. She thinks he must miss that. She'd miss it herself. Soon she and David "can do everything." She knows that she and David are "darker inside" than Catherine, and sexual experiments don't "belong" to Catherine just "because she did them first." Whereas Catherine was "compelled" by her own desires, Marita decides she is compelled by David's desires.

244:17 I think you should go to town. . . . club . . . where you met your friends: Jenks's editing is highly misleading here. These lines have been moved from seventeen chapters earlier in the manuscript *(3.28.47)*, and Jenks turns a casual onetime suggestion ("You go to town and get the papers and have a drink. . . .") into a piece of advice about how David should lead his life. Jenks adds "I think you should," and he adds "every day." These additions are not justified by what Hemingway wrote.

244:22 You've been over-run with girls: In the manuscript, Marita says this directly after she's just asked David, "*Do I make a good boy?*" (*3.45.17;* my emphasis). Needless to say, Jenks's editing in the Scribner's edition produces a very false impression that Marita intends to reestablish and reinforce traditional gender roles in their relationship.

244:23 I'm always going to see you have your men friends: This line has been moved here from its actual location in the manuscript seventeen chapters earlier (see *[163:31] 3.28.18*). From thirty pages later in that same chapter, Jenks imports the passage running from "I'm going to see you have your men friends" through "Not on purpose and it was my own fault" (244:25). The effect again is to produce the false impression that the novel ends with David's retrenchment in conventional masculinity.

(244:23) 3.45.17 "*fix up Catherine . . . hit Kenya. . . .*" "*have to be married*": In the manuscript, David promises Marita that Catherine will be cured and they will all be together in Kenya by Christmas. When Marita wonders if they'd have to be married to live in Kenya, David replies, "Good God, no." That would make them too "conspicuous." To understand David's joke, one needs to recognize that colonial settlers in Kenya's "Happy Valley" in the 1920s had established such a reputation for sexual hijinks that a stock joke in Britain ran, "Are you married, or do you live in Kenya?" (Farson 234).

David tells Marita that, to get married, he wouldn't mind being a "registered Mohammedan." After all, it can't be any worse than being in the RAF. Marita isn't thinking about herself, she explains, but being married would be "better for children." David and Marita then discuss what their children might be like, and Marita hopes for a daughter who will be both like her and like David.

(244:25) 3.45.19 like Kim and the bazaars: In the manuscript, as David and Marita discuss what an interesting life their daughter would have, Marita suggests that the girl would be "like Kim and the bazaars." The allusion to *Kim,* Kipling's novel about the orphaned son of an Irish soldier in Imperial India, advances the colonial rhetoric of the preceding pages, where Marita has been calling David "Effendi" and "Sahib" and he has called her "Ali" (see *[244:2] 3.45.1*). It also implies their daughter would be like a son—one who, like Kim, can pass as a native in the bazaars of India.

(244:25) 3.45.20 "*new car. . . .*" "*Lancia. . . .*" "*Mercedes 200*": Marita promises that they'll buy a new car that will feel entirely their own. David wants a Lancia, and

Marita wants to use it to destroy an "enormous white Mercedes 200." It could happen, David says, but only if the Mercedes is "sick." In 1927, David and Marita would be looking at a Lancia Lambda series VII, but it isn't clear what their car would look like. The Lambda was celebrated for several innovations—most famously the first use of a load-bearing unitary body—but with the series VII, Lancia also began offering a separate chassis version for custom coachwork. David could be thinking of anything from a two-seater sport model to a more conservative Berlina. The comparatively light Lancia, even with the new and larger engine of the series VII, is a contrast with the heavy but faster Mercedes-Benz Typ Stuttgart 200.[5]

The impetus for David's interest in a Lancia probably stems from Hemingway's experience touring Europe in 1953, 1954, and 1956 in different Lancia Aurelias—cars praised for their high quality, "advanced engineering, and road manners" (Cain). In May 1959, Hemingway decided to use his Italian royalties (which couldn't be repatriated) to buy a new Lancia Flaminia Berlina.[6] Self-conscious about the expense of his new luxury car, Hemingway nicknamed it "La Barata, the cheap one" (V. Hemingway 50).

(244:25) 3.45.22 "scandalous. . . . head clipped. . . . Catherine nonsense. . . ." "Gobi Desert. . . ." "dinosaur eggs": In the manuscript, Marita wonders if they look "too scandalous" to go to Turin to buy a Lancia. They look "too scandalous to go anywhere," David answers. He plans to get his hair clipped short tomorrow, he tells her, to remove all that "Catherine nonsense." Inspired by David's plan, Marita comes up with perhaps the wildest of the novel's many fetishistic fantasies of racial and ethnic transformation: "We can be people from the Gobi Desert." In reply, David promises to bring his "dinosaur eggs."

By "people of the Gobi Desert," Marita seems to mean Kazakhs (who inhabit the region along with Mongols and Uyghurs), but she confuses them with Cossacks (a different people, whose name nonetheless derives from the same root word for "wanderer"). As David would know from his reading of Gogol (see next entry), a shaved head with a remaining long forelock (called an *oseledets*) was formerly the signifier of true male Ukrainian Cossack identity.[7]

More interesting is David's immediate leap from "Gobi Desert" to "dinosaur eggs." The oddest of the novel's many egg references (see 4:9), David's association is rooted in the famous 1923 discovery by a team from the American Museum of Natural History of twenty-five fossilized dinosaur eggs in the Gobi Desert. In what was described as "the largest find of the remains of prehistoric animals in the history of paleontology," the team found over seventy-two skulls and twelve complete skeletons, but the press was most fascinated by the eggs—the first ever found, and which established for the first time that dinosaurs laid eggs ("Find"). The fossil find was so large that, in a stunning leap of scientific reasoning, Roy Chapman Andrews, leader of the expedition, thought he had discovered the "original home" of all life on the planet and the "cradle of the human race" ("Beginnings"). He told the *New York Times:* "The expedition had proved Central Asia to have been the paleontological Garden of Eden, the center of life in the world." And he "predicted that the skeletons of the ancestors of man would some day be discovered in the Gobi Desert" ("Scientists"). Andrews repeated this claim about "a paleontological Garden of Eden" on the first page of his book *On the Trail of Ancient Man,* which Hemingway read in 1927 (vii).[8] To be "people from the Gobi Desert," then, would be to be people from Eden—perhaps even Adam and Eve. (See also *[210:16] 3.38.16.*)

(244:25) 3.45.22 "non-singing Cossack . . . girl disguised as a young officer. . . ." "Taras Bulba": In the manuscript, Marita suggests that they can be Cossacks (see above), but David protests that he can't sing. Marita tells him he can be a "non-singing Cossack," and she'll be his "girl disguised as a young officer." The idea of cross-dressing Cossacks inspires David to ask Marita if she has read Gogol's *Taras Bulba.* David doesn't think a girl could remain disguised for long amongst that sort of Cossack.

The jokes about singing are inspired by two groups of former soldiers displaced by the Russian Revolution: the Don Cossack Choir and the Kuban Cossack Chorus.[9] Both groups toured Europe to critical acclaim throughout the 1920s.

David's association of cross-dressing Cossacks with Gogol's novel celebrating Cossack warrior hypermasculinity stems from a scene in which Taras Bulba's youngest son, Andrei, falls in love with a Polish beauty and climbs up a tree onto the roof of her house and then down a chimney into her room. Once inside, stunned by her beauty, he stands mute as she playfully hangs earrings on him, dresses him in her "transparent muslin chemisette with ruffles embroidered in gold," and crowns him with her "glittering diadem" (Gogol 36). Later, when his love for the beautiful maiden leads him to fight for the Polish against the Cossacks, he appears on the battlefield in a resplendent golden uniform and is killed by his own father. In *Hemingway's Fetishism,* I suggest that Gogol's novel and Théophile Gautier's *Mademoiselle de Maupin* (see below) demonstrate how transvestic narratives, counterintuitive as it may seem, are largely about sustaining and reinforcing masculinity (249–56). The historical setting of *Taras Bulba* is unclear, but Hemingway probably associated its conflict between the Poles and Cossacks with both the Polish-Soviet War of 1919–21 and the partitioning of Poland during the reign of Catherine the Great (see *[244:2] 3.44.25*).

(244:25) 3.45.22 "Mademoiselle de Maupin. . . ." "pornography. . . . Did it give you an erection": In the manuscript, David's claim that it would be difficult for a girl to remain disguised as an officer amongst Cossacks (see above) leads Marita to ask, "What about *Mademoiselle de Maupin?*" Rather than answering directly, in some deleted lines, David claims Gautier's novel was just written to make "erections," though it wasn't "dirty like pornography." In his undeleted response, he claims the

novel is just "what we do made into musical comedy." David then asks Marita if it gave her "an erection." "Of course," she answers. Didn't it give him one? Yes, David answers. That's what it was written for.

The title character of Théophile Gautier's 1835 novel, Madelaine de Maupin, disguises herself as a male cavalier and, together with her servant (also a young girl disguised as a boy), rides off to seek adventure and discover what men are truly like when unaccompanied by women. The male hero of the novel, d'Albert, initially pursues a passionate affair with the beautiful Rosette—yet she is not his ideal, which he finds instead embodied in the Greek god Hermaphrodite: "It is indeed among the most subtle creations of the pagan genius, this son of Hermes and Aphrodite. You can't imagine anything more ravishing in the world than these two bodies, both of them perfect, harmoniously fused together" (Gautier 196). (For Hermaphrodite's importance to *Eden*, see *[17:22] 1.1.21.*) Needless to say, when d'Albert encounters Madelaine successfully disguised as the cavalier Théodore de Sérannes, he falls passionately in love with him (her)—as does Rosette.

David's deleted assertion that the novel isn't pornographic—even if it was written to produce erections—responds, in part, to an important legal case, *Halsey v. New York,* that Hemingway would have read about in the newspapers and in his copy of Morris Ernst and William Seagle's *To the Pure . . . : A Study of Obscenity and the Censor* (1928). In 1917, Raymond Halsey, a New York bookseller, was arrested after an agent of the New York Society for Suppression of Vice, posing as a customer, purchased a copy of *Mademoiselle de Maupin*. In his own defense, Halsey sued for malicious prosecution and in 1920 secured a $2,500 verdict against the New York Society for Suppression of Vice. The decision was upheld in 1922 by the New York Court of Appeals, and in 1929 Morris Ernst, cofounder of the American Civil Liberties Union, used this case as the central precedent in his successful defense of the publisher in the famous American *Well of Loneliness* trial (see *[54:23] 3.9.14*).

Yet Hemingway had a special sort of "radar" for stories of fetishism and fetishistic cross-dressing (see entry above), and though he also tried to disavow the "dirtiness" of *Mademoiselle de Maupin* in *Islands in the Stream,* it represents for David and Marita "what we do" (even if in musical comedy form), and it produced erections—including in women (see 15:13). The question of what was and what wasn't pornographic must have been on Hemingway's mind because, as he explained in a 1948 letter to Mary Hemingway, he dreamed of *The Garden of Eden* producing half a million erections (*HF* 246).[10]

(245:11) 3.45.25bis **Feb. 17:** This page in the manuscript, where Marita again tells David she's his "street Arab" and will be something entirely new—something he never had, even in Madrid—is dated in the margin 17 February. On 18 February 1959, Hemingway's friend Taylor Williams died. As he told Slim Hayward, in a 7 April 1959 letter, he had been on the verge of finishing his novel, but Taylor's death "upset things entirely" (JFK). On 10 April, he told Alfred Rice he had kept working on the novel "but had to throw it away" (JFK). The manuscript does continue for one more chapter, but it is comparatively unpolished. It is important to note how different these remaining pages are from the spirit of the ending produced by Jenks for the Scribner's edition of the novel.

In the next few manuscript pages, Marita, at dinner, wants to be David's girl and his boy too, but he predicts she'll eventually tire of it. Only when *he* does, she promises, and she assures him he won't suffer remorse. But David isn't optimistic: nobody, he tells her, can understand anyone else's remorse. Undismayed, Marita tells David she enjoys "corrupting" him. She likes to hear his voice change when he is excited. But David tells her she doesn't have to invent games to take his mind off his troubles as if he were an "idiot child." They then get ready to eat dinner.

245:22 **In the dark:** In the manuscript, as they lie in the dark, Marita apologizes to David for being "silly" about "corruption" *(3.45.31)*. She wants him the way that he is. The way *they* are, he answers. And yet how is that? Marita says she will be however he wants her to be—or, correcting herself, however they *both* want to be. "Can we then?" David asks. "Yes," Marita answers, assuring him it won't be like Madrid. Their lovemaking dialogue is cryptic, but Marita says they "both are." They both are *what?* David asks—but Marita tells him he already knows. A deleted line in the manuscript tells us they had "everything of Madrid." This implies that they are both "boys," and it is clear that this is what they both wanted *(3.45.33)*.

245:25 **I'm your girl:** Jenks's editing here is highly misleading. He condenses two different lines in the manuscript to produce the impression that Marita is insisting on the stability of her identity as a girl. In doing so, he deletes David's admonition that she doesn't need to "change so soon." In other words, Marita is insisting upon her girlhood here, not because she will restore heteronormativity in David's life but because as they have just made love *she has been a boy*. And when David asks her how she knows about remorse, she answers with a line that sounds disconcertingly like Catherine: "Because I'm you as well as me" (3.45.33).

245:31 **He was sleeping on his side:** In the manuscript, the chapter continues. There, in the next line, as Marita watches the sleeping David, she hopes their lovemaking was "better than Madrid" *(3.45.34)*. Marita thinks that she must be better in bed than Catherine, because she really *is* both a "better boy" and a "better girl." That's why she doesn't need to "change back and forth" (see 192:25). Yet as she pities Catherine, she thinks about how much she owes her. She hopes her lovemaking with David will help him to write in the morning. She wishes she could have gone to sleep as a boy, but she thinks this would have given David remorse. She knows David loves their gender-bending sexuality as much as she does, and, she thinks, it can't be a sin if it feels so good. It's a miracle that she is just "the same" as David, and yet she never would have known about it if she hadn't read the Madrid section of the narrative. She knows she shouldn't tease David about "corruption," but she finds it exciting. They share the "same tribal things," and they don't need to worry about "Hebrew laws" or taboos. She knows she has to take care of David, confining their sexual games to the dark.

NOTES

1. For a more extensive treatment of fetish words and naming (which will add to this list Maria in *For Whom the Bell Tolls,* whose nickname "rabbit" aligns her with *hare*), see HF 110–18.

2. Thomas Campbell's line reworks an earlier one from Coleridge's 1794 sonnet "To Kosciusko," where a "loud and fearful shriek" greets the "Fall'n Kosciusko." Leigh Hunt and Keats also wrote sonnets "To Kosciusko."

3. Hemingway owned a copy of Katherine Anthony's *Catherine the Great* (Knopf 1925). He also knew the story of Catherine the Great, Kościuszko, and the partition of Poland from his copy of Bernard Pares's *A History of Russia* (Knopf 1947). While he was working on *Eden,* Hemingway developed a friendship with his Polish translator, Bronislaw Zielinsky, who visited him in Ketchum in November 1958. This may have inspired him to think about things Polish.

4. This is not necessarily an anachronism. Images of Falconetti from the filming had appeared in newspapers as early as July 1927. See, for instance, "Le Procès de Jeanne d'Arc."

5. There is a minor anachronism here. Though Mercedes-Benz began making the Typ 200 in 1927, they did not begin calling it the "Typ 200" until a rebranding of the car in 1929.

6. For Hemingway's decision, see letter to Harry Brague, 24 May 1959 (PUL).

7. See, for instance, Gogol 112, 124.

8. Hemingway checked Andrews's book out of Sylvia Beach's lending library in October 1926 and returned it in February 1927 (Reynolds, *Hemingway's Reading* 91). In later years, Hemingway apparently still thought enough of Andrews to buy his 1945 book *Meet Your Ancestors: A Biography of Primitive Man* (Brasch and Sigman 52).

9. The Kuban Cossack Chorus of the 1920s is distinct from the Kuban Cossack Chorus formed in 1811, dissolved by the Bolshevik authorities under their de-Cossackization program in 1921, and then revived by the Soviet state in 1936.

10. For an extended discussing of this moment in *Eden* and Hemingway's engagement with *Mademoiselle de Maupin,* see HF 249–56.

CHAPTER 30 *(MSS. CHAPTER 46)*

247:15 **He was fortunate, just now, that his father was not a simple man:** This sentence in the Scribner's edition has been moved seven chapters away from its original context in the manuscript (see *[211:8] 3.39.2ii*). Needless to say, it means something quite different in its original context.

247:23 **there was no sign that any of it would ever cease returning to him intact:** This line does appear on the fourth page of the manuscript's final chapter, but it carries no sense of an ending, and the chapter continues for another thirty-eight pages.

(247:24) 3.46.5 **"You're like Mazeppa. . . ." "Héros XII":** In the manuscript, David puts away his writing implements and goes out to the garden to find Marita. Thrilled with David's success, she calls him a "wonderful weight carrying horse" and compares him once again to Mazeppa (see *[140:29] 3.24.9*). This time, however, the reference is less to the hero of Byron's poem than it is to a successful French steeplechaser of the 1920s, Mazeppa II. David replies that he feels "like Héros XII after last year's Grand Steeple." David even looks like him, Marita says. After all, he was "a blond horse." When she kisses David, she feels like she's kissing "a great animal," and several pages later in the manuscript he still is not fully human again. Marita is glad he isn't owned by the Duke of Decazes, owner of one of the largest racing stables in France *(3.46.12)*. Needless to say, this scene fits into a larger pattern of cross-species identifications in the novel (see 62:28, 180:11, *[194:4] 3.36.5*, and 199:20).

Described by Hemingway's horse aficionado friend, poet Evan Shipman, as "the greatest steeplechase horse of his time on the continent," Héros XII won the Paris Grand Steeplechase in 1922 (with the Duke of Decazes's Corot placing second) and finished third when Hemingway bet on him and attended the 1923 race, which was won by the Duke of Decazes's horse L'Yser (Mandel, *Hemingway's* 209). David's reference to "last year's" race is a notable anachronism, but Hemingway was always happy to exercise poetic license to honor a favorite horse. For instance, as Mandel notes, Frederic Henry, in *A Farewell to Arms*, bets on Light for Me at San Siro in 1917 even though the real Light for Me wasn't foaled until 1918 and didn't begin winning prizes until the 1920s ("Dating" 5).

(247:24) 3.46.9 **But where's Catherine?. . . . You broke me loose:** In the manuscript, after some loving and encouraging conversation with David, Marita brings him some hardboiled eggs with Savora and a beer. He is still so disoriented from being deeply immersed in his writing that he asks, "But where's Catherine?" When Marita answers that she's probably in Saint-Jean-de-Luz or Hendaye, he asks, "Where are we?" "Here at the bar," Marita answers, but David considers that answer too simple. He's more satisfied when she answers, "We're anywhere." Hoping that going into town might snap him out of his mental state, they decide to go into Cannes. Marita isn't sure how to help him in his present state of mind, but he insists that she already has. "You broke me loose," he tells her. Marita replies that he's done the same for her.

(247:24) 3.46.11 **book of all the cuttings:** As they talk in the manuscript about writing and critics, Marita promises to keep a scrapbook of his press clippings—a notable contrast with Catherine. David jokes that they can keep it on a chain in the bathroom. If organizing the clippings is too big a job, Marita decides, she can always hire someone to help. She thinks in any case she probably should hire a secretary to help David with letters. David doesn't want to be too "domesticated," but Marita says this is how she can help him.

Page 3.46.12 in the manuscript is dated 24 February [1959], but the page raising the possibility of hiring a secretary *(3.46.11i)* is an insert probably added during or after the "dangerous summer" of 1959, when Hemingway decided to hire Valerie Danby-Smith as a secretary, first for his summer entourage following the taurine mano a mano between matadors Antonio Ordóñez and Luis Miguel Dominguín and then to help him in Cuba. (For Hemingway's work on *Eden* while he was writing *The Dangerous Summer,* see appendix C.)

(247:24) 3.46.16 **It ends with the fire:** As they lunch at the café in Cannes, David and Marita compare Cannes to Monte Carlo, dismissing the latter as a city built in the spirit of menopause. All the towns they really love, opines David, are built on death. Marita protests, telling him that you can really only be young in an "old place" like the Mediterranean. Enjoying the day but still in the grip of his post-writing frame of mind, David feels as if he has "no identity at all." It's something that happens to him when through work he gets "too far out" and then "can't come back into [him]self."

David tells Marita he never wrote anything "worth a damn" during his marriage to Catherine until Marita arrived—calling the honeymoon narrative a "bloody corvée" (a day's unpaid labor owed by a vassal to his lord)—but Marita encourages him to finish it. Couldn't he at least "write it up to the fire?" He supposes so, admitting, with clear metatextual implications, that this is the story's natural conclusion.

David then thinks that he ought to try to find out where Catherine is and how she is doing, and Marita promises to do that for him tomorrow so he can stay focused on his writing.

(247:24) 3.46.20 **"I try to write simply...." "Who do you write for really?"** After paying up at the café, Marita and David swim at the cove, but it is too windy and cold. As they drive back to the hotel, they can feel the "summer blowing away." Back at the bar of the hotel, they talk about writing. David explains that he aspires to write "simply," so he can make regular readers "find something" or "see and feel what they would never have seen or felt." When Marita tells him she would have thought that he wrote for "an elite," he replies that he does: "I write for you and me" *(3.46.20)*. In a deleted sentence, he adds that he writes for "~~all the dead ... everyone who ever flew or ever lived in Africa and loved it~~." He also writes for "~~all those who feel and understand and know but are not articulate~~." But he dismisses his "speech" as "pretentious." When Marita presses him further on who he really writes for, he has a one-word answer: "Me." He can't try to please other people, because he has to try to *be* them. Marita approves. Does he care about anyone else's opinions? "Yours," David answers, and he also cares about those who know about his subject and who know about writing. Do these readers know about the "*Mystère?*" Marita asks. Yes, David answers. They can feel its presence, or they "try to find out how it is done.... But mostly they try to explain it" *(3.46.20iv)*.

(247:24) 3.46.20vi **had Africa together and I've never been there:** In the manuscript, David says the only place you "have" is the place where you are at the moment, but Marita disagrees. She says they've "had Africa together"—presumably both in the bedroom and through David's fiction—even though she's "never been there." (It is noteworthy that this passage contradicts an earlier passage that indicates she *has* been to Africa [see *(205:11) 3.37.32]*; Hemingway was never able to revise and reconcile these pages.) David notes that he has to return to his difficult mission in Africa in the morning. As David mixes two big martinis and reminds her of the first one he made her, Marita says that seems a "hundred years ago." They have known each other, in fact, for eighteen days.

(247:24) 3.46.21 **never loved anyone but you ... except my brother.... Girls are nothing.... Any more than queers would be for you:** In the manuscript, as David and Marita compare their loneliness at this time of day, Marita tells him that she never loved anyone before him, except her brother (see *[162:4]* 422.4 3.27.8). Not even girls? David asks. No, the girls had been fun, and were "better than nothing," but they meant nothing "if you're not that way"—any more "than queers" would mean for him. David says he tries not to be rude, but "queers" give him the "creeps." Marita says her brother "wasn't at all that way," but she thinks he never loved anyone but her (see 126:12).

This homophobic disavowal of homosexuality by both David and Marita (which clearly elides the initial power of Marita's attraction to Catherine) should be understood in the context of the previous evening's lovemaking, when they were both "boys" and had "~~everything of Madrid~~" (see 245:22). In fetishistic sexuality, where both the subject and partner may oscillate between male and female identifications, homophobic anxiety frequently accompanies same-sex combinations. The fetishist both recognizes and disavows a current of homosexual desire in the self—insisting on a difference, since he understands himself and his partner as biologically heterosexual, however much they may identify as boy/girls. We see this sort of homophobic anxiety clearly in the *Eden* manuscript when Nick asks Andy if his haircut makes him look like a "bloody sodomite" *(422.2 2.5).*

(247:24) 3.46.25 **worried about Catherine. . . . the oldest story:** In the manuscript, David and Marita move from the bar out onto the terrace, which is "cool with the end of summer." David brings out coats for them both, and Marita can see he is "worried about Catherine." Marita "misses her too," though she's "glad she's gone." The topic is sensitive, and Marita can feel they're about to quarrel, but instead they go back to the bar to make martinis.

As he looks at Marita in the bar mirror, David invites her to tell him sometime about her brother, but she thinks it must be too familiar already. "It's probably the oldest story," she thinks, though she admits she's never read a version of it. (For Hemingway, sibling romance was the "oldest story." See 6:6.) Her family experience was "hateful," with many terrible fights. The chapter and the manuscript end with no sense of closure, with David enjoying the way the martini makes him feel "so marvelous and powerful and so successful."

APPENDIX A

The Sheldon Ending

Written in June 1958, the four manuscript folders of the Sheldon ending (Item 422.2, folders 2–5, in the Hemingway Collection at the JFK Library—distinct from the main body of the *Eden* manuscript, Item 422.1) have been described by scholars as "fragments," and as an alternate ending for the novel, but together they constitute a single, unified (albeit messy) narrative that Hemingway, at least as late as September 1958, meant to revise and use to complete the Sheldon subplot before returning to the Bournes and completing the novel with the already-written provisional ending (appendix B).[1] For more on the composition and placement of these pages, see appendix C.

ITEM 422.2, FOLDER 2

422.2 2.1 **What happened to them finally?** The story begins with Andrew Murray (see *[51:2] 3.9.1*) talking to an unnamed female interlocutor many years after the events described in the novel. The interlocutor has apparently read a story Andy has written about the Sheldons (see *[44:33] 3.5.6*) and asks, "And what happened to them finally?" She thinks it's a "very strange story" and wonders how Andy came to know it. Barbara told him, he replies, adding that he "made up what she didn't tell."[2] "You did very well about the girl I thought," she said. "But it isn't like a girl now. Nobody would believe it now because everything is changed. Just technically. Things aren't done that way anymore. It's all so primitive." Andy answers, with an implicit nod to the Edenic, "Things were primitive then." The Sheldons were beautiful, he remembers, and like Adam and Eve, "they didn't know there was anyone in the world except themselves."

The girl wonders if there was anything "queer" about Nick, but Andy is sure that there wasn't. He had "a dark sort of go to hell look and women were crazy about him," but he only had eyes for Barbara, who was "heartbreak beautiful." They talk about Nick's talent as a painter (see *[42:17] 3.5.1*), and the girl asks again to hear what finally happened to them. Andy tells her that her curiosity and the way she feels about the Sheldons is why he stopped the story where he did.

Hemingway in Alpini Hat, 1928. (Ernest Hemingway Collection. Photographs. John F. Kennedy Presidential Library and Museum. Photo by Man Ray, © Man Ray 2015 Trust / Artists Rights Society, ARS, NY / ADAGP, Paris, 2022.)

Andy remembers running into them around Paris and having drinks with both of them at Deux Magots (see 42:15 and *[44:33]* 3.5.6). They had recently been in the Alps, where Nick was painting the high mountain snows, and Nick was wearing an old Alpine hunter's hat, something like an Alpini hat. They were obviously very much in love. He remembers running into Nick next late in the spring, again at Deux Magots. This time Nick is sitting by himself behind a pile of saucers, with his hat pulled down. Andy notices that his hair is as long as Barbara's "and cut the same way." (A deleted line on the previous page of the manuscript tells us that women weren't wearing their hair as long as Barbara's then. The contrast, almost like a photographic negative, be tween Barbara and Catherine is noteworthy [see 16:17].) The girl thinks the Sheldons must have "looked very strange," but Andy demurs. "Right after the war lots of young men in Italy wore their hair that way," he tells her. "Italo Balbo was one."

422.2 2.4i **Italo Balbo:** Andy's seemingly offhand reference to the smiling poster-boy of Italian fascism, Italo Balbo, is probably inspired by an association with Nick's Alpini hat, but it resonates with several major themes in *Eden*. A lieutenant in the Italian Alpini during WWI, Balbo participated in the bloody fighting on Monte Grappa with a platoon associated with the elite Arditi shock troops.[3] After the war, he joined the Associazione Arditi and edited the fiercely nationalistic and pro-D'Annunzio military publication *L'Alpino* before joining the fascists and becoming a leader of Mussolini's Blackshirts. Dressed in his *ardito*-style jacket, with his Alpini hat pulled over his "wild mop of hair," he was a one of the central organizers of the 1922 March on Rome and was subsequently named commander of the fascist militia (Segrè 41). In 1926, Balbo was appointed undersecretary, and in 1929 minister, of Italy's air ministry. In these roles, he was responsible for all aspects of Italian aviation and began his own series of daring flights. According to his biographer Claudio Segrè, his highly publicized "achievements as an aviator transformed him from a provincial Italian politician with a dubious Blackshirt past into an international celebrity" (145). A vocal proponent of Italy's colonial ambitions who would eventually be appointed governor of Libya, he declared in 1926, "Europe must peacefully grant us some colonies, or we will sooner or later take them by force" ("Italy"). While his WWI experience with the Arditi on Monte Grappa resonates with Hemingway's youthful war fantasies,[4] and his leadership in the Golden Age of Flight aligns him with fellow pilot David Bourne (see 112:12 and 204:20), his role as an aggressive colonialist aligns him with Colonel Boyle (see 61:5 and *[214:22] 3.39.9*).

422.2 2.5 **bloody sodomite:** When Andy sits down, Nick wants to ask him a question:

"Do you think I look like some bloody sodomite?"
"No. Of course not. Who thinks you look like a bloody sodomite?"
"I do."
"You don't," I said. "You look like a condottiere out of work...."
"Don't ever start anything you can't finish," he said.

In fact, Nick is afraid that he's into something that can't be finished. When Andy asks about the pile of saucers, Nick answers that he's been "trying to make up [his] mind" about something. (For a consideration of this passage, see *[247:24] 3.46.21*.)

Barbara soon appears, radiant and excited, announcing that she and Nick are late for an appointment. But Nick says he can't go through with it—whatever *it* is. As Barbara begins to plead with him, Andy tries to excuse himself, but Barbara urges him to stay. It isn't as "shameless" or "awful" as it sounds, she promises. Telling them to wait, Barbara says that she'll go back to the shop and tell them Nick won't be able to make it. Alone at the table again with Andy, Nick tells Andy he knows that must have sounded "complicated," but it wasn't. It was just about a haircut Barbara wanted him to get—something that "means a lot to her" but means nothing to him. Andy urges him to go catch up with Barbara, and Nick decides he will.

Andy doesn't see them in town in the next week. He then hears they have left town, presumably for the Basque Coast, where Nick said they were going.

422.2 2.6bis3 **the hell of it is now I like it too:** There are six different page 6s ending this folder in the manuscript—none clearly deleted. Several are consecutive, so they comprise three distinct passages.

In addition to the passage already described above, which seems to be the final version, there is a version where Nick pulls off his hat to reveal his long hair. In another version, Nick remembers seeing Andy at the coiffeurs with them that February when he and Barbara had cut their hair together the first time (see *[32] 2.1.17*). Nick had been "sort of shocked" by the haircut but had liked it. But now he is uncomfortable with it. "This is Paris," Andy tells him. He can wear his hair however he likes—or he can just cut his hair short for the summer. It's more complicated than that, Nick explains. Barbara cares about this deeply, and he wants to please her; "And the hell of it is now I like it too." He just doesn't want to look like a "sodomite."

ITEM 422.2, FOLDER 3

422.2 3.7 **Re-do all of this . . . Sept 20:** This manuscript folder begins with page 7 and represents a continuation of the previous folder. A note from Hemingway at the top of the first page indicates that this is to be placed "after David and Catherine's story stops in September"—which would still place it before the provisional ending (appendix B). On a separate sheet at the beginning of the folder, Hemingway writes: "Re-do all of this. . . . September 20." While this note implies that he still intended to use this material long after adding David's African stories and Marita to the novel, there is no evidence that he rewrote it in November 1958 when he rewrote chapters 20 through 36 of manuscript book III.

422.2 3.7 **So what happened?** Still speaking with his unnamed interlocutor, Andy tells her that he next saw the Sheldons in August at Hendaye. Much like the Bournes in Le Grau-du-Roi, they are tanned the color of "Indians"; they wear Basque fisherman's shirts, shorts, and espadrilles; and they sport identical haircuts—though their hair is long enough to touch their shoulders. Inviting Andy to join them at their table, where they are drinking real Pernod (see *[36:12] 3.1.3*), Barbara proudly announces, "We're a scandal." They had tried to get their hair cut in Saint-Jean-de-Luz, but the coiffeur wouldn't serve them. Nick adds, "Everybody thinks we're queer. But who cares?"

422.2 3.8 ~~**Catherine**~~ **Barbara:** For most of the rest of the Sheldon ending, Nick calls his wife *Catherine*, which is then struck through and replaced with *Barbara*. This is jarring, and it might be tempting to think that Hemingway actually began to confuse his two heroines since they have so much in common,[5] but the real explanation can be found in the manuscript to *A Moveable Feast* (JFK Item 123). There, in a draft of the Voralberg chapter, a loose page of notes blends text about the pilot fish with text from this folder of the *Eden* manuscript concerning Nick's "Indian trick" (see *422.2 3.15*). On the page, Hemingway tries out some potential titles and subtitles for

Eden, one of which is "The Sand Castle"—a subtitle that clearly refers to these pages from the Sheldon ending (see *422.2 3.10*). More importantly, Hemingway experiments with a new title for *Eden:* "The Two Catherines." Above this, he has written (and partially struck through), "~~I have called both of these women Catherine because I have the most pleasant name~~." So in June 1958, Hemingway briefly played with the idea of naming *both* of his heroines Catherine. (Marita had not significantly entered the novel yet.) That he even momentarily entertained such an impossible idea underscores the crucial importance to him of this special name (see 17:23).

422.2 3.10 **Why didn't you marry them?** Exasperated by the way Andy goes on about the beauty and shining hair of the Sheldons, his interlocutor asks why he didn't marry them both. When he responds by telling her to go to hell, she walks off to join a crowd at another table. This is the last we see of her, but Nick, unfazed, continues to narrate the story.

422.2 3.10 **Undiscovered Country. . . . sand castle:** Andy remembers at the café in Hendaye asking Nick about his paintings, which Nick promises to show him. Barbara asks to see Andy's writing, but he doubts she could decipher his handwriting. In Paris, he let her read part of "The Undiscovered Country" (see 7:7 and 189:2), she says, but that, he reminds her, was in typescript. Nick tells Andy that he and Barbara have been painting in Cambo-les-Bains and in the Pyrenees at Les Aldudes. He boasts that Barbara can paint the houses without reducing them to the picturesque. Meanwhile, he's been concentrating on the hills. Barbara wants to paint them, too—"the other side of Roncevaux" (see *[44:28] 3.5.6*)—but to avoid talking about her own painting, she shifts the topic to how wonderful it will be when they're all famous. Then they can go to the Met and the Louvre and the Art Institute and admire Nick's paintings of Barbara, and they can have Andy's book about them. Before Andy publishes "the definitive book," Barbara wants him to write a short one about them as a "sort of memorial." Much like Catherine with David's honeymoon narrative, she wants it illustrated with snapshots and color plates (see 189:2). Under the influence of absinthe, her plans grow wildly for a snapshot of them beside an enormous sand castle with an incoming tide. Afterwards, as she stares out to sea, Nick looks at Andy and "[shakes] his head barely perceptibly."

They invite Andy to join them for dinner at their pension, and he reflects sadly that for the first time since he's known them, they actually seem to want someone else in their world. Barbara decides to change her clothes for dinner, and Andy watches her stroll "down the beach road with her thumbs in her pockets." A phallic woman, like Catherine (see 17:23), she is "walking cocky like a boy."

"Absinthe isn't good for her," Nick says. It probably isn't good for anyone, replies Andy, but he and Nick both love it and agree that it's good for making you "not give a damn."

422.2 3.15 **Systeme Colonel William T. Cody:** Talk of not giving a damn serves as a segue for Andy to ask what it's like for Nick to travel in Spain with his hair so long. Grinning, Nick shows Andy his "old Indian trick," hiding his hair under his hat. He calls it "*Systeme* Colonel William T. Cody," explaining that this was what Cody would do when he went out nights. Barbara likes (a deleted line says "needs") his hair to match hers, and it's little enough for him to do to please her. When Andy replies that he couldn't do it himself, Nick answers, "Nobody could unless they liked it," and Nick has discovered that he likes it "plenty."

In *Hemingway's Fetishism*, I suggest that Buffalo Bill Cody serves here as a stand-in for General George Armstrong Custer, a perennial background figure in Hemingway's novels and fetishistic associations—someone he could alternately, or even simultaneously, both identify and disidentify with to negotiate his own gender identity and the bigendered rift in his ego.[6]

422.2 3.16 **I'd be spooked. . . . her hand in my pocket:** At dinner, Nick suggests that Barbara get Andy to cut his hair like theirs, too, and Barbara immediately begins to plead for it. She'd be glad to cut it, she tells him, and "it's quite long already." But, using the same word Hemingway employed to describe his own reaction after dyeing his own hair bright red, as well as the one David uses after Catherine dyes his hair blond, Andy tells her he would be too "spooked" (see 17:23, *[168:3] 3.29.19*, and *[178:7] 3.31.10*). Nick explains that this is just how he felt when he did it, but like Catherine, he says there's no fun without danger (see *[178:7] 3.31.10*). Barbara continues to plead until Andy finally agrees. Nick suggests that Barbara cut it before the absinthe wears off, but dinner lasts too long, and walking back along the sea wall with them Andy says he can't go through with it. His hair needs to grow some more anyway, Barbara admits. When Andy tells her he's still "spooked," she tells him that "everybody's spooked." She admits to feeling spooked about her imaginary sand castle.

As Nick stands on the beach staring out at the sand, Barbara slides her hand into Andy's pocket. As her hand explores, confirming how they feel about each other, she asks Andy to stay, and he agrees that he will. She wants to know if he'll do the haircut, too. He will "if it ever makes sense," but he knows it won't. As they walk over to Nick, still staring at the sea, Andy gently removes Barbara's hand from his pocket.

422.2 3.19 **stay through September:** Andy decides to stay on in Hendaye through September and settles into his writing routine while Nick and Barbara continue to paint. Nick is painting well, but Barbara's work is "very close to the edge" and worries Andy. He suspects it worries her too. His mornings writing are productive, and some days he runs into Nick or Barbara or both of them at the café. They often swim before lunch. It all sounds very much like the Bournes on the Riviera.

One day, Nick, deeply tanned and with salt water drying in his tangled hair, comes into the café from painting on the beach, alive with the challenge of trying to capture the bulge of feeding mullet in the changing tide on the sandbar. Such things are very difficult, he reports, but sometimes he does "some Jongkind" to cheer himself up (see *[42:17]* *3.5.1*). Andy asks about Barbara's painting, but Nick says she isn't painting now. He worries about her, and so does Andy. But Nick says she's been better since Andy has been in town. Nick is afraid that he's too absorbed by his painting to really be good company for her himself. (The parallel with Catherine's mental fragility and David's artistic preoccupation is obvious.) Andy suggests—as if it would be a "cure"—that they're doing well enough financially for Barbara to have a baby, but Nick explains that she can't have one. She has ridden into Saint-Jean-de-Luz to get her hair washed, and they decide to have an absinthe and some shrimp while they wait for her to return and join them for lunch.

Andy can see that something is on Nick's mind, and Nick asks if he saw David and Catherine in Madrid. Nick mentions that they came through Hendaye, and Andy says he spent time with them in Madrid and meant to tell him. Nick asks him to tell Barbara.

ITEM 422.2, FOLDER 4

422.2 4.19vii **Another day. . . . devilled:** The previous folder ends with a long insert between pages 19 and 20 of the Sheldon ending. This eleven-holograph-page folder picks up where that folder leaves off and is composed entirely of a continuation of that insert.

Another day, Andy is sitting at the café when Barbara shows up and joins him. She asks about his writing and is clearly and sincerely glad to hear it has gone so well he is "spooked." She tells him that Nick is out on the sand painting, trying to capture the moment the tide changes. They're both sure he'll succeed.

September is half-gone, and Andy already misses it. Barbara orders herself a Pernod, knowing that Andy doesn't approve, and asks him why he's worried about her. When he lies and says that he isn't, she doesn't believe him. She wonders if he thought she was "crazy" when he saw her at Deux Magots in the spring (see 42:15 and *[44:33]* *3.5.6*). "A little bit," Andy admits, but "Nick explained." She gives us some more details of that day: Nick had already been to the coiffeurs to have his hair washed, which has to be done before the cutting, and the coiffeurs were waiting to cut it by special appointment after closing up the shop for the day. When Andy says he doesn't need the details, Barbara—sounding very much like Catherine and realizing that Andy is aroused—apologizes for "devilling" him. She asks if she's "devilled" him "very much." Andy lies and says she hasn't.

Barbara wonders if Andy thinks she's "harmful to Nick." No, he answers, nothing can hurt Nick. She loves Nick deeply, she tells Andy, but she can't help doing "crazy things." Andy says he "understand[s] about the things," and she knows that he does. She promises to stop devilling him, too, claiming that she's "thought it all out." They can't swim with the tide so far out, so Andy decides to cross the Spanish border to Irun to eat *percebes* (see *[54:23] 3.10.7*). Barbara wants to join him if Nick is still working, asking Andy how he got to be her best friend. By hanging around Hendaye Plage trying to keep her from absinthe, he replies. Barbara doesn't accept that answer. No, she tells him, it's because he let her put her hand in his pocket. Ignoring her promise not to devil him, she tells him that she likes to make his voice change—and in some deleted lines, she tries to put her hand in his pocket again. When Andy's voice changes, she laughs and tells him *that's* why he's her best friend. "I only have you and Nicky," she says, though she "nearly had something else." This is clearly a reference to Catherine, but Barbara gave that up "to be good and . . . not to have a bad effect on her." Like Catherine Bourne, who feels like "two persons" (see *[66:11] 3.14.4*), Barbara tells Andy, "There's two of me and there are two of you. You and Nicky. Nicky makes three because I made him two. . . . At first I thought it would be nicer if you could be two like Nicky. But now I know better." In a deleted line after this, Andy thinks of Nick, "The poor lost bastard"; instead, he tells Barbara that he's "no good at being two." Barbara realizes this, though she thought it would be better for all of them, or at least fun, if he could be. She wonders how things can be "so simple and wonderful and then get so complicated."

Andy suggests the absinthe is what's making things complicated for Barbara, but she disagrees. The reverse is the case. She drinks absinthe because her situation is so complicated, and she says it started with Catherine. Andy tells her he saw Catherine in Madrid. Barbara wants to know if she was beautiful. She was, Andy answers. But she's "destructive," Barbara says. She may not mean to be, but she is.

ITEM 422.2, FOLDER 5

422.2 4.19xviii She came into the room. . . . remorse. . . . "take it back. . . ." Hispano Suiza: One day when Nick has gone off to paint across the river at Cape Higuer, Barbara comes to Andy's room and they make love. Afterwards, she suffers from nearly suicidal "remorse," and Andy takes her to the café to get her drunk before Nick returns. It is the first time she has been unfaithful to Nick, and she asks Andy desperately if she can "take it back . . . like something I said." She can't, of course, though Andy assures her she can. He promises "it never happened," and she hopes he can "make it that way."

Nevertheless, on another late September day, with Nick painting in the hills, she returns to Andy's room and kisses him. He reminds her how she felt last time, but she insists this time is different. Last time she did it for him, but this time will be for her. Last time didn't happen, he tells her. He tries to talk her out of his room, telling her there will be no "this time." Instead, she sits down on his bed and eventually seduces him. Last time, she tells Andy, she "wanted to die," but now she doesn't see a problem. She's clear that she really loves Nick, and she doesn't think her behavior can touch him. She doesn't want to talk about it, though, because she couldn't stand a return of the remorse.

Afterwards, Andy and Barbara go swimming, and Barbara is clearly disturbed. Her wet hair is "full of sand like a drowned girl," and she worries that they never built the sand castle she imagined for the snapshots for Andy's book. Later, they shower up and meet at the café.

Looking back on it, Andy realizes that by then Nick must already have been dead. On his bicycle, returning from painting, he had been hit by a small Renault dodging a speeding, road-hogging luxury Hispano Suiza that suddenly appeared over the crest of a hill. He had died before he could reach a hospital, and he was buried in Biarritz. Andy drove Barbara to the cemetery, but she was too distraught to go to the gravesite. The painful memory of caring for Barbara throughout the entire ordeal, Andy reflects, is why he had ended the story where he did in the version read by his interlocutor (see 422.2 2.1).

422.2 4.23 ***Re-do properly. . . . Ruined. . . . EH Jun 25:*** Hemingway left a note in the manuscript here, dated "Jun 25," complaining that he had been interrupted by visitors and instructing himself to rework what remained of the Sheldon ending. This must have been 25 June 1958 (see appendix C.)

422.2 4.24 ***nursing home with a good doctor:*** Racked with guilt, Barbara "did not talk for more than a week. She was in a nursing home with a good doctor and day and night nurses." She would hold Andy's hand but wouldn't look at him. Meanwhile, he dealt with the lawyers and attended to necessities. The story is almost too painful for Andy to remember, and he wonders that he ever wrote it.

Trying to help Barbara, he takes her first to Paris and then to Italy. Paris is too full of painful memories, but in Bergamo she starts to speak again, "mostly at night," and Andy thinks she's starting to get better.

422.2 4.25 ***Venice . . . old Luna. . . . Switzerland:*** Andy next takes Barbara to Venice, where they stay in adjoining rooms at the venerable Hotel Luna, the oldest hotel in Venice. (Around the corner from what would become Harry's Bar, overlooking the Giardini Reali, and steps away from the Piazza San Marco, the Hotel Luna was a fashionable first-class hotel.)

In retrospect, Andy thinks he should have taken Barbara to Switzerland, but she absolutely didn't want to go to a sanatorium (see appendix B). Andy was committed to taking care of her, and, to his own surprise, he was writing better than ever.

One day, after stepping out for a while, Andy returns to find a suicide note—a letter which in some respects mirrors Catherine's final letter to David. In it, Barbara tells him she is sure he'll write their story very well. She's sorry they never took the snapshots, but she's sure they built their castle. She thanks Andy for making her well enough to see what she has to do. Nothing was his fault. With the clear implication that she intends to drown herself (an implication confirmed in the provisional ending, appendix B), she writes that she'll pretend the waters of Venice are absinthe: "It's just about the same color and I never minded how it tasted." She has kept her "legal sleep things" for the past month, she writes, so there shouldn't be any legal difficulties, implying that she will take the pills before drowning herself. She knows what she has to do. The Sheldon story ends with her note.

NOTES

1. Scholars are to be excused for finding this story fragmentary. In a few places, Hemingway has revised pages without clearly deleting superseded pages, and the proper placement of a confusingly numbered eighteen-page insert between pages 19 and 20 of the manuscript is crucial to revealing its narrative unity. Page *422.2 4.19* in the manuscript is the top part of a page sliced in two with scissors; page *422.2 4.19xviii*, the final page is the insert, has also been sliced in two with scissors and is the bottom half of the original *422.2 4.19*.

2. The passages from the *Eden* manuscript quoted in this appendix have all been previously published in Fleming ("Endings") and Spilka.

3. Technically, the unit did not belong to the *arditi*, but it performed similar tasks as was commonly referred to by that title (Segrè 24).

4. See Reynolds, *Young Hemingway* 18, 32, 56.

5. Spilka and Fleming ("Endings") both come to this conclusion.

6. For Custer's role in Hemingway's imagination, see *HF* 216–38. There, I link Hemingway's fascination with Custer to his fascination with the Italian proto-fascist poet Gabriele D'Annunzio. If Cody is a stand-in for Custer, proximity of reference suggests that Italo Balbo may function as a similar sort of stand-in for D'Annunzio (see *422.2 2.4i*).

APPENDIX B

The Provisional Ending

Item 422.2, folder 1, in the Hemingway Collection at the JFK Library (distinct from the main body of the Eden manuscript, Item 422.1): Hemingway intended to use this ending for the novel at least as late as the autumn of 1958, when he had brought the novel up to the death of the elephant. For the composition history and a more complete consideration of Hemingway's intentions for this ending, see appendix C.

What Hemingway called the "provisional ending" opens with a couple sunning on the yellow sand of a cove, sheltered by the red rocks of the Estérel, the blue sea before them. "It seems so long ago," the girl says, remembering a time when they were "strange children" *(422.2 1.1)*.[1] Coming to this ending from the final chapters of the main *Eden* manuscript (which, in fact, were written long after the provisional ending, see appendix C), it is only when the woman asks if the man remembers when they "were both virginal in Madrid" that we realize the couple is Catherine and David, not David and Marita *(422.2 1.2)*. Catherine remembers that she had had to "seduce" David then, and she hadn't even known what she had been seducing him into. She thinks they were "comic then." Yes, David agrees, "We were a yell of laughter" *(422.2 1.2)*. The word "comic" becomes a sort of refrain running throughout the chapter.

After they cool off in the sea, they lie down again, and David gently oils Catherine, including her breasts, which have been covered with a scarf. "They're still good," Catherine says, though she's no longer sure what they're good for. She tries but can't remember the name of the hair product that had worked "such miracles" for them. David asks if she's "had enough sun," but that's one thing, she tells him, she could "never have enough of." She adds, ominously, that she's had enough of everything else. "Why did we run out of things?" she asks. "There was everything and we ran through it in a year" *(422.2 1.4)*. Thinking of Madrid, she asks David if he remembers the "comic colonel." Then, revealing more of a psychic fragility that has so far lurked just beneath the surface of the chapter, she asks if they'd seen him again. They had, and David assures her that she remembers. Catherine is happy enough to tell David she remembers, but she assures him she doesn't. She feels more confident remembering that they never went to Africa, but David again corrects her. They did—though it is unclear if David means this literally or figuratively.

334

David talks her into moving out of the sun to rest her head in the shade, and it is clear he is functioning as her caretaker.

Shutting her eyes, she asks David if he wants to swim. She won't "try anything comic," she promises *(422.2 1.7)*. Clearly, she has attempted suicide before. When David assures her that they can swim before lunch, she decides to entertain him by talking: "Remember when I used to talk about anything and everything and we owned the world?" Like Eve talking with Adam, she tells David that once "all we had to do was see it and we owned it." But, more like God, Catherine tells him she had "made everything in [her own] image. Remember? I could change everything. Change me change you change us both change the seasons change everything for my delight. And then it speeded up and speeded up and then it went away and then I went away" *(422.2 1.7)*.

"Then you came back," David tells her. "Not really," answers Catherine. She has recovered, she will recover, David assures her. But she doesn't believe it. "They don't know," she answers. "They just say they know. That's all Switzerland is except cows and timepieces and goiters is people that don't know saying they know" (see 158:12). David answers with faith in the progress of psychiatry, but Catherine can't be swayed. "Next time it will be worse. . . . Don't let's be comic" *(422.2 1.8)*. To change the topic, David reminds her that they'll swim soon. Catherine appreciates that he was always good to her. When David tells her that he loves her, she finds the word "comic." She'd rather avoid it.

As David watches Catherine with her eyes closed, as he had watched her "on the beach at le Grau du Roi," she tells him she loves him. She then asks, "Now can I have a surprise like in the old days?" *(422.2 1.10)*. Of course, David answers. Would he really promise "without knowing?" Yes, David answers, already knowing. The conversation grows still more ominous. Catherine asks,

> "If it goes bad again so I'd have to go back to the place can I, may I do it the way Barbara did? I don't mean in a dirty place like Venice."
> "I couldn't let you."
> "Would you do it with me."
> "Sure."
> "I knew you would," she said. "That's why I didn't like to ask."
> "Probably it would never happen."
> "Probably. Who knows? Now should we have the nice swim before lunch?" *(422.2 1.10)*

So, with this implicit suicide pact, ends the provisional ending. Needless to say, in spirit it is strikingly different than the ending of the Scribner's volume—an ending Hemingway never contemplated. *The Garden of Eden* that Hemingway wrote— whether we look at this ending or at the chapters he wrote in the main body of the manuscript to cover the period after Catherine's departure—is simply *not* about the restoration of David's masculinity and the reestablishment of heteronormativity.

NOTE

1. The passages from the *Eden* manuscript quoted in this appendix have all been previously published in Comley and Scholes, Fleming ("Endings"), Spilka, and Strong ("Go to Sleep").

APPENDIX C

Dating the Composition of *The Garden of Eden*

The *Eden* manuscript, or rather its composition—despite a few admirable attempts to date it and many confident but mistaken pronouncements about it (some of them my own)—has long been something of a mystery. In her memoir *How It Was,* Mary Hemingway recalls that Ernest began his "new novel set in the south of France" as a short story in the months before their marriage in March 1946, and there is good circumstantial evidence to support this (181, 452). Mary's letters from the summer and fall of 1945 compare Ernest's Cuban home to the French Riviera and often describe the joys of sunning Bourne-like "in the altogether."[1] Ernest was "working steadily every morning,"[2] and at Ernest's request, Mary agreed to "lighten her hair from peanut butter to platinum blonde" (Christian 107). Ernest's pleas for this bleaching must have been pronounced enough to generate tension in their relationship, for in an early 1946 letter, he assures Mary that he loves her as she is and that he never means to pressure her to do anything she doesn't want to about her hair. He refers to what he calls their "hair adventures" as a sort of experimental "holiday" that he hopes will be fun for them both and signs the letter with love, "E. (C.) H."[3] And who can this enigmatic and oddly parenthesized "C" be if not Ernest's alter ego, Catherine? (His middle name was Miller.) By May 1947, at least, what Ernest called his nighttime "jollities and secrecies" with Mary closely mirrored the lovemaking practiced by David and Catherine Bourne in Le Grau-du-Roi. In a series of remarkable letters, he urges Mary to variously cut and dye her hair and repeatedly calls her "Pete"; he then dyes his own hair "as red as a French polished copper pot or a newly minted penny" and refers to himself as Mary's "girl Catherine" (see 17:23).[4] A year later, in a long letter to Mary instructing her how to get her hair done, he promises that "the girl in my book will have her hair the way you are fixing yours now and ... some 500,000 up people will have d'erections about it" (qtd. in *HF* 246). Meanwhile, he told his friend Colonel Buck Lanham that he was writing about "the happiness of the Garden man must lose" (Baker 460).[5]

This much is clear: Hemingway began the novel long before he wrote the bulk of what we now have. At least, in a July 1958 letter to Harry Brague, he explains that he "had written the first chapters" of *Eden* at some point before he began work on *A Moveable Feast* in the spring of 1957. Yet it is difficult to say with any precision

337

how far these chapters extended, because we have no manuscript material dating to this period of the novel's evolution.[6] While Hemingway's letters throughout the late 1940s describe a novel that first swelled from four hundred pages in February 1946 to nine hundred pages that June, this was not, as has sometimes been speculated, *The Garden of Eden*. Rather, this was the Land, Sea, and Air Book that Hemingway began before going to Europe in 1944 and that eventually evolved into *Islands in the Stream* and *Old Man and the Sea*.[7] Rose Marie Burwell has speculated that *The Garden of Eden* originally began as part of this Land, Sea, and Air Book—which she suggests was a single ur-text that also supposedly spun off *Across the River and Intro the Trees*—but this ignores Mary Hemingway's memory that *Eden* began as a short story, and Burwell's theory is based on little more than a few thematic similarities between the texts. By the same logic, *A Farewell to Arms, For Whom the Bell Tolls,* and *A Moveable Feast* would have also begun as part of this same ur-text. It seems far more likely that the thematic similarities between these texts are the result of Hemingway's interests and preoccupations, not their origin in a common text. Given the subject matter of *Eden* and the time when Hemingway was writing, it is not surprising that his letters from the 1940s say little about the project. Describing how Ernest had worked "intermittently" on *Eden* since the 1940s, Mary Hemingway recalls that he "did not invite me to read this new work each evening, as I had done with other books, and I did not press him about it" (*HIW* 452). This was an intensely personal and revealing, almost private, work.

It seems to have been his intensive work on *A Moveable Feast* in the fall and winter of 1957–58—"crowding on a good streak of writing"—that brought Hemingway back to *The Garden of Eden*.[8] As he worked on *Feast*'s chapter about the pilot fish and the end of his marriage to Hadley, he explained, "The second part of Paris . . . . the part with Pauline, I have not eliminated but have saved for the start of another book. It is a start rather than an ending" (*MF-RE* 235). In August 1958, Mary Hemingway recalled that in the early spring of that year, as she was busy typing what Ernest had written of *Feast,* he "started on a new thing which grew and grew" and soon "enslaved him."[9] This "new thing"—which wasn't entirely new—was *The Garden of Eden*. Hemingway put aside "the Paris stuff" (even though he thought he might add two chapters to it) and devoted himself instead—morning, noon, and evening—to the story of David and Catherine Bourne.[10]

The entirety of the *Eden* manuscript that we have (with the exception of a few late inserts) seems to date from this period between the early spring of 1958 and February 1959. It does, however, show traces of its prehistory. The early chapters of the manuscript set in Le Grau-du-Roi, Hendaye, and Madrid (manuscript book I, chapters 1–4, and book III, chapters 1–11) are written either entirely or partially in typescript (typed by Hemingway) with pencil corrections.[11] With Hemingway, this is almost always a sign of a manuscript late in the composition process. His usual practice was to write one or two initial drafts in longhand before producing a typescript for further pencil correction. A statistical comparison of deleted words in *Eden*'s typescript and holograph pages demonstrates that these typescript pages are more polished, and they were doubtlessly preceded by holograph pages that are now missing. Indeed, in spite of Hemingway's reputation for never throwing away a scrap of paper, this novel about the destruction of David Bourne's manuscripts is an exception, and Hemingway was clearly self-conscious of this fact and its resulting ironies (see *[122:17]* 422.4 3.21.42 and 215:23). These early chapters with typescript pages—unlike the entirely holograph portion of the novel that follows them—carry no composition or revision dates, and it might be tempting to speculate that they date to the 1940s. Attention to the paper on which they were written, however, demonstrates that this cannot be the case. With the exception of the first chapter, they are typed on the same onionskin watermark paper (or onionskin lacking watermark) used for later holograph sections of the novel, and chapters that begin in typescript before switching to holograph (book III, chapters 5, 6, 9, and 11)—implying significant revision—generally use the same paper for both typescript and holograph pages.[12] (The paper used for the first chapter reappears briefly in chapter 4 in a context that suggests that it does not significantly predate the rest of that chapter.) What does seem clear is that Hemingway typed and revised these early chapters by the middle of May 1958. The entirely holograph section of the manuscript begins with book III, chapter 12, and a steady stream of composition dates begins to appear with the next chapter on May 18.

What is surprising is how close Hemingway thought he was to completing his novel at this time. A separate item in the Hemingway Collection at the John F. Kennedy Library in Boston (item 422.2, folder 1), distinct from the primary *Eden* manuscript (item 422.1), contains an eleven-page holograph text with the following heading:

^Provisional Ending^ ^May^
Chapter F̶i̶f̶t̶e̶e̶n̶ ^probably 36^

This provisional ending (see appendix B) was once kept in the same envelope with book II of the manuscript (the Sheldon backstory, now in item 422.1) and the Sheldon ending (item 422.2, folders 2–5; see appendix A), and a note on the envelope flap in Hemingway's hand reads: "written in May '58 when thought something might happen before book could be finished." Another note on the envelope flap instructs, "insert in Book III following chapter twentysome. EH June 28." This is then changed to "insert in Book III following chapter 2? 34 (tentative arrangement) Sept. 20 58." (The number 2? has been erased and the second digit is not legible; this is what is indicated by the question mark.)[13]

This evidence alone tells us a great deal about the evolution of *The Garden of Eden*. For one thing, Hemingway originally imagined a much shorter novel. In May

1958—probably fearing the dangers of the Cuban Revolution—Hemingway felt intimations of mortality. In the safe at the Finca Vigía, he left a note dated 20 May 1958 with instructions to his literary executors; he placed it in an envelope dated 24 May 1958, explaining that it was to be "opened in case of my death." It was during this time, when he "thought something might happen," that Hemingway wrote the provisional ending. In the main *Eden* manuscript (item 422.1), book III, chapter 15 (the equivalent of chapter 8 in the Scribner's edition) begins with the header: "Chapter 15 ^(Really Chap 1/ Last Book)^," and a note on that folder of the manuscript is dated May 23. The provisional ending, originally labeled "Chapter Fifteen," must have been written a few days before this. So, when Hemingway wrote it (on the same onionskin paper without watermark that he used for the other manuscript chapters in May 1958), he planned to end his story soon after the Madrid chapters. The result would have been a novella in which Marita and the African stories never appear. (Marita doesn't appear in the manuscript until the very end of book III, chapter 19, and David begins his first African story in chapter 20.) In May 1958, Hemingway had no idea that he would continue writing steadily through February 1959, adding another thirty manuscript chapters to his novel.

Yet, though Hemingway wrote the provisional ending early in his composition process, he didn't abandon it. As indicated by the June 28 and Sept. 20 '58 dates and the thrice-revised directions to insert the ending around chapters "twentysome," 34, or 36, Hemingway wrote with this ending in mind long after Marita enters the novel and David begins his African stories, and he still intended to use this ending when he organized his manuscript materials before leaving Cuba for Ketchum at the beginning of October 1958.

In June, Hemingway worked on a conclusion to the Sheldon subplot (see appendix A), and this seems also to have been when he wrote (or perhaps rewrote) the single-chapter manuscript book II, as a backstory for the Sheldons to be inserted before David and Catherine meet them in Hendaye.[14] A note in the Sheldon ending indicates that he meant to place it "after David and Catherine's story stops in September," but before the action of the provisional ending (appendix B), which takes place a good while later. On 25 June, four pages from the ending of the Sheldon subplot, Hemingway was interrupted by the arrival of visitors and felt he had to rush his work. A note in the manuscript reminds him to rewrite these pages, which consist of three versions (one clearly deleted) of Barbara's suicide note. Writing the next day to Juanito Quintana, he said he was close to finishing but needed to write at least six more chapters.[15] So when Hemingway wrote his note on 28 June about the placement of the provisional ending somewhere around chapter "twentysome," he probably was imagining a novel with a very minor role (if any) for Marita and without David's African stories.[16]

But that summer Ernest couldn't stop writing. At the beginning of July, Mary wrote to Bill Horne that work had "been driving Ernest like a fiend. . . . He's busy without breakfast about 6 o'clock, doesn't knock off until time to swim a minute before lunch at 2, and all too often I keep finding him silently back at work at 4." She feared he was overworking himself and knew they couldn't go anywhere "until the dragon lets him loose."[17] But it never did. Getting ready to leave Cuba for Ketchum, on 21 September, Ernest told Harvey Breit that he'd been writing all summer as if in a "fever."[18] A week earlier, he'd told Buck Lanham that, after "a year of all work no play," he'd written 160,000 words on the novel and had finally reached a point where he could take a break. Once again, he thought he was "close to the end."[19]

On 20 September, trying to organize the massive manuscript before leaving for Ketchum, Hemingway still intended to use both the Sheldon ending and the provisional ending he had written in May, though what he meant by its new placement—"following chapter 34" or "probably 36"—requires careful thought.[20] Today's book III manuscript chapters 27 and 28 were once a single chapter with consecutive page numbering, as were chapters 30 and 31; and chapters 32 through 36 were once a single mammoth chapter (begun 25 August, with composition dates running through 11 September) with sixty-six consecutively numbered pages. Thus, the header of chapter 37 reads: "Thirty One? Thirty Two? Chapter Thirty-Seven." When Hemingway wrote his 20 September note, it seems very likely that he had written to at least page twenty of what is now chapter 37—the conclusion of David's elephant story. As he'd told Lanham, this was a little over 160,000 words into the manuscript, and it was a natural place to take a break. But he still would have *thought* of this as chapter 31 or 32, imagining that he could wrap the novel up with the provisional ending in a few more chapters. The division of these chapters into their present numbering and organization probably happened when Hemingway revised what are now chapters 20 through 36 during the second half of November, carefully dating the rewrite on the first page of each chapter.[21] Thus, when composition dates reappear in the manuscript for the first time since September on 5 December, forty-three pages into what is now manuscript chapter 37, all indications are that Hemingway expected to build quickly to the provisional ending.

Indeed, although Hemingway may have entertained other ideas to end the novel, there is no clear indication that he ever conclusively abandoned either the Sheldon ending or the provisional ending. The ending he wrote in May 1958 could still work well after Catherine's destruction of David's stories and David's recovery, the writing of which occupied Hemingway through February 1959. In these ten late chapters, Marita, though she supports David's writing unwaveringly, comes to more and more clearly resemble Catherine (see *[244:25] 3.45.22* and 245:22), and when David and Marita discuss taking Catherine to Switzerland for treatment (see *[242:26] 3.44.17*), Hemingway seems to be laying further groundwork for the provisional ending. He certainly never intended to end the novel as Jenks did in the Scribner's edition. Whatever he was planning for the conclusion, though, was upset by the 18 February 1959 death of his friend Taylor Williams. He kept writing after the death of Williams, but as he later told Slim Hayward, he "had to throw... away" what he wrote.[22] The final composition date in the margin of the manuscript's final chapter is 24 February. That final chapter contains a metatextual suggestion that the honeymoon narrative really ends with the fire (see *[247:24] 3.46.16*); yet Hemingway told Alfred Rice that April that he hoped to finish the novel with three more chapters before undertaking the process of revision. First, he told him, he needed to go to Europe, where in addition to researching an updated appendix for a new edition of *Death in the Afternoon* (which under the influence of a lucrative serialization offer from *Life* magazine, eventually morphed into *The Dangerous Summer*), he hoped to conduct final research for *The Garden of Eden* and the book "Scribner's will be publishing before it" (*A Moveable Feast*)—clearly implying that he intended to publish *Eden*.[23]

As disheartening and disruptive as the death of Taylor Williams must have been, preparations in the spring of 1959 for the move from Ketchum to Cuba, from Cuba to New York, and from New York to Europe must have been far more disruptive. Before leaving Ketchum, on 13 March Hemingway sent the *Eden* manuscript by registered mail (insured for $100,000) to his wealthy friend, bibliographer, and manuscript manager, Lee Samuels, in New York for photostating.[24] A little over a month later, he picked it up in New York before sailing for Europe on 25 April.[25] That summer, he was distracted by the nonstop travel necessary to document the taurine mano a mano unfolding between Luis Miguel Dominguín and Antonio Ordóñez, but Valerie Hemingway remembers reading the *Eden* manuscript, at Ernest's invitation, in Nîmes that October before they visited Aigues-Mortes and Le Grau-du-Roi (68–69). On 15 October, he wrote to Mary that he'd made notes on Hendaye and Spain and everywhere the Bournes drove, with the exception of the Riviera, which was so transformed that its present incarnation could only be deceptive.[26] Far from abandoning *Eden*, he told Hotchner, "Am very anxious to get this bull stuff wrapped up so I will be free to go back + to finish the novel.... It is all done but the end + I should have the advantage of coming to that from a long way away" (*DPDH* 268–69). He told Harry Brague that this "could very easily be one of the best" novels he'd ever written.[27]

Unfortunately, Hemingway never got a chance to return to the *Eden* manuscript. Though he repeatedly protested that he could focus on only one project at a time, he was now juggling three book projects. Feeling morally compelled by the $10,000 advance he had taken from *Life* magazine (which he now regretted) and pressured by their deadline, he put aside his two nearly finished manuscripts and devoted himself to the bullfighting narrative that continued to grow and grow, far beyond the desires of *Life*. He had shared a draft of *A Moveable Feast* with Scribner's in November 1959, but on 31 March 1960, he told them to scratch it from their fall list because he didn't have the time to complete the revisions.[28] He hoped, instead, he could have it for them in 1961. By the end of May 1960, he had completed a hundred-thousand-word draft of *The Dangerous Summer*, having worked, he told Rice, as hard as he ever had in his life, but to finish the book he would have to return to Spain.[29] There, in August, his mental health began to deteriorate. Soon he was in the Mayo Clinic for the first of two stays. In the months before Hemingway took his life, on July 2, 1961, he added another fifty thousand words to *The Dangerous Summer* and tried to finish *A Moveable Feast*, but he was never able to return to *Eden*.

NOTES

1. See letter to Pamela Churchill, 4 July 1945 (JFK); see also letter to Parthy Vanderwicken, 20 Dec. 1945 (JFK).
2. Mary Hemingway, letter to Patrick Hemingway 11 Nov. 1945 (JFK).
3. Letter to Mary Hemingway, c.1946 (JFK).
4. For an extended discussion of these letters, see Eby, *HF* 200–3.
5. As Burwell notes, the letter Baker cites (12 June 1948) does not appear in Lanham's papers at Princeton, nor is it in the JFK. She speculates that it may have been among the "uninventoried papers . . . taken from Baker's office after his death." She notes, however, that Hemingway used the same phrase in a different context in a letter of the same date to Charles Scribner Sr. (97).
6. Letter to Brague, 31 July 1958 (PUL). For the beginning of *Moveable Feast*, see letter to Harvey Breit, 16 June 1957 (JFK).
7. See, for instance, Hemingway's 14 October 1944 and 5 March 1947 letters to Max Perkins, in Bruccoli, *Only Thing* 333, 339.
8. Hemingway letter to Wirt Williams, 20 Jan. 1958 (JFK).
9. Mary Hemingway, letter to Bill Seward, 22 Aug. 1958 (JFK). Burwell cites a 16 Dec. 1957 letter from Hemingway to Buck Lanham that claims he had fourteen chapters completed on one book (*Feast*) and was simultaneously working on another (*Eden*) (98). I have been unable to locate this letter. There is a 15 Dec. 1957 letter to Lanham (PUL) that mentions the fourteen chapters on one book; it does not, however, mention work on any other book.
10. See letter to Harry Brague, 31 July 1958 (PUL). For Hemingway's morning, noon, and evening work habits, see his letter to Juanito Quintana, 26 June 1958 (JFK), and Mary Hemingway's letter to Bill and Bunny Horne, 1 July 1958 (JFK).
11. Hemingway's typing can be distinguished by the use of an extra space before the final period of a sentence. We also know that Hemingway typed these pages because he makes frequent emendations and insertions as he types.
12. The three papers of the *Eden* manuscript—Millers Falls onionskin, onion skin without watermark, and Esleeck onionskin—all appear in the *Moveable Feast* manuscript, suggesting the temporal contiguity of these projects. With the exception of book I, chapter 1 (on Millers Falls onionskin), book I, chapters 2–3 (on Esleeck onionskin), and the occasional stray page (usually a later insert), Hemingway wrote on onionskin without watermark until early June 1958, bringing the manuscript up to book III, chapter 20. He then switched to Esleeck onionskin for the remainder of the manuscript (including book II, which was later inserted in its present position). My thanks to Hilary Justice for her assistance with this.
13. Burwell, following Spilka, misdates this provisional ending, suggesting it was written in May 1950, instead of May 1958 (202). This plays a large role in her mistaken argument about *Eden*'s link to Hemingway's Land, Sea, and Air Book.

14. The typescript first page of book II, on the onionskin paper without watermark that Hemingway used in May 1958, suggests that book II was first drafted before the Hendaye chapters of book III—a conclusion bolstered by the fact that Nick Sheldon's name in book II appears to originally have been Michael. Yet the fact that book II was originally kept in a separate folder with the Sheldon ending (see appendix A)—and the fact that it is written on paper Hemingway used from June 1958 to February 1959—suggests that it may have been a later insert, written in June 1958. It seems likely that it was drafted in or before May 1958 but was heavily rewritten in June.

15. Letter to Quintana, 26 June 1958 (JFK).

16. Marita and Nina appear in the manuscript *(3.19.20)* six pages after a margin note dated June 8. This is written on the onionskin paper without watermark that Hemingway used in May and early June 1958, but the same manuscript page where Catherine actually brings Marita home *(3.20.4)* marks a change to the Esleeck watermark onionskin paper that Hemingway began using in June and used for the rest of the manuscript. It is difficult to date these early chapters with Marita because there are no more composition dates in the manuscript of the Bourne plot until 15 July—but this is five chapters later in the Bourne narrative. Given the pace at which Hemingway was writing, it is likely that Marita had, at least, entered the Bournes' lives by the time Hemingway wrote his note on 28 June.

17. Mary Hemingway, letter to Bill and Bunny Horne, 1 July 1958 (JFK).

18. Letter to Breit, 21 Sept. 1958 (JFK).

19. Letter to Lanham, 13 Sept. 1958 (PUL).

20. For Hemingway's intentions regarding the Sheldon ending, see appendix A *(422.2 3.7)*.

21. Instead of bringing the manuscript with him on the drive to Ketchum, Hemingway entrusted Lee Samuels to ship it to him. It arrived in Ketchum sometime before 2 November, and Hemingway began his rewrites on 16 November. See letters to Christopher Janus, 21 Oct. 1958 (IndU) and Lee Samuels, 2 Nov. 1958 (UT).

22. Letter to Hayward, 7 Apr. 1959 (JFK).

23. Letter to Rice, 10 Apr. 1959 (JFK).

24. Letters to Samuels, 5 Feb. 1959 (UT), and Charles Scribner Jr., 12 Apr. 1959 (PUL).

25. For Hemingway's 22 April arrival in New York and 25 April departure for Europe, see Mary Hemingway's 19 April letter to Waldo and Ellen Peirce (LOC).

26. Letter to Mary Hemingway, 15 Oct. 1959 (JFK).

27. Letter to Brague, 26 Aug. 1959 (PUL).

28. Letter to Charles Scribner Jr., 31 March 1960 (PUL).

29. Letter to Rice, 31 May 1960 (JFK).

WORKS CITED

"African Women Provide New Hair-Cut Styles; Toque of Clay and Castor Oil the Most Popular." *New York Times,* 30 Dec. 1928, p. 39.

Allen, Frederick Lewis. *Only Yesterday: An Informal History of the 1920s.* Perennial Classic, 2000.

"All France Agog over Landru Trial: Bluebeard, Accused of Killing 11 Women, on Trial at Versailles Tomorrow. Tragi-comic Character." *New York Times,* 6 Nov. 1921, p. 19.

"*An American at Large*" [Review]. *Kirkus Review,* 18 Apr. 1947.

"The American Volunteers in Morocco." *Christian Science Monitor,* 31 July 1925, p. 16.

Amory, Cleveland. *The Proper Bostonians.* Dutton, 1955.

"And Now Tilton's Present That Popular New Fabric 'Sharkskin.'" *Los Angeles Times,* 2 Apr. 1929, p. 11.

Andrews, Roy Chapman. *On the Trail of Ancient Man: A Narrative of the Field Work of the Central Asiatic Expeditions.* G. P. Putnam's Sons, 1926.

"À Nice, hier matin, une jeune femme a été tuée d'un coup de couteau dans son appartement." *L'Éclaireur de Nice et du Sud-Est,* 20 Oct. 1927, p. 1.

Annuaire des grands cercles et du grand monde: Sports et clubs. A. Lahure, 1927, pp. 29–61.

Anonymous. *Immortalia: An Anthology of American Ballads, Sailors' Songs, Cowboy Songs, College Songs, Parodies, Limericks, and Other Humorous Verses and Doggerel Now for the First Time Brought Together in Book Form.* Edited by A Gentleman About Town, For Subscribers, 1927.

Anselmi, Angelo Tito. *Isotta Fraschini.* Milani, 1977.

Arnaud, Claude. *Jean Cocteau: A Life.* Yale UP, 2016.

"Au Bar du Carlton." *La Gazette de Bayonne, du Pays Basque, & des Landes,* 26 Apr. 1935, p. 2.

Automobile Quarterly. *Automobile Quarterly's World of Cars.* Dutton, 1971.

"Autumn Health Parades: An Open-Air 'Gym' of the Riviera." *The Sketch,* 2 Nov. 1927, p. 224.

Aveline, Françoise. *Chanel: Parfum.* Éditions Assouline, 2003.

"'Away with Clothing,' Cry the Back to Nature Crusaders: Europe Has 3,000,000 Sun Worshippers Who Even Invade the Restaurants without a Rag of Clothing—Had a Presidential Candidate in Last German Election." *The Boston Globe,* 20 Sept. 1925, p. C8.

Baedeker, Karl. *The Riviera: South-Eastern France and Corsica, the Italian Lakes and Lake of Geneva.* Baedeker, 1931.

Baker, Carlos. *Ernest Hemingway: A Life Story.* Collier, 1969.

Barker, Ronald. *Bugatti.* Ballantine Books, 1971.

Baroja, Pio. *El aprendiz de conspirador. Memorias de un hombre de acción.* Rafael Caro Raggio, 1920.

"Beginnings of Man Sought in Mongolia: Andrews Is Returning to New York to Prepare for New Expeditions: Saw Signs of Bigger Find: Region of Dinosaur Eggs Is Indicated as the Seat of Animal Life." *New York Times,* 7 Nov. 1923, p. 17.

Bell, W. D. M. *The Wanderings of an Elephant Hunter.* Scribner's, 1923.

Berne, Pierre. "Aigues-Mortes et ses environs: Etude de géographie humaine." *Société de Géographie Bulletin,* Bibliothéque de la Société Languedocienne de Géographie, 1935, pp. 61–96.

Bertaux, Émile. *Les guides bleus: Espagne et Portugal.* Librairie Hachette, 1921.

Bettonica, Luis, and Luis Bosch. *Palace Hotel, Madrid.* Sociedad General del Libreria, 1987.

Bichsel, Rolf. *Tavel: Des hommes et des vins.* Éditions Féret, 2011.

"Birthplace of Modern Man Put in East Africa." *New York Times,* 25 July 1933, p. 21.

Bisch, Louis Edward. *Be Glad You're Neurotic.* 2nd ed., McGraw-Hill, 1946.

Blair, Fredrika. *Isadora: Portrait of the Artist as a Woman.* Equation, 1986.

Blas Vega, José. *Vida y cante de Don Antonio Chacón: Le edad de oro del flamenco (1869–1929).* Editorial Cinterco, 1990.

Blume, Mary. *Côte d'Azur: Inventing the French Riviera.* Thames and Hudson, 1992.

Blunt, David Enderby. *Elephant.* Neville Spearman, 1933.

"Bobbed Hair and Curls to Be 1927 Style, Coiffeurs Declare at Vienna Exposition." *New York Times,* 4 Jan. 1927, p. 27.

"Boom Fortunes Made and Unmade as Casino Craze Sweeps Riviera." *New York Herald* (Paris edition), 23 Sept. 1926, p. 6.

Boone, Joseph. *The Homoerotics of Orientalism.* Columbia UP, 2014.

Booth, Howard J. "Kipling, 'Beastliness' and Soldatenliebe." *In Time's Eye: Essays on Rudyard Kipling,* edited by Jan Montefiore, Manchester UP, 2013, pp. 225–49.

Boswell, James. *The Life of Samuel Johnson, LL. D.* Vol. 2, Dent, 1906.

Bouzonviller, Elisabeth. "A Decisive Stopover in 'an Antiseptic Smelling Land': Switzerland as a Place of Decision and Recovery in F. Scott Fitzgerald's Fiction." *F. Scott Fitzgerald Review,* vol. 3, 2004, pp. 27–42.

"Boyish Bob Is Banned by Paris Hairdressers." *New York Times,* 9 June 1927, p. 1.

"Boyish Bob Is Now Ruled Out: Paris Decrees the 'Joan of Arc.'" *New York Times,* 28 Mar. 1927, p. 23.

Brasch, James. "'Christ, I wish I Could Paint': The Correspondence between Ernest Hemingway and Bernard Berenson." *Hemingway in Italy and Other Essays,* edited by Robert W. Lewis, Praeger, 1990, pp. 49–68.

Brasch, James, and Joseph Sigman. *Hemingway's Library: A Composite Record.* Electronic Edition, John F. Kennedy Library, 2000.

Broer, Lawrence R. *Vonnegut and Hemingway: Writers at War.* U of South Carolina P, 2011.

Bronson, Edgar Beecher. *In Closed Territory.* A. C. McClurg, 1910.

Bruccoli, Matthew J. *Hemingway at Auction 1930–1973.* Gale, 1973.

———, editor. *The Only Thing that Counts: The Ernest Hemingway-Maxwell Perkins Correspondence.* Scribner's, 1996.

———. *Some Sort of Epic Grandeur: The Life of F. Scott Fitzgerald.* 2nd revised ed., U of South Carolina P, 2002.

Brun, Maurice. "Palavas perle du littoral." *La Tribune de Marseille,* Aug. 1926, p. 2.

Bryden, H. A. "African Big Game." *Big Game Shooting,* edited by Horace G. Hutchinson, vol. 2, Country Life, 1905, pp. 3–220.

Buchanan, Lucile. "Fashion Gives Approval of Trousers for Women: Many Versions Now Find Favor in Today's Mode." *St. Louis Star,* 20 Apr. 1927, p. 19.
"Building Bungalows on the Riviera." *New York Herald* (Paris edition), 19 Dec. 1926, p. 5.
Burnett, Robert. *The Life of Paul Gauguin.* Cobden-Sanderson, 1936.
Bürgi, H., Z. Supersaxo, and B. Selz. "Iodine Deficiency Diseases in Switzerland One Hundred Years after Theodore Kocher's Survey: A Historical Review with Some New Goitre Prevalence." *Acta Endocrinol,* vol. 126, no. 6, 1990, pp. 577–90.
Burns, Louis F. *A History of the Osage People.* U of Alabama P, 2004.
Burwell, Rose Marie. *Hemingway: The Postwar Years and the Posthumous Novels.* Cambridge UP, 1996.
Butchart, Amber Jane. *Nautical Chic.* Abrams, 2015.
Butler, Frank Hedges. *Wine and the Wine Lands of the World: With Some Account of Places Visited.* T. Fisher Unwin, 1926.
Butler, Judith. *Gender Trouble: Feminism and the Subversion of Identity.* Routledge, 1990.
"Buys a Volcano for Hunting Game: Sir Charles Ross Purchases in Africa Largest Crater in World." *New York Herald,* 12 Nov. 1922, p. 35.
Byron, George Gordon. *The Complete Poetical Works.* Houghton Mifflin, 1905.
Cain, Donald Peter. "Franco and the Aurelia: Lancia's Pioneering V-6." *Automobile Quarterly,* vol. 34, no. 3, 1995, p. 29.
Calabi, Silvio, Steve Helsley, and Roger Sanger. *Hemingway's Guns.* Shooting Sportsman Book, 2010.
"Cannes Summer Season Popular." *New York Herald* (Paris edition), 28 Aug. 1926, p. 8.
Carroll, Raymond G. "Paris by Day: Seen and Heard." *Los Angeles Times,* 22 June 1924, p. 20.
Caswell, John. *Sporting Rifles and Rifle Shooting.* D. Appleton, 1920.
"Cervecería del pasaje." *Heraldo de Madrid,* 17 May 1924, p. 6.
Cheatle, Joseph James Nefey. "Between Oscar Wilde and Stonewall: Representations of Homosexuality in Twentieth-Century British and American Literature." 2014. Miami U, PhD dissertation.
"Choses et autres." *La Vie Parisienne,* 1 Sept. 1928, p. 721.
"Choses et gens." *Le Cri de Paris,* 31 Aug. 1919, pp. 6–7.
Christian, Timothy. *Hemingway's Widow: The Life and Legacy of Mary Welsh Hemingway.* Pegasus Books, 2022.
"Christopher Morley Roams Fancyland." *Charlotte News,* 20 Nov. 1927, p. 10B.
Cierplikowski, Antoine. *Antoine.* Prentice Hall, 1945.
Cloud, Yvonne. "The News in the Holiday Mail Bag: Letters from 'The Cap' and le Touquet." *The Graphic,* 28 Aug. 1926, p. 339.
Cocteau, Jean. *The Journals of Jean Cocteau.* Edited by Wallace Fowlie, Criterion Books, 1956.
Cogniat, Raymond. "Les peintres de la femme." *Femme de France,* 2 June 1929, p. 24.
Colonial Office. *Confidential Correspondence Relating to Affairs in the East Africa Protectorate, April 7, 1905 to June 8, 1906.* African no. 771, Colonial Office, April 1907.
"Comienza la feria de Abril sevillana." *El Liberal,* 19 Apr. 1927, p. 5.
Comley, Nancy. "The Light from Hemingway's Garden: Regendering Papa." *Hemingway and Women: Female Critics and the Feminine Voice,* edited by Lawrence Broer and Gloria Holland, U of Alabama P, 2002, pp. 204–17.
Comley, Nancy, and Robert Scholes. *Hemingway's Genders: Rereading the Hemingway Text.* Yale UP, 1994.

Courthion, Pierre. "Panorama de la painture: Marie Laurencin." *Comoedia,* 6 June 1927, p. 3.
"Cropped Waitresses Banned by Manager." *The Daily Record,* 11 Sept. 1926, p. 5.
Cruz, Teresa. "Percebes?" *Guerreiros do Mar / Warriors of the Sea,* edited by João Mariano, Grupo Forum, 1998.
Culot, Maurice, Geneviève Mesuret, Dominique Delaunay, and Institute Français d'Architecture. *Hendaye, Irún, Fontarabie: Villes de la frontière.* Éditions Norma, 1998.
"The Cult of Beauty." *Gentlewoman and Modern Life,* 27 Mar. 1926, p. 514.
"Curls and Waves Are Eclipsing Sleek Bob." *San Bernadino County Sun,* 6 Nov. 1927, p. 2.
Curtis, Verna Posever, and Selma Reuben Holo. *La Tauromaquia: Goya, Picasso and the Bullfight.* Milwaukee Art Museum, 1986.
Cushman, Stephen. "Why Didn't Hemingway Mention This Crater?" *Southwest Review,* vol. 94, no. 4, 2009, pp. 462–77.
Dale, Philip Marshall. *Medical Biographies: The Ailments of Thirty-Three Famous Persons.* U of Oklahoma P, 1952.
Daly, Ann. *Done into Dance: Isadora Duncan in America.* Indiana UP, 1995.
Danchev, Alex. *Georges Braque: A Life.* Arcade, 2005.
Darrow, Clarence. "The Edwardses and the Jukeses." *The American Mercury,* vol. 6, Oct. 1925, pp. 147–57.
"Death of the Eton Crop." *The Northern Whig and Belfast Post,* 16 Aug. 1927, p. 11
del Gizzo, Suzanne. "Going Home: Hemingway, Primitivism, and Identity." *Modern Fiction Studies,* vol. 49, no. 3, 2003, pp. 496–523.
del Gizzo, Suzanne, and Kirk Curnutt, editors. *The New Hemingway Studies.* Cambridge UP, 2020.
"Delightful 'Kiki' Coming to Strand." *The Hartford Courant,* 19 Apr. 1926, p. C2.
Dery, Gaston. "Heures de Deauville." *La Femme de France,* 21 Aug. 1927, p. 20.
"Deserting Eton Crop." *Hastings and St. Leonards Observer,* 8 Oct. 1925, p. 26.
Dick, Robert. *Auto Racing Comes of Age: A Transatlantic View of the Cars, Drivers and Speedways, 1900–1925.* McFarland, 2013.
Diliberto, Gioia. *Hadley.* Ticknor and Fields, 1992.
Domenichino, Jean, Xavier Daumalin, and Jean-Marie Guillon. *Paul Ricard et "le vrai pastis de Marseille."* Éditions Jeanne Laffitte, 2009.
Dominé, André, editor. *Culinaria France.* Könemann, 1999.
"¿Donde . . . ? en la Gran Cervecería J. Alvarez." *ABC,* 16 Apr. 1927, p. 34.
Dos Passos, John. *The Best Times.* New American Library, 1966.
———. "The Republic of Honest Men." *Travel Books and Other Writings, 1916–1941,* Library of America, 2003, pp. 338–68.
Dudley, Marc. *Hemingway, Race, and Art: Bloodlines and the Color Line.* Kent State UP, 2012.
Duffield, Edgar N. "Motoring and Motorists: Trials of the Times: No. 4, the 45 H. P. Isotta Fraschini." *The Graphic,* 13 Aug. 1927, p. 266.
Duménil, Renaud. *Antibes, Juan-les-Pins: Le plaisir déployé, 1900–1960.* Editions Équinoxe, 2002.
Duncan, David Douglas. *The Private World of Pablo Picasso.* Harper, 1958.
Dupouy, Alexandre. *Pascin.* Parkstone Press, 2014.
Earle, David. *All Man! Hemingway, 1950s Men's Magazines, and the Masculine Persona.* Kent State UP, 2009.
Eby, Carl. "'Come Back to the Beach Ag'in, David Honey!': Hemingway's Fetishization of

Race in *The Garden of Eden* Manuscripts." *The Hemingway Review*, vol. 14, no. 2, 1995, pp. 98–118.

———. "Gardens of *Eden* and *Earthly Delights*: Hemingway, Bosch, and the Divided Self." *The Hemingway Review*, vol. 37, no. 2, 2018, pp. 65–79.

———. "'He Felt the Change So That It Hurt Him All Through': Sodomy and Transvestic Hallucination in Late Hemingway." *The Hemingway Review*, vol. 25, no. 1, 2005, pp. 77–95.

———. *Hemingway's Fetishism: Psychoanalysis and the Mirror of Manhood*. SUNY Press, 1999.

———. "Hemingway's Truth and Tribal Politics." *The Hemingway Review*, vol. 19, no. 1, 1999, pp. 24–27.

———. "'In the Year of the Maji Maji': Settler Colonialism, the Nandi Resistance, and Race in *The Garden of Eden*," *The Hemingway Review*, vol. 39, no. 1, 2019, pp. 9–39.

———. "Reading Hemingway Backwards: Teaching *A Farewell to Arms* in Light of *The Garden of Eden*." *Teaching Hemingway and Gender*, edited by Verna Kale, Kent State UP, 2016, pp. 104–14.

———. "The Sea Change." *Reading Hemingway's* Winner Take Nothing, Kent State UP, 2021, pp. 83–98.

———. "Who Is 'the Destructive Type'?: Re-reading Literary Jealousy and Destruction in *The Garden of Eden*." *The Hemingway Review*, vol. 33, no. 2, 2014, pp. 99–106.

"Eddie Cantor, Noted Comedian, Stars at Orpheum." *San Francisco Examiner*, 9 May 1927, p. 16L.

"El 'buffet' italiano." *Mundo Gráfico*, 28 March 1923.

Elder, Robert K., Aaron Vetch, and Mark Cirino. *Hidden Hemingway: Inside the Archives of Oak Park*. Kent State UP, 2016.

Elliott, Bridget. "Arabesque: Marie Laurencin, Decadence and Decorative Excess." *Modernist Sexualities*, edited by Hugh Stevens and Caroline Howlett, Manchester UP, 2000, pp. 92–113.

Ellis, Henry Havelock. "The Development of the Sexual Instinct." *Studies in the Psychology of Sex*, vol. 1, Random House, 1942.

"Emile Prunier, of Restaurant Fame, Is Dead: Paris Specialist in Sea-Food Known to Many Americans." *New York Herald* (Paris edition), 8 Nov. 1925, p. 3.

"English and American News: Biarritz Notes." *Gazette de Biarritz*, 15 Aug. 1926, p. 2.

"Entre le ciel et l'eau." *Le Temps*, 17 Aug. 1926, p. 1.

Epstein, Louis. "Impresario Interrupted: Comte Étienne de Beaumont and the Soirées de Paris." *Revue de Musicologie*, vol. 102, no. 1, 2016, pp. 91–130.

"Ernest Hemingway Shown at His Best." *Hartford Courant*, 20 Nov. 1927, E5.

Ernst, Morris L., and William Seagle. *To the Pure . . . : A Study of Obscenity and the Censor*. Viking, 1928.

"Estadistica roja de 1926." *La Lidia*, no. 424, 18 Oct. 1926, p. 8.

"Eton Crop Ban." *Yorkshire Evening Post*, 14 Aug. 1926, p. 6.

"Eton Crop Banned: French Barbers Vote Down 'Skinned Rabbit' Coiffures." *Decatur Herald*, 24 Nov. 1928, p. 7.

"Eton Crop Doomed." *Leeds Mercury*, 17 Sept. 1927, p. 7.

"The Eton Crop Goes." *Aberdeen Press and Journal*, 12 Sept. 1927, p. 7.

"Eton Crop Going." *Nottingham Evening Post*, 14 May 1926, p. 6.

"Eton Crop Is Latest British Designation of That Boyish Shingle." *Chicago Tribune*, 27 Nov. 1925, p. 17.

"The Eton Crop Peril." *Sunderland Daily Echo,* 8 Dec. 1926, p. 3

"Eton Crop Scare." *Sunday Post,* 30 Aug. 1925, p. 8.

"The Eton Crop Will Die." *Northern Whig and Belfast Post,* 5 Feb. 1927, p. 11.

"Exaggerated Bob Is London Rage: Curls Ironed Out with Machines." *Washington Post,* 7 Dec. 1924, p. A7A.

F. A. M. "Diary of a Young Colonial." *Manchester Guardian,* 11 Oct. 1957, p. 6.

Fantina, Richard. *Ernest Hemingway: Machismo and Masochism.* Palgrave, 2005.

Farson, Negley. *Behind God's Back.* Victor Gollancz, 1940.

Faucigny-Lucinge, Jean-Louis de. *Un gentilhomme cosmopolite: Mémoires.* Perrin, 1990.

Feibleman, Peter. *The Cooking of Spain and Portugal.* Time-Life, 1969.

Fernandez, Jeanne Ramon [published as J. R. F]. "Quelques jours de printemps à Biarritz." *Vogue* (French), 1 June 1925, pp. 3–5, 60, 62.

Finamore, Michelle Tolini. *Hollywood before Glamour: Fashion in American Silent Film.* Palgrave MacMillan, 2013.

"Find 25 Big Eggs in Dinosaurs' Nests: Natural History Museum Men Make Notable Discoveries in Mongolia." *New York Times,* 26 Sept. 1923, p. 1.

Fitzgerald, F. Scott. *A Life in Letters.* Simon and Schuster, 1995.

———. *Tender Is the Night.* Scribner's, 1995.

"Fleet Cossack Conquered by Fleeter Plane: Air Service Protects Polish Borders." *Chicago Tribune* (Paris edition), 23 May 1921, p. 5.

Fleming, Robert. "The Endings of Hemingway's *Garden of Eden.*" *American Literature,* vol. 61, no. 2, 1989, pp. 261–70.

———. *The Face in the Mirror: Hemingway's Writers.* U of Alabama P, 1994.

Ford, Richard. *Gatherings from Spain.* John Murray, 1846.

"A Forecast of the Bathing Mode for Palm Beach." *Vogue* (American), 7 Dec. 1929, pp. 76–77.

"Fortunes in Land on the Riviera: Boom Follows Casinos: Wild Scramble for Inches." *Leeds Mercury,* 2 Nov. 1926, p. 6.

Foster, Jeanne Robert. "A Parisienne's Philosophy of Coiffures: The Chic Coiffure of Paris, Expressing the Restless Spirit of the Modern Age, Changes to Conform to Each Type of Beauty." *Vogue* (American), 15 July 1923, p. 35.

"French Murder Reveals Unclad Mountain Colony: Marriage Barred by Zarathostras." *Atlanta Constitution,* 26 Oct. 1927, p. 1.

Freud, Sigmund. "Fetishism." *The Standard Edition of the Complete Psychological Works of Sigmund Freud,* translated by James Strachey, vol. 21, Hogarth, 1963, pp. 147–58.

———. "Splitting of the Ego in the Defensive Process." *The Standard Edition of the Complete Psychological Works of Sigmund Freud,* translated by James Strachey, vol. 23, Hogarth, 1964, pp. 271–78.

"From Dawn to Dinner Paris Says—." *Philadelphia Inquirer* (magazine section), 19 Aug. 1928, p. 10.

"From Trousers to Shorts! A Century of Women's Sports Dress." *The Sketch,* 16 Mar. 1927, p. 499.

Funchal, Domingos António de Sousa Coutinho. *La Guerre de la péninsule sous son véritable point de vue.* Weissenbruch, 1819.

Gajdusek, Robert E. "The Cost of Sin in the Garden: A Study of An Amended Theme in *The Garden of Eden.*" *Resources for American Literary Study,* vol. 19, no. 1, 1993, pp. 1–21.

Gamman, Lorraine, and Merja Makinen. *Female Fetishism.* NYU Press, 1994.

Garfield, Brian. *The Meinertzhagen Mystery: The Life and Legend of a Colossal Fraud.* Potomac Books, 2007.
Gautier, Théophile. *Mademoiselle de Maupin.* Translated by Joanna Richardson, Penguin, 1981.
Gibbons, Herbert Adams. *Riviera Towns.* Robert M. McBride, 1920.
Girard, Xavier. *The French Riviera in the 1920s.* Assouline, 2002.
GLAAD. "GLAAD Media Reference Guide—Glossary of Terms: Transgender." *GLAAD Media Reference Guide,* 11th edition, https://www.glaad.org/reference/trans-terms.
Gogol, Nikolai. "Taras Bulba." *The Complete Tales of Nikolai Gogol,* edited by Leonard J. Kent, translated by Constance Garnett, vol. 2, U of Chicago P, 1985, pp. 22–132.
Gold, Arthur, and Robert Fizdale. *Misia: The Life of Misia Sert.* Knopf, 1980.
González Gordon, Manuel M. *Sherry: The Noble Wine.* Cassell, 1972.
Goodrich, Lloyd. *Record of Works by Winslow Homer.* Vols. 4.2 and 5, Goodrich-Homer Art Education Project, 2012 and 2014.
Gosselin, Chris C., and S. B. C. Eysenck. "The Transvestite 'Double Image': A Preliminary Report." *Personality and Individual Differences,* vol. 1, no. 2, 1980, pp. 172–73.
Greenacre, Phyllis. *Emotional Growth: Psychoanalytic Studies of the Gifted and a Great Variety of Other Individuals.* Vol. 1, International UP, 1971.
Grissom, C. Edgar. *Ernest Hemingway: A Descriptive Bibliography.* Oak Knoll Press, 2011.
Gruyer, Paul. *Saint-Germain, Poissy, Maisons, Marly-le-Roi.* Henri Laurens, 1922.
Guillet, Jean-Luc. *American's Riviera: "Les années folles."* Éditions Équinoxe, 2005.
Gwynne, Erskine. "Around Biarritz." *New York Herald Tribune* (Paris edition), 20 Apr. 1938, p. 5.
"A Haig & Haig Message to the Discriminating Public." *The Manchester Guardian,* 1 Sept. 1921, p. 9.
"Hair Dresser's Exhibition." *The Age,* 23 Feb. 1927, p. 16.
Hale, Julian. *The French Riviera: A Cultural History.* Oxford UP, 2009.
Harmon, Dudley. "Family to Be Tested for Heredity's Law." *New York Times,* 24 June 1923, p. xxii.
Harris, Frank. *My Life and Loves.* Grove Press, 1963.
Harp, Stephen L. *Au Naturel: Naturism, Nudism, and Tourism in Twentieth-Century France.* LSU Press, 2014.
Hawkins, Ruth. *Unbelievable Happiness and Final Sorrow: The Hemingway-Pfeiffer Marriage.* U of Arkansas P, 2012.
Hediger, Ryan. "The Elephant in the Writing Room: Sympathy and Weakness in Hemingway's 'Masculine Text,' *The Garden of Eden.*" *The Hemingway Review,* vol. 31, no. 1, 2011, pp. 79–95.
"He Drank with Them, Played with Them, Wrote a Book about Them." *Boston Daily Globe,* 18 Dec. 1927, p. B3.
"The Hemingway Cult." *Des Moins Sunday Register,* 29 Jan. 1928, p. G8.
Hemingway, Ernest. *Across the River and into the Trees.* Scribner's, 1950.
———. "The Art of the Short Story." *The Paris Review,* vol. 79, Spring 1981, pp. 85–102.
———. *By-Line: Ernest Hemingway.* Edited by William White, Scribner's, 1967.
———. *The Complete Short Stories of Ernest Hemingway: The Finca Vigía Edition.* Scribner's, 1987.
———. *Dateline: Toronto: The Complete Toronto Star Dispatches, 1920–1924.* Scribner's, 1985.
———. *Death in the Afternoon.* Scribner's, 1932.
———. *Ernest Hemingway: Selected Letters 1917–1961.* Edited by Carlos Baker, Scribner's, 1981.

---. "Ernest Hemingway." *Writers at Work: The Paris Review Interviews: Second Series,* edited by George Plimpton, Penguin, 1977, pp. 215–39.
---. *A Farewell to Arms.* Scribner's, 1995.
---. *The Fifth Column and the First Forty-Nine Stories.* Scribner's, 1938.
---. *For Whom the Bell Tolls.* Scribner's, 1940.
---. *The Garden of Eden.* Scribner's, 1986.
---. *Green Hills of Africa.* Scribner's 1935.
---. *Hemingway and the Mechanism of Fame: Statements, Public Letters, Introductions, Forewords, Prefaces, Blurbs, Reviews, and Endorsements.* Edited by Matthew J. Bruccoli with Judith S. Baughman, U of South Carolina P, 2006.
---. *Islands in the Stream.* Scribner's, 1970.
---. *The Letters of Ernest Hemingway, 1907–1922.* Vol. 1, edited by Sandra Spanier and Robert Trogdon, Cambridge UP, 2011.
---. *The Letters of Ernest Hemingway, 1923–1925.* Vol. 2, edited by Sandra Spanier, Albert J. Defazio III, and Robert Trogdon, Cambridge UP, 2013.
---. *The Letters of Ernest Hemingway, 1926–1929.* Vol. 3, edited by Rena Sanderson, Sandra Spanier, and Robert Trogdon, Cambridge UP, 2015.
---. *The Letters of Ernest Hemingway, 1929–1931.* Vol. 4, edited by Sandra Spanier and Miriam Mandel, Cambridge UP, 2017.
---. *The Letters of Ernest Hemingway, 1932–1934.* Vol. 5, edited by Sandra Spanier and Miriam Mandel, Cambridge UP, 2020.
---. *Men at War: The Best War Stories of All Time.* Edited by Ernest Hemingway, Wing Books, 1992.
---. *A Moveable Feast: The Restored Edition.* Edited by Sean Hemingway, Scribner's, 2009.
---. *The Nick Adams Stories.* Edited by Philip Young, Scribner's, 1973.
---. "Safari." *Look,* 26 Jan. 1954, pp. 19–34.
---. *The Sun Also Rises.* Scribner's, 1995.
---. *The Sun Also Rises: A Facsimile Edition, part I.* Edited by Matthew Bruccoli, Omnigraphics, 1990.
---. *To Have and Have Not.* Scribner's, 1970.
---. "Torcello Piece." *Hemingway and Italy: Twenty-First-Century Perspectives,* edited by Mark Cirino and Mark P. Ott, UP of Florida, 2017, pp. xi–xii.
---. *Der Unbesiegte, mit 28 Graphiken von Pablo Picasso.* Translated by Annemarie Horschitz-Horst, Fackelträger-Vert, 1958.
---. *Under Kilimanjaro.* Kent State UP, 2005.
Hemingway, Ernest, and A. E. Hotchner. *Dear Papa, Dear Hotch: The Correspondence of Ernest Hemingway and A. E. Hotchner.* Edited by Albert J. DeFazio III, U of Missouri P, 2005.
Hemingway, Gregory. *Papa: A Personal Memoir.* Houghton Mifflin, 1976.
"Hemingway Legend Forming." *Hartford Courant,* 27 Apr. 1927, p. 6D.
Hemingway, Mary. East Africa Journal. Mary Hemingway Papers, John F. Kennedy Library, Boston.
---. *How It Was.* Knopf, 1976.
---. "The Making of a Book: A Chronicle and a Memoir." *New York Times Book Review,* 10 May 1964, pp. 26–27.

Hemingway, Valerie. *Running with the Bulls: My Years with the Hemingways.* Ballantine Books, 2004.
"The Hemingways in Sun Valley: The Novelist Takes a Wife." *Life,* 6 Jan. 1941, pp. 52–57.
Hendrickson, Paul. *Hemingway's Boat: Everything He Loved in Life, and Lost, 1934–1961.* Knopf, 2011.
Hermann, Thomas. *"Quite a Little about Painters": Art and Artists in Hemingway's Life and Work.* Francke, 1997.
Herrin, Judith. *Ravenna: Capital of Empire, Crucible of Europe.* Princeton UP, 2020.
Higley, Stephen Richard. *The Geography of the American Upper Class.* Rowman & Littlefield, 1995.
Hofmann, Paul. "Spain's Summer Capital: San Sebastian Plays Host to Franco, Who Arrived in Truly Royal Fashion." *New York Times,* 1 Aug. 1964, p. 3.
Hotchner, A. E. *Papa Hemingway.* Random House, 1966.
Huard, Raymond, and Pierre Maillot. *Jules Desbois, 1851–1935: Une celebration tragique de la vie.* Le Cherche Midi Éditeur, 2000.
Hudson, W. H. *Far Away and Long Ago: A History of My Early Life.* Dutton, 1918.
———. *Nature in Downland.* Dent, 1951.
Hunt, Carl de Vidal. "Should Women Strive to Look Like Men? The Question of 'La Garçonne.'" *The Washington Post,* 18 Apr. 1926, p. SM1.
Hyland, Douglas, and Heather McPherson. *Marie Laurencin, Artist and Muse.* Birmingham Museum of Art, 1989.
"In the Margin." *Paris Times,* 8 Aug. 1925, p. 2.
"Indians Lavish Spenders." *New York Times,* 14 Nov. 1920, p. E20.
International Game Fish Association. *1985, World Record Game Fishes: Freshwater, Saltwater, and Fly Fishing.* IGFA, 1985.
"Italy Said to Plan Mobilization in June." *Washington Post,* 26 Apr. 1926, p. 1.
James, Ed. "Adah Isaacs Menken: A Tribute." *New York Clipper,* 14 Nov. 1863, p. 243.
James, Edwin. "Airmen Marvel at Skill." *New York Times,* 28 May 1927, p. 1.
"Jelke to Take Stand in Vice Charge Defense: 'Poor Little Rich Boy' Picture Planned; Press Presence at New Phase Undecided." *Los Angeles Times,* 24 Feb. 1953, p. 21.
Jenks, Tom. *"The Garden of Eden* at Twenty-five." *Hemingway's* The Garden of Eden: *Twenty-five Years of Criticism,* edited by Suzanne del Gizzo and Frederic J. Svoboda, Kent State UP, 2012, pp. 1–12.
Johnson, Douglas Wilson. *Battlefields of the World War: Western and Southern Fronts: A Study in Military Geography.* Oxford UP, 1921.
Johnson, Frederick. *A Standard Swahili-English Dictionary.* Oxford UP, 1939.
Jones, Robert B. "Mimesis and Metafiction in Hemingway's *The Garden of Eden.*" *The Hemingway Review,* vol. 7, no. 1, 1987, pp. 2–13.
Jouenne, Lucien. *Pendant vos vacances, pêchez au bord de la mer.* Ernest Flammarion, 1922.
Justice, Hilary. *The Bones of the Others: The Hemingway Text from the Lost Manuscripts to the Posthumous Novels.* Kent State UP, 2006.
Juta, René. "Mediterranean Blues: The Riviera Sun-Worshippers." *The Graphic,* 20 Aug. 1927, p. 302.
Kaplan, Louise. *Female Perversions.* Anchor, 1991.
Kennedy, J. Gerald. "Life as Fiction: The Lure of Hemingway's *Garden.*" *The Southern Review,* vol. 24, fall 1987, pp. 451–61.

Kert, Bernice. *The Hemingway Women*. Norton, 1983.
Khan, Badruddin. "Not-So-Gay Life in Pakistan in the 1980s and 1990s." *Islamic Homosexualities: Culture, History, and Literature,* edited by Stephen O. Murray and Will Roscoe, NYU Press, 1997, pp. 275–96.
Kilgallen, Dorothy. "Kilgallen on Broadway." *The Charleston Gazette,* 4 Sept. 1951, p. 7.
"King Alfonso Tells of Race to Madrid: 300-Mile Dash from San Sebastian Made in Six Hours at Night to Combat Revolt." *New York Times,* 15 Sep. 1926, p. 19.
Kladstrup, Don, and Petie Kladstrup. *Champagne: How the World's Most Glamorous Wine Triumphed over War and Hard Times.* William Morrow, 2005.
Kospoth, B. J. "Impressions of André Derain." *Chicago Tribune* (Paris edition), 2 May 1926, p. 4.
Kozodoy, Ruth. *Isadora Duncan.* Chelsea House, 1988.
"Krim Puts Price on Americans." *New York Times,* 24 Sept. 1925, p. 27.
Kurth, Peter. *Isadora: A Sensational Life.* Little, Brown and Co., 2001.
Kuzminskaya, Tatyana. *Tolstoy as I Knew Him: My Life at Home and at Yasnaya Polyana.* Macmillan, 1948.
"La beauté à la mer et à la montagne." *Femina,* Aug. 1927, pp. 25–30.
"La nueva cervecería de Alvarez." *Mundo Gráfico,* 11 May 1927.
"La peinture Française en Allemagne." *Cahiers d'art,* 1930, pp. 153–57.
"La pose de la première pierre de l'Hôtel Provençal à Juan-les-Pins." *L'Èclaireur du Dimanche,* 20 June 1926, pp. 17–18.
"La quatrième exposition de l'automobile à Nice et ses plus beaux stands." *L'Eclaireur du Dimanche,* 22 Mar. 1925, p. 19.
"La Saison." *Le Figaro,* 5 Apr. 1927, p. 2.
"La Saison à Hendaye." *Femina,* 1930, p. 35.
"La Saison de Juan-les-Pins." *Le Figaro,* 30 May 1926, p. 4.
Lacan, Jacques, and Wladimir Granoff. "Fetishism: The Symbolic, the Imaginary, and the Real." *Perversions: Psychodynamics and Therapy,* edited by Sandor Lorand, Gramercy, 1956, pp. 265–76.
"L'ancien capitaine russe qui a tué Mme. Lord-Vernet aurait frappé par jalousie." *Le Petit Parisien,* 22 Oct. 1927, p. 1.
Laplanche, J., and J.-B. Pontalis. *The Language of Psychoanalysis.* Norton, 1973.
Laporte, Jean. "The Maecenas of Paris Entertains." *Vogue* (American), 1 Sept. 1924, pp. 48–49.
Lardner, John. "If Sparrow Is in Heaven It Must Be Open All Night." *Daily Boston Globe,* 14 June 1941, p. 9.
Lasserre, Jean. "Connaissez-vous Ernest Hemingway grand romancier coureur de terres boxeur et aficionado." *Comoedia,* 7 Nov. 1933, p. 1.
Laver, James. *The House of Haig.* John Haig & Co., 1958.
"Le cinema: Ombres fuyantes." *L'Homme Libre,* 22 July 1932, p. 2.
Le Gallienne, Richard. *The Romance of Perfume.* Richard Hudnut, 1928.
"Le procès de Jeanne d'Arc." *Excelsior,* 15 July 1927, p. 4.
"Le quinze aout a la mer." *Le Monde illustré,* 23 Aug. 1919, p. 605.
Lerner, Preston, and Matt Stone. *History's Greatest Automotive Mysteries, Myths, and Rumors Revealed.* Motorbooks, 2012.
"Les costumes de plage." *Vogue* (French), July 1930, pp. 47, 74.
"Les parfums des grands couturiers rencontrent la faveur des femmes." *Vogue* (French), 1 Dec. 1925, pp. 28–29, 52.

Lever, Maurice. *Isadora: roman d'une vie*. Press de la Renaissance, 1987.
Liedtke, Walter. "Three Paintings by El Greco." *Metropolitan Museum Journal*, vol. 50, 2015, pp. 12–41.
Lorenzi, Fabius. "Croquis de plage." *Le journal amusant*, 14 July 1923, p. 10.
"L'ouverture de l'Hôtel Provençal à Juan-les-Pins." *L'Èclaireur du Dimanche*, 10 July 1927, p. 6.
"Love Cult Colony Cultivates Cabbages in Its Modern Eden; Inmates 'Wear' Nature's Garb." *The Times* (Shreveport, LA), 26 Oct. 1927, p. 1.
Luján, Néstor. "Don Salchichón: Historia de un viejo amigo del hombre." *El Salchichón de Vic: De la despensa del payés a la mesa del rey,* Casa Riere Ordeix, 1992, pp. 3–13.
Lynn, Kenneth. *Hemingway.* Simon and Schuster, 1987.
Lynn-Allen, B. G. *Shot-Gun and Sunlight: The Game Birds of East Africa.* Batchworth Press, 1951.
MacLeish, Archibald. *Letters of Archibald MacLeish, 1907–1982.* Houghton Mifflin, 1983.
———. *Streets in the Moon.* Houghton Mifflin, 1926.
Mairie du Grau-du-Roi. *Un siècle d'histoire: 1900–2002: Le Grau-du-Roi—Port Camargue.* Marie du Grau-du-Roi, 2003.
"Makes Art of Bobbing Hair: Antoine, Who Wanted to Be a Sculptor, Here from Paris to Open Shop." *New York Times*, 12 Mar. 1927, p. 16.
Mandel, Miriam. "Dating the Narration of Hemingway's *A Farewell to Arms:* San Siro." *The Hemingway Review*, vol. 35, no. 1, 2015, pp. 53–62.
———. *Hemingway's* Death in the Afternoon: *The Complete Annotations*. Scarecrow Press, 2002.
Mankowitz, Wolf. *Mazeppa: The Lives, Loves, and Legends of Adah Isaacs Menken.* Stein and Day, 1982.
Mannoni, Octave. *Clefs pour l'imaginaire ou l'autre scène.* Editions de Seuil, 1969.
Marande, Emmanuelle de. *Mandelieu la Napoule: Jadis, naguère, et aujourd'hui.* Editions Serre, 1988.
Maris, Faith. "A Day's Trip through Book Shops of Paris." *New York Herald* (Paris edition), 25 July 1926, p. 3.
Maroto, Pilar Silva. "Extracting the Stone of Madness." *Bosch: The 5th Centenary Exhibition,* edited by Pilar Silva Maroto, Museo del Prado, 2016, pp. 356–63.
———. "*The Haywain* Triptych." *Bosch: The 5th Centenary Exhibition,* edited by Pilar Silva Maroto, Museo del Prado, 2016, pp. 283–91.
Marsh, Terry. *French Riviera: The Green Guide.* Michelin, 2015.
Martin, Richard, and Harold Koda. *Haute Couture.* Metropolitan Museum of Art, 1995.
Masson, Charles. *Museé National du Luxembourg: Catalogue des peintures, sculptures et miniatures.* Musées Nationaux, 1927.
Matson, A. T. *Nandi Resistance to British Rule: The Volcano Erupts.* Cambridge African Studies Center, 1993.
Mazzeo, Tilar J. *The Secret of Chanel No. 5: The Intimate History of the World's Most Famous Perfume.* Harper, 2010.
McCormick, Donald. *One Man's Wars: The Story of Charles Sweeny: Soldier of Fortune.* Arthur Barker, 1972.
McMullin, John [published as "As Seen by Him"]. "Antibes and Venice." *Vogue* (American), 28 Sept. 1929, pp. 68–70, 126, 128.
Meinertzhagen, Richard. *Kenya Diary, 1902–1906.* Oliver and Boyd, 1957.
Mencken, H. L. *Prejudices: Third Series.* Knopf, 1922.
Messent, Peter. *Ernest Hemingway.* St. Martin's, 1992.

Meyers, Jeffrey. *Hemingway: A Biography.* Harper and Row, 1985.
M. H. "Paris Tempts the Summer with New Fads and Fabrics." *Vogue* (American), 1 June 1923, p. 42–44, 126.
Mintler, Catherine R. "Economic Power and the Female Expatriate Consumer Artist in *The Garden of Eden.*" *Teaching Hemingway and Gender,* edited by Verna Kale, Kent State UP, 2016, pp. 115–26.
Mitchell, Perry. "Denies Killing Wives: Suspected Bluebeard in Paris Challenges Police." *Washington Post,* 11 May 1919, p. 10.
Moddelmog, Debra A. "Queer Families in Hemingway's Fiction." *Hemingway and Women: Female Critics and the Female Voice,* edited by Lawrence Broer and Gloria Holland, U of Alabama P, 2002, pp. 173–89.
———. *Reading Desire: In Pursuit of Ernest Hemingway.* Cornell UP, 1999.
———. "'Who's Normal? What's Normal?': Teaching *The Garden of Eden* through the Lens of Normality Studies." *The Hemingway Review,* vol. 30, no. 1, 2010, pp. 142–51.
"The Mode Goes Mannish: Slacks, Shirts, Shorts, among Beach Styles Borrowed from the Men." *New York Times,* 13 Dec. 1931, p. X12.
Monmarché, Marcel. *Les guides bleus: Pyrénées.* Librairie Hachette, 1928.
Moore, Ernst. *Ivory: Scourge of Africa.* Harper, 1931.
Moreira, Peter. *Hemingway on the China Font: His World War II Spy Mission with Martha Gellhorn.* Potomac Books, 2006.
Morley, Christopher. "The Bowling Green." *The Saturday Review of Literature,* 18 Dec. 1928, p. 451.
———. *The Romany Stain.* Doubleday, Page and Co., 1926.
Morrison, Toni. *Playing in the Dark: Whiteness and the Literary Imagination.* Vintage, 1994.
Moss, Peter. *The Race Goes On . . . : A Millennium Retrospect of Racing in Hong Kong.* The Hong Kong Jockey Club, 2000.
Muirhead, Findlay, and Marcel Monmarché, editors. *The Blue Guides: Southern France.* MacMillan, 1926.
Mulligan, Elizabeth. "Lydia Pinkham Was Ahead of Her Time." *Saint Louis Post-Dispatch,* 13 Jan. 1974, pp. 1K, 8K.
Museo del Prado. *Catálogo.* Museo del Prado, 1933.
———. *Catálogo de los cuadros.* Museo del Prado, 1952.
Naether, Carl A. *The Book of the Pigeon.* David McKay, 1944.
Nesmith, Chris. "'The Law of an Ancient God' and the Editing of Hemingway's *Garden of Eden:* The Final Corrected Typescript and Galleys." *The Hemingway Review,* vol. 20, no. 2, 2001, pp. 16–36.
Neumann, Arthur H. *Elephant-Hunting in East Equatorial Africa; Being an Account of Three Years' Ivory-Hunting under Mount Kenia and among the Ndorobo Savages of the Lorugi Mountains, including a Trip to the North End of Lake Rudolph.* Ward, 1898.
"New Process on Sharkskin." *Leavenworth New Era,* 5 Nov. 1920, p. 1.
"Nice Is Becoming A Summer Resort." *New York Herald* (Paris edition), 1 May 1926, p. 7.
Nicholson, Tim. *Isotta-Fraschini: The Noble Pride of Italy.* Ballentine, 1971.
———. *The Isotta Fraschini Tipo 8 Series.* Profile Publications, 1967.
Normand-Romain, Antoinette le. *Rodin: The Gates of Hell.* Musée Rodin, 2002.
"Nos echos." *L'Instransigeant,* 5 Aug. 1920, p. 2.
"Nos echos." *L'Instransigeant,* 30 July 1925, p. 2.

"Nous vivons de plus en plus sur la plage." *Vogue* (French), 1 July 1927, p. 19.
"Nouvelles Inventions." *Le cuir technique,* vol. 17, no. 6, 15 Mar. 1925, pp. 122–23.
"Nude Cult Found in Murder Probe." *Chattanooga Times,* 26 Oct. 1927, p. 3.
"On the Riviera, Whither Fashionables Flock in April." *New York Times,* 26 Apr. 1914, p. SM12.
"Ordeal of an 'Eton Crop': An Onlooker's Glimpse of Dame Fashion's Next Whim for the Hair." *Yorkshire Evening Post,* 6 Mar. 1925, p. 8.
O'Rourke, Sean. *Grace Under Pressure: The Life of Even Shipman.* Harvardwood, 2010.
———. "Who Was with Pascin at the Dôme?" *Journal of Modern Literature,* vol. 26, no. 2, 2003, pp. 160–63.
Ortega Rubio, Juan. *Historia de Madrid y de los pueblos de su provincia.* Imprenta Municipal, 1921.
Ory, Pascal. *L'Invention du bronzage: Essai d'une histoire culturelle.* Editions Complexe, 2008.
Ostrom, Lizzie. *Perfume: A Century of Scents.* Pegasus, 2016.
Ovid. *The Metamorphoses.* Translated by Horace Gregory, Viking, 1958.
Paris, Jean de. "Inauguration à Nîmes de l'Imperator." *Figaro,* 4 Oct. 1930, p. 3.
"Paris Clubs Exclude Idle Aristocrats as Members." *The Washington Post,* 27 Oct. 1921, p. 6.
"Paris Frowns on Boyish Bob: Hairdressers Assert Feminizing Influence of Styles Has Doomed the Vogue of the Close Crop." *New York Times,* 24 Apr. 1927, p. 14.
"Paris Has New Fad: Sharkskin on Hats, Shoes." *Des Moines Sunday Register,* 17 Oct. 1926, p. G5.
Partridge, Eric. *A Dictionary of Slang and Unconventional English.* 3rd ed., Routledge and Kegan Paul, 1937.
Payne, Stanley G. *Spain's First Democracy: The Second Republic, 1931–1936.* U of Wisconsin P, 1993.
Peters, K. J. "The Thematic Integrity of *The Garden of Eden.*" *The Hemingway Review,* vol. 10, no. 2, 1991, pp. 17–29.
Philips, Arthur, and Henry F. Morris. *Marriage Laws in Africa.* Oxford UP, 1971.
Phillipps-Wolley, Clive. *Big Game Shooting.* Vol. 1, Longmans Green, 1894.
Picard, Gaston. "Un Eden à sauver: Plaidoyer pour Théoule." *Comoedia,* 8 Jan. 1927, p. 3.
Pickard, Henri. "A Trade in Beauty." *Cincinnati Enquirer,* 23 Mar. 1923, p. 6.
Poiret, Paul. "Will Skirts Disappear?: A Thirty-year Prophecy by Paris Arbiter of Fashion." *Forum,* vol. 77, no. 1, 1 Jan. 1927, pp. 30–40.
Powell, Tamara M. "Lilith Started It!: Catherine as Lilith in *The Garden of Eden.*" *The Hemingway Review,* vol. 15, no. 2, 1996, pp. 79–88.
Praviel, Armand. *Biarritz, Pau, and the Basque Country.* Medici Society, 1928.
"Prospects for Settlers in British East Africa." *The Southern Reporter,* 18 May 1905, p. 4.
Proust, Marcel. *Remembrance of Things Past.* Vol. 1, Random House, 1934.
Prunier, Simone. *La Maison: The History of Prunier's.* Longmans, Green, and Co., 1957.
Putnam, Ann. "On Defiling Eden: The Search for Eve in the Garden of Sorrows." *Hemingway and Women: Female Critics and the Female Voice,* edited by Lawrence Broer and Gloria Holland, U of Alabama P, 2002, pp. 109–30.
Quétel, Claude. *History of Syphilis.* Translated by Judith Braddock and Brian Pike, Johns Hopkins UP, 1990.
Quintanilla, Paul. *Waiting at the Shore: Art, Revolution, War, and Exile in the Life of the Spanish Artist Luis Quintanilla.* Sussex Academic Press, 2014.
Raab, David. *Battle of the Piave: Death of the Austro-Hungarian Army, 1918.* Dorrance, 2003.
Raeburn, John. *Fame Became of Him: Hemingway as Public Writer.* Indiana UP, 1984.
"Resorts on Riviera Delightful in Summer." *New York Herald* (Paris edition), 16 Aug. 1925, p. 4.

Raynal, Maurice. "Les Arts." *L'Intransigeant,* 23 May 1923, p. 2.
Reynolds, Michael. *Hemingway: The American Homecoming.* Blackwell, 1992.
———. *Hemingway: The Final Years.* Norton, 1999.
———. *Hemingway: The Paris Years.* Norton, 1999.
———. *Hemingway's Reading 1910–1940: An Inventory.* Princeton UP, 1981.
———. *The Young Hemingway.* Norton, 1986.
Reynolds, Quentin. *They Fought for the Sky: The Dramatic Story of the First War in the Sky.* Rinehart, 1959.
Richardson, John. *A Life of Picasso: The Triumphant Years, 1917–1932.* Knopf, 2007.
Richter, Charles de. "La Riviera mondaine." *La Rampe,* 15 Feb. 1927, pp. 62–63.
Río López, Ángel del. *Plaza Mayor de Madrid: Cuatrocientos años de historia.* La Librería, 2016.
Rittenhouse, Anne. "Dress." *Atlanta Constitution,* 28 Dec. 1921, p. 8.
"Riviera Developers Plan a Palm Beach at Juan-les-Pins to Rival Deauville." *New York Times,* 15 Feb. 1925, p. 1.
Riviere, Joan. "Womanliness as Masquerade." *Formulations of Fantasy,* edited by Victor Burgin, James Donald, and Cora Kaplan, Methuen, 1986, 35–44.
Rivkin, Mike. *Big-Game Fishing Headquarters: A History of the IGFA.* IGFA Press, 2005.
Roberts, Charley, and Charles P. Hess. *Charles Sweeny, the Man Who Inspired Hemingway.* McFarland, 2017.
Roberts, Mary Louise. *Civilization without Sexes: Reconstructing Gender in Postwar France, 1917–1927.* U of Chicago P, 1994.
Roe, Steven Charles. *The Artist as Bluebeard: Hemingway Critiques Hemingway in* The Garden of Eden *Manuscript.* 1994. U of British Columbia, PhD dissertation.
———. "Opening Bluebeard's Closet: Writing and Aggression in Hemingway's *The Garden of Eden* Manuscript." *The Hemingway Review,* vol. 12, no. 1, 1992, pp. 52–66.
Rohy, Valerie. *Anachronism and Its Others: Sexuality, Race, Temporality.* SUNY Press, 2009.
Roosevelt, Theodore. *African Game Trails.* Narrative Press, 2001.
Ross, Lillian. "How Do You Like It Now, Gentlemen?" *New Yorker,* 13 May 1950, pp. 36–62.
Rothschild, Deborah. "Masters of the Art of Living." *Making It New: The Art and Style of Sara and Gerald Murphy,* edited by Deborah Rothschild, U of California P, 2007, pp. 11–87.
Ruark, Robert. "Stupidity Is Dooming African Garden of Eden." *The Press Democrat* (Santa Rosa, CA), 14 Feb. 1956, p. 4.
"Russian Captain Admits Killing American's Wife: Says She Tried to Stop Him Ending Own Life." *Chicago Daily Tribune,* 21 Oct. 1927, p. 7.
"Russian Princess, Reduced to Poverty, Drinks Poison on Promenade at Nice." *New York Times,* 26 Apr. 1925, p. 1.
Saks Fifth Avenue. "Announcing the Return of Antoine." *New York Times,* 2 Dec. 1927, p. 5.
Sanford, Marcelline Hemingway. *At the Hemingways.* Little Brown, 1962.
Scafella, Frank. "Clippings from *The Garden of Eden.*" *The Hemingway Review,* vol. 7, no. 1, 1987, pp. 20–29.
Schillings, C. G. *In Wildest Africa.* Vol. 1, Hutchinson and Co., 1907.
Schmid, Howard A. *And a River Went out of Eden: The Estuarial Motif in Hemingway's* The Garden of Eden. 1994. U of Montana, PhD dissertation.
"Scientists Motor to a Mystery Land: Century-Old Secrets Wrested from Heart of Ancient Mongolia by Famous Little Auto: A Garden of Eden Found." *New York Times,* 11 Nov. 1923, p. S8.

Segrave, Kerry. *Suntanning in 20th Century America*. McFarland, 2005.
Segrè, Claudio G. *Italo Balbo: A Fascist Life*. U of California P, 1987.
Sénat [of France]. "Rapport." No. 94., 26 Feb. 1929, 1–2.
"Septembre sur la Côte d'Argent: Les plaisirs et les sports alternant à Biarritz." *L'Intransigeant*, 9 Sept. 1935, p. 2.
Seymour, James William Davenport, editor. *History of the American Field Service in France, "Friends of France," 1914–1917*. Vol. 1, Houghton Mifflin, 1920.
"Sharkskin Is Favored by Fashion: Dresses and Jackets of New Material Popular for Summer." *Mason City Globe-Gazette*, 15 July 1936, p. 6.
Sheean, Vincent. "Love of French Spurs Aviators: Case for American Flyers in Morocco Given." *Los Angeles Times*, 14 Nov. 1925, p. 5.
———. *Personal History: Youth and Revolution: The Story of One Person's Relationship to Living History*. Garden City Publishing Co., 1937.
———. "Yankee Air Unit Hit: Part in Rif War Denounced: Bombing Unarmed Villages Condemned as Crime by Statement." *Los Angeles Times*, 18 Oct. 1925, p. 1.
———. "Yankee Flyers Regret Bombs: Americans in Morocco Slay Women and Children: Discover Truth Only after Several Bombardments: Sheshuan Objective Proves to Be Noncombatant Town." *Los Angeles Times*, 13 Nov 1925, p. 4.
Shipman, Evan. "Mazeppa." *The New Caravan*, edited by Alfred Kreymborg, Lewis Mumford, and Paul Rosenfeld, Norton, 1936, pp. 290–96.
Silbergleid, Robin. "Into Africa: Narrative and Authority in Hemingway's *The Garden of Eden*." *The Hemingway Review*, vol. 27, no. 2, 2008, pp. 96–116.
Simien, Frédéric. *Memoire en images: Le Grau-du-Roi*. Alan Sutton, 2007.
Sinclair, Gail. "Carol and Ernest Hemingway: The Letters of Loss." *The Hemingway Review*, vol. 24.1, no. 1, 2004, pp. 37–48.
"Skeleton Called the Earliest Modern Man Is Dug Up in Kenya and Removed Intact." *New York Times*, 12 Jan. 1929, p. 9.
"Smart Women Now Cultivate the Sun-Bronzed Complexion." *Ithaca Journal News*, 30 Jan. 1928, p. 2.
Smith, Rex Alan. *The Carving of Mount Rushmore*. Abbeville, 1985.
"The Social World." *Chicago Tribune* (Paris edition), 23 June 1927, p. 4.
"Soleil, Soleil." *Vogue* (French), Oct. 1927, p. 35.
Solomon, Barbara Probst. "Where's Papa?: Scribner's *The Garden of Eden* Is Not the Novel Hemingway Wrote." *The New Republic*, 9 Mar. 1987, pp. 30–34.
Spilka, Mark. *Hemingway's Quarrel with Androgyny*. U of Nebraska P, 1990.
Stamelman, Richard. *Perfume: Joy, Obsession, Scandal, Sin: A Cultural History of Fragrance from 1750 to the Present*. Rizzoli, 2006.
Stigand, C. H. *Hunting the Elephant in Africa: And Other Recollections of Thirteen Years' Wanderings*. Macmillan, 1913.
Stoller, Robert. *Observing the Erotic Imagination*. Yale UP, 1985.
Stoneback, H. R. "From the Rue Saint-Jacques to the Pass of Roland to the 'Unfinished Church on the Edge of the Cliff.'" *The Hemingway Review*, vol. 6, no. 1, 1986, pp. 2–29.
———. "Memorable Eggs 'in Danger of Getting Cold' and Mackerel 'Perilous with Edge-Level Juice': Eating in Hemingway's Garden." *The Hemingway Review*, vol. 8, no. 2, 1989, pp. 22–29.
———. "Pilgrimage Variations: Hemingway's Sacred Landscapes." *Religion and Literature*, vol. 35, nos. 2–3, 2003, pp. 49–65.

———. *Reading Hemingway's* The Sun Also Rises. Kent State UP, 2007.
Strong, Amy. "'Go to Sleep, Devil': The Awakening of Catherine's Feminism in *The Garden of Eden.*" *Hemingway and Women: Female Critics and the Feminine Voice,* edited by Lawrence Broer and Gloria Holland, U of Alabama P, 2002, pp. 190–203.
———. *Race and Identity in Hemingway's Fiction.* Palgrave Macmillan, 2008.
Strychacz, Thomas. *Hemingway's Theaters of Masculinity.* LSU Press, 2003.
Sueiro, Daniel. "Hemingway o la solidaridad." *ABC,* 19 Aug. 1959, p. 5.
"The Sun-Bronzed Complexion Latest Fad of the Smart." *The Wisconsin State Journal,* 22 Jan. 1928, p. 4.
"Sun Tan Is So Smart!" *Wilkes-Barre Record,* 28 Dec. 1928, p. 11.
"The Sun-Tan Vogue Makes Back and Arms Important." *The Daily Argus-Leader,* Sioux Falls, S. D., 1 Aug. 1928, p. 5.
Tadié, Jean-Yves. *Marcel Proust.* Translated by Euan Cameron, Viking, 2000.
"Tailleur in Big Role: O'Rossen Stresses the Simple Tailor-Made—English Materials are Featured." *New York Times,* 18 Feb 1934, p. X9.
Tériade, E. "Documentaire sur la jeune peinture." *Cahiers d'art,* 1930, pp. 69–84.
"That Eton Crop." *Northern Daily Mail,* 1 Sept. 1926, p. 5.
Thierry de Ville d'Avray, Henri-Charles. *Histoire de Cannes: Documents et détails sur la Provence.* F. Robaudy, 1909.
Titler, Dale. *The Day the Red Baron Died.* Ballantine Books, 1970.
Tolstoy, Leo. *Anna Karenina.* Translated by Constance Garnett, Barnes and Noble Classics, 2003.
———. *Anna Karenina.* Translated by Louise Maude and Aylmer Maude, Vintage, 2010.
———. *Anna Karenina.* Translated by Nathan Dole, Thomas Crowell, 1914.
———. *Anna Karenina.* Translated by Richard Pevear and Larissa Volokhonsky, Penguin, 2012.
———. *Anna Karenina.* Translated by Rosemary Edmonds, Penguin, 1978.
Torres, R. Peyronnet de. "Michel Detroyat, virtuose de l'air." *L'Intransigeant,* 28 Sept. 1933, p. 2.
Train, Daniel. "'Reading Slowly to Make It Last': Reading Readers in Hemingway's *The Garden of Eden.*" *The Hemingway Review,* vol. 36, no. 1, 2016, pp. 31–48.
Trévières, Pierre de. "La chasse aux requins." *Le Pêle-mêle,* 6 Feb. 1927, p. 17.
Troyat, Henri. *Tolstoy.* Translated by Nancy Amphoux, Doubleday, 1967.
Tucci, Douglass Shand. *The Art of the Scandal: The Life and Times of Isabella Stewart Gardner.* HarperCollins, 1997.
Tuohy, Ferdinand. "The Golden Fleece on the Riviera: Types of a Hard-up Season: The Cromwell Roaders and the Montparnassians." *The Graphic,* 26 Feb. 1927, p. 312.
Turudich, Daniela. *Art Deco Hair: Hairstyles from the 1920s & 1930s.* Streamline Press, 2013.
Twomey, Lisa. "Ernest Hemingway—¿Amigo de España?" *Hemingway's Spain: Imagining the Spanish World,* edited by Carl Eby and Mark Cirino, Kent State UP, 2016, pp. 28–43.
"Un danger public: La fraude sur les similaires d'absinthe." *Mercure Africain,* 5 Nov. 1924, p. 1374.
"Une decoration au Colonel Sweeney" [sic]. *Paris-soir,* 3 Feb. 1926, p. 4.
"Une formule nouvelle de l'élégance féminine." *Vogue* (French), 1 Sept. 1927, p. 10.
Updike, John. "The Sinister Sex." *New Yorker,* 30 June 1986, pp. 85–88.
Vaill, Amanda. *Everybody Was So Young: Gerald and Sara Murphy: A Lost Generation Love Story.* Broadway Books, 1998.
Van Gogh, Vincent. *The Complete Letters of Vincent Van Gogh.* Vol. 3, Bulfinch Press, 1958.
Vega, Jesus E. "The Influence of Spanish Writers on Hemingway." *The Hemingway Review,* vol. 39, no. 2, 2020, pp. 63–77.

Viertel, Peter. *Dangerous Friends: At Large with Hemingway and Huston in the Fifties.* Doubleday, 1992.

Ward, James Rowland. *Rowland Ward's Records of Big Game with Their Distribution Characteristics, Dimensions, Weights and Horn and Tusk Measurements.* Edited by Guy Dollman and J. B. Burlace, Ward, 1928.

Weber, Ronald. *News of Paris: American Journalists in the City of Light between the Wars.* Ivan R. Dee, 2006.

Weiss, Pierre. "L'exploit magnifique." *Revue Aéronautique de France,* July 1927, p. 4.

Widower, A. Grass. "Friday to Monday—and Juan-les-Pins." *The Illustrated Sporting and Dramatic News,* 20 June 1925, p. 809.

Wildenstein, Georges. *Paul Gauguin.* Vol. 1, Éditions Les Beaux Arts, 1964.

Williams, Valentine. "New-Rich and New-Poor on the Riviera." *The Living Age,* 4 July 1925, p. 52.

Willingham, Kathy. *Ernest Hemingway and the Surrealist Garden.* 1995. Texas Tech U, PhD dissertation.

———. "Hemingway's *The Garden of Eden:* Writing with the Body." *The Hemingway Review,* vol. 12, no. 2, 1993, pp. 46–61.

Winnicott, D. W. *Playing and Reality.* Routledge, 1989.

Wittels, Betina. *Absinthe, Sip of Seduction.* Speck Press, 2008.

Wolfe, Cary. "Father's, Lovers, and Friend Killers: Rearticulating Gender and Race via Species in Hemingway." *boundary 2,* vol. 29, no. 1, 2002, pp. 223–57.

Wolfe, Thomas. *Look Homeward Angel: A Story of a Buried Life.* Modern Library, 1929.

Wrangel, Baron George. "European Chatter." *The Cincinnati Enquirer,* 19 Apr. 1931, p. 8F.

Wyatt, David. *Hemingway, Style, and the Art of Emotion.* Cambridge UP, 2015.

Zdatny, Steve. *Fashion, Work, and Politics in Modern France.* Palgrave Macmillan, 2006.

———. "Hairstyles." *Encyclopedia of Clothing and Fashion,* edited by Valerie Steele, vol. 2, Scribner's, 2005, pp. 161–65.

INDEX

Page references in *italics* refer to illustrations.

ABC, 120, 141, 299, 305
Abd el-Krim, 142, 146, 291
Abraham, Karl, 233
absinthe, 61, 89–90, 99, 101, 106–7, 224, 328–31, 333; Pernod, 84–85, 88, 109, 124, 157, 327, 330
Across the River and into the Trees (Hemingway): allusions/character inspirations in, 130, 146, 240, 275; aristocratic titles in, 180; fetishistic elements in, 31, 37, 41, 50n31, 96, 307; French jingoism in, 151; themes of, 338; Torcello in, 300–301; *Vogue* in, 48n11
Africa: birds of, 253–54; British East, 145, 191–92, 204–5, 219, 223, 228, 231–32, 254; Edenic nature of, 4, 204–5, 254, 271, 288–89, 308; German East, 188, 204–5, 231–32; Hemingway's plane crashes in, 57–58, 205, 242–43, 250; Hemingway's safaris, 46, 64–65, 150, 204–6, 212n1, 233–34, 247, 250; landscape of, 150, 204–5, 213, 247–48, 253; memory/deep past and, 13, 164, 322; North, 309, 311, 326; Pyrenees, 116; safari clothes and, 177–78. *See also* colonialism; Debba; elephants; Kenya
Aigues-Mortes, 10–13, *11, 13,* 15, 28, 266, 312
airplanes/aviation: in Africa, 142, 146, 152, 225, 233–34, 289, 291, 310; Australian Flying Corps (WWI), 302; *chasse* pilots (WWI), 133; "chivalry of the air," 192, 290–92; Golden Age of Flight, 192, 199, 275–76, 326; Hemingway's plane crashes, 57–58, 64, 205, 242, 250, 289; knowledge of winds and, 34; Lafayette Escadrille (WWI/Rif War), 145–46, 291, 310; pilots, 32, 34, 64, 133, 142, 145–47, 192, 194n2, 203, 225, 237, 275–76, 291, 302, 310, 326, 397; Royal Air Force, 145, 155n5, 286, 314; Spad (WWI plane), 203, 237–38, 276; warplanes, 290, 302

Alba, Duchess of, 121
alcohol. *See* absinthe; champagne; food and drink; wine
Alfonso XII, King, 156
Alfonso XIII, King, 84, 112
Allen, Frederick Lewis, 37–38
Alvarez, José, 137n1
Álvarez del Vayo, Julio, 142
American Ambulance Field Service (AFS), 126–27
American Mercury, 185
American Museum of Natural History, 315–16
Amory, Cleveland, 289
Anderson, Sherwood, 49n24, 169
Andrews, Roy Chapman, 315–16
animals: baboons, 204, 214; beaver, 311; "crazy pigeon," 269; cuckoos, 269–70; dogs, 233–34, 242–43; donkeys, 167; francolin birds, 253–54; hoopoe birds, 118; kongoni (antelope), 213; nightingales/larks, 309–10; pheasant/snipe/woodcock, 282; rabbit, 125; seals/sea mammals, 308; vultures, 215, *216*. *See also* cats/lions; elephants; horses
Antheil, George, 241
Anthony, Katherine, 319n3
Apollinaire, Guillaume, 99, 238
Araquistáin Quevedo, Luis, 142
Arles, 14–15, *15,* 25, 30
Arnaud, Claude, 261
Art Institute of Chicago, 93, 328
Atlantic Monthly, 297–98
Australian Flying Corps, 302
Avignon, 29, 33–34, 67, 87
Avocourt Wood, 126

Baedeker guides, 176, 208, 233
Bairnsfather, Bruce, 300
Baker, Carlos, 96–97, 246n5

Baker, Josephine, 33, 51–52, 144, 211
Balbo, Italo, 325–26, 333n6
Balestier, Wolcott, 308
"Ballad of Lydia Pinkham," 276–78
ballet: American Ballet Theatre, 241; Ballets Russes, 48n12, 238–41, 286; based on Byron's "Mazeppa," 215; *The Capital of the World*, 241; *Les soirées de Paris*, 239–40; Murphys as "figures in a ballet," 240
bars, cafés, and restaurants: Bar Basque (Biarritz), 102, 108–9; Brasserie Lipp (Paris), 75–76, 98, 112–13, 188, 225; Buffet Italiano (Madrid), 142–43, 154nn2–3; Café Continental (Le Grau-du-Roi), 14; Café de Flore (Paris), 76, 98; Café des Allées (Cannes), 178, 185, 225, 279, 299; Café les Deux Magots (Paris), 75–76, 92, 98–99, 325, 330; Café Weber (Paris), 112–13; Closerie des Lilas (Paris), 93, 98; Harry's Bar (Venice), 332; Maison Prunier (Paris), 113, 179, 199–200, 201n5, 252; Sonny's Bar (Biarritz), 101–2
Barnes, Djuna, 98–99, 266
Barney, Natalie, 99, 266
Baroja, Pio, 114–15, 137n3
Barry, Ellen, 20
Basque coast, 82, 84, 88–90, 96, 327. See also Hendaye Plage
"Battler, The" (Hemingway), 22
Baudelaire, Charles, 42, 85
Beach, Sylvia, 183, 319n8
Beaumont, Étienne de, Comte, 23, 180, 239–40. See also Bonnin de la Bonninière de Beaumont family
Beaumont, Monique de, 240–41, 246n5. See also Bonnin de la Bonninière de Beaumont family
Beaumont, Paule, 240–41. See also Bonnin de la Bonninière de Beaumont family
Beaux, Ernest, 105
Bedwell, Bettina, 20, 141, 292
Bell, Walter "Karamojo," 205, 234, 253
Belmonte, Juan, 93
belote (card game), 303
Berenson, Bernard, 12, 16, 134–35, 289
Berlin, Irving, 243
Biarritz: fashions in, 21, 25, 84; overdevelopment of, 83–84, 101–2, 108
bicycling, 9, 33–34, 68, 87, 98, 118, 207, 256, 292, 332

Binswanger, Ludwig, 233
Bisch, Louis, 220
Bishop, John Peale, 23
"bitch," 157, 173, 185, 215
Black Hills, 143–44
Blas Vega, José, 125
Blixen-Finecke, Bror von, 65, 205, 275
Bleuler, Eugen, 233
Bluebeard, 58–59, 213
Blue Guide, 16, 34, 118, 175–76, 185–86, 290
Blunt, David Enderby, 255–56
blushing, 180, 202, 217
boats/ships, 12, 14, 48n3, 93, 178, 217, 237, 278–79; destroyers, 18, 200, 275–76, 290–91
Bonaparte, Pauline, 249
Bonnin de la Bonninière de Beaumont family, 310–11
Bookman, 144
bookplates, 238–39, 241
Booth, Howard, 119
Borrow, George Henry, 117–18, 137n4
Bosch, Hieronymus, 16, 111, 129–30, 140, 274–75; *Extraction of the Stone of Madness*, 130, *131*; *The Garden of Earthly Delights*, 3, 17, 118, 121–24, *122–23*, 130, 275, 301, 305; *The Haywain*, 129–30, *132*; *The Temptation of Saint Anthony*, 130, 134
Boston Herald, 277
Boswell, James, 62
Boulton, Prudence, 210
Bow, Clara, 179, 286
Boyle, Kay, 106, 292
Brague, Harry, 337, 342
Braque, Georges, 16, 135, 268–69, 287
Breit, Harvey, 66–67, 97, 121, 242, 294, 341
Brenan, Gerald, 118
Brentano's bookstore, 183
Breton, André, 98, 240
Britishisms, 224, 228
British Museum, 255
Bronson, Edgar Beecher, 204
Brooklyn Bridge, 288
Brooks Brothers, 215
Bruccoli, Matthew, 246n5
Bruegel, Pieter, the Elder, 111, 130, 274–75
Bryant, Louise, 151
Buchanan, Lucile, 74
Buen Retiro (Madrid), 156
Bugatti T35 (car), 67–68, 127–29, *128*, 133, 137n8, 163, 167, 179, 225, 242

bullfighting: famous matadors, 93, 125, 261, 321; Hemingway and, 56, 95, 246n1, 261, 342; in Madrid, 65, 111, 137n2, 141; in Nîmes, 34–35; visual depictions of, 95, 134, 246n1, 261, 285, 286
Bunyan, John, 224
Burke, Edmund, 62
Burnett, Robert, 51, 228
Burns, Louis, 190
Burton, Richard Francis, 119
Burwell, Rose Marie: on Hemingway's letters to Lanham, 343n5, 343n9; reading of *GOE*, 40, 117, 208–9, 259, 294; ur-text theory, 295n4, 338, 343n13
Busch, Wilhelm M., 110n5
Butler, Judith, 110n12
Byron, Lord: "The Island," 62, 63n4; "Mazeppa," 63n4, 215–16, *217*, 320

Cagnes-sur-Mer, 176, 193
Cahiers d'art, 228
Callaghan, Morley, 201n5
Calvinists, 210–11, 220
Camargue, 10, 115, 118. *See also* Le Grau-du-Roi
Campbell, Thomas, 309–10
canals, 10, *11, 12, 13,* 14, 27, 244–45
"Canary for One, A" (Hemingway), 220
Cancionera (Madrid), 114
Cannes, 16, 19, 23–24, 83–84, 101, 161, 175, 193, 274; Edenic nature of, 3
Cantor, Eddie, 285–86, *285*
Cap d'Antibes, 20, 22–24, 32, 139, 176, 225, 237, 240, 274; Eden Roc, 3
"Capital of the World, The" (Hemingway), 241
capital punishment, 59, 186–87, 195, 223
Carlton Hotel (Biarritz), 102
Carmelites, 114
cars/driving: Amilcar, 137n8; Cadillac, 190, 210; corniches (cliffside roads), 185–86, 208, 241; dangers of, 128–29, 133, 137n9, 139, 147, 185–86, 210, 305, 332; Duesenberg, 128–29; Edenic countryside and, 176, 183; Hispana Suiza, 112, 331–32; Lancia, 189, 314–15; Mercedes-Benz, 314–15; N7 (road), 207–8, 299; Spain's roads, 112, 167–68. *See also* Bugatti T35 (car); Isotta Fraschini (car)
casinos: in Hendaye Plage, 81, *82*; in Juan-les-Pins, 23–24, 175, 191, 199; in Le Grau-du-Roi, *10–11,* 24–25, *25*; in Palavas-les-Flots, 16

castration: anxiety about, 37, 50n42, 100, 131, 259–60, 277; symbolic, 40, 131, 195, 226, 230. *See also* female phallus
Cathedral of Santa Maria Assunta (Torcello), 300–301
Catherine of Siena, Saint, 34
Catherine the Great, 310, 316
Catholic Church, 25–26, 34, 114, 141, 210–11, 220, 305–6. *See also* Crusades
cats/lions: cat, 45, 59–60, 153, 157; kitten/kitty, 30, 45–46, 49n24, 54, 59–60, 237; lion, 58–60, 65–67, 99, 259, 288
Cerutti family, 108
Cervecería Alvarez (Madrid), 111–12, 114, 137n1, 143
Cézanne, Paul, 15–16, 94, 129, 135, 137n3, 158, 279
Chacón, Antonio, 125–26
champagne, 16, 124, 151, 179, 189, 207, 290; Bollinger, 199–200; Lanson, 108; Perrier-Jouët, 61, 108, 256–57, 287
Chanel, Gabrielle "Coco," 19, 32, 48n12, 49n26, 84, 101, 104–5, 177, 239–40
Chanel No. 5 (perfume), 104–5
change: as both/and, 136, 172, 198, 222, 267–68, 270, 312–13, 318; endless, 154, 209–10, 335; fetishistic excitement and, 30–31, 33, 65–67, 76–77; mutual/shared, 193, 252, 311, 318; ominous/sinister undertones of, 87, 92, 220–21; physical manifestations of, 104, 107, 152, 156, 190, 193, 256; psychological charge of, 30–31, 40–41, 52, 64, 181, 263–64; ritual questions and, 52–53, 174, 176, 252; wind as symbol of, 34–35; wrenching, 157, 209–10, 214, 267–68; writing as experience of, 207. *See also* sea changes
Charenton, 85, 249
Charlemagne, King, 96
Charleston dance craze, 144
Chasseur Français, 141
Chemin des Dames, 126
Cherokee, 250
chess, 202
Chevalier, Maurice, 144
Chicago Tribune, 141, 285, 292
"Christmas Gift, The" (Hemingway), 212n2
Cierplikowski, Antoine, Monsieur, 101, 110n14
Cigognes, 237–38
Circuito Nacional de Firmes Especiales, 112
"Clark's Fork Valley, Wyoming, The" (Hemingway), 48n11

clippings. *See* press clippings
Cocteau, Jean, 35, 48n12, 99, 101, 238–40, 261–62
Cody, William T. "Buffalo Bill," 329
Coleridge, Samuel, 319n2
colonialism: critique of, 4, 68, 147, 151–52, 223, 228, 231–32; Edenic naming of species and, 253–54; extractive, 146–47, 255, 255, 271–72, 272, 292; French jingoism and, 150–52; romantic, 51; settler, 140, 143–44, 191, 204–5, 223, 248, 288–89, 314; tourism and, 161, 176, 311; in United States, 143–44, 190–91. *See also* Africa; Kenya; Morocco
"comic," 334–35
Comité des forges, 244–45
Comley, Nancy, 40, 148, 158, 208
Comoedia, 4, 161
consumerism: automobiles 127–28, 179, 315, 332; fashion, 150, 177; luxury food and drink, 108, 124, 163, 178, 199–200, 207; luxury hotels, 35, 65, 81, 107, 119–20; and social class 180. *See also* wealth
Cook, James, Captain, 188–89, 228
Coolidge, Calvin, 143–44, *143*
Cooper, Dick, 275
Cooper, Duff, 309
corruption, 68–69, 133, 208, 222, 224, 318–19
Cossacks, 310, 315–16
Côte d'Azur. *See* French Riviera (Côte d'Azur)
Council of Trent, 116
Coutinho, Domingos António de Sousa, 116
"craziness": in art, 130; and *chasse* pilots, 133; colors and, 15, 242; compulsive cruelty and, 106–7; "crazy pigeon," 269; dysphoria/disorientation, 242, 321, 334–35; erraticism as sign of, 249, 265, 329–30; fetishism as work of, 236, 252, 330–31; hatred and, 305; mental deterioration and, 220, 243–44; "monstrous" crime and, 303; postwar era and, 270; riven ego and, 211–12, 222, 229–30; as something hurried, 251–52, 335. *See also* sanatoriums/asylums
creativity: conflicting forces and, 3, 69, 208–9; destruction and, 18–19, 70, 140, 193, 200–201, 209, 213–14, 249, 276, 293, 296, 321; frustrated, 55–56, 93–94, 117, 157–58, 164, 213, 229; gender/sexual experimentation and, 139, 208–9, 231, 249; "inventing" and, 18, 154, 157, 172, 209, 222, 243, 267; jealousy of, 56–57, 139, 164, 263; people's lives as

artistic medium for, 36, 62, 117, 158, 267; procreation and, 62–63, 149, 157–58, 208–9, 230–31, 269, 274, 277, 300, 304, 314, 330
Croix de Guerre, 135, 145
Crusades, 12–13, 28
Cuba, 135, 321, 337, 340–42
Cuir de Russie (perfume), 104–5
Custer, George Armstrong, 329
Cyber, Madame, 39

Daisy Miller (James), 220
Dale, Philip Marshall, 231
Danby-Smith, Valerie. *See* Hemingway, Valerie Danby-Smith (daughter-in-law of EH)
Dangerous Summer, The (Hemingway), 4, 137n2, 342–43
D'Annunzio, Gabriele, 325, 333n6
Dante Alighieri, 42
Darrow, Clarence, 185
David and Goliath, 224, 253, 307
Death in the Afternoon (Hemingway): on Madrid/Prado, 99, 111, 115, 125, 142; morality/immorality in, 53; publication/text of, 134, 167, 170n5, 246n1, 342; real people/events in, 125, 261, 266; syphilis in, 12–13, 235n5; on writing and the "iceberg principle," 92, 137n4, 256, 272
Deauville, 16, 25, 32, 49n26, 51, 84, 101, 175
Debba, 63, 66–67, 183, 186, 199, 206, 219, 273–74. *See also* Kamba identity
Decazes, Duke of, 320
Degas, Edgar, 85
de la Claras, Marquise, 102
del Sarto, Andrea, 16, 111, 120–21, 152
depression/despair, 36, 156, 224, 226, 245, 307. *See also* remorse
Derain, André, 16, 239, 265–66
Desbois, Jules, *148*, *149*
Deschanel, Paul, 249
desire: agency of, 47, 53, 64, 173–74; compulsivity of, 60–61, 100, 139, 153, 227; consent vs. coercion and, 76, 224, 226, 251, 263–64, 265, 311, 326, 334; discovered, 329; Hemingway as agent of, 168–69, 222; hunger as metaphor for, 16–17, 28–29; inexplicable nature of, 65–66; and merging with other half, 31, 42–43, *43*, 47, 76–77; oscillation of, 197, 264; perversion and, 198; "true," 197; unsatiated, 76–77. *See also* lesbian desire; sex/sexuality

destruction: biblical/locust, 150, 182, 195–96, 248; burning of manuscripts, 26, 59, 213, 223, 229, 231, 281, 294, 296, 299, 303, 305, 312; compensation for, 229; creation and, 18–19, 193, 200–201, 208–9, 213–14, 276, 293, 296, 321; destroyers (ships) and, 18, 200, 275–76, 290–91; driving's dangers and, 128–29, 133, 139, 147, 185–86, 210, 305, 332; looming, 70, 220–21, 224; loss and, 196, 214, 219, 243, 259; massacre/killing and, 182, 188, 207, 223, 232, 243, 260, 262, 272, 291–92, 332; pleasure as cause of, 100, 219; press clippings' potential of, 56–60, 70; rebuilding/cure and, 140, 218, 281, 300–301, 330; "ruin" and, 18–19, 211, 287, 313; self-, 58, 70, 147, 212, 332–33; tossing/tearing up manuscripts, 207, 229–30, 293, 339, 342; verbal insults and, 286–88
Détroyat, Michel, 275–76
devil, 3, 18, 63, 101, 211–12, 330–31. *See also* hell
Diaghilev, Sergei, 48n12, 99, 238–40, 262
Dial, 144
Dietrich, Marlene, 275
"Dilatory Domicile," 288
Diliberto, Gioia, 219
Dinesen, Isak (Karen Blixen), 65
dinosaur eggs, 315–16
disavowal, 37, 40, 45, 69, 124, 156–57, 198, 230, 268, 313, 322. *See also* fetishism
Dole, Nathan Haskell, 282
Domínguín, Luis Miguel, 137n2, 321, 342
Donaldson, Walter, 144
Don Cossack Choir, 316
Dorman-Smith, Chink, 97
Dos Passos, John, 20, 23, 146, 154n3, 292
Doughty, Charles Montagu, 167, 170n5
Dowson, Ernest, 278, 280
Dreyer, Carl Theodor, 312
Dufy, Raoul, 16, 265–67, 297
Dugdale, R. L., 185
Dumas, Alexandre, 107, 116, 288
Duncan, David Douglas, 286
Duncan, Isadora, 128, 137n8
Dunikowski, Xavier, 101
Dunoyer de Segonzac, André, 16, 266–67, 297
Durville, André, 32
Durville, Gaston, 32

Earle, David, 57
Eastman, Max, 23, 144

ecstasy, 100, 157–58, 163
Eden: allegorizing readings of novel and, 3–4, 129, 140, 157, 209–11, 324, 335; in Bosch's paintings, 122–24, *122–23*, 130, *132*; forbidden fruit and, 58–59; naming of beasts in, 254, 271; original site of, 289, 315–16; profound loss and, 157, 196, 271, 337
Edenic places: French Riviera, 10; Garden of Hôtel Biron, 3, 42; Gobi Desert, 316–17; Grasse, 105; Hendaye, 83; Juan-les-Pins, 175–76; Kenya, 254; La Napoule/Théoule, 4, 161; Le Grau-du-Roi, 14, 16, 24, 31; Magadi Desert, 204; Ngorongoro Crater, 4, 288–89, 308; Novastoshnah, 308; Saint-Jean-de-Luz, 108; Zarathustra colony, 262. *See also* Africa
Edmonds, Rosemary, 282
Edward VII, King, 84
eggs, 17; birds', 269–70; caviar, 16, 199, 201n5, 207, 251–52; dinosaur, 315–16; eaten, 73, 89, 176, 214, 300, 303, 321; Humpty Dumpty, 273, 300, 304; twinning and, 148
ego. *See* riven ego
El Debate, 141
Elder, Robert K., 246n1
elephants: eye of, 27, 272–73; hunting of, 17, 138n10, 205, 233–34, 247, 253–56, *255*, 259–60, 271–73, *272*; old bull, 233–34, 242–43, 248, 254–56, 259. *See also* ivory
El Escorial, 122, 130
El Gallo, 261
El Greco, 15–16, 111, 116–17
Eliot, T. S., 17, 208, 272, 310
El Liberal, 141
Ellis, Havelock, 119
Encina, Juan de la, 142
Ernst, Morris, 317
Estabrook, Arthur H., 185
Estérel, the, 49n27, 65, 67, 83, 161–63, *162*, 185–86, 208, 256, 334
eugenics, 184–85

Falconetti, Renée Jeanne, 19, 312, *312*
Farewell to Arms, A (Hemingway): brandy in, 61–62; "craziness" in, 211–12, 252; fetish words/names in, 45, 59, 307; hair in, 19, 30, 36–37, 100; Hemingway's themes in, 17, 35, 320, 338; merged lovers in, 31, 86, 95–96, 258; nurse figure in, 41, 218; publication/reception of, 94, 144

fashion/clothing: Alpini hat, 325–26, *325;* Andalusian *traje corto* (short suit), 125; Basque shirt, 76, 88, 327; beach pajamas, 189; *boina* (beret), 88; elephant hair and, 282n1; espadrilles, 20–21, 267, 327; fisherman's shirts, 19–21, 88, 327; "gamin," 267; *garçonne* (flapper), 21, 39, 105, 158, 177; high/Parisian, 19–21, 84, 104, 150, 177; "high stiff collar," 143, *143;* men's earrings, 206, 250; modesty/decency and, 19–20, 25, 32, 38–39, 102–3, 105, 183, 189, 215; nautical chic, 20–21, 48n12; safari clothes, 177–78; shorts, 19–21, 25, 267, 327; skiing clothes, 73–74; sweaters, 20–21, 26, 63–64, 89, 100, 104–5, 177, 186, 221n2, 267; white linen dress, 251–52; white sharkskin, 13, 150, 177, 209; women's polos, 19–21, 214–15, 222, 306; women's slacks/trousers, 19–21, 25, 74–75, 177, 189. *See also specific designers*

"Fathers and Sons" (Hemingway), 273–74

father-son relations, 182, 191–92, 207, 222–23, 227, 259, 272–73, 281, 289–90, 292

Fauntleroy, Cedric E., 310

female masquerade, 99–101, 106–9, 120, 158

female phallus: breast erection, 40, 104, 256, 264, 308; claimed by woman, 99–100, 264, 308, 317; cropped hair and, 40, 131; fetish as, 37, 45, 230; mouth/lip erection, 99, 104, 107, 136, 156–57, 190; "walking cocky," 328. *See also* castration

Femina, 33, 39, 52

feminine hysteria, 158

femme fatales, 130–31, *133,* 194, 202, 251, 264

Fenichel, Otto, 258n1

fetish: as something worn, 66–67, 95–96, 149, 168, 206, 250–51; as tool of fetishist, 29–30

fetishism: color contrast and, 89, 100, 150, 186, 237, 252; disavowal of sexual difference, 37–38, 40, 45, 69, 212, 260, 268, 312–13, 322–23; fantasy vs. real person, 180–81; hair and, 29–31, 33, 35, 53, 59–60, 85–86, 136, 165–66, 219, 222; misrecognition and, 95–96, 100–101, 136–37, 170, 193; "normality" and, 86, 220; onset in young adulthood, 50n42; ruination and, 18–19; sin and, 17–18. *See also* cats/lions; disavowal; hair; mirrors; riven ego; sunbathing/suntan

fetishistic cross-dressing: Cossacks and, 316; in "dirty" novels, 316–17; exhibitionism and, 245; *garçonne* (flapper) era and, 21, 39; glossed, 45; masculinity/femininity and, 18–19, 31, 168, 260; mirrors and, 95–96; named alter egos and, 30–31, 41, 45–47, 67, 77, 151, 153, 217, 252. *See also* female masquerade; gender transformation; racial transformation

fetishistic excitement: anxiety and, 38, 75, 168–69, 261, 323; change and, 30–31, 33, 65–67, 76–77; fashion and, 21, 26, 214–15; feeling vs. thinking and, 57, 152–53; fright of/"spooked," 46, 54–55, 75, 84, 86, 96, 165, 236, 251, 257, 261, 329–30; swollen throats and, 36–37, 252, 318, 331; taboos/transgression and, 37–38, 64, 77, 84, 86, 90, 139, 156–57, 198, 203, 206, 211, 220–21; trauma and, 38, 41, 45, 170, 251, 258. *See also* gender transformation; racial transformation

fetishistic narratives, 18–19, 30–31, 45, 68, 168, 173, 251–52, 316

fetishistic sexuality: "darker taste," 105; nighttime, 47, 52, 54–55, 67, 73, 95, 153–54, 172, 193, 200, 313; pederasty, 64, 225, 273, 311; ritualized erotic scenarios and, 52–53, 95, 174, 252, 257. *See also* sex/sexuality

fetishistic surprises, 29–31, 37, 45–46, 75, 96, 100, 139, 236

fetish words, 60, 198–99, 307. *See also* cats/lions

Field and Stream, 27

Fifth Column, The (Hemingway), 282

"Fifty Grand" (Hemingway), 298

Finca Vigía, 170n5, 246n1, 246n6, 340

fish/fishing: cities/villages, 10, 12, 14, 16, 27, 175; Coolidge and, 143–44, *143;* fashion and, 19–21, 88; *loup de mer* (European sea bass), 27–28, 257; mackerel, 14, 16–17, 28, 188–89; rouget, 172; trout, 143–44; world records in, 27, 48n18

Fitzgerald, F. Scott, 18, 23, 56, 165, 201n5, 220, 225, 274, 293; *Tender Is the Night,* 176, 178–80, 233, 240

Fitzgerald, Zelda, 18, 23, 56, 57, 211, 220, 233, 249, 274

flamenco, 125–26, 134–35, 139, 238

Flaubert, Gustave, 135

Fleming, Robert, 26, 35–36, 294, 333n5

food and drink: aphrodisiacs, 125, 207; Armagnac, 61–62, 172, 224; artichokes, 17, 29, 257; beer, 75–76, 111–13, 124–25, 142, 188, 207, 321; caviar, 16, 124, 199, 207, 252; chicken, 176, 308; cocktails/martinis, 142, food and drink (*cont.*) 163, 251, 322–23; Cognac, 61–62; *crab Mexicaine*, 113; figs, 204, 214; flageolets (beans), 39; fois gras, 189; French fries, 151; garlic olive, 195; "giant killer," 224, 228, 307; Grey Poupon mustard, 176; "hero drink," 61–62, 172; melon, 118–19, 176; pastis (anise-based alcohol), 61; *percebes* (barnacles), 124–25, 331; Perrier water, 61, 172, 224, 278; potato salad, 75, 188; sauerkraut, 75; sausage, 75, 116; Savora mustard, 176, 321; shellfish, 84, 111–13, 124–25, 134, 172, 279, 330; sherry, 98, 115, 137, 140, 174, 299; Suze liqueur, 209; truffles, 176; whiskey, 178, 224. *See also* absinthe; champagne; eggs; fish/fishing; hunger; wine

Ford, Richard, 116–18, 137n4

For Whom the Bell Tolls (Hemingway): fetishistic elements in, 21–22, 31, 37, 96, 312, 319n1; "giant killer" in, 224; Hemingway's themes in, 35, 230, 244, 338

fossils, 315–16

Frank, Waldo, 137n4

Franklin, Sidney, 286

French Riviera (Côte d'Azur): artistic depictions of, 48n12, 238, 240, 267; Edenic nature of, 3–4, 10, 22–24, 161, 176, 193, 262; hanging villages, 176; land boom, 175, 183; "launching fashions" and, 19–21, 189, 215; nationalities at, 22, 180, 190–91, 249–50; summer "season" at, 19, 22–24, 32–33, 51–52, 139, 175–76, 189, 199, 215, 225; Train Bleu, 22

Freud, Sigmund, 37, 40, 45, 100, 108, 120, 260, 267

Friderich, Ernest, 68

Froissard, Jean, 12

Fuenterrabía (Hondarribia), 82

Gajdusek, Robert, 17, 277

Galignani's bookstore, 183, 252

"Gambler, the Nun, and the Radio, the" (Hemingway), 224

Garden, Mary, 22

Gardénia (perfume), 104–5

Garden of Eden, The (Hemingway): anachronisms in, 9, 35, 61, 102–3, 125, 140, 146, 150, 184, 231, 301, 309–10, 319nn4–5; 320; character ages in, 39, 60, 106, 220, 231, 242; character names in, 26, 46–47, 60, 217–18, 344n14; dating the composition of, 317–18, 321, 327, 332, 334, 337–43; Hemingway's intention to publish, 166, 342; Hemingway's project in, 119, 317; "provisional ending" of, 5, 31, 129, 212, 233, 304, 333, 334–36, 340–41; Scribner's ending of, 4–5, 236, 246, 264, 273, 309, 314, 318, 320, 335–36; Sheldon ending, 324–33, 339–41; timeline of, 9, 14, 33, 65, 82–83, 140–41, 148, 161, 172, 185, 201–2, 225, 236, 263, 322; title of, 3–4, 266, 269, 327–28; writing process of, 68, 166, 180, 196, 200–201, 242, 279, 293–94, 300, 327, 342. *See also* Eden; Jenks, Tom

Gardner, Ava, 35

Gardner, Carol Hemingway (sister of EH), 289–90

Gardner, Isabella Stewart (Mrs. Jack), 289–90

Garfield, Brian, 232

Garnett, Constance, 282

Gauguin, Paul, 16, 30, 51, 62, 129, 228, 245

Gautier, Théophile, 316–17

Gellhorn, Martha (third wife of EH), 166, 169

Gendarmerie Nationale, 88

gender roles: disrupted, 127–28, 309; fashion and, 19–21, 25, 102–3, 177, 189, 267

gender transformation: compulsivity of, 136; facilitated by fetish, 37–38, 40–41, 74, 147–48, 174, 309; fetishistic excitement of, 30–31, 33, 104, 107, 152–54; mirrors and, 95–96, 136–37; nighttime, 54–55, 67, 73, 153–54, 157, 172, 181, 193, 318–19; in pigeons, 269; Rodin's *Metamorphoses* and, 30, 41–43, 43, 73, 101

Gentlewoman and Modern Life, 39

George, Lloyd, 243

Ghiberti, Lorenzo, 42

Gide, André, 121, 239, 262, 311

Gilbert, Sandra, 229

Girard, Xavier, 267

Gobi Desert, 315–16

Gogol, Nikolai, 315–16

goiters, 233, 235n7, 335

Goldberg, Reuben "Rube," 300

Golfe-Juan, 175, 290

Goncharova, Natalia, 240

Gould, Frank Jay, 175–76

Goya, Francisco, 16, 111, 121, 124, 129, 152–53

Gramont, Élisabeth de, Duchesse, *103*

Grant, C. H. B., 253

Graphic, 23–24

Grave di Papadopoli, 306

Great Rift Valley, 188, 191, 204–5, 223

Greco-Turkish War, 145, 276
Greenacre, Phyllis, 186, 260
Green Hills of Africa (Hemingway), 55, 76, 167, 250, 282
Gregory XI, 34
Gris, Juan, 16, 134
Gubar, Susan, 229
guillotine, 59, 186–87, 195
"gypsies," 90, 112, 118, 137n4

Haig & Haig, 178
hair: "African haircut," 19, 64, 66, 167, 236–37, 309, 311; Alberto-Culver-V05, 166, 168; barbering as erotic act, 21, 38, 75–76, 108, 166, 168–69, 218, 312; "Bizerte street urchin," 51, 64, 66, 225, 311; blonde, 165–66; *cendre* (ashen) rinse, 218; Cossack, 315; coverings, 26; cropped to scalp, 312, *312*; Danish girl's, 53, 66–67, 165, 169, 172–74; dyeing, 30, 41, 45–46, 54–55, 69, 165–66, 168–70, 237, 256–57, 261; "embarrassing," 106–7, 245, 250, 257, 261, 326–27; Eton crop, 19, 37–39, 102–3, *103*, 211; exhibitions for, 39, 103; fashion trendsetting and, 19, 37–39, 74, 102–3, 185; *garçonne* (flapper), 21, 39, 158; hairdressers vs. barbers, 37–38, 75–76, 101, 103, 218; hairdressing trade unions and, 168–69; "heiress" and, 198–99, 307; "Indian"/"Indian trick," 75–76, 327, 329; ivory, 22, 229–30, 252, 256, 257; "jailbait," 106, 265; long, 86, 148, 325, 327, 329–30; "Madrid," 170, 236–37, 311; matching haircuts, 21, 37, 74–75, 84, 86, 165, 170, 172–73, 230, 256–57, 261, 325, 329; ruination and, 18–19, 313; Samson's, 226; sand/salt in, 329–30, 332; sibling romance and, 22, 73–76, 165, 256–57; sterility and, 158; "strange," 109; sun-streaked, 21, 29, 35, 68–69; "Tahitian," 245; "wet seal," 211, 225, 308, 311; white, 250–51
Hall, Radclyffe, 119
hallucinations, 30–31, 40–41, 53, 156, 212, 270
Halsey, Raymond, 317
Halsey v. New York, 317
Harp, Stephen, 32
Harper's Bazaar, 74, 297–98
Harris, Frank, 231, 235n5
Hartford Courant, 56
Hawkins, Ruth, 60
Hayward, Leland, 194n2
Hayward, Slim, 250, 274, 317–18, 342

Hediger, Ryan, 259
hell, 114–15, 211; artistic visions of, 3, 42, *44*, 121–24, *123*, 130, *132*, 301. *See also* devil
Hemingway, Ernest (EH), *325*; aging/death of, 145, 242–43, 343; art owned by, 135, 228; ballet and, 240–41; bookplate of, 238, 246n1; ear piercing and, 206, 250; estranged sister and, 289–90; as hairstylist, 41, 45, 108, 165–66, 168–69, 170n4, 237, 337; hair of, 41, 46, 54, 257, 329, 337; "iceberg principle," 29, 87, 92, 152, 249, 256; journalism and, 141–42, 144, 288, 292; legend of, 56–58, 152, 166, 194n2, 206, 236–37, 259; marriages of, 23, 41, 45–47, 49n24, 54–55, *103*; reading practices of, 170n5; second honeymoon of, 9–12, 20, 26, 49n19; sexuality of, 41, 52, 54–55, 67, 174, 208, 237; talismans carried by, 195; traumas and, 38, 41, 45, 170, 258, 305. *See also* Debba; Gellhorn, Martha (third wife of EH); Sanford, Marcelline Hemingway (sister of EH); *and individual works*
Hemingway, Grace Hall (mother of EH), 18, 22, 38, 60, 267
Hemingway, Gregory (son of EH), 64, 260
Hemingway, Hadley Richardson (first wife of EH): divorce of, 55, 98, 139, 194, 338; EH's names for, 45, 49n24, 54, 59–60; freckles/hair of, 29, 74, 169; loss of manuscripts by, 18, 213–14; marriage to EH, 9, 106, 113, 119, 219; Riviera vacation of, 9, 23, 33, 139, 161, 176, 237, 274
Hemingway, Leicester (brother of EH), 296
Hemingway, Mary Welsh (fourth wife of EH): African travels of, 46, 64, 66–67, 150, 186, 204–6, 219, 237, 250, 279, 311; EH's letters to, 45–46, 54, 137n9, 237, 257, 317, 337, 342; EH's names for, 41, 45–46, 49n24, 54–55, 59, 199, 337; on EH's tastes/vices, 58, 121; on EH's writing practices, 166, 214, 263, 293–94, 337–38, 340–41; European travels of, 12, 111, 113, 115, 118, 237, 256, 301; hair of, 30, 41, 45–46, 54–55, 64, 66, 165–66, 169, 237, 252n1, 256, 311, 337; *How It Was*, 15, 206, 240, 289–90, 294n2, 301, 337; illness/injuries of, 64, 250; US travels of, 93, 116
Hemingway, Patrick (son of EH), 64, 70n1
Hemingway, Pauline Pfeiffer (second wife of EH): affair with EH, 106, 155n9, 194; death of, 260; family of, 155n8; hair and, 30, 69, *103*, 165–66; honeymoon of, 9–12, 20, 26,

INDEX · 369

Hemingway, Pauline Pfeiffer (*cont.*) 34, 49n19, 56, 90, 118, 152, 168; as merged with EH, 49n24, 86, 258; Riviera vacation of, 9, 23, 33, 139, 161, 176, 237, 274; at *Vogue*, 20, 33, 177; wealth of, 55, 60, 198–99; wedding of, 148, 305–6

Hemingway, Valerie Danby-Smith (daughter-in-law of EH), 15, 35, 49n20, 129, 195, 296, 306, 321, 342

Hendaye Plage: casino in, 81, *82;* Hemingway's vacations at, 69, 81; Pauline's hair dyeing in, 30; site/layout of, 65, 81–83, *82*, 108, 137n9

Henry, Barklie McKee, 58

Henry IV, King, 107

Hermaphrodite, 42–43, *43*, 317

Héros XII (horse), 320

Her Privates We (Manning), 26

Herrick, Robert, 144

Herrin, Judith, 301

Hickok, Guy, 112

highlands, 248, 271

"Hills Like White Elephants" (Hemingway), 10, 36, 168

holograph pages, 87, 118, 278, 293, 330, 339

"Homage to Switzerland" (Hemingway), 307

Homer, Winslow, 16, 92–94

Hong Kong, 197

Horne, Bill, 214, 294, 340–41

horses: Cossack/war, 97, 310; on marshes/beaches, 115, 118, 227–28; in Mazeppa legend, 215–16, *217*; nervousness of, 270; racing, 197–99, 215, 244, 320. *See also* Humpty Dumpty

Hotchner, A. E., 48n3, 141–42, 188–89, 241, 342

hotels: Grand Hôtel Pommier (Le Grau-du-Roi), 12; Hôtel Bellevue d'Angleterre (Le Grau-du-Roi), *10*, 12, 14, 24, *25*; Hôtel Biron (Paris), 3, 42, 73, 123, 262 (*see also* Musée Rodin); Hôtel Crillon (Paris), 65, 107, 140; Hôtel du Cap (Antibes), 22–23, 225; Hôtel Eskualduna (Hendaye), 81–83, *82*, 104; Hotel Luna (Venice), 332; Imperator (Nîmes), 35; Maïon Longa (La Napoule), 161–63, *162;* Palace Hotel (Madrid), 119–20, *120*, 124–25, 127, 137n6, 141–42, 154, 179; Pavillon Henri IV (Saint-Germain-en-Laye), 102, 107, 140; Pensión Aguilar (Madrid), 142; Ondarraïtz Hotel (Hendaye), 81, 91n1; Ritz Hotel (Paris), 87, 101, 120, 213–14

Houk, Nita, 166, 169, 170n4

Houk, Walter, 170n4

Hudson, Thomas, 155n5

Hudson, W. H., 13, 163–64, 200, 254, 269–70

Hugo, Victor, 215

Humpty Dumpty, 273, 300, 304

hunger, 16–17, 28–29. *See also* food and drink

Hunt, Leigh, 319n2

hunting: big-game, 133–34, 204–5, 241, 246n1, 253–55, 259, 271, 275, 288; birds, 253–54; guns, 205, 212n6, 247, 253; gunbearers and, 205, 247; periodicals on, 141; spears, 234; wing shooting, 281–82. *See also* elephants

Hutchinson, Horace, 253

Hutton, Barbara, 184

Immortalia, 277

Indianapolis 500, 129

Ingram, Rex, 23

innocence, 3, 42, 69, 99, 124, 222, 224; as naivete of world, 135–36, 193, 291, 324

In Our Time (Hemingway), 56–57, 144

International Game Fish Association, 27

Iseult/Isolde, 218

Isidro Labrador, San (festival of), 9, 65

Islamic law, 219, 314

Islands in the Stream (Hemingway): art in, 93; on "dirty" novel, 317; fetishistic elements in, 21–22, 37, 41, 198, 307; *GOE* and, 4, 295n4, 338; hair in, 30, 50n37, 77n1; people/places named in, 76, 164, 266; RAF and, 155n5

Isotta Fraschini (car), 179, 186, 210, 217, 225, 238, 242, 306

Ivancich, Adriana, 240–41, 252n1

Ivancich, Gianfranco, 48n11

ivory: elephant tusks, 22, 147, 233–34, 255–56, *255*, 259, 271–72, *272*, 292; erotic smoothness of, 43, 233, 252; hair color, 22, 229–30, 256–57, 280; Hemingway's nickname for Marcelline, 22, 230, 259–60

"I Will Sing of My Redeemer," 276

Jacobsen, Carl, 42

"jailbait," 106, 265

James, Henry, 113

Jelke, Mickey (and family), 183–84

Jenks, Tom: achievement of, 4–5; chapter deletions by, 4, 9, 73, 81, 89, 109, 118, 119, 126, 174, 244, 256; corrections by, 231; line/word deletions by, 28, 41–42, 51, 95, 104, 178, 203, 229, 268, 273, 305; muting/reshaping by, 30, 51,

65–66, 87, 92, 95, 150, 154, 236–37, 268, 273, 307, 309, 313, 314, 318, 341; transpositions by, 4, 47, 52, 54, 84, 107, 109, 140, 172, 179–80, 245–46, 267, 290, 297, 313, 314, 320; word insertions by, 40, 81, 154, 174–75, 203, 214, 314; word substitutions by, 28, 176, 207, 214, 231
Joan of Arc, 19, 312, *312*
jockey clubs, 244
Johnson, Frederick, 182, 218, 247
Johnson, Samuel, 62
Joinville, Jean de, 48n5
Jongkind, Johan Barthold, 16, 92–93, 330
Jouenne, Lucien, 27
journalism, 141–42, 144, 184, 192, 262, 285, 291–92. *See also individual periodicals*
Joyce, James, 98, 121
Juan de la Cruz, San, 114
Juan-les-Pins: casino in, 23–24, 175, 191, 199; Edenic nature of, 3, 175–76; fashions in, 20, 189; Hemingway's 1926 vacation in, 9, 23, 98, 161, 176, 199, 274; sunbathing at, 32, 52, 175
Jukes family, 183–85
Junek, Elizabeth, 127–28
Jung, Carl, 233
Justice, Hilary, 29, 140, 158

Kahn, Gus, 144
Kahnweiler, Daniel-Henry, 135
Kamba identity, 41, 51, 205–6, 236–37, 309. *See also* Debba
"Kanaka," 51, 60, 66, 88, 188, 210, 228
Kaplan, Louise, 110n12
Keats, John, 319n2
Kenya: bird species of, 253–54; colonial conflicts in, 191, 205, 223, 231–32, 248; landscape of, 204–5, 213, 223, 248, 253; marital laws in, 219, 314; seas of, 278–79
Ketchum (ID), 98, 282, 319n3, 340–42
Khokhlova, Olga, 286–87
Kibo, 243, 271
Kid Boots, 286
Kid from Spain, The, 285, 286
Kienné de Mongeot, Marcel, 32
Kiki, 267
Kilgallen, Dorothy, 184
King's African Rifles (KAR), 183, 232, 304
Kipling, Rudyard: "If—," 280–81; *Kim*, 314; *The Naulahka*, 308; and sexuality, 118–19; *Soldiers Three*, 119; "The White Seal," 308

kissing: opposite-sex, 18, 47, 57, 190, 192, 224, 303, 306, 308, 320, 331; same-sex, 42, 153, 190, 193
Kissling, Moïse, 101
Klee, Paul, 16, 134, 228
Klupfell, Wlatchylas de, 262
Kościuszko, Andrzej Tadeusz Bonawentura, 309–11
Kościuszko Squadron, 310
Krohg, Per, 266
Kuban Cossack Chorus, 316
Kurth, Peter, 128
Kuzminskaya, Tatyana, 287

Lacan, Jacques, 117, 120
Lacloche, Anne-Marie, 241
Lacoste, René, 215
Lafayette Escadrille (Sharifian Squadron), 145–46, 291, 310
La Femme de France, 33
Lake Magadi, 150, 204, 212n2, 213, 253–54
L'Alpino, 325
La Napoule, 34, 65, 82–83, 148, 161–63, *162*, 185, 208. *See also* Théoule
Land, Sea, and Air Book (Hemingway), 155n5, 338, 343n13
Landru, Henri Désiré, 58–59
Lange, Monique, 246n5
Lanham, Buck, 45, 155n8, 282n3, 337, 341, 343n9
La Nouvelle Revue Française, 297–98
La passion de Jeanne d'Arc, 19, 312, *312*
Lardner, John, 292
Larousse, Pierre, 133–34
Lasserre, Jean, 194n2
"Last Good Country, The" (Hemingway), 22, 30, 273
Last Judgment (mosaic), 301
La Torre del Oro, 114
La Tribune de Marseille, 16
Laurencin, Marie, 16, 99, 239, 265–66, 297
L'Auto, 292
La Vie Parisienne, 191
La vie sage, 32
Lawrence, T. E., 170n5
Leakey, Louis, 4
Leakey, Richard, 289
L'Éclaireur de Nice, 141, 181n1, 192, 209, 262
Le Cri de Paris, 49n26
Leda and the Swan, 148, *149*
Le Figaro, 163

INDEX · 371

Le Gallienne, Richard, 110n21
Legion of Honor, 135, 145–46
Le Grau-du-Roi: casino in, *10–11*, 24–25, *25*; Edenic nature of, 3, 16, 24–25, 27, 140; fishing in, 10, 12, 14, 27; foreigners in, 24, 48n15; Hemingway's honeymoon in, 9–12, 20, 26, 34, 36, 4919, 56, 118; location/site of, 10–14, *10–11, 13*, 24, 29, 61, 68, 115; name of, 28
Le journal amusant, 49n27
Le Miroir des Sports, 141, 192
Lempicka, Tamara de, 128
Le Provençal (Juan-les-Pins), 175–76
lesbian desire, 180–81, 186, 190, 193–94, 202–3, 266–67; pathologized, 197–98, 245, 249; proxy experiences of, 224; transvestic fantasy and, 172–74, 182
Les Saintes-Maries-de-la-Mer, 9, 48n18, 90, 114, 118
Le Temps, 175
Le Train Bleu, 48n12, 238, 240
Life, 142, 184, 342
Lindbergh, Charles, 192, 275
Litri (Manuel Báez), 125
London Daily Mail, 141
Look, 58, 150
Lord, Horace Wilfred, 262
Lord-Vernet, Marcelle, 262
Louis IX, Saint, 12, 28
Louis Vuitton, 213, 263
Louis XIV, King, 107
Louvre, 93, 328
Lozano, Alberto, 142
Lutherans, 210–11, 220
Luxembourg Gardens, 148
Lydia Pinkham's Vegetable Compound, 276–78
Lynn-Allen, B. G., 253–54

MacDarby, Gabriel, 306
Machakos, 204–5
Mackworth-Praed, C. W., 253
MacLeish, Archibald, 97–98, 110n9, 164, 276, 278, 293
MacLeish, Kenneth, 97, 276
Madrid: festivals in, 9, 65; Hell's Alley in, 114–15; Hemingway's haunts in, 111, 125–26, 141–42; parks in, 156; roads around, 112, 167, 242. *See also* Prado
magnolia trees, 82–83
maharajas, 134, 190–91
mairie (town hall), 305–6

Maji Maji Rebellion, 59, 188, 205, 223, 231–32
Mallarmé, Stéphane, 98
Malmaison, 249
Mandel, Miriam, 125, 320
Manet, Édouard, 85
Mangin, Charles, 126
Mann, Thomas, 163–64, 200
Manning, Frederic, 26
Mannoni, Octave, 37
Margueritte, Victor, 158
Marismas, 115
marriage laws, 219, 305–6, 314
Marseille, 12, 16, 20, 28, 48n3
Martinet, Henry, 82–83
Masai people, 66–67, 206, 237, 274
masculinity: critiqued, 182; emasculated, 192, 229, 245–46, 251, 261; hyper-, 316; "intact," 268; shored up/retrenchment of, 182, 245–46, 251, 280–81, 314, 316
Massine, Léonide, 239–40
Masson, André, 216
Maude, Louise and Aylmer, 282
Mau Mau crisis, 191, 223, 231–32, 248
Maupassant, Guy de, 94, 230–31, 235n5
Mayo Clinic, 343
Mazepa, Ivan, 215
Mazeppa, legend of, 215–16, *217*
Mazeppa II (horse), 320
Mazzeo, Tilar J., 110n20
Médaille Militaire, 145
Meinertzhagen, Richard, 134, 182–83, 232
memory: deep past and, 13; dual directionality of, 164, 182, 202, 207, 222, 227, 248, 259, 272–73; of events not lived, 302, 322, 334–35; forgetting as denial, 200–201, 249, 251, 331
Men at War (Hemingway), 26, 48n5
Mencken, H. L., 119, 228
Menken, Adah Isaacs, 215
Menton, 208, 241, 249
Men without Women (Hemingway), 56, 217
merging/merged lovers: fetishistic desire and, 38, 258; in *GOE*, 31, 45, 55, 76–77, 257–58; Hermaphrodite, 42–43, *43*, 317. *See also* riven ego
Messent, Peter, 40
Metropolitan Museum of Art, 116, 328
Milhaud, Darius, 239–40
Milman, Henry Hart, 229
mimosa trees, 82–83
Mintler, Catherine R., 229

372 · INDEX

Miró, Joan, 228
mirrors, 261, 306; dissociative misrecognition in, 45, 68, 95, 170, 173, 222, 250; in Hemingway's other texts, 45, 68, 95–96; Hemingway's own confrontation with, 242–43; as motif in *GOE,* 33, 67, 75–76, 95–96, 117, 136–37, 170, 172–74, 190, 203, 222, 250, 256–57, 261, 306; riven ego and, 95–96, 173, 250–51, 258
Mistinguett (Jeanne Florentine Bourgeois), 23, 303
Moddelmog, Debra, 40, 158, 220, 236–37
Modigliani, Amedeo, 101
"Mohammedan," 219, 314
Molyneux, Edward Henry, 19, 150, 177
Moncrieff, C. K. Scott, 13
Monet, Claude, 93
Monte Carlo, 84, 189, 321
Montparnasse, 104, 106, 266
Moore, Ernst, 255, 271–72
Morgan, J. P., 183
Morley, Christopher, 90
Morocco, 142, 145–47, 151–52, 225, 291–92, 310
Mount Kilimanjaro, 234, 243, 247–48, 253, 255
Moveable Feast, A (Hemingway): food/hunger in, 16, 188; hair fetish in, 74; Hemingway's wives in, 9, 74, 113, 139, 194, 338; people/places named in, 56, 75, 98, 113, 188, 216, 238, 249, 266; themes in, 42, 151, 338; writing/publication of, 70n4, 87, 214, 262, 266, 327–28, 337–38, 342–43, 343n12; on writing/writers, 55, 65, 307
"Mr. and Mrs. Eliot" (Hemingway), 229
Murphy, Gerald and Sara, 20, 22–24, 139, 176, 199, 225, 239–40, 261, 274
Murray, John, 117–18
Musée du Luxembourg, 148, 245
Musée Rodin, 30, 41–43, *43–44,* 73, 262. *See also* Rodin, Auguste
Museum of Modern Art (MoMA), 109n2, 228
Music Box, 243
Mussolini, Benito, 291, 325
mutiny on the Bounty, 62
"My Own Life" (Hemingway), 235n5

Naether, Carl, 269
Nandi Resistance, 205, 223, 231–32
Napoleon I, Emperor, 116, 303–4, 310
narcissism, 31, 55, 99, 104, 106, 257–58, 280, 299, 335

narrative focalization, 112, 127, 219, 225–26, 264, 307–8
"Natural History of the Dead, A" (Hemingway), 164
naturist movement, 31–32
Negrín López, Juan, 142
Neumann, Arthur Henry, 138n10, 205, 247, 253
New Caravan, 216
New Republic, 144, 298
New York Clipper, 215
New York Herald, 23, 113, 141, 162, 285, 292
New York Times, 25, 175, 190, 237, 243, 267, 289, 291, 316
Ngorongoro Crater, 4, 288–89, 308
Nguruman Escarpment, 204, 207, 223, 253–54
Nice, 23–24, 68, 83–84, 101, 128, 175–76, 262
Nice, Hellé, 128
Nick Adams stories (Hemingway), 64, 210, 273–74. *See also individual stories*
Nîmes, 24–25, 33–35, 68, 342
Nivelle, Robert, 126
Nobel Prize, 57, 135
normal schools, 220
nudist free-love colony, 262
nurse figures, 41, 218

obituaries, 17, 58, 145
obscenity trials, 119, 317
Occitan, 28
Oklahoma, 190–91, 210, 243, 260, 304
Old Man and the Sea (Hemingway), 184, 338
Ol Doinyo Orok Mountain, 248, 253
Olduvai Gorge, 4, 289
onionskin paper, 339–40
"On the Quai at Smyrna" (Hemingway), 276
Ordóñez, Antonio, 137n2, 321, 342
"original Romeike," 57, 294. *See also* press clippings
O'Rossen, Louis, 19, 177
Ory, Pascal, 49n26
Osage tribe, 190, 210
overdrafts, 289
Ovid, 30, 42–43, *43*
Oxford English Dictionary, 304

Pacific islands, 51, 62, 228, 245
Palavas-les-Flots, 12, 16
Pamplona, 96–97, 240, 268, 274
Pares, Bernard, 319n3
Paris Herald, 285

Paris Review, 129
Paris Times, 303
Partridge, Eric, 224
Pasaje Alvarez, 111
Pascin, Jules, 16, 95, 265–66
Patinir, Joachim, 16, 129–30, 134
Patou, Jean, 33, 84
Payot's (Paris), 76
paysage (landscape), 231
Peirce, Waldo, 16, 93, 99, 225
Pepe-Hillo, 95
Percival, Philip, 205, 212n1
perfume, 104–6, 110n21
Perkins, Max, 10, 57–58, 94, 144, 170n5, 294, 298
Perlmutter, Bronia and Tylia, 266
Pernod, Henri Louis, 157. See also absinthe
Perrault, Charles, 58
perversion, 69, 99, 197–98, 303, 312–13
Pétain, Marshal, 276
Peters, K. J., 208, 222–23, 299
Petrarch, 34
Pfeiffer, Karl, 178
Pfeiffer, Pauline. *See* Hemingway, Pauline Pfeiffer (second wife of EH)
Pfeiffer family, 60
Phelan, Janet, 219
Phillipps-Wolley, Clive, 271
Physiopolis, 32
Picard, Gaston, 161
Picasso, Pablo, 16, 262, 279; abstraction of, 110n20, 269; book illustrations by, 93–95, 110nn4–5, 265–66, 287; bookplates by, 238, 241; designs for ballet, 48n12, 99, 238–40; personality/life of, 285–88; summers on the Riviera, 22–23, 35, 175, 274–75, 285–86; war and, 135, 287
pillar of salt, 13, 150, 155n9, 177, 209, 211
Pinkham, Lydia, 276–78, 288
Pius XI, Pope, 25, 179
plane trees, 172, 178, 279, 299
Plimpton, George, 15, 129, 137n1
Pointe de l'Aiguille, 161, 237
Poiret, Paul, 74, 84, 189
Polish-Soviet War, 310, 316
Poniatowski, Józef (and family), 310–11
Pont du Gard, 33–34
pornography, 119, 183, 251, 266, 316–17
Porquerolles, 291
Porter, Cole, 22
Pound, Ezra, 15, 27–28, 98, 146, 154n3, 278

Prado: emotional experience of visiting, 113, 135, 152, 154, 226; Hemingway's love for, 111, 118; location of, 120, 124, 156; paintings at, 118, 120–22, 124, 129–31, 134, 152–53, 275, 305; sculpture not at, 148; visiting as a "boy," 148, 152–54
Pradt, Dominique de, 116
press clippings, 56–60, 70, 88–89, 109, 192, 200, 294, 296, 321
Primo de Rivera, Miguel, 112, 126, 136, 143, 146, 151, 154n3
Prometheus, 215, *216*
Proust, Marcel, 135, 262; *Guermantes' Way,* 239; *A Remembrance of Things Past,* 13–14, 90, 113, 163–64, 200, 244; *Sodome et Gomorrhe* (*Cities of the Plain*), 13–14, 113, 150, 239; *Swann's Way,* 113
Provence, 34, 49n20, 61
Prunier, Émile Alfred, 199
Psalms, 304
pseudosibling romance. *See* sibling romance
psychoanalytic theory, 40, 95–96, 117, 120, 149. *See also* castration; female phallus; fetishism; mirrors; riven ego
publishing, 55, 117–18, 134, 166, 297–98
Pyrenees, 89, 116, 328

Quétel, Claude, 230–31
Quintana, Juanito, 340
Quintanilla, Luis, 109n2, 134, 137n3, 142–43
Quintanilla, Paul, 142

racial otherness: "dusky paramour," 229; fetishization of, 51, 64, 66–68, 205–6, 219, 233, 236–37, 250, 264, 265, 274; "savage friend," 286; stereotyped, 60–61, 64, 88, 95, 190–91, 210–11, 237, 311, 327, 329; "tribal marks," 66, 250
racial transformation: fantasies of, 51–52, 64–67, 118, 147, 186, 205–6, 228, 245, 250, 314–17; fetishistic excitement of, 65–67, 245, 274, 309; sunbathing and, 31, 33, 49n26, 51–52, 89, 112, 116, 228, 327
Radiguet, Raymond, 239, 261, 266
Raeburn, John, 56
Rasmusson, Daniel, 94, 109n3
Ravenna, 300–301
Red Baron (Manfred von Richthofen), 302
red buttes/rocks, 167–68, 208, 334
remorse: alcohol's ameliorating of, 53–54, 62,

75, 195, 224, 323, 328, 331–32; "badness"/sin and, 36, 53, 75, 106–7, 119, 140, 153, 195, 202, 226; elephant hunting and, 260; fear of, 202; intense, 210–11, 222; lack of, 137, 140, 154, 174, 176–77, 263–64; postcoital, 36, 156–57, 195, 202, 225–26, 251, 261, 331; successful avoidance of, 311, 313, 318; wormwood and, 157, 209. *See also* depression/despair

Renoir, Pierre-Auguste, 94

Revue Aéronautique de France, 276

Reynolds, Michael, 57, 230, 239

Reynolds, Quentin, 302n3

Ricard, Paul, 61

Rice, Alfred, 302n1, 318, 342

Richardson, Hadley. *See* Hemingway, Hadley Richardson (first wife of EH)

Richardson, John, 239, 286

Richthofen, Manfred von, "Red Baron," 302

rifles, 205, 247, 253

Rif War, 142–43, 145–47, 151–52, 225, 291–92, 310

Rikli, Arnold, 32

Rimbaud, Arthur, 85, 98, 149–50

riven ego: authorial, 18, 30–31, 36, 55–57, 150–51, 191, 232, 268, 329; bigendered, 31, 33, 36–37, 45, 156–57, 299, 331; as catalyst to cruelty, 230, 232; dissociation/misrecognition and, 100–101, 192, 195–97, 222, 232, 250, 257, 321; envy between, 19, 56, 120; fetishism's effect on, 232–33; hallucinatory moments and, 41, 156, 212; Hemingway's alter ego (Catherine), 45–46, 54, 60, 166, 211–12, 257, 260, 296, 310, 328, 337; identity vs. roots and, 207, 260, 304; Lacanian registers and, 117; merger and, 55, 257–58; mirrors and, 95–96, 173, 250–51, 258; named alter egos and, 30–31, 41, 45–47, 66–67, 77, 151, 153, 217–18, 252, 260; narcissism and, 55; oscillating vs. simultaneously bigendered, 267–68, 318, 322–23; proxy sexuality and, 224, 250; Rodin's *Metamorphoses* and, 41–43, *43*; self-division and, 99, 107, 150–51, 153, 219, 268, 310

Riviere, Joan, 110n12

Rivkin, Mike, 48n18

Roberts, Mary Louise, 19–20, 38–39, 158

Robertson, Sparrow, 141, 292

Robinson, Sonny, 102

Robinson, W. Heath, 300

Rockefeller family, 184, 238

Rodin, Auguste, 16, 148, 262; *The Metamorphoses of Ovid*, 30, 41–43, *43–44*, 47, 53, 73,

101, 123, 148, 262; *The Gates of Hell*, 3, 42, 44, 123, 262

Roe, Steven, 59

Rollin, Léon, 142

Romany Stain, 89–90, 118

Romeike, Henry (and family), 57, 294

Roncevaux, 89, 96–97, 268, 328

Roosevelt, Theodore, 134, 247

Rorschach, Hermann, 233

Rosenberg, Léonce, 135

Ross, Charles, 288

Ross, Lillian, 116

Royal Air Force (RAF), 145, 286, 314

Ruark, Robert, 294n1

Rubens, Peter Paul, 111, 215, *216*

ruin. *See* destruction

Russian Revolution, 250, 316

Sacco, Nicola, 187

Sade, Marquis de, 249

"Safari" (Hemingway), 150

Saint Elizabeths Hospital, 98, 278

Saint-Germain-des-Prés, 76, 98

Saint-Germain-en-Laye, 102, 107, 140

Saint-Jean-de-Luz, 108–9

Saint-Raphaël, 23, 67, 161, 165, 208, 225, 244

Samson and Delilah, 131, 226

Samuels, Lee, 342, 344n21

sanatoriums/asylums, 14–15, 98, 220, 233, 236, 249, 278, 308, 332, 335. *See also* "craziness"

Sandburg, Carl, 277

Sanford, Marcelline Hemingway (sister of EH), 22, 38, 101, 105, 113, 170n5, 177, 230, 258–59, 267

San Sebastian, 84, 112

Santiago de Compostela, 114

Sarah, Saint, 9, 118

Satie, Erik, 239–40

Saturday Review of Literature, 90

scandal, 19, 84, 102, 189, 215, 219, 312, 315, 327

Schillings, Carl, 271

Scholes, Robert, 40, 148, 208

Scribner, Charles, 12, 94, 343n5

scripting, 18, 94, 117, 158, 185–86, 189, 229, 299, 335

"Sea Change, The" (Hemingway), 21, 26, 37, 68, 108, 190, 198

sea changes, 21, 30, 68–69, 156

Seagle, William, 317

Segrave, Kerry, 49n26

Segrè, Claudio, 326
Seldes, Gilbert, 23
Sella, Antoine, 22
Sert, Misia, 239–40
Seville (festival of), 9, 65
Seward, Bill, 294
sex/sexuality: anal penetration, 40–41; bisexuality, 225, 237, 266; "bloody sodomite," 99, 323, 326–27; celibate marriage and, 185, 202–3; debauchery, 28, 188–89; female physiology and, 158, 224, 276–77; heteronormativity, 5, 211, 236, 246, 264, 273, 280, 309, 318, 336; homosexuality, 98–99, 118–19, 153–54, 156–57, 172–74, 239, 261, 263–64, 322–23; hunger as desire and, 16–17, 28–29; impotence, 307; "inner journey" and, 167, 186, 188, 212; jealousy and, 243, 245, 263–64, 268; love triangles, 9, 68, 194, 202–3, 224–26, 262–63, 278; masturbation, 293–94; pathologizing of, 39, 197–98, 221n3, 245, 249; polygamy, 64, 189, 219–21, 242, 252, 314, 328; postcoital clarity and, 35, 174–75; postcoital ruminations and, 47, 52, 75–77, 172, 174, 219, 264, 318–19; proxy/"understudy," 224, 242–43, 248, 250; "queer," 87, 100, 322, 324, 327; sex/sleep/death aligned, 304; syphilis/clap, 12–13, 48n6, 230–31, 273; "understudy," 242–43, 248, 252; unfaithfulness, 193, 195–99, 219, 279–80, 286, 293–94, 331–32. *See also* fetishistic sexuality; lesbian desire; merging/merged lovers; sibling romance
Shakespeare, William: *Cymbeline,* 309–10; *Hamlet,* 26, 309; *Henry IV, Part One,* 277–78; *Romeo and Juliet,* 239–40; *The Tempest,* 21, 68–69
Sharifian Squadron (Lafayette Escadrille), 145–46, 225, 291, 310
Sheean, Vincent, 126, 141, 146–47, 151–52, 291–92
Sherard, Robert Harborough, 235n5
Shipman, Evan, 215–17, 320
Shompole Conservancy, 204, 213, 253
"shoot with shits," 280–81
"Short Happy Life of Francis Macomber, The" (Hemingway), 224
sibling romance: "brotherhood" and, 54–55, 85–86, 206, 256–57, 261; dead brother and, 203, 237–38, 276, 301–2, 322–23; estranged sister and, 290; haircuts and, 22, 73–76,

165, 170, 222, 256–57; as "oldest story," 323; taboo of incest, 203, 301–2
Silbergleid, Robin, 272–73, 294
Simmons, Isabelle, 219
sin: as catalyst for writing, 222–23, 318–19; crime as, 193; in daytime, 172; erotic charge of, 69, 73, 312; fetish of, 26, 36, 101, 211, 225, 256–57; innocence and, 3; Judeo-Christian understandings of, 210–11; shamba as site of, 182–83, 274; taboo and, 198; vice and, 17–18, 69, 108; writer's isolation as, 293–94. *See also* remorse
Sioux, 143–44
skiing, 73–74, 133, 242
Smith, Bill, 121
Smith's bookstore, 183
"Snows of Kilimanjaro, The" (Hemingway), 55, 156, 307
Social Register, 288
Sociéte Naturiste, 32
Sodom and Gomorrah, 13–14, 113, 150, 211
"Soldier's Home" (Hemingway), 22, 307
Solomon, Barbara Probst, 17
Somali men/women, 64, 210–11, 214, 219, 264, 279
Sommer, François, 241
Song of Roland, The, 89, 96–97, 268, 276, 307
Souders, George, 129
Southard, Addison, 197
Southern Reporter, 191
Spanish Civil War, 111, 122, 142, 148
Spilka, Mark, 26, 42, 167, 208, 333n5, 343n13
SS Mystique, 163, 304
station climatique et balnéaire (beach resort town), 24
Steeplechase Park, 199
Stein, Gertrude, 135, 146, 169, 240
sterility, 230–31
Stevenson, Robert Louis, 167, 170n5
Stewart, Don Ogden, 23, 240
St. Honoré d'Eylau (Paris), 306
Stigand, Chauncey H., 205, 247, 259, 271
St. Joseph's (Paris), 305–6
Stoller, Robert, 18, 31, 38, 52, 251
Stoneback, H. R., 17, 28, 96–97, 114, 188, 208, 273
Stravinsky, Igor, 134, 239–40
St. Tropez, 249
"Summer People, The" (Hemingway), 35
Sun Also Rises, The (Hemingway): bicycle racing in, 292; fetishistic elements in, 45,

50n42, 102, 218, 307; kept artists in, 229; morality/immorality in, 53, 85; print run/reception of, 55–56, 90, 119, 298; settings in, 65, 84, 96, 180; W. H. Hudson in, 164; writing of, 87, 137n1; WWI pilot in, 192, 276

sunbathing/suntan: dangers of, 52; "enough of," 334–35; fad of, 19–22, 25, 32–33, 49n26, 49n27, 51–52, 175–76, 267; erotically exciting, 33, 66–67, 74, 99; freckles and, 29; hair bleaching and, 21, 29, 222; nude/naturist, 31–32, 186; racially coded, 31, 33, 49n26, 51–52, 89, 112, 116, 228, 327; and suntan as "grown," 110n13; and suntan as "worn," 67, 149; and suntan from skiing, 74

Swahili: *askari* (soldier), 232, 234, 254; *bibi* (woman/concubine), 182; *haya* (shame/modesty), 180, 217; Juma (name), 247; *magadi* (soda), 213; *ndiyo* (yes, it is so), 223; *ngoma* (drum), 273; *penda* (love), 245; *samahani* (I'm sorry), 245; *shamba* (farm), 182–83, 274; *shauri* (show), 257; *sota* (move along on the buttocks), 217–18; *toto* (child), 254

Sweeny, Charles, 145–48, 291, 310

swimming: cliff diving, 237; drowning and, 212, 332–33, 335; nude, 186; seals and, 308; summer season and, 9, 16, 106, 226, 228, 322; swimwear, 25, 267; tides and, 331

Switzerland, 113, 157, 198, 220, 233, 235n7, 236, 240, 308, 310, 332, 335, 341

Symonds, John Addington, 119

ta gueule (shut your trap), 293
Tahitian identity, 66, 228, 245
talisman, 195, 282n1
Talmadge, Norma, 267
Taylor, Pondoro, 205
Teniers, David, the Younger, 16, 134
"Ten Indians" (Hemingway), 10, 36, 273
tennis, 215
Teresa of Avila, Saint, 114
Théoule, 106, 161–63, 237, 256; Edenic nature of, 4, 161. *See also* La Napoule
"There Is a Name I Love to Hear," 47
"thief girl," 107–8, 120
Thomas, Norman, 291
Tilyou, Eddy, 199
Tintoretto, Jacopo Robusti, 16, 121, 129–31, *133*
Tio Pepe, 115, 178, 299
Titler, Dale, 302
"Today Is Friday" (Hemingway), 261

To Have and Have Not (Hemingway), 21, 35, 37, 50n37, 170, 229, 307
Tolstoy, Leo, 282, 287
Torcello, 300–301
Toronto Daily Star, 243
Toronto Star Weekly, 235n7
Torrents of Spring (Hemingway), 55
Toulouse-Lautrec, Henri de, 85, 94
Tour de France, 292
Train, Daniel, 57, 296–97
Transatlantic Review, 240, 261, 297
transvestic narrative. *See* fetishistic cross-dressing
trauma: elephant mourning and, 259; fetishistic excitement and, 38, 41, 45, 170, 251, 258; of World War I, 126–27, 135–36, 192, 287–88
trepanation, 130, *131*, 135, 287–88
"tribal," 64, 66, 68, 249–51, 257, 280, 319
Tristan and Iseult/Isolde, 218
True at First Light (Hemingway), 4
Tucci, Douglass Shand, 289
Turgenev, Ivan, 282
twinning, 22, 37–38, 148, 165, 170, 256–58, 259, 261, 267. *See also* sibling romance
Twomey, Lisa, 305
Tyburn Hill (London), 223
Tzara, Tristan, 240

Udet, Ernst, 275
Unamuno, Miguel de, 154n3
"Undefeated, The" (Hemingway), 94–95, 144, 261, 266
Under Kilimanjaro (Hemingway): on books/writing, 164, 309; elephant hunting in, 233–34, 247, 259–60; fetishistic elements in, 30, 41, 155n9, 183, 206, 211, 237, 307; "giant killer" in, 224; writing/publication of, 4, 64–65, 232
USS MacLeish, 276

Valencia (fair of), 28
Valentino, Rudolph, 23, 179
Valle-Inclán, Ramón del, 142
Valois, Achille, 148
Vanderbilt family, 184
Van Gogh, Theo, 14
Van Gogh, Vincent, 14–16, *15*, 30, 129
Vanzetti, Bartolomeo, 187
Vega, Jesus E., 137n3
Velázquez, Diego, 111

INDEX · 377

Venice, 21, 130, 241, 300–301, 332–33
Verdun, 126
Verlaine, Paul, 85, 98, 149
Vernet, Horace, 215, *217*
"Very Short Story, A" (Hemingway), 41
Vevey, 220
vice: addiction and, 17, 58, 100, 124–25; new money and, 184; obscenities and, 119, 317; sin and, 17–18, 69, 108; taboo and, 198
Victoria, Queen, 84
Viertel, Peter, 48n3
Villa Rosa (Madrid), 125–26, 134, 139
Viollet-le-Duc, Eugène, 12
Virgil, 304
visual arts: art criticism and, 134–35; art dealers and, 88, 93, 135; exhibitions of, 92–93, 301; "hair sculpture," 101, 139, 169; landscape paintings, 94, 116–17, 231, 279, 328; mosaics, 300–301; portraits, 120–21; sculpture, 41–43. *See also individual artists*
Viviani, René, 249
Vivre Intégralement, 32
Vogue: bobbed hair in, 37–39, 102–3, *103*, 169; Bugattis in, 127; fashions in, 20–21, 25, 141, 177, 215, 267; Hemingway as regular reader of, 48n11; Pauline at, 20, 33, 177; on perfumes, 105; tans in, 49n26
volunteer ambulance service, 126–27
Vu, 99

Wagner, Richard, 218
Walpole, Hugh, 119
Walsh, Ernest, 106
Walter, Marie-Thérèse, 286
Ward, James Rowland, 133–34, 138n10, 255
Washington Post, 39, 102
wealth: aversion to, 241, 280–81, 288; dangers of, 55, 108, 163, 229; as liberating, 60, 69–70, 93–94, 119–20, 185; new money and, 127, 180, 183–85, 190, 239; vs. poverty, 73–74, 113; profiteering and, 244–45, 289; status symbols of, 127–29, 179, 220, 238–40, 244, 314–15; as topic of conversation, 88–89, 241, 287. *See also* consumerism
weather: cool breezes, 34–35, 245; end of summer, 322–23; "insane," 183; monsoons, 278–79; rain, 88–89; winds/mistral, 33–35, 174, 177, 270, 322
Well of Loneliness trial, 119, 317

Welsh, Mary. *See* Hemingway, Mary Welsh (fourth wife of EH)
Whitfield, Frederick, 47
Wilde, Oscar, 85, 98
"wild girl," 107–9
Williams, Taylor, 302n1, 317–18, 341–42
Willingham, Kathy, 15, 60, 117, 195
Wilson, Edmund, 144
Winchell, Walter, 184
wine: "African," 116; Beaujolais, 89, 279; Burgundy, 90; Chateau Yquem, 89–90; Irouléguy, 89; light Provençal rosés, 176; "Romany Stain," 89–90; Rosé de Béarn, 89; Sancerre, 113, 279; Tavel, 17, 29, 49n20, 172, 257; Valdepeñas, 116. *See also* champagne
Winnicott, D. W., 19, 38, 258
Wister, Owen, 119
Wolfe, Cary, 155n7, 259, 269, 272
Wolfe, Thomas, 140
Woolworth, F. W., 183–84
World War I: AFS in, 126–27; alcohol production/laws, 85, 178, 200; Arditi shock troops in, 325–26; bawdy songs of, 276–78; bombings during, 301; Bourne's surname in *GOE* and, 26; cartoons during, 300; casualties of, 97, 126, 135, 287–88; change and, 34, 177, 183, 244, 249–50, 270, 325; decorated veterans of, 135, 145; fertility debated after, 158, 230–31; gender relations and, 19–20, 38–39, 102–3, 183, 189; "giant killer," 224; Hemingway's wounding in, 41, 45, 306; naval warfare of, 290–91; postwar treaties, 107; profiteering in, 244–45; Riviera tourism and, 22; trauma of, 126–27, 135–36, 192, 287–88. *See also* airplanes/aviation
World War II, 51, 155n5, 200, 275–76, 301
Wrangel, George, Baron, 108
writing: authentic support for, 306, 308, 321; as autobiographical experience, 207, 249, 290; commodification of, 180, 229, 297–98; as defensive process, 182, 188, 202, 209, 223, 227, 229–30, 259; economic authority over, 55, 229, 241, 297; emotional/marital costs of, 35–36, 163–64, 192, 194, 200–201, 227; enforced isolation and, 35–36, 166, 188, 194, 200–201, 213–14, 259, 263, 280, 290, 338; as exploration/discovery, 164, 182, 196, 200–201, 209, 227, 248–49, 259, 263; as frenzied ride, 215, 242, 294, 338, 340–41; "iceberg

principle," 29, 87, 92, 152, 249, 256; illustrations for, 93–95, 99, 166, 216, 238, 242, 261, 265–69, 287, 297, 328; jealousy of, 55–56, 62–63, 157–58, 263, 309; as life's work, 149–50, 290; loss/sorrow and, 157, 226, 248, 251, 259, 272–73, 281; as masturbatory, 293–94; *mystère* of, 280, 282, 322; as process of "living in" a story, 207, 214, 263, 268; in sand, 26, 309, 329; sex/sin as catalyst for, 35, 174–75, 208, 222–23, 230–31, 249, 318–19; as souvenir, 28–29; with the body, 62–63, 117, 139; travel literature, 117–18, 167; writer's block and, 307–8; writer's public persona and, 56–59, 192, 293; writer's self-righteousness and, 88–89, 98, 163, 238, 322. *See also* press clippings

Zaphiro, Dennis, 204, 243
Zaragoza, 96–98, 167–68
Zdatny, Steve, 39
Ziegfeld Follies, 243, 286
Zielinsky, Bronislaw, 319n3